Lecture Notes in Computer Science 3156

Commenced Publication in 1973
Founding and Former Series Editors:
Gerhard Goos, Juris Hartmanis, and Jan van Leeuwen

Marc Joye Jean-Jacques Quisquater (Eds.)

Cryptographic Hardware and Embedded Systems – CHES 2004

6th International Workshop
Cambridge, MA, USA, August 11-13, 2004
Proceedings

 Springer

Volume Editors

Marc Joye
Gemplus, Card Security Group
La Vigie, Avenue du Jujubier, ZI Athélia IV
13705 La Ciotat Cedex, France
E-mail: marc.joye@gemplus.com

Jean-Jacques Quisquater
Université Catholique de Louvain
UCL Crypto Group
Place du Levant 3
1348 Louvain-la-Neuve, Belgium
E-mail: jjq@dice.ucl.ac.be

Library of Congress Control Number: 2004109601

CR Subject Classification (1998): E.3, C.2, C.3, B.7, G.2.1, D.4.6, K.6.5, F.2.1, J.2

ISSN 0302-9743
ISBN 3-540-22666-4 Springer Berlin Heidelberg New York

Springer is a part of Springer Science+Business Media

springeronline.com

© International Association for Cryptologic Research 2004
Printed in Germany

Typesetting: Camera-ready by author, data conversion by PTP-Berlin, Protago-TeX-Production GmbH
Printed on acid-free paper   SPIN: 11307204   06/3142   5 4 3 2 1 0

Preface

These are the proceedings of CHES 2004, the 6th Workshop on Cryptographic Hardware and Embedded Systems. For the first time, the CHES Workshop was sponsored by the International Association for Cryptologic Research (IACR).

This year, the number of submissions reached a new record. One hundred and twenty-five papers were submitted, of which 32 were selected for presentation. Each submitted paper was reviewed by at least 3 members of the program committee. We are very grateful to the program committee for their hard and efficient work in assembling the program. We are also grateful to the 108 external referees who helped in the review process in their area of expertise.

In addition to the submitted contributions, the program included three invited talks, by Neil Gershenfeld (Center for Bits and Atoms, MIT) about "Physical Information Security", by Isaac Chuang (Medialab, MIT) about "Quantum Cryptography", and by Paul Kocher (Cryptography Research) about "Physical Attacks". It also included a rump session, chaired by Christof Paar, which featured informal talks on recent results.

As in the previous years, the workshop focused on all aspects of cryptographic hardware and embedded system security. We sincerely hope that the CHES Workshop series will remain a premium forum for intellectual exchange in this area.

This workshop would not have been possible without the involvement of several persons. In addition to the program committee members and the external referees, we would like to thank Christof Paar and Berk Sunar for their help on local organization. Special thanks also go to Karsten Tellmann for maintaining the Web pages and to Julien Brouchier for installing and running the submission and reviewing softwares of K.U. Leuven. Last but not least, we would like to thank all the authors who submitted papers, making the workshop possible, and the authors of accepted papers for their cooperation.

August 2004   Marc Joye and Jean-Jacques Quisquater

6th Workshop on Cryptographic Hardware and Embedded Systems

August 11–13, 2004, Boston/Cambridge, USA
http://www.chesworkshop.org/

Organizing Committee

Christof Paar (Publicity Chair) .... Ruhr-Universität Bochum, Germany
Berk Sunar (General Chair) .... Worcester Polytechnic Institute, USA

Program Committee

Roberto Avanzi .... Institute for Experimental Mathematics, Germany
Benoît Chevallier-Mames .... Gemplus, France
Claude Crépeau .... McGill University, Canada
Marc Girault .... France Telecom, France
Jovan Golić .... Telecom Italia, Italy
Marc Joye (Co-chair) .... Gemplus, France
Seungjoo Kim .... Sungkyunkwan University, Korea
Çetin Koç .... Oregon State University, USA
Paul Kocher .... Cryptography Research, USA
François Koeune .... K2Crypt, Belgium
Tanja Lange .... Ruhr-Universität Bochum, Germany
Ruby Lee .... Princeton University, USA
Pierre-Yvan Liardet .... ST Microelectronics, France
Thomas Messerges .... Motorola, USA
Jean-Jacques Quisquater (Co-chair) .... Université Catholique
de Louvain, Belgium
Josyula R. Rao .... IBM T.J. Watson Research, USA
Kouichi Sakurai .... Kyushu University, Japan
Erkay Savaş .... Sabanci University, Turkey
Werner Schindler .... Bundesamt für Sicherheit in
der Informationstechnik, Germany
Jean-Pierre Seifert .... Infineon Technologies, Germany
Joseph Silverman .... Brown University, USA
Tsuyoshi Takagi .... Technische Universität Darmstadt, Germany
Frédéric Valette .... DCSSI, France
Serge Vaudenay .... EPFL, Switzerland
Colin Walter .... Comodo Research Lab, UK
Sung-Ming Yen .... National Central University, Taiwan

Steering Committee

Burton Kaliski .... RSA Laboratories, USA
Çetin Koç .... Oregon State University, USA
Christof Paar .... Ruhr-Universität Bochum, Germany
Jean-Jacques Quisquater .... Université Catholique de Louvain, Belgium
Colin Walter .... Comodo Research Lab, UK

External Referees

Onur Acıiçmez	Darrel Hankerson	Pascal Paillier
Kazumaro Aoki	Clemens Heuberger	Eric Peeters
Toru Akishita	Chun Pyo Hong	Gerardo Pelosi
Gildas Avoine	Keijirou Ike	Gilles Piret
Thomas Baignères	Joshua Jaffe	Arash Reyhani-Masoleh
Claude Barral	Antoine Joux	Ottavio Rizzo
Lejla Batina	Pascal Junod	Francisco
Florent Bersani	Charanjit Jutla	Rodrìguez-Henrìquez
Guido Bertoni	Vangelis Karatsiolis	Pankaj Rohatgi
Eric Brier	Masanobu Katagi	Fabrice Romain
Philippe Bulens	Minho Kim	Yasuyuki Sakai
Benoît Calmels	Shinsaku Kiyomoto	Akashi Satoh
Julien Cathalo	Doug Kuhlman	Daniel Schepers
Guy Cathébras	Sébastien Kunz-Jacques	Katja Schmidt-Samoa
Suresh Chari	Soonhak Kwon	Adi Shamir
Jung Hee Cheon	Sandeep Kumar	Atsushi Shimbo
Chien-ning Chen	Gwenaelle Martinet	Nicolas Sklavos
Che Wun Chiou	Donghoon Lee	Nigel Smart
Mathieu Ciet	Sangjin Lee	Jung Hwan Song
Christophe Clavier	Kerstin Lemke	Fabio Sozzani
Jean-Sébastien Coron	Yi Lu	Martijn Stam
Magnus Daum	Philippe Manet	François-Xavier
Guerric	Stefan Mangard	Standaert
Meurice de Dormale	Natsume Matsuzaki	Michael Steiner
Jean-François Dhem	Renato Menicocci	Daisuke Suzuki
Christophe Doche	Jean Monnerat	Alexei Tchoulkine
Reouven Elbaz	Christophe Mourtel	Yannick Teglia
Wieland Fischer	Frédéric Muller	Alexandre F. Tenca
Jacques Fournier	Michaël Nève	Thomas Tkacik
Pasqualina Fragneto	Kim Nguyen	Lionel Torres
Henri Gilbert	Philippe Oechslin	Eran Tromer
Louis Goubin	Francis Olivier	Michael Tunstall
Johann Großschädl	Kenji Ohkuma	Ingrid Verbauwhede
Jorge Guajardo	Takeshi Okamoto	Karine Villegas
Eric Hall	Katsuyuki Okeya	Andrew Weigl
DongGuK Han	Sıddıka Berna Örs	Kai Wirt
Helena Handschuh	Elisabeth Oswald	Chi-Dian Wu

Previous CHES Workshop Proceedings

CHES 1999: Çetin K. Koç and Christof Paar (Editors). *Cryptographic Hardware and Embedded Systems*, vol. 1717 of *Lecture Notes in Computer Science*, Springer-Verlag, 1999.

CHES 2000: Çetin K. Koç and Christof Paar (Editors). *Cryptographic Hardware and Embedded Systems – CHES 2000*, vol. 1965 of *Lecture Notes in Computer Science*, Springer-Verlag, 2000.

CHES 2001: Çetin K. Koç, David Naccache, and Christof Paar (Editors). *Cryptographic Hardware and Embedded Systems – CHES 2001*, vol. 2162 of *Lecture Notes in Computer Science*, Springer-Verlag, 2001.

CHES 2002: Burton S. Kaliski, Jr., Çetin K. Koç, and Christof Paar (Editors). *Cryptographic Hardware and Embedded Systems – CHES 2002*, vol. 2523 of *Lecture Notes in Computer Science*, Springer-Verlag, 2002.

CHES 2003: Colin D. Walter, Çetin K. Koç, and Christof Paar (Editors). *Cryptographic Hardware and Embedded Systems – CHES 2003*, vol. 2779 of *Lecture Notes in Computer Science*, Springer-Verlag, 2003.

Table of Contents

Collision Attacks

Side Channels II

Fault Attacks

Hardware Implementation I

Side Channels III

Low Resources II

Hardware Implementation II

Authentication and Signatures

Towards Efficient Second-Order Power Analysis

Jason Waddle and David Wagner

University of California at Berkeley

Abstract. Viable cryptosystem designs must address power analysis attacks, and masking is a commonly proposed technique for defending against these side-channel attacks. It is possible to overcome simple masking by using higher-order techniques, but apparently only at some cost in terms of generality, number of required samples from the device being attacked, and computational complexity. We make progress towards ascertaining the significance of these costs by exploring a couple of attacks that attempt to efficiently employ second-order techniques to overcome masking. In particular, we consider two variants of second-order differential power analysis: Zero-Offset 2DPA and FFT 2DPA.

1 Introduction

Power analysis is a major concern for designers of smartcards and other embedded cryptosystems. The advance of Differential Power Analysis (DPA) in 1998 by Paul Kocher [1] made power analysis attacks even more practical since an attacker using DPA did not need to know very much about the device being attacked.

The technique of masking or duplication is commonly suggested as a way to stymie first-order power attacks, including DPA. In order to defeat masking, attacks would have to correlate the power consumption at multiple times during a single computation. Attacks of this sort were suggested and investigated (for example, by Thomas Messerges [2]), but it seems that the attacker was once again required to know significant details about the device under analysis.

This paper attempts to make progress towards a second-order analog of Differential Power Analysis. To this end, we suggest two second-order attacks, neither of which require much more time than straight DPA, but which are able to defeat some countermeasures. These attacks are basically preprocessing routines that attempt to correlate power traces with themselves and then apply standard DPA to the results.

In Section 2, we give some background and contrast first-order and second-order power analysis techniques. We also discuss the apparently inherent costs of higher-order attacks.

In Section 3, we present our model and give the intuition behind our techniques.

In Section 4, we give some techniques for second-order power analysis. In particular, we present some algorithms and analyze them in terms of limitations and requirements: generality, runtime, and number of required traces.

M. Joye and J.-J. Quisquater (Eds.): CHES 2004, LNCS 3156, pp. 1–15, 2004.

Section 5 contains some closing remarks, and Appendix A gives the formal derivations for the noise amplifications that are behind the limitations of the attacks in Section 4.

2   First-Order and Second-Order Power Analysis

We consider a cryptosystem that takes an input, performs some computations that combine this input and some internally stored secret, and produces an output. For concreteness, we will refer to this computation as an *encryption*, an input as a *plaintext*, the secret as a *key*, and the output as a *ciphertext*, though it is not necessary that the device actually be encrypting. An attacker would like to extract the secret from this device. If the attacker uses only the input and output information (i.e., the attacker treats the cryptosystem as a "black box"), it is operating in a traditional private-computation model; in this case, the secret's safety is entirely up to the algorithm implemented by the device.

In practice, however, the attacker may have access to some more *side-channel* information about the device's computation; if this extra information is correlated with the secret, it may be exploitable. This information can come from a variety of observables: timing, electromagnetic radiation, power consumption, etc. Since power consumption can usually be measured by externally probing the connection of the device with its power supply, it is one of the easiest of these side-channels to exploit, and it is our focus in this discussion.

2.1   First-Order Power Analysis Attacks

First-order attacks are characterized by the property that they exploit highly local correlation of the secret with the power trace. Typically, the secret-correlated power draw occurs at a consistent time during the encryption and has consistent sign and magnitude.

Simple Power Analysis (SPA). In simple first-order power analysis attacks, the adversary is assumed to have some fairly explicit knowledge of the analyzed cryptosystem. In particular, he knows the time at which the power consumption is correlated with part of the secret. By measuring the power consumption at this time (and perhaps averaging over a few encryptions to reduce the ambiguity introduced by noise), he gains some information about the key.

As a simple example, suppose the attacker knows that the first bit of the key k_0 is loaded into a register at $100\mu s$ into the encryption. The average power draw at $100\mu s$ is m, but when the k_0 is 0 this average is $m - \delta$ and when k_0 is 1, this average is $m + \delta$. Given enough samples of the power draw at $100\mu s$ to distinguish these means (where the number of samples required depends on the level of noise relative to δ), he can determine the first bit of the key.

Differential Power Analysis (DPA). One of the most amazing and trouble-some features of differential power analysis is that, unlike with SPA, the attacker does not need such specific information about how the analyzed device implements its function. In particular, she can be ignorant of the specific times at which the power consumption is correlated with the secret; it is only necessary that the correlation is reasonably consistent.

In differential power analysis attacks, the attacker has identified some intermediate value in the computation that is 1) correlated with the power consumption, and 2) dependent only on the plaintext (or ciphertext or both) and some small part of the key. She gathers a collection of *power traces* by sampling power consumption at a very high frequency throughout a series of encryptions of different plaintexts. If the intermediate value is sufficiently correlated with the power consumption, the adversary can use the power traces to verify guesses at the small part of the key.

In particular, for each possible value of relevant part of the key, the attacker will divide the traces into groups according to the intermediate value predicted by current guess at the key and the trace's corresponding plaintext (or ciphertext); if the averaged power trace of each group differs noticeably from the others (the averaged differences will have a large difference at the time of correlation), it is likely that the current key guess is correct. Since incorrectly predicted intermediate value will not be correlated with the measured power traces, incorrect key guesses should result in all groups having very similar averaged power traces.

2.2   Higher-Order Attacks

A higher-order attack addresses a situation where there is some intermediate value (or set of values) that depends only on the plaintext and some small part of the key, but it is not correlated directly with the power consumption at any particular time. Instead, this value contributes to the joint distribution of the power consumption at a few times during the computation.

An important example of such a situation comes about when the *masking* (or duplication) technique is employed to protect against first-order attacks. As a typical example of masking, consider an implementation that wishes to perform a computation using some intermediate, key-dependent bit b. Rather than computing directly with b and opening itself up to DPA attacks, however, it performs the computation twice: once with a random bit r, then with the *masked bit* $(r + b)$.[1] The implementation is designed to use these two masked intermediate results as inputs to the rest of the computation.

In this case, knowledge of either r or $r + b$ alone is not of any use to the attacker. Since the first-order attacks look for local, linear correlation of b with the power draw, they are stymied. If, however, an attack could correlate the power

---

[1] Though we use the symbol '+' to denote the masking operation, we require nothing from it other than that $c = a + b$ implies $(-1)^c = (-1)^{a+b}$; for our purposes, it is convenient to just assume that '+' is exclusive-or.

consumption at the time r is present and the time $r+b$ is present (e.g., by multiplying the power consumptions at these times), it could gain some information on b.

For example, suppose a cryptographic device employs masking to hide some intermediate bit b that is derived directly from the key, but displays the following behavior: at $100\mu s$, the average power draw is $m + \delta(-1)^r$ and at $210\mu s$ it is $m + \delta(-1)^{(r+b)}$. An attacker aware of this fact could multiply the samples at these times for each trace and obtain a product value with expected value[2]

$$\mathbb{E}[\text{product of samples}] = \begin{cases} m^2 + \delta^2 & \text{if } b = 0 \\ m^2 - \delta^2 & \text{if } b = 1 \end{cases} \tag{1}$$

Summing the samples over n encryptions, the means would be $n(m^2+\delta^2)$ for $b = 0$ and $n(m^2-\delta^2)$ for $b = 1$. By choosing n large enough to reduce the relative effect of noise, the attacker could distinguish these distributions and deduce b. An attack of this sort is the second-order analog of an SPA attack.

But how practical is this really? A higher-order attack seems to face two major problems:

 - How much does the process of correlation amplify the noise, thereby increasing standard deviation and requiring more samples to reliably differentiate distributions?
 - How does it identify the times when the power consumption is correlated with an intermediate value?

The first issue is apparent when calculating the standard deviation of the product computed in the above attack. If the power consumption at times $100\mu s$ and $210\mu s$ both have standard deviation σ, then the product has standard deviation

$$\sigma_{\text{product}} = \begin{cases} \sqrt{\sigma^4 + 2\sigma^2 m^2 + 4\delta^2 m^m + 2\delta^2\sigma^2} & \text{if } b = 0, \\ \sqrt{\sigma^4 + 2\sigma^2 m^2 + 2\delta^2\sigma^2} & \text{if } b = 1 \end{cases} \tag{2}$$

effectively squaring the standard deviation of zero-mean noise. This means that substantially many more samples are required to distinguish the $b = 0$ and $b = 1$ distributions than would be required in a first-order attack, if one were possible.

The second issue is essentially the higher-order analog of the problem with SPA: attackers require exact knowledge of the time at which the intermediate value and the power consumption are correlated. DPA resolves this problem by considering many samples of the power consumption throughout an encryption. Unfortunately, the natural generalization of this approach to even second-order attacks, where a product would be accumulated for each (t_1, t_2) time pair, is extremely computationally taxing. The second-order attacks discussed in this paper avoid this overhead.

---

[2] Here the expectation is taken over both the random noise and the value of the masking bit r, and the noise components at times $100\mu s$ and $210\mu s$ are assumed independent.

3   The Power Analysis Model

Both of the attacks we present are second-order attacks which are essentially preprocessing steps applied to the power traces followed by standard DPA.

In this section, we develop our model and present standard DPA in this framework, both as a point of reference and as a necessary subroutine for our attacks, which are described in Section 4.

3.1   The Model

We assume that the attacker has guessed part of the key and has predicted an intermediate bit value b for each of the power traces, grouping them into a $b = 0$ and a $b = 1$ group. For simplicity, we assume there are n traces in each of these groups: trace i from group b is called T_i^b, where $0 \leq i < n$. Each trace contains samples at m evenly spaced times; the sample at time t from this trace is denoted $T_i^b(t)$, where $0 \leq t < m$.

Each sample has a *noise* component and possibly a *signal* component, if it is correlated with b. We assume that each noise component is Gaussian with equal standard deviation and independent of the noise in other samples in its own trace and other traces. For simplicity, we also assume that the input has been normalized so that each noise component is a 0-mean Gaussian with standard deviation one (i.e., $\sim \mathcal{N}(0, 1)$). The random variable for the noise component in trace i from group b at time t is $S_i^b(t)$, for $0 \leq t < m$.

We assume that the device being analyzed is utilizing masking so that there is a uniformly distributed independent random variable for each trace that corresponds to the masking bit; it will be more convenient for us to deal with $\{\pm 1\}$ bit values, so if the random bit in trace i from group b is r, we define the random variable $R_i^b = (-1)^r$.

Finally, if the guess for b is correct, the power consumption is correlated with the random masking bit and the intermediate value b at the same times in each trace. Specifically, we assume that there is some parameter d (in units of the standard deviation of the noise) and times c_0 and c_1 such that the random bit makes a contribution of dR_i^b to the power consumption at time c_0 and the masked bit makes a contribution of $d(-1)^b R_i^b$ at time c_1.

We can now characterize the trace sample distributions in terms of these noise and signal components:

- If the guess of the key is correct, then for $0 \leq i < n$, $0 \leq t < m$, and $b \in \{0, 1\}$, we have:

$$T_i^b(t) = \begin{cases} S_i^b(t) + dR_i^b & \text{if } t = c_0 \\ S_i^b(t) + d(-1)^b R_i^b & \text{if } t = c_1 \\ S_i^b(t) & \text{otherwise} \end{cases} \tag{3}$$

- If the key is predicted incorrectly, however, then the groups are not correlated with the true value of b in each trace and hence there is no correlation between the grouping and the power consumption in the traces, so, for $0 \leq i < n$, $0 \leq t < m$, and $b \in \{0, 1\}$:

$$T_i^b(t) = S_t^b(t) \tag{4}$$

Given these traces as inputs, the algorithms try to decide whether the groupings (and hence the guess for the key) are correct by distinguishing these distributions.

3.2   The Generic DPA Subroutine

Both algorithms use a subroutine DPA after their preprocessing step. For our purposes, this subroutine simply takes the two groups of traces, T^0 and T^1, a threshold value τ, and determines whether the groups' totalled traces differ by more than τ at any sample time. If the difference of the totalled traces is greater than τ at any point, DPA returns 1, indicating that T^0 and T^1 have different distributions; if the difference is no more than τ at any point, DPA returns 0, indicating that it thinks T^0 and T^1 are identically distributed.

$\text{DPA}(T^0, T^1, \tau)$
1 :   for each $t \in \{0, \ldots, m - 1\}$:
2 : $s \leftarrow 0$
3 :   for each $i \in \{0, \ldots, n - 1\}$:
4 : $s \leftarrow s + T_i^0(t) - T_i^1(t)$
5 :   if $|s| > \tau$ return 1
6 :   return 0

When using the DPA subroutine, it is most important to pick the threshold, τ, appropriately. Typically, to minimize the impact of false positives and false negatives, τ should be half the difference. This is perhaps unexpected since false positives are actually far more likely than false negatives when using a midpoint threshold test since false positives can occur if *any* of the m times' samples sum deviates above τ, while false negatives require exactly the correlated time's samples to deviate below τ. The reason for not choosing τ to equalize the probabilities is that false negatives are far more detrimental than false positives: an attack suggesting two likely subkeys is more helpful than an attack suggesting none.

An equally important consideration in using DPA is whether τ is large enough compared to the noise to reduce the probability of error. Typically, the samples' noise components will be independent and the summed samples' noise will be Gaussian, so we can can achieve negligible probability of error by using n large enough that τ is some constant multiple of the standard deviation.

DPA runs in time $\Theta(nm)$. Each run of DPA decides the correctness of only one guessed grouping, however, so an attack that tries l groupings runs in time $\Theta(nml)$.

4   Our Second-Order Attacks

The two second-order variants of DPA that we discuss are Zero-Offset 2DPA and FFT 2DPA. The former is applied in the special but not necessarily unlikely situation when the power correlation times for the two bits are coincident (i.e., the random bit r and the masked bit $r + b$ are correlated with the power consumption at the same time). The latter attack applies to the more general situation where the attacker does not know the times of correlation; it discovers the correlation with only slight computational overhead but pays a price in the number of required samples.

4.1   Zero-Offset 2DPA

Zero-Offset 2DPA is a very simple variation of ordinary first-order DPA that can be applied against systems that employ masking in such a way that both the random bit r and the masked intermediate bit $r + b$ correlate with the power consumption at the same time. In the language of our model, $c_0 = c_1$.

The coincident effect of the two masked values may seem to be too specialized of a circumstance to occur in practice, but it does come up. The motivation for this attack is the claim by Coron and Goubin [3] that some techniques suggested by Messerges [4] were insecure due to some register containing the multi-bit intermediate value a or its complement $\bar{a}$. Since Messerges assumes a power consumption model based on Hamming weight, it was not clear how a first-order attack would exploit this register. However, we observe that such a system can be attacked (even in the Hamming model) by a Zero-Offset 2DPA that uses as its intermediate value the exclusive-or of the first two bits of a. Another example of a situation with coincident power consumption correlation is in a paired circuit design that computes with both the random and masked inputs in parallel.

Combining $c_0 = c_1$ with Equation (3), we see that in a correct grouping:

$$T_i^b(t) = \begin{cases} S_i^b(t) + dR_i^b + d(-1)^b R_i^b & \text{if } t = c_0 \\ S_i^b(t) & \text{otherwise} \end{cases} \qquad (5)$$

In an incorrect grouping, $T_i^b(t)$ is distributed exactly as in the general uncorrelated case in Equation (4).

Note that in a correct grouping, when $b = 1$, the influence of the two bits cancel, leaving $T_i^1(c_0) = S_i^1(c_0)$, while when $b = 0$, the influences of the two bits combine constructively and we get $T_i^0(c_0) = S_i^0(c_0) + 2dR_i^0$. In the former case, there appears to be no influence of the bits on the power consumption distribution, but in the latter case, the bits contribute a bimodal component. The bimodal component has mean 0, however, so it would not be apparent in a first-order averaging analysis.

Zero-offset 2DPA exploits the bimodal component for the $b = 0$ case by simply squaring the samples in the power traces before running straight DPA.

```
Zero-Offset-2DPA(T⁰, T¹)
1 :     for each b ∈ {0,1}, i ∈ {0, ... , n}, t ∈ {0, ... , m}:
2 :         Tᵢᵇ(t) ← (Tᵢᵇ(t))²
3 :     return DPA(T⁰, T¹, 2nd²)
```

Why does this work? Suppose we have a correct grouping and consider the expected values for the sum of the squares of the samples at time c_0 in the two groups:

– if $b = 0$,

$$\mathbb{E}\left[\sum_{i=0}^{n-1}[T_i^0(c_0)]^2\right] = \sum_{i=0}^{n-1}\mathbb{E}[(S_i^0(c_0))^2 + 4dS_i^0(c_0)R_i^0 + 4d^2(R_i^0)^2]$$

$$= \sum_{i=0}^{n-1}\left(\mathbb{E}[(S_i^0(c_0))^2] + \mathbb{E}[4dS_i^0(c_0)R_i^0] + \mathbb{E}[4d^2(R_i^0)^2]\right)$$

$$= \sum_{i=0}^{n-1}(1 + 0 + 4d^2)$$

$$= 4nd^2 + n \tag{6}$$

– if $b = 1$,

$$\mathbb{E}\left[\sum_{i=0}^{n-1}[T_i^1(c_0)]^2\right] = \sum_{i=0}^{n-1}\mathbb{E}[(S_i^1(c_0))^2]$$

$$= \sum_{i=0}^{n-1}1$$

$$= n \tag{7}$$

The above derivations use the fact that if $S \sim \mathcal{N}(0,1)$ then $S^2 \sim \chi^2(1,0)$ (i.e., S^2 has χ^2 distribution with $\nu = 1$ degree of freedom and non-centrality parameter $\delta^2 = 0$), and the expected value of a $\chi^2(\nu, \delta^2)$ random variable is $\nu + \delta^2$.

Thus, the expected difference of the sum of products for the c_0 samples is $4nd^2$, while the expected difference for incorrect groupings is clearly 0. In Section A.1, we show that the difference of the groups' sums of products is essentially Gaussian with standard deviation

$$\sigma = \sqrt{n(16d^2 + 4)}. \tag{8}$$

For an attack that uses a DPA threshold value at least k standard deviations from the mean, we will need at least $k^2 \cdot \frac{(4d^2+1)}{4d^4}$ traces. This $\frac{(4d^2+1)}{4d^4}$ blowup factor may be substantial; recall that d is in units of the standard deviation of the noise, so it may be significantly less than 1.

The preprocessing in Zero-Offset-DPA takes time $\Theta(nm)$. After this preprocessing, each of l subsequent guessed groupings can be tested using DPA in time $\Theta(nm)$, for a total runtime of $\Theta(nm + nml) = \Theta(nml)$. It is important to keep in mind when comparing these run times that the number n of required traces for Zero-Offset-DPA can be somewhat larger than would be necessary for first-order DPA—if a first-order attack were possible.

A Natural Variation: Known-Offset 2DPA. If the difference $s = c_1 - c_0$ is non-zero but known, a similar attack may be mounted. Instead of calculating the squares of the samples, the adversary can calculate the lagged product:

$$L_i^b(t, s) = T_i^b(t) \cdot T_i^b(t + s), \tag{9}$$

where the addition $t + s$ is intended to be cyclic in $\{0, \ldots n - 1\}$.

This lagged product at the correct offset $s = c_1 - c_0$ has properties similar to the squared samples discussed above, and can be used in the same way.

4.2 FFT 2DPA

Fast Fourier Transform (FFT) 2DPA is useful in that it is more general than Zero-Offset 2DPA: it does not require that the times of correlation be coincident, and it does not require any particular information about c_0 and c_1.

To achieve this, it uses the FFT to compute the *correlation* of a trace with itself—an *autocorrelation*. The autocorrelation A_i^b of a trace T_i^b is also defined on values $t \in \{0, \ldots, m - 1\}$, but this argument is considered an *offset* or *lag* value rather than an absolute time. Specifically, for $b \in \{0, 1\}$, $0 \le i < n$, and $0 \le t < m$,

$$A_i^b(t) = \sum_{j=0}^{m-1} T_i^b(j) \cdot T_i^b(j + t) \tag{10}$$

The argument $t + j$ in $T_i^b(j + t)$ is understood to be cyclic in $\{0, \ldots, m - 1\}$, so that $A_i^b(t) = A_i^b(m - t)$, and we really only need to consider $0 \le t \le m/2$.

To see why $A_i^b(t)$ might be useful, recall Equation (3) and notice that most of the terms of $A_i^b(t)$ are of the form $S_i^b(j) \cdot S_i^b(j + t)$; in fact, the only terms that differ are where j or $j + t$ is c_0 or c_1. This observation suggests a way to view the sum for $A_i^b(t)$ by splitting it up by the different types of terms from Equation (3), and in fact it is instructive to do so. To simplify notation, let $Q = \{c_0 - t, c_0, c_1 - t, c_1\}$, the set of "interesting" indices, where the terms of $A_i^b(t)$ are "unusual" when $j \in Q$. Assuming $t \ne c_1 - c_0$,

$$\begin{aligned}
A_i^b(t) = {} & S_i^b(c_0 - t) \cdot [S_i^b(c_0) + dR_i^b] \\
& + [S_i^b(c_0) + dR_i^b] \cdot S_i^b(c_0 + t) \\
& + S_i^b(c_1 - t) \cdot [S_i^b(c_1) + d(-1)^b R_i^b] \\
& + [S_i^b(c_1) + d(-1)^b R_i^b] \cdot S_i^b(c_1 + t) \\
& + \sum_{j \notin Q} S_i^b(j) \cdot S_i^b(j + t)
\end{aligned} \tag{11}$$

and we can distribute and recombine terms to get

$$A_i^b(t) = [S_i^b(c_0 - t) + S_i^b(c_0 + t)] \cdot dR_i^b$$
$$+ [S_i^b(c_1 - t) + S_i^b(c_1 + t)] \cdot d(-1)^b R_i^b$$
$$+ \sum_{j=0}^{m-1} S_i^b(j) \cdot S_i^b(j + t). \tag{12}$$

Using Equation (12) and the fact that $\mathbb{E}[XY] = \mathbb{E}[X] \cdot \mathbb{E}[Y]$ when X and Y are independent random variables, it is straightforward to verify that $\mathbb{E}[A_i^b(t)] = 0$ when $t \neq c_1 - c_0$; its terms in that case are products involving some 0-mean independent random variable (this is exactly what we show in Equation (15)). On the other hand, $A_i^b(c_1 - c_0)$ involves terms that are products of dependent random variables, as can be seen by reference to Equation (10). We make frequent use of Equation (12) in our derivations in this section and in Appendix A.2.

This technique requires a subroutine to compute the autocorrelation of a trace:

Autocorrelate(T)
1 : $F \leftarrow \text{FFT}(T)$
2 :   for each $t \in \{0, \ldots, m - 1\}$:
3 : $F(t) \leftarrow |F(t)|^2$
4 :   return Inv-FFT(F)

The $|F(t)|^2$ in line 3 is the squared $\mathcal{L}_2$-norm of the complex number $F(t)$ (i.e., $|F(t)|^2 = \overline{F(t)} \cdot F(t)$, where $\overline{\alpha}$ denotes the complex conjugate of α).

The subroutine FFT computes the usual Discrete Fourier Transform:

$$(\text{FFT}(T))(x) = \sum_{j=0}^{m-1} T(j) \cdot \omega^{-xj} \tag{13}$$

and Inv-FFT computes the Inverse Discrete Fourier Transform:

$$(\text{Inv-FFT}(T))(y) = \frac{1}{m} \sum_{j=0}^{m-1} T(j) \cdot \omega^{xj} \tag{14}$$

In the above equations, ω is a complex primitive mth root of unity (i.e., $\omega \in \mathbb{C}$, $\omega^m = 1$, and $\omega^k \neq 1$ for all $0 < k < m$).

The subroutines FFT, Inv-FFT, and therefore Autocorrelate itself all run in time $\Theta(m \log m)$.

We can now define the top-level FFT-2DPA algorithm:

FFT-2DPA(T^0, T^1, τ)
1 :   for each $b \in \{0, 1\}$, $t \in \{0, \ldots, m - 1\}$:
2 : $Z^b(t) \leftarrow 0$
3 :   for each $b \in \{0, 1\}$, $i \in \{0, \ldots, n - 1\}$:
4 : $A^b \leftarrow \text{Autocorrelate}(T_i^b)$

5 :   for each $t \in \{0, \ldots, m-1\}$:
6 : $Z^b(t) \leftarrow Z^b(t) + A^b(t)$
7 :   return $\text{DPA}(Z^0, Z^1, nd^2)$

What makes this work? Assuming a correct grouping, the expected sums are:

$- \; t \neq c_1 - c_0$:

$$
\begin{aligned}
\mathbb{E}[Z^b(t)] &= \mathbb{E}\left[\sum_{i=0}^{n-1} \sum_{j=0}^{m-1} (T_i^b(j) \cdot T_i^b(j+t)) \right] \\
&= n \sum_{j=0}^{m-1} \mathbb{E}[T_0^b(j) \cdot T_0^b(j+t)] \\
&= n\,\mathbb{E}\left[[S_0^b(c_0 - t) + S_0^b(c_0 + t)] \cdot dR_0^b \right] \\
&\quad + n\,\mathbb{E}\left[[S_0^b(c_1 - t) + S_0^b(c_1 + t)] \cdot d(-1)^b R_0^b \right] \\
&\quad + nm\,\mathbb{E}\left[S_0^b(0) \cdot S_0^b(0+t) \right] \\
&= 0
\end{aligned}
\tag{15}
$$

$- \; t = (c_1 - c_0)$:

$$
\begin{aligned}
\mathbb{E}[Z^b(t)] &= \mathbb{E}\left[\sum_{i=0}^{n-1} \sum_{j=0}^{m-1} (T_i^b(j) \cdot T_i^b(j+t)) \right] \\
&= n \sum_{j=0}^{m-1} \mathbb{E}[T_0^b(j) \cdot T_0^b(j+t)] \\
&= n\,\mathbb{E}\left[[S_0^b(c_0 - t) + S_0^b(c_1)] \cdot dR_0^b \right] \\
&\quad + n\,\mathbb{E}\left[[S_0^b(c_0) + S_0^b(c_1 + t)] \cdot d(-1)^b R_0^b \right] \\
&\quad + n\,\mathbb{E}[d^2 (R_0^b)^2 (-1)^b] \\
&\quad + nm\,\mathbb{E}\left[S_0^b(0) \cdot S_0^b(0+t) \right] \\
&= 0 + 0 + n\,\mathbb{E}[d^2 (R_0^b)^2 (-1)^b] + 0 \\
&= nd^2(-1)^b
\end{aligned}
\tag{16}
$$

So in a correct grouping, we have

$$
\mathbb{E}[Z^0(t) - Z^1(t)] = \begin{cases} 2nd^2 & \text{if } t = c_1 - c_0 \\ 0 & \text{otherwise.} \end{cases}
\tag{17}
$$

In incorrect groupings, however, $\mathbb{E}[Z^0(t) - Z^1(t)] = 0$ for all $t \in \{0, \ldots, m-1\}$.

In Section A.2, we see that this distribution is closely approximated by a Gaussian with standard deviation $\sigma = \sqrt{n(8d^2 + 2m)}$, so that an attacker who wishes to use a threshold at least k standard deviations away from the mean needs n to be at least about $k^2 \cdot \frac{(4d^2+m)}{2d^4}$.

Note that the noise from the other samples contributes significantly to the standard deviation at $Z^b(c_1 - c_0)$, so this attack would only be practical for relatively short traces and a significant correlated bit influence (i.e., when m is small and d is not much smaller than 1).

The preprocessing in FFT-2DPA runs in time $\Theta(nm \log m)$. After this preprocessing, however, each of l guessed groupings can be tested using DPA in time $\Theta(nm)$, for a total runtime of $\Theta(nm \log m + nml)$, amortizing to $\Theta(nml)$ if $l = \Omega(\log m)$. Again, when considering this runtime, it is important to keep in mind that the number n of required traces can be substantially larger than would be necessary for first-order DPA—if a first-order attack were possible.

FFT and Known-Offset 2DPA. It might be very helpful in practice to use the FFT in second-order power analysis attacks for attempting to determine the offset of correlation. With a few traces, it could be possible to use an FFT to find the offset s of repeated computations, such as when the same function is computed with the random bit r at time c_0 and with the masked bit $r + b$ at time $c_0 + s$.

With even a few values of s suggested by an FFT on these traces, a Known-Offset 2DPA attack could be attempted, which could require far fewer traces than straight FFT 2DPA since Known-Offset 2DPA suffers from less noise amplification.

5   Conclusion

We explored two second-order attacks that attempt to defeat masking while minimizing computation resource requirements in terms of space and time.

The first, Zero-Offset 2DPA, works in the special situation where the masking bit and the masked bit are coincidentally correlated with the power consumption, either canceling out or contributing a bimodal component. It runs with almost no noticeable overhead over standard DPA, but the number of required power traces increases more quickly with the relative noise present in the power consumption.

The second technique, FFT 2DPA, works in the more general situation where the attacker knows very little about the device being analyzed and suffers only logarithmic overhead in terms of runtime. On the other hand, it also requires many more power traces as the relative noise increases.

In summary, we expect that Zero-Offset 2DPA and Known-Offset 2DPA can be of some practical use, but FFT 2DPA probably suffers from too much noise amplification to be generally effective. However, if the traces are fairly short and the correlated bit influence fairly large, it can be effective.

References

1. Paul Kocher, Joshua Jaffe, and Benjamin Jun, "Differential Power Analysis," in proceedings of *Advances in Cryptology—CRYPTO '99*, Springer-Verlag, 1999, pp. 388-397.
2. Thomas Messerges, "Using Second-Order Power Analysis to Attack DPA Resistant Software," *Lecture Notes in Computer Science*, 1965:238-??, 2001.
3. Jean-Sébastien Coron and Louis Goubin, "On Boolean and Arithmetic Masking against Differential Power Analysis", in *Proceedings of Workshop on Cryptographic Hardware and Embedded Systems*, Springer-Verlag, August 2000.
4. Thomas S. Messerges, "Securing the AES Finalists Against Power Analysis Attacks," in *Proceedings of Workshop on Cryptographic Hardware and Embedded Systems*, Springer-Verlag, August 1999, pp. 144-157.

A   Noise Amplification

In this section, we attempt to characterize the distribution of the estimators that we use to distinguish the target distributions. In particular, we show that the estimators have near-Gaussian distributions and we calculate their standard deviations.

A.1   Zero-Offset 2DPA

As in Section 4.1, we assume that the times of correlation are coincident, so that $c_0 = c_1$. From this, we get that the distribution of the samples in a correct grouping follows Equation (5):

$$T_i^b(t) = \begin{cases} S_i^b(t) + dR_i^b + d(-1)^b R_i^b & \text{if } t = c_0 \\ S_i^b(t) & \text{otherwise} \end{cases} \tag{18}$$

The sum

$$\sum_{i=0}^{n-1} [T_i^0(c_0)]^2 = \sum_{i=0}^{n-1} [S_i^0(c_0) + 2dR_i^0]^2 \tag{19}$$

is then a $\chi^2(\nu, \delta^2)$-distributed random variable with $\nu = n$ degrees of freedom and non-centrality parameter $\delta^2 = \sum_{i=0}^{n-1}(2dR_i^0)^2 = 4nd^2$. It has mean $\nu + \delta^2 = 4nd^2 + n$ and standard deviation $\sqrt{2(\nu + 2\delta^2)} = \sqrt{2(n + 8nd^2)} = \sqrt{n(16d^2 + 2)}$.

A common rule of thumb is that χ^2-distributed random variables with over thirty degrees of freedom are closely approximated by Gaussians. We expect $n \gg 30$, so we say

$$\sum_{i=0}^{n-1} [T_i^0(c_0)]^2 \sim \mathcal{N}\left(4nd^2 + n, \sqrt{n(16d^2 + 2)}\right). \tag{20}$$

Similarly, we obtain $\sum_{i=0}^{n-1}[T_i^1(c_0)]^2 \sim \chi^2(n, 0)$, which, since $n \gg 30$, we approximate with

$$\sum_{i=0}^{n-1}[T_i^1(c_0)]^2 \sim \mathcal{N}\left(n, \sqrt{2n}\right). \tag{21}$$

The difference of the summed squares is then

$$\sum_{i=0}^{n-1}\left[(T_i^0(c_0))^2 - (T_i^1(c_0))^2\right] \sim \mathcal{N}\left(4nd^2, \sqrt{n(16d^2 + 4)}\right). \tag{22}$$

A.2   FFT 2DPA

Recalling our discussion from Section 4.2, we want to examine the distribution of

$$Z^b(t) = \sum_{i=0}^{n-1}\sum_{j=0}^{m-1} T_i^b(j) \cdot T_i^b(j+t). \tag{23}$$

when $t = c_1 - c_0$. Its standard deviation should dominate that of $Z^b(t')$ for $t' \neq c_1 - c_0$ (for simplicity, we assume $c_1 - c_0 \neq c_0 - c_1$).

In Section 4.2, we saw that $\mathbb{E}[Z^b(t)] = nd^2(-1)^b$. We would now like to calculate its standard deviation.

In the following, we liberally use the fact that

$$\mathrm{Var}[X + Y] = \mathrm{Var}[X] + \mathrm{Var}[Y] + 2\,\mathrm{Cov}[X, Y], \tag{24}$$

where $\mathrm{Cov}[X, Y]$ is the *covariance* of X and Y ($\mathrm{Cov}[X, Y] \triangleq \mathbb{E}[XY] - \mathbb{E}[X]\,\mathbb{E}[Y]$). We would often like to add variances of random variables that are not independent; Equation (24) says we can do so if the random variables have 0 covariance.

Since the traces are independent and identically distributed,

$$\begin{aligned}
\mathrm{Var}[Z^b(t)] &= \sum_{i=0}^{n-1} \mathrm{Var}\left[\sum_{j=0}^{m-1} T_i^b(j) \cdot T_i^b(j+t)\right] \\
&= n\,\mathrm{Var}\left[\sum_{j=0}^{m-1} T_0^b(j) \cdot T_0^b(j+t)\right] \\
&= n\,\mathrm{Var}\left[dR_0^b([S_i^b(c_0 - t) + S_0^b(c_1)] + (-1)^b[S_0^b(c_0) + S_0^b(c_1 + t)])\right] \\
&\quad + n\,\mathrm{Var}\left[\sum_{j=0}^{m-1} S_0^b(j) \cdot S_0^b(j+t)\right]
\end{aligned} \tag{25}$$

where we were able to split the variance in the last line since the two terms have 0 covariance.

To calculate $\operatorname{Var}\left[dR_0^b([S_0^b(c_0 - t) + S_0^b(c_1)] + (-1)^b[S_0^b(c_0) + S_0^b(c_1 + t)])\right]$, note that its terms have 0 covariance. For example:

$$
\begin{aligned}
\operatorname{Cov}[dR_0^b S_0^b(c_0 - t), dR_0^b S_0^b(c_1)] &= \mathbb{E}[(dR_0^b)^2 S_0^b(c_0 - t) \cdot S_0^b(c_1)] \\
&\quad - \mathbb{E}[dR_0^b S_0^b(c_0 - t)] \mathbb{E}[dR_0^b S_0^b(c_1)] \\
&= 0 - 0 = 0
\end{aligned}
\tag{26}
$$

since the expectation of a product involving an independent 0-mean random variable is 0. Furthermore, it is easy to check that each term has the same variance, and

$$
\begin{aligned}
\operatorname{Var}[dR_0^b S_0^b(c_1)] &= \mathbb{E}\left[[dR_0^b S_0^b(c_1)]^2\right] - \mathbb{E}[dR_0^b S_0^b(c_1)]^2 \\
&= d^2 \, \mathbb{E}\left[[S_0^b(c_1)]^2\right] - 0 \\
&= d^2,
\end{aligned}
\tag{27}
$$

for a total contribution of

$$
\operatorname{Var}\left[dR_0^b([S_0^b(c_0 - t) + S_0^b(c_1)] + (-1)^b[S_0^b(c_0) + S_0^b(c_1 + t)])\right] = 4d^2.
\tag{28}
$$

The calculation of $\operatorname{Var}\left[\sum_{j=0}^{m-1} S_0^b(j) \cdot S_0^b(j + t)\right]$ is similar since its terms also have covariance 0 and they all have the same variance. Thus,

$$
\begin{aligned}
\operatorname{Var}\left[\sum_{j=0}^{m-1} S_0^b(j) S_0^b(j + t)\right] &= m \operatorname{Var}[S_0^b(0) S_0^b(0 + t)] \\
&= m \left(\mathbb{E}\left[[S_0^b(0)]^2 [S_0^b(t)]^2\right] - \mathbb{E}[S_0^b(0) S_0^b(t)]^2\right) \\
&= m(1 + 0) = m.
\end{aligned}
\tag{29}
$$

Finally, plugging Equations (28) and (29) into Equation (25), we get the result

$$
\operatorname{Var}[Z^b(t)] = n(m + 4d^2)
\tag{30}
$$

and the corresponding standard deviation is $\sqrt{n(m + 4d^2)}$.

As in Section A.1, we expect n to be large and we say

$$
Z^b(t) \sim \mathcal{N}\left(nd^2(-1)^b, \sqrt{n(4d^2 + m)}\right).
\tag{31}
$$

Finally, we get the distribution of the difference:

$$
Z^0(t) - Z^1(t) \sim \mathcal{N}\left(2nd^2, \sqrt{n(8d^2 + 2m)}\right).
\tag{32}
$$

Correlation Power Analysis with a Leakage Model

Eric Brier, Christophe Clavier, and Francis Olivier

Gemplus Card International, France
Security Technology Department
{eric.brier, christophe.clavier, francis.olivier}@gemplus.com

Abstract. A classical model is used for the power consumption of cryptographic devices. It is based on the Hamming distance of the data handled with regard to an unknown but constant reference state. Once validated experimentally it allows an optimal attack to be derived called Correlation Power Analysis. It also explains the defects of former approaches such as Differential Power Analysis.

Keywords: Correlation factor, CPA, DPA, Hamming distance, power analysis, DES, AES, secure cryptographic device, side channel.

1 Introduction

In the scope of statistical power analysis against cryptographic devices, two historical trends can be observed. The first one is the well known differential power analysis (DPA) introduced by Paul Kocher [12,13] and formalized by Thomas Messerges et al. [16]. The second one has been suggested in various papers [8,14,18] and proposed to use the correlation factor between the power samples and the Hamming weight of the handled data. Both approaches exhibit some limitations due to unrealistic assumptions and model imperfections that will be examined more thoroughly in this paper. This work follows previous studies aiming at either improving the Hamming weight model [2], or enhancing the DPA itself by various means [6,4].

The proposed approach is based on the Hamming distance model which can be seen as a generalization of the Hamming weight model. All its basic assumptions were already mentioned in various papers from year 2000 [16,8,6,2]. But they remained allusive as possible explanation of DPA defects and never leaded to any complete and convenient exploitation. Our experimental work is a synthesis of those former approaches in order to give a full insight on the data leakage. Following [8,14,18] we propose to use the correlation power analysis (CPA) to identify the parameters of the leakage model. Then we show that sound and efficient attacks can be conducted against unprotected implementations of many algorithms such as DES or AES. This study deliberately restricts itself to the scope of secret key cryptography although it may be extended beyond.

This paper is organized as follows: Section 2 introduces the Hamming distance model and Section 3 proves the relevance of the correlation factor. The

M. Joye and J.-J. Quisquater (Eds.): CHES 2004, LNCS 3156, pp. 16–29, 2004.

model based correlation attack is described in Section 4 with the impact on the model errors. Section 5 addresses the estimation problem and the experimental results which validate the model are exposed in Section 6. Section 7 contains the comparative study with DPA and addresses more specifically the so-called "ghost peaks" problem encountered by those who have to deal with erroneous conclusions when implementing classical DPA on the substitution boxes of the DES first round: it is shown there how the proposed model explains many defects of the DPA and how the correlation power analysis can help in conducting sound attacks in optimal conditions. Our conclusion summarizes the advantages and drawbacks of CPA versus DPA and reminds that countermeasures work against both methods as well.

2   The Hamming Distance Consumption Model

Classically, most power analyses found in literature are based upon the Hamming weight model [13,16], that is the number of bits set in a data word. In a m-bit microprocessor, binary data is coded $D = \sum_{j=0}^{m-1} d_j 2^j$, with the bit values $d_j = 0$ or 1. Its Hamming weight is simply the number of bits set to 1, $H(D) = \sum_{j=0}^{m-1} d_j$. Its integer values stand between 0 and m. If D contains m independent and uniformly distributed bits, the whole word has an average Hamming weight $\mu_H = m/2$ and a variance $\sigma_H^2 = m/4$.

It is generally assumed that the data leakage through the power side-channel depends on the number of bits switching from one state to the other [6,8] at a given time. A microprocessor is modeled as a state-machine where transitions from state to state are triggered by events such as the edges of a clock signal. This seems relevant when looking at a logical elementary gate as implemented in CMOS technology. The current consumed is related to the energy required to flip the bits from one state to the next. It is composed of two main contributions: the capacitor's charge and the short circuit induced by the gate transition. Curiously, this elementary behavior is commonly admitted but has never given rise to any satisfactory model that is widely applicable. Only hardware designers are familiar with simulation tools to foresee the current consumption of microelectronic devices.

If the transition model is adopted, a basic question is posed: what is the reference state from which the bits are switched? We assume here that this reference state is a constant machine word, R, which is unknown, but not necessarily zero. It will always be the same if the same data manipulation always occurs at the same time, although this assumes the absence of any desynchronizing effect. Moreover, it is assumed that switching a bit from 0 to 1 or from 1 to 0 requires the same amount of energy and that all the machine bits handled at a given time are perfectly balanced and consume the same.

These restrictive assumptions are quite realistic and affordable without any thorough knowledge of microelectronic devices. They lead to a convenient expression for the leakage model. Indeed the number of flipping bits to go from R to D is described by $H(D \oplus R)$ also called the Hamming distance between D

and R. This statement encloses the Hamming weight model which assumes that $R = 0$. If D is a uniform random variable, so is $D \oplus R$, and $H(D \oplus R)$ has the same mean $m/2$ and variance $m/4$ as $H(D)$.

We also assume a linear relationship between the current consumption and $H(D \oplus R)$. This can be seen as a limitation but considering a chip as a large set of elementary electrical components, this linear model fits reality quite well. It does not represent the entire consumption of a chip but only the data dependent part. This does not seem unrealistic because the bus lines are usually considered as the most consuming elements within a micro-controller. All the remaining things in the power consumption of a chip are assigned to a term denoted b which is assumed independent from the other variables: b encloses offsets, time dependent components and noise. Therefore the basic model for the data dependency can be written:

$$W = aH(D \oplus R) + b$$

where a is a scalar gain between the Hamming distance and W the power consumed.

3   The Linear Correlation Factor

A linear model implies some relationships between the variances of the different terms considered as random variables: $\sigma_W^2 = a^2 \sigma_H^2 + \sigma_b^2$. Classical statistics introduce the correlation factor ρ_{WH} between the Hamming distance and the measured power to assess the linear model fitting rate. It is the covariance between both random variables normalized by the product of their standard deviations. Under the uncorrelated noise assumption, this definition leads to:

$$\rho_{WH} = \frac{\mathrm{cov}(W, H)}{\sigma_W \sigma_H} = \frac{a\sigma_H}{\sigma_W} = \frac{a\sigma_H}{\sqrt{a^2\sigma_H^2 + \sigma_b^2}} = \frac{a\sqrt{m}}{\sqrt{ma^2 + 4\sigma_b^2}}$$

This equation complies with the well known property: $-1 \leq \rho_{WH} \leq +1$: for a perfect model the correlation factor tends to ± 1 if the variance of noise tends to 0, the sign depending on the sign of the linear gain a. If the model applies only to l independent bits amongst m, a partial correlation still exists:

$$\rho_{WH_{l/m}} = \frac{a\sqrt{l}}{\sqrt{ma^2 + 4\sigma_b^2}} = \rho_{WH}\sqrt{\frac{l}{m}}$$

4   Secret Inference Based on Correlation Power Analysis

The relationships written above show that if the model is valid the correlation factor is maximized when the noise variance is minimum. This means that ρ_{WH} can help to determine the reference state R. Assume, just like in DPA, that a set of known but randomly varying data D and a set of related power consumption W are available. If the 2^m possible values of R are scanned exhaustively they can be ranked by the correlation factor they produce when combined with the observation W. This is not that expensive when considering an 8-bit micro-controller, the case with many of today's smart cards, as only 256 values are to be tested. On 32-bit architectures this exhaustive search cannot be applied as such. But it is still possible to work with partial correlation or to introduce prior knowledge.

Let R be the true reference and $H = H(D \oplus R)$ the right prediction on the Hamming distance. Let R' represent a candidate value and H' the related model $H' = H(D \oplus R')$. Assume a value of R' that has k bits that differ from those of R, then: $H(R \oplus R') = k$. Since b is independent from other variables, the correlation test leads to (see [5]):

$$\rho_{WH'} = \frac{\mathrm{cov}(aH + b, H')}{\sigma_W \sigma'_H} = \frac{a}{\sigma_W} \frac{\mathrm{cov}(H, H')}{\sigma'_H} = \rho_{WH}\rho_{HH'} = \rho_{WH} \frac{m - 2k}{m}$$

This formula shows how the correlation factor is capable of rejecting wrong candidates for R. For instance, if a single bit is wrong amongst an 8-bit word, the correlation is reduced by $1/4$. If all the bits are wrong, i-e $R' = \neg R$, then an anti-correlation should be observed with $\rho_{WH'} = -\rho_{WH}$. In absolute value or if the linear gain is assumed positive ($a > 0$), there cannot be any R' leading to a higher correlation rate than R. This proves the uniqueness of the solution and therefore how the reference state can be determined.

This analysis can be performed on the power trace assigned to a piece of code while manipulating known and varying data. If we assume that the handled data is the result of a XOR operation between a secret key word K and a known message word M, $D = K \oplus M$, the procedure described above, i-e exhaustive search on R and correlation test, should lead to $K \oplus R$ associated with $\max(\rho_{WH})$. Indeed if a correlation occurs when M is handled with respect to R_1, another has to occur later on, when $M \oplus K$ is manipulated in turn, possibly with a different reference state R_2 (in fact with $K \oplus R_2$ since only M is known).

For instance, when considering the first *AddRoundKey* function at the beginning of the AES algorithm embedded on an 8-bit processor, it is obvious that such a method leads to the whole key masked by the constant reference byte R_2. If R_2 is the same for all the key bytes, which is highly plausible, only 2^8 possibilities remain to be tested by exhaustive search to infer the entire key material. This complementary brute force may be avoided if R_2 is determined by other means or known to be always equal to 0 (on certain chips).

This attack is not restricted to the $\oplus$ operation. It also applies to many other operators often encountered in secret key cryptography. For instance, other arithmetic, logical operations or look-up tables (LUT) can be treated in the same manner by using $\mathrm{H}(\mathrm{LUT}(M \star K) \oplus R)$, where $\star$ represents the involved function i.e. $\oplus$, $+$, $-$, OR, AND, or whatever operation. Let's notice that the ambiguity between K and $K \oplus R$ is completely removed by the substitution boxes encountered in secret key algorithms thanks to the non-linearity of the corresponding LUT: this may require to exhaust both K and R, but only once for R in most cases. To conduct an analysis in the best conditions, we emphasize the benefit of correctly modeling the whole machine word that is actually handled and its transition with respect to the reference state R which is to be determined as an unknown of the problem.

5   Estimation

In a real case with a set of N power curves W_i and N associated random data words M_i, for a given reference state R the known data words produce a set of N predicted Hamming distances $H_{i,R} = H(M_i \oplus R)$. An estimate $\hat{\rho}_{WH}$ of the correlation factor ρ_{WH} is given by the following formula:

$$\hat{\rho}_{WH}(R) = \frac{N \sum W_i H_{i,R} - \sum W_i \sum H_{i,R}}{\sqrt{N \sum W_i^2 - (\sum W_i)^2} \sqrt{N \sum H_{i,R}^2 - (\sum H_{i,R})^2}}$$

where the summations are taken over the N samples ($i = 1, N$) at each time step within the power traces $W_i(t)$.

It is theoretically difficult to compute the variance of the estimator $\hat{\rho}_{WH}$ with respect to the number of available samples N. In practice a few hundred experiments suffice to provide a workable estimate of the correlation factor. N has to be increased with the model variance $m/4$ (higher on a 32-bit architecture) and in presence of measurement noise level obviously. Next results will show that this is more than necessary for conducting reliable tests. The reader is referred to [5] for further discussion about the estimation on experimental data and optimality issues. It is shown that this approach can be seen as a maximum likelihood model fitting procedure when R is exhausted to maximize $\hat{\rho}_{WH}$.

6   Experimental Results

This section aims at confronting the leakage model to real experiments. General rules of behavior are derived from the analysis of various chips for secure devices conducted during the passed years.

Our first experience was performed onto a basic XOR algorithm implemented in a 8-bit chip known for leaking information (more suitable for didactic purpose). The sequence of instructions was simply the following:

 − load a byte D_1 into the accumulator
 − XOR D_1 with a constant D_2
 − store the result from the accumulator to a destination memory cell.

The program was executed 256 times with D_1 varying from 0 to 255. As displayed on Figure 1, two significant correlation peaks were obtained with two different reference states: the first one being the address of D_1, the second one the opcode of the XOR instruction. These curves bring the experimental evidence of leakage principles that previous works just hint at, without going into more detail [16,8,6,17]. They illustrate the most general case of a transfer sequence

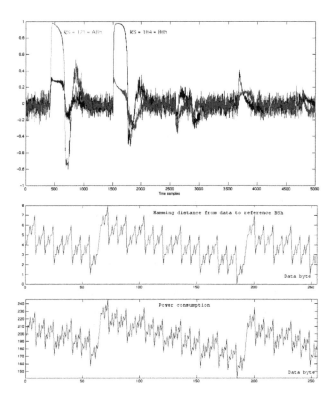

Fig. 1. Upper: consecutive correlation peaks for two different reference states. Lower: for varying data (0-255), model array and measurement array taken at the time of the second correlation peak.

on a common bus. The address of a data word is transmitted just before its value that is in turn immediately followed by the opcode of the next instruction which is fetched. Such a behavior can be observed on a wide variety of chips even those implementing 16 or 32-bit architectures. Correlation rates ranging from 60% to more than 90% can often be obtained. Figure 2 shows an example of partial correlation on a 32-bit architecture: when only 4 bits are predicted among 32, the correlation loss is in about the ratio $\sqrt{8}$ which is consistent with the displayed correlations.

This sort of results can be observed on various technologies and implementations. Nevertheless the following restrictions have to be mentioned:

- Sometimes the reference state is systematically 0. This can be assigned to the so-called pre-charged logic where the bus is cleared between each transferred value. Another possible reason is that complex architectures implement separated busses for data and addresses, that may prohibit certain transitions. In all those cases the Hamming weight model is recovered as a particular case of the more general Hamming distance model.

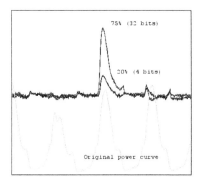

Fig. 2. Two correlation peaks for full word (32 bits) and partial (4 bits) predictions. According to theory the 20% peak should rather be around 26%.

- The sequence of correlation peaks may sometimes be blurred or spread over the time in presence of a pipe line.
- Some recent technologies implement hardware security features designed to impede statistical power analysis. These countermeasures offer various levels of efficiencies going from the most naive and easy to bypass, to the most effective which merely cancel any data dependency.

There are different kinds of countermeasures which are completely similar to those designed against DPA.

- Some of them consist in introducing desynchronization in the execution of the process so that the curves are not aligned anymore within a same acquisition set. For that purpose there exist various techniques such as fake cycles insertion, unstable clocking or random delays [6,18]. In certain cases their effect can be corrected by applying appropriate signal processing.
- Other countermeasures consist in blurring the power traces with additional noise or filtering circuitry [19]. Sometimes they can be bypassed by curves selection and/or averaging or by using another side channel such as electromagnetic radiation [9,1].
- The data can also be ciphered dynamically during a process by hardware (such as bus encryption) or software means (data masking with a random [11,7,20,10]), so that the handled variables become unpredictable: then no correlation can be expected anymore. In theory sophisticated attacks such as higher order analysis [15] can overcome the data masking method; but they are easy to thwart in practice by using desynchronization for instance.

Indeed, if implemented alone, none of these countermeasures can be considered as absolutely secure against statistical analyses. They just increase the amount of effort and level of expertise required to achieve an attack. However combined defenses, implementing at least two of these countermeasures, prove to be very efficient and practically dissuasive. The state of the art of countermeasures in the design of tamper resistant devices has made big advances in the recent years.

It is now admitted that security requirements include sound implementations as much as robust cryptographic schemes.

7   Comparison with DPA

This section addresses the comparison of the proposed CPA method with Differential Power Analysis (DPA). It refers to the former works done by Messerges et al. [16,17] who formalized the ideas previously suggested by Kocher [12,13]. A critical study is proposed in [5].

7.1   Practical Problems with DPA: The "Ghost Peaks"

We just consider hereafter the practical implementation of DPA against the DES substitutions (1st round). In fact this well-known attack works quite well only if the following assumptions are fulfilled:

1. Word space assumption: within the word hosting the predicted bit, the contribution of the non-targeted bits is independent of the targeted bit value. Their average influence in the curves pack of 0 is the same as that in the curves pack of 1. So the attacker does not need to care about these bits.
2. Guess space assumption: the predicted value of the targeted bit for any wrong sub-key guess does not depend on the value associated to the correct guess.
3. Time space assumption: the power consumption W does not depend on the value of the targeted bit except when it is explicitly handled.

But when confronted to the experience, the attack comes up against the following facts.

- *Fact A*. For the correct guess, DPA peaks appear also when the targeted bit is not explicitly handled. This is worth being noticed albeit not really embarrassing. However this contradicts the third assumption.
- *Fact B*. Some DPA peaks also appear for wrong guesses: they are called "ghost peaks". This fact is more problematic for making a sound decision and comes in contradiction with the second assumption.
- *Fact C*. The true DPA peak given by the right guess may be smaller than some ghost peaks, and even null or negative! This seems somewhat amazing and quite confusing for an attacker. The reasons must be searched for inside the crudeness of the optimistic first assumption.

7.2   The "Ghost Peaks" Explanation

With the help of a thorough analysis of substitution boxes and the Hamming distance model it is now possible to explain the observed facts and show how wrong the basic assumptions of DPA can be.

Fact A. As a matter of fact some data handled along the algorithm may be partially correlated with the targeted bit. This is not that surprising when looking at the structure of the DES. A bit taken from the output nibble of a SBox has a lifetime lasting at least until the end of the round (and beyond if the left part of the IP output does not vary too much). A DPA peak rises each time this bit and its 3 peer bits undergo the following P permutation since they all belong to the same machine word.

Fact B. The reason why wrong guesses may generate DPA peaks is that the distributions of an SBox output bit for two different guesses are deterministic and so possibly partially correlated. The following example is very convincing about that point. Let's consider the leftmost bit of the fifth SBox of the DES when the input data D varies from 0 to 63 and combined with two different sub-keys : $\mathrm{MSB}(\mathrm{SBox}_5(D \oplus 0x00))$ and $\mathrm{MSB}(\mathrm{SBox}_5(D \oplus 0x36))$. Both series of bits are respectively listed hereafter, with their bitwise XOR on the third line:

11011010100101100010010110010011101010010110110101010100100010101101
10011010110101100010010111010010101011010110100101010010100010111001
01000000010000000000000001000001000001000000010000000000000010100

The third line contains 8 set bits, revealing only eight errors of prediction among 64. This example shows that a wrong guess, say 0, can provide a good prediction at a rate of $56/64$, that is not that far from the correct one $0x36$. The result would be equivalent for any other pair of sub-keys K and $K \oplus 0x36$. Consequently a substantial concurrent DPA peak will appear at the same location than the right one. The weakness of the contrast will disturb the guesses ranking especially in presence of high SNR.

Fact C. DPA implicitly considers the word bits carried along with the targeted bit as uniformly distributed and independent from the targeted one. This is erroneous because implementation introduces a deterministic link between their values. Their asymmetric contribution may affect the height and sign of a DPA peak. This may influence the analysis on the one hand by shrinking relevant peaks, on the other hand by enhancing meaningless ones. There exists a well known trick to bypass this difficulty as mentioned in [4]. It consists in shifting the DPA attacks a little bit further in the processing and perform the prediction just after the end of the first round when the right part of the data (32 bits) is XORed with the left part of the IP output. As the message is chosen freely, this represents an opportunity to re-balance the loss of randomness by bringing new refreshed random data. But this does not fix *Fact B* in a general case .

To get rid of these ambiguities the model based approach aims at taking the whole information into account. This requires to introduce the notion of algorithmic implementation that DPA assumptions completely occult.

When considering the substitution boxes of the DES, it cannot be avoided to remind that the output values are 4-bit values. Although these 4 bits are in principle equivalent as DPA selection bits, they live together with 4 other bits in the context of an 8-bit microprocessor. Efficient implementations use to exploit those 4 bits to save some storage space in constrained environments like smart card chips. A trick referred to as "SBox compression" consists in storing 2 SBox values within a same byte. Thus the required space is halved. There are different ways to implement this. Let's consider for instance the 2 first boxes: instead of allocating 2 different arrays, it is more efficient to build up the following look-up table: $LUT_{12}(k) = SBox_1(k) \parallel SBox_2(k)$. For a given input index k, the array byte contains the values of two neighboring boxes. Then according to the Hamming distance consumption model, the power trace should vary like:

- $H(LUT_{12}(D_1 \oplus K_1) \oplus R_1)$ when computing $SBox_1$.
- $H(LUT_{12}(D_2 \oplus K_2) \oplus R_2)$ when computing $SBox_2$.

If the values are bind like this, their respective bits cannot be considered as independent anymore. To prove this assertion we have conducted an experiment on a real 8-bit implementation that was not protected by any DPA countermeasures. Working in a "white box" mode, the model parameters had been previously calibrated with respect to the measured consumption traces. The reference state $R = 0xB7$ had been identified as the Opcode of an instruction transferring the content of the accumulator to RAM using direct addressing. The model fitted the experimental data samples quite well; their correlation factor even reached 97%. So we were able to simulate the real consumption of the Sbox output with a high accuracy. Then the study consisted in applying a classical single bit DPA to the output of $SBox_1$ in parallel on both sets of 200 data samples: the measured and the simulated power consumptions.

As figure 3 shows, the simulated and experimental DPA biases match particularly well. One can notice the following points:

- The 4 output bits are far from being equivalent.
- The polarity of the peak associated to the correct guess 24 depends on the polarity of the reference state. As $R = 0xB7$ its leftmost nibble aligned with $SBox_1$ is $0xB = $ '1011' and only the selection bit 2 (counted from the left) results in a positive peak whereas the 3 others undergo a transition from 1 to 0, leading to a negative peak.
- In addition this bit is a somewhat lucky bit because when it is used as selection bit only guess 50 competes with the right sub-key. This is a particular favorable case occurring here on $SBox_1$, partly due to the set of 200 used messages. It cannot be extrapolated to other boxes.
- The dispersion of the DPA bias over the guesses is quite confuse (see bit 4).

The quality of the modeling proves that those facts cannot be incriminated to the number of acquisitions. Increasing it much higher than 200 does not help: the level of the peaks with respect to the guesses does not evolve and converges to the same ranking. This particular counter-example proves that the ambiguity of DPA does not lie in imperfect estimation but in wrong basic hypotheses.

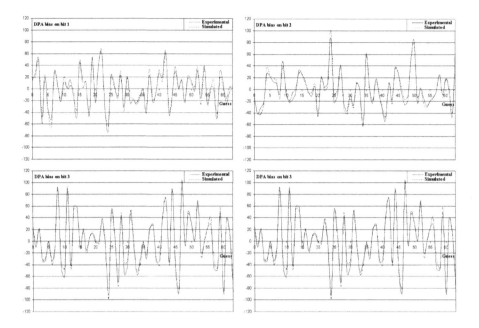

Fig. 3. DPA biases on SBox$_1$ versus guesses for selection bits 1, 2, 3 and 4, on modeled and experimental data; the correct guess is 24.

7.3   Results of Model Based CPA

For comparison the table hereafter provides the ranking of the 6 first guesses sorted by decreasing correlation rates. This result is obtained with as few as only 40 curves! The full key is 11 22 33 44 55 66 77 88 in hexadecimal format and the corresponding sub-keys at the first round are 24, 19, 8, 8, 5, 50, 43, 2 in decimal representation.

SBox$_1$		SBox$_2$		SBox$_3$		SBox$_4$		SBox$_5$		SBox$_6$		SBox$_7$		SBox$_8$	
K	ρ_{max}	K	ρ_{max}	K	ρ_{max}	K	ρ_{max}	K	ρ_{max}	K	ρ_{max}	K	ρ_{max}	K	ρ_{max}
24	92%	19	90%	8	87%	8	88%	5	91%	50	92%	43	89%	2	89%
48	74%	18	77%	18	69%	44	67%	32	71%	25	71%	42	76%	28	77%
01	74%	57	70%	05	68%	49	67%	25	70%	05	70%	52	70%	61	76%
33	74%	02	70%	22	66%	02	66%	34	69%	54	70%	38	69%	41	72%
15	74%	12	68%	58	66%	29	66%	61	67%	29	69%	0	69%	37	70%
06	74%	13	67%	43	65%	37	65%	37	67%	53	67%	30	68%	15	69%

This table shows that the correct guess always stands out with a good contrast. Therefore a sound decision can be made without any ambiguity despite a rough estimation of ρ_{max}.

A similar attack has also been conducted on a 32-bit implementation, in a white box mode with a perfect knowledge of the implemented substitution tables and the reference state which was 0. The key was 7C A1 10 45 4A 1A 6E 57 in hexadecimal format and the related sub-keys at the 1st round were 28, 12, 43, 0, 15, 60, 5, 38 in decimal representation. The number of curves is 100. As next table shows, the contrast is good between the correct and the most competing wrong guess (around 40% on boxes 1 to 4). The correlation rate is not that high on boxes 5 to 8, definitely because of partial and imperfect modeling, but it proves to remain exploitable and thus a robust indicator. When the number of bits per machine word is greater, the contrast between the guesses is relatively enhanced, but finding the right model could be more difficult in a black box mode.

SBox$_1$		SBox$_2$		SBox$_3$		SBox$_4$		SBox$_5$		SBox$_6$		SBox$_7$		SBox$_8$	
K	ρ_{max}	K	ρ_{max}	K	ρ_{max}	K	ρ_{max}	K	ρ_{max}	K	ρ_{max}	K	ρ_{max}	K	ρ_{max}
28	77%	12	69%	43	73%	0	82%	15	52%	60	51%	5	51%	38	47%
19	36%	27	29%	40	43%	29	43%	03	33%	10	34%	15	40%	05	29%
42	35%	24	27%	36	35%	20	35%	58	30%	58	33%	6	29%	55	26%
61	31%	58	27%	06	33%	60	32%	10	30%	18	31%	12	29%	39	25%

8   Conclusion

Our experience on a large set of smart card chips over the last years has convinced us on the validity of the Hamming distance model and the advantages of the CPA method against DPA, in terms of efficiency, robustness and number of experiments. An important and reassuring conclusion is that all the countermeasures designed against DPA offer the same defensive efficiency against the model based CPA attack. This is not that surprising since those countermeasures aim at undermining the common prerequisites that both approaches are based on: side-channel observability and intermediate variable predictability.

The main drawback of CPA regards the characterization of the leakage model parameters. As it is more demanding than DPA, the method may seem more difficult to implement. However it may be objected that:

- A statistical power analysis of any kind is never conducted blindly without any preliminary reverse engineering (process identification, bit tracing): this is the opportunity to quantify the leakage rate by CPA on known data.
- DPA requires more sample curves anyway since all the unpredicted data bits penalize the signal to noise ratio (see [5]).
- If DPA fails by lack of implementation knowledge (increasing the number of curves does not necessarily help), we have shown how to infer a part of this information without excessive efforts: for instance the reference state is to be found by exhaustive search only once in general.
- There exists many situations where the implementation variants (like SBox implementation in DES) are not so numerous because of operational constraints.
- If part of the model cannot be inferred (SBox implementation in DES, hardware co-processor), partial correlation with the remainder may still provide exploitable indications.

Eventually DPA remains relevant in case of very special architectures for which the model may be completely out of reach, like in certain hard wired co-processors.

References

1. D. Agrawal, B. Archambeault, J.R. Rao, and P. Rohatgi. The EM side channel(s): Attacks and assessment methodologies. In *Cryptographic Hardware and Embedded Systems — CHES 2002*, LNCS 2523, pp. 29–45, Springer-Verlag, 2002. See also http://www.research.ibm.com.intsec/emf-paper.ps.
2. M.L. Akkar, R. Bévan, P. Dischamp, and D. Moyart. Power analysis, what is now possible... In *Advances in Cryptology — ASIACRYPT 2000*, LNCS 1976, pp. 489–502, Springer-Verlag, 2000.
3. M.L. Akkar and C. Giraud. An Implementation of DES and AES secure against some attacks. In *Cryptographic Hardware and Embedded Systems — CHES 2001*, LNCS 2162 pp. 309–318, Springer-Verlag, 2001.
4. R. Bévan and R. Knudsen. Ways to enhance differential power analysis. In *Information Security and Cryptology — ICISC 2002*, LNCS 2587, pp. 327–342, Springer-Verlag, 2002.
5. E. Brier, C. Clavier, and F. Olivier. Optimal statistical power analysis. http://eprint.iacr.org/2003/152/.
6. C. Clavier, J.-S. Coron, and N. Dabbous. Differential power analysis in the presence of hardware countermeasures. In *Cryptographic Hardware and Embedded Systems — CHES 2000*, LNCS 1965, pp. 252–263, Springer-Verlag, 2000.
7. J.-S. Coron and L. Goubin. On Boolean and arithmetic masking against differential power analysis. In *Cryptographic Hardware and Embedded Systems — CHES 2000*, LNCS 1965, pp. 231–237, Springer-Verlag, 2000.
8. J.-S. Coron, P. Kocher, and D. Naccache. Statistics and secret leakage. In *Financial Cryptography (FC 2000)*, LNCS 1972, pp. 157–173, Springer-Verlag, 2001.
9. K. Gandolfi, C. Mourtel, and F. Olivier. Electromagnetic attacks: Concrete results. In *Cryptographic Hardware and Embedded Systems — CHES 2001*, LNCS 2162, pp. 252–261, Springer-Verlag, 2001.
10. J. Golić and C. Tymen. Multiplicative masking and power analysis of AES. In *Cryptographic Hardware and Embedded Systems — CHES 2002*, LNCS 2523, pp. 198–212, Springer-Verlag, 2002.
11. L. Goubin and J. Patarin. DES and differential power analysis. In *Cryptographic Hardware and Embedded Systems (CHES '99)*, LNCS 1717, pp. 158–172, Springer-Verlag, 1999.
12. P. Kocher, J. Jaffe, and B. Jun. Introduction to differential power analysis and related attacks. http://www.cryptography.com.
13. P. Kocher, J. Jaffe, and B. Jun. Differential power analysis. In *Advances in Cryptology — CRYPTO '99*, LNCS 1666, pp. 388–397, Springer-Verlag, 1999.
14. R. Mayer-Sommer. Smartly analysing the simplicity and the power of simple power analysis on smartcards. In *Cryptographic Hardware and Embedded Systems — CHES 2000*. LNCS 1965, pp. 78–92, Springer-Verlag, 2000.
15. T.S. Messerges. Using second-order power analysis to attack DPA resistant software. In *Cryptographic Hardware and Embedded Systems — CHES 2000*. LNCS 1965, pp. 238–252, Springer-Verlag, 2000.

16. T. Messerges, E. Dabbish, and R. Sloan. Investigation of power analysis attacks on smartcards. In *Usenix Workshop on Smartcard Technology 1999*. `http://www.usenix.org`.
17. T. Messerges, E. Dabbish, and R. Sloan. Examining smart-card security under the threat of power analysis attacks. *IEEE Transactions on Computers*, 51(5): 541–552, May 2002.
18. E. Oswald. On Side-Channel Attacks and the Application of Algorithmic Countermeasures. PhD Thesis, Faculty of Science of the University of Technology Graz (IAIK-TUG), Austria, May 2003.
19. A. Shamir. Protecting smart cards from passive power analysis with detached power supplies. In *Cryptographic Hardware and Embedded Systems — CHES 2000*. LNCS 1965, pp. 71–77, Springer-Verlag, 2000.
20. E. Trichina, D. De Seta, and L. Germani. Simplified adaptive multiplicative masking for AES. In *Cryptographic Hardware and Embedded Systems — CHES 2002*, LNCS 2523, pp. 187–197, Springer-Verlag, 2002.

Power Analysis of an FPGA

Implementation of Rijndael:
Is Pipelining a DPA Countermeasure?

François-Xavier Standaert[1], Sıddıka Berna Örs[2] , and Bart Preneel[2]

[1] UCL Crypto Group, Laboratoire de Microélectronique
Université Catholique de Louvain,
Place du Levant, 3, B-1348 Louvain-La-Neuve, Belgium standaert@dice.ucl.ac.be
[2] Katholieke Universiteit Leuven, Dept. ESAT/SCD-COSIC,
Kasteelpark Arenberg 10, B-3001 Leuven-Heverlee, Belgium.
siddika.bernaors,bart.preneel@esat.kuleuven.ac.be

Abstract. Since their publication in 1998, power analysis attacks have attracted significant attention within the cryptographic community. So far, they have been successfully applied to different kinds of (unprotected) implementations of symmetric and public-key encryption schemes. However, most published attacks apply to smart cards and only a few publications assess the vulnerability of hardware implementations. In this paper we investigate the vulnerability of Rijndael FPGA (Field Programmable Gate Array) implementations to power analysis attacks. The design used to carry out the experiments is an optimized architecture with high clock frequencies, presented at CHES 2003. First, we provide a clear discussion of the hypothesis used to mount the attack. Then, we propose theoretical predictions of the attacks that we confirmed experimentally, which are the first successful experiments against an FPGA implementation of Rijndael. In addition, we evaluate the effect of pipelining and unrolling techniques in terms of resistance against power analysis. We also emphasize how the efficiency of the attack significantly depends on the knowledge of the design.

1 Introduction

Side-channel analysis is becoming a classical topic in cryptographic design, but although numerous papers investigate Differential Power Analysis (DPA) from a theoretical point of view, only a few articles focus on their practical implementation. Moreover, most of the published research is related to smart cards and only a few papers assess the context of hardware and FPGA implementations.

As soon as hardware design is concerned, the questions of effectiveness, clock frequency and area requirements are of primary importance. In this paper,

* Sıddıka Berna Örs is funded by research grants of the Katholieke Universiteit Leuven, Belgium. This work was supported by Concerted Research Action GOA-MEFISTO-666 of the Flemish Government and by the FWO "Identification and Cryptography" project (G.0141.03).

M. Joye and J.-J. Quisquater (Eds.): CHES 2004, LNCS 3156, pp. 30–44, 2004.

we demonstrate that they also have a very substantial impact on the feasibility of power analysis attacks. For this purpose, we investigated an optimized FPGA implementation of the Advanced Encryption Standard Rijndael [1,2], presented at CHES 2003. In addition to the practical evaluation of the attack, we present a number of original observations concerning: (*i*) the effect of pipelining and unrolling techniques in terms of resistance against power analysis attacks; (*ii*) the relationship between the knowledge of a hardware design and the efficiency of power analysis attacks. (*iii*) the effect of high clock frequencies on the measurement setup. Moreover, we characterized some design components (*e.g.* the registers) in terms of *predictablility* and *leakage*. This results in tools that could be used to analyze power analysis attacks in general. Finally, we compare our results with the only published attack against a hardware implementation of Rijndael that we are aware of [3] to validate our conclusions.

This paper is structured as follows. Section 2 presents the hypothesis used to carry out the power analysis attack and Section 3 gives a short description of our Rijndael implementation. Section 4 describes how to perform theoretical predictions on the power consumption in a pipeline design and Section 5 explains how to use these predictions in order to mount a practical attack. Section 6 presents theoretical predictions of the attack and their practical implementation is discussed in Sect. 7. Additional considerations about pipeline and unrolled designs are presented in Sect. 8. Section 9 re-discusses the hypothesis. Finally, conclusions are in Sect. 10.

2   Hypothesis

In Differential Power Analysis, an attacker uses a hypothetical model of the device under attack to predict its power consumption. These predictions are then compared to the real measured power consumption in order to recover secret information (*e.g.* secret key bits). The quality of the model has a strong impact on the effectiveness of the attack and it is therefore of primary importance.

While little information is available on the design and implementation of FPGAs (much of the information is proprietary), we can make assumptions about how commercial FPGAs behave at the transistor level. The most popular technology used to build programmable logic is static RAM[1], where the storage cells, the logic blocks and the connection blocks are made of CMOS gates. For these circuits, it is reasonable to assume that the main component of the power consumption is the dynamic power consumption. For a single CMOS gate, we can express it as follows [5]:

$$P_{\mathrm{D}} = C_{\mathrm{L}} V_{\mathrm{DD}}^2 \ P_{0 \to 1} f \tag{1}$$

where C_{L} is the gate load capacitance, V_{DD} the supply voltage, $P_{0 \to 1}$ the probability of a $0 \to 1$ output transition and f the clock frequency.

---

[1] For all the experiments, we used a Xilinx Virtex XCV800 FPGA [4].

Equation (1) specifies that the power consumption of CMOS circuits is data-dependent. However, for the attacker, the relevant question is to know if this data-dependent behavior is observable. This was confirmed by the following test.

Let three 4096-bit vectors be defined as follows. Initially, $a_0 = 00000...001$ and $b_0, c_0 = 00000...000$. Then:

$$a_{i+1} = SL(a_i), \quad b_{i+1} = b_i \oplus a_i, \quad c_{i+1} = c_i \oplus b_i,$$

where SL is the shift left operator and consecutive values (x_i, x_{i+1}) are separated by a register. It is easy to see that:

- a is a bit-vector with a constant Hamming weight ($H(a) = 1$). The position of the 1-bit inside the vector is incremented/decremented from 0 to 4095.
- b is a bit-vector for which the Hamming weight is incremented/decremented from 0 to 4095.
- c is a bit-vector for which the number of bit switches between two consecutive states is incremented/decremented from 0 to 4095.

A design that generates these three vectors was implemented in the FPGA.

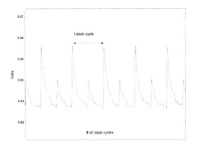

Fig. 1. One single power trace

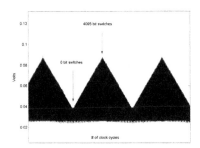

Fig. 2. Preliminary test

Figure 1 illustrates[2] a single power trace. Figure 2 illustrates the power consumption of vectors a, b and c during about 20 000 clock cycles. From this experiment, we conclude that the power consumption clearly depends on the number of transitions in registers.

Based on these considerations, we used the following **hypothesis** to mount power analysis attacks against FPGAs: "an estimation of a device power consumption at time t is given by the number of bit transitions inside the device registers at this time". Predicting the transitions in registers is reasonable since registers usually consume the largest part of the power in a design.

---

[2] Measurement setups for DPA have already been intensively described in the open literature. In Fig. 1, we observe the voltage variations over a small resistor inserted in the supply circuit of the FPGA. Every trace was averaged 10 times in order to remove the noise from our measurements.

3   Hardware Description

A short description of the Rijndael algorithm is given in the Appendix A. The architecture used to investigate DPA against Rijndael was presented last year at CHES 2003 [6]. We briefly describe its significant details.

SubBytes: The substitution box (S-box) is implemented as a 256 x 8 multiplexer and takes advantage of specific properties of the FPGA. Note that two pipeline stages are inserted for efficiency purposes, as represented in Appendix B. In SubBytes, this S-box is applied to the 16 bytes of the state in parallel.

MixAdd: In [6], an efficient combination of MixColums and the key addition is proposed, based on an optimal use of the FPGA resources. The resulting MixAdd transform allows MixColumns and AddRoundKey to be computed in two clock cycles, the key addition being embedded with MixColumns in the second cycle.

Complete architecture: The complete architecture is represented in Fig. 3, where all the registers are 128-bit long[3]. It is a loop architecture with pipeline, designed for optimizing the ratio $Throughput\ (Mbits/s)/Area$ $(slices)$. It is important to remark that the multiplexer model for the S-box implies that its first part uses four 128-bit registers. The resulting design implements the round (and key round) function in 5 clock cycles and the complete cipher in 52 clock cycles.

4   Predictions in a Pipeline Design

The question we assess in this paper is to know whether pipelining has any influence on DPA resistance. We also investigate a practical design that is the result of efficiency optimizations. Loop architectures are a relevant choice for investigation because they satisfy the usual area and throughput requirements for block cipher applications. However, unrolled architectures will also be explored in a further section.

Based on the hypothesis of Sect. 2, the first step in a power analysis attack is to make theoretical predictions on the power consumption. This can be done using a selection function D that we define as follows. Let X_i and X_{i+1} be two consecutive values inside a target register. An estimation of the register power consumption at the time of the transition is given by the function $D = H(X_i \oplus X_{i+1})$. An attacker who has to predict the transitions inside the registers of an implementation therefore needs to answer two basic questions:

1. Which register transitions can we predict?
2. Which register transitions leak information?

Answering these questions determines which registers will be targeted during the attack. As an attacker can use the plaintexts (*resp.* ciphertexts) and predict transitions by partial encryption (*resp.* decryption), it is also important to evaluate both scenarios.

---

[3] Except the first part of Mixadd that is 176-bit long.

4.1   Definitions

i. The *predictability* of a register is related to the number of key bits one should know to predict its transitions. For block ciphers, this depends on the size of the S-boxes and the diffusion layer. In practice, it is assumed that it is possible to guess up to 16 key bits, and the diffusion layer usually prevents guessing of more than one block cipher round. In Rijndael, S-boxes are 8-bit wide and their outputs are thus *predictable* after the first (*resp.* final) key addition. However, every MixColumns output bit depends on 32 key bits and is therefore computationally intensive to guess.

ii. We denote a register as a *full* (*resp. empty*) register if its transitions leak (*resp.* do not leak) secret information. For example, it is obvious that an input (*resp.* output) register does not leak any secret information as it only contains the plaintext (*resp.* ciphertext). A surprising consequence of the hypothesis introduced in Sect. 2 is that the registers following an initial (*resp.* final) key addition do not leak information either. To illustrate this statement, we use the following key addition:

AddKey
{ *result = input ⊕ key*; }

Let assume that the *result* is actually stored in an FPGA register R. Let two consecutive inputs of the key addition be denoted as $input_1$ and $input_2$. Using the previously defined selection function, the register power consumption may be estimated by:

$$P_R \propto H(result_1 \oplus result_2) = H(input_1 \oplus key \oplus input_2 \oplus key)$$
$$= H(input_1 \oplus input_2) \qquad (2)$$

Equation 2 clearly specifies that the register R is *empty*. In practice, registers of our Rijndael implementation will actually remain *empty* as long as the state has not passed through the non-linear S-box. Thereafter, the power consumption depends on $H(sbox(input_1 \oplus key) \oplus sbox(input_2 \oplus key))$ and therefore on the key.

Remark that this observation strongly depends on the hypothesis and selection functions used to perform the attack, what we will discuss further in Sect. 9. Another surprising observation is that the register R may still leak secret information if reset signals are used. This is due to the constant state that reset signals introduce. Then, we have:

$$P_R \propto H(\text{"all zeroes"} \oplus result_1) = H(\text{"all zeroes"} \oplus input_1 \oplus key)$$
$$= H(input_1 \oplus key) \qquad (3)$$

which makes the power consumption dependent on the key again. As a consequence, a secure hardware implementation should not apply reset signals to its inner registers in order to delete this additional information leakage. Note that a similar observation has been used to attack smart card implementations, where the constant state actually corresponds to a constant instruction address.

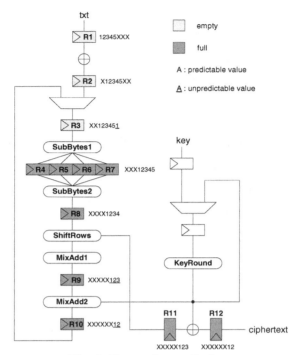

Fig. 3. Encryption predictions.

4.2 Predictions in Rijndael

Figure 3 illustrates *predictable* and *full* registers when our AES design is filled with 5 different texts, denoted 1,2,...,5, during the first eight clock cycles of an encryption. As an example, during the first cycle, register $R1$ contains the plaintext 1 while all the other registers are undefined. During the second cycle, $R1$ contains the plaintext 2, $R2$ contains the plaintext 1 and the other registers are undefined. Remark that in the eighth cycle, the multiplexer starts to loop and register $R3$ therefore contains data corresponding to plaintext 1 again.

Similarly, Figure 4 illustrates *predictable* and *full* registers when our AES design is filled with 5 different texts, denoted 1,2,...,5, during the last six clock cycles of an encryption. As an example, the register $R12$ contains the first ciphertext in the second cycle, ciphertext 2 in the third cycle and ciphertext 3 in the fourth cycle.

In the next section, we explain how theoretical predictions of the power consumption can be used to attack an FPGA implementation of Rijndael.

5 Description of a Correlation Attack

A correlation attack [3,7] against an FPGA implementation of Rijndael is divided into three steps. Let N be the number of plaintext/ciphertext pairs for which the

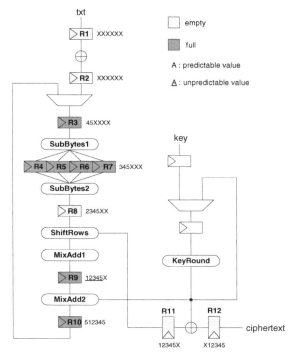

Fig. 4. Decryption predictions.

power consumption measurements are accessible. Let K be the secret encryption key. When simulating the attacks, we assume that K is known to the attacker. In case of practical attacks, it is of course unknown.

Prediction phase: For each of the N encrypted plaintexts, the attacker first selects the target registers and clock cycle for the previously defined selection function D. In Fig. 3, we see that between cycles 7 and 8, registers $R4, R5, R6, R7, R8, R11$ and $R12$ are *full* and have *predictable* and defined values. Similarly, in Fig. 4, we observe that between cycles 1 and 2, registers $R3, R4, R5, R6, R7$ and $R10$ are *full* and have *predictable* and defined values. Depending on the knowledge of the design, these registers can therefore be targeted. Due to the size of the Rijndael S-box, the predictions are performed on 8 bits and may be repeated for every 8-bit part of a register R_i.

Let t be the number of 8-bit registers targeted by the attacker. Then, he predicts the value of D (*i.e.* the number of bit switches inside the target registers in the targeted clock cycle) for the 2^8 possible key guesses and N plaintexts. The result of the prediction phase is an $N \times 2^8$ **selected prediction matrix**, containing integers between 0 and $8 \times t$. For simulation purposes, it is also interesting to produce the **global prediction matrix** that contains the number of bit switches inside all the 12 registers[4] of the design, for all the cycles. That is, if the encryption is performed in 52 clock cycles, we obtain a $N \times 52$ matrix, containing integers between 0 and $12 \times 128 = 1536$. This is only feasible if the key is known. In accordance with the hypothesis of Sect. 2, these matrices give estimations for the power consumption of the device.

Measurement phase: During the measurement phase, we let the FPGA encrypt the same N plaintexts with the same key, as we did in the prediction phase. While the chip is operating, we measure the power consumption for the 52 consecutive clock cycles. Then, the power consumption trace of each encryption is averaged 10 times in order to remove the noise from our measurements and we store the maximum values of each encryption cycle so that we produce an $N \times 52$ matrix with the power consumption values for all the texts, cycles. We denote it as the **global consumption matrix**.

Correlation phase: In the correlation phase, we compute the correlation coefficient between a column of the global consumption matrix (corresponding to the cycle targeted by the prediction phase) and all the columns of the selected prediction matrix (corresponding to all the 2^8 key guesses). If the attack is successful, we expect that only one value, corresponding to the correct key guess, leads to a high correlation coefficient.

An efficient way to perform the correlation between theoretical predictions and real measurements is to use the Pearson coefficient. Let M_i denote the ith measurement data (*i.e.* the ith trace) and M the set of traces. Let P_i denote the prediction of the model for the ith trace and P the set of such predictions. Then we calculate:

$$C(M, P) = \frac{E(M.P) - E(M).E(P)}{\sqrt{Var(M).Var(P)}}. \tag{4}$$

where $E(M)$ denotes the mean of the set of traces M and $Var(M)$ its variance. If this correlation is high, it is usually assumed that the prediction of the model, and thus the key hypothesis, is correct.

Finally, theoretical predictions of the attack can be performed by using the global prediction matrix instead of the global consumption matrix. As the global prediction matrix contains the number of bit switches inside all the registers, it represents a theoretical noise free measurement and may help to determine the minimum number of texts needed to mount a successful attack, *i.e.* an attack where the correct key guess leads to the highest correlation coefficient. This is investigated in the next section.

---

[4] Remark that since the same key is used for all the measurements, the power consumption of the key schedule is fixed and may be considered as a DC component that we can neglect as a first approximation.

6   An Attack Using Simulated Data

In this section, we study the influence of the number of registers predicted on the efficiency of the attack. Different scenarios can be considered that correspond to different abilities of the attacker. In the most basic case, the attacker does not have any information about the design and has to make assumptions about its implementation. A reasonable assumption is that the S-box outputs will be stored in registers[5]. Therefore, the attacker will only predict the switching activity of 8 bits in $R8$ (in encryption) or $R3$ (in decryption). In the first step of the simulated attack, we produce the **selected prediction matrix** and **global prediction matrix** as defined in the previous section. Thereafter, we perform the correlation phase between these two matrixes. If the attack is successful, we expect that only one value, corresponding to the correct key guess, leads to a high correlation coefficient.

As the attacker is interested to determine the minimum number of plaintexts necessary to extract the correct key, we calculated this correlation coefficient for different values of $N : 1 \leq N \leq 4096$. As shown in Fig. 5.(A), after approximately 1500 plaintexts the right 8 key bits can be distinguished from a wrong guess. We may therefore say that the attack is **theoretically successful** after about 1500 texts.

In a more advanced scenario, the attacker has access to some implementation details (for example the scheme of Fig. 3) and may determine the *predictable* and *full* registers. Based on the complete predictions of Fig. 3, the correlation coefficient values for every key guess and different numbers of traces are represented in Fig. 5.(B). We observe that the correct key guess is distinguishable after about 500 plaintexts, but stays closely correlated to 3 other candidates. The explanation of this phenomenon can be found in the implementation details of the substitution box represented in the annexes (Figure 6). As the S-box is a large multiplexer with two pipeline stage, 6 input bits are actually used to select the values in registers $R4, R5, R6, R7$. Thereafter, two last bits select the final result of $R8$. As a consequence, if the key guess is such that the first 6 input bits of the S-box remain unchanged, the values stored in registers $R4, R5, R6, R7$ will be the same. Only the S-box output in register $R8$ will differ. As there are 4 such key guesses, we will have 4 closely correlated candidates, including the correct one, what we can clearly observe in Fig. 5.(B).

A solution to this problem is to use the decryption predictions of Fig. 4. Then, even if only one bit differs at the output of the S-box (in $R8$), it will not result in the same intermediate register transitions. Based on these predictions, the correlation coefficient values for every key guess and different number of traces are represented in Fig. 5.(C), where the correct key candidate is clearly distinguishable after about 500 traces.

---

[5] This is usually the case in Rijndael because S-boxes are the most time (and space) -consuming parts of the algorithm.

7   An Attack Using Practical Measurements

When attacking a device practically, the selected prediction matrix remains unchanged while we replace the global prediction matrix by the real measured global consumption matrix. Therefore, we let the FPGA encrypt 4096 plaintexts with the same key as we did in the previous section and produced the matrix as described in Sect. 5.

To evaluate the quality of our theoretical predictions, we made a preliminary experiment and computed the correlation coefficient between one (in practice the 26th) column of the **global prediction matrix** and every column of the **global consumption matrix**. Figure 5.(D) clearly illustrates that the highest correlation value appears for the predicted round, and therefore confirms that our predictions are correlated with real measurements.

In order to identify the correct 8 MSBs of the final round key, we used the correlation coefficient again. As it is shown in Fig. 5.(E), the correct key guess is distinguishable after about 1000 traces. As a consequence, the attack is **practically successful**, *i.e.* the selected prediction matrix is sufficiently correlated with the real measurements and we can extract the key information. Remark that comparing Figures 5.(C) and 5.(E) allows us to evaluate the effect of the measurement phase. Compared with smart cards, the sampling process was made more difficult by the high clock frequency of the Rijndael design (around 100 MHz). Note also that the noise was removed from the measurements by an averaging process, but this step could be removed or reduced if the measurement setup was improved. Nevertheless, due to the specificities of our acquisition device[6], the averaging was directly done during the measurement step and did not increase the memory requirements of the attack. If we compare these results with the only published power analysis attack against ASIC implementations of Rijndael [3], the quality of our measurements seems to be better. Moreover, we need significantly less plaintexts for the attack to be practically successful.

Finally, it is important to note that more key bits may be found using exactly the same set of measurements. The attacker only has to modify the **selected prediction matrix** and target different key bits. The full key can therefore be recovered computing the correlation between the **global consumption matrix** and 16 predictions, each one revealing 8 key bits.

8   Adding More Pipeline

Previous sections emphasized that pipelining a loop implementation of Rijndael does not provide any efficient protection against DPA. However, the predictions of Sect. 6 also reveal that when only one register (*e.g.* R8 in Fig. 4.(A)) is predicted, we need significantly more traces than when several registers

---

[6] Tektronix TDS 7104 oscilloscope.

are predicted. The efficiency of an attack against a loop implementation is notably due to the fact that most registers are predictable, because only one round is implemented. In case of unrolled and pipelined implementations, the situation strongly differs, as only the outer rounds are partially predictable. As a consequence, the inner rounds may be viewed as noise generators and therefore act as a well known DPA countermeasure. Although noise addition does not fundamentally counteract power analysis attacks (the signal is still present and may still be recovered), it has the advantage of decreasing the correlation between predictions and measurements. Moreover, if the noise is added in the form of unrolled pipeline stages, it does not reduce the efficiency of an implementation. Finally, the method introduced in Sect. 5, allows us to theoretically predict the effect of unrolled architectures with pipelining on resistance against DPA.

A first step to predict the effect of pipeline stages is to investigate the theoretical number of bit switches in a register. In the following, we will assume that the rounds of a block cipher behave like a random number generator. In practice, this is only true after a few rounds, when the diffusion is complete. Based on this hypothesis, we may predict the probability $P(x, n)$ of having x bit switches between two states S_1, S_2 in an n-bit register:

$$P(x, n) = P(H(S_1 \oplus S_2) = x) = \frac{C_{n,x}}{2^n} \tag{5}$$

As a consequence, the number of bit switches is distributed as a binomial which can be approximated by a Gaussian distribution with parameters $\mu = n/2$ and $\sigma^2 = n/4$. It is therefore possible to predict the number of bit switches in registers of arbitrary size.

For example, in the design of Fig. 3, we observe that one round is implemented in 5 cycles, using eight 128-bit registers. Its transitions may be simulated as a Gaussian distributed random noise with parameters $\mu = 512$ and $\sigma^2 = 256$. In general, if an n-round unrolled implementation is considered, we can add Gaussian distributed random noise with parameters $\mu = (n - 1).512$ and $\sigma^2 = (n - 1).256$ to our previously computed global prediction matrix and then compute the correlation with the selected prediction matrix.

The result of an attack using simulated data with 10 rounds unrolled and 5 pipeline stages per round is illustrated in Fig. 5.(F), where we used the same **selected prediction matrix** as in the previous section. While the correct key guess still has the best correlation value, we clearly observe that the correlation value was significantly reduced if we compare with Fig. 5.(C), making a practical attack much more difficult.

9   Hypothesis (2)

Looking back at the hypothesis of Sect. 2, it is important to evaluate how the work presented in this paper could be improved and how representative are our

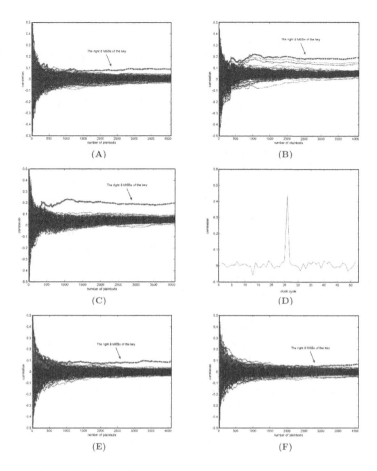

Fig. 5. (A) A simulated attack using register R8 only.
(B) A simulated attack using complete encryption predictions (R4,R5,R6,R7,R8,R11,R12).
(C) A simulated attack using complete decryption predictions (R3,R4,R5,R6,R7,R10).
(D) Correlation between global predictions for cycle 26 and measurements (N = 4096).
(E) A correlation attack with real measurements.
(F) A simulated attack against an unrolled implementation.

results. To the question "Are power analysis attacks realistic against efficient FPGA implementations of Rijndael?" we may certainly answer "yes". While attackers usually investigate "toy" implementations for side-channel attacks, we took a real and optimized design with high clock frequencies and evaluated the significance of pipelining techniques in terms of DPA resistance. From an attacker's point of view, we have investigated the simplest possible hypothesis and built a practical attack based on these simple assumptions. However, the question "How to counteract these power analysis attacks?" is still open in different ways. When countermeasures are considered, it is important to note that our measurements can be improved in several ways; moreover, the attack model should be taken into account.

As an illustration, we limited the transition predictions to the registers of the Rijndael design. However, it is clear that registers are not the only leaking parts in FPGAs and transitions in other components could be predicted in order to improve the attack. Similarly, looking back at Equation (1), a more accurate prediction of the FPGA power consumption could be done by evaluating the load capacitance values. A notifiable feature of FPGAs is that they are made of different resources (*e.g.* logic blocks, connections) of which the power consumption differs because of different effective load capacitances. As a consequence, the power consumption of FPGA designs does not only depend on their switching activity but also on the internal resources used. In practice, more accurate estimations about the most consuming components of an FPGA design can be derived from the delay information that is generated by most implementation tools [8]. As an input delay represents the delay seen by a signal driving that input due to the capacitance along the wire, large (*resp.* small) delay values indicate that the wire has a large (*resp.* small) capacitance. Based on the reports automatically generated by implementation tools, one may expect to recover a very accurate information about the signals that are driving high capacitances. The knowledge of the implementation netlists with delay information is therefore relevant; it will allow an attacker to improve the attack.

Finally, more advanced attack scenarios are possible, *e.g.* taking the key scheduling into account, or using more complex power consumption models. The measurement setup could also be improved and therefore the gap between theoretical predictions of the attacks and practical results would be reduced. To conclude, this paper used a simple leakage model and we could already recover secret information. However, as far as Boolean masking (or other countermeasures) are concerned, it is certainly not sufficient to mask the transitions in registers only and there are other leakage sources to investigate and prevent.

10   Conclusions

We have investigated a power analysis attack against a practical FPGA implementation of Rijndael and have exhibited the effect of pipelining and unrolling techniques in this context. It is first demonstrated that pipelining a loop implementation does not provide an effective countermeasure if an attacker has access to the design details because most of the registers in the pipeline remain predictable. Then we illustrate how the combination of pipelining and unrolling techniques may counteract power analysis attacks as a random noise generator. We also provide a theoretical model allowing the simulation and comparison of the attacks in different contexts. In practice, we have mounted the first successful attack against an efficient FPGA implementation of Rijndael. Finally, a clear discussion of the hypothesis used to perform power analysis is provided with some proposals for further improvements.

References

1. J. Daemen, V. Rijmen, *"The Design of Rijndael. AES – The Advanced Encryption Standard,"* Springer-Verlag, 2001.
2. FIPS 197, *"Advanced Encryption Standard,"* Federal Information Processing Standard, NIST, U.S. Dept. of Commerce, November 26, 2001.
3. S.B.Ors, F.Gurkaynak, E. Oswald, B. Preneel *Power-Analysis Attack on an ASIC AES implementation*, in the proceedings of ITCC 2004, Las Vegas, April 5-7 2004.
4. Xilinx: *Virtex 2.5V Field Programmable Gate Arrays Data Sheet*, http://www.xilinx.com.
5. J.M.Rabaey, *Digital Integrated Circuits*, Prentice Hall International, 1996.
6. F.-X.Standaert, G.Rouvroy, J.-J.Quisquater, J.-D.Legat, *Efficient Implementation of Rijndael Encryption in Reconfigurable Hardware: Improvements and Design Tradeoffs*, in the proceedings of CHES 2003, Lecture Notes in Computer Science, vol 2779, pp 334-350, Springer-Verlag, 2003.
7. E.Brier, C.Clavier, F.Olivier, *Optimal Statistical Power Analysis* , IACR e-print archive 2003/152.
8. L.T. Mc Daniel, *An Investigation of Differential Power Analysis Attacks on FPGA-based Encryption Systems*, Master Thesis, Virginia Polytechnic Insitute and State University, May 29, 2003.
9. P.Kocher, J.Jaffe, B.Jun, *Differential Power Analysis*, in the proceedings of CRYPTO 99, Lecture Notes in Computer Science 1666, pp 398-412, Springer-Verlag.

A   Short Description of Rijndael

Rijndael is an iterated block cipher with a variable block length and a variable key length. The block length and the key length can be independently specified to 128, 192 and 256 bit. This paper focusses on the 128-bit version. The algorithm consists of a serial of 10 applications of a key-dependent round transformation to the cipher state and the round is composed of four different operations. In pseudo C, we have:

Round(state,roundkey)
```
{
SubBytes(state);
ShiftRows(state);
MixColumns(state);
AddRoundKey(state,roundkey);
}
```

SubBytes is a non-linear byte substitution operating on each byte of the state independently. ShiftRows is a cyclic shift of the bytes of the state. In MixColumns, the columns (1 column = 4 bytes) of the state are considered as polynomials over $GF(2^8)$ and multiplied modulo $x^4 + 1$ with a fixed polynomial. Finally, AddRoundKey is a bitwise XOR with the bits of the key.

Rijndael's initial 128-bit key is expanded to eleven 128-bit roundkeys by means of a key scheduling algorithm. Although the key scheduling is also implemented in hardware, its description is not necessary for the understanding of the paper and we will consider it as a black box.

Finally, the complete cipher consists of an initial roundkey addition, 10 rounds and a final round where MixColumns has been removed. In pseudo C, we have:

Rijndael(state,cipherkey)

```
{
KeyExpansion(cipherkey,expandedkey[0..10]);
AddRoundKey(state,expandedkey[0]);
for (i=1;i<10;i++)
    {
    Round(state,expandedkey[i]);
    }
SubBytes(state);
ShiftRows(state);
AddRoundKey(state,expandedkey[10]);
}
```

A more detailed view of the Rijndael algorthm can be found in [1].

B   Implementation of the Substitution Box

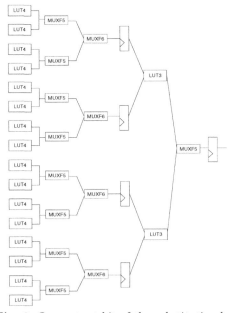

Fig. 6. One output bit of the substitution box.

Long Modular Multiplication for Cryptographic Applications[1]

Laszlo Hars

Seagate Research, 1251 Waterfront Place, Pittsburgh PA 15222, USA
Laszlo@Hars.US

Abstract. A digit-serial, multiplier-accumulator based cryptographic co-processor architecture is proposed, similar to fix-point DSP's with enhancements, supporting long modular arithmetic and general computations. Several new "column-sum" variants of popular quadratic time modular multiplication algorithms are presented (Montgomery and interleaved division-reduction with or without Quisquater scaling), which are faster than the traditional implementations, need no or very little memory beyond the operand storage and perform squaring about twice faster than general multiplications or modular reductions. They provide similar advantages in software for general purpose CPU's.

Keywords: Computer Arithmetic, Cryptography, Modular multiplication, Modular reduction, Montgomery multiplication, Quisquater multiplication, Optimization, Multiply-accumulate architecture, Reciprocal

1 Introduction

Long exponentiation based cryptographic operations are performed infrequently in secure client devices like smart cards or OSD disk drives [15] and it is not economical to include a large piece of HW dedicated only to that task. A DSP-like architecture with minor enhancements for speeding up long modular arithmetic can be used for many other tasks, too, providing an almost free long modular arithmetic engine. A digit-serial, multiplier-accumulator based cryptographic co-processor architecture is proposed, like fix-point DSP's, with inexpensive enhancements for speeding up long modular arithmetic.

Internal fast memory is expensive (storage for eight 2K-bit integers costs about twice as much as the whole arithmetic engine), but only a portion of this memory is needed for processing other than RSA or Diffie-Hellman type operations, so we try to keep this memory small. Several new variants of popular modular multiplication algorithms are presented (Montgomery and interleaved division-reduction with-, or without Quisquater scaling), which either don't need extra memory beyond the parameters or, for extra speed, use one or two additional pre-computed parameters of the size of the modulus. All of these algorithms perform squaring about twice faster than general multiplications and modular reductions. The speed and memory usage advantages of these algorithms are preserved for SW for general purpose CPU's as well.

---

[1] The full version of the paper is at: http://www.hars.us/Papers/ModMult.pdf

M. Joye and J.-J. Quisquater (Eds.): CHES 2004, LNCS 3156, pp. 45–61, 2004.

1.1 Notations

- Long integers are denoted by $A = \{a_{n-1}...a_1a_0\} = \sum d^i a_i$ in a d-ary number system, where a_i ($0 \leq a_i \leq d-1$) are called the **digits**. We consider here $d = 2^{16} = 65,536$, that is 16 bits, but our results directly translate to other digit sizes, like $d = 2^{32}$
- $|A|$ or $|A|_d$ denotes the number of digits, the length of a d-ary number
- $[x]$ stands for the integer part of x.
- $DO(Q)$ refers to the Least Significant digit (digit 0) of an integer or accumulator Q
- $MS(Q)$ refers to the content of the accumulator Q, shifted to the right by one digit
- LS stands for **L**east **S**ignificant, the low order bit/s or digit/s of a number
- MS stands for **M**ost **S**ignificant, the high order bit/s or digit/s of a number
- (*Grammar*) *School multiplication*: the digit-by-digit-multiplication algorithms, as taught in schools. It has 2 variants in the order the digit-products are calculated:
  - Row-order: $for_{i=0...|a|-1} \; for_{j=0...|b|-1} \; ...a_i b_j...$
  - Column-order: $for_{k=0...|a|+|b|-2} \; for_{i,j: \, i+j=k} \; ...a_i b_j...$

2 Computing Architecture

Our experimental HW is clocked at 150 MHz. It is designed around a 16×16-bit single cycle **multiplier**. This is the largest, the most expensive part of the HW after the memory (0.13μm CMOS: 16,000 μm^2). Such circuits have been designed for 300 MHz clock rate and beyond in even for CMOS 0.18 μm technology, often used in smart cards, but they are large and expensive. There are much faster or longer multipliers at smaller feature sizes, like the 370 MHz 36×36-bit multipliers in ALTERA FPGA's [1].

We concentrate on algorithms, which accumulate digit-products in column order, although many of the speed-up techniques are applicable to row multiplications, too [17]. The digits of both multiplicands are constantly reloaded to the multiplier: $C = A \cdot B = \{a_0b_0, \; a_1b_0+a_0b_1, \; a_2b_0+a_1b_1+a_0b_2...\}$. The digit-products are summed in columns. High-speed 40-bit CMOS adders have 5 gates delay, can perform 4 additions in a single clock cycle with time for loading and storing the results in RAM. After a digit-multiplication the 32-bit result is added to the accumulator and the multiplier starts working on the next product. When all digit-products are accumulated for the current digit of C the LS digit from the accumulator is shifted out and stored. By feeding the multiplier and accumulator constantly we achieve sustained single cycle digit multiply-accumulate operations.

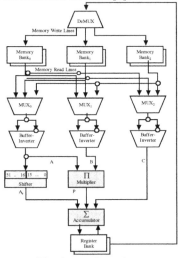

Fig. 1. Dataflow diagram

Memory. To avoid access conflicts separate RAM banks are needed for the operands and the result. Optimal space efficiency requires the ability to change the value of a digit, i.e., read and write to the same memory location within the same clock cycle. It can be done easily at low speed (smart cards), but faster systems need tricky designs. The algorithms presented here would benefit from this read/write capability, which is only needed in one memory bank, holding the temporary results.

At higher clock frequencies some data buffering, pipelining is necessary to run the algorithms at full speed, causing address *offsets* between the read and write phase of the memory update. Because the presented algorithms access their data *sequentially*, *circular* addressing can be used. The updated digit is written to the location where the next digit is being read from, not where the changed digit was originated from. At each update this causes a shift of loci in data storage. The corresponding circular address offset has to be considered at the next access to the data.

This way, one address decoder for this memory bank is enough, with some registers and a little faster memory cells – still less expensive than any other solution. However, it is a custom design; no off-the-shelf (library) memory blocks can be used.

A dual ported memory bank offer simultaneous read/write capabilities, but two single ported RAM banks cost the same and provide double the storage room and more options to optimize algorithms. With 2 banks, data is read from one and the changed data is written to another memory bank, not being accessed by the read logic.

The **accumulator** consists of a couple of 50-bit registers (48 data bits with 2 additional bits for sign and carry/borrow), a barrel shifter and a fast 48-bit adder. It can be laid out as a 32-bit adder and an 18-bit counter for most of our algorithms, performing together up to 3 additions in a clock cycle. One of the inputs is from a 50-bit 2's complement internal register, the other input is selected from the memory banks (can be shifted), from the multiplier or from a (shifted) accumulator register. At the end of the additions, the content of the register can be shifted to the left or (sign extended) to the right and/or the LS digit stored in RAM.

Since only the LS digit is taken out from the accumulator, it can still work on carry propagation while the next addition starts, allowing cheaper designs (0.13µm CMOS: $2,000µm^2$, 12.5% of the area of the multiplier). Some algorithms speed up with one or two internal shift-add operations, effectively implementing a fast multiplier with multiplicands of at most 2 nonzero bits (1, 2, 3, 4, 5, 6; 8, 9,10; 12; 17…).

3 Basic Arithmetic

Addition/Subtraction: In our algorithms digits are generated, or read from memory, from *right to left* to handle carry propagation. The sign of the result is not known until all digits are processed; therefore, 2's complement representation is used.

Multiplication: Cryptographic applications don't use negative numbers; therefore our digit-multiplication circuit performs only unsigned multiplications. The products are accumulated (added to a 32…50-bit register) but only single digits are extracted from these registers and stored in memory.

For operand sizes in cryptographic applications the school multiplication is the best, requiring simple control. Some speed improvement can be expected from the more complicated Karatsuba method, but the Toom-Cook 3-way (or beyond) multiplication is actually slower for these lengths [6]. An FFT based multiplication takes even longer until much larger operands (in our case about 8 times slower).

Division: The algorithms presented here compute long divisions with the help of short ones (one- or two-digit divisors) performed by multiplications with reciprocals. The reciprocals are calculated with only a small constant number of digit-operations. In our test system linear approximations were followed by 3 or 4 Newton iterations. [9]

4 Traditional Modular Multiplication Algorithms

We assume $m = \{m_{n-1} m_{n-2} \ldots m_0\}$ is normalized, that is $\frac{1}{2}d \le m_{n-1} < d$ or $\frac{1}{2}d^{n-1} \le m < d^n$. It is normally the case with RSA moduli. If not, we have to normalize it: replace m with $2^k m$. A modular reduction step (discussed below) fixes the result: having $R_k = a \bmod 2^k m$ calculated, $R \leftarrow R_k - q \cdot m$, where q is computed from the leading digits of R_k and $2^k m$. These de/normalization steps are only performed at the beginning and end of the calculations (in case of an exponentiation chain), so the amortized cost is negligible.

There are a basically 4 algorithms used in memory constrained, digit serial applications (smart card, secure co-processors, consumer electronics, etc.): Interleaved row multiplication and reduction, Montgomery, Barrett and Quisquater multiplications. [1], [3], [12], [13]. We present algorithmic and HW speedups for them, so we have to review their basic versions first.

Montgomery multiplication. It is simple and fast, utilizing right-to-left divisions (sometimes called exact division or odd division [7]). In this direction there are no problems with carries (which propagate away from the processed digits) or with estimating the quotient digit wrong, so no correction steps are necessary. This gives it some 6% speed advantage over Barrett's reduction and more than 20% speed advantage over

```
for i = 0 … n-1
    t = x_i·m' mod d
    x = x + t·m·d^i
x = x / d^n
if( x ≥ m )
    x = x - m
```

Fig. 2. Montgomery reduction of x

division based reductions [3]. The traditional Montgomery multiplication calculates the product in "row order", but it still can take advantage of a speedup for squaring. (This is commonly believed not to be the case, see e.g. in [11], Remark 14.40, but the trick of Fig. 7 works here, too.) The main *disadvantage* is that the numbers have to be converted to a special form before the calculations and fixed at the end, that is, significant pre- and post-processing and extra memory is needed.

In Fig. 2 the Montgomery reduction is described. The constant $m' = -m_0^{-1} \bmod d$ is a pre-calculated single digit number. It exists if m_0 is odd, which is the case in cryptography, since m is prime or a product of odd primes.

The rational behind the algorithm is to represent a long integer a, $0 \le a < m$, as $aR \bmod m$ with the constant $R = d^n$. A modular product of these $(aR)(bR) \bmod m$ is not in the proper form. To correct it, we have to multiply with R^{-1}, because $(aR)(bR)R^{-1} \bmod m = (ab)R \bmod m$. This

```
x = 0^n
for i = 0 … n-1
    t = (x_0+a_i b_0)m' mod d
    x = (x + a_i b + t·m)/d
if( x ≥ m )
    x = x - m
```

Fig. 3. Montgomery multiplication

$x \rightarrow xR^{-1}$ mod m correction step is called ***Montgomery reduction***, taking about the same time as the school multiplication.

The product AB can be calculated interleaved with the reduction, called the ***Montgomery multiplication*** (Fig. 3). It needs squaring-speedup as noted above. The instruction $x = (x+a_i b+t \cdot m)/d$ is a loop through the digits of B and m from right to left, keeping the carry propagating to the left.

Barrett multiplication. It can take advantage of double speed squaring, too, but calculates and stores the quotient $q = [ab/m]$, although it is not needed later. (During the calculations q and the remainder r cannot be stored in the same memory bank.) To avoid slow divisions, Barrett uses μ, a pre-computed reciprocal of m. These result in an extra storage need of $2n$ digits.

```
(A₁dⁿ + A₀) ← a b
q ← MS n digits of A₁μ
r ← A₀- LS n digits of qm
if r < 0: r ← r + dⁿ⁺¹
while r ≥ m: r ← r - m
```

Fig. 4. Barrett's multiplication

The modular reduction of a product is ab mod $m = ab - [ab/m]\,m$. Division by m is slower than multiplication, therefore $\mu = 1/m$ is calculated beforehand to multiply with. It is scaled to make it suitable for integer arithmetic, that is, $\mu = [d^{2n}/m]$ is calculated (μ is 1 bit longer than m). Multiplying with that and keeping the most significant n bits only, the error is at most 2, compared to the larger result of the exact division. The subtraction gives at most n-digit results, i.e. the most significant digits of ab and $[ab/m]\,m$ agree, therefore only the least significant n digits of both are needed. These yield the algorithm given in Fig. 4.

The half products can be calculated in half as many clock cycles as the full products with school multiplication. In practice a few extra bits precision is needed to guarantee that the last "while" cycle does not run too many times. This increase in operand length makes the algorithm slightly slower than Montgomery's multiplication.

Quisquater's multiplication is a variant of Barrett's algorithm. It multiplies the modulus with a number S, resulting in many leading 1 bits. This makes μ unnecessary, and the corresponding MS-half division becomes trivial. The conversion steps and the calculation with longer modulus could offset the time savings, but in many cases this algorithm is faster. [5]

Interleaved row-multiplication and reduction
Long division (modular reduction) steps can be interleaved with the multiplication steps. The advantage is that we don't need to store $2n$-digit full products before the division starts. Furthermore, as the digit-products are calculated, we can keep them in short (32-bit) registers and subtract the digits calculated for the modular reduction, making storing and re-loading unnecessary. During accumulation of the partial products if an intermediate result becomes too large we subtract an appropriate multiple of the modulus.

```
C = 0   // long integer
for i = n-1 … 0
    C = C·d + A·bᵢ
    q = MS( MS(C)·μ )
    C = C-q·M
    if( C ≥ M )
        C = C-M
```

Fig. 5. Interleaved row multiplication & modular reduction

- Multiply one of the operands, A, by the digits of the other one, from *left to right*: $C_{n-1} = Ab_{n-1}$, $C_{n-2} = Ab_{n-2}$...$C_0 = Ab_0$. (Here each C_i can be $n+1$-digit long, implicitly padded with i zeros to the right.)
- $C \leftarrow C_{n-1} - q_{n-1}m$, with such a q_{n-1}, that reduces the length of C to n digits. (Multiply the MS digit of C with the pre-computed $\mu = d^2/m_{n-1}$ to get the ratio. A few extra guard bits ensure an error of q_{n-1} to be at most 1.)
- For $i = n-2...0$: add C_i to C, shifted to the right by one digit. Again, C can become $n+1$ digits long (excluded the trailing 0's), so $C \leftarrow C - q_i m$, with such a q_i, that reduces the length of C to n digits. If the implicit padding is taken into consideration, we actually subtracted $d^{i-1}qm$.

If the reduction $C \leftarrow C - q_i m$ is not sufficient to reduce the length of C to n digits (q is off by 1), we need a subtraction of m (equivalent to setting $q_i \leftarrow q_i + 1$). With guard bits it is very rare, so the average time for modular multiplications is only twice longer than what it takes to normally multiply 2 numbers. The result is AB mod m, and the digits q_i form the quotient $q = \Sigma d^i q_i = [AB/m]$. (When not needed, don't store them.) It is a left-right version of the Montgomery multiplication. The products $\mathtt{A \cdot b_i}$ and $\mathtt{q \cdot M}$ are calculated with loops collecting digit-products in an accumulator, storing the LS digit of the accumulator in memory shown in Fig. 6.

```
Q = 0  //32-bit accu
for k = 0 … n-1
    Q = MS(Q) + a_k b_i
    c_k = D0(Q)
c_n = MS(Q)
```

Fig. 6. Row products
$\mathtt{C = A \cdot b_i}$

Memory access. If the number of read/write operations is a concern, the MS digits of $\mathtt{C \cdot d + A \cdot b_i}$ could be calculated first, giving a good estimate for q. A single loop calculates $\mathtt{C' + A \cdot b_i - q \cdot M}$, there is no need to store and retrieve the digits of C in between.

```
Q = 0  //33-bit accu
for k = 0 … i-1
    Q = MS(Q) + 2a_k a_i
    c_k = D0(Q)
Q = MS(Q) + a_i^2
c_{i,i+1} = Q
```

Fig. 7. Row-squaring

Squaring. In row i the product $a_k a_i$ is calculated, which has the weight d^{k+i}. The same product is calculated in row k, too. Instead of repeating the work, we accumulate $2a_k a_i$ in row i. In order to keep track of which product is calculated when, in row i we consider only $a_k a_i$ with $k \leq i$. Because of the multiplier 2 the product is accumulated 1 bit shifted, but the result is still at most $i+1$ digits. (The worst case if all the digits are $d-1$ gives $d^{i+2} - d^i - 2d + 2 < d^{i+2}$.) We can accumulate half products faster: $a_k a_i$ and $a_k^2/2$, and double the final result. When a_0 was odd we accumulate $(a_0^2 - 1)/2$, with a final correction step [17].

5 New Multiplication Algorithms

Below new variants of popular modular multiplication algorithms are presented, tailored to the proposed HW, which was in turn designed, to allow speeding up these algorithms. Even as microprocessor *software* these algorithms are faster than their traditional counterparts. Their running time comes from two parts, the multiplication and the modular reduction. On the multiply-accumulate HW the products are calculated in n^2 clock cycles for the general case, and $n(n+1)/2$ clock cycles for squaring (loop j in Fig. 10 ignores repeated products, double the result and adds the square term). The modular reduction phase differentiates the algorithms, taking $(1+s)n^2 + t \cdot n + constant$ clock cycles.

5.1 Row- or Column-Multiplication

At modular reduction a multiple of m: $q \cdot m$ is subtracted from the partial results. q is computed from the MS digits. At row-multiplication they get calculated last, which forces us to save/load partial results, or process the MS digits out of order. It slows down the algorithms and causes errors in the estimation of q, to be fixed with extra processing time. Calculating the product-digits in columns, the MS digits are available when they are needed, but with the help of longer or bundled accumulators. Both techniques lead to algorithms of comparable complexities. Here we deal with *column multiplications*, while the row multiplication results are presented in [17].

5.2 Left-Right-Left Multiplication with Interleaved Modular Reduction

The family of these algorithms is called LRL (or military-step) algorithms. They don't need special representation of numbers and need only a handful of bytes extra memory.

Short reciprocal. The LRL algorithms replace division with multiplication with the reciprocal. For approximate 2-digit reciprocals, $\mu \approx d^{n+2}/2m$, only the MS digits are used, making the calculation fast. Since m is normalized, $\frac{1}{2}d^n \leq m < d^n$, the exact reciprocal $\frac{1}{2}d^2 < [d^{n+2}/2m] \leq d^2$ is 2 digits, except at the minimum of $m = \frac{1}{2}d^n$. Decreasing the overflowed values, to make $\mu \leq d^2 - 1$, does not affect the overall accuracy of the approximation. Most algorithms work well with this approximate reciprocal, calculated with a small constant number of digit operations (around 20 with Newton iteration). If the *exact* 2-digit reciprocal is needed, compare $d^{n+2}/2$ and μm. If the approximation is done according to Note R below, adding m if needed makes the error $0 \leq err < m$. When this addition was necessary, $\mu+1$ is the exact reciprocal, and it can be calculated in $2n + O(1)$ clock cycles, in the average ($4n + const$ worst case).

Lemma 1 The 2-digit approximate reciprocal calculated from the 2 MS digits of m $\mu = [d^4/(2dm_{n-1}+2m_{n-2})]$ has an error $-2 < \gamma < 1$ from to the true ratio $d^{n+2}/2m$.
Proof $d^{n+2}/2m = d^4/(2dm_{n-1}+2m_{n-2}+2m')$ with $0 \leq m' < 1$, m' representing the omitted digits. $d^4 - \mu \cdot 2(dm_{n-1}+m_{n-2}) = r$, the remainder of the division. $0 \leq r < 2(dm_{n-1}+m_{n-2})$. From $d^4/(2dm_{n-1}+2m_{n-2}+2m') = \mu + \gamma$ we get $d^4 = 2(dm_{n-1}+m_{n-2}+m')(\mu + \gamma)$, or

$$\gamma = (r/2 - \mu m')/(dm_{n-1}+m_{n-2}+m'). \tag{1}$$

It is decreased by setting $r = 0$, giving a negative expression, which is decreasing with m'. Putting $m' = 1$, larger than its maximum, gives $-\mu/(dm_{n-1}+m_{n-2}+1) < \gamma$. μ is largest when the denominator is the smallest, resulting in $-2 < -(d^4/d^2)/(d^2/2+1) < \gamma$.

The other side of the inequality is proved by setting r to $2(dm_{n-1}+m_{n-2})$ larger than its maximum. If the expression in (1) is positive, it is decreasing with m', so setting it to its minimum $m' = 0$ gives the maximum: $(dm_{n-1}+m_{n-2}-\mu \cdot 0)/(dm_{n-1}+m_{n-2}+0) = 1 > \gamma$. []

Let's denote the 2-digit reciprocals by $\mu=[d^{n+2}/2m]$, $\mu^{(0)}=[d^4/(2dm_{n-1}+2m_{n-2})]$, and $\mu^{(1)}=[d^4/(2dm_{n-1}+2m_{n-2}+2)]$ (subtracting 1 if needed to make them exactly 2-digit). From the definition: $\mu^{(1)} \leq \mu \leq \mu^{(0)}$.
Lemma 2   a) If $(dm_{n-1}+m_{n-2}) \cdot (dm_{n-1}+m_{n-2}+1) \leq \frac{1}{2}d^4$: $\mu^{(0)} - \mu^{(1)} = 1$ or 2 and
b) if $(dm_{n-1}+m_{n-2}) \cdot (dm_{n-1}+m_{n-2}+1) \geq \frac{1}{2}d^4$: $\mu^{(0)} - \mu^{(1)} = 0$ or 1.
Proof $d^4/(2dm_{n-1}+2m_{n-2})-d^4/(2dm_{n-1}+2m_{n-2}+2) = \frac{1}{2}d^4/((dm_{n-1}+m_{n-2}) \cdot (dm_{n-1}+m_{n-2}+1))$.
In case a) the difference is less than 2, so the integer parts are at most 2 apart. In case b) the difference is less than 1, making the integer part differ at most by 1. []

Corollary $\mu = [d^4/2m]$, the 2-digit reciprocal of m can be calculated from its 2 MS digits with an error of ≤ 2, with desired sign of the error, knowing $\mu^{(1)} \leq \mu \leq \mu^{(0)}$.

Lemma 3 If $d = 2^{16}$ and $m \geq 0xB504\ C417... > d^n/\sqrt{2}$, the error $\mu^{(0)} - \mu^{(1)} = 0$ or 1.

Proof Easily verified by computing the values not covered by Lemma 2, case b). []

Corollary If $d = 2^{16}$ and $m > d^n/\sqrt{2} = 0xB504\ F333...$, the error $\mu^{(0)} - \mu^{(1)} = 0$ or 1. (Similar results hold for other practical digit sizes, like 24, 32, 48 or 64 bits.)

Note R. In Lemma 2 Case a) we can look at the next bit (MS bit of m_{n-3}). If it is 0, $\mu^{(0)}$ is closer to μ than $\mu^{(1)}$, so an approximation with an error at most 1 is provided by $\mu^{(1)}+1 \leq \mu \leq \mu^{(0)}$. If the MS bit of m_{n-3} is 1, $\mu^{(1)}$ is closer to μ, then $\mu^{(1)} \leq \mu \leq \mu^{(0)}-1$ provides an error of at most 1.

Note T. Dropping some LS bits, the truncated $\mu^{(1)}$ is never too large and has an error at most 1 in the LS bit kept. This approximation of the reciprocal can be calculated with only a small constant number of digit operations. Adding 1 in the last bit-position of the truncated reciprocal yields another approximate reciprocal, which is never too small and has an error of at most one in this bit-position.

Algorithm LRL4

- Calculate $a_{n-1}b_{n-1}$, padded with $n-1$ zeros to the right. Subtract a multiple of the modulus m, such that the result becomes n digits long (it was at most $n+1$ digits long): Multiply the MS digit with twice the pre-computed $\mu = [d^{n+2}/2m]$ to get the ratio q_{n-1}. (A few extra guard bits ensure an error of at most 1.)
- Calculate the next MS digit from the product: $a_{n-1}b_{n-2} + a_{n-2}b_{n-1}$, pad, and add to the n-digit partial remainder calculated before, giving at most $n+1$ digits. A multiplication with μ of the MS digit(s) gives q_{n-2}, such that subtracting $q_{n-2}m$ reduces the partial result again to n digits. Multiplication the digits of m (taken from right-to-left) with the single digit q_{n-2} and their subtraction from the partial remainder is done in parallel (pipelined).

```
Rn-1…n-3 = ana-1bnb-1d + ana-1bnb-2 + ana-2bnb-1
for k = na+nb-4…n-3    // products downward
    Rn…n-4 += Σi+j==k aibj
    if (overflow) R -= m
q = (Rn-1μ1d² + Rn-1μ0d + Rn-2μ1d + Rn-2μ0) /d³·2
R = (R-q·m)d
for k = 0…n-4          // LS product-digits
    Rn…k += Σi+j==k aibj
while( Rn > 0 ) R -= m // overflow
```

Fig. 8. The LRL4 modular multiplication algorithm

- Continue this way until the new digit-products summed in columns do not increase the length of the partial product (the LS $n-2$ digits of the product). The rest is calculated from *right-to-left* and added normally to the product, with a possible final reduction step.

The reduction step is better delayed until the MS 3 digits of the product are calculated. This way adding the next product-digit can cause a carry at the MS bit at most 1: the possible maximum is $n(d-1)^2 \ll d^3$. The overflowed digit need not be stored, the situation can be fixed immediately by subtracting m. This overflow happens if the new digit is large, and the first digit of the partial result is larger than $d-n$. This digit is the result of the

```
c = 0  // 1 digit temp
store
Q = 0  // 33-bit
accumulator
for k = 0 … n-1
    Q = MS(Q) + c - q·m_k
    c = r_k
    r_k = D0(Q)
```

Fig. 9. Inner loop of modular reduction $R = (R-q·m)d$

modular reduction, so it is very close to uniformly distributed random. The probability of an overflow is less than n/d, about 1 in 1,000 at 16-bit digits, practically 0 for 32-bit digits.

This way we need not store $2n$-digit-products, the partial remainders only grow to n digits (plus an occasional over/under-flow bit). Although the used column-sums of digit-products add only to the 3 MS digits of the partial product (no long carry propagation), the subtraction of $q_i m$ still needs n-digit arithmetic (the LS digits further to the right are implicit 0's). All together a handful (t) steps are needed to calculate an

```
Q = 0                  // 50bit accumulator
for k = 0 … n-4
    Q = MS(Q) + r_k
    for j = max(0,k+1-
n_a)…min(k+1,n_b)
        Q += a_{k-j}b_j
    r_k = D0(Q)
for i = n-3 … n  // storing digits
    Q = MS(Q) + r_i
    r_i = D0(d)
```

Fig. 10. Calculation the digits of $a·b$
for k = 0 … n-4: $R_{n…k}$ += $\Sigma_{i+j==k}$ $a_i b_j$

approximate quotient q_i, which makes $n^2 + tn$ clock cycles for the modular reduction. $\{\mu_1, \mu_0\}$ is a 2-digit pre-computed reciprocal of m. The implementation details are shown in Fig. 9 and Fig. 10. If the quotient $[ab/m]$ is needed, too, we store the sequence of q_i's. There is a minor difficulty with the occasional $q \leftarrow q+1$ correction steps, which might cause repeated carry propagation. Since it happens rarely, it does not slow down the process noticeably, but we could store the locations of the correction steps (a few bytes storage) and do a final right-to-left scan of the quotient, to add one to the digits where the correction occurred.

Time complexity $\mu = [d^{n+2}/2m]$ the 2-digit reciprocal is at most 1 smaller than the true ratio $d^{n+2}/2m$. The quotient q is calculated from the 2 MS digits of the dividend x and the reciprocal μ:

$$q = [2(\mu_1 x_n d^2 + (\mu_1 x_{n-1} + \mu_0 x_n)d + \mu_0 x_{n-1})/d^3].$$ (LRL4q)

Proposition: q is equal to or at most 1 less than the integer part of the true quotient.

Proof: At the reduction steps the true ratio was $q' = [(x_n d^n + x_{n-1} d^{n-1} + \xi d^{n-1})/m]$ with some $0 \leq \xi < 1$, representing the rest of the digits of x. The approximate reciprocal μ has an error γ, at most 1 from the rational $d^{n+2}/2m$, so our estimated ratio

$$q = [2(x_n d + x_{n-1}) \cdot (d^{n+2}/2m - \gamma)/d^3]$$
$$= [(x_n d^n + x_{n-1} d^{n-1} + \xi d^{n-1})/m - \xi d^{n-1}/m - 2(x_n d + x_{n-1})\gamma/d^3]$$

The subtracted error term, $\xi d^{n-1}/m + 2(x_n d + x_{n-1})\gamma/d^3$ is increased if we put $\gamma = 1$, $\xi = 1$, x_n, $x_{n-1} = d - 1$, and m to its smallest possible value, $\frac{1}{2} d^n$. The error is smaller than the resulting $2d^{n-1}/d^n + 2(d^2 - 1)/d^3 = (4d^2 - 2)/d^3$, which is less than 1 if $d \geq 4$. []

If the reciprocal was calculated from the 2 MS digits of m (error $-2 < \gamma < 1$), the partial remainder could become negative, having an error of at most roughly $\pm 4/d$. Most of the time the added new digit-products fix the partial results, but sometimes an *add-back* correction step is necessary. The running time of the modular reduction in SW is less than $\boxed{1.0001n^2 + 4n}$, in the average; $\boxed{n^2 + 4n}$ with extra HW.

LRL3 From the calculation of q we can drop $\mu_0 x_{n-1}$. It causes an additional error of at most $2(d-1)^2/d^3 < 2/d$. The approximate quotient digit is calculated with

$$q = [2(\mu_1 x_n d + \mu_1 x_{n-1} + \mu_0 x_n)/d^2]. \tag{LRL3q}$$

It takes 3 clock cycles with our multiply-accumulate HW, with a 1 bit left-shift and extracting the MS digit. In pure software implementation the occasional addition-subtraction steps add $0.0001n^2$ to the running time, in the average. Alternatively, the overflow can be handled at the next reduction step, where the new quotient will be larger, $q = d + q'$, with $q' < d$. In the proposed HW the extra shifted additions of the modulus digits can be done in parallel to the multiplications, so the worst case running time is $\boxed{n^2 + 3n}$ for the modular reduction, in SW we need $\boxed{1.0001n^2 + 3n}$ steps.

Note If the reduction step fails to reduce the length of the remainder, the second MS digit is very small $(0...\pm 6)$. In this case, adding the subsequent digit of the product (the next column-sum) cannot cause an overflow, so the reduction can be safely delayed after the next digit is calculated and added. It simplifies the algorithm but does not change its running time.

LRL2 Shifting μ a few bits to the right, does not help. E.g. 8 bits give $\mu_1 \approx \sqrt{d}$ which still does not make any of the terms in calculation of q small, like $\mu_1 x_{n-1} < 2d^{3/2}$. Dropping it anyway makes the resulting

$$q = [(\mu_1 x_n d + \mu_0 x_n)/d^{3/2}] \tag{LRL2q}$$

not very good, giving often an error of 1, sometimes 2. The average running time of the SW version is large, $\boxed{2n^2 + 2n}$; but with extensive use of HW it is $\boxed{n^2 + 2n}$.

LRL1 Instead of dropping terms from (LRL3q), we can use shorter reciprocals and employ shift operations to calculate some of the products. Without first shifting the modulus to make the reciprocal normalized we get $\mu = [d^3/(dm_{n-1} + m_{n-2})]$, with $\mu_1 = 1$, which reduces some multiplications to additions. Unfortunately, at least 1 more bit is needed to the right of μ_0. Its effects can be accommodated by a shift-addition with the content of the accumulator. This leads to LRL1, the fastest of the LRL algorithms.

Keep the last results in the 50-bit accumulator $Q = cd^3 + x_n d^2 + x_{n-1} d + x_{n-2}$ (3 digits + carry). Use 1 digit + 2 bits reciprocals in the form $\mu = \frac{1}{2}[2d^{n+1}/m] = d + \mu_0 + \delta$, with $\delta = 0, \frac{1}{2}$. The multiplication with d needs no action when manipulating the content of the accumulator. Multiplication with $\delta > 0$ is also done inside the accumulator parallel to the multiplication with μ_0: add the content of the accumulator to itself, shifted right by 17 bits.

What remains is to calculate $\mu_0(cd^2 + x_n d + x_{n-1})$. If c is 0 or 1 then $\mu_0 cd^2$ is computed by a shift/add, parallel to the $\mu_0 x_n$ multiplication. We drop the term $\mu_0 x_{n-1}/d^2$ from the approximation of q. The LRL1 algorithm still works, using only one digit-multiplication ($\mu_0 x_n$) for the quotient estimate with two shift-adds, $\mu_0 cd$ and the accumulator times δ/d. All aditions are done in the LS 32 bits of the accumulator.

$$q = \left[\left(Q + Q \delta/d \right) / d^2 + \mu_0 c + \mu_0 x_n /d \right] \qquad \text{(LRL1}q\text{)}$$

Similar reasoning as at LRL4 assures that the conditions $c = 0$ or 1, and $0 \le q < 3d$ is maintained during the calculations. The probability of the corrections is $\approx \frac{1}{4}$, giving an average SW running time $\boxed{1.25n^2 + n}$; in the accumulator-shift HW $\boxed{n^2 + n}$.

Computer experiments. A C program simulating the algorithm was tested against the results of GMP (GNU Multi Precision library [6]). 55 million modular multiplications of random 8192×8192 mod 8192 bits were tried, in addition to several billion shorter ones. The digit $n+1$ of the partial results in the modular reduction was always 0 or 1 and $0 \le q < 3d$ remained true.

Note. The last overflow correction (after the right-to-left multiplication phase) can be omitted, if we are in an exponentiation chain. At overflow the MS digit is 1, the second digit is small, and so at the beginning of the next modular multiplication there is no more overflow (the MS digit stays as 1), and it can be handled the normal way.

5.3 Modulus Scaling

The last algorithm uses only one digit-multiplication to get the approximate quotient for the modular reduction steps. We can get away with even fewer (0), but with a cost in preprocessing. It increases the length of the modulus. To avoid increasing the length of the result, the final modular reduction step in the modular multiplications is done with the original modulus. Preprocessing the modulus is simple and fast, so the algorithms below are competitive to the standard division based algorithms even for a single call. If a chain of calculations is performed with the same modulus (exponentiation) the preprocessing becomes negligible compared to the overall computation time.

The **main idea** is that the calculation of q becomes easier if the MS digit is 1 and the next digit is 0. Almost the same good is if all the bits of the MS digit are 1. In these cases ***no*** multiplication is needed for finding the approximate q [5], [15].

We can convert the modulus to this form by multiplying it with an appropriate 1-digit scaling factor. This causes one-time extra costs at converting the modulus in the beginning of the calculation chain, but the last modular reduction is done with the original modulus, and so the results are correct at the end of the algorithms (no postprocessing). The modified modulus is one digit longer, which could require extra multiply-accumulate steps at each reduction sweep, unless SW or HW changes take advantage of the special MS digits. These modified longer reduction sweeps are performed 1 fewer times than the original modulus would require. The final reduction with the original modulus makes the number of reduction sweeps the same as before.

There are two choices for the scaled modulus, $\{m_{n+1}, m_n\} = \{1, 0\}$ and $m_n = d-1$. The corresponding modular reduction algorithms are denoted by S10 and S0F. In both cases $q = r_{n+1}$ gives the estimate. Both algorithms need to store and process only the LS n digits of the scaled modulus, the processing of the MS digits can be hardwired.

Algorithm S0F The initial conversion step changed the modulus, such that $|m| = n+1$ and $m_n = d-1$. The current remainder R is shifted up (logically, that is only the indexing is changed) to make it $n+2$ digits long, such that $R = \{r_{n+1}, r_n..., r_1, 0\}$.

Proposition: $q = r_{n+1}$ is never too large, sometimes it is 1 too small.
Proof: (similar to the proof under S10 below) []

Correction steps q is *often* off by 1. It results in an overflow, i.e., the bit is not cleared from above the MS digit of the partial results. We have to correct them immediately (by subtracting m), otherwise the next q will be 17 bits long, and the error of the ratio estimation is doubled, so there could be a still larger overflow next.

These frequent correction steps cannot be avoided with one digit scaling. It corresponds to a division of single digits and they don't provide good quotient estimates. The S10 algorithm below uses an extra bit, so it is better in this sense.

Algorithm S10: The initial conversion step changed the modulus, such that $|m| = n+2$ and $m_{n+1} = 1$, $m_n = 0$. The current remainder R is shifted to the left (logically, that is only the indexing is changed) to make it also $n+2$ digits long, such that $R = \pm\{r_{n+1}, r_n,..., r_1, 0\}$. We use signed remainders and have to handle overflows, that is, a sign and an overflow bit could temporarily precede the digits of R. The algorithm will add/subtract m to fix the overflow if it occurs.

Now there are $|d|_2+1$ bits of the modulus fixed, and the signed R is providing also $|d|_2+1$ bits of information for q. With them correction steps will rarely be needed.
Proposition: $q = r_{n+1}$ for $R \geq 0$, and $q = d-1-r_{n+1}$ for $R < 0$ assignment gives an estimate of the quotient, which is never too small, sometimes 1 too large.
Proof: When $R \geq 0$ the extreme cases are:

1. Minimum/maximum: $R=\{r_{n+1},0,...0\}$, and $m=\{1, 0, d-1,...d-1\}=d^{n+1}+d^n-1$. The true quotient is $[r_{n+1}d^{n+1}/(d^{n+1} + d^n - 1)] = [r_{n+1} - r_{n+1}(d^n-1)/(d^{n+1} + d^n - 1)]$ $\geq [r_{n+1} - (d-1)(d^n-1)/(d^{n+1} + d^n - 1)] = r_{n+1}-1$, because r_{n+1} is integer and the subtracted term inside the integer part function is positive and less than 1: $(d^{n+1} - d^n - d + 1)/(d^{n+1} + d^n - 1) < 1$.

2. Maximum/minimum: $R = \{r_{n+1}, d-1, d-1,...d-1\} = r_{n+1}d^{n+1}+d^{n+1}-1$, and $m = \{1, 0, 0,...0\} = d^{n+1}$ give $[(r_{n+1}d^{n+1}+ d^{n+1} -1)/d^{n+1}] = [r_{n+1} + (d^{n+1} -1)/d^{n+1}] = r_{n+1}$. These show that the estimated q is never too small.

When R is negative, the modular reduction step is done with adding $q \cdot m$ to R. The above calculations can be repeated with the absolute value of R. However, the estimated (negative) quotient would be sometimes 1 too small, so we increase its value by one. This is also necessary to keep q a single-digit number. []

Correction steps. Overflow requiring extra correction steps, almost never occurs. Computer experiments showed that, during over 10 million random 8192×8192 mod 8192-bit modular multiplications there were only 5 subtractive corrections step performed, no underflow was detected. During over 10^{10} random 1024×1024 mod 1024-bit modular multiplications there were 2 overflows and no underflow. Accordingly, the use of only software corrections does not slow down S10.

```
R_{n-1 ... n-3} = a_{na-1}b_{nb-1}d + a_{na-1}b_{nb-2} + a_{na-2}b_{nb-1}
for k = n_a+n_b-4 ... n-3           // products down
    R_{n ... n-4} += Σ_{i+j==k} a_i b_j
    if ( R_n > 0 )  R -= m          // overflow
    if ( R_n <-1 )  R += m          // underflow
    if ( R_n == 0 )                 // positive rem
        q = R_{n-1}
        R =(R - q·m)d
    else                            // nagative rem
        q = d-1-R_{n-1}
        R =(R + q·m)d
for k = 0 ... n-4                   // LS digits
    R_{n ... k} += Σ_{i+j==k} a_i b_j
while( R_n > 0 )  R -= m            // overflow
while( R_n <-1 )  R += m            // underflow
```

Fig. 11. Basic structure of the S10 modular multiplication algorithm

The remainder is rarely longer than $n+1$, because at the start, there is no overflow: the MS digits of the products, even together with all the others don't give longer than $|A| + |B|$ -digit results. After a modular reduction

-   if the estimated quotient q was correct, the remainder R is less than mS, that is, either $|R| = n+1$, or R = $\{1, 0, r_{n-1}, ...\}$, where the third digit is smaller than that of mS. This last case is very unlikely (less than $1/(4d)$).

-   if the estimated quotient q was one too large, the remainder R changes sign. If the correct quotient $q-1$ would reduce R to a number of smaller magnitude than $\{0, 0, r_{n-1}, ...\}$, with the third digit at most as large as that of mS, then the actual q could cause an overflow. Again, it is a very unlikely combination of events.

Implementation. The MS 3 digits and the sign/overflow bits of the partial results can be kept in the accumulator. Because the multiplier is not used with the special MS digits of the scaled modulus, they can be manipulated together in the accumulator. Adding the next product-digit is done also in the accumulator in a single cycle.

Proposition: There is no need for longer than 50-bit accumulator.

Proof. The added product-digit could cause a carry less than n to the $n+1^{st}$ digit. If there was already an overflow, this digit is 0, so there will be no further carry propagation. If the $n+1^{st}$ digit was large, we know, the $n+2^{nd}$ digit of R was zero. These show that the MS digit of R can be $-2, -1, 0, 1$ — exactly what can be represented by the carry and sign, as a 2-bit 2's complement number. []

Computing the scaling factor. S Let n, n_a, n_b denote the length of m, A and B respectively. Let us calculate $S = [(d-1)d/m_{n-1}]$ for SOF, and $S = [d^2/m_{n-1}]$ for S10. With normalized m: $\frac{1}{2}d \leq m_{n-1} < d$, so we get S one bit and one digit long. If the short division estimated the long one inaccurately, we may need to add or subtract m, but at most a couple of times suffice, providing an $O(n)$ process. Adding/subtracting m changes the MS digit by at most 1, so it gets the desired value at the end.

5.4 Montgomery Multiplication with Multiply-Accumulate Structure

We can generate the product-digits of AB from right to left and keep updating R, an $n+1$-digit partial remainder, initialized to 0. The final result will be also in R. When the next digit of AB has been generated with its carry (all necessary digit-products accumulated), it is added to R, followed by adding an appropriate multiple of the modulus $t \cdot m$, such that the **last digit** is cleared: $t = r_0 \cdot m'$ with $m' = -m_0^{-1} \bmod d$. It can be done in a single sweep over R. The result gets stored in R shifted by 1 digit to the right (suppressing the trailing 0). The new product-digit, when calculated in the next iteration, is added again to the LS position of R.

```
R = 0^{n+1}
for i = 0 … 2n-1
    Q = r_0
    for_{j,k} 0 ≤ (j,k) < n, j+k == i
        Q += a_j b_k
    t = Q·m' mod d
    Q += t·m_0
    for j = 1 … n-1
        Q = MS(Q) + r_j + t·m_j
        r_{j-1} = D0(Q)
    r_{n,n-1} = MS(Q)
if( R ≥ m )
    R = R - m
```

Fig. 12. Montgomery multiplication with multiply-accumulate structure

Proposition after each reduction sweep (loop i) the remainder is R $\leq m+n(d-1)$.

This fact ensures, that the intermediate results do not grow larger than $n+1$ digits, and a single final correction step is enough to reduce the result R into $[0, m)$. If $n \geq 3$ and any of the MS digits $m_k < d-1$, $k = 2, 3, 4\ldots$, then R remains always n-digit long. (The case where each but the 2 LS digits of m is $d-1$ is trivial to handle.)

Proof by induction. At start it is true. At a later iteration c_i is the new product-digit, R $\leftarrow [(R+c_i+t\cdot m)/d] \leq [(m+n(d-1)+(d-1)^2\cdot n+(d-1)\cdot m)/d] = m+n(d-1)$. []

We don't need correction steps or processing the accumulator, so some HW costs can be saved. The final reduction step can be omitted during a calculation chain [5], since the next modular reduction produces a result R $\leq m+n(d-1)$ from n-digit inputs, anyway. Only the final result has to be fixed. Also, double-speed squaring can be easily done in the loop (j,k).

Montgomery-T (Tail Tailoring) The Montgomery reduction needs one multiplication to compute the reduction factor t. Using Quisquater's scaling, this time to transform the LS, instead of the MS digit to a special value, we can get rid of this multiplication. The last modular reduction step is performed with the original modulus m to reduce the result below m.

If $m' = 1$, the calculation of $t = LS(r_0 \cdot m')$ becomes trivial: $t = r_0$. It is the case if $m_0 = d - 1$, what we want to achieve with scaling.

The first step in each modular reduction sweep, $Q = r_0 + t m_0$, has to be performed even though we now the LS digit of the result (0), because the carry, the MS digit is needed. If $m_0 = d - 1$, we know the result without calculation: $Q = r_0 + t m_0 = r_0 + r_0(d - 1) = r_0 d$. Accordingly, we can start the loop 1 digit to the left, saving one multiplication there, too. Therefore, the modular reduction step is not longer than what it was with the sorter modulus.

To make $m_0 = d - 1$ we multiply (scale) m with an appropriate one-digit factor S, which happens to be the familiar constant $m' = -m_0^{-1} \bmod d$, because $m_0 S = m_0 m' \equiv -m_0 m_0^{-1} \bmod d = d - 1$. Multiplying m with S increases its length by 1 digit, but as we have just seen, the extra trailing digit does not increase the number of digit-multiplications during modular reduction.

The modular reduction performs $n - 1$ iterations with the modulus mS: $n(n-1)$ digit-multiplications, and one iteration with the modulus m: $n + 1$ digit-multiplications. We saved $n - 1$ digit-multiplications during the modular reduction steps. The price is the need to calculate S, mS and store both m and mS.

Proof of correctness: One Montgomery reduction step calculates $A_1 = (A + k \cdot mS)/d$, with such a k, that ensures no remainder of the division. Taking this equation modulo m, we get $A_1 \equiv A \cdot d^{-1} \bmod mS$. After $n - 1$ iterations the result is $A_{n-1} \equiv A \cdot d^{-(n-1)} \bmod mS$. The final step is a reduction mod m: $A_n \equiv A_{n-1} \cdot d^{-1} \bmod m$. In general $(a \bmod b \cdot c) \bmod c = a \bmod c$, (for integers a, b and c), so we get $A_n = A \cdot d^{-n} \bmod m$, or m larger than that (the result is of the same length as m). This is the result of the original Montgomery reduction. []

6 Summary

There is no single "best" modular multiplication algorithm, for all circumstances.

- In *software* for general purpose microprocessors
  - For very long operands sub-quadratic multiplications are the best, like Karatsuba, Toom-Cook or FFFT-based methods [6]
  - For cryptographic applications
    - If memory is limited (or auxiliary data does not fit to a memory cache): LRL3 or LRL1 (dependent on the instruction timing)
    - If memory is of no concern: S10 or Montgomery-T (needs pre/post-process)
- If some *HW* enhancements can be designed:
  - If there is enough memory: S10 (simpler)
  - Otherwise: LRL1.

The table below summarizes the running time of the *modular reduction phase* of our modular multiplication algorithms (without the n^2 steps of the multiplication phase).

Algorithm	Storage beyond operands	Preprocessing	Postprocessing	#Digit-products + fixes in SW	Extra HW	#Digit-products with extra HW
Barrett	$2n$	$O(n^2)$	–	n^2+5n	–	n^2+5n
LRL4	–	–	–	$1.0001n^2+4n$	Shifter	n^2+4n
LRL3	–	–	–	$1.0001n^2+3n$	Shifter	n^2+3n
LRL2	–	–	–	$2n^2+2n$	Shifter	n^2+2n
LRL1	–	–	–	$1.25n^2$	Shifter Accu-adder	n^2+n
SOF	n	n	–	$1.25n^2$	Shifter, Accu-adder	n^2
S10	n	n	–	$(1+\varepsilon)n^2$ (signed)	Shifter Accu-adder	n^2
S10-2	n	n	–	$(1+\varepsilon)n^2$ (signed)	Accu-adder	$n^2 + \varepsilon n^2$ adds
Montgomery	–	$O(n^2)$	$O(n^2)$	n^2+n	–	n^2+n
Montgomery-T	n	$O(n^2)$	$O(n^2)$	n^2	–	n^2

References

1. ALTERA Literature: Stratix II Devices http://www.altera.com/literature/lit-stx2.jsp
2. P.D.Barrett, *Implementing the Rivest Shamir Adleman public key encryption algorithm on standard digital signal processor*, In Advances in Cryptology-Crypto'86, Springer, 1987, pp.311-323.
3. Bosselaers, R. Govaerts and J. Vandewalle, *Comparison of three modular reduction functions*, In Advances in Cryptology-Crypto'93, LNCS 773, Springer-Verlag, 1994, pp.175-186.
4. E. F. Brickell. *A Survey of Hardware Implementations of RSA*. Proceedings of Crypto'89, Lecture Notes in Computer Science, Springer-Verlag, 1990.
5. J.-F. Dhem, J.-J. Quisquater, *Recent results on modular multiplications for smart cards*, Proceedings of CARDIS 1998, Volume 1820 of Lecture Notes in Computer Security, pp 350-366, Springer-Verlag, 2000
6. GNU Multiple Precision Arithmetic Library http://www.swox.com/gmp/gmp-man-4.1.2.pdf
7. K. Hensel, *Theorie der algebraische Zahlen*. Leipzig, 1908
8. J. Jedwab and C. J. Mitchell. *Minimum weight modified signed-digit representations and fast exponentiation*. Electronics Letters, 25(17):1171-1172, 17. August 1989.
9. D. E. Knuth. *The Art of Computer Programming*. Volume 2. Seminumerical Algorithms. Addison-Wesley, 1981. Algorithm 4.3.3R
10. W. Krandick, J. R. Johnson, *Efficient Multiprecision Floating Point Multiplication with Exact Rounding*, Tech. Rep. 93-76, RISC-Linz, Johannes Kepler University, Linz, Austria, 1993.
11. A.Menezes, P.van Oorschot, S.Vanstone, *Handbook of Applied Cryptography*, CRC Press, 1996.
12. P.L. Montgomery, *Modular Multiplication without Trial Division*, Mathematics of Computation, Vol. 44, No. 170, 1985, pp. 519-521.
13. J.-J. Quisquater, *Presentation at the rump session of Eurocrypt'90*.
14. R. L. Rivest; A. Shamir, and L. Adleman. 1978. *A method for obtaining digital signatures and public key cryptosystems*. Communications of the ACM 21(2):120--126

15. SNIA OSD Technical Work Group http://www.snia.org/tech_activities/workgroups/osd/
16. C. D. Walter, *Faster modular multiplication by operand scaling*, Advances in Cryptology, Proc. Crypto'91, LNCS 576, J. Feigenbaum, Ed., Springer-Verlag, 1992, pp. 313—323
17. L. Hars, *manuscript*, 2003.

Leak Resistant Arithmetic

Jean-Claude Bajard[1], Laurent Imbert[2], Pierre-Yvan Liardet[3], and
Yannick Teglia[3]

[1] LIRMM, CNRS, Université Montpellier II
161 rue Ada, 34392 Montpellier cedex 5, France
bajard@lirmm.fr
[2] LIRMM, CNRS, France, and
ATIPS[†], CISaC[‡], University of Calgary
2500 University drive N.W, Calgary, T2N 1C2, Canada
Laurent.Imbert@lirmm.fr,
[3] STMicroelectronics, Smartcard ICs
Z.I. Rousset, 13106 Rousset Cedex, France
{Pierre-Yvan.Liardet,Yannick.Teglia}@st.com

Abstract. In this paper we show how the usage of Residue Number
Systems (RNS) can easily be turned into a natural defense against many
side-channel attacks (SCA). We introduce a Leak Resistant Arithmetic
(LRA), and present its capacities to defeat timing, power (SPA, DPA)
and electromagnetic (EMA) attacks.

Keywords: Side channel attacks, residue number systems, RNS Montgomery multiplication.

1 Introduction

Side-channel attacks rely on the interactions between the component and the
real world. Those attacks formerly appeared in the network security world and
eventually came within the smartcard and embedded system world to become
the most pertinent kind of attacks on secure tokens. Some attacks monitor the
computation through its time execution or its power consumption in order to
discover secrets, as shown by P. Kocher in [19,18]. Some others try to modify
the component's behavior or data, through fault injection as pointed out first
by D. Boneh, R. A. DeMillo, and R. J. Lipton in [6] in the case of public-key
protocols, and extended to secret-key algorithms by E. Biham and A. Shamir
in [5]. From noise adding to whole algorithm randomization, different ways have
been considered to secure the implementations against side channels [19], and
especially against power analysis [18,12]. One difficult task when preventing from
SCA is to protect from differential power analysis (DPA) introduced by P. Kocher
in [18] and its equivalent for electromagnetic attacks (EMA) [9,1], and recent

---

[†] Advanced Technology Information Processing Systems
[‡] Center for Information Security and Cryptography

M. Joye and J.-J. Quisquater (Eds.): CHES 2004, LNCS 3156, pp. 62–75, 2004.

multi-channel attacks [2]. These specific attacks take advantage of correlations between the internal computation and the side channel information.

The purpose of Leak Resistant Arithmetic (LRA) is to provide a protection at the arithmetic level, i.e. in the way we represent the numbers for internal computations. We show how the usage of Residue Number Systems (RNS), through a careful choice of the modular multiplication algorithm, can easily be turned into a natural defense against SCA. In the same time, our solution provides fast parallel implementation and enough scalability to support key-size growth induced by the progress of classical cryptanalysis and computational power. In addition, another advantage of LRA is that classical countermeasures still apply at the upper level. We illustrate this fact in Sect. 3.3 through an adaptation to LRA of the Montgomery ladder [23], which has been analyzed in the context of side-channels [15], and which features (C safe-error and M safe-error protected) make it a first-class substitute to the square-and-multiply algorithm.

This paper puts together previous works from J.-C. Bajard and L. Imbert on RNS Montgomery multiplication and RSA implementation [3,4], and P.-Y. Liardet original idea of addressing SCA using RNS, proposed in September 2002 in [20]. The same idea has been independently investigated by M. Ciet, M. Neeve, E. Peeters, and J.-J. Quisquater, and recently published in [8]. In Sect. 3.1, we address the problem of the Montgomery factor when RNS bases are randomly chosen, and we propose solutions which make it possible to randomly select new RNS bases during the exponentiation in Sect. 3.3.

2   The Residue Number Systems

In RNS, an integer X is represented according to a base $\mathcal{B} = (m_1, m_2, \dots, m_k)$ of relatively prime numbers, called moduli, by the sequence $(x_1, x_2, \dots, x_k)$, where $x_i = X \bmod m_i$ for $i = 1 \dots k$. The conversion from radix to RNS is then easily performed. The Chinese Remainder Theorem (CRT) ensures the uniqueness of this representation within the range $0 \leqslant X < M$, where $M = \prod_{i=1}^{k} m_i$. The constructive proof of this theorem provides an algorithm to convert X from its residue representation to the classical radix representation:

$$X = \sum_{i=1}^{k} x_i \, T_i \left| T_i^{-1} \right|_{m_i} \bmod M, \qquad (1)$$

where $T_i = M/m_i$ and $\left| T_i^{-1} \right|_{m_i}$ is the inverse of T_i modulo m_i. In the rest of the paper, $|X|_m$ denotes the remainder of X in the division by m, i.e. the value $(X \bmod m) < m$.

One of the well known advantages of RNS is that additions, subtractions and multiplications are very simple and can be efficiently implemented on a parallel architecture [17]. Furthermore, only the dynamic range of the final result has to be taken into account since all the intermediate values can be greater than M.

On the other hand, one of the disadvantages of this representation is that we cannot easily decide whether $(x_1, \dots, x_k)$ is greater or less[1] than $(y_1, \dots, y_k)$.

For cryptographic applications, modular reduction ($X \bmod N$), multiplication ($XY \bmod N$) and exponentiation ($X^E \bmod N$) are the most important operations. Many solutions have been proposed for those operations. For example, it is well known that they can be efficiently computed without trial division using Montgomery algorithms [22].

Let us briefly recall the principles of Montgomery multiplication algorithm. Given two integers β^k, N such that $\gcd(\beta^k, N) = 1$, and $0 \leqslant XY < \beta^k N$, Montgomery multiplication evaluates $XY(\beta^k)^{-1} \bmod N$ by computing the value $Q < \beta^k$ such that $XY + QN$ is a multiple of β^k. Hence, the quotient $(XY + QN)/\beta^k$ is exact and easily performed. The result is less than $2N$. More detailed discussions on Montgomery reduction and multiplication algorithms can be found in [21,7].

2.1   RNS Montgomery Multiplication

In this section we recall a recent RNS version of the Montgomery multiplication algorithm, previously proposed in [3,4]. In the RNS version of the Montgomery multiplication, the value

$$M_1 = \prod_{i=1}^{k} m_i, \tag{2}$$

is chosen as the Montgomery constant (instead of β^k in the classical representation). Hence, the RNS Montgomery multiplication of A and B yields

$$R = ABM_1^{-1} \bmod N, \tag{3}$$

where R, A, B and N are represented in RNS according to a predefined base $\mathcal{B}_1$. As in the classical Montgomery algorithm we look for an integer Q such that $(AB + QN)$ is a multiple of M_1. However, the multiplication by M_1^{-1} cannot be performed in the base $\mathcal{B}_1$. We define an extended base $\mathcal{B}_2$ of k extra relatively prime moduli and perform the multiplication by M_1^{-1} within this new base $\mathcal{B}_2$. For simplicity we shall consider that both $\mathcal{B}_1$ and $\mathcal{B}_2$ are of size k. Let us define $\mathcal{B}_1 = (m_1, \dots, m_k)$ and $\mathcal{B}_2 = (m_{k+1}, \dots m_{2k})$, with $M_2 = \prod_{i=1}^{k} m_{k+i}$, and $\gcd(M_1, M_2) = 1$.

Now, in order to compute Q, we use the fact that $(AB + QN)$ must be a multiple of M_1. Clearly $Q = -ABN^{-1} \bmod M_1$, and thus

$$q_i = -a_i b_i n_i^{-1} \bmod m_i, \ \forall i = 1 \dots k. \tag{4}$$

As a result, we have computed a value $Q < M_1$ such that $Q = -ABN^{-1} \bmod M_1$. As pointed out previously we compute $(AB + QN)$ in the extra base $\mathcal{B}_2$. Before we can evaluate $(AB + QN)$ we have to know the product AB in base $\mathcal{B}_2$ and extend Q, which has just been computed in base $\mathcal{B}_1$ using (4), in base

---

[1] According to the CRT testing the equality of two RNS numbers is trivial.

$\mathcal{B}_2$. We then compute $R = (AB + QN)M_1^{-1}$ in base $\mathcal{B}_2$, and extend the result back to the base $\mathcal{B}_1$ for future use (the next call to Montgomery multiplication). Algorithm 1 describes the computations of our RNS Montgomery multiplication. It computes the Montgomery product $ABM_1^{-1} \bmod N$, where A, B, and N are represented in RNS in both bases $\mathcal{B}_1$ and $\mathcal{B}_2$.

Algorithm 1 : $\mathrm{MM}(A, B, N, \mathcal{B}_1, \mathcal{B}_2)$, *RNS Montgomery Multiplication*

Input : Two RNS bases $\mathcal{B}_1 = (m_1, \dots, m_k)$, and $\mathcal{B}_2 = (m_{k+1}, \dots, m_{2k})$, such that $M_1 = \prod_{i=1}^{k} m_i, M_2 = \prod_{i=1}^{k} m_{k+i}$ and $\gcd(M_1, M_2) = 1$; a positive integer N represented in RNS in both bases such that $0 < 4N < M_1, M_2$ and $\gcd(N, M_1) = 1$; (Note that M_1 can be greater or less than M_2.) two positive integers A, B represented in RNS in both bases, with $AB < M_1 N$.

Output : A positive integer R represented in RNS in both bases, such that $R \equiv ABM_1^{-1} \pmod{N}$, and $R < 2N$.

1: $T \leftarrow A \otimes_{RNS} B$ in $\mathcal{B}_1 \cup \mathcal{B}_2$
2: $Q \leftarrow T \otimes_{RNS} (-N^{-1})$ in $\mathcal{B}_1$
3: Extend Q from $\mathcal{B}_1$ to $\mathcal{B}_2$
4: $R \leftarrow (T \oplus_{RNS} Q \otimes_{RNS} N) \otimes_{RNS} M_1^{-1}$ in $\mathcal{B}_2$
5: Extend R back from $\mathcal{B}_2$ to $\mathcal{B}_1$

Steps $1, 2$ and 4 of algorithm 1 consist of full RNS operations and can be performed in parallel. As a consequence the complexity of the algorithm clearly relies on the two base extensions of lines 3 and 5.

Many different methods have been proposed to perform the base extension. Among those based on the CRT, [24] and [16] use a floating-point like dedicated unit, [26] proposes a version with an extra modulo greater than k (this method is not valid for the first extension of Algorithm 1), [25] perform an approximated extension, and [3] allow an offset for the first base extension which is compensated during the second one. Other solutions have been proposed which use the mixed radix system (MRS) [10]. The great advantage of the MRS approach is that the modification of one modulus, only requires the computation of at most k new values.

In [8], Posch and Posch's RNS Montgomery algorithm [25] is used, together with J.-C. Bajard *et al.* base extensions [3], which requires the computation of T_i and T_i^{-1} for each modulus m_i, where $T_i = M/m_i$ is about the same size as M, i.e. about 512 bits. In the context of random bases, precomputations are inconceivable (their choices of parameters lead to more than 2^{35} possible values for M). So we suppose that they evaluate these values at each base selection. Note that our algorithm uses the MRS conversion to avoid this problem.

2.2   Modular Exponentiation

The RNS Montgomery multiplication easily adapts to modular exponentiation algorithms. Since the exponent is not represented in RNS, we can consider any classic method for modular exponentiation, from the basic binary (square-and-multiply) algorithm to other fast exponentiation methods [11]. As with any Montgomery based exponentiation algorithm, the first step in the evaluation of $X^E \bmod N$, is to transform the input X into the so-called Montgomery representation: $X' = XM_1 \bmod N$ (X' is sometimes referred to as the N-residue of x according to M_1). This is done using a Montgomery multiplication with X and ($M_1^2 \bmod N$) as inputs. This representation has the advantage of being stable over Montgomery multiplication:

$$MM(X', Y', N, \mathcal{B}_1, \mathcal{B}_2) \equiv XYM_1 \bmod N.$$

At the end of the exponentiation, the value $Z' = X^E M_1 \bmod N$ is converted back into the expected result $Z = X^E \bmod N$ using a last call to Montgomery multiplication with Z' and 1 as inputs.

3   Leak Resistant Arithmetic

One advantage of the RNS algorithms presented in previous sections is to offer many degrees of freedom for the randomization of processed data. In this section we propose two approaches based on the random selection of the RNS bases, which provides randomization, both at the circuit level (spatial randomization) and the data level (arithmetic masking). They represent a good trade-off between randomization strength and implementation cost. We consider two approaches:

- **Random choice of the initial bases:** Randomization of the input data is provided by randomly choosing the elements of $\mathcal{B}1$ and $\mathcal{B}2$ before each modular exponentiation.
- **Random change of bases before and during the exponentiation:** A generic algorithm is proposed offering many degrees of freedom in the implementation and at the security level.

3.1   Solving the Problem of the Montgomery Factor

A random draw of $\mathcal{B}_1$ and $\mathcal{B}_2$ is seen as a permutation γ, over the predefined set $\mathcal{B}$ of size $2k$. The first k elements give $\mathcal{B}_{1,\gamma} = \left(m_{\gamma(1)}, \ldots, m_{\gamma(k)}\right)$, and the next k ones give $\mathcal{B}_{2,\gamma} = \left(m_{\gamma(k+1)}, \ldots, m_{\gamma(2k)}\right)$. We denote $M_{1,\gamma}$ and $M_{2,\gamma}$ the products of the elements of $\mathcal{B}_{1,\gamma}$ and $\mathcal{B}_{2,\gamma}$ respectively:

$$M_{1,\gamma} = \prod_{i=1}^{k} m_{\gamma(i)}, \quad M_{2,\gamma} = \prod_{i=k+1}^{2k} m_{\gamma(i)}.$$

Before we give more details on SCA aspects, we solve an important problem due to the random choice of $\mathcal{B}_1$ and $\mathcal{B}_2$. As pointed out before, modular exponentiation of any input X usually starts with an initial modular multiplication to get into the Montgomery representation, according to the so-called Montgomery factor. As mentioned before, we would have to perform the Montgomery multiplication of X and $(M_{1,\gamma}^2 \bmod N)$. But since $M_{1,\gamma}$ is the product of k randomly chosen moduli, we do not know $(M_{1,\gamma}^2 \bmod N)$ beforehand. The huge number of possibilities for $M_{1,\gamma}$ (further evaluated) makes the precomputation of the products of all the subsets of k elements of $\mathcal{B}$ unconceivable. On-the-fly evaluation of $(M_{1,\gamma}^2 \bmod N)$, after the random choice of $\mathcal{B}_{1,\gamma}$, would be very expensive and would require dedicated hardware.

The solution we propose is achieved through a call to our RNS Montgomery multiplication where the roles of the bases $\mathcal{B}_{1,\gamma}$ and $\mathcal{B}_{2,\gamma}$ are exchanged. The following proposition holds:

Proposition 1. *For every permutation γ over $\mathcal{B}$, the Montgomery representation of X according to $\mathcal{B}_{1,\gamma}$, i.e. the value $X M_{1,\gamma} \bmod N$, is obtained with (note the order of $\mathcal{B}_{1,\gamma}$ and $\mathcal{B}_{2,\gamma}$ in the call to MM):*

$$MM(X, M \bmod N, N, \mathcal{B}_{2,\gamma}, \mathcal{B}_{1,\gamma}), \tag{5}$$

where $M = \prod_{i=1}^{2k} m_i$.

Proof. It suffices to remark that $\forall \gamma$, we have $M = M_{1,\gamma} M_{2,\gamma}$. Thus:

$$MM(X, M \bmod N, N, \mathcal{B}_{2,\gamma}, \mathcal{B}_{1,\gamma}) = X M_{1,\gamma} M_{2,\gamma} M_{2,\gamma}^{-1} \bmod N = X M_{1,\gamma} \bmod N.$$

□

It is important to note that $M \bmod N$ does not depend on γ. This value is precomputed for each m_i. We obtain the result in RNS for the two bases, and we continue the exponentiation, with the two bases $\mathcal{B}_{1,\gamma}$ and $\mathcal{B}_{2,\gamma}$ playing their usual role as in $MM(.,.,N,\mathcal{B}_{1,\gamma},\mathcal{B}_{2,\gamma})$. This solution only requires the precomputation of $2k$ small constants, of the size of the m_js: for $j = 1...2k$, we store the values $|M \bmod N|_{m_j}$, where $M = \prod_{j=1}^{2k} m_j$.

We remark that this problem of the Montgomery factor is not mentioned in [8]. Using their notations, the precomputation of $\widetilde{M}^2 \bmod p$ and $\widetilde{M}^2 \bmod q$ for all the possible RNS bases would require the precomputation of $\binom{69}{9} > 2^{35}$ values of 512 bits each (more than 6.5 TBytes). We must then assume that $\widetilde{M}^2 \bmod p$ and $\widetilde{M}^2 \bmod q$ (or $X \widetilde{M} \bmod p$ and $X \widetilde{M} \bmod q$) are computed using other techniques, like Barrett or Quisquater, as precisely pointed out in [13]. This would require dedicated hardware (protected against SCA), and thus, drastically increase the size of the circuitry. In this case, the advantages of the RNS solution seems very limited. Using the same parameters, our algorithm only requires 144 Kbytes of memory, and one call to RNS Montgomery (which has to be done anyway).

3.2   Initial Random Bases

Taking into account the order of the elements within the bases, a set $\mathcal{B}$ of $2k$ moduli, leads to $2k!$ different bases $\mathcal{B}_{1,\gamma}$ and $\mathcal{B}_{2,\gamma}$ of k moduli each. Since two consecutive exponentiations are performed with two different permutations, γ and γ', identical input data leak different information through the side-channel. Actually, after step 2 of algorithm 1, we have computed $Q = (q_{\gamma(1)}, \ldots, q_{\gamma(2)})$ in $\mathcal{B}_{1,\gamma}$, where $q_{\gamma(i)} = q \bmod m_{\gamma(i)}$ for $i = 1...k$. Then, for each $m_{\gamma(j)}$ in $\mathcal{B}_{2,\gamma}$, we evaluate

$$|q|_{m_{\gamma(j)}} = \left|t_1 + m_{\gamma(1)}(t_2 + m_{\gamma(2)}(t_3 + \cdots + m_{\gamma(k-1)}t_k)\cdots)\right|_{m_{\gamma(j)}}, \qquad (6)$$

where the t_is are evaluated as follows, with $\mu_{s,t} = m_{\gamma(s)}^{-1} \bmod m_{\gamma(t)}$:

$$t_1 = |q|_{m_{\gamma(1)}} = q_{\gamma(1)} \qquad (7)$$

$$t_2 = \left|(q_{\gamma(2)} - t_1)\mu_{1,2}\right|_{m_{\gamma(2)}} \qquad (8)$$

$$\vdots$$

$$t_k = \left|(\cdots (q_{\gamma(k)} - t_1)\mu_{1,k} - \cdots - t_{k-1})\mu_{k-1,k}\right|_{m_{\gamma(k)}} \qquad (9)$$

From (6) to (9), we remark the influence of γ on the computations. It is clear that the values $\mu_{s,t}$ used to evaluate the t_is are different for each new permutation. Moreover, although all of them need to be precomputed, only about half of them (those with $s > t$) are used in (7) to (9). The same remark applies for (6) where all the operands differ from one permutation to another. It is also important to note that equations (6) to (9) require modular arithmetic to be performed modulo different values at each permutation. Initial random bases will thus give very different traces through the side-channel, even with identical input data. This significantly increases the number of experiments the attacker should try in order to retrieve secret information.

Initial random bases also provides data randomization. Selecting two bases of k moduli each within a set of exactly $2k$ moduli, gives $\binom{2k}{k} = \frac{(2k)!}{k!k!}$ pairs $(M_{1,\gamma}, M_{2,\gamma})$, i.e. $\binom{2k}{k}$ different Montgomery representations. Let us explain why this parameter corresponds to the level of randomization of the input data provided by our arithmetic. Randomizations of the message and the exponent are well known techniques to defeat DPA [19]. These randomizations prevent from chosen and known plain-text SCA targeting a secret carried out by the exponent during the exponentiation. In classical arithmetic solutions, such a masking can be obtained by choosing a pair of random values (r_i, r_f), with $r_i \equiv r_f^{-1} \pmod{N}$, and by multiplying (modulo N) the message X by r_i before the exponentiation, such that $Xr_i \bmod N$ has a uniform distribution[2]. Similar techniques are used to randomize the exponent and the modulus. The size of the random factor(s) must be chosen large enough to ensure a good level of randomization.

In our case, $M_{1,\gamma}$ plays the same role as the random factor r_i. The first step of the exponentiation which converts X into $XM_{1,\gamma} \bmod N$, thus provides message randomization. Since $M_{1,\gamma}$ is the product of randomly selected moduli, and can

---

[2] A final multiplication by $r_f^e \bmod N$ is required at the end.

take $\binom{2k}{k}$ different values, we can consider that the output $XM_{1,\gamma} \bmod N$ has a uniform distribution (if k is large enough). It is important to note that the randomization of X is free since the first call to $MM(...)$ must be performed anyway.

Table 1 gives randomization rates of different base sizes, and the corresponding size of the factor r_i in classic arithmetic solutions, computed as $\lfloor \log_2(\binom{2k}{k}) \rfloor$. For example, we remark that $k = 34$ ($|\mathcal{B}| = 68$), provides about the same randomization level as a random factor r_i of 64 bits.

Table 1. Randomization level of different base sizes, and their equivalent in classic arithmetic masking solutions.

size of $\mathcal{B}$	$\binom{2k}{k}$	equiv. size of r_i (in bits)
36	9075135300	33
44	2104098963720	40
52	495918532948104	48
60	118264581564861424	56
68	28453041475240576740	64
80	107507208733336176461620	76

In terms of memory requirements, initial random bases require the precomputation of $2k$ moduli m_i of n bits each, $2k-1$ modular inverses $|m_i^{-1}|_{m_j}$ ($i \neq j$) for each m_j, and $2k$ values $|M \bmod N|_{m_i}$; a total of $2k(2k+1)$ n-bit integers. Table 2 gives the total memory requirements for different values of k and n and the corresponding RSA equivalent dynamic range (computed as $k(n-1)$, which is the size of the lower bound of $M_{1,\gamma}$ considering $2^{n-1} \leq m_i < 2^n$). For example, a set $\mathcal{B}$ of $2k = 68$ moduli of 32 bits each (which correspond to approximately 1054-bit numbers in classical binary representation) requires about 18 Kbytes of memory.

Table 2. Memory requirements for various parameters k and n, and the corresponding RSA equiv. size.

k	n = size of the m_is (in bits)	memory (in KBytes)	dynamic range
30	18	8	> 510
25	32	10	> 775
34	32	18	> 1054
17	64	9.5	> 1071
32	64	33	> 2016

We remark that the space complexity is in $O(k^2n)$. Thus, it is better to consider smaller bases with larger moduli. Of course, the complexity of the basic cells which perform the arithmetic over each m_i increases at the same time. A tradeoff between the two parameters k and n has to be found, according to the hardware resources.

3.3 Random Bases During Exponentiation

In this section, we show how we can randomly change the RNS bases during the exponentiation. As for the initial random bases version presented in the previous section, we must solve another problem, the on-the-fly conversion between two different Montgomery representations.

Let us assume that initial random bases have been selected and that the exponentiation algorithm has computed until, say $Y = X^\alpha M_{1,\gamma} \bmod N$ over the two bases $(\mathcal{B}_{1,\gamma}, \mathcal{B}_{2,\gamma})$. In order to continue with two new random bases $(\mathcal{B}_{1,\gamma'}, \mathcal{B}_{2,\gamma'})$, we have to switch from the old Montgomery representation (according to $M_{1,\gamma}$) to the new one (according to $M_{1,\gamma'}$). In other words, the question is: given $X^\alpha M_{1,\gamma} \bmod N$, how can we compute $X^\alpha M_{1,\gamma'} \bmod N$?

A straightforward solution is to get out of the old Montgomery representation with

$$MM(Y, 1, N, \mathcal{B}_{1,\gamma}, \mathcal{B}_{2,\gamma}) = X^\alpha \bmod N = Z,$$

and to enter into the new Montgomery representation with

$$MM(Z, M \bmod N, N, \mathcal{B}_{2,\gamma'}, \mathcal{B}_{1,\gamma'}) = X^\alpha M_{1,\gamma'} \bmod N$$

using the solution proposed in Sect. 3.2. The exponentiation can then continue according to $M_{1,\gamma'}$ until the next base change. The main drawback of this solution is that we loose the randomization of $X^\alpha \bmod N$ between the two calls to $MM(...)$.

A better solution consists in inverting the order of the two calls to $MM(...)$. Actually, if we first call (note the order of $\mathcal{B}_{1,\gamma}$ and $\mathcal{B}_{2,\gamma}$)

$$MM(X^\alpha M_{1,\gamma} \bmod N, M \bmod N, N, \mathcal{B}_{2,\gamma'}, \mathcal{B}_{1,\gamma'}),$$

we obtain

$$X^\alpha M_{1,\gamma} M_{1,\gamma'} \bmod N.$$

We then call

$$MM(X^\alpha M_{1,\gamma} M_{1,\gamma'} \bmod N, 1, N, \mathcal{B}_{1,\gamma}, \mathcal{B}_{2,\gamma})$$

and get the expected result

$$X^\alpha M_{1,\gamma'} \bmod N.$$

As a result, the value $X^\alpha \bmod N$ is always masked by a random quantity.

In order to illustrate the fact that our arithmetic easily adapts to existing countermeasures at the upper level, Algorithm 2 is a RNS variant of an exponentiation algorithm (adapted from the Montgomery ladder [23]), proposed by M. Joye and S.-M. Yen [15]. The permutations are indiced according to the bits of the exponent. We start with the initial random permutation γ_l and we use γ_i and γ_{i+1} to represent the old and new ones at each iteration (note that γ_{i+1} can be equal to γ_i if no new permutation is selected.). Note that this generic algorithm offers many implementation options in the frequency of base exchange. Although it is always possible to pay the price for a new permutation of $\mathcal{B}$ at each iteration, this is our feeling that such an ultimate option does not necessarily provides a better security, although this seems difficult to prove at the algorithmic level.

Algorithm 2 : $RME(X, C, N, \mathcal{B})$, *Randomized Modular Exponentiation*

Input : A set $\mathcal{B} = \{m_1, \ldots, m_k, m_{k+1}, \ldots, m_{2k}\}$ of relatively prime integers ; an
  integer X less than N represented in RNS for all $m_j \in \mathcal{B}$, with $4N < M_{1,\gamma}$, where
  $M_{1,\gamma} = \prod_{i=1}^{k} m_{\gamma(i)}$ for all permutation γ of $\mathcal{B}$; a positive exponent $E = \sum_{i=0}^{l-1} e_i 2^i$.
Output : A positive integer $Z = X^E \mod N$ represented in RNS over $\mathcal{B}$.
  1: Select randomly γ_l
  2: $U_0 \leftarrow MM(1, M \mod N, N, \mathcal{B}_{2,\gamma_l}, \mathcal{B}_{1,\gamma_l})$
  3: $U_1 \leftarrow MM(X, M \mod N, N, \mathcal{B}_{2,\gamma_l}, \mathcal{B}_{1,\gamma_l})$
  4: **for** $i = l - 1$ **down to** 0 **do**
  5:   $b \leftarrow \overline{e_i}$
  6:   $U_b \leftarrow MM(U_b, U_{e_i}, N, \mathcal{B}_{1,\gamma_{i+1}}, \mathcal{B}_{2,\gamma_{i+1}})$
  7:   **if** new γ_i randomly selected **then**
  8:     $U_0 \leftarrow MM(U_0, M \mod N, N, \mathcal{B}_{2,\gamma_i}, \mathcal{B}_{1,\gamma_i})$
  9:     $U_0 \leftarrow MM(U_0, 1, N, \mathcal{B}_{1,\gamma_{i+1}}, \mathcal{B}_{2,\gamma_{i+1}})$
  10:     $U_1 \leftarrow MM(U_1, M \mod N, N, \mathcal{B}_{2,\gamma_i}, \mathcal{B}_{1,\gamma_i})$
  11:     $U_1 \leftarrow MM(U_1, 1, N, \mathcal{B}_{1,\gamma_{i+1}}, \mathcal{B}_{2,\gamma_{i+1}})$
  12:   **else**
  13:     $\gamma_i = \gamma_{i+1}$
  14:   **end if**
  15:   $U_{e_i} \leftarrow MM(U_{e_i}, U_{e_i}, N, \mathcal{B}_{1,\gamma_i}, \mathcal{B}_{2,\gamma_i})$
  16: **end for**
  17: $Z \leftarrow MM(U_0, 1, N, \mathcal{B}_{1,\gamma_0}, \mathcal{B}_{2,\gamma_0})$

---

4 Implementation Aspects

In this section we propose an efficient addressing scheme which shows that our
algorithms can be implemented rather efficiently at a reasonable hardware cost.

In a highly parallel implementation, the circuit can be built with $2k$ identical
basic cells. If k is large it might not be possible to build a circuit having actually
$2k$ cells. In this case, it is always possible to implement the algorithms with
fewer cells, at the price of less parallelization, by adding control to deal with the
available cells. Each elementary cell can perform the basic modular arithmetic
operations. It receives three operands x, y, m, one control bit and return either
the sum or the product[3] (depending on the control bit) of x and y modulo m
(see Fig. 1).

The precomputed values are stored in a multiple access memory and are
addressed through a permutation table which implements γ. Each elementary cell
has an identification number and performs the operation modulo the value given
by γ for this number. For example, in Fig. 1, the jth cell performs the modular
multiplication $x \mu_{i,j} \mod m_{\gamma(j)}$, where $\mu_{i,j}$ (see 3.2 for details) is retrieved from
the memory through the permutation table. When the value $\mu_{i,j} = |m_{\gamma(i)}^{-1}|_{m_{\gamma(j)}}$
is required, the indices i, j are passed to γ which returns the value stored at
the address $(\gamma(i), \gamma(j))$. When $i = j$, the memory blocks can be used to store
the $|M \mod N|_{m_i}$. The advantage of using a permutation table is that the cells

---

[3] We can also consider a multiply-and-add operation which returns $xy + z \mod m$.

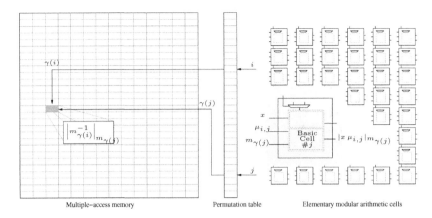

Multiple–access memory   Permutation table   Elementary modular arithmetic cells

Fig. 1. Sketch of a RNS-based cryptoprocessor with a network of elementary cells exchanging data with the memory through a permutation table.

do not have to deal with the permutations themselves. Each time we randomly select a new couple of bases, we just need to reconfigure the permutation table.

5   Side-Channel Analysis

In LRA, timing attacks are prevented by masking the input data. Actually, since $M_{1,\gamma}$ comes from a randomly chosen subset of $\mathcal{B}$, the first Montgomery multiplication provides randomization of the message at no extra cost[4]. Note also that timing attacks can still be prevented at the algorithmic level with LRA as presented in Sect. 3.3 with the adaptation of the exponentiation method proposed in [15].

LRA provides natural resistance to SPA, DPA and EMA, by generating a very high level of randomization, both at the data level and the order of the computations.

The first feature brought by the proposed LRA is the randomization of the bases. If we assume that the architecture has exactly $2k$ elementary cells, each cell performs its computations with a randomly drawn modulo. Hence, if the same computation is performed several times, a given cell never computes the same calculation. This leads to protections that act at different levels. First, we have the so-called spatial protection, since a given location, i.e. a cell, behaves differently for the same calculation (same input data); this helps to foil EMA focusing on the activity of an elementary cell. Moreover, the random choice of the bases leads to the randomization of the message. This is a well known technique to defeat DPA as well as SPA.

---

[4] If further masking is required, a random multiple of $\phi(N)$ can easily be added to the exponent (represented in classical binary representation) before each modular exponentiation.

The second feature, which acts against SPA and DPA, is due to the random bases changes during the exponentiation. Actually, the values from an iteration to another within the exponentiation algorithm are no longer correlated. By the way, it thwarts classical DPA in iterative attacks e.g. on RSA algorithms. Moreover, many implementation options in the frequency of base exchange allow the user to easily increase the level of randomization.

Previous attacks on public key protocols using Fault injection [6] works well when the values are stored in the classic positional binary number representation. For example, the attack on non-CRT implementation of RSA makes the assumption that the flip of one bit of a register during the exponentiation changes a value z to $z \pm 2^b$ for an unknown bit b. Since RNS is not such a positional number system, this assumption is not valid anymore and known fault attacks do not apply. Moreover, the use of (redundant) residue number and polynomial systems for error checking/correcting has been investigating in the past (see [14], [27]) and would apply perfectly to our system in order to reinforce the resistance against fault-based attacks (in the case of the CRT signature scheme for example). Even though fault injection issues has not been addressed here, it is not unreasonable to think that the LRA could also be used to defeat them. A deeper analysis is required in order to see how this goal can be accurately achieved.

6   Conclusions

We presented a new defense against side channel analysis adapted to public key cryptosystems operating over large finite rings or field (RSA, ElGamal, ECC over large prime fields, etc). For that purpose we introduced a Leak Resistant Arithmetic (LRA) based on Residue Number Systems (RNS). We provided concrete algorithms together with example of implementation. Our approach allows the usage of many implementation optimizations at the field operator level without introducing weaknesses. The computation overhead due to our technique is shown to be negligible regarding to the overall computation time. We have shown that the LRA provides self robustness against EMA, DPA and SPA at the field implementation level. Moreover, at an upper level, usual protections against SCA easily adapt.

References

[1] D. Agrawal, B. Archambeault J. R. Rao, and P. Rohatgi. The EM side-channel(s). In B. S. Kaliski Jr., Ç. K. Koç, and C. Paar, editors, *Cryptographic Hardware and Embedded Systems - CHES 2002*, volume 2523 of *LNCS*, pages 29–45, Redwood Shores, CA, USA, August 2002. Springer-Verlag.

[2] D. Agrawal, J. R. Rao, and P. Rohatgi. Multi-channel attacks. In C. D. Walter and C. Paar, editors, *Cryptographic Hardware and Embedded Systems - CHES 2003*, volume 2779 of *LNCS*, pages 2–16, Köln, Germany, September 2003. Springer-Verlag.

[3] J.-C. Bajard, L.-S. Didier, and P. Kornerup. Modular multiplication and base extension in residue number systems. In N. Burgess, editor, *Proceedings 15th IEEE symposium on Computer Arithmetic*, pages 59–65, Vail, Colorado, USA, June 2001.

[4] J.-C. Bajard and L. Imbert. A full RNS implementation of RSA. *IEEE Transactions on Computers*, 53(6):769–774, June 2004.

[5] E. Biham and A. Shamir. Differential fault analysis of secret key cryptosystems. In *Advances in Cryptology – CRYPTO'97*, number 1294 in LNCS, pages 513–525. Springer-Verlag, 1997.

[6] D. Boneh, R. A. DeMillo, and R. J. Lipton. On the importance of checking cryptographic protocols for faults. In W. Fumy, editor, *Advances in Cryptology – Eurocrypt'97: International Conference on the Theory and Application of Cryptographic Techniques*, volume 1233 of *LNCS*, pages 37–51, Konstanz, Germany, May 1997. Springer-Verlag.

[7] Ç. K. Koç, T. Acar, and B. S. Kaliski Jr. Analyzing and comparing montgomery multiplication algorithms. *IEEE Micro*, 16(3):26–33, June 1996.

[8] M. Ciet, M. Neve, E. Peeters, and J.-J. Quisquater. Parallel FPGA implementation of RSA with residue number systems – can side-channel threats be avoided? In *46th IEEE International Midwest Symposium on Circuits and Systems (MWSCAS-2003)*, Cairo, Egypt, December 2003.

[9] K. Gandolfi, C. Mourtel, and F. Olivier. Electromagnetic analysis: Concrete results. In Ç. K. Koç, D. Naccache, and C. Paar, editors, *Cryptographic Hardware and Embedded Systems – CHES 2001*, volume 2162 of *LNCS*, pages 251–272, Paris, France, May 2001. Springer-Verlag.

[10] H. L. Garner. The residue number system. *IRE Transactions on Electronic Computers*, EC-8:140–147, June 1959.

[11] D. M. Gordon. A survey of fast exponentiation methods. *Journal of Algorithms*, 27(1):129–146, April 1998.

[12] L. Goubin and J. Patarin. DES and differential power analysis – the duplication method. In *Cryptographic Hardware and Embedded Systems – CHES 99*, number 1717 in LNCS, pages 158–172. Springer-Verlag, 1999.

[13] G. Hachez and J.-J. Quisquater. Montgomery multiplication with no final subtraction: Improved results. In Ç. K. Koç and C. Paar, editors, *Cryptographic Hardware and Embedded Systems - CHES 2000*, volume 1965 of *LNCS*, pages 293–301. Springer-Verlag, 2000.

[14] W. K. Jenkins. The design of error checkers for self-checking residue number arithmetic. *IEEE Transactions on Computers*, C-32(4):388–396, April 1983.

[15] M. Joye and S.-M. Yen. The montgomery powering ladder. In *Cryptographic Hardware and Embedded Systems – CHES 2002*, volume 2523 of *LNCS*, pages 291–302, 2002.

[16] S. Kawamura, M. Koike, F. Sano, and A. Shimbo. Cox-rower architecture for fast parallel montgomery multiplication. In *Advances in Cryptology - EUROCRYPT 2000*, number 1807 in LNCS, pages 523–538, May 2000.

[17] D. E. Knuth. *The Art of Computer Programming, Vol. 2: Seminumerical Algorithms*. Addison-Wesley, Reading, MA, third edition, 1997.

[18] P. Kocher, J. Jaffe, and B. Jun. Differential power analysis. In M. Wiener, editor, *Advances in Cryptology – CRYPTO'99*, volume 1666 of *LNCS*, pages 388–397, Santa-Barbara, CA, USA, August 1999. Springer-Verlag.

[19] P. C. Kocher. Timing attacks on implementations of diffie-hellman, RSA, DSS, and other systems. In N. Koblitz, editor, *Advances in Cryptology - CRYPTO '96*, volume 1109 of *LNCS*, pages 104–113, Santa-Barbara, CA, USA, August 1996. Springer-Verlag.

[20] P.-Y. Liardet. Masquage de données décomposées dans un système de résidus. Patent, September 2002. Dépôt Français numéro FR0211671, dépôt Européen numéro EP03300126.

[21] A. J. Menezes, P. C. Van Oorschot, and S. A. Vanstone. *Handbook of applied cryptography*. CRC Press, 2000 N.W. Corporate Blvd., Boca Raton, FL 33431-9868, USA, 1997.

[22] P. L. Montgomery. Modular multiplication without trial division. *Mathematics of Computation*, 44(170):519–521, April 1985.

[23] P. L. Montgomery. Speeding the pollard and elliptic curve methods of factorization. *Mathematics of Computation*, 48(177):243–264, January 1987.

[24] H. Nozaki, M. Motoyama, A. Shimbo, and S. Kawamura. Implementation of RSA algorithm based on RNS montgomery multiplication. In *Cryptographic Hardware and Embedded Systems - CHES 2001*, number 2162 in LNCS, pages 364–376, September 2001.

[25] K. C. Posch and R. Posch. Modulo reduction in residue number systems. *IEEE Transactions on Parallel and Distributed Systems*, 6(5):449–454, May 1995.

[26] A. P. Shenoy and R. Kumaresan. Fast base extension using a redundant modulus in RNS. *IEEE Transactions on Computers*, 38(2):292–297, February 1989.

[27] P. R. Turner. Residue polynomial systems. *Theoretical Computer Science*, 279(1-2):29–49, May 2002.

Efficient Linear Array for Multiplication in $GF(2^m)$ Using a Normal Basis for Elliptic Curve Cryptography

Soonhak Kwon[1], Kris Gaj[2], Chang Hoon Kim[3], and Chun Pyo Hong[3]

[1] Inst. of Basic Science and Dept. of Mathematics, Sungkyunkwan University,
Suwon 440-746, Korea
shkwon@math.skku.ac.kr
[2] Dept. of Electrical and Computer Engineering, George Mason University,
University Drive, Fairfax, VA 22030, USA
kgaj@gmu.edu
[3] Dept. of Computer and Information Engineering, Daegu University,
Kyungsan 712-714, Korea
chkim@dsp.taegu.ac.kr,cphong@daegu.ac.kr

Abstract. We present a new sequential normal basis multiplier over $GF(2^m)$. The gate complexity of our multiplier is significantly reduced from that of Agnew et al. and is comparable to that of Reyhani-Masoleh and Hasan, which is the lowest complexity normal basis multiplier of the same kinds. On the other hand, the critical path delay of our multiplier is same to that of Agnew et al. Therefore it is supposed to have a shorter or the same critical path delay to that of Reyhani-Masoleh and Hasan. Moreover our method of using a Gaussian normal basis makes it easy to find a basic multiplication table of normal elements. So one can easily construct a circuit array for large finite fields, $GF(2^m)$ where $m = 163, 233, 283, 409, 571$, i.e. the five recommended fields by NIST for elliptic curve cryptography.

Keywords: Massey-Omura multiplier, Gaussian normal basis, finite field, elliptic curve cryptography, critical path delay.

1 Introduction

Finite field multiplication finds various applications in many cryptographic areas such as ECC and AES. Though one may design a finite field multiplier in a software implementation, a hardware arrangement has a strong advantage when one wants a high speed multiplier. Moreover arithmetic of $GF(2^m)$ is easily realized in a circuit design using a few logical gates. A good multiplication algorithm depends on the choice of a basis for a given finite field. Especially a normal basis is widely used [5,10,11] because it has some good properties such as simple squaring. A multiplication in $GF(2^m)$ can be classified into two types, a parallel (two dimensional) [4,5,8,10] and a sequential (linear) [1,3,9,11] architectures. Though a parallel multiplier is well suited for high speed applications, ECC requires large m for $GF(2^m)$ (at least $m = 163$) to support a sufficient security. In other words, since the parallel architecture has an area complexity of $O(m^2)$, it

M. Joye and J.-J. Quisquater (Eds.): CHES 2004, LNCS 3156, pp. 76–91, 2004.

is not suited for this application. On the other hand, a sequential multiplier has an area complexity of $O(m)$ and therefore is applicable for ECC. Since it takes m clock cycles to produce one multiplication result using a sequential multiplier, it is slower than a parallel multiplier. Consequently reducing the total delay time of a sequential multiplier is very important.

A normal basis multiplier of Massey and Omura [7] has a parallel-in, serial-out structure and has a quite long critical path delay proportional to $\log_2 m$. Agnew et al. [1] proposed a sequential multiplier which has a parallel-in, parallel-out structure. It is based on the multiplication algorithm of Massey and Omura, however the critical path delay of the multiplier of Agnew et al. is significantly reduced from that of Massey and Omura. Recently, Reyhani-Masoleh and Hasan [3] presented two sequential multipliers using a symmetric property of multiplication of normal elements. Both multipliers in [3] have roughly the same area complexity and critical path delay. These multipliers have the reduced area complexity from that of Agnew et al. with a slightly increased critical path delay. In fact, the exact critical path delay of the multipliers of Reyhani-Masoleh and Hasan is difficult to estimate in terms of m and is generally believed to be slightly longer or equal to that of Agnew et al. For example, for the case of a type II ONB, the critical path delay of Reyhani-Masoleh and Hasan [3] is $T_A + 3T_X$ while that of Agnew et al. [1] is $T_A + 2T_X$, where T_A, T_X are the delay time of a two input AND gate and a two input XOR gate, respectively. However since we are dealing with a sequential (linear) multiplier, even a small increment of critical path delay such as T_X results in a total delay of mT_X where m is the size of a field.

Our aim in this paper is to present a sequential multiplier using a Gaussian normal basis in $GF(2^m)$ for odd m. Since choosing an odd m is a necessary condition for cryptographic purposes and since a low complexity normal basis is frequently a Gaussian normal basis of type (m, k) for low k, our restriction in this paper does not cause any serious problem for practical purposes. In fact all the five recommended fields $GF(2^m)$ by NIST [16] for ECC where $m = 163, 233, 283, 409, 571$ can be dealt using our Gaussian normal basis, and the corresponding circuits are easy to construct if one follows a simple arithmetic rule of a Gaussian normal basis. We will show that the area complexity of our sequential multiplier is reduced from that of the multiplier of Agnew et al. [1] and thus comparable to that of the multiplier of Reyhani-Masoleh and Hasan [3]. Moreover the critical path delay of our multiplier is same to that of Agnew et al. and therefore is believed to be shorter or equal to that of Reyhani-Masoleh and Hasan.

2 Review of the Multipliers of Agnew et al. and Reyhani-Masoleh and Hasan

Let $GF(2^m)$ be a finite field with characteristic two. $GF(2^m)$ is a vector space of dimension m over $GF(2)$. A basis of the form $\{\alpha, \alpha^2, \alpha^{2^2}, \cdots, \alpha^{2^{m-1}}\}$ is called a normal basis for $GF(2^m)$. It is well known [6] that a normal basis exists for all $m \geq 1$. Let $\{\alpha_0, \alpha_1, \cdots, \alpha_{m-1}\}$ be a normal basis in $GF(2^m)$ with $\alpha_i = \alpha^{2^i}$. Let

$$\alpha_i \alpha_j = \sum_{s=0}^{m-1} \lambda_{ij}^{(s)} \alpha_s, \qquad (1)$$

where $\lambda_{ij}^{(s)}$ is in $GF(2)$. Then for any integer t, we have

$$\alpha_i \alpha_j = (\alpha_{i-t}\alpha_{j-t})^{2^t} = \sum_{s=0}^{m-1} \lambda_{i-t,j-t}^{(s)} \alpha_{s+t} = \sum_{s=0}^{m-1} \lambda_{i-t,j-t}^{(s-t)} \alpha_s, \qquad (2)$$

where the subscripts and superscripts of λ are reduced (mod m). Therefore comparing the coefficients of α_s, we find

$$\lambda_{ij}^{(s)} = \lambda_{i-t,j-t}^{(s-t)}. \qquad (3)$$

In particular, we have

$$\lambda_{ij}^{(s)} = \lambda_{i-s,j-s}^{(0)}. \qquad (4)$$

Letting $A = \sum_{i=0}^{m-1} a_i \alpha_i$ and $B = \sum_{j=0}^{m-1} b_j \alpha_j$ in $GF(2^m)$, we have the multiplication $C = AB = \sum_{s=0}^{m-1} c_s \alpha_s$ where

$$C = \sum_{i,j} a_i b_j \alpha_i \alpha_j = \sum_{i,j} a_i b_j \sum_{s=0}^{m-1} \lambda_{ij}^{(s)} \alpha_s = \sum_{s=0}^{m-1} (\sum_{i,j} a_i b_j \lambda_{ij}^{(s)}) \alpha_s. \qquad (5)$$

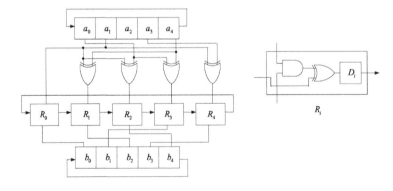

Fig. 1. A circuit of Agnew et al. in $GF(2^5)$

Therefore, using (4), we have the coefficients c_s of $C = AB$ as

$$c_s = \sum_{i,j} a_i b_j \lambda_{ij}^{(s)} = \sum_{i,j} a_i b_j \lambda_{i-s,j-s}^{(0)} = \sum_{i,j} a_{i+s} b_{j+s} \lambda_{ij}^{(0)}, \qquad (6)$$

where the subscripts of a, b and λ are reduced (mod m). The circuit of Agnew et al. [1] is a straightforward realization of the above equation with the information of the m by m matrix $(\lambda_{ij}^{(0)})$. When there is a type II ONB (optimal normal basis), it is easy to find $\lambda_{ij}^{(0)}$ as is explained in [1]. That is,

$$\lambda_{ij}^{(0)} = 1 \quad \text{iff} \quad 2^i \pm 2^j \equiv \pm 1 \pmod{2m+1}. \tag{7}$$

Figure 1 shows the circuit of Agnew et al. for the case $m = 5$ where a type II ONB is used. For arbitrary finite field, finding $\lambda_{ij}^{(0)}$ may not be so easy. However if we have a Gaussian normal basis, one can easily find $\lambda_{ij}^{(0)}$ by following a simple arithmetic rule. A Gaussian normal basis and a type II ONB will be discussed briefly in the following sections.

Recently, Reyhani-Masoleh and Hasan [3] suggested a new normal basis multiplication algorithm which significantly reduces the area complexity compared with the multiplier of Agnew et al. They used $\alpha\alpha_i$ instead of $\alpha_i\alpha_j$ and wisely utilized the symmetric property between $\alpha\alpha_i$ and $\alpha\alpha_{m-i}$. In fact they proposed two sequential multiplication architectures, so called XESMPO and AESMPO [3]. Since the hardware complexity of AESMPO is higher than that of XESMPO and both architectures have the same critical path delay, we will sketch the idea in [3,4] for the case of XESMPO. In [3,4], the multiplication $C = AB$ is expressed as

$$\sum_{i,j} a_i b_j \alpha_i \alpha_j = \sum_{i=0}^{m-1} a_i b_i \alpha_{i+1} + \sum_{i=0}^{m-1} \sum_{j \neq i} a_i b_j (\alpha\alpha_{j-i})^{2^i}$$
$$= \sum_{i=0}^{m-1} a_i b_i \alpha_{i+1} + \sum_{i=0}^{m-1} \sum_{j \neq 0} a_i b_{j+i} (\alpha\alpha_j)^{2^i}. \tag{8}$$

When m is odd, the second term of the right side of the above equation is written as

$$\sum_{i=0}^{m-1} \sum_{j=1}^{\nu} a_i b_{j+i} (\alpha\alpha_j)^{2^i} + \sum_{i=0}^{m-1} \sum_{j=m-\nu}^{m-1} a_i b_{j+i} (\alpha\alpha_j)^{2^i}, \tag{9}$$

and when m is even, it is written as

$$\sum_{i=0}^{m-1} \sum_{j=1}^{\nu} a_i b_{j+i} (\alpha\alpha_j)^{2^i} + \sum_{i=0}^{m-1} \sum_{j=m-\nu}^{m-1} a_i b_{j+i} (\alpha\alpha_j)^{2^i} + \sum_{i=0}^{m-1} a_i b_{\nu+1+i} (\alpha\alpha_{\nu+1})^{2^i}, \tag{10}$$

where $\nu = \lfloor \frac{m-1}{2} \rfloor$, i.e. $m = 2\nu + 1$ or $m = 2\nu + 2$. Also the second term of (9) and (10) is written as

$$\sum_{i=0}^{m-1} \sum_{j=m-\nu}^{m-1} a_i b_{j+i} (\alpha\alpha_j)^{2^i} = \sum_{i=0}^{m-1} \sum_{j=1}^{\nu} a_i b_{m-j+i} (\alpha\alpha_{m-j})^{2^i}$$

$$= \sum_{i=0}^{m-1} \sum_{j=1}^{\nu} a_{i+j} b_i (\alpha\alpha_{m-j})^{2^{i+j}} \quad (11)$$

$$= \sum_{i=0}^{m-1} \sum_{j=1}^{\nu} a_{i+j} b_i (\alpha\alpha_j)^{2^i},$$

where the first (resp. second) equality comes from the rearrangement of the summation with respect to j (resp. i) and all the subscripts are reduced to (mod m). Therefore we have the basic multiplication formula of Reyhani-Masoleh and Hasan depending on whether m is *odd* or m is *even* as

$$AB = \sum_{i=0}^{m-1} a_i b_i \alpha_{i+1} + \sum_{i=0}^{m-1} \sum_{j=1}^{\nu} (a_i b_{j+i} + a_{j+i} b_i)(\alpha\alpha_j)^{2^i}, \quad (12)$$

or

$$AB = \sum_{i=0}^{m-1} a_i b_i \alpha_{i+1} + \sum_{i=0}^{m-1} \sum_{j=1}^{\nu} (a_i b_{j+i} + a_{j+i} b_i)(\alpha\alpha_j)^{2^i} + \sum_{i=0}^{m-1} a_i b_{\nu+1+i} (\alpha\alpha_{\nu+1})^{2^i}. \quad (13)$$

Using these formulas, they derived a sequential multiplier where the gate complexity is significantly reduced from that of [1]. The circuit of the multiplier is shown in Figure 2 for $m = 5$ where a type II ONB is used.

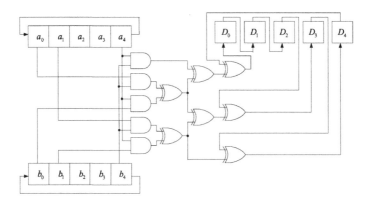

Fig. 2. A circuit of Reyhani-Masoleh and Hasan in $GF(2^5)$

3   Gaussian Normal Basis of Type k in $GF(2^m)$

We will briefly explain basic multiplication principle in $GF(2^m)$ with a Gaussian normal basis of type k over $GF(2)$ (See [6,12].). Let m, k be positive integers such that $p = mk + 1$ is a prime $\neq 2$. Let $K = \langle \tau \rangle$ be a unique subgroup of order k in $GF(p)^{\times}$. Let β be a primitive pth root of unity in $GF(2^{mk})$. The following element

$$\alpha = \sum_{j=0}^{k-1} \beta^{\tau^j} \tag{14}$$

is called a Gauss period of type (m, k) over $GF(2)$. Let $ord_p 2$ be the order of 2 (mod p) and assume $gcd(mk/ord_p 2, m) = 1$. Then it is well known [6] that α is a normal element in $GF(2^m)$. That is, letting $\alpha_i = \alpha^{2^i}$ for $0 \leq i \leq m - 1$, $\{\alpha_0, \alpha_1, \alpha_2, \cdots, \alpha_{m-1}\}$ is a basis for $GF(2^m)$ over $GF(2)$. It is called a Gaussian normal basis of type k or (m, k) in $GF(2^m)$. Since $K = \langle \tau \rangle$ is a subgroup of order k in the cyclic group $GF(p)^{\times}$, the quotient group $GF(p)^{\times}/K$ is also a cyclic group of order m and the generator of the group is $2K$. Therefore we have a coset decomposition of $GF(p)^{\times}$ as a disjoint union,

$$GF(p)^{\times} = K_0 \cup K_1 \cup K_2 \cdots \cup K_{m-1}, \tag{15}$$

where $K_i = 2^i K, 0 \leq i \leq m - 1$, and an element in $GF(p)^{\times}$ is uniquely written as $\tau^s 2^t$ for some $0 \leq s \leq k - 1$ and $0 \leq t \leq m - 1$. For each $0 \leq i \leq m - 1$, we have

$$\alpha\alpha_i = \sum_{s=0}^{k-1} \beta^{\tau^s} \sum_{t=0}^{k-1} \beta^{\tau^t 2^i} = \sum_{s=0}^{k-1}\sum_{t=0}^{k-1} \beta^{\tau^s(1+\tau^{t-s}2^i)} = \sum_{s=0}^{k-1}\sum_{t=0}^{k-1} \beta^{\tau^s(1+\tau^t 2^i)}. \tag{16}$$

From (15), there are unique $0 \leq u \leq k - 1$ and $0 \leq v \leq m - 1$ such that $1 + \tau^u 2^v = 0 \in GF(p)$. If $t \neq u$ or $i \neq v$, then we have $1 + \tau^t 2^i \in K_{\sigma(t,i)}$ for some $0 \leq \sigma(t, i) \leq m - 1$ depending on t and i. Thus we may write $1 + \tau^t 2^i = \tau^{t'} 2^{\sigma(t,i)}$ for some t'. Now when $i \neq v$,

$$\alpha\alpha_i = \sum_{s=0}^{k-1}\sum_{t=0}^{k-1} \beta^{\tau^s(1+\tau^t 2^i)} = \sum_{s=0}^{k-1}\sum_{t=0}^{k-1} \beta^{\tau^s(\tau^{t'} 2^{\sigma(t,i)})}$$

$$= \sum_{t=0}^{k-1}\sum_{s=0}^{k-1} \beta^{\tau^{s+t'} 2^{\sigma(t,i)}} = \sum_{t=0}^{k-1} \alpha^{2^{\sigma(t,i)}} = \sum_{t=0}^{k-1} \alpha_{\sigma(t,i)}. \tag{17}$$

Also when $i = v$,

$$\alpha\alpha_v = \sum_{s=0}^{k-1}\sum_{t=0}^{k-1} \beta^{\tau^s(1+\tau^t 2^v)} = \sum_{t\neq u}\sum_{s=0}^{k-1} \beta^{\tau^s(\tau^{t'} 2^{\sigma(t,v)})} + \sum_{s=0}^{k-1} \beta^{\tau^s(1+\tau^u 2^v)}$$

$$= \sum_{t\neq u}\sum_{s=0}^{k-1} \beta^{\tau^{s+t'} 2^{\sigma(t,v)}} + \sum_{s=0}^{k-1} 1 = \sum_{t\neq u} \alpha^{2^{\sigma(t,v)}} + k = \sum_{t\neq u} \alpha_{\sigma(t,v)} + k. \tag{18}$$

Therefore $\alpha\alpha_i$ is computed by the sum of at most k basis elements in $\{\alpha_0, \alpha_1, \cdots, \alpha_{m-1}\}$ for $i \neq v$ and $\alpha\alpha_v$ is computed by the sum of at most $k-1$ basis elements and the constant term $k \equiv 0, 1 \in GF(2)$.

4   New Multiplication Algorithm Using a Gaussian Normal Basis in $GF(2^m)$ for m Odd

4.1   Symmetry of $(\lambda_{ij}^{(s)})$ and (λ_{ij})

Efficient implementation of ECC over a binary field $GF(2^m)$ requires that m is *odd*, or more strongly m is *prime*. These conditions are necessary to avoid Pohlig-Helllman type attacks. For example, all the five binary fields $GF(2^m)$, $m = 163, 233, 283, 409, 571$ suggested by NIST [16] for ECDSA have the property that $m = prime$. Therefore it is not so serious restriction to assume that m is odd for a fast multiplication algorithm if one is interested in this kind of applications. For odd values of m, it is well known [15] that a Gaussian normal basis of type k or (m, k) always exists for some $k \geq 1$. Since $mk + 1$ is a prime with $m = odd$, it follows that k is even. Thus it is enough to study the multiplication in $GF(2^m)$ for odd m with a Gaussian normal basis of type k for even k. To derive a low complexity architecture, in view of the multiplication formulas (17) and (18), one should choose a small k, i.e. low complexity Gaussian normal basis. The least possible even $k \geq 1$ is $k = 2$. This is so called a type II ONB (optimal normal basis) or more specifically a type 2 Gaussian normal basis. Among the five binary fields recommended by NIST, $m = 233$ is the only case where a type II ONB exists. On the other hand, the lowest complexity Gaussian normal basis for the rest of the fields are type 4 Gaussian normal basis when $m = 163, 409$, type 6 Gaussian normal basis when $m = 283$, and type 10 Gaussian normal basis when $m = 571$ (See [12]).

Let $\{\alpha_0, \alpha_1, \cdots, \alpha_{m-1}\}$ be any normal basis in $GF(2^m)$ with $\alpha_i = \alpha^{2^i}$ and let

$$\alpha\alpha_i = \sum_{j=0}^{m-1} \lambda_{ij}\alpha_j, \qquad (19)$$

where λ_{ij} is in $GF(2)$. Taking repeated powers of 2 for both sides of the above equation, one finds

$$\lambda_{ij}^{(s)} = \lambda_{i-j,s-j}, \qquad (20)$$

where $\lambda_{ij}^{(s)}$ is defined in (1). An explicit table of $\lambda_{ij}^{(s)}$ is necessary for construction of the multipliers of Agnew et al. and also of Reyhani-Masoleh and Hasan. Finding $\lambda_{ij}^{(s)}$ may not be so easy unless one has a sufficient information on the given normal basis. Also note that $(\lambda_{ij}^{(s)})$ is a symmetric matrix but (λ_{ij}) is not in general. However, it turns out that (λ_{ij}) is a symmetric matrix if a Gaussian normal basis of type k with k even is used. More precisely, we have the following.

Lemma 1. *If $\{\alpha_0, \alpha_1, \cdots, \alpha_{m-1}\}$ is a Gaussian normal basis of type k where k is even, then we have*

$$\lambda_{ij}^{(0)} = \lambda_{ij}.$$

Proof. From (20), it is enough to show that $\lambda_{ij} = \lambda_{i-j,-j}$. From the formulas (17) and (18), it is clear that $\lambda_{ij} = 1$ if and only there exist odd pairs of (s, s') (mod k) such that

$$1 + \tau^s 2^i = \tau^{s'} 2^j, \tag{21}$$

where $\langle \tau \rangle$ is a unique multiplicative subgroup of order k in $GF(p)^\times$ with $p = mk + 1$. Let S be the set of all pairs (s, s') (mod k) satisfying (21) and same way define T as the set of all pairs (t, t') (mod k) satisfying $1 + \tau^t 2^{i-j} = \tau^{t'} 2^{-j}$. To prove $\lambda_{ij} = \lambda_{i-j,-j}$, it suffices to show that the sets S and T have the same cardinality. Dividing both sides of the equation (21) by $\tau^{s'} 2^j$, we get

$$\tau^{-s'} 2^{-j} + \tau^{s-s'} 2^{i-j} = 1. \tag{22}$$

Since the order of τ is k where k is even, we have $-1 = \tau^{\frac{k}{2}}$ and therefore

$$\tau^{-s'} 2^{-j} = 1 + \tau^{\frac{k}{2}+s-s'} 2^{i-j}. \tag{23}$$

Since the map $f_S : S \to T$ defined by $f_S(s, s') = (\frac{k}{2} + s - s', -s')$ and the map $f_T : T \to S$ defined by $f_T(t, t') = (\frac{k}{2} + t - t', -t')$ give one to one correspondence, i.e. $f_S \circ f_T = id = f_T \circ f_S$, we are done. □

4.2 Construction of a Sequential Multiplier and Complexity Analysis

Now from (6) and also from Lemma 1, we have c_s of $C = \sum_{i=0}^{m-1} c_s \alpha_s = AB$ as

$$c_s = \sum_{i,j} a_{i+s} b_{j+s} \lambda_{ij}^{(0)} = \sum_{i,j} a_{i+s} b_{j+s} \lambda_{ij} = \sum_{j=0}^{m-1} \left(\sum_{i=0}^{m-1} a_{i+s} \lambda_{ij} \right) b_{j+s}. \tag{24}$$

Let us define an element x_{st}, $0 \le s, t \le m-1$, in $GF(2)$ as

$$x_{st} = \left(\sum_{i=0}^{m-1} a_{i+s} \lambda_{it} \right) b_{t+s}, \tag{25}$$

with corresponding matrix $X = (x_{st})$. Then the tth column vector X_t of X is

$$X_t = (x_{0t}, x_{1t}, \cdots, x_{m-1,t})^T, \tag{26}$$

where $(x_{0t}, x_{1t}, \cdots, x_{m-1,t})^T$ is the transposition of the row vector $(x_{0t}, x_{1t}, \cdots, x_{m-1,t})$. Also the sum of all column vectors X_t, $t = 0, 1, \cdots, m-1$, is exactly

$$(c_0, c_1, \cdots, c_{m-1})^T, \tag{27}$$

because $\sum_{t=0}^{m-1} x_{st} = c_s$. Our purpose is to reduce the gate complexity of our multiplier by rearranging the column vectors X_t and reusing partial sums in the computation. Let $m - 1 = 2\nu$ and define m by m matrix $Y = (y_{st})$ by the following permutation of the column vectors of X as follows; When ν is odd, define Y as

$$(X_\nu, \cdots, X_3, X_1, X_{m-1}, X_{m-3}, \cdots, X_{m-\nu}, X_{\nu-1}, \cdots, X_2, X_0, X_{m-2}, \cdots, X_{m-\nu+1}),$$
(28)

and when ν is even, Y is defined as

$$(X_\nu, \cdots, X_2, X_0, X_{m-2}, \cdots, X_{m-\nu}, X_{\nu-1}, \cdots, X_3, X_1, X_{m-1}, X_{m-3}, \cdots, X_{m-\nu+1}).$$
(29)

Then the sum of all column vectors Y_t, $0 \le t \le m - 1$, of Y with $Y_t = (y_{0t}, y_{1t}, \cdots, y_{m-1,t})^T$ is same to the sum of all column vectors X_t, $0 \le t \le m-1$, of X which is $(c_0, c_1, \cdots, c_{m-1})^T$.

To derive a parallel-in, parallel-out multiplication architecture, we will compute the sum of shifted diagonal vectors of Y, instead of computing the sum of column vectors of Y. This can be done from the following observations. In the expression of the matrix Y, there are exactly $t - 1$ columns between the vectors X_t and X_{m-t}. Also, sth entry of X_t and $s + t$th entry of X_{m-t} have the same terms of a_is in their summands. In other words, from (25), we have

$$x_{s+t,m-t} = \left(\sum_{i=0}^{m-1} a_{i+s+t}\lambda_{i,-t}\right)b_s = \left(\sum_{i=0}^{m-1} a_{i+s}\lambda_{i-t,-t}\right)b_s = \left(\sum_{i=0}^{m-1} a_{i+s}\lambda_{it}\right)b_s, \quad (30)$$

where the third expression comes from the rearrangement of the summation on the subscript i and the last expression comes from Lemma 1 saying $\lambda_{ij} = \lambda_{i-j,-j}$. Thus x_{st} and $x_{s+t,m-t}$ have the same term $\sum_{i=0}^{m-1} a_{i+s}\lambda_{it}$ in their expression and this will save the number of XOR gates during the computation of AB.

Table 1. New multiplication algorithm

---

1. $A = \sum_{i=0}^{m-1} a_i\alpha_i$ and $B = \sum_{i=0}^{m-1} b_i\alpha_i$ are loaded in m-bit registers respectively. Also intermediate values $D_0, D_1, \cdots, D_{m-1}$ of the multiplication are all set to zero.
2. For $t = 0$ to $m - 1$, do the following;

$$y_{s,s+t} + D_{s+t} \longrightarrow D_{s+t+1}, \quad (31)$$

where the above computation is done in parallel for all $0 \le s \le m - 1$.
3. After mth iteration, we have $D_i = c_i$ for all $0 \le i \le m-1$, where $AB = \sum_{i=0}^{m-1} c_i\alpha_i$.

Let us explain the above algorithm in detail. At the first cycle ($t = 0$), $D_{s+1} = D_s + y_{ss}$ are simultaneously computed for all $0 \le s \le m - 1$, i.e. $D_1 = y_{00}, D_2 = y_{11}, \cdots, D_0 = y_{m-1,m-1}$. When $t = 1$, $D_{s+2} = D_{s+1} + y_{s,s+1}$ are simultaneously computed for all $0 \le s \le m - 1$, i.e. $D_2 = D_1 + y_{01} = y_{00} + y_{01}, D_3 = D_2 + y_{12} = $

$y_{11}+y_{12}, \cdots, D_1 = D_0+y_{m-1,0} = y_{m-1,m-1}+y_{m-1,0}$. Finally, at mth $(t = m-1)$ cycle, $D_s = D_{s-1} + y_{s,s-1}$ are simultaneously computed. That is,

$$D_0 = D_{m-1} + y_{0,m-1} = y_{00} + y_{01} + \cdots + y_{0,m-1} = c_0,$$
$$D_1 = D_0 + y_{10} = y_{11} + y_{12} + \cdots + y_{10} = c_1,$$
$$\cdots \cdots$$
$$\cdots \cdots$$
$$D_{m-1} = D_{m-2} + y_{m-1,m-2} = y_{m-1,m-1} + y_{m-1,0} + \cdots + y_{m-1,m-2} = c_{m-1}. \tag{32}$$

In other words, for a fixed s, the final value D_s is sequentially computed in the following order

$$D_s = \overbrace{y_{ss}}^{D_{s+1}} + \underbrace{y_{s,s+1}}_{D_{s+2}} + y_{s,s+2} + \cdots + y_{s,s-1} = \sum_{i=0}^{m-1} y_{s,s+i} = c_s. \tag{33}$$

Note that $y_{s-1,s}$ and y_{ss}, $0 \le s \le m - 1$, in the equation (32), are from the same column Y_s of the matrix Y. Since Y is obtained by a column permutation of a matrix X, we conclude that $y_{s-1,s} = x_{s-1,s'}$ and $y_{ss} = x_{ss'}$ for some s' depending on s. Moreover from the equation (25), we get

$$x_{ss'} = (\sum_{i=0}^{m-1} a_{i+s}\lambda_{is'})b_{s'+s}, \quad and \quad x_{s-1,s'} = (\sum_{i=0}^{m-1} a_{i+s-1}\lambda_{is'})b_{s'+s-1}, \tag{34}$$

which implies that $x_{s-1,s'}$ $(= y_{s-1,s})$ is obtained by right cyclic shifting by one position of the vectors a_is and b_is from the expression $x_{s,s'}$ $(= y_{s,s})$. Since this can be done without any extra cost, all the necessary gates to construct a circuit from the algorithm in Table 1 are the gates needed to compute the first (i.e. $t = 0$) clock cycle of the step 2 of the algorithm,

$$D_{s+1} = D_s + y_{ss}, \quad 0 \le s \le m - 1. \tag{35}$$

Recall that, for each s, there is a corresponding (because of a permutation) s' such that

$$y_{ss} = x_{ss'} = (\sum_{i=0}^{m-1} a_{i+s}\lambda_{is'})b_{s'+s}. \tag{36}$$

If $s' \ne 0$, i.e. if $x_{ss'}$ is not in the 0th column of X, then from the equations (25) and (30), we find that the necessary XOR gates to compute $x_{ss'}$ and $x_{s+s',m-s'}$ (which are the diagonal entries of the matrix Y) can be shared. Note that $x_{ss'} = (\sum_{i=0}^{m-1} a_{i+s}\lambda_{is'})b_{s'+s}$ can be computed by one AND gate and at most $k-1$ XOR gates since the multiplication matrix (λ_{ij}) of a Gaussian normal basis of type k has at most k nonzero entries for each column (row) in view of the equation (17). Thus the total number of necessary gates to compute all $y_{ss} = x_{ss'}$ with $s' \ne 0$ is $m - 1$ AND gates plus $\frac{m-1}{2}(k - 1)$ XOR gates.

Table 2. Comparison with previously proposed architectures

	Critical path delay (Type II ONB case)	AND	XOR (Type II ONB case)	flip-flop
Massey and Omura [7]	$\leq T_A + \lceil \log_2 (mk) \rceil T_X$ $(T_A + \lceil \log_2 (2m) \rceil T_X)$	C_N	$\leq C_N - 1$ $(2m - 2)$	$2m$
Agnew et al. [1]	$\leq T_A + (1 + \lceil \log_2 k \rceil) T_X$ $(T_A + 2T_X)$	m	$\leq C_N$ $(2m - 1)$	$3m$
Reyhani-Masoleh and Hasan [3]	$\leq T_A + (1 + \lceil \log_2 (k + 2) \rceil) T_X$ $(T_A + 3T_X)$	m	$\leq \frac{1}{2}(C_N + 1) + \lfloor \frac{m}{2} \rfloor$ $(\frac{3m-1}{2})$	$3m$
This paper	$\leq T_A + (1 + \lceil \log_2 k \rceil) T_X$ $(T_A + 2T_X)$	m	$\leq m + \frac{m-1}{2}(k - 1)$ $(\frac{3m-1}{2})$	$3m$

When $s' = 0$, then the number of nonzero entries of λ_{i0}, $0 \leq i \leq m - 1$, is one because $\alpha\alpha_0 = \alpha^2 = \alpha_1$. Therefore we need one AND gate and no XOR gate to compute $x_{ss'}$ with $s' = 0$. Since the addition $D_s + y_{ss}$, $0 \leq s \leq m - 1$, in (35) needs one XOR gate for each $0 \leq s \leq m - 1$, the total gate complexity of our multiplier is m AND gates plus at most $m + \frac{m-1}{2}(k-1)$ XOR gates. The critical path delay can also be evaluated easily. It is clear from (35) and (36) that the critical path delay is at most $T_A + (1 + \lceil \log_2 k \rceil) T_X$. We compare our sequential multiplier with other multipliers of the same kinds in Table 2. In the table, C_N denotes the number of nonzero entries in the matrix $(\lambda_{ij}^{(0)})$. It is well known [6] that $C_N \leq mk + m - k$ if k is odd and $C_N \leq mk - 1$ if k is even. In our case of $GF(2^m)$ with $m = odd$, it is easy, from (17) and (18), to see that C_N has a more strong bound $C_N \leq mk - k + 1$. Thus the bounds $\leq \frac{C_N+1}{2} + \lfloor \frac{m}{2} \rfloor$ in [3] is same to $\leq \frac{mk-k+2}{2} + \frac{m-1}{2} = \frac{2m+mk-m-k+1}{2} = m + \frac{m-1}{2}(k - 1)$. Consequently the circuit in [3] and our multiplier have more or less the same hardware complexity.

4.3   Gaussian Normal Basis of Type 2 and 4 for ECC

Let $p = 2m + 1$ be a prime such that $gcd(2m/ord_p2, m) = 1$, i.e. either 2 is a primitive root (mod p) or $ord_p2 = m$ and $m = odd$. Then the element $\alpha = \beta + \beta^{-1}$ where β is a primitive pth root of unity in $GF(2^{2m})$ forms a normal basis $\{\alpha_0, \alpha_1, \cdots, \alpha_{m-1}\}$ in $GF(2^m)$, which we call a Gaussian normal basis of type 2 (or a type II ONB). A multiplication matrix (λ_{ij}) of $\alpha\alpha_i$ has the following property; $\lambda_{ij} = 1$ if and only if $1 \pm 2^i \equiv \pm 2^j$ (mod p) for any choice of $\pm$ sign. This is obvious from the basic properties of Gaussian normal basis in Section 3. Since m divides ord_p2, $i = 0$ is a unique value (mod m) satisfying $1 \pm 2^i \equiv 0$ (mod p). That is, $\alpha\alpha_0 = \alpha_1$ and the 0th row of (λ_{ij}) is $(0, 1, 0, \cdots, 0)$. If $i \neq 0$, then $1 \pm 2^i \not\equiv 0$ (mod p) and thus ith $(i \neq 0)$ row of (λ_{ij}) contains exactly two nonzero entries. Therefore for the case of a type II optimal normal basis, we need m AND gates and $m + \frac{m-1}{2} = \frac{3m-1}{2}$ XOR gates. Also the critical path delay is $T_A + 2T_X$, while that of [3] is $T_A + 3T_X$. Let us give a more explicit example for the case $m = 5$.

Example 1. Let β be a primitive 11th root of of unity in $GF(2^{10})$ and let $\alpha = \beta + \beta^{-1}$ be a type II optimal normal element in $GF(2^5)$. The computations of $\alpha\alpha_i$, $0 \leq i \leq 4$, are easily done from the following table. For each block regarding K and K', (s,t) entry with $0 \leq s \leq 1$ and $0 \leq t \leq 4$ has the value $\tau^s 2^t$ and $1 + \tau^s 2^t$ respectively, where $\langle \tau \rangle = \langle -1 \rangle$ is a unique multiplicative subgroup of order 2 in $GF(11)^\times$.

Table 3. Computation of K_i and K'_i using a type II ONB in $GF(2^m)$ for $m = 5$

K_0	K_1	K_2	K_3	K_4	K'_0	K'_1	K'_2	K'_3	K'_4
1	2	4	8	5	2	3	5	9	6
-1	-2	-4	-8	-5	0	-1	-3	-7	-4

From the above table, it can be found that $\alpha\alpha_0 = \alpha_1$ and

$$\alpha\alpha_1 = \alpha_0 + \alpha_3, \quad \alpha\alpha_2 = \alpha_3 + \alpha_4, \quad \alpha\alpha_3 = \alpha_1 + \alpha_2, \quad \alpha\alpha_4 = \alpha_2 + \alpha_4. \tag{37}$$

For example, the computation of $\alpha\alpha_3$ can be done as follows. See the block K'_3 and find $9 \equiv -2 \pmod{11}$ is in K_1 and $-7 \equiv 4$ is in K_2. Thus we have $\alpha\alpha_3 = \alpha_1 + \alpha_2$. In fact, for the case of type II ONB, there is a more regular expression called a palindromic representation which enables us to find the multiplication table more easily. However for the general treatments of all Gaussian normal bases of type k for arbitrary k, we are following this rule. Note that for all other type II ONB where $m \neq 5$, the multiplication table can be derived exactly the same manner. From (37), the corresponding matrix (λ_{ij}) for $m = 5$ is

$$(\lambda_{ij}) = \begin{pmatrix} 0 & 1 & 0 & 0 & 0 \\ 1 & 0 & 0 & 1 & 0 \\ 0 & 0 & 0 & 1 & 1 \\ 0 & 1 & 1 & 0 & 0 \\ 0 & 0 & 1 & 0 & 1 \end{pmatrix}, \tag{38}$$

and using (24),(25),(28),(29), we find that the multiplication $C = \sum_{i=0}^{4} c_i \alpha_i$ of $A = \sum_{i=0}^{4} a_i \alpha_i$ and $B = \sum_{i=0}^{4} b_i \alpha_i$ is written as follows.

$$c_0 = \underline{(a_3 + a_4)b_2} + a_1 b_0 + (a_1 + a_2)b_3 + (a_0 + a_3)b_1 + (a_2 + a_4)b_4$$
$$c_1 = (a_4 + a_0)b_3 + \underline{a_2 b_1} + (a_2 + a_3)b_4 + (a_1 + a_4)b_2 + (a_3 + a_0)b_0$$
$$c_2 = (a_0 + a_1)b_4 + a_3 b_2 + \underline{(a_3 + a_4)b_0} + (a_2 + a_0)b_3 + (a_4 + a_1)b_1 \tag{39}$$
$$c_3 = (a_1 + a_2)b_0 + a_4 b_3 + (a_4 + a_0)b_1 + \underline{(a_3 + a_1)b_4} + (a_0 + a_2)b_2$$
$$c_4 = (a_2 + a_3)b_1 + a_0 b_4 + (a_0 + a_1)b_2 + (a_4 + a_2)b_0 + \underline{(a_1 + a_3)b_3}$$

From this, one has the shift register arrangement of $C = AB$ using a type II ONB in $GF(2^m)$ for $m = 5$ and it is shown in Figure 3. Note that the underlined entries are the first terms to be computed. Also note that the (shifted) diagonal entries have the common terms of a_is.

As is mentioned before, there exists only one field $GF(2^{233})$ for which a type II ONB exists in $GF(2^m)$ among the recommended five fields $GF(2^m)$, $m = 163, 233, 283, 409, 571$, by NIST. Though the circuits of multiplication using a type II ONB are presented in many places [1,3,10,11], the authors could not find an explicit example of a circuit design using a Gaussian normal basis of

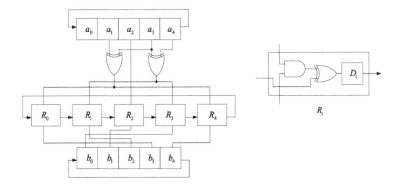

Fig. 3. A new multiplication circuit using a type II ONB in $GF(2^m)$ for $m = 5$

type $k > 2$. Since there are two fields $GF(2^{163}), GF(2^{409})$ for which a Gaussian normal basis of type 4 exists, it is worthwhile to study the multiplication and the corresponding circuit for this case. For the clarity of exposition, we will explain a Gaussian normal basis of type $k = 4$ in $GF(2^m)$ for $m = 7$. Note that the general case can be dealt in the same manner as in the following example.

Example 2. Let $p = 29 = mk + 1$ with $m = 7, k = 4$ where a Gauss period α of type $(7, 4)$ exists in $GF(2^7)$. In this case, the unique cyclic subgroup of order 4 in $GF(29)^\times$ is $K = \{1, 2^7, 2^{14}, 2^{21}\} = \{1, 12, 28, 17\}$. Let β be a primitive 29th root of unity in $GF(2^{28})$. Thus letting $\tau = 12$, a normal element α is written as $\alpha = \beta + \beta^{12} + \beta^{17} + \beta^{28}$ and $\{\alpha_0, \alpha_1, \cdots, \alpha_6\}$ is a normal basis in $GF(2^7)$. The computations of $\alpha\alpha_i$, $0 \le i \le 6$, are done from the following table. For each block regarding K and K', (s, t) entry with $0 \le s \le 3$ and $0 \le t \le 6$ has the value $\tau^s 2^t$ and $1 + \tau^s 2^t$ respectively.

Table 4. Computation of K_i and K'_i using a Gaussian normal basis of type $k = 4$ in $GF(2^m)$ for $m = 7$

K_0	K_1	K_2	K_3	K_4	K_5	K_6	K'_0	K'_1	K'_2	K'_3	K'_4	K'_5	K'_6
1	2	4	8	16	3	6	2	3	5	9	17	4	7
12	24	19	9	18	7	14	13	25	20	10	19	8	15
28	27	25	21	13	26	23	0	28	26	22	14	27	24
17	5	10	20	11	22	15	18	6	11	21	12	23	16

From the above table, we find $\alpha\alpha_0 = \alpha_1$ and

$$\alpha\alpha_1 = \alpha_0 + \alpha_2 + \alpha_5 + \alpha_6, \quad \alpha\alpha_2 = \alpha_1 + \alpha_3 + \alpha_4 + \alpha_5, \quad \alpha\alpha_3 = \alpha_2 + \alpha_5,$$
$$\alpha\alpha_4 = \alpha_2 + \alpha_6, \quad \alpha\alpha_5 = \alpha_1 + \alpha_2 + \alpha_3 + \alpha_6, \quad \alpha\alpha_6 = \alpha_1 + \alpha_4 + \alpha_5 + \alpha_6. \tag{40}$$

For example, see the block K'_2 for the expression of $\alpha\alpha_2$. The entries of K'_2 are $5, 20, 26, 11$. Now see the blocks of K_is and find $5 \in K_1, 20 \in K_3, 26 \in K_5, 11 \in K_4$. Thus we get $\alpha\alpha_2 = \alpha_1 + \alpha_3 + \alpha_4 + \alpha_5$. From (40), the multiplication matrix (λ_{ij}) is written as

$$(\lambda_{ij}) = \begin{pmatrix} 0\,1\,0\,0\,0\,0\,0 \\ 1\,0\,1\,0\,0\,1\,1 \\ 0\,1\,0\,1\,1\,1\,0 \\ 0\,0\,1\,0\,0\,1\,0 \\ 0\,0\,1\,0\,0\,0\,1 \\ 0\,1\,1\,1\,0\,0\,1 \\ 0\,1\,0\,0\,1\,1\,1 \end{pmatrix}, \tag{41}$$

and again using the relations (24),(25),(28),(29), we get the following multiplication result $C = AB = \sum_{i=0}^{6} c_i \alpha_i$. In the following table, a_{ijkl} is defined as $a_{ijkl} = a_i + a_j + a_k + a_l$. For example, we have $c_0 = (a_2 + a_5)b_3 + (a_0 + a_2 + a_5 + a_6)b_1 + (a_1 + a_4 + a_5 + a_6)b_6 + (a_2 + a_6)b_4 + (a_1 + a_3 + a_4 + a_5)b_2 + a_1 b_0 + (a_1 + a_2 + a_3 + a_6)b_5$.

$$\begin{aligned}
c_0 &= \underline{(a_2 + a_5)b_3} + a_{0256}b_1 + a_{1456}b_6 + (a_2 + a_6)b_4 + a_{1345}b_2 + a_1 b_0 + a_{1236}b_5 \\
c_1 &= (a_3 + a_6)b_4 + \underline{a_{1360}b_2} + a_{2560}b_0 + (a_3 + a_0)b_5 + a_{2456}b_3 + a_2 b_1 + a_{2340}b_6 \\
c_2 &= (a_4 + a_0)b_5 + a_{2401}b_3 + \underline{a_{3601}b_1} + (a_4 + a_1)b_6 + a_{3560}b_4 + a_3 b_2 + a_{3451}b_0 \\
c_3 &= (a_5 + a_1)b_6 + a_{3512}b_4 + a_{4012}b_2 + \underline{(a_5 + a_2)b_0} + a_{4601}b_5 + a_3 b_3 + a_{4562}b_1 \quad (42) \\
c_4 &= (a_6 + a_2)b_0 + a_{4623}b_5 + a_{5123}b_3 + (a_6 + a_3)b_1 + \underline{a_{5012}b_6} + a_4 b_4 + a_{5603}b_2 \\
c_5 &= (a_0 + a_3)b_1 + a_{5034}b_6 + a_{6234}b_4 + (a_0 + a_4)b_2 + a_{6123}b_0 + \underline{a_6 b_5} + a_{6014}b_3 \\
c_6 &= (a_1 + a_4)b_2 + a_{6145}b_0 + a_{0345}b_5 + (a_1 + a_5)b_3 + a_{0234}b_1 + a_0 b_6 + \underline{a_{0125}b_4}
\end{aligned}$$

The corresponding shift register arrangement of $C = AB$ using a Gaussian normal basis of type 4 in $GF(2^m)$ for $m = 7$ is shown in Figure 4. Also note that the underlined entries are the first terms to be computed and the (shifted) diagonal entries have the common terms of a_is. The critical path delay of the circuit using a type 4 Gaussian normal basis is only $T_A + 3T_X$ and can be effectively realized for the case $GF(2^{163})$ and $GF(2^{409})$ also.

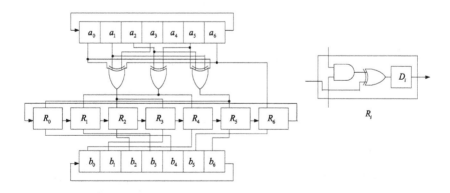

Fig. 4. A new multiplication circuit using a Gaussian normal basis of type 4 in $GF(2^m)$ for $m = 7$

5   Conclusions

In this paper, we proposed a low complexity sequential normal basis multiplier over $GF(2^m)$ for odd m using a Gaussian normal basis of type k. Since, in many cryptographic applications, m should be an odd integer or a prime, our assumption on m is not at all restrictive for a practical purpose. We presented a general method of constructing a circuit arrangement of the multiplier and showed explicit examples for the cases of type 2 and 4 Gaussian normal bases. Among the five binary fields, $GF(2^m)$ with $m = 163, 233, 283, 409, 571$, recommended by NIST [16] for ECC, our examples cover the cases $m = 163, 233, 409$ since $GF(2^{233})$ has a type II ONB and $GF(2^{163}), GF(2^{409})$ have a Gaussian normal basis of type 4. Our general method can also be applied to other fields $GF(2^{283})$ and $GF(2^{571})$ since they have a Gaussian normal basis of type 6 and 10, respectively. Compared with previously proposed architectures of the same kinds, our multiplier has a superior or comparable area complexity and delay time. Thus it is well suited for many applications such as VLSI implementation of elliptic curve cryptographic protocols.

References

1. G.B. Agnew, R.C. Mullin, I. Onyszchuk, and S.A. Vanstone, "An implementation for a fast public key cryptosystem," *J. Cryptology*, vol. 3, pp. 63–79, 1991.
2. G.B. Agnew, R.C. Mullin, and S.A. Vanstone, "Fast exponentiation in $GF(2^n)$," *Eurocrypt 88, Lecture Notes in Computer Science*, vol. 330, pp. 251–255, 1988.
3. A. Reyhani-Masoleh and M.A. Hasan, "Low complexity sequential normal basis multipliers over $GF(2^m)$," *16th IEEE Symposium on Computer Arithmetic*, vol. 16, pp. 188–195, 2003.
4. A. Reyhani-Masoleh and M.A. Hasan, "A new construction of Massey-Omura parallel multiplier over $GF(2^m)$," *IEEE Trans. Computers*, vol. 51, pp. 511–520, 2002.
5. A. Reyhani-Masoleh and M.A. Hasan, "Efficient multiplication beyond optimal normal bases," *IEEE Trans. Computers*, vol. 52, pp. 428–439, 2003.
6. A.J. Menezes, I.F. Blake, S. Gao, R.C. Mullin, S.A. Vanstone, and T. Yaghoobian, *Applications of Finite Fields*, Kluwer Academic Publisher, 1993.
7. J.L. Massy and J.K. Omura, "Computational method and apparatus for finite field arithmetic," *US Patent No. 4587627*, 1986.
8. C. Paar, P. Fleischmann, and P. Roelse, "Efficient multiplier architectures for Galois fields $GF(2^{4n})$," *IEEE Trans. Computers*, vol. 47, pp. 162–170, 1998.
9. E.R. Berlekamp, "Bit-serial Reed-Solomon encoders," *IEEE Trans. Inform. Theory*, vol. 28, pp. 869–874, 1982.
10. B. Sunar and Ç.K. Koç, "An efficient optimal normal basis type II multiplier," *IEEE Trans. Computers*, vol. 50, pp. 83–87, 2001.
11. H. Wu, M.A. Hasan, I.F. Blake, and S. Gao, "Finite field multiplier using redundant representation," *IEEE Trans. Computers*, vol. 51, pp. 1306–1316, 2002.
12. S. Gao, J. von zur Gathen, and D. Panario, "Orders and cryptographical applications," *Math. Comp.*, vol. 67, pp. 343–352, 1998.
13. J. von zur Gathen and I. Shparlinski, "Orders of Gauss periods in finite fields," *ISAAC 95, Lecture Notes in Computer Science*, vol. 1004, pp. 208–215, 1995.

14. S. Gao and S. Vanstone, "On orders of optimal normal basis generators," *Math. Comp.*, vol. 64, pp. 1227–1233, 1995.
15. S. Feisel, J. von zur Gathen, M. Shokrollahi, "Normal bases via general Gauss periods," *Math. Comp.*, vol. 68, pp. 271–290, 1999.
16. NIST, "Digital Signature Standard," *FIPS Publication*, 186-2, February, 2000.

Low-Power Elliptic Curve Cryptography Using Scaled Modular Arithmetic

E. Öztürk[1], B. Sunar[1], and E. Savaş[2]

[1] Department of Electrical & Computer Engineering, Worcester Polytechnic Institute, Worcester MA, 01609, USA,
erdinc, sunar@wpi.edu
[2] Faculty of Engineering and Natural Sciences, Sabanci University, Istanbul, Turkey
TR-34956
erkays@sabanciuniv.edu

Abstract. We introduce new modulus scaling techniques for transforming a class of primes into special forms which enables efficient arithmetic. The scaling technique may be used to improve multiplication and inversion in finite fields. We present an efficient inversion algorithm that utilizes the structure of scaled modulus. Our inversion algorithm exhibits superior performance to the Euclidean algorithm and lends itself to efficient hardware implementation due to its simplicity. Using the scaled modulus technique and our specialized inversion algorithm we develop an elliptic curve processor architecture. The resulting architecture successfully utilizes redundant representation of elements in $GF(p)$ and provides a low-power, high speed, and small footprint specialized elliptic curve implementation.

1   Introduction

Modular arithmetic has a variety of applications in cryptography. Many public-key algorithms heavily depend on modular arithmetic. Among these RSA encryption and digital signature schemes, discrete logarithm problem (DLP) based schemes such as the Diffie-Helman key agreement [4] and El-Gamal encryption and signature schemes [8], and elliptic curve cryptography [6,7] play an important role in authentication and encryption protocols. The implementation of RSA based schemes requires the arithmetic of integers modulo a large integer, that is in the form of a product of two large primes $n = p \cdot q$. On the other hand, implementations of Diffie-Helman and El-Gamal schemes are based on the arithmetic of integers modulo a large prime p. While ECDSA is built on complex algebraic structures, the underlying arithmetic operations are either modular operations with respect to a large prime modulus ($GF(p)$ case) or polynomial arithmetic modulo a high degree irreducible polynomial defined over the finite field $GF(2)$ ($GF(2^k)$ case). Special moduli for $GF(2^k)$ arithmetic were also proposed [2,10]. Low Hamming-weight irreducible polynomials such as trinomials and pentanomials became a popular choice [10,1] for both hardware and software implementations of ECDSA over $GF(2^k)$. Particularly, trinomials

M. Joye and J.-J. Quisquater (Eds.): CHES 2004, LNCS 3156, pp. 92–106, 2004.

of the form $x^k + x + 1$ allow efficient reduction. For many bit-lengths such polynomials do not exist; therefore less efficient trinomials, i.e. $x^k + x^u + 1$ with $u > 1$, or pentanomials, i.e. $x^k + x^u + x^v + x^z + 1$, are used instead. Hence, in many cases the performance suffers degradation due to extra additions and alignment adjustments.

In this paper we utilize integer moduli of special form, which is reminiscent of low-Hamming weight polynomials. Although the idea of using a low-Hamming weight integer modulus is not new [3], its application to Elliptic Curve Cryptography was limited to only elliptic curves defined over Optimal Extension Fields (i.e. $GF(p^k)$ with mid-size p of special form), or non-optimal primes such as those utilized by the NIST curves. In this work we achieve moduli of Mersenne form by introducing a modulus scaling technique. This allows us to develop a fast inversion algorithm that lends itself to efficient inversion hardware. For proof of concept we implemented a specialized elliptic curve processor. Besides using scaled arithmetic and the special inversion algorithm, we introduced several innovations at the hardware level such as a fast comparator for redundant arithmetic and shared arithmetic core for power optimization. The resulting architecture requires extremely low power at very small footprint and provides reasonable execution speed.

2   Previous Work

A straightforward method to implement integer and polynomial modular multiplications is to first compute the product of the two operands, $t = a \cdot b$, and then to reduce the product using the modulus, $c = t \bmod p$. Traditionally, the reduction step is implemented by a division operation, which is significantly more demanding than the initial multiplication. To alleviate the reduction problem in integer modular multiplications, Crandall proposed [3] using *special primes*, primes of the form $p = 2^k - u$, where u is a small integer constant. By using special primes, modular reduction turns into a multiplication operation by the small constant u, that, in many cases, may be performed by a series of less expensive shift and add operations:

$$t = t_h 2^k + t_l$$
$$c = t_h 2^k + t_l \pmod{p}$$
$$c = t_h \cdot u + t_l \pmod{2^k - u} .$$

It should be noticed that $t_h \cdot u$ is not fully reduced. Depending on the length of u, a few more reductions are needed. The best possible choice for a special prime is a Mersenne prime, $p = 2^k - 1$, with k fixed to a word-boundary. In this case, the reduction operation becomes a simple modular addition $c = t_h + t_l \bmod p$. Similarly primes of the form $2^k + 1$ may simplify reduction into a modular subtraction $c = t_l - t_h \bmod p$. Unfortunately, Mersenne primes and primes of the form $2^k + 1$ are scarce. For degrees up to 1000 no primes of form $2^k + 1$ and only the two Mersenne primes $2^{521} - 1$ and $2^{607} - 1$ exist. Moreover, these primes are too large for ECDSA which utilizes bit-lengths in the range $160 - 350$. Hence, a more practical choice is to use primes of the form $2^k - 3$. For a constant larger than $u = 3$, and a degree k that is not aligned to a word boundary, some extra shifts and additions may be needed. To relax the restrictions, Solinas [11] introduced a generalization for special primes. His technique is based on signed bit recoding. While increasing the number of possible special primes, additional low-level operations are needed. The special modulus reduction technique introduced by Crandall [3] restricts the constant u in $p = 2^k - u$ to a small constant that fits into a single word.

3   Modulus Scaling Techniques

The idea of modulus scaling was introduced by Walter [13]. In this work, the modulus was scaled to obtain a certain representation in the higher order bits, which helped the estimation of the quotient in Barrett's reduction technique. The method works by scaling to the prime modulus to obtain a new modulus, $m = p \cdot s$ Reducing an integer a using the new modulus m will produce a result that is congruent to the residue obtained by reducing a modulo p. This follows from the fact that reduction is a repetitive subtraction of the modulus. Subtracting m is equivalent to s times subtracting p and thus $(a \bmod m) \bmod p \equiv a \bmod p$. When a scaled modulus is used, residues will be in the range $[m - 1, 0] = [s \cdot p - 1, 0]$. The number is not fully reduced and essentially we are using a redundant representation where an integer is represented using $\lceil \log_2 s \rceil$ more bits than necessary. Consequently, it will be necessary that the final result is reduced by p to obtain a fully reduced representation. Here we wish to use scaling to produce moduli of special form. If a random pattern appears in a modulus, it will not be possible to use the low-weight optimizations discussed in Section 2. However, by finding a suitable small constant s, it may be possible to scale the prime p to obtain a new modulus of special form, that is either of low-weight or in a form that allows efficient recoding. To keep the redundancy minimal, the scaling factor must be small compared to the original modulus. Assuming a random modulus, such a small factor might be hard or even impossible to find. We concentrate again on primes of special forms. We present two heuristics that form a basis for efficient on-the-fly scaling:

Heuristic 1 *If the base B representation of an integer contains a series of repeating digits, scaling the integer with the largest possible digit, produces a string of repeating zero digits in the scaled and recoded integer.*

The justification of the heuristic is quite simple. Assume the representation of the modulus in base B contains a repeating digit of arbitrary value D. We use the constant scaling factor $s = B - 1$ to compute m. When a string of repeating D-digits is multiplied with the scaling factor, and written in base B we obtain the following

$$(DDDD \ldots DDD)_B \cdot (B - 1) = (DDDD \ldots DDD0)_B - (DDDD \ldots DDD)_B$$
$$= (D000 \ldots 000\bar{D})_B.$$

The bar over the least significant digit denotes a negative valued digit.

The presented scaling technique is simple, efficient, and only requires the modulus to have repeating digits. Since the scaling factor is fixed and only depends on the length of the repeating pattern – not its value –, a modulus with multiple repeating digits can be scaled properly at the cost of increasing the length of the modulus by a single digit. We present another heuristics for scaling, this technique is more efficient but more restrictive on the modulus.

Heuristic 2 *Given a modulus containing repeating D-digits in base B representation, if $B - 1$ is divisible by the repeating digit, then the modulus can be efficiently scaled by the factor $\frac{B-1}{D}$.*

As earlier the heuristic is verified by multiplying a string of repeating digits with the scaling factor and then by recoding.

$$(DDD\ldots DDD)_B \cdot \frac{B-1}{D} = ((B-1)(B-1)(B-1)\ldots(B-1))_B$$
$$= (1000\ldots 0\bar{1})_B.$$

We provide two examples for the heuristics in Appendix A. We have compiled a list of primes that when scaled with a small factor produce moduli of the form $2^k \pm 1$ in Table 4 (see Appendix A). These primes provide a wide range of perfect choices for the implementation of cryptographic schemes.

4   Scaled Modular Inversion

In this section we consider the application of scaled arithmetic to implement more efficient inversion operations. An efficient way of calculating multiplicative inverses is to use binary extended Euclidean based algorithms. The Montgomery inversion algorithm proposed by Kaliski [5] is one of the most efficient inversion algorithms for random primes. Montgomery inversion, however, is not suitable when used with scaled primes since it does not exploit our special moduli. Furthermore, it can be used only when Montgomery arithmetic is employed. Therefore, what we need is an algorithm that takes advantage of the proposed special moduli. Thomas et al. [12] proposed the Algorithm X for Mersenne primes of the form $2^q - 1$ (see Appendix B).

Due to its simplicity Algorithm X is likely to yield an efficient hardware implementation. Another advantage of Algorithm X is the fact that the carry-free arithmetic can be employed. The main problem with other binary extended Euclidean algorithms is that they usually have a step involving comparison of two integers. The comparison in Algorithm X is much simpler and may be implemented easily using carry-free arithmetic.

The algorithm can be modified to support the other types of special moduli as well. For instance, changing Step 4 of the algorithm to $b := -(2^{q-e}b) \pmod{p}$ will make the algorithm work for special moduli of the form $2^q + 1$ with almost no penalty in the implementation. The only problem with a special modulus, m is the fact that it is not prime (but multiple of a prime, $m = sp$) and therefore inverse of an integer $a < m$ does not exist when $\gcd(a, m) \neq 1$. With a small modification to the algorithm this problem may be solved as well. Without loss of generalization the solution is easier when s is a small prime number. Algorithm X normally terminates when $u = 1$ for integers that are relatively prime to the modulus, m. When the integer a is not relatively prime to the modulus, then Algorithm X must terminate when $u = \gcd(a, m) = s$ resulting $b = a^{-1} \cdot s$ (mod m). In order to obtain the inverse of a when $\gcd(a, m) \neq 1$, an extra multiplication at the end is necessary:

$$b = b \cdot (s^{-1} \pmod{p}) \pmod{m}$$

where $s^{-1} \pmod{p}$ needs to be precomputed. This precomputation and the task of checking $y = s$ as well as $y = 1$, on the other hand, may be avoided utilizing the following technique. The integer a, whose inverse is to be computed, is first multiplied by the scale s before the inverse computation: $\bar{a} = a \cdot s$. When the inverse computation is completed we have the following equality

$$\bar{a} \cdot b + m \cdot k = s$$

and thus

$$a \cdot s \cdot b + p \cdot s \cdot k = s .$$

When both sides of the equation is divided by s we obtain

$$a \cdot b + p \cdot k = 1.$$

Therefore, the algorithm automatically yields the inverse of a as $b = a^{-1}$ if the input is taken as $s \cdot a \bmod m$ instead of a. Although this technique necessitates an extra multiplication before the inversion operation independent of whether a is relatively prime to modulus m or not, eliminating the precomputation and a comparison is a significant improvement in a possible hardware implementation. Furthermore, this multiplication will reduce to several additions when the scale is a small integer such as the $s = 3$ in $p = (2^{167} + 1)/3$. Another useful modification to Algorithm X is to transform it into a division algorithm to compute operations of the form d/a. The only change required is to initialize b with d instead of 1 in Step 1 of the algorithm. This simple modification saves one multiplication in elliptic curve operations. The Algorithm X modified for division with scaled modulus is shown below:

Algorithm X - modified for division with scaled modulus

Input: $a \in [1, m - 1]$, $d \in [1, m - 1]$, m, and q where $m = 2^q \pm 1$
Output: $b \in [1, m - 1]$, where $b = d/a \pmod{m}$
1:       $a := a \cdot s \pmod{m}$;
2:       $(b, c, u, v) := (d, 0, a, m)$;
3:       Find e such that $2^e \| u$
4:       $u := u/2^e$; // shift off trailing zeros
5:       $b := \mp(2^{q-e} b) \pmod{m}$; // circular left shift

6:      if $u = s$ return b;
7:      $(b, c, u, v) := (b + c, b, u + v, u)$;
8:      go to Step 3

One can easily observe that the Algorithm X has the loop invariant b/u (mod m) $\equiv d/a$ (mod m) . Note that the Step 5 of Algorithm X can be performed using simple circular left shift operations. The advantage of performing the Step 5 with simple circular shifts may dissappear for moduli of the form $2^q - c$ with even a small c. Many inversion algorithms consist of a big loop and the efficiency of an inversion algorithm depends on the number of iterations in this loop, k, which, in turn, determines the total number of additions, shift operations to be performed. The number of iterations are usually of random nature (but demonstrates a regular and familiar distribution) and only statistical analysis can be given. In order to show that Algorithm X is also efficient in terms of iteration number, we compared its distribution for k against that of Montgomery inversion algorithm. We computed the inverses of 10000 randomly chosen integers modulo $m = 2^{167} + 1$ using Algorithm X. Since $p = m/3$ is a 166-bit prime we repeated the same experiment with the Montgomery inversion algorithm using p. Besides having much easier operations in each iteration we observed that the average number of iterations of Algorithm X is slightly lower than the total number of iterations of the Montgomery inversion algorithm.

5   The Elliptic Curve Architecture

We build our elliptic curve scheme over the prime field $GF((2^{167} + 1)/3)$. This particular prime allows us to utilize a very small scaling factor $s = 3$. To implement the field operations we use Algorithm X as outlined in Section 4. Our simulation for this particular choice of prime showed that our inversion technique is only by about three times slower than a multiplication operation. Furthermore, the inversion is implemented as a division saving one multiplication operation. Thus the actual ratio is closer to two. Since inversion is relatively fast, we prefer to use affine coordinates. Besides faster implementation, affine coordinates provide a significant amount of reduction in power and circuit area since projective coordinates require a large number of extra storage. For an elliptic curve of form $y^2 = x^3 + ax + b$ defined over $GF(2^{167} + 1)/3$ we use the standard point addition operation defined in [7].

For power efficiency we optimize our design to include minimal hardware. An effective strategy in reducing the power consumption is to spread the computation to a longer time interval via serialization which we employ extensively. On the other hand, a reasonable time performance is also desired. Since the elliptic curve is defined over a large integer field $GF(p)$ (168-bits) carry propagations are critical in the performance of the overall architecture. To this end, we build the entire arithmetic architecture using the carry-save methodology. This design choice regulates all carry propagations and delivers a very short critical path delay, and thus a very high limit for the operating frequency.

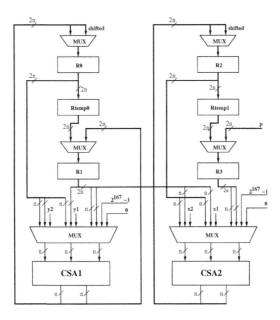

Fig. 1. Block diagram of the arithmetic unit

The redundant representation doubles all registers in the arithmetic unit, i.e. we need two separate registers to hold both the carry part and the sum part of a number. Furthermore, the inherent difficulty in comparing numbers represented in carry-save notation is another challenge. In addition, shifts and rotate operations become more cumbersome. Nevertheless, as evident from our design it is possible to overcome these difficulties.

In developing the arithmetic architecture we primarily focus on finding the minimal circuit to implement Algorithm X efficiently. Since the architecture is built around the idea of maximizing hardware sharing among various operations, the multiplication, squaring and addition operations are all achieved by the same arithmetic core. The control is hierarchically organized to implement the basic arithmetic operations, point addition, point doubling, and the scalar point multiplication operation in layers of simple state machines. The simplicity of Algorithm X and scaled arithmetic allows us to accomplish all operations using only a few small state machines. Since we lack the space we do not discuss the control circuit any further but focus on the basic functionality and describe the innovations in the arithmetic core.

The arithmetic unit shown in Figure 1 is built around four main registers $R0, R1, R2, R3$, and two extra registers Rtemp0, Rtemp1 which are used for temporary storage. Note that these registers store both the sum and carry parts due to the carry-save representation. For the same purpose the architecture is built around two (almost) parallel data paths.

We briefly outline the implementation of basic arithmetic operations as follows:

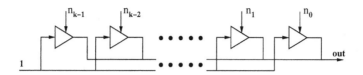

Fig. 2. Comparator unit built using tri-state buffers

Comparison. Comparing two numbers in carry-save architecture is difficult since the redundant representation hides the actual values. On the positive side, the comparison in Algorithm X is only with a constant value of $s = 3$. Such a comparator may be built using a massive OR tree with $2k$ inputs. Unfortunately, such an OR tree would cause serious latency ($O(\log_2 k)$ gate delays) and significantly increase the critical path delay. We instead prefer a novel comparator design that works only for comparing a number with zero. In order to compare a number with 3, extra logic is needed for the first two bits, which is nothing more than a pair of XOR gates. The rest of the bits are connected directly to the comparator. The comparator is built by connecting three-state buffers together as shown in Figure 2. The input lines are connected together and set to logic 1. Similarly the output lines are connected together and taken as the output of the comparator. We feed the bits of the data input in parallel to the enable inputs of the three-state buffers. Hence, if one or more of the bits of the data input is logic 1, which means the number is not equal to 0, we see logic 1 at the output of the comparator. If the number is 0, none of the three-state buffers is enabled and therefore we see a Hi-Z (high impedance) output. Note that our comparator design works in constant time (O(1) gate delays) regardless of the length of the operands.

Modulo Reduction. Since the hardware works for $m = 2^{167} + 1$, 168-bit registers would be sufficient. However, we use an extra bit to detect when the number becomes greater than m. If one of the left-most bits of the number (carry or sum) is one, the number is reduced modulo m. Note that

$$2^{168} = 2 \cdot (2^{167} + 1) - 2 = 2m - 2 = m - 2 \pmod{m}.$$

Hence, the reduction is achieved by subtracting 2^{168} (or simply deleting this bit) and adding $m - 2 = (11 \ldots 11111)_2$ (167 bits) to the number. If both of the leftmost bits are 1 then: $2 \cdot (2^{168}) = 4 \cdot (2^{167} + 1) - 4 = 4m - 4 = m - 4$ (mod m) . Therefore $m - 4 = (111 \ldots 11101)_2$ (167 bits) has to be added to the number and both of the leftmost bits are deleted.

Subtraction. Suppose k is a 168 bit number which we want to subtract from another number modulo m. The bitwise complement of k is found as

$$k' = (2^{168} - 1) - k = 2 \cdot (2^{167} + 1) - 3 - k = -3 - k \pmod{m} .$$

Thus $-k = k'+3 \bmod m$. This means that to subtract k from a number we simply add the bitwise complement of k and 3 to the number. There is a caveat though. Remember that our numbers are kept in carry save representation, there are two

168-bit numbers representing k. Let k_s and k_c denote the sum and carry parts of k, respectively. Since $k = k_s + k_c$ then $-k = -k_s - k_c = (k'_s + 3) + (k'_c + 3) = k_s' + k_c' + 6 \bmod m$. Therefore the constant value 6 has to be added to the complements of the carry and sum registers in order to compute $-k$.

Multiplication. We serialize our multiplication algorithm by processing one bit of one operand and all bits of the second operand in each iteration. The standard multiplication algorithm had to be modified to make it compatible with the carry save representation. Due to the redundant representation, the value of the leftmost bit of the multiplier is not known. Hence, the left to right multiplication algorithm may not be used directly. We prefer to use the right to left multiplication algorithm. With this change, instead of shifting the product we multiply the multiplicand by two (or shift left) in each iteration step.

There are 3 registers used for the multiplication: R0 (multiplicand), R1 (product) and R2 (multiplier). The multiplication algorithm has 3 steps :

1. Initialization: This is done by the control circuit. The multiplicand is loaded to R0, the multiplier is loaded to R2 and R1 is reset.
2. Addition: This step is only done when the rightmost bit of register R2 is 1. The content of register R0 is added to R1.
3. Shifting: The multiplier has to be processed bit by bit starting from the right. We do this by shifting register R2 to the right in each iteration of the multiplication. Since the register R2 is connected to the comparator, the algorithm terminates after this step if the number becomes 0 else the algorithm continues with Step 2. Note that no counters are used in the design. This eliminates potential increases in the critical path delay. The multiplicand needs to be doubled in each iteration as well. This is achieved by shifting register R0 to the left. This operation is performed in parallel with shifting R2, so no extra clock cycles are needed. However, shifting to the left can cause overflow. Therefore, the result needs to be reduced modulo m if the leftmost bit of the register R0 is 1.

Division. To realize the division operation there are four registers used to hold b, c, u and v, two temporary registers are used for the addition of two numbers in carry-save architecture. Two carry-save adders, multiplexers and comparator architecture are also utilized.

The division algorithm shown in Algorithm X has 5 steps:

1. Initialization: This is done by the control circuit. Load registers with $b = d, c = 0, u = a$ (the data input) and $v = m = (2^{167} + 1)$.
2. $u = u/2^e$: This operation is done by shifting u to the right until a 1-bit is encountered. However, due to the carry-save architecture this operation requires special care. The rightmost bit of the carry register is always zero since there is no carry input. Thus just checking the rightmost bit of the sum register is sufficient. Also, the carry has to be propagated to the left in each iteration. This is done by adding 0 to the number. If a 1-bit is encountered, the operation proceeds to the next step.

3. $b = (-2^{q-e} \cdot b) \bmod m$: Assume u holds a random pattern, e will be very small (not more than 3 for most of the cases). Thus, $q - e$ is most likely a large number. Therefore, multiplication by 2^{q-e} would require many shifts to left. To compute this operation more efficiently, this step is rewritten using the identity $2^q = -1 \bmod m$ as $b = 2^{-e} \cdot b \pmod{m}$. Therefore, b needs to be halved e-times. If b is even we may shift it to the right and thereby divide it by two. Otherwise, we add m to it to make it even and then shift. Since this step takes e iterations, it can be performed concurrently with the 2nd step of the algorithm. Hence no extra clock cycles are needed for this step.

4. Compare u with $s = 3$: The comparator architecture explained above is used to implement this step. There are two cases when $u = 3$: $u_s = (11)_2, u_c = (00)_2$ and $u_s = (01)_2, u_c = (10)_2$. Therefore, the rightmost two bits need a special logic for the comparison, and the rest of the bits are connected directly to the three-state comparator shown in Figure 2.

5. Additions in $(b, c, u, v) := (b + c, b, u + v, u)$. Two clock cycles are needed to add two numbers in carry-save architecture, since a carry-save adder has 3 inputs and there are 4 numbers to add. During the addition operation to preserve the values of b and u the two temporary registers are used.

6 Performance Analysis

In this section we analyze the speed performance of the overall architecture and determine the number of cycles required to perform the elliptic curve operations. The main contributors to the delay are field multiplications and division operations. Field additions are performed in 1 cycle (or 2 cycles if both operands are in the carry-save representation). Therefore field additions which take place outside of the multiplication or division operations are neglected.

The multiplication operation iterates over the bits of one operand. On average half of the bits will be ones and will require a 2 cycle addition. Hence, 168 clock cycles will be needed. The multiplicand will be shifted in each cycle and modulo reduced in about half of the iterations. Hence another $1.5 \cdot 168 = 252$ cycles are spent. The multiplication operation takes on average a total of 420 cycles.

The steps of the division algorithm are reorganized in Figure 3 according to the order and concurrency of the operations. Note the two concurrent operations shown in Step 2. In fact this is the only step in the algorithm which requires multiple clock cycles, hence the concurrency saves many cycles. In Step 2, u is shifted until all zero bits in the LSB are removed. Each shift operation takes place within one cycle. For a randomly picked value of u the probability of the last e bits all being zeroes is $(1/2)^e$, hence the expected value of e is $E(e) = \sum_{i=1}^{\infty} i(1/2)^i = 2$. In each iteration of the algorithm we expect on average of 2 cycles to be spent. Step 3 does not spend any cycles since the comparator architecture is combinational. The additions in Step 4 require 2 clock cycles. Hence a total of 4 cycles is spent in each iteration of the division algorithm. Our simulation results showed that the division algorithm would iterate on average about 320 times. The total time spent in division is found as $1,280$ cycles. This is very close to our hardware simulation results which gave an average of $1,288$ cycles.

1: Initialize all registers
$(b, c, u, v) \leftarrow (d, 0, a, m)$
2: Shift off all trailing zeros and rotate b
$u \leftarrow u >> e \quad b \leftarrow b >> e \pmod{m}$
3: Check terminate condition
if $u = s$ return b
4: Update variables
$(b, c, u, v) \leftarrow (b + c, b, u + v, u);$
go back to Step 2

Fig. 3. Hardware algorithm for division.

The total number of clock cycles for point addition and doubling is found as $2,120$ and $2,540$, respectively. The total time required for computing a point multiplication is found as $545,440$ cycles.

7   Results and Comparison

The presented architecture was developed into Verilog modules and synthesized using the Synopsys tools Design Compiler and Power Compiler. In the synthesis we used the TSMC $0.13\,\mu m$ ASIC library, which is characterized for power. The global operating voltage is 1 V. The resulting architecture was synthesized for three operating frequencies. The implementation results are shown in Table 1. As seen in the table the area varies around 30 Kgates. The circuit achieves its intended purpose by consuming only 0.99 mW at 20 Mhz. In this mode the point multiplication operation takes about 31.9 msec. Although this is not very fast, this operating mode might be useful for interactive applications with extremely stringent power limitations. On the other hand, when the circuit is synthesized for 200 Mhz operation, the area is slightly increased to 34 Kgates, and the power consumption increased to 9.89 mW. However, a point multiplication takes now only 3.1 msec.

Table 1. Implementation Results.

Op. Freq. (MHz)	Area (gates)	Power (mW)	Avg. Delay (msec)
20	30,333	0.99	31.9
100	30,443	4.34	6.3
200	34,390	9.89	3.1

We compare our design with another customized low-power elliptic curve implementation presented by Schroeppel et al. in CHES 2002 [9]. Their design employed an elliptic curve defined over a field tower $GF(2^{178})$ and used specialized field arithmetic to minimize the design. A point halving algorithm was used in place of the traditional point doubling algorithm. The design was power optimized through clock gating and other standard methods of power optimization. The main contribution was the clever minimization of the gate logic through efficient tower field arithmetic. Note that their design includes a fully functional signature generation architecture whereas our design is limited to point multiplication. Although a side by side comparison is not possible, we find it useful to state their results: The design was synthesized for 20 Mhz operation using 0.5 μm ASIC technology. The synthesized design occupied an area of 112 Kgates and consumed 150 mW. The elliptic curve signature was computed in 4.4 msec.

An architectural comparison of the two designs shows that our design operates bit serially in one operand whereas their design employs a more parallel implementation strategy. This leads to lower critical paths and much smaller area in our design. The much shorter critical path allows much higher operating frequencies requiring more clock cycles to compute the same operation. However, due to the smaller area, when operated at similar frequencies our design consumes much less power.

8   Conclusions

In this paper we demonstrated that scaled arithmetic, which is based on the idea of transforming a class of primes into special forms that enable efficient arithmetic, can be profitably used in elliptic curve cryptography. To this end, we implemented an elliptic curve cryptography processor using scaled arithmetic. Implementation results show that the use of scaled moduli in elliptic curve cryptography offers a superior performance in terms of area, power, and speed. We proposed a novel inversion algorithm for scaled moduli that results in an efficient hardware implementation. It has been observed that the inversion algorithm eliminates the need for projective coordinates that require prohibitively a large amount of extra storage. The successful use of redundant representation (i.e. carry-save notation) in all arithmetic operations including the inversion with the introduction of an innovative comparator design leads to a significant reduction in critical path delay resulting in a very high operating clock frequency. The fact that the same data path (i.e. arithmetic core) is used for all the field operations leads to a very small chip area. Comparison with another implementation demonstrated that our implementation features desirable properties for resource-constrained computing environments.

References

1. G. B. Agnew, R. C. Mullin, and S. A. Vanstone. An Implementation of Elliptic Curve Cryptosystems over $F_{2^{155}}$. *IEEE Journal on Selected Areas in Communications*, 11(5):804–813, June 1993.

2. E. Berlekamp. *Algebraic Coding Theory.* McGraw-Hill, New York, NY, 1968.
3. R. E. Crandall. Method and Apparatus for Public Key Exchange in a Cryptographic System. U.S. Patent Number 5,159,632, October 1992.
4. W. Diffie and M. E. Hellman. New Directions in Cryptography. *IEEE Transactions on Information Theory*, 22:644–654, November 1976.
5. B. S. Kaliski Jr. The Montgomery Inverse and its Applications. *IEEE Transactions on Computers*, 44(8):1064–1065, 1995.
6. N. Koblitz. Elliptic Curve Cryptosystems. *Mathematics of Computation*, 48(177):203–209, January 1987.
7. A. J. Menezes. *Elliptic Curve Public Key Cryptosystems.* Kluwer Academic Publishers, Boston, MA, 1993.
8. National Institute for Standards and Technology. Digital Signature Standard (DSS). *Federal Register*, 56:169, Auguts 1991.
9. R. Schroeppel, C. Beaver, R. Miller, R. Gonzales, and T. Draelos. A Low-Power Design for an Elliptic Curve Digital Signature Chip. In B. S. Kaliski Jr., C. K. Koc, and C. Paar, editors, *Cryptographic Hardware and Embedded Sytems — CHES 2002*, Lecture Notes in Computer Science, pages 366–380. Springer-Verlag Berlin, 2002.
10. R. Schroeppel, H. Orman, S. O'Malley, and O. Spatscheck. Fast Key Exchange with Elliptic Curve Systems. In D. Coppersmith, editor, *Advances in Cryptology — CRYPTO 95*, Lecture Notes in Computer Science, No. 973, pages 43–56. Springer-Verlag, 1995.
11. J. A. Solinas. Generalized Mersenne Numbers. CORR-99-39, CACR Technical Report, University of Waterloo, 1999.
12. J. J. Thomas, J. M. Keller, and G. N. Larsen. The Calculation of Multiplicative Inverses over $GF(p)$ Efficiently where p is a Mersenne Prime. *IEEE Transactions on Computers*, 5(35):478–482, 1986.
13. C. D. Walter. Faster Modular Multiplication by Operand Scaling. In J. Feigenbaum, editor, *Advances in Cryptology — CRYPTO'91*, Lecture Notes in Computer Science, No. 576, pages 313–323. Springer-Verlag, 1992.

Appendix

A   Modulus Scaling

Example 1. We select the following prime

$$p = (5123456781234567812345678123456781234567812345678123456807)_{16}.$$

By inspection we identify $(12345678)_{16}$ as a repeating pattern. By selecting the base $B = 2^{32}$, the repeating pattern becomes a digit. The scaling factor is the largest digit $s = B - 1 = 2^{32} - 1 = (\text{FFFFFFFF})_{16}$. The scaled modulus is computed as

$$m = s \cdot p$$

$$= (5123456730000000000000000000000000000000000000000085DCBA97F9)_{16}$$

The representation may contain more than one repeating digit. For instance, the prime $p = (57777777777777333333333338B)_{16}$ has two repeating digits 7 and 3. Since both fit into a digit in base $B = 16$, scaling with $B - 1 = 15$ will work on both strings:

$$m = p \cdot s$$
$$= (5200000000000004\overline{0}0000000000525)_{16}.$$

Example 2. Let the prime p be

$$p = (D79435E50D79435D79435E50D79435E50D79435E50D79435E50D79435E50\|$$
$$D79435E50D79435E50D79435E50D79435E5)_{16}$$

By inspection the repeating pattern is detected as $D = (0D79435E5)_{16}$. The digit D fits into 36-bits, thus the base is selected as $B = 2^{36}$. Since $D|(B - 1)$ the scaling factor is computed as $s = \frac{2^{36}-1}{(0D79435E5)_{16}} = 19$. The scaled modulus becomes $m = s \cdot p = 2^{384} - 2^{320} - 1$.

A table of special primes is given below. Each row lists all degrees up to $i = 1024$ for which a prime exists in the form specified at the beginning of the row.

In the following table a list of scaled moduli of the form $2^k \pm 1$ is shown. The scaling factor and the prime modulus is provided in the same row.

Table 2. List of special primes up to degree 1024.

PRIME	$0 < i < 1024$
$2^i + 1$	$1, 2, 4, 8, 16$
$2^i + 3$	$1, 2, 3, 4, 6, 7, 8, 16, 12, 15, 16, 18, 28, 30, 55, 67, 84, 228, 390, 784$
$2^i + 5$	$1, 3, 5, 11, 47, 53, 141, 143, 191, 273, 341$
$3 \cdot 2^i + 1$	$1, 2, 5, 6, 8, 12, 18, 30, 36, 41, 66, 189, 201, 209, 276, 353, 408, 438, 534$
$5 \cdot 2^i + 1$	$1, 3, 7, 13, 15, 25, 39, 55, 75, 85, 127$
$3 \cdot 2^i + 5$	$1, 2, 3, 4, 5, 6, 7, 8, 14, 16, 19, 22, 24, 27, 29, 32, 38, 54, 57, 60, 76, 94, 132, 139, 175,$ $187, 208, 230, 379, 384, 632$
$5 \cdot 2^i + 3$	$1, 2, 3, 4, 5, 7, 8, 11, 12, 18, 20, 26, 28, 32, 34, 43, 44, 50, 52, 58, 65, 66, 107, 140, 197$ $274, 280, 380, 393, 506, 664, 738, 875, 944, 1016$
$2^i - 1$	$2, 3, 5, 7, 13, 17, 19, 31, 61, 89, 107, 127, 521, 607$
$2^i - 3$	$3, 4, 5, 6, 9, 10, 12, 14, 20, 22, 24, 29, 94, 116, 122, 150, 174, 213, 221, 233, 266, 336,$ $452, 545, 689, 694, 850$
$2^i - 5$	$3, 4, 6, 8, 10, 12, 18, 20, 26, 32, 36, 56, 66, 118, 130, 150, 166, 206, 226, 550, 706, 810$
$3 \cdot 2^i - 1$	$1, 2, 3, 4, 6, 7, 11, 18, 34, 38, 43, 55, 64, 76, 94, 103, 143, 206, 216, 306, 324, 391, 458, 470, 827$
$5 \cdot 2^i - 1$	$2, 4, 8, 10, 12, 14, 18, 32, 48, 54, 72, 148, 184, 248, 270, 274, 420$
$3 \cdot 2^i - 5$	$2, 3, 4, 7, 9, 10, 13, 15, 25, 31, 34, 48, 52, 64, 109, 145, 162, 204, 207, 231, 271, 348, 444, 553, 559$
$5 \cdot 2^i - 3$	$1, 2, 3, 5, 6, 8, 9, 12, 17, 20, 27, 29, 30, 36, 62, 72, 83, 117, 119, 137, 149, 152, 176, 201, 243, 470,$ $540, 590, 611, 887, 996$

Table 3. Scaled moduli of the form $2^k \pm 1$.

Modulus	Scale	Prime Modulus (hexadecimal)
$2^{83} - 1$	167	C4372F855D824CA58E9
$2^{92} + 1$	17	F0F0F0F0F0F0F0F0F0F0F1
$2^{97} - 1$	11447	B73493DECFD9B68318EF9
$2^{101} + 1$	3	AAAAAAAAAAAAAAAAAAAAAAAAB
$2^{104} + 1$	257	FF00FF00FF00FF00FF00FF01
$2^{107} + 1$	1929	10FCAEA5E3998C02A77B49EB9
$2^{116} + 1$	1009681	109DC950DA32FC88E84D688F1
$2^{127} + 1$	3	2AAAAAAAAAAAAAAAAAAAAAAAAAAAAAAB
$2^{131} - 1$	263	7C97D9108C2AD4329DB02EB8F166349
$2^{148} + 1$	17	F0F0F0F0F0F0F0F0F0F0F0F0F0F0F0F0F1
$2^{167} + 1$	3	2AAAAAAAAAAAAAAAAAAAAAAAAAAAAAAAAAAAAAAAB
$2^{179} - 1$	514447	104E5A80A157457ABC6482776A0E7EE78C616DA91
$2^{191} + 1$	3	2AAAAAAAAAAAAAAAAAAAAAAAAAAAAAAAAAAAAAAAAAAAAAB
$2^{197} - 1$	7487	1181B149E3E4C85E5F1FB2507D481CB8C6DD39E358BAD41
$2^{199} + 1$	3	2AAAAAAAAAAAAAAAAAAAAAAAAAAAAAAAAAAAAAAAAAAAAAAAAB
$2^{233} + 1$	39173361	DB47AE1104FD220D294905CAD4166DB817CE5936FBFBCAC5B411
$2^{281} - 1$	80929	19E9D9CE852ACD5A5A35C4EAA034F0BFF8EA0E7187964BD94B554C27D831862B81F
$2^{313} + 1$	3	AAAAAAAAAAAAAAAAAAAAAAAAAAAAAAAAAAAAAAAAAAAAAAAAAAAAAAAAAAAAAAAAAAAAAAAAAAAAAAAB
$2^{356} + 1$	17	F0F0F0F0F0F0F0F0F0F0F0F0F0F0F0F0F0F0F0F0F0F0F0F0F0F0F0F0F0F0F0F0F0F0F0F0F0F0F0F0F0F0F0F1

B   Inversion Algorithm for Mersenne Primes of the Form $2^q - 1$

Algorithm X

Input: $a \in [1, p-1]$, p, and q where p is prime and $p = 2^q - 1$
Output: $b \in [1, p-1]$, where $b = a^{-1} \pmod{p}$
1:        $(b, c, u, v) := (1, 0, a, p)$;
2:        Find e such that $2^e \| u$
3:        $u := u/2^e$; // shift off trailing zeros
4:        $b := (2^{q-e}b) \pmod{p}$; // circular left shift
5:        if $u = 1$ return b;
6:        $(b, c, u, v) := (b + c, b, u + v, u)$;
7:        go to Step 2

A Low-Cost ECC Coprocessor for Smartcards

Harald Aigner[1], Holger Bock[2], Markus Hütter[2], and Johannes Wolkerstorfer[3]

[1] D. Swarovski & Co.,
6112 Wattens, Austria.
Ches04@Aigner.name

[2] Infineon Technologies,
Development Center Graz, Austria.
{Holger.Bock,Huetter.External}@infineon.com, http://www.infineon.com/

[3] Institute for Applied Information Processing and Communications,
Graz University of Technology, Inffeldgasse 16a, 8010 Graz, Austria.
Johannes.Wolkerstorfer@iaik.at, http://www.iaik.at/

Abstract. In this article we present a low-cost coprocessor for smartcards which supports all necessary mathematical operations for a fast calculation of the Elliptic Curve Digital Signature Algorithm (ECDSA) based on the finite field $GF(2^m)$. These ECDSA operations are $GF(2^m)$ addition, 4-bit digit-serial multiplication in $GF(2^m)$, inversion in $GF(2^m)$, and inversion in $GF(p)$. An efficient implementation of the multiplicative inversion which breaks the 11:1 limit regarding multiplications makes it possible to use affine instead of projective coordinates for point operations on elliptic curves. A bitslice architecture allows an easy adaptation for different bit lengths. A small chip area is achieved by reusing the hardware registers for different operations.

Keywords: Elliptic Curve Cryptography (ECC), digital signature, multiplicative inverse, hardware implementation.

1 Introduction

Smartcards offer a high-quality identification method by means of digital signatures. This identification provides legally effective authenticity, confidentiality, integrity, and non-repudiation of transactions in e-business, e-government, m-commerce, and Internet applications.

The Digital Signature Algorithm based on elliptic curves (ECDSA) is commonly used for achieving authenticity. Elliptic curve cryptography allows to use short key sizes compared to other cryptographic standards such as RSA. Short keys are especially favourable for targeting smartcards because smartcards typically offer very limited resources. These limited resources also motivate usage of a coprocessor to accelerate the time-consuming calculations of ECDSA and other cryptographic operations.

This paper presents a coprocessor which can be integrated into the Infineon SLE66CXxxxP family and allows a significant speed-up of ECDSA calculation.

M. Joye and J.-J. Quisquater (Eds.): CHES 2004, LNCS 3156, pp. 107–118, 2004.

This is achieved by a fast and compact implementation of the underlying arithmetic operations. We identified mainly three operations that are crucial for performance. These operations are multiplication in the finite field $GF(2^m)$ and the computation of the multiplicative inverses in $GF(p)$ and $GF(2^m)$.

In particular, accelerated $GF(2^m)$ inversion, presented in this paper, allows to use affine coordinates instead of projective coordinates. Affine coordinates become attractive when the calculation of the $GF(2^m)$ inversion requires less time than about 11 multiplications. This relation origins from the additional multiplications that become necessary when using projective coordinates. More details can be found in Section 3. Affine coordinates use simpler formulas for calculating EC operations. They consist of less finite field operations and require a smaller number of auxiliary variables. Therefore, the usage of affine coordinates saves memory, registers and reduces the number of bus transfers, all of which are scarce resources on smartcards.

The remainder of this article is structured as follows: the next section gives an overview over related work. Section 3 introduces the mathematical background of elliptic curve cryptography, point operations on elliptic curves, and the ECDSA. The target smartcard architecture and the coprocessor hardware is presented in Section 4. Section 5 summarizes implementation results of the coprocessor. Conclusions are drawn in Section 6.

2   Related Work

The recently published book *Guide to Elliptic Curve Cryptography* gives a comprehensive overview on the state-of-art of implementing elliptic-curve cryptosystems in hardware and in software [2]. In this article we will narrow our view on related hardware implementations. Unfortunately, none of the published hardware implementations is targeted towards an ECC coprocessor for 8-bit smartcards. This is unpleasant because the intended application has an enormous impact on the design of an optimized ECC hardware. The target application fixes many parameters for which a circuit can be optimized. For instance the parameter *throughput*: a server application might demand several thousand EC operations per second, whereas a smartcard may be contented with ten operations per second or even less. Other parameters influencing efficiency are scalability (the ability to adopt to other operand sizes or other finite fields), energy efficiency, the desired target technology (FPGA, ASIC, or ASSP), the amount of hardware resources required (gate count), and last-but-not-least security aspects (robustness against side channel attacks like timing attacks, SPA, and DPA).

Different design parameters will lead to different ECC implementations. The range of possible ECC implementations is large: starting from pure software implementations, instruction-set extensions (ISE) became popular for 16-bit and 32-bit platforms to accelerate ECC over $GF(2^m)$ [3]. ISE are not useful for 8-bit platforms because slow data transport in 8-bit systems will deteriorate accelerated field operations. Alternatives are heavy-weight accelerators for complete EC operations [4,5,7,8] or hardware-software co-design approaches where computational intensive tasks are done by an EC coprocessor [9]. These coprocessors can either calculate all finite field operations [12] or support only multiplication as the most demanding finite field operation [10,11]. Circuits for calculating the multiplicative inverse in the finite fields $GF(p)$ and $GF(2^m)$ are rare [12,13].

The most obvious operation to support in hardware is multiplication because multiplication contributes most to the runtime of EC operations. Fast multiplication even helps to speedup the calculation of the multiplicative inverse when using Fermat's theorem. Fermat's theorem allows to calculate the inverse by exponentiation. Exponentiation, in turn, can be calculated by repeated multiplications [1]. Even than, exponentiation takes more than 100 times longer than multiplication which makes the use of affine coordinates for EC operations unattractive. Useful multipliers which can operate both in $GF(p)$ and $GF(2^m)$ were presented by J. Großschädl [11] and E. Savaş et al. [10]. J. Großschädl's approach uses a dual-field bit-serial multiplier utilizing interleaved modular reduction. The achieved $GF(p)$ performance is slower than the $GF(2^m)$ performance. E. Savaş et al. approach bases on a Montgomery multiplier for both fields and allows to handle arbitrarily large operands due to a scalability feature which is achieved by a pipelined array of processing elements. Both approaches use a redundant representation for $GF(p)$ results to circumvent critical-path problems caused by carry propagation in the $GF(p)$ mode of operation.

Hardware accelerators for modular inversion usually base on the extended Euclidean algorithm or variants of it. The dual-field inversion circuit by A. Gutub et al. is no exception [13]. Their circuit is scalable which means it can calculate inverses of any length. This feature seems to come at a high price because performance is lower than attainable and the architecture seems to have interconnect penalties due to a large number of wide buses getting multiplexed. J. Wolkerstorfer manages to embed the inversion functionality for $GF(p)$ and $GF(2^m)$ into a dual-field arithmetic unit at negligible additional cost compared to the cost of a mere dual-field multiplication unit [12]. Nevertheless, inversion takes 70 times longer than multiplication.

Some implementations of EC processors have no hardware support for inversion [9]. For other implementations it remains unclear whether they have or not [6]. EC processors with very fast high-radix multipliers (which require substantial hardware resources) often lack dedicated inversion circuitry. They calculate inverses via Fermat's theorem to reuse the multiplier. The EC processor of G. Orlando et al. is an example for this [7]. A counter-example is the fastest known EC processor by N. Gura et al. [8]. This EC processor for server applications has a 256×64-bit multiplier and a separate inversion unit which calculates inverses in $2m$ clock cycles by running a variant of the extended Euclidean algorithm. In comparison, inversion calculated by exponentiation would take three times longer in the worst case. EC processors trimmed for energy-efficient operation have usually smaller multipliers with either bit-serial processing or a moderate degree of parallelization. Hence, inversion calculated via exponentiation would become slow too. Therefore, they often have hardware support for calculating the modular inverse using the extended Euclidean algorithm. An example is the so-called Domain-Specific Reconfigurable Cryptographic Processor by J. Goodman et al. [4] and the $GF(2^{178})$-EC-processor by R. Schroeppel et al. [5]. The latter can calculate inverses only in $GF(2^{178})$. The calculation of the $GF(p)$ inverses for signature generation is avoided by using a modified signature scheme.

3   Mathematical Background

This section describes the point operations on elliptic curves and compares the use of affine coordinates with projective coordinates for point representation. It also gives an overview of the mathematical operations in the finite field $GF(2^m)$. The section will end with a short description of the Elliptic Curve Digital Signature Algorithm (ECDSA).

The use of elliptic curves in cryptography was proposed first by Victor Miller [15] and Neal Koblitz [16] in 1985. The mathematical basis for the security of elliptic-curve cryptosystems is the computational intractability of the Elliptic Curve Discrete Logarithm Problem (ECDLP) leading to smaller key-sizes (compared to, e.g., RSA) which make elliptic curves attractive especially for smartcards where a small hardware implementation is desired.

3.1   Point Operations on Elliptic Curves

The points on an elliptic curve E together with the point at infinity $\mathcal{O}$ form an *abelian group* under an *addition* operation. Two distinct points $P, Q \in E$ can be added to $R = P + Q$. Performing this calculation involves several operations (addition, multiplication, and inversion) in the underlying field $GF(2^m)$. In case $P = Q$, the addition turns into point *doubling* and uses slightly different formulas.

The *scalar multiplication* of a point $P \in E$ by an integer k is the sum

$$\overbrace{P + P + \cdots + P}^{k \text{ times}} = \sum_k P = kP \tag{1}$$

In cryptographic applications k can be very large (usually 163 or 191 bits) which would lead to an enormous computing time using repeated point addition. However, scalar multiplication can be performed more efficiently by the *double-and-add method* [17].

3.2   Point Representation on Elliptic Curves

There are two commonly used representations of points on elliptic curves: *affine coordinates* and *projective coordinates*. Various types of projective coordinates exist. Within this paper, the main focus is on *Jacobian* projective coordinates because they allow the fastest implementation of point doubling compared with other types like *standard* projective coordinates or *Chudnovsky* projective coordinates.

An affine point on an elliptic curve E is specified by a pair of finite field elements (x, y) which are called the *affine coordinates* for the point. The point at infinity $\mathcal{O}$ has no affine representation. It may be more efficient to compute numerators and denominators separately if division is expensive to calculate. For this reason, the affine coordinates are transformed into *projective coordinates* which consist of three elements (X, Y, Z).

The number of operations in the underlying finite field $GF(2^m)$ for calculating point operations strongly depends on the chosen coordinate representation. Table 1 shows the number of additions, multiplications, and inversions in the finite field $GF(2^m)$ and the number of auxiliary variables needed for an implementation according to [18].

Table 1. Comparison of operations on elliptic curves over $GF(2^m)$

	#Add.	#Mult.	#Inv.	#Var.
Point addition (affine)	9	3	1	2
Point doubling (affine)	6	3	1	2
Point addition (projective)	7	14	0	5
Point doubling (projective)	4	10	0	4

Table 1 shows that, e.g., a point addition takes 3 multiplications and 1 inversion in the underlying field with affine coordinates. It takes 14 multiplications using projective coordinates. Additions are not considered because they are very easy to calculate. Nearly all implementations of elliptic curves use projective coordinates. This leads to more multiplications but the costly calculation of the inverse can be avoided and calculation is still faster than using affine coordinates. However, calculating the multiplicative inverse at least as fast as $14 - 3 = 11$ multiplications makes it economical to use affine coordinates instead of projective coordinates with all advantages as described in the introduction. Affine coordinates become a little bit less attractive when they are compared with the projective version of Montgomery's ladder. This approach was proposed by Lopez and Dahab [14]. It uses only 11 multiplications for a combined point-addition and point-doubling operation. Thus, inversion has to be faster than 8 multiplications to make affine coordinates competitive. When comparing the affine version of Montgomery's method against the projective variant, inversion has to break a 5-to-1 limit.

3.3 Berlekamp's Variant of the Extended Euclidean Algorithm

E. Berlekamp introduced a variant of the binary extended Euclidean algorithm for calculating the multiplicative inverse in $GF(2^m)$ in [20] along with a proposal for an efficient hardware implementation. A slight modification of this algorithm makes it possible to calculate the multiplicative $GF(2^m)$ inverse in a constant time of $2m + 1$ clock cycles.

Using a bit-serial $GF(2^m)$ multiplier, a multiplication takes m clock cycles. With a 4-bit digit-serial multiplier this value is reduced to $\lceil \frac{m}{4} \rceil$ clock cycles.

Thus, it is possible to perform an inversion faster than 11 multiplications both, with a bit-serial and a 4-bit digit-serial multiplier. This allows the use of affine coordinates instead of projective coordinates which avoids the use of coordinate transformations and reduces the number of auxiliary variables. Using the affine version of Montgomery's ladder is preferable when a bit-serial multiplier or a 2-bit-digit serial multiplier is used. Otherwise, the projective version will be faster.

3.4   Elliptic Curve Digital Signature Algorithm

Algorithm 1 shows the creation of an elliptic-curve digital signature. The inputs of the algorithm are the so called domain parameters (see [21]), a message m, and the key pair (d, Q). Random number generation and the SHA-1 hash-function are also needed but are usually calculated within a dedicated coprocessor and, therefore, are not considered in the following.

Algorithm 1 Elliptic Curve Digital Signature Algorithm - generation

---
Require: Message m, domain parameters
Ensure: Signature (r, s) of m
 1: Select a random integer k, $1 \le k \le n - 1$.
 2: Compute $kP = (x_1, y_1)$.
 3: Compute $r = x_1 \bmod n$. If $r = 0$ go to step 1.
 4: Compute $k^{-1} \bmod n$.
 5: Compute $e = \text{SHA-1}(m)$.
 6: Compute $s = k^{-1}(e + dr) \bmod n$. If $s = 0$ go to step 1.
 7: **return** (r, s)

The remaining two main operations are the scalar multiplication (line 2 of Algorithm 1) which is calculated by means of addition, multiplication, and inversion in the finite field $\text{GF}(2^m)$ and $\text{GF}(p)$ inversion (line 4 of Algorithm 1). The coprocessor provides these functions and therefore allows a fast calculation of the ECDSA.

4   Architecture

This section introduces the SLE66 smart card family of Infineon and shows how we extended the existing architecture with our new elliptic-curve coprocessor. We designed the elliptic-curve module to optimally fit into the given architecture and to achieve maximum speed when calculating digital signatures. Very low area requirements account for low cost.

Section 4.1 presents our target architecture, the SLE66XxxxP smartcard family. Section 4.2 shows the new ECC coprocessor architecture in detail.

4.1   Target Smartcard Architecture

Figure 1 shows the block diagram of the Infineon SLE66XxxxP smartcard [19]. A multiplexed address and data bus connects various modules like memories (ROM, XRAM, NVRAM), a Random Number Generator (RNG) or the UART to the CPU. In the actual design also a RSA coprocessor called Advanced Crypto Engine(ACE) is used to accelerate cryptographic operations. However, the ACE requires much resources since it is designed to operate with key lengths of 1024 bits and beyond. With our design we target low-cost elliptic-curve applications that rely on much smaller key lengths. Typical key lengths in such a scenario are 163 or 191 bits.

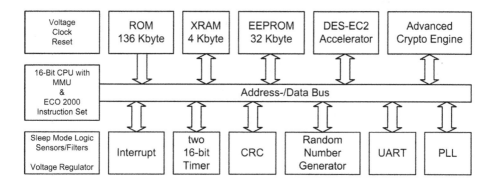

Fig. 1. Block diagram of the Infineon SLE66XxxxP smartcard family

According to this overall architecture we designed the coprocessor to communicate via the bus with the ECO 2000 CPU. The 8-bit CPU bus uses time multiplexing for address and data transport. It is able to deliver maximum 4 data bits within each clock cycle. To achieve maximum throughput we designed our architecture to process 4 bits in each clock cycle to avoid any wait states. We designed a 4-bit serial parallel multiplier to process 4 bits in each clock cycle.

To achieve low cost the new coprocessor needs to be small in terms of area. Having our new coprocessor we are able to omit the actual RSA coprocessor that can handle up to 1024 bit multiplication including registers of the same size.

The RSA coprocessor efficiently performs arithmetic operations in $GF(p)$. The calculation of an ECDSA as it was described in section 3.4 requires efficient calculation of an inversion in $GF(p)$. Therefore, we need to support inversion in $GF(p)$ in our new architecture to be able to omit the actual RSA architecture. Section 4.2 shows the implementation of our architecture.

Our new architecture supports all operations required to build a low cost smartcard system based on elliptic curve cryptography. The presented architecture is very competitive in terms of area and performance.

4.2   Elliptic-Curve Coprocessor

The coprocessor integrates four basic operations: $GF(2^m)$ addition, 4-bit digit-serial multiplication in $GF(2^m)$, and calculation of the multiplicative inverse in $GF(2^m)$ and $GF(p)$. Figure 2 shows the overall system structure. The coprocessor consists of three major parts:

- Bus Decoder: The bus decoder is the interface between the multiplexed address and data bus (X-bus) of the SLE66 CPU and the coprocessor.
- Data Path: The main part of the data path consists of *leaf cells* which integrate the basic functionality of multiplication, addition, and calculation of the inverse. It also contains an adder and an up/down counter which performs $GF(p)$ addition (adder) and is used for Berlekamp's version of the Euclidean Algorithm (counter).
- Control Logic: The control logic is a core component of the coprocessor. Its state machine generates the control signals for the data path to implement the two algorithms for $GF(p)$ inversion and $GF(2^m)$ inversion and sets the proper functions of the leaf cells.

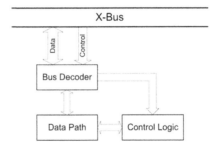

Fig. 2. Overall structure

The leaf cell (shown in Figure 3) is the main part of the data path. It is instantiated 192 times (24 slices of eight cells each, see Figure 4). The cell consists of four registers (A to D), combinational logic for achieving the necessary functionality (e.g. inversion, multiplication), and multiplexing. The grey box marks the 4-bit digit-serial multiply and reduce part. The implemented functions are as follows:

- Each register can perform a *shift-left* operation. This is essential for a fast $GF(2^m)$ inversion.
- Register C can perform the *shift-right* operation necessary for the binary extended Euclidean algorithm.
- C and D can both do an *8-bit shift left* and an *8-bit shift right* which is used for loading register C (with bus values or addition result) and reading register D.

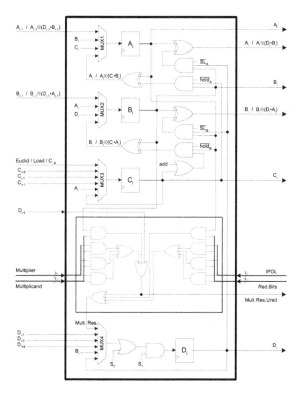

Fig. 3. Leaf cell

- Since only register C can be loaded and do a shift right, register contents must be distributed. So A can load the values of B or C, B can load the values of A or D, C the value of A, and D the value of B. This allows each register contents to be loaded to each other register.
- A and B store the calculation results of the $GF(2^m)$ inversion.
- B is used to store the $GF(2^m)$ addition result and
- D is used to store the $GF(2^m)$ multiplication result.
- Of course, each register can *hold* its actual value.

The presented architecture is fully scalable with regard to operand length. The VHDL model of the coprocessor was carefully developed to support various operand lengths. This can be achieved by inserting additional slices to the architecture which is possible by simple parameter adjustment in the VHDL model.

As a countermeasure against side channel attacks it is possible to implement the leaf cells using a secure logic style. Such a full custom implementation of the comparably small leaf cell together with a generator tool for placement and routing of m leaf cells can be used to implement the whole architecture using a secure logic style.

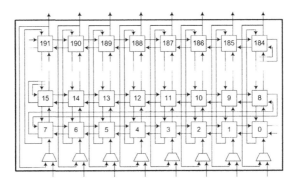

Fig. 4. Leaf cell array

5   Results

The coprocessor has been synthesized on a 0.13 µm CMOS process from Infineon. The synthesis was done with worst-case speed parameters and clock constraints of 10 MHz. The resulting chip area is 0.16 mm^2. Table 2 gives a more detailed overview of the area allocation. The values in the data path row include the leaf cell array, the adder/counter, and the bus decoder. The total size corresponds to a gate count of approximately 25,000 NAND gates. A leaf cell without support for GF(2^m) inversion would have a size of 496.0 µm^2 which saves about 30% area.

Table 2. Chip area of the coprocessor

Part	Area in µm^2	%
(Leaf cell	692.8	0.4)
Control unit	10,649.6	6.7
Data path	148,784.2	93.3
Total	159,433.8	100.0

All performance results are based on the finite field GF(2^{191}) on a hardware implementation of 192 leaf cells (24 slices of 8 cells each). To get a reasonable performance estimation some assumptions must be made:

- The scalar multiplication has average-case characteristics (190 point doubling and 95 point addition) using the double-and-add method.
- A software overhead of 30% for scalar multiplication is added
- GF(p) inversion cannot be calculated in constant time. Therefore, an average value obtained from numerous simulations is taken.
- A software overhead of 5% for GF(p) inversion is added.
- Other operations needed for ECDSA calculation (besides GF(p) inversion and scalar multiplication) are not considered because they denote only a very small part of the whole algorithm.

The 'software overhead' results are based on Infineon-internal experiences. The overhead covers operations like loading operands or storing intermediate results which are necessary for an assembler implementation in the smartcard.

Table 3. ECDSA performance for 191 bit

Operation	clock cycles
Scalar Multiplication	341,430
30% overhead	102,429
GF(p) inversion	24,310
5% overhead	1,216
Total	**469,385**

Table 3 summarizes the run time of the main parts of an ECDSA calculation. A comparison with Infineon's SLE66 smartcard family shows that the coprocessor can achieve a speed-up of 4.13 compared to smartcards with the Advanced Crypto Engine (ACE) and 7.44 on smartcards without ACE.

6   Conclusion

In this article we presented a low-cost ECC smartcard coprocessor which allows a fast calculation of the Elliptic Curve Digital Signature Algorithm (ECDSA) over the finite field GF(2^m). The coprocessor supports all basic operations needed for the ECDSA. These operations are GF(2^m) addition, 4-bit digit-serial multiplication in GF(2^m) and calculation of the multiplicative inverse in GF(p) and GF(2^m). Particularly, the fast GF(2^m) inversion makes it possible to use affine instead of projective coordinates for elliptic-curve point operations. This results in a simplified control on the software level and smaller storage effort.

References

1. A. Menezes, P. Oorschot, S. Vanstone, *Handbook of Applied Cryptography*, CRC Press, 1997.
2. D. Hankerson, A. Menezes, S. Vanstone, *Guide to Elliptic Curve Cryptography*, ISBN 0-387-95273-X, Springer Verlag, 2004.
3. J. Großschädl, G. Kamendje, *Instruction Set Extension for Fast Elliptic Curve Cryptography over Binary Finite Fields GF(2^m)*, Application-Specific Systems, Architectures, and Processors—ASAP 2003, pp. 455–468, IEEE Computer Society Press,, 2003.
4. J. Goodman, A. P. Chandrakasan, *An Energy-efficient Reconfigurable Public-Key Cryptography Processor*, IEEE Journal of Solid-State Circuits, pp. 1808–1820, November 2001.
5. R. Schroeppel, Ch. Beaver, R. Gonzales, R. Miller, T. Draelos, *A Low-Power Design for an Elliptic Curve Digital Signature Chip*, Cryptographic Hardware and Embedded Systems—CHES 2002, LNCS 2523, pp. 366–380, Springer Verlag, Berlin, 2003.

6. S. Okada, N. Torii, K. Itoh, M. Takenaka, *A High-performance Reconfigurable Elliptic Curve Processor for GF(2^m)*, Cryptographic Hardware and Embedded Systems—CHES 2000, LNCS 1965, pp. 25–40, Springer Verlag, Berlin, 2000.

7. G. Orlando, Ch. Paar, *A High-performance Reconfigurable Elliptic Curve Processor for GF(2^m)*, Cryptographic Hardware and Embedded Systems—CHES 2000, LNCS 1965, pp. 41–56, Springer Verlag, Berlin, 2000.

8. N. Gura, S. Chang Shantz, H. Eberle, D. Finchelstein, S. Gupta, V. Gupta, D. Stebila, *An End-to-End Systems Approach to Elliptic Curve Cryptography*, Cryptographic Hardware and Embedded Systems—CHES 2002, LNCS 2523, pp. 349–365, Springer Verlag, Berlin, 2003.

9. M. Ernst, M. Jung, F. Madlener, S. Huss, R. Blümel, *A Reconfigurable System on Chip Implementation for Elliptic Curve Cryptography over GF(2^m)*, Cryptographic Hardware and Embedded Systems—CHES 2002, LNCS 2523, pp. 381–399, Springer Verlag, Berlin, 2003.

10. E. Savaş, A. Tenca, Ç. Koç, *A Scalable and Unified Multiplier Architecture for Finite Fields GF(p) and GF(2^m)*, Cryptographic Hardware and Embedded Systems—CHES 2000, LNCS 1965, pp. 277–292, Springer Verlag, Berlin, 2000.

11. J. Großschädl, *A Bitserial Unified Multiplier Architecture for Finite Fields GF(p) and GF(2^m)*, Cryptographic Hardware and Embedded Systems—CHES 2001, LNCS 2162, pp. 206–223, Springer Verlag, 2001.

12. J. Wolkerstorfer, *Dual-Field Arithmetic Unit for GF(p) and GF(2^m)*, Cryptographic Hardware and Embedded Systems—CHES 2002, LNCS 2523, pp. 500–514, Springer Verlag, Berlin, 2003.

13. A. Gutub, A. Tenca, E. Savaş, Ç. Koç, *Scalable and Unified Hardware to Compute Montgomery Inverse in GF(p) and GF(2^m)*, Cryptographic Hardware and Embedded Systems—CHES 2002, LNCS 2523, pp. 484–499, Springer Verlag, Berlin, 2003.

14. J. Lopez and R. Dahab, *Fast Multiplication on Elliptic Curves over GF (2^m) without Precomputation*, Cryptographic Hardware and Embedded Systems—CHES 1999, LNCS 1717, pp. 316–327, Springer Verlag, 1999.

15. Victor S. Miller, *Use of Elliptic Curves in Cryptography*, LNCS 218, Springer Verlag, Berlin, 1985.

16. Neal Koblitz, *Elliptic Curve Cryptosystems*, Mathematics of Computation, Volume 48, 1987.

17. Éric Brier and Marc Joye, *Weierstraß Elliptic Curves and Side-Channel Attacks*, LNCS 2274, Springer Verlag, Berlin, 2001.

18. IEEE P1363, *Standard Specifications for Public-Key Cryptography*, IEEE standard, 2000.

19. Infineon Technologies, *Security and Chip Card ICs, SLE 66CX322P*, Product Information, 2002.

20. Elwyn R. Berlekamp, *Algebraic Coding Theory*, Aegean Park Press, revised 1984 edition, 1984.

21. Don B. Johnson, Alfred J. Menezes, and Scott Vanstone, *The Elliptic Curve Digital Signature Algorithm (ECDSA)*, International Journal of Information Security, Volume 1, 2001.

Comparing Elliptic Curve Cryptography and RSA on 8-Bit CPUs

Nils Gura, Arun Patel, Arvinderpal Wander, Hans Eberle, and
Sheueling Chang Shantz

Sun Microsystems Laboratories
{Nils.Gura, Arun.Patel,Arvinderpal.Wander,Hans.Eberle,
Sheueling.Chang}@sun.com
http://www.research.sun.com/projects/crypto

Abstract. Strong public-key cryptography is often considered to be too computationally expensive for small devices if not accelerated by cryptographic hardware. We revisited this statement and implemented elliptic curve point multiplication for 160-bit, 192-bit, and 224-bit NIST/SECG curves over GF(p) and RSA-1024 and RSA-2048 on two 8-bit microcontrollers. To accelerate multiple-precision multiplication, we propose a new algorithm to reduce the number of memory accesses.

Implementation and analysis led to three observations: 1. Public-key cryptography is viable on small devices without hardware acceleration. On an Atmel ATmega128 at 8 MHz we measured 0.81s for 160-bit ECC point multiplication and 0.43s for a RSA-1024 operation with exponent $e = 2^{16} + 1$. 2. The relative performance advantage of ECC point multiplication over RSA modular exponentiation increases with the decrease in processor word size and the increase in key size. 3. Elliptic curves over fields using pseudo-Mersenne primes as standardized by NIST and SECG allow for high performance implementations and show no performance disadvantage over optimal extension fields or prime fields selected specifically for a particular processor architecture.

Keywords: Elliptic Curve Cryptography, RSA, modular multiplication, sensor networks.

1 Introduction

As the Internet expands, it will encompass not only server and desktop systems, but also large numbers of small devices ranging from PDAs and cell phones to appliances and networked sensors. Inexpensive radio transceivers, integrated or attached to small processors, will provide the basis for small devices that can exchange information both locally with peers and, through gateway devices, globally with entities on the Internet. Deploying these devices in accessible environments exposes them to potential attackers that could tamper with them, eavesdrop communications, alter transmitted data, or attach unauthorized devices to the network. These risks can be mitigated by employing strong cryptography to ensure authentication, authorization, data confidentiality, and data

M. Joye and J.-J. Quisquater (Eds.): CHES 2004, LNCS 3156, pp. 119–132, 2004.

integrity. Symmetric cryptography, which is computationally inexpensive, can be used to achieve some of these goals. However, it is inflexible with respect to key management as it requires pre-distribution of keys. On the other hand, public-key cryptography allows for flexible key management, but requires a significant amount of computation. However, the compute capabilities of low-cost CPUs are very limited in terms of clock frequency, memory size, and power constraints.

Compared to RSA, the prevalent public-key scheme of the Internet today, Elliptic Curve Cryptography (ECC) offers smaller key sizes, faster computation, as well as memory, energy and bandwidth savings and is thus better suited for small devices. While RSA and ECC can be accelerated with dedicated cryptographic coprocessors such as those used in smart cards, coprocessors require additional hardware adding to the size and complexity of the devices. Therefore, they may not be desirable for low-cost implementations. Only few publications have considered public-key cryptography on small devices without coprocessors. Hasegawa et al. implemented ECDSA signature generation and verification on a 10MHz M16C microcomputer [11]. The implementation requires 4KB of code space and uses a 160-bit field prime $p = 65112 * 2^{144} - 1$ chosen to accommodate the 16-bit processor architecture. Signatures can be generated in 150ms and verified in 630ms. Based on the ECC integer library, the authors also estimate 10s for RSA-1024 signature generation and 400ms for verification using $e = 2^{16} + 1$. Bailey and Paar suggest the use of optimal extension fields (OEFs) that enable efficient reduction when subfield primes are chosen as pseudo-Mersenne primes close to the word size of the targeted processor [2]. An implementation of this concept for elliptic curve point multiplication over $GF((2^8 - 17)^{17})$ on an 8-bit 8051 processor architecture is described by Woodbury, Bailey and Paar in [17]. On a 12MHz 8051 with 12 clock cycles per instruction cycle, the authors measured 8.37s for general point multiplication using the binary method and 1.83s for point multiplication with a fixed base point. The code size was 13KB and 183 bytes of internal and 340 bytes of external RAM were used. Pietiläinen evaluated the relative performance of RSA and ECC on smart cards [16].

This paper focuses on implementation aspects of standardized RSA and ECC over NIST/SECG $GF(p)$ curves and evaluates the algorithms with respect to performance, code size, and memory usage. We consider software and hardware optimization techniques for RSA and ECC based on implementations on two exemplary 8-bit microcontroller platforms: The 8051-based Chipcon CC1010 [6], and the Atmel AVR ATmega128 [1].

2   Public-Key Algorithms ECC and RSA

ECC and RSA are mature public-key algorithms that have been researched by the academic community for many years; RSA was conceived by Rivest, Shamir and Adleman in 1976 and Koblitz and Miller independently published work on ECC in 1985. The fundamental operation underlying RSA is modular exponentiation in integer rings and its security stems from the difficulty of factoring large integers. ECC operates on groups of points over elliptic curves and derives its security from the hardness of the elliptic curve discrete logarithm problem (ECDLP). While sub-exponential algorithms can solve the integer factorization problem, only exponential algorithms are known for the ECDLP. This allows ECC to achieve the same level of security with smaller key sizes and higher computational efficiency; ECC-160 provides comparable security to RSA-1024 and ECC-224 provides comparable security to RSA-2048.

2.1   Implementing RSA

RSA operations are modular exponentiations of large integers with a typical size of 512 to 2048 bits. RSA encryption generates a ciphertext C from a message M based on a modular exponentiation $C = M^e \mod n$. Decryption regenerates the message by computing $M = C^d \mod n$ [1]. Among the several techniques that can be used to accelerate RSA [3], we specifically focused on those applicable under the constraints of 8-bit devices.

Chinese Remainder Theorem. RSA private-key operations, namely decryption and signature generation, can be accelerated using the Chinese Remainder Theorem (CRT). RSA chooses the modulus n as the product of two primes p and q, where p and q are on the order of $\sqrt{n}$ (e.g. for a 1024-bit n, p and q are on average 512 bits long). Using the CRT, a modular exponentiation for decryption $M = C^d \mod n$ can be decomposed into two modular exponentiations $M_1 = C_1^{d_1} \mod p$ and $M_2 = C_2^{d_2} \mod q$, where C_1, d_1, C_2 and d_2 are roughly half the size of n. Assuming schoolbook multiplication with operands of size $\frac{m}{2} = \frac{\lceil log_2(n) \rceil}{2}$, modular multiplications can be computed in roughly $\frac{1}{4}$ of the time as m-bit modular multiplications. Thus the CRT reduces computation time by nearly $\frac{3}{4}$ resulting in up to a 4x speedup.

Montgomery Multiplication. An efficient reduction scheme for arbitrary moduli n is Montgomery reduction which computes $C' * r^{-1} \mod n$ instead of $C' \mod n$. Appendix B shows a simple algorithm for Montgomery reduction of a $2m$-bit integer C' to an m-bit integer C on a processor with a word size of k bits. Using schoolbook multiplication, an $m \times m$-bit multiplication requires $\lceil \frac{m}{k} \rceil^2$ $k \times k$-bit multiplications and Montgomery reduction requires $\lceil \frac{m}{k} \rceil^2 + \lceil \frac{m}{k} \rceil$ $k \times k$-bit multiplications. Therefore, the total cost of an $m \times m$-bit Montgomery multiplication is $2\lceil \frac{m}{k} \rceil^2 + \lceil \frac{m}{k} \rceil$.

Optimized Squaring. The squaring of a large integer A, decomposed into multiple k-bit words $(A_{n-1}, ..., A_0)$, can take advantage of the fact that partial products $A_i A_j, i \neq j$ occur twice. For example, a squaring of $A = (A_1, A_0)$ needs to compute the partial product $A_1 A_0$ only once since $A^2 = (A_1 * 2^k + A_0) = A_1 A_1 * 2^{2k} + 2A_1 A_0 * 2^k + A_0 A_0$. Thus $m \times m$-bit squarings including Montgomery reduction require only $\frac{3}{2}\lceil \frac{m}{k} \rceil^2 + \frac{3}{2}\lceil \frac{m}{k} \rceil$ $k \times k$-bit multiplications, reducing computational complexity by up to 25%.

---

[1] A detailed description and a proof of mathematical correctness can be found e.g. in [3].

2.2   Implementing ECC

The fundamental operation underlying ECC is *point multiplication*, which is defined over finite field operations[2]. All standardized elliptic curves are defined over either prime integer fields $GF(p)$ or binary polynomial fields $GF(2^m)$. In this paper we consider only prime integer fields since binary polynomial field arithmetic, specifically multiplication, is insufficiently supported by current microprocessors and would thus lead to lower performance. The point multiplication kP of an integer k and a point P on an elliptic curve $C : y^2 = x^3 + ax + b$ over a prime field $GF(p)$ with curve parameters $a, b \in GF(p)$ can be decomposed into a sequence of *point additions* and *point doublings*. Numerous techniques have been proposed to accelerate ECC point multiplication. Since we do not make assumptions about the point P in a point multiplication kP, optimization methods for fixed points cannot be applied. In the following, we will describe the most important optimization techniques for general point multiplication on elliptic curves over $GF(p)$ standardized by either NIST or SECG.

Projective Coordinate Systems. Cohen et al. found that mixed coordinate systems using a combination of modified Jacobian and affine coordinates offer the best performance [7]. A point addition of one point in modified Jacobian coordinates $P_1 = (X_1, Y_1, Z_1, aZ_1^4)$ and one point in affine coordinates $P_2 = (x_2, y_2)$ resulting in $P_3 = (X_3, Y_3, Z_3, aZ_3^4)$ is shown in Formula 1 and a point doubling of a point in modified Jacobian coordinates P_1 is shown in Formula 2.

$$X_3 = -H^3 - 2X_1H^2 + r^2, Y_3 = -Y_1H^3 + r(X_1H^2 - X_3), Z_3 = Z_1H$$
$$aZ_3^4 = aZ_3^4 \quad \text{with} \quad H = x_2Z_1^2 - X_1, r = y_2Z_1^3 - Y_1 \tag{1}$$

$$X_3 = T, Y_3 = M(S - T) - U, Z_3 = 2Y_1Z_1, aZ_3^4 = 2U(aZ_1^4)$$
$$\text{with} \quad S = 4X_1Y_1^2, U = 8Y_1^4, M = 3X_1^2 + (aZ_1^4), T = -2S + M^2 \tag{2}$$

Using the above formulas, point addition requires 9 multiplications and 5 squarings and point doubling requires 4 multiplications and 4 squarings as the most expensive operations.

Non-Adjacent Forms. Non-adjacent forms (NAFs) are a method of recoding the scalar k in a point multiplication kP in order to reduce the number of non-zero bits and thus the number of point additions [14]. This is accomplished by using digits that can be either 0, 1 or -1. For example, $15P = (1\,1\,1\,1)_2P$ can be represented as $15P = (1\,0\,0\,0\,\text{-}1)_2P$. The NAF of a scalar k has the properties of having the lowest Hamming weight of any signed representation of k, being unique, and at most one bit longer than k. By definition, non-zero digits can never be adjacent resulting in a reduction of point additions from $\frac{m-1}{2}$ for the binary method to $\frac{m}{3}$ for NAF-encoded scalars. Negative digits translate into point subtractions, which require the same effort as point additions since the inverse of an affine point $P = (x, y)$ is simply $-P = (x, -y)$.

---

[2] For a detailed introduction to ECC the reader is referred to [10].

Curve-Specific Optimizations. NIST and SECG specified a set of elliptic curves with verified security properties that allow for significant performance optimizations [15] [4]. For all NIST and most SECG curves, the underlying field primes p were chosen as pseudo-Mersenne primes to allow for optimized modular reduction. They can be represented as $p = 2^m - \omega$ where ω is the sum of a few powers of two and $\omega \ll 2^m$. Reduction of a $2m$-bit multiplication result C' split into two m-bit halves c_1' and c_0' can be computed based on the congruence $2^m \equiv \omega$:

$$C' = (c_1', c_0') = A * B$$
$$\texttt{while } (c_1' \neq 0)$$
$$(c_1', c_0') = c_1' * \omega + c_0'$$
$$C = c_0' \bmod p$$

Since pseudo-Mersenne primes are sparse, multiplication by ω is commonly implemented with additions and shifts. It is important to note that compared to Montgomery reduction, reduction for pseudo-Mersenne primes requires substantially less effort on devices with small processor word sizes k. As described in Section 1, Montgomery reduction of a $2m$-bit product to an m-bit result requires $\lceil \frac{m}{k} \rceil^2 + \lceil \frac{m}{k} \rceil$ $k \times k$-bit multiplications. The ratio $\lceil \frac{m}{k} \rceil^2$ grows by the square as the processor word size k is decreased. Reduction for NIST/SECG pseudo-Mersenne primes, however, typically only requires two multiplications with a sparse ω. The number of corresponding additions and shifts scales linearly with the decrease of k. For example, if n multiplications were needed for Montgomery reduction on a 32-bit processor, $16n$ multiplications would be needed on an 8-bit processor. On the other hand, if a additions were needed for pseudo-Mersenne prime reduction on a machine with a 32-bit processor, only $4a$ additions would be needed on an 8-bit processor. Other ECC operations such as addition and subtraction also scale linearly. As a result, implementations of ECC exhibit a relative performance advantage over RSA on processors with small word sizes. Assuming a constant number of addends in the pseudo-Mersenne field primes, the advantage of ECC over RSA on devices with small word sizes likewise grows with the key size.

All NIST and some SECG curves further allow for optimization based on the curve parameter a being $a = -3$. Referring to point doubling Formula 2, M can be computed as $M = 3X_1^2 - 3Z_1^4 = 3(X_1 - Z_1^2) * (X_1 + Z_1^2)$ and aZ_3^4 as $aZ_3^4 = 6UZ_1^4$. As a result, aZ_3^4 does not have to be computed in point addition Formula 1 such that point doublings can be performed with 4 multiplications and 4 squarings and point additions can be performed with 8 multiplications and 3 squarings. Similar optimizations were used by Hitchcock et al. [12] and Hasegawa et al. [11].

3   Optimizing Multiplication for Memory Operations

Modular multiplication and squaring of large integers are the single performance-critical operations for RSA and ECC as we will show in Section 4. Therefore, high-performance implementations need to focus specifically on optimizing these operations. On small processors, multiple-precision multiplication of large integers not only involves arithmetic operations, but also a significant amount of data transport to and from memory due to limited register space. To reduce computational complexity, we considered Karatsuba Ofman [13] and FFT multiplication, but found that the recursive nature of these algorithms leads to increased memory consumption and frequent memory accesses to intermediate results and stack structures. In addition, Karatsuba Ofman and FFT multiplication cannot be applied to Montgomery reduction due to dependencies of the partial products. We therefore decided to focus on optimizing schoolbook multiplication. For schoolbook multiplication of m-bit integers on a device with a word size of k bits, the multiplication effort for m-bit integers is fixed to $n^2 = \lceil \frac{m}{k} \rceil^2$ $k \times k$-bit multiplication operations plus appendant additions.

Therefore, computation time can mainly be optimized by reducing the number of non-arithmetic operations, specifically memory operations. Table 1 illustrates and analyzes three multiplication strategies with respect to register usage and memory operations. It shows exemplary multiplications of n-word integers $(a_{n-1}, \ldots, a_1, a_0)$ and $(b_{n-1}, \ldots, b_1, b_0)$. The analysis assumes that multiplicand, multiplier and result cannot fit into register space at the same time such that memory accesses are necessary.

3.1   Row-Wise Multiplication

The row-wise multiplication strategy keeps the multiplier b_i constant and multiplies it with the entire multiple-precision multiplicand $(a_{n-1}, \ldots, a_1, a_0)$ before moving to the next multiplier b_{i+1}. Partial products are summed up in an accumulator consisting of n registers $(r_{n-1}, \ldots, r_1, r_0)$. Once a row is completed, the last register of the accumulator (r_0 for the first row) can be stored to memory as part of the final result and can be reused for accumulation of the next row. Two registers are required to store the constant b_i and one variable a_j. In the above implementation, row-wise implementation requires $n + 2$ registers and performs $n^2 + 3n$ memory accesses[3]. That is, for each $k \times k$ multiplication one memory load operation is needed. On processor architectures that do not have sufficient register space for the accumulator, up to $n^2 + 1$ additional load and $n^2 - n$ additional store operations are required. On the other hand, processors that can hold both the accumulator and the entire multiplicand in register space can perform row-wise multiplication with $2n + 1$ registers and only $4n$ memory accesses. In addition to memory accesses, pointers to multiplicand, multiplier and result may have to be adjusted on implementations using indexed addressing. If multiplicand and multiplier are indexed, one pointer increment/decrement is needed for each load operation, which is true for all three multiplication algorithms.

3.2   Column-Wise Multiplication

The column-wise multiplication strategy sums up columns of partial products $a_j * b_i$, where $i + j = l$ for column l. At the end of each column, one k-bit word

---

[3] Additional registers may be required for pointers, multiplication results and temporary data storage. We do not consider them in the analysis since they depend on the processor architecture.

is stored as part of the final multiplication result. Column-wise multiplication requires $4 + \lceil log_2(n)/k \rceil$ registers, the fewest number of all three algorithms. It is interesting to note that the number of registers grows only negligibly with the increase of the operand size n. Column-wise multiplication is thus well suited for architectures with limited register space. However, $2n^2 + 2n$ memory operations have to be performed, which corresponds to two memory load operations per $k \times k$ multiplication. Implementations of column-wise multiplication require advancing pointers to both multiplicand a_j and multiplier b_i once for every $k \times k$-bit multiplication.

3.3   Hybrid Multiplication

We propose a new hybrid multiplication strategy that combines the advantages of row-wise and column-wise multiplication. Hybrid multiplication aims at optimizing for both the number of registers and the number of memory accesses. We employ the column-wise strategy as the "outer algorithm" and the row-wise strategy as the "inner algorithm". That is, hybrid multiplication computes columns that consist of rows of partial products. The savings in memory bandwidth stem from the fact that k-bit operands of the multiplier are used in several multiplications, but are loaded from memory only once. Looking at column 0 in the example, b_0 and b_1 are used in two multiplications, but have to be loaded only once. Register usage and memory accesses depend on the the number of partial products per row (or column width) d. The hybrid method equals the column-wise strategy for $d = 1$ and it equals the row-wise strategy for $d = n$, where the entire multiplicand is kept in registers. d can be chosen according to the targeted processor; larger values of d require fewer memory operations, but more registers to store operands and to accumulate the result. To optimize the algorithm performance for r available registers, d should be chosen such that $d = max\{i | 1 \leq i \leq n, r \geq 3i + \lceil log_2(n/i)/k \rceil\}$. Note that the number of registers grows only logarithmically with the increase in operand size n. Therefore, for a fixed value of d, hybrid multiplication scales to a wide range of operand sizes n without requiring additional registers. This is important for implementations that have to support algorithms such as RSA and ECC for multiple key sizes. The hybrid multiplication algorithm is shown in pseudo code in Appendix A.

4   Implementation and Evaluation

We implemented ECC point multiplication and modular exponentiation on two exemplary 8-bit platforms in assembly code. As the first processor, we chose a Chipcon CC1010 8-bit microcontroller which implements the Intel 8051 instruction set. The CC1010 contains 32KB of FLASH program memory, 2KB of external data memory and 128 bytes of internal data memory. As part of the 8051 architecture, 32 bytes of the internal memory are used to form 4 banks of 8 8-bit registers for temporary data storage. One 8-bit accumulator is the destination register of all arithmetic operations. The CC1010 is clocked at 14.7456MHz with one instruction cycle corresponding to 4 clock cycles such that the clock frequency adjusted for instruction cycles is 3.6864MHz.

Table 1. Multiple-precision multiplication of integers with $n = 4$ words.

Row-Wise Multiplication	Column-Wise Multiplication	Hybrid Multiplication ($d = 2$)
row 0: a_0b_0, a_1b_0, a_2b_0, a_3b_0	col 0: a_0b_0 col 1: a_1b_0, a_0b_1 col 2: a_2b_0, a_1b_1, a_0b_2	col 0, row 0: a_0b_0, a_1b_0, a_0b_1
row 1: a_0b_1, a_1b_1, a_2b_1, a_3b_1	col 3: a_3b_0, a_2b_1, a_1b_2, a_0b_3	row 1: a_1b_1, a_2b_0
a_0b_2, a_1b_2, a_2b_2, a_3b_2	... a_3b_1, a_2b_2, a_1b_3	col 1, row 0: a_3b_0, a_2b_1
a_0b_3, a_1b_3, a_2b_3, a_3b_3	a_3b_2, a_2b_3	row 1: a_3b_1
	a_3b_3	row 2: a_0b_2, a_1b_2, a_0b_3 row 3: a_1b_3, a_2b_2 a_3b_2, a_2b_3 a_3b_3
accumulator: ... $r_2\,r_1\,r_0\,r_3\,r_2\,r_1\,r_0$	accumulator: $\leftarrow\ r_2\,r_1\,r_0$	accumulator: $\leftarrow\ r_4\,r_3\,r_2\,r_1\,r_0$

	Row-Wise	Column-Wise	Hybrid
accumulator registers	n	$2 + \lceil log_2(n)/k \rceil$	$2d + \lceil log_2(n/d)/k \rceil$
operand registers	2	2	$d+1$
memory loads	$n^2 + n$	$2n^2$	$2\lceil n^2/d \rceil$
memory stores	$2n$	$2n$	$2n$
registers	$n + 2$	$4 + \lceil log_2(n)/k \rceil$	$3d + \lceil log_2(n/d)/k \rceil$
memory ops	$n^2 + 3n$	$2n^2 + 2n$	$2\lceil n^2/d \rceil + 2n$

Table 2. Average ECC and RSA execution times on the ATmega128 and the CC1010.

Algorithm	ATmega128 @ 8MHz			CC1010 @ 14.7456MHz		
	time	data mem	code	time	data mem	code
	s	bytes	bytes	s	ext+int, bytes	bytes
ECC secp160r1	0.81s	282	3682	4.58s	180+86	2166
ECC secp192r1	1.24s	336	3979	7.56s	216+102	2152
ECC secp224r1	2.19s	422	4812	11.98s	259+114	2214
Mod. exp. 512	5.37s	328	1071	53.33s	321+71	764
RSA-1024 public-key $e = 2^{16} + 1$	0.43s	542	1073	> 4.48s		
RSA-1024 private-key w. CRT	10.99s	930	6292	~ 106.66s		
RSA-2048 public-key $e = 2^{16} + 1$	1.94s	1332	2854			
RSA-2048 private-key w. CRT	83.26s	1853	7736			

The execution time for the RSA-1024 private-key operation on the CC1010 was approximated as twice the execution time of a 512-bit Montgomery exponentiation and the execution time for the RSA-1024 public-key operation was estimated as four times the execution time of a 512-bit Montgomery exponentiation using $e = 2^{16} + 1$. Since only one 512-bit operand and no full 1024-bit operand can be kept in internal memory, an actual implementation of the RSA-1024 public-key operation would be even less efficient.

As the second processor, we chose an Atmel ATmega128, a popular processor used for sensor network research, for example on the Crossbow motes platform [8]. The ATmega128 is an 8-bit microcontroller based on the AVR architecture and contains 128KB of FLASH program memory and 4KB of data memory. Unlike the CC1010, the ATmega128 implements a homogeneous data memory that can be addressed by three 16-bit pointer registers with pre-decrement and post-increment functionality. The register set consists of 32 8-bit registers, where all registers can be destinations of arithmetic operations. The ATmega128 can be operated at frequencies up to 16MHz, where one instruction cycle equals one clock cycle.

Given the limited processor resources, we chose to focus our implementation efforts on a small memory footprint using performance optimizations applicable to small devices without significant increases in either code size or memory usage. For ECC, we implemented point multiplication for three SECG-standardized elliptic curves, secp160r1, secp192r1, and secp224r1, including optimized squarings and the techniques described in section 2.2. Inversion was implemented with the algorithm proposed by Chang Shantz [5]. We evaluated the three multiplication strategies with respect to processor capabilities. The CC1010 can access only one bank of 8 registers at a time, where switching register banks requires multiple instruction cycles. Looking at the hybrid multiplication strategy, at least 7 registers are required for the smallest column width of $d = 2$ and two registers are needed to store pointer registers exceeding the number of available registers. We therefore resolved to implementing the row-wise multiplication strategy and unrolled parts of the inner multiplication loop[4]. On the ATmega128, the hybrid multiplication method can be applied with a column width of up to $d = 6$ requiring 19 registers. We chose $d = 5$ for secp160r1 accomodating a 20-byte operand size and $d = 6$ for secp192r1 and secp224r1.

For RSA, we implemented RSA-1024 on both processors and RSA-2048 on the ATmega128 incorporating the optimizations described in section 2.1. The CC1010 implementation of Montgomery multiplication uses row-wise multiplication, where the ATmega128 implementation employs the hybrid strategy using the maximal column width of $d = 6$. Since the operand word size of 64 bytes for RSA-1024 with CRT is not a multiple of $d = 6$, the implementation performs a 528×528-bit Montgomery multiplication, where optimizations could be made at the cost of increased code size. For the RSA public-key operations we used a small exponent of $e = 2^{16} + 1$.

Table 2 summarizes performance, memory usage, and code size of the ECC and RSA implementations. For both the CC1010 and the ATmega128, ECC-160 point multiplication outperforms the RSA-1024 private-key operation by an order of magnitude and is within a factor of 2 of the RSA-1024 public-key operation. Due to the performance characteristics of Montgomery reduction and pseudo-Mersenne prime reduction, this ratio favors ECC-224 even more when compared to RSA-2048.

---

[4] A later analysis showed that implementing the column-wise strategy would save 9.5% cycles in the inner multiplication loop by reducing the number of memory accesses.

For point multiplication over secp160r1, over 77% of the execution time on the ATmega128 and over 85% of the execution time on the CC1010 are spent on multiple-precision multiplications and squarings not including reduction. This underlines the need for focusing optimization efforts primarily on the inner multiplication and squaring loops. Confirming this observation, we found that an optimized implementation on the CC1010 that unrolled loops for addition, subtraction, reduction and copy operations required 35% more code space while decreasing execution time by only 3%. Our numbers further show that on processor architectures with small word sizes, the use of pseudo Mersenne primes reduces the time spent on reduction to a negligible amount. Replacing the column-wise with the hybrid method, we measured a performance improvement for ECC point multiplication of 24.8% for secp160r1 and 25.0% for secp224r1 on the ATmega128. Non-adjacent forms accounted for an 11% performance increase on both devices. Comparing the memory requirements, it is interesting to note that while modular exponentiation requires relatively little memory, a full RSA implementation with CRT requires additional routines and several precomputed constants significantly increasing the memory requirements.

Table 3 shows the instruction decomposition for a 160-bit multiplication and a 512/528-bit Montgomery multiplication on both platforms. Looking at the amount of time spent on arithmetic operations, the small register set and the single destination register for arithmetic operations lead to a low multiplication efficiency on the CC1010. Multiplication and addition instructions account for only 38.2% of a 160-bit multiplication and 28.7% for a 512-bit Montgomery multiplication. Despite the high multiplication cost of 5 instruction cycles, register pressure results in frequent memory accesses and a large overhead of non-arithmetic instructions. In comparison, 69.6% of the time for a 160-bit multiplication and 72.6% of the time for a 528-bit Montgomery multiplication is spent on arithmetic instructions on the ATmega128. This increase in efficiency can be mostly attributed to the large register file and variable destination registers for arithmetic operations. Furthermore, the homogeneous memory architecture and post-increment and pre-decrement functionality for memory operations lead to performance advantages for large key sizes.

We expect that performance improvements for ECC and RSA could be achieved by employing window techniques for point multiplication / modular exponentiation and by using Karatsuba Ofman multiplication. However, these techniques would lead to significant increases in data memory usage and code size and add to the complexity of the implementation.

5   Instruction Set Extensions

Table 3 shows that addition and multiplication instructions account for the majority of the execution time for both processors. Significant performance improvements can be achieved by combining one multiplication and two additions into one instruction as proposed by Großschädl [9]. We refer to this instruction as "MULACC" and define it to perform the following operation on a source register r_s, a destination register r_d, a fixed architectural register r_c and a non-architectural register exc (all of bit-width k):

Table 3. Decomposition of 160x160-bit multiplication and 512x512/528x528-bit Montgomery multiplication on the Chipcon CC1010 and the ATmega128.

			Chipcon CC1010			
			160x160 mult.		512x512 Montg. mult.	
Instruction type	Opcodes	Cycles/instr.	Instr. cycles	%	Instr. cycles	%
Register swap	XCH A, B	2	2280	24.46	32512	12.60
Multiplication	MUL	5	2000	21.46	41280	16.00
Addition	ADD/ADDC	1	1560	16.74	32723	12.68
Data stores	MOV ADDR, RX	1	1220	13.09	17057	6.61
Data loads	MOV RX, ADDR	1	1025	11.00	41938	16.25
Pointer inc./dec.	INC/DEC	1	895	9.60	33656	13.04
Dec. + branch	DJNZ	3	297	3.19	24957	9.67
Data loads (ext.)	MOVX	2	40	0.43	16934	6.56
Data stores (ext.)	MOVX	2	0	0.00	16678	6.46
Other			4	0.04	307	0.12
Total			9321	100.00	258042	100.00
Time @ 14.7456MHz			2.53ms		70.00ms	
			ATmega128			
			160x160 mult.		528x528 Montg. mult.	
Instruction type	Opcodes	Cycles/instr.	Instr. cycles	%	Instr. cycles	%
Addition	ADD/ADC	1	1360	43.79	29766	45.67
Multiplication	MUL	2	800	25.76	17556	26.94
16-bit Register move	MOVW	1	335	10.79	7262	11.14
Data loads	LD/LDI	2	334	10.75	6169	9.47
Data stores	ST	2	80	2.58	524	0.80
Jumps	RJMP/IJMP	2	66	2.12	0	0.00
Function calls/rets	CALL/RET	4	0	0.00	1452	2.23
Other			131	4.22	2442	3.75
Total			3106	100.00	65171	100.00
Time @ 8MHz			0.39ms		8.15ms	
			ATmega128 with MULACC instruction			
			160x160 mult.		528x528 Montg. mult.	
Instruction type	Opcodes	Cycles/instr.	Instr. cycles	%	Instr. cycles	%
Multiply-accumulate	MULACC	2	960	48.34	20328	51.27
Data loads	LD/LDI	2	334	16.82	6169	15.56
Addition	ADD/ADC	1	320	16.11	6292	15.87
Data stores	ST	2	80	4.03	524	1.32
Jumps	RJMP/IJMP	2	66	3.32	0	0.00
Function calls/rets	CALL/RET	4	0	0.00	1452	3.66
Multiplication	MUL	2	0	0.00	924	2.33
16-bit Register move	MOVW	1	15	0.76	2	0.01
Other			211	10.62	3960	9.99
Total			1986	100.00	39651	100.00
Time @ 8MHz			0.25ms		4.96ms	
Time reduction			36.06%		39.16%	

Reduction for 160-bit multiplication and the conditional subtraction of the prime for Montgomery multiplication are not included in the instruction counts.

$$
\begin{aligned}
\text{MULACC } r_d, r_s : \quad r_d &\leftarrow (r_s * r_c + exc + r_d)[k - 1..0] \\
exc &\leftarrow (r_s * r_c + exc + r_d)[2k - 1..k]
\end{aligned}
\tag{3}
$$

MULACC multiplies the source register r_s with an implicit register r_c, adds registers exc and r_d and stores the lower k bits of the $2k$-bit result in register r_d. The upper k bits are stored in register exc, from where they can be used in a subsequent MULACC operation. We refer to exc as the "extended carry register" since its function resembles the carry bit used for additions. Applied to the row-wise or hybrid multiplication strategy, MULACC can generate a partial product $a_j * b_i$, add the upper k bits of the previous partial product $a_{j-1} * b_i$, add k bits from an accumulator register and store the result in the accumulator register in a single instruction. Since MULACC uses only two variable registers and r_c, exc are fixed, it is compatible with both the 8051 and AVR instruction sets. Table 3 shows the instruction decomposition for a 160-bit multiplication and 528-bit Montgomery multiplication using the MULACC instruction on the ATmega128. Implemented as a 2-cycle instruction, MULACC reduces the execution time of a 160-bit multiplication by more than 36% resulting in a total reduction of point multiplication time of 27.6% to 0.59s. The execution time for 528-bit Montgomery multiplication is reduced by 39%. MULACC further reduces the number of registers needed for the inner multiplication loop such that the hybrid multiplication method could be implemented with a column width of $d = 8$, which would result in even higher performance gains. On the CC1010, we measured a reduction in execution time of 39% to 2.78s for secp160r1 point multiplication and 38% to 33.06s for 512-bit Montgomery exponentiation.

6   Conclusions

We compared elliptic curve point multiplication over three SECG/NIST curves secp160r1, secp192r1, and secp224r1 with RSA-1024 and RSA-2048 on two 8-bit processor architectures. On both platforms, ECC-160 point multiplication outperforms the RSA-1024 private-key operation by an order of magnitude and is within a factor of 2 of the RSA-1024 public-key operation.

We presented a novel multiplication algorithm that significantly reduces the number of memory accesses. This algorithm led to a 25% performance increase for ECC point multiplication on the Atmel AVR platform.

Our measurements and analysis led to fundamental observations: The relative performance of ECC over RSA increases as the word size of the processor decreases. This stems from the fact that the complexity of addition, subtraction and optimized reduction based on sparse pseudo-Mersenne primes grows linearly with the decrease of the word size whereas Montgomery reduction grows quadratically. As a result, ECC point multiplication on small devices becomes comparable in performance to RSA public-key operations and we expect it to be higher for large key sizes.

In contrast to Hasegawa et al. and Woodbury, Bailey and Paar, our observations do not support the claim that field primes chosen specifically for a particular processor architecture or OEFs lead to significant performance improvements over prime fields using pseudo-Mersenne primes as recommended by NIST and SECG. Using pseudo-Mersenne primes as specified for NIST/SECG curves, more than 85% of the time for secp160r1 point multiplication on the 8051 architecture and more than 77% on the AVR architecture was spent on integer multiplication not including reduction. Therefore, further optimizing reduction would not lead to significant performance improvements. Woodbury, Bailey and Paar represent field elements $GF((2^8 - 17)^{17}$ as polynomials with 17 8-bit integer coefficients. Polynomial multiplication in this field requires the same number of 8x8-bit multiplications as 17-byte integer multiplication. The algorithm for polynomial multiplication corresponds to integer multiplication using the column-wise method, where optimized reduction is performed at the end of each column. The hybrid or row-wise methods cannot be applied such that we expect the performance of ECC over OEFs to be lower on architectures such as the Atmel AVR.

We plan to continue our work on small devices towards a complete lightweight implementation of the security protocol SSL/TLS.

References

1. Atmel Corporation. http://www.atmel.com/.
2. D. V. Bailey and C. Paar. Optimal Extension Fields for Fast Arithmetic in Public-Key Algorithms. In *Advances in Cryptography — CRYPTO '98*, volume 1462 of *Lecture Notes in Computer Science*, pages 472–485. Springer-Verlag, 1998.
3. Ç. K. Koç. High-Speed RSA Implementation. Technical report, RSA Laboratories TR201, November 1994.
4. Certicom Research. SEC 2: Recommended Elliptic Curve Domain Parameters. Standards for Efficient Cryptography Version 1.0, September 2000.
5. S. Chang Shantz. From Euclid's GCD to Montgomery Multiplication to the Great Divide. Technical report, Sun Microsystems Laboratories TR-2001-95, June 2001.
6. Chipcon AS. http://www.chipcon.com/.
7. H. Cohen, A. Miyaji, and T. Ono. Efficient elliptic curve exponentiation using mixed coordinates. In *ASIACRYPT: Advances in Cryptology*, volume 1514 of *Lecture Notes in Computer Science*, pages 51–65. Springer-Verlag, 1998.
8. Crossbow Technology, Inc. http://www.xbow.com/.
9. J. Großschädl. Instruction Set Extension for Long Integer Modulo Arithmetic on RISC-Based Smart Cards. In *14th Symposium on Computer Architecture and High Performance Computing*, pages 13–19. IEEE Computer Society, October 2002.
10. D. Hankerson, A. J. Menezes, and S. Vanstone. *Guide to Elliptic Curve Cryptography*. Springer-Verlag, 2004.
11. T. Hasegawa, J. Nakajima, and M. Matsui. A practical implementation of elliptic curve cryptosystems over GF (p) on a 16-bit microcomputer. In *Public Key Cryptography PKC '98*, volume 1431 of *Lecture Notes in Computer Science*, pages 182–194. Springer-Verlag, 1998.
12. Y. Hitchcock, E. Dawson, A. Clark, and P. Montague. Implementing an efficient elliptic curve cryptosystem over GF(p) on a smart card. *ANZIAM Journal*, 44(E):C354–C377, 2003.
13. A. Karatsuba and Y. Ofman. Multiplication of Many-Digital Numbers by Automatic Computers. *Doklady Akad. Nauk*, (145):293–294, 1963. Translation in Physics-Doklady 7, 595-596.
14. F. Morain and J. Olivos. Speeding up the computations on an elliptic curve using addition-subtraction chains. *Theoretical Informatics and Applications*, 24:531–543, 1990.
15. National Institute of Standards and Technology. Recommended Elliptic Curves for Federal Government Use, August 1999.
16. H. Pietiläinen. *Elliptic curve cryptography on smart cards*. Helsinki University of Technology, Faculty of Information Technology, October 2000. Master's Thesis.
17. A. D. Woodbury, D. V. Bailey, and C. Paar. Elliptic Curve Cryptography on Smart Cards without Coprocessors. In *The Fourth Smart Card Research and Advanced Applications (CARDIS2000) Conference*, September 2000. Bristol, UK.

A   Algorithm for Hybrid Multiplication

The two outer nested loops describe column-wise multiplication and the two inner nested loops describe row-wise multiplication. Multiplicand and multiplier are located in memory locations mem_a and mem_b and are temporarily loaded into registers $a_{d-1}, \ldots, a_0$ and b. The result is accumulated in registers $r_{2d-1+\lceil log2(n/d)/k \rceil}, \ldots, r_0$, where the lower d registers are stored to result memory location mem_c at the end of each column.

```
Input:
n                        : operand size in words
d                        : column width
mem_a [⌈ n/d ⌉*d-1..0] : multiplicand A
mem_b [⌈ n/d ⌉*d-1..0] : multiplier B

Output:
mem_c [⌈ n/d ⌉*2d-1..0] : result C = A * B

for i=0 to ⌈ n/d ⌉-1
  for j=0 to i
    (a_{d-1},..., a_0) = mem_a[(i-j+1)*d-1..(i-j)*d]
    for s=0 to d-1
      b = mem_b[j*d+s]
      for t=0 to d-1
        (r_{2d-1+⌈ log2(n/d)/k ⌉},..., r_0) = (r_{2d-1+⌈ log2(n/d)/k ⌉},..., r_0) +
                                                a_t * b * 2^{k*(t+s)}
  mem_c[(i+1)*d..i*d] = (r_{d-1},..., r_0)
  (r_{d-1+⌈ log2(n/d)/k ⌉},..., r_0) = (r_{2d-1+⌈ log2(n/d)/k ⌉},..., r_d)
  (r_{2d-1+⌈ log2(n/d)/k ⌉},..., r_d) = 0
for i=⌈ n/d ⌉ to 2⌈ n/d ⌉-2
  for j=i-⌈ n/d ⌉+1 to ⌈ n/d ⌉-1
    (a_{d-1},..., a_0) = mem_a[(i-j+1)*d-1..(i-j)*d]
    for s=0 to d-1
      b = mem_b[j*d+s]
      for t=0 to d-1
        (r_{2d-1+⌈ log2(n/d)/k ⌉},..., r_0) = (r_{2d-1+⌈ log2(n/d)/k ⌉},..., r_0) +
                                                a_t * b * 2^{k*(t+s)}
  mem_c[(i+1)*d ..i*d] = (r_{d-1},..., r_0)
  (r_{d-1+⌈ log2(n/d)/k ⌉},..., r_0) = (r_{2d-1+⌈ log2(n/d)/k ⌉},..., r_d)
  (r_{2d-1+⌈ log2(n/d)/k ⌉},..., r_d) = 0
mem_c[(i+1)*d ..i*d] = (r_{d-1},..., r_0)
```

B   Algorithm for Montgomery Reduction

The algorithm below describes Montgomery reduction of a $2m$-bit multiplication result $C' = A * B$ of two m-bit numbers A and B to $C = C' * r^{-1} \mod n$ on a processor with a k-bit word size.

```
n' = -1/n mod 2^k
for i=0 to ⌈ m/k ⌉-1
    s=C'*n' mod 2^k
    C'=C'+ s * n      // last k bits of C' become 0
    C'=C' >> k        // division by 2^k
if C'>=n
    C'=C'- n
return C=C'
```

Instruction Set Extensions for Fast Arithmetic in Finite Fields GF(p) and GF(2^m)

Johann Großschädl[1] and Erkay Savaş[2]

[1] Institute for Applied Information Processing and Communications
Graz University of Technology, Inffeldgasse 16a, A–8010 Graz, Austria
Johann.Groszschaedl@iaik.at
[2] Faculty of Engineering and Natural Sciences
Sabanci University, Orhanli-Tuzla, TR–34956 Istanbul, Turkey
erkays@sabanciuniv.edu

Abstract. Instruction set extensions are a small number of custom instructions specifically designed to accelerate the processing of a given kind of workload such as multimedia or cryptography. Enhancing a general-purpose RISC processor with a few application-specific instructions to facilitate the inner loop operations of public-key cryptosystems can result in a significant performance gain. In this paper we introduce a set of five custom instructions to accelerate arithmetic operations in finite fields GF(p) and GF(2^m). The custom instructions can be easily integrated into a standard RISC architecture like MIPS32 and require only little extra hardware. Our experimental results show that an extended MIPS32 core is able to perform an elliptic curve scalar multiplication over a 192-bit prime field in 36 msec, assuming a clock speed of 33 MHz. An elliptic curve scalar multiplication over the binary field GF(2^{191}) takes only 21 msec, which is approximately six times faster than a software implementation on a standard MIPS32 processor.

1 Introduction

The customization of processors is nowadays widely employed in the embedded systems field. An embedded system consists of both hardware and software components, and is generally designed for a given (pre-defined) application or application domain. This makes a strong case for tweaking both the hardware (i.e. processor) and the software with the goal to find the "best" interface between them. In recent years, multimedia instruction set extensions became very popular because they enable increased performance on a range of applications for the penalty of little extra silicon area [11]. Various micro-processor vendors developed architectural enhancements for fast multimedia processing (e.g. Intel's MMX and SSE, Hewlett-Packard's MAX, MIPS Technologies' MDMX, or Altivec/VMX/Velocity Engine designed by Motorola, IBM and Apple).

Not only multimedia workloads, but also public-key cryptosystems are amenable to processor specialization. Most software algorithms for multiple-precision arithmetic spend the vast majority of their running time in a few performance-critical sections, typically in inner loops that execute the same operation using

M. Joye and J.-J. Quisquater (Eds.): CHES 2004, LNCS 3156, pp. 133–147, 2004.

separate data in each iteration [14]. Speeding up these loops through dedicated instruction set extensions can result in a tremendous performance gain.

In this paper, we explore the potential of instruction set extensions for fast arithmetic in finite fields on an embedded RISC processor. The performance of elliptic curve cryptosystems is primarily determined by the efficient implementation of arithmetic operations in the underlying finite field [8,2]. Augmenting a general-purpose processor with a few custom instructions for fast arithmetic in finite fields has a number of benefits over using a hardware accelerator such as a cryptographic co-processor. First, the concept of instruction set extensions eliminates the communication overhead given in processor/co-processor systems. Second, the area of a cryptographic co-processor is generally much larger than the area of a functional unit that is tightly coupled to the processor core and directly controlled by the instruction stream. Third, instruction set extensions offer a degree of flexibility and scalability that goes far beyond of fixed-function hardware like a co-processor.

Instruction set extensions offer a high degree of flexibility as they permit to use the "best" algorithm for the miscellaneous arithmetic operations in finite fields. For instance, squaring of a long integer can be done almost twice as fast as multiplication of two different integers [14]. Hardware multipliers normally do not take advantage of special squaring algorithms since this would greatly complicate their architecture. Another example is modular reduction. Montgomery's algorithm [19] is very well suited for hardware and software implementation as it replaces the trial division with simple shift operations. However, certain special primes, like the so-called *generalized Mersenne* (GM) primes used in elliptic curve cryptography, facilitate much faster reduction methods. For instance, the reduction of a 384-bit integer modulo the GM prime $p = 2^{192} - 2^{64} - 1$ can be simply realized by additions modulo p [26]. A modular multiplier which performs the reduction operation according to Montgomery's method is not able to take advantage from GM primes.

1.1   Related Work

Contrary to multimedia extensions, there exist only very few research papers concerned with optimized instruction sets for public-key cryptography. Previous work [5] and [23] focussed on the ARMv4 architecture and proposed architectural enhancements to support long integer modular arithmetic. Our work [6] presents two custom instructions to accelerate Montgomery multiplication on a MIPS32 core. A 1024-bit modular exponentiation can be executed in 425 msec when the processor is clocked at 33 MHz. This result confirms that instruction set extensions allow fast yet flexible implementations of public-key cryptography. The commercial products [17] and [27] primarily target the market for multi-application smart cards. Both are able to execute a 1024-bit modular exponentiation in less than 350 msec (at 33 MHz). The product briefs claim that these processors also feature instruction set extensions for elliptic curve cryptography. However, no details about the custom instructions and the achieved performance figures have been released to the public.

1.2   Contributions of This Work

In this paper, we introduce a set of five custom instructions to accelerate arithmetic operations in prime fields $GF(p)$ and binary extension fields $GF(2^m)$. The custom instructions can be easily integrated into the MIPS32 instruction set architecture [16]. We selected MIPS32 for our research because it is one of the most popular architectures in the embedded systems area.

Designing instruction set extensions for arithmetic in finite fields requires to select the proper algorithms for the diverse arithmetic operations and to select the proper custom instructions (out of a huge number of candidate instructions) so that the combination of both gives the best result. The selection of the proper algorithms is necessary since most arithmetic operations can be implemented in different ways. For instance, multiple-precision multiplication can be realized according the pencil-and-paper method [14], Comba's method [4], Karatsuba's method, etc. Our first contribution in this paper is a "guide" through the algorithm selection process. We discuss several arithmetic algorithms and identify those which are most suitable for the design of instruction set extensions.

A major problem when designing instruction set extensions is that a number of (micro-)architectural constraints have to be considered, e.g. instruction size and format, the number of source and destination addresses within an instruction word, the number of general-purpose registers, etc. Our second contribution in this paper is to demonstrate that it is possible to find custom instructions which support the processing of arithmetic algorithms in an efficient manner, and, at the same time, are simple to integrate into the MIPS32 architecture.

2   Arithmetic in Prime Fields

The elements of a prime field $GF(p)$ are the residue classes modulo p, typically represented by the set $\{0, 1, \ldots, p-1\}$. Arithmetic in $GF(p)$ is nothing else than conventional modular arithmetic, i.e. addition and multiplication modulo the prime p. In this section we briefly review some basic algorithms for long integer arithmetic and discuss minor modifications/adaptions to facilitate the processing of these algorithms on an extended MIPS32 core.

2.1   Notation

Throughout this paper, we use uppercase letters to denote long integers whose precision exceeds the word-size w of the processor. In software, the long integers may be stored in multi-word data structures, e.g. arrays of single-precision integers. We can write a non-negative n-bit integer A as a sequence of $d = \lceil n/w \rceil$ words, each consisting of w bits, i.e. $A = (A_{d-1}, \ldots, A_1, A_0)$. In the following, the w-bit words are denoted by indexed uppercase letters, whereas indexed lowercase letters represent the individual bits of an integer.

$$A = \sum_{i=0}^{n-1} a_i \cdot 2^i = \sum_{j=0}^{d-1} A_j \cdot 2^{j \cdot w} \quad \text{with} \quad A_j = \sum_{k=0}^{w-1} a_{j \cdot w + k} \cdot 2^k \quad (1)$$

Algorithm 1. Comba's method for multiple-precision multiplication

---

Input: Two n-bit integers, $A = (A_{d-1}, \ldots, A_0)$ and $B = (B_{d-1}, \ldots, B_0)$, represented
by $d = \lceil n/w \rceil$ words each.
Output: Product $Z = A \cdot B = (Z_{2d-1}, \ldots, Z_0)$.
  1: $S \leftarrow 0$
  2: **for** i from 0 by 1 to $d - 1$ **do**
  3:     **for** j from 0 by 1 to i **do**
  4:         $S \leftarrow S + A_j \cdot B_{i-j}$
  5:     **end for**
  6:     $Z_i \leftarrow S \bmod 2^w$
  7:     $S \leftarrow \lfloor S/2^w \rfloor$ $\{w$-bit right-shift of $S\}$
  8: **end for**
  9: **for** i from d by 1 to $2d - 2$ **do**
 10:     **for** j from $i - d + 1$ by 1 to $d - 1$ **do**
 11:         $S \leftarrow S + A_j \cdot B_{i-j}$
 12:     **end for**
 13:     $Z_i \leftarrow S \bmod 2^w$
 14:     $S \leftarrow \lfloor S/2^w \rfloor$ $\{w$-bit right-shift of $S\}$
 15: **end for**
 16: $Z_{2d-1} \leftarrow S \bmod 2^w$
 17: **return** $Z = (Z_{2d-1}, \ldots, Z_0)$

2.2   Multiple-Precision Multiplication and Squaring

The elementary algorithm for multiplying two multiple-precision integers is the
so-called *operand scanning method*, which is nothing else than a reorganization
of the standard pencil-and-paper multiplication taught in grade school [14]. A
different technique for multiple-precision multiplication, commonly referred to
as *Comba's method* [4], outperforms the operand scanning method on most processors, especially when implemented in assembly language. Comba's method
(Algorithm 1) accumulates the inner-product terms $A_j \cdot B_{i-j}$ on a column-by-
column basis, as illustrated in Figure 1. The operation performed in the inner
loops of Algorithm 1 is *multiply-and-accumulate*, i.e. two w-bit words are multiplied and the $2w$-bit product is added to a cumulative sum S. Note that S can be
up to $2w + \lceil \log_2(d) \rceil$ bits long, and thus we need three w-bit registers to accommodate the sum S. The operation at line 6 and 13 of Algorithm 1 assigns the w
least significant bits of S to the word Z_i. Both the operand scanning technique
and Comba's method require exactly d^2 single-precision multiplications, but the
latter forms the product Z by computing each word Z_i at a time, starting with
the least significant word Z_0 (*product scanning*). Comba's method reduces the
number of memory accesses (in particular STORE instructions) at the expense
of more costly address calculation and some extra loop overhead.

The square A^2 of a long integer A can be computed almost twice as fast as
the product $A \cdot B$ of two distinct integers. Due to a "symmetry" in the squaring
operation, the inner-product terms of the form $A_x \cdot A_y$ appear once for $x = y$
and twice for $x \neq y$, which is easily observed from Figure 1. However, since all

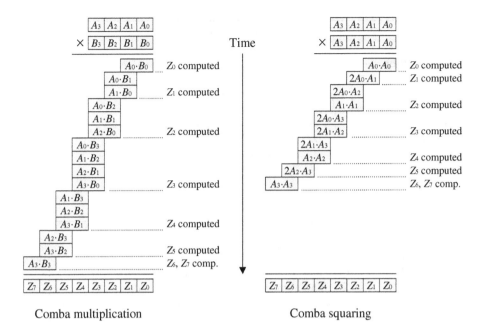

Fig. 1. Comparison of running times for Comba multiplication and Comba squaring

inner-products $A_x \cdot A_y$ and $A_y \cdot A_x$ are equivalent, they need only be computed once and then left shifted in order to be doubled. Therefore, squaring a d-word integer requires only $(d^2 + d)/2$ single-precision multiplications.

2.3   Modular Reduction

One of the most most widely used generic algorithms for modular reduction was introduced by Montgomery in 1985 [19]. Reference [10] describes several methods for efficient software implementation of Montgomery multiplication. One of these is the *Finely Integrated Product Scanning* (FIPS) method, which can be viewed as Comba multiplication with "finely" integrated Montgomery reduction, i.e. multiplication and reduction steps are carried out in the same inner loop.

Certain primes of a special (customized) form facilitate much faster reduction techniques. Of particular importance are the *generalized Mersenne* (GM) primes [26] that have been proposed by the National Institute of Standards and Technology (NIST) [21]. GM primes can be written as $p = f(2^k)$, where f is a low-degree polynomial with small integer coefficients and k is a multiple of the word-size w. The simplest example is the 192-bit GM prime $P = 2^{192} - 2^{64} - 1$. By using the relation $2^{192} \equiv 2^{64} + 1 \bmod P$, the reduction of a 384-bit integer $Z < P^2$ modulo the prime P can be easily carried out by means of three 192-bit modular additions [26]. These modular additions are typically realized through conventional multiple-precision additions, followed by repeated conditional subtractions of P until the result within the range of $(0, P - 1)$.

Algorithm 2. Fast reduction modulo the GM prime $P = 2^{192} - 2^{64} - 1$ (for $w = 32$)

Input: A 384-bit number $Z = (Z_{11}, \ldots, Z_0)$ with $0 \leq Z_i < 2^{32}$.
Output: 192-bit number $R \equiv Z \bmod P$ (R may not be fully reduced).
 1: $S \leftarrow Z_5 + Z_9 + Z_{11}$; $T \leftarrow S \bmod 2^{32}$; $q \leftarrow \lfloor S/2^{32} \rfloor$
 2: $S \leftarrow Z_0 + Z_6 + Z_{10} + q$; $R_0 \leftarrow S \bmod 2^{32}$; $S \leftarrow \lfloor S/2^{32} \rfloor$
 3: $S \leftarrow S + Z_1 + Z_7 + Z_{11}$; $R_1 \leftarrow S \bmod 2^{32}$; $S \leftarrow \lfloor S/2^{32} \rfloor$
 4: $S \leftarrow S + Z_2 + Z_6 + Z_8 + Z_{10} + q$; $R_2 \leftarrow S \bmod 2^{32}$; $S \leftarrow \lfloor S/2^{32} \rfloor$
 5: $S \leftarrow S + Z_3 + Z_7 + Z_9 + Z_{11}$; $R_3 \leftarrow S \bmod 2^{32}$; $S \leftarrow \lfloor S/2^{32} \rfloor$
 6: $S \leftarrow S + Z_4 + Z_8 + Z_{10}$; $R_4 \leftarrow S \bmod 2^{32}$; $S \leftarrow \lfloor S/2^{32} \rfloor$
 7: $S \leftarrow S + T$; $R_5 \leftarrow S \bmod 2^{32}$; $q \leftarrow \lfloor S/2^{32} \rfloor$
 8: $R \leftarrow (R_5, R_4, R_3, R_2, R_1, R_0)$
 9: **if** $q > 0$ **then** $R \leftarrow (R + 2^{64} + 1) \bmod 2^{192}$ **end if**
10: **return** R

Algorithm 2 shows a concrete implementation of the fast reduction modulo $P = 2^{192} - 2^{64} - 1$. We assume that Z is a 384-bit integer represented by twelve 32-bit words $Z_{11}, \ldots, Z_0$. The algorithm integrates the conditional subtractions of P into the multiple-precision additions instead of performing them thereafter. Moreover, the result R is computed one word at a time, starting with the least significant word R_0. The algorithm first estimates the quotient q that determines the multiple of P to be subtracted. Note that the subtraction of $q \cdot P$ is actually realized by addition of the two's complement $q \cdot (2^{192} - P) = q \cdot 2^{64} + q$. In some extremely rare cases, a final subtraction (i.e. two's complement addition) of P may be necessary to guarantee that the result is less than 2^{192} so that it can be stored in an array of six 32-bit words. However, this final subtraction has no impact on the execution time since it is virtually never performed.

3   Arithmetic in Binary Extension Fields

The finite field $\mathrm{GF}(2^m)$ is isomorphic to $\mathrm{GF}(2)[t]/(p(t))$ whereby $p(t)$ is an irreducible polynomial of degree m with coefficients from $\mathrm{GF}(2)$. We represent the elements of $\mathrm{GF}(2^m)$ as *binary polynomials* of degree up to $m - 1$. Addition is the simple logical XOR operation, while the multiplication of field elements is performed modulo the irreducible polynomial $p(t)$.

3.1   Notation

Any binary polynomial $a(t)$ of degree $m - 1$ can be associated with a bit-string of length m. Splitting this bit-string into $d = \lceil m/w \rceil$ chunks of w bits each leads to a similar array-representation as for integers, i.e. $a(t) = (A_{d-1}, \ldots, A_1, A_0)$. We use indexed uppercase letters to denote w-bit words and indexed lowercase letters to denote the individual coefficients of a binary polynomial.

$$a(t) = \sum_{i=0}^{m-1} a_i \cdot t^i = \sum_{j=0}^{d-1} A_j \cdot t^{j \cdot w} \quad \text{with} \quad A_j = \sum_{k=0}^{w-1} a_{j \cdot w + k} \cdot t^k \tag{2}$$

3.2   Multiplication and Squaring of Binary Polynomials

Multiplication in $GF(2^m)$ involves multiplying two binary polynomials and then finding the residue modulo the irreducible polynomial $p(t)$. The simplest way to compute the product $a(t) \cdot b(t)$ is by scanning the coefficients of $b(t)$ from b_{m-1} to b_0 and adding the partial product $a(t) \cdot b_i$ to a running sum. Several variants of this classical shift-and-xor method have been published, see e.g. [13,8] for a detailed treatment. The most efficient of these variants is the *comb method* in conjunction with a window technique to reduce the number of both shift and XOR operations [13]. However, the major drawback of the shift-and-xor method (and its variants) is that only a few bits of $b(t)$ are processed at a time.

To overcome this drawback, Nahum *et al.* [20] (and independently Koç and Acar [9]) proposed to equip general-purpose processors with a fast hardware multiplier for $(w \times w)$-bit multiplication of binary polynomials, giving a $2w$-bit result. The availability of an instruction for word-level multiplication of polynomials over $GF(2)$, which we call MULGF2 as in [9], greatly facilitates the arithmetic in $GF(2^m)$. All standard algorithms for multiple-precision multiplication of integers, such as the operand scanning technique or Comba's method, can be applied to binary polynomials as well [7]. In the polynomial case, the inner loop operation of Algorithm 1 translates to $S \leftarrow S \oplus A_i \otimes B_{i-j}$, whereby $\otimes$ denotes the MULGF2 operation and $\oplus$ is the logical XOR. The word-level algorithms utilize the full precision of the processor's registers and datapath, respectively, and therefore they are more efficient than the shift-and-xor method.

The complexity of squaring a binary polynomial $a(t)$ scales linearly with its degree. A conventional software implementation employs a pre-computed look-up table with 256 entries to convert 8-bit chunks of $a(t)$ into their expanded 16-bit counterparts [8]. The availability of the MULGF2 instruction allows to realize a more efficient word-level version of the squaring algorithm. Note that the sum of two identical products vanishes over $GF(2)$, i.e. $A_x \otimes A_y \oplus A_y \otimes A_x = 0$, and hence only d MULGF2 operations are necessary to square a d-word polynomial.

3.3   Reduction Modulo an Irreducible Polynomial

Once the product $z(t) = a(t) \cdot b(t)$ has been formed, it must be reduced modulo the irreducible polynomial $p(t)$ to get the final result. This reduction can be efficiently performed when $p(t)$ is a sparse polynomial such as a trinomial or a pentanomial [25,8]. As an example, let us consider the finite field $GF(2^{191})$ and the irreducible polynomial $p(t) = t^{191} + t^9 + 1$, which is given in Appendix J.2.1 of [1]. Furthermore, let $z(t)$ be a binary polynomial represented by twelve 32-bit words. The simple relation $t^{191} \equiv t^9 + t \bmod p(t)$ leads to the word-level reduction technique specified in Algorithm 3. This algorithm requires only shifts of 32-bit words (indicated by the symbols $\ll$ and $\gg$) and logical XORs.

A generic reduction algorithm that works for any irreducible polynomial is the adaption of Montgomery's method for binary polynomials [9]. Both the operand scanning and the product scanning technique require to carry out $2d^2 + d$ MULGF2 operations for d-word operands. We refer to [9,10] for further details.

Algorithm 3. Fast reduction modulo the trinomial $p(t) = t^{191} + t^9 + 1$ (for $w = 32$)

Input: A binary polynomial $z(t) = (Z_{11}, \ldots, Z_0)$ of degree at most 383.
Output: Result $r(t) \equiv z(t) \bmod p(t)$ of degree ≤ 191 ($r(t)$ may not be fully reduced).
 1: $Z_6 \leftarrow Z_6 \oplus (Z_{11} \gg 22) \oplus (Z_{11} \gg 31)$
 2: $R_5 \leftarrow Z_5 \oplus (Z_{11} \ll 10) \oplus (Z_{11} \ll 1) \oplus (Z_{10} \gg 22) \oplus (Z_{10} \gg 31)$
 3: $R_4 \leftarrow Z_4 \oplus (Z_{10} \ll 10) \oplus (Z_{10} \ll 1) \oplus (Z_9 \gg 22) \oplus (Z_9 \gg 31)$
 4: $R_3 \leftarrow Z_3 \oplus (Z_9 \ll 10) \oplus (Z_9 \ll 1) \oplus (Z_8 \gg 22) \oplus (Z_8 \gg 31)$
 5: $R_2 \leftarrow Z_2 \oplus (Z_8 \ll 10) \oplus (Z_8 \ll 1) \oplus (Z_7 \gg 22) \oplus (Z_7 \gg 31)$
 6: $R_1 \leftarrow Z_1 \oplus (Z_7 \ll 10) \oplus (Z_7 \ll 1) \oplus (Z_6 \gg 22) \oplus (Z_6 \gg 31)$
 7: $R_0 \leftarrow Z_0 \oplus (Z_6 \ll 10) \oplus (Z_6 \ll 1)$
 8: **return** $r(t) = (R_5, R_4, R_3, R_2, R_1, R_0)$

---

4   The MIPS32 Architecture and Proposed Extensions

The MIPS32 architecture is a superset of the previous MIPS I and MIPS II instruction set architectures and incorporates new instructions for standardized DSP operations like "multiply-and-add" (MADD) [16]. MIPS32 uses a load/store data model with 32 general-purpose registers (GPRs) of 32 bits each. The fixed-length, regularly encoded instruction set includes the usual arithmetic/logical instructions. MIPS32 processors implement a *delay slot* for load instructions, which means that the instruction immediately following a load cannot use the value loaded from memory. The branch instructions' effects are also delayed by one instruction; the instruction following the branch instruction is always executed, regardless of whether the branch is taken or not. Optimizing MIPS compilers try to fill load and branch delay slots with useful instructions.

The 4Km processor core [15] is a high-performance implementation of the MIPS32 instruction set architecture. Key features of the 4Km are a five-stage pipeline with branch control, a fast multiply/divide unit (MDU) supporting single-cycle (32×16)-bit multiplications, and up to 16 kB of separate data and instruction caches. Most instructions occupy the execute stage of the pipeline only for a single clock cycle. The MDU works autonomously, which means that the 4Km has a separate pipeline for all multiply, multiply-and-add, and divide operations (see Figure 2). This pipeline operates in parallel with the integer unit (IU) pipeline and does not necessarily stall when the IU pipeline stalls. Long-running (multi-cycle) MDU operations, such as a (32×32)-bit multiply or a divide, can be partially masked by other IU instructions.

The MDU of the 4Km consists of a (32×16)-bit Booth recoded multiplier, two result/accumulation registers (referenced by the names HI and LO), a divide state machine, and the necessary control logic. MIPS32 defines the result of a multiply operation to be placed in the HI and LO registers. Using MFHI (move from HI) and MFLO (move from LO) instructions, these values can be transferred to general-purpose registers. As mentioned before, MIPS32 also has a "multiply-and-add" (MADD) instruction, which multiplies two 32-bit words and adds the product to the 64-bit concatenated values in the HI/LO register pair. Then, the resulting value is written back to the HI and LO registers.

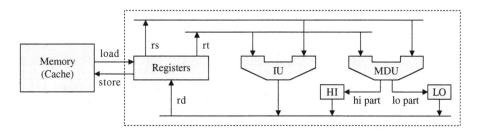

Fig. 2. 4Km datapath with integer unit (IU) and multiply/divide unit (MDU)

4.1   Unified Multiply/Accumulate Unit

The MADDU instruction performs essentially the same operation as MADD, but treats the 32-bit operands to be multiplied as unsigned integers. At a first glance, it seems that MADDU implements exactly the operation carried out in the inner loop of Comba multiplication (i.e. two unsigned 32-bit words are multiplied and the product is added to a running sum, see line 4 and 11 of Algorithm 1). However, the problem is that the accumulator and HI/LO register pair of a standard MIPS32 core is only 64 bits wide, and therefore the MDU is not able to sum up 64-bit products without overflow and loss of precision. In this subsection, we present two simple MDU enhancements to better support finite field arithmetic on a MIPS32 processor.

Firstly, we propose to equip the MDU with a 72-bit accumulator and to extend the precision of the HI register to 40 bits so that the HI/LO register pair is able to accommodate 72 bits altogether. This little modification makes Comba's method (Algorithm 1) very efficient on MIPS32 processors. A "wide" accumulator with eight *guard bits* means that we can accumulate up to 256 double-precision products without overflow, which is sufficient for cryptographic applications. The extra hardware cost is negligible, and a slightly longer critical path in the MDU's final adder is irrelevant for smart cards.

Secondly, we argue that a so-called "unified" multiplier is essential for the efficient implementation of elliptic curve cryptography over $GF(2^m)$. A unified multiplier is a multiplier that uses the same datapath for both integers and binary polynomials [24]. In its simplest form, a unified multiplier is composed of *dual-field adders*, which are full adders with some extra logic to set the carry output to zero. Therefore, a unified multiplier is an elegant way to implement the MULGF2 instruction on a MIPS32 processor, the more so as the area of a unified multiplier is only slightly larger than that of a conventional multiplier [24].

4.2   Instruction Set Extensions

In this subsection, we present five custom instructions to accelerate the processing of arithmetic operations in finite fields $GF(p)$ and $GF(2^m)$. We selected the custom instructions with three goals in mind, namely to maximize performance of applications within the given application domain, to minimize the required

Table 1. Useful instructions for finite field arithmetic on a MIPS32 processor

Format	Description	Operation
MULTU rs, rt	Multiply Unsigned	$(HI/LO) \leftarrow rs \times rt$
MADDU rs, rt	Multiply and ADD Unsigned	$(HI/LO) \leftarrow (HI/LO) + rs \times rt$
M2ADDU rs, rt	Multiply, Double and ADD Unsigned	$(HI/LO) \leftarrow (HI/LO) + 2rs \times rt$
ADDAU rs, rt	ADD to Accumulator Unsigned	$(HI/LO) \leftarrow (HI/LO) + rs + rt$
SHA	SHift Accumulator	$(HI/LO) \leftarrow (HI/LO) \gg 32$
MULGF2 rs, rt	Multiply over GF(2)	$(HI/LO) \leftarrow rs \otimes rt$
MADDGF2 rs, rt	Multiply and ADD over GF(2)	$(HI/LO) \leftarrow (HI/LO) \oplus rs \otimes rt$

hardware resources, and to allow for simple integration into the base architecture (MIPS32 in our case). After careful analysis of a variety of candidate instructions and different hardware/software interfaces, we found that a set of only five custom instructions represents the best trade-off between the goals mentioned before. These instructions are summarized in Table 1, together with the native MIPS32 instructions MULTU and MADDU.

The MADDU instruction computes $rs \times rt$, treating both operands as unsigned integers, and accumulates the 64-bit product to the concatenated values in the HI/LO register pair. This is exactly the operation carried out in the inner loop of both Comba's method and FIPS Montgomery multiplication. The wide accumulator and the extended precision of the HI register help to avoid overflows.

Our first custom instruction, M2ADDU, multiplies two 32-bit integers $rs \times rt$, doubles the product, and accumulates it to HI/LO. This instruction is very useful for multiple-precision squaring of integers. The multiplication by 2 can be simply realized via a hard-wired left shift and requires essentially no additional hardware (except for a few multiplexors).

MIPS32 has no "add-with-carry" instruction. The instruction ADDAU ("add to accumulator unsigned") was designed to support multiple-precision addition and reduction modulo a GM prime (see Algorithm 2). ADDAU computes the sum $rs + rt$ of two unsigned integers and accumulates it to the HI/LO registers. Multiple-precision subtraction also profits from ADDAU since a subtraction can be easily accomplished through addition of the two's complement.

The instruction SHA shifts the concatenated values in the HI/LO register pair 32 bits to the right (with zeroes shifted in), i.e. the contents of HI is copied to LO and the eight guard bits are copied to HI. Thus, SHA implements exactly the operation at line 7 and 14 of Algorithm 1 and is also useful for Algorithm 2.

The MULGF2 instruction is similar to the MULTU, but treats the operands as binary polynomials of degree ≤ 31 and performs a multiplication over GF(2). The product $rs \otimes rt$ is written to the HI/LO register pair. MULGF2 facilitates diverse algorithms for multiplication and squaring of binary polynomials.

Finally, the instruction MADDGF2, which is similar to MADDU, multiplies two binary polynomials and adds (i.e. XORs) the product $rs \otimes rt$ to HI/LO. The availability of MADDGF2 allows for an efficient implementation of both Comba's method and FIPS Montgomery multiplication for binary polynomials.

```
label: LW    $t0, 0($t1)        # load A[j] into $t0
       LW    $t2, 0($t3)        # load B[i-j] into $t2
       ADDIU $t1, $t1, 4        # increment pointer $t1 by 4
       MADDU $t0, $t2           # (HI|LO)=(HI|LO)+($t0*$t2)
       BNE   $t3, $t4, label    # branch if $t3 != $t4
       ADDIU $t3, $t3, -4       # decrement pointer $t3 by 4
```

Fig. 3. MIPS32 assembly code for the inner loop of Comba multiplication

5   Performance Evaluation

SystemC is a system-level design and modelling platform consisting of a collection of C++ libraries and a simulation kernel [22]. It allows accurate modelling of mixed hardware/software designs at different levels of abstraction.

We developed a functional, cycle-accurate SystemC model of a MIPS32 core in order to verify the correctness of the arithmetic algorithms and to estimate their execution times. Our model implements a subset of the MIPS32 instruction set architecture, along with the five custom instructions introduced in Subsection 4.2. While load and branch delays are considered in our model, we did not simulate the impact of cache misses, i.e. we assume a perfect cache system. Our MIPS32 has a single-issue pipeline and executes the IU instructions in one cycle. The two custom instructions MADDAU and SHA are very simple, and therefore we define that they also execute in one cycle. The number of clock cycles for the diverse multiply and multiply-and-add instructions depends on the dimension of the unified multiplier. For instance, performing a (32×32)-bit multiplication on a (32×16)-bit multiplier requires two passes through the multiplier. However, we will demonstrate in the following subsection that the inner loop operation of Comba's method allows to mask the latency of a multi-cycle multiplier.

5.1   Inner Loop Operation

We developed hand-optimized assembly routines for the arithmetic algorithms presented in Section 2 and 3, respectively, and simulated their execution on our extended MIPS32 core. Figure 3 depicts an assembly implementation of the inner loop of Comba's method (see line 4 of Algorithm 1). Before entering the loop, registers $t1 and $t3 are initialized with the current address of A_0 and B_{i-j}, respectively. Register $t4 holds the address of B_0. Our assembly routine starts with two LW instructions to load the operands A_j and B_{i-j} into general-purpose registers. The MADDU instruction computes the product $A_j \cdot B_{i-j}$ and accumulates it to a running sum stored in the HI/LO register pair. Note that the extended precision of the accumulator and the HI register guarantee that there is no overflow or loss of precision.

Two ADDIU ("add immediate unsigned") instructions, which perform simple pointer arithmetic, are used to fill the load and branch delay slot, respectively. Register $t3 holds the address of B_{i-j} and is decremented by 4 each time the

Table 2. Simulated execution times (in clock cycles) of arithmetic operations. Some operations in GF(p) need a final subtraction of p; the according time is set in brackets

Arithmetic operation	GF(p), $|p| = 192$	GF(2^m), $m = 191$
Modular addition	74 (155)	62
Comba multiplication w/o red.	347	347
Comba squaring w/o red.	238	74
Fast reduction (loop unrolled)	65	75
Montgomery multiplication	594 (675)	594
Montgomery squaring	447 (528)	306
Scalar multiplication (generic)	$1668 \cdot 10^3$	$1040 \cdot 10^3$
Scalar multiplication (optimized)	$1178 \cdot 10^3$	$693 \cdot 10^3$

loop repeats, whereas the pointer to the word A_j (stored in register $\$t1$) is incremented by 4. The loop finishes when the pointer to B_{i-j} reaches the address of B_0, which is stored in $\$t4$. Note that the loop termination condition of the second inner loop (line 11 of Algorithm 1) differs slightly from the first one.

A MIPS32 core with a (32×16)-bit multiplier and a 72-bit accumulator executes the instruction sequence shown in Figure 3 in six clock cycles, provided that no cache misses occur. The MADDU instruction writes its result to the HI/LO register pair (see Figure 2) and does not occupy the register file's write port during the second clock cycle. Therefore, other arithmetic/logical instructions can be executed during the latency period of the MADDU operation, i.e. the inner loop of Comba's method does not need a single-cycle multiplier to reach peak performance. For example, a (32×12)-bit multiplier, which requires three clock cycles to complete a (32×32)-bit multiplication, allows to achieve the same performance as a fully parallel (32×32)-bit multiplier [6].

5.2   Experimental Results

In the following, we briefly sketch how the arithmetic algorithms described in Section 2 can be implemented efficiently on an extended MIPS32 core, taking advantage of our custom instructions. Comba's method (Algorithm 1) performs d^2 iterations of the inner loop, whereby one iteration takes six clock cycles. The operation at line 7 and 14 of Algorithm 1 is easily accomplished with help of the SHA instruction. Multiple-precision squaring according to Comba's method (see Figure 1) benefits from the M2ADDU instruction. The two custom instructions ADDAU and SHA facilitate the implementation of multiple-precision addition as well as reduction modulo a GM prime (Algorithm 2). Last but not least, the inner loop of FIPS Montgomery multiplication and squaring is very similar to the inner loop of Comba multiplication and squaring, respectively, and therefore profits from the availability of MADDU, M2ADDU, as well as SHA. Table 2 shows the simulated execution times of these algorithms for 192-bit operands.

The implementation of the arithmetic algorithms for binary fields GF(2^m) is also straightforward. Comba's method can be applied to the multiplication of binary polynomials as well, provided that the instruction set includes MULGF2 and MADDGF2 (see Section 3). The instructions executed in the inner loop are exactly the same as shown in Figure 3, with the exception that MADDU is replaced by MADDGF2. Polynomial squaring is supported by MULGF2, while the word-level reduction modulo a sparse polynomial, such as performed by Algorithm 3, can be done efficiently with native MIPS32 instructions (assuming that the processor is equipped with a fast barrel shifter). The inner loop of FIPS Montgomery multiplication in $GF(2^m)$ is similar to the inner loop of Comba's method. Table 2 details the simulated running times of these algorithms. Unless denoted otherwise, the timings were achieved without loop unrolling.

Besides the timings for the finite field arithmetic, Table 2 also includes the execution times for a scalar multiplication over the specified prime and binary field, respectively. We used projective coordinates and implemented the scalar multiplication over $GF(2^{191})$ as described in [12]. On the other hand, the scalar multiplication over $GF(p)$ was realized with help of the binary NAF method [2] and the Jacobian coordinates presented in [3].

Table 2 shows the execution times for both a *generic* implementation and an *optimized* implementation. The generic version uses Montgomery multiplication and squaring, respectively, and can process operands of any length. There is no restriction regarding the prime p or the irreducible polynomial $p(t)$, i.e. the generic implementation works for any field $GF(p)$ and $GF(2^m)$. On the other hand, the optimized version takes advantage of the fast reduction techniques according to Algorithm 2 and 3, respectively. In both the prime field case and the binary field case, the optimized implementation is more than 30% faster.

Comparison to Conventional Software Implementation. In our context, the phrase "conventional software implementation" refers to an implementation that uses only native MIPS32 instructions. A recent white paper by MIPS Technologies recommends to implement multiple-precision multiplication according to the operand scanning method [18]. However, the inner loop of the operand scanning method requires at least 11 MIPS32 instructions (see [18]), which is almost twice as much as for the Comba inner loop on an extended MIPS32 core with a wide accumulator. Our simulations show that the operand scanning method needs 620 cycles for a multiplication of 192-bit integers. An optimized implementation of the fast reduction for GM primes is almost as slow as the Montgomery reduction since MIPS32 lacks an add-with-carry instruction.

The situation is even worse for arithmetic in binary extension fields. If MULGF2 and MADDGF2 are not available, one is forced to use the shift-and-xor algorithm or one of its optimized variants [8]. The most efficient of these variants is, according to our experiments, more than ten times slower than Comba's method with MULGF2 and MADDGF2. Despite our best effort, we were not able to implement the multiplication in $GF(2^{191})$ in less than 3600 cycles, even when we fully unrolled the loops. In summary, the presented instruction set extensions accelerate the optimized scalar multiplication over $GF(p)$ by a factor of almost two, and make the scalar multiplication over $GF(2^m)$ about six times faster.

6 Discussion and Conclusions

The presented instruction set extensions allow to perform a scalar multiplication over $GF(2^{191})$ in 693k clock cycles, and a scalar multiplication over a 192-bit prime field in 1178k cycles, respectively. Assuming a clock frequency of 33 MHz, which is a typical frequency for multi-application smart cards, these cycle counts correspond to an execution time of 21 msec and 36 msec, respectively. Note that these timings were achieved without loop unrolling (except for the fast reduction algorithms) and without pre-computation of points. The proposed instructions accelerate both generic arithmetic algorithms (e.g. Montgomery multiplication) as well as special algorithms for certain fields like GM prime fields or binary extension fields with sparse irreducible polynomials. We verified the correctness of the presented concepts (i.e. the extended MIPS32 processor and the software routines running on it) with help of a cycle-accurate SystemC model.

A look "under the hood" of our instruction set extensions reveals further advantages. MIPS32, like most other RISC architectures, requires that arithmetic/logical instructions have a three-operand format (two source registers and one destination register). The five custom instructions presented in this paper fulfill this requirement, and thus they can be easily integrated into a MIPS32 core. Moreover, the extended core remains fully compatible to the base architecture (MIPS32 in our case). All five custom instructions are executed in one and the same functional unit, namely the MDU. Another advantage of our approach is that a fully parallel (32×32)-bit multiplier is not necessary to reach peak performance. Therefore, the hardware cost of our extensions is marginal.

Acknowledgements. The first author was supported by the Austrian Science Fund (FWF) under grant number P16952-N04 ("Instruction Set Extensions for Public-Key Cryptography"). The second author was supported by The Scientific and Technical Research Council of Turkey under project number 104E007.

References

1. American National Standards Institute. X9.62-1998, Public key cryptography for the financial services industry: The elliptic curve digital signature algorithm, 1999.
2. M. K. Brown et al. Software implementation of the NIST elliptic curves over prime fields. In *Topics in Cryptology — CT-RSA 2001*, LNCS 2020, pp. 250–265. Springer Verlag, 2001.
3. H. Cohen, A. Miyaji, and T. Ono. Efficient elliptic curve exponentiation using mixed coordinates. In *Advances in Cryptology — ASIACRYPT '98*, LNCS 1514, pp. 51–65. Springer Verlag, 1998.
4. P. G. Comba. Exponentiation cryptosystems on the IBM PC. *IBM Systems Journal*, 29(4):526–538, Oct. 1990.
5. J.-F. Dhem. *Design of an efficient public-key cryptographic library for RISC-based smart cards*. Ph.D. Thesis, Université Catholique de Louvain, Belgium, 1998.
6. J. Großschädl and G.-A. Kamendje. Architectural enhancements for Montgomery multiplication on embedded RISC processors. In *Applied Cryptography and Network Security — ACNS 2003*, LNCS 2846, pp. 418–434. Springer Verlag, 2003.

7. J. Großschädl and G.-A. Kamendje. Instruction set extension for fast elliptic curve cryptography over binary finite fields GF(2^m). In *Proceedings of the 14th IEEE International Conference on Application-specific Systems, Architectures and Processors (ASAP 2003)*, pp. 455–468. IEEE Computer Society Press, 2003.

8. D. Hankerson, J. López Hernandez, and A. J. Menezes. Software implementation of elliptic curve cryptography over binary fields. In *Cryptographic Hardware and Embedded Systems — CHES 2000*, LNCS 1965, pp. 1–24. Springer Verlag, 2000.

9. Ç. K. Koç and T. Acar. Montgomery multiplication in GF(2^k). *Designs, Codes and Cryptography*, 14(1):57–69, Apr. 1998.

10. Ç. K. Koç, T. Acar, and B. S. Kaliski. Analyzing and comparing Montgomery multiplication algorithms. *IEEE Micro*, 16(3):26–33, June 1996.

11. R. B. Lee. Accelerating multimedia with enhanced microprocessors. *IEEE Micro*, 15(2):22–32, Apr. 1995.

12. J. López and R. Dahab. Fast multiplication on elliptic curves over $GF(2^m)$ without precomputation. In *Cryptographic Hardware and Embedded Systems*, LNCS 1717, pp. 316–327. Springer Verlag, 1999.

13. J. López and R. Dahab. High-speed software multiplication in $\mathbb{F}_{2^m}$. In *Progress in Cryptology — INDOCRYPT 2000*, LNCS 1977, pp. 203–212. Springer Verlag, 2000.

14. A. J. Menezes, P. C. van Oorschot, and S. A. Vanstone. *Handbook of Applied Cryptography*. CRC Press, 1996.

15. MIPS Technologies, Inc. MIPS32 4Km^{TM} Processor Core Datasheet. Available for download at http://www.mips.com/publications/index.html, Sept. 2001.

16. MIPS Technologies, Inc. MIPS32^{TM} Architecture for Programmers. Available for download at http://www.mips.com/publications/index.html, Mar. 2001.

17. MIPS Technologies, Inc. SmartMIPS Architecture Smart Card Extensions. Product brief, available for download at http://www.mips.com, Feb. 2001.

18. MIPS Technologies, Inc. 64-bit architecture speeds RSA by 4x. White Paper, available for download at http://www.mips.com, June 2002.

19. P. L. Montgomery. Modular multiplication without trial division. *Mathematics of Computation*, 44(170):519–521, Apr. 1985.

20. E. M. Nahum et al. Towards high performance cryptographic software. In *Proceedings of the 3rd IEEE Workshop on the Architecture and Implementation of High Performance Communication Subsystems (HPCS '95)*, pp. 69–72. IEEE, 1995.

21. National Institute of Standards and Technology. Digital Signature Standard (DSS). Federal Information Processing Standards Publication 186-2, 2000.

22. The Open SystemC Initiative (OSCI). *SystemC Version 2.0 User's Guide*, 2002.

23. B. J. Phillips and N. Burgess. Implementing 1,024-bit RSA exponentiation on a 32-bit processor core. In *Proceedings of the 12th IEEE International Conference on Application-specific Systems, Architectures and Processors (ASAP 2000)*, pp. 127–137. IEEE Computer Society Press, 2000.

24. E. Savaş, A. F. Tenca, and Ç. K. Koç. A scalable and unified multiplier architecture for finite fields $GF(p)$ and $GF(2^m)$. In *Cryptographic Hardware and Embedded Systems — CHES 2000*, LNCS 1965, pp. 277–292. Springer Verlag, 2000.

25. R. Schroeppel et al. Fast key exchange with elliptic curve systems. In *Advances in Cryptology — CRYPTO '95*, LNCS 963, pp. 43–56. Springer Verlag, 1995.

26. J. A. Solinas. Generalized Mersenne numbers. Technical Report CORR-99-39, University of Waterloo, Canada, 1999.

27. STMicroelectronics. ST22 SmartJ Platform Smartcard ICs. Available online at http://www.st.com/stonline/products/families/smartcard/insc9901.htm.

Aspects of Hyperelliptic Curves over Large Prime Fields in Software Implementations

Roberto Maria Avanzi[*]

Institute for Experimental Mathematics (IEM) — University of Duisburg-Essen
Ellernstraße 29, D-45326 Essen, Germany
mocenigo@exp-math.uni-essen.de

Department of Electrical Engineering and Information Sciences
Ruhr University of Bochum, Universitätsstraße 150, D-44780 Bochum, Germany

Abstract. We present an implementation of elliptic curves and of hyperelliptic curves of genus 2 and 3 over prime fields. To achieve a fair comparison between the different types of groups, we developed an ad-hoc arithmetic library, designed to remove most of the overheads that penalize implementations of curve-based cryptography over prime fields. These overheads get worse for smaller fields, and thus for larger genera for a fixed group size. We also use techniques for delaying modular reductions to reduce the amount of modular reductions in the formulae for the group operations.

The result is that the performance of hyperelliptic curves of genus 2 over prime fields is much closer to the performance of elliptic curves than previously thought. For groups of 192 and 256 bits the difference is about 14% and 15% respectively.

Keywords: Elliptic and hyperelliptic curves, cryptography, efficient implementation, prime field arithmetic, lazy and incomplete modular reduction.

1 Introduction

In 1988 Koblitz [21] proposed to use hyperelliptic curves (HEC) as an alternative to elliptic curves (EC) for designing cryptosystems based on the *discrete logarithm problem* (DLP). EC are just the genus 1 HEC. Cryptosystems based on EC need a much shorter key than RSA or systems based on the DLP in finite fields: A 160-bit EC key is considered to offer security equivalent to that of a 1024-bit RSA key [25]. Since the best known methods to solve the DLP on EC and on HEC of genus smaller than 4 have the same complexity, these curves offer the same security level, but HEC of genus 4 or higher offer less security [12,38].

Until recently, HEC have been considered not practical [36] because of the difficulty of finding suitable curves and their poor performance with respect to EC. In the subsequent years the situation changed.

Firstly, it is now possible to efficiently construct genus 2 and 3 HEC whose Jacobian has almost prime order of cryptographic relevance. Over prime fields one can either

---

[*] This research has been supported by the Commission of the European Communities through the IST Programme under Contract IST-2001-32613 (see http://www.arehcc.com).

M. Joye and J.-J. Quisquater (Eds.): CHES 2004, LNCS 3156, pp. 148–162, 2004.

count points in genus 2 [13], or use the complex multiplication (CM) method for genus 2 [29,39] and 3 [39].

Secondly, the performance of the HEC group operations has been considerably improved. For genus 2 the first results were due to Harley [17]. The state of the art is now represented by the explicit formulae of Lange: see [23,24] and further references therein. For genus 3, see [32,33] (and also [14]).

HEC are attractive to designers of embedded hardware since they require smaller fields than EC: The order of the Jacobian of a HEC of genus g over a field with q elements is $\approx q^g$. This means that a 160-bit group is given by an EC with $q \approx 2^{160}$, by an HEC of genus 2 with $q \approx 2^{80}$, and genus 3 with $q \approx 2^{53}$. There has been also research on securing implementations of HEC on embedded devices against differential and Goubin-type power analysis [2].

The purpose of this paper is to present a thorough, fair and unbiased comparison of the relative performance merits of generic EC and HEC of small genus 2 or 3 over prime fields. We are not interested in comparing against very special classes of curves or in the use of prime moduli of special form.

There have been several software implementations of HEC on personal computers and workstations. Most of those are in even characteristic (see [35,32], [33], and also [40, 41]), but some are over prime fields [22,35]. It is now known that in *even characteristic*, HEC can offer performance comparable to EC.

Until now there have been no concrete results showing the same for prime fields. Traditional implementations such as [22] are based on general purpose software libraries, such as gmp [16]. These libraries introduce overheads which are quite significant for small operands such as those occurring in curve cryptography, and get worse as the fields get smaller. Moreover, gmp has no native support for fast modular reduction techniques. In our modular arithmetic library, described in § 2.1, we made every effort to avoid such overheads. On a PC we get a speed-up from 2 to 5 over gmp for operations in fields of cryptographic relevance (see Table 1). We also exploit techniques for reducing the number of modular reductions in the formulae for the group operations.

We thus show that the performance of genus 2 HEC over prime fields is much closer to the performance of EC than previously thought. For groups of 192 resp. 256 bits the difference is approximately 14%, resp. 15%. The gap with genus 3 curves has been significantly reduced too. See Section 3 for more precise results.

While the only significant constraint in workstations and commodity PCs may be processing power, the results of our work should also be applicable to other more constrained environments, such as Palm platforms, which are also based on general-purpose processors. In fact, a port of our library to the ARM processor has been recently finished and yields similar results.

In Section 2, we describe the implementation of the arithmetic library and of the group operations. In Section 3, we give timings and draw our conclusions.

2   Implementation

We use the following abbreviations: w is the bit length of the characteristic of the prime field. M, S and I denote a multiplication, a squaring and an inversion in the field. m and s denote a multiplication and a squaring, respectively, of two w-bit integers with a $2w$-bit result. R denotes a modular (or Montgomery) reduction of a $2w$-bit integer with a w-bit result.

2.1 Prime Field Library

We already said that standard long integer software libraries introduce several types of overheads. One is the fixed function call overhead. Other ones arise from the processing of operands of variable length in loops, such as branch mispredictions at the beginning and end of the loops, and are negligible for very large operands. For operands of size relevant for curve cryptography the CPU will spend more time performing jumps and paying branch misprediction penalties than doing arithmetic. Memory management overheads can be very costly, too.

Thus, the smaller the field becomes, the higher will be the time wasted in the overheads. Because of the larger number of field operations in smaller fields, HEC suffer from a much larger performance loss than EC.

Design. Our software library nuMONGO has been designed to allow efficient reference implementations of EC and HEC over prime fields. It implements arithmetic operations in rings $\mathbb{Z}/N\mathbb{Z}$ with N odd, with the elements stored in Montgomery's representation [31], and the reduction algorithm is Montgomery's REDC function – see § 2.1 for some more details. Many optimization techniques employed are similar to those in [6].

nuMONGO is written in C++ to take advantage of inline functions, overloaded functions statically resolved at compile time for clarity of coding, and operator overloading for I/O only. All arithmetic operations are implemented as imperative functions. nuMONGO contains no classes. All data structures are minimalistic. All elements of $\mathbb{Z}/N\mathbb{Z}$ are stored in vectors of fixed length of 32-bit words. All temporary memory is allocated on the stack. No data structure is ever dynamically resized or relocated. This eliminates memory management overheads.

The routines aim to be as simple as possible. The least possible number of routines are implemented which still allow to perform all desired field operations: They are built from elementary operations working on single words, available as generic C macros as well as assembler macros for x86-compatible CPUs. A CPU able to process 32-bit operands is assumed, but not necessarily a 32-bit CPU – the library in fact compiled also on an Alpha. Inlining was used extensively, most loops are unrolled; there are very few conditional branches, hence branch mispredictions are rare. There are separate arithmetic routines for all operand sizes, in steps of 32 bits from 32 to 256 bits, as well as for 48–bit fields (80 and 112-bit fields have been implemented too, but gave no speed-up over the 96 and 128-bit routines).

Multiplication. We begin with two algorithms to multiply "smallish" multi-precision operands: Schoolbook multiplication and Comba's method [10].

The next two algorithms take as input two ℓ-word integers $u = (u_{\ell-1}, \ldots, u_1, u_0)$ and $v = (v_{\ell-1}, \ldots, v_0)$, and output the 2ℓ-word integer $r = (r_{2\ell-1}, \ldots, r_0)$ such that $r = uv$.

Schoolbook multiplication	Comba's method
1. $\quad r_0 \leftarrow 0, \ldots, r_{2\ell-1} \leftarrow 0$	1. $\quad s_0 \leftarrow 0, s_1 \leftarrow 0, s_2 \leftarrow 0$
2. $\quad$ for i from 0 to $\ell - 1$ do {	2. $\quad$ for k from 0 to $2(\ell - 1)$ do {
3. $\quad\quad c \leftarrow 0$	3. $\quad\quad$ for each pair (i, j) such that $i + j = k$
4. $\quad\quad$ for j from 0 to $\ell - 1$ do {	$\quad\quad\quad$ and $0 \leqslant i, j < \ell$, do {
5. $\quad\quad\quad (c, r_{j+i}) \leftarrow u_i v_j + r_{j+i} + c$ }	4. $\quad\quad\quad (s_2, s_1, s_0) \leftarrow (s_2, s_1, s_0) + u_i v_j$ }
6. $\quad\quad r_{i+\ell} \leftarrow c$ }	5. $\quad\quad r_k \leftarrow s_0, s_0 \leftarrow s_1, s_1 \leftarrow s_2, s_2 \leftarrow 0$ }
7. $\quad$ return(r)	6. $\quad r_{2\ell-1} \leftarrow s_0$
	7. $\quad$ return(r)

The schoolbook method multiplies the first factor by each digit of the second factor, and accumulates the results. Comba's method instead, for each digit of the result, say the kth one, computes the partial products $u_i v_j$ on the *diagonals* $i + j = k$, adding these double precision results to a triple precision accumulator. It requires fewer memory writes and more reads than the schoolbook multiplication. This is the method adopted in [6]. For both methods, several optimizations have been done. They can both be used with Karatsuba's trick [20].

In our experience, Comba's method did not perform better than the schoolbook method (on the ARM the situation is different). This may be due to the fact that the Athlon CPU has a write-back level 1 cache [1], hence several close writes to the same memory location cost little more than one generic write. For $n = 192$ and $n = 256$ we reduced a n-bit multiplication to three $n/2$-bit multiplications by means of Karatsuba's trick. For smaller sizes and for 224-bit operands, the schoolbook method was still faster.

For the considered operand sizes, squaring routines did not bring a significant improvement over the multiplication routines, hence they were not included.

Montgomery's reduction without trial division. Montgomery [31] proposed to speed up modular reduction by replacing the modulus N by a larger integer R coprime to N for which division is faster. In practice, if β is the machine radix (in our case $\beta = 2^{32}$) and N is an odd ℓ-word integer, then $R = \beta^\ell$. Division by R and taking remainder are just shift and masking operations.

Let $\text{REDC}(x)$ be a function which, for $0 \leqslant x < NR$, computes $xR^{-1} \bmod N$.

The modular residue x is represented by its *r-sidu* $\bar{x} = xR \bmod N$. Addition, subtraction, negation and testing for equality are performed on r-sidus as usual.

Note that $x = \text{REDC}(\bar{x})$. To get the r-sidu of an integer x, compute $\text{REDC}(xR^2)$, hence $R^2 \bmod N$ should be computed during system initialization. Now $\bar{x} \bar{y} \equiv xR yR \equiv \overline{xy}R \bmod N$, so $\overline{xy} = \text{REDC}(xy)$ can be computed without any division by N. We implemented REDC by the following method [5], which requires the inverse n_0' of N modulo the machine radix $\beta = 2^{32}$.

Function $\text{REDC}(\mathbf{x})$

INPUT: A 2ℓ-word integer $x = (x_{2\ell-1}, \ldots, x_1, x_0)$, and N, n_0' and β as above.
OUTPUT: The ℓ-word integer y such that $y = xR^{-1} \bmod N$ and $0 \leqslant y < N$.

1. $\quad y = (y_{2\ell-1}, \ldots, y_1, y_0) \leftarrow x$
2. $\quad$ for i from 0 to $\ell - 1$ do {
3. $\quad\quad t \leftarrow y_0 \cdot n_0' \bmod \beta, \quad y \leftarrow y + t \cdot N, \quad y \leftarrow y \div \beta$ }
4. $\quad$ if $y \geqslant N$ then $y \leftarrow y - N$
5. $\quad$ return(y)

This algorithm is, essentially, Hensel's odd division for computing inverses of 2-adic numbers to a higher base: At each iteration of the loop, a multiple of N is added to y such that the result is divisible by β, and then y is divided by β (a one word shift). After the loop, $y \equiv x/\beta^\ell \equiv xR^{-1} \bmod N$ and $y < 2N$. If $y \geqslant N$, a subtraction corrects the result. The cost of REDC is, at least in theory, that of a schoolbook multiplication of ℓ-word integers, some shifts and some additions; In practice it is somewhat more expensive, but still much faster than the naive reduction involving long divisions. We did not use the interleaved multiplication with reduction [31]: It usually performs better on DSPs [11], but not on general-purpose CPUs with few registers.

Inversion. With the exception of 32-bit operands, inversion is based on the extended binary GCD, and uses an almost-inverse technique [19] with final multiplication from a table of precomputed powers of 2 mod N. This was the fastest approach up to about 192 bits. For 32-bit operands we got better performance with the extended Euclidean algorithm and special treatment of small quotients to avoid divisions. Inversion was not sped up further for larger input sizes because of the intended usage of the library: For elliptic curves over prime fields, inversion-free coordinate systems are much faster than affine coordinates, so there is need, basically, only for one inversion at the end of a scalar multiplication. For hyperelliptic curves, fields are quite small (32 to 128 bits in most cases), hence our inversion routines have optimal performance anyway. Therefore, Lehmer's method or the improvements by Jebelean [18] or Lercier [26] have not been included in the final version of the library.

Performance. In Table 1 we show some timings of basic operations with gmp version 4.1 and nuMONGO. The timings have been measured on a PC with a 1 GHz AMD Athlon Model 4 processor, under the Linux operating system (kernel version 2.4). Our programs have been compiled with the GNU C Compiler (gcc) versions 2.95.3 and 3.3.1. For each test, we took the version that gave the best timings. nuMONGO always performed best with gcc 3.3.1, whereas some gmp tests performed better with gcc 2.95.3[1]. We describe the meaning of the entries. There are two groups of rows, grouped under the name of library used to benchmark the following operations: multiplication of two integers (m), modular or Montgomery reduction (R), modular or Montgomery inversion (I). The ratios of a reduction to a multiplication and of an inversion to the time of a multiplication together with a reduction are given, too: The first ratio tells how many "multiplications" we save each time we save a reduction using the techniques described in the next subsection; the second ratio is the cost of a field inversion in field multiplications. The columns correspond to the bit lengths of the operands. A few remarks:

1. nuMONGO can perform better than a far more optimized, but general purpose library. In fact, the kernel of gmp is entirely written in assembler for most architectures, including the one considered here.

---

[1] In some cases gcc 2.95.3 produced the fastest code when optimizing nuMONGO for size (-Os), not for speed! This seems to be a strange but known phenomenon. gcc 3.3.1 had a more orthodox behavior and gave the best code with -O3, i.e. when optimizing aggressively for speed. In both cases, additional compiler flags were used for fine-tuning.

Table 1. Timings of basic operations in μsec (1 GHz AMD Athlon PC) and ratios

Lib/Op/Bits		32	48	64	96	128	160	192	224	256
numONGO	m	0.0079	0.0201	0.0267	0.054	0.11	0.146	0.198	0.361	0.392
	R	0.0298	0.0536	0.0487	0.097	0.159	0.241	0.319	0.416	0.493
	I	0.61	1.85	1.987	4.457	7.6	11.2	16.3	22.3	28.8
	R/m	3.77	2.667	1.824	1.796	1.445	1.651	1.61	1.152	1.258
	I/(R+m)	16.19	25.102	26.35	29.52	28.25	28.94	31.53	28.7	32.55
gmp v. 4.1	m	0.094	0.155	0.16	0.206	0.238	0.308	0.354	0.44	0.508
	R	0.234	0.419	0.423	0.65	0.81	0.986	1.154	1.264	1.528
	I	2.53	4.74	6.41	9.77	13.3	17.2	21.26	25.84	29.6
	R/m	2.489	2.703	2.644	3.155	3.403	3.201	3.26	2.873	3.008
	I/(R+m)	7.713	8.258	10.99	11.41	12.69	13.29	14.1	15.16	14.54

2. For larger operands gmp catches up with numONGO, the modular reduction remaining slower because it is not based on Montgomery's algorithm.
3. numONGO has a higher I/(m+R) ratio than gmp. This shows how big the overheads in general purpose libraries are for such small inputs.

2.2 Lazy and Incomplete Reduction

Lazy and incomplete modular reduction are described in [3]. Here, we give a short treatment. Let $p < 2^w$ be a prime, where w is a fixed integer. We consider expressions of the form $\sum_{i=1}^{d} a_i b_i \bmod p$ with $0 \leqslant a_i, b_i < p$. Such expressions occur in the explicit formulae for HEC. To use most modular reduction algorithms, including Montgomery's, at the *end* of the summation, we have to make sure that all partial sums of $\sum a_i b_i$ are smaller than $p\, 2^w$. Some authors (for example [27]) suggested to use *small* primes, to guarantee that the condition $\sum a_i b_i < p\, 2^w$ is always satisfied. Note that [27] exploited the possibility of accumulating several partial results before reduction for the extension field arithmetic, but not at the group operation level. The use of small primes at the group operation level has been considered also in [14] after the present paper appeared as a preprint. However, "just" using primes which are "small enough" would contradict one of our design principles, which is to have no restriction on p except its word length.

What we do, additionally, is to ensure that the number obtained by removing the least significant w bits of any intermediate result remains $< p$. We do this by adding the products $a_i b_i$ in succession, and checking if there has been an overflow or if the most significant half of the intermediate sum is $\geqslant p$: if so we subtract p from the number obtained ignoring the w least significant bits of the intermediate result. If the intermediate result is $\geqslant 2^{2w}$, the additional bit can be stored in a carry. Since all intermediate results are bounded by $p2^{w+1} < (p+2^w)2^w$, upon subtraction of $p\, 2^w$ the carry will always be zero. This requires as many operations as allowing intermediate results in triple precision, but less memory accesses are needed: In practice this leads to a faster approach, and at the end we have to reduce a number x bounded by $p\, 2^w$, making the modular reduction easier.

This technique of course works with any *classical modular reduction algorithm. That it works with Montgomery's r-sidus and with* REDC *is a consequence of the linearity of the operator* REDC *modulo p.*

nuMONGO supports Lazy (i.e. delayed) and Incomplete (i.e. limited to the number obtained by removing the least significant w bits) modular reduction. Thus, an expression of the form $\sum_{i=0}^{d-1} a_i b_i \bmod p$ can be evaluated by d multiplications but only one modular reduction instead of d. A modular reduction is at least as expensive as a multiplication, and often much more, see Table 1.

Remark 1. We *cannot* add a reduced element to an unreduced element in Montgomery's representation. In fact, Montgomery's representation $\overline{a}$ of the integer a is $aR \bmod p$ (R as in § 2.1 with $N = p$). Now, $\overline{bc}$ is congruent to $bcR^2 \bmod p$, not to $\overline{bc} = bcR \bmod p$. Hence, a and bc have been multiplied by different constants $\bmod p$ to obtain $\overline{a}$ and $\overline{bc}$, and $\overline{a} + \overline{bc}$ bears no fixed relation to $a + bc$.

2.3   Implementation of the Explicit Formulae

We assume that the reader is acquainted with elliptic and hyperelliptic curves.

Elliptic Curves. We consider elliptic curves defined over a field F of odd characteristic greater than 3 given by a Weierstrass equation

$$E \ : \ y^2 = x^3 + a_4 x + a_6 \tag{1}$$

where the polynomial $x^3 + a_4 x + a_6$ has no multiple roots. The set of points of E over (any extension of) the field F and the point at infinity $\mathcal{O}$ form a group.

There are 5 different coordinate systems [9]: *affine* ($\mathcal{A}$), the finite points "being" the pairs (x, y) that satisfy (1); *projective* ($\mathcal{P}$), also called *homogeneous*, where a point $[X, Y, Z]$ corresponds to $(X/Z, Y/Z)$ in affine coordinates; *Jacobian* ($\mathcal{J}$), where a point (X, Y, Z) corresponds to $(X/Z^2, Y/Z^3)$; and two variants of $\mathcal{J}$, namely, *Chudnowski Jacobian* ($\mathcal{J}^c$), with coordinates (X, Y, Z, Z^2, Z^3), and *modified Jacobian* ($\mathcal{J}^m$), with coordinates $(X, Y, Z, a_4 Z^4)$. They are accurately described in [9], where the formulae for all group operations are given. It is possible to add two points in any two different coordinate systems and get a result in a third system. For example, when doing a scalar multiplication, it is a good idea to keep the base point and all precomputed points in $\mathcal{A}$, since adding those points will be less expensive than using other coordinate systems.

For EC, only few savings in REDCs are possible.

Let us work out an example, namely, how many REDCs can be saved in the addition $\mathcal{A} + \mathcal{P} = \mathcal{P}$. Let $P_1 = (X_1, Y_1)$, $P_2 = [X_2, Y_2, Z_2]$ and $P_3 = [X_3, Y_3, Z_3]$. Then, $P_3 = P_1 + P_2$ is computed as follows [9]:

$$u = Y_2 - Y_1 Z_2 \quad v = X_2 - X_1 Z_2, \quad A = u^2 Z_2 - v^3 - 2v^2 X_1 Z_2,$$
$$X_3 = vA, \quad Y_3 = u(v^2 X_1 Z_2 - A) - v^3 Y_1 Z_2, \quad Z_3 = v^3 Z_2.$$

For the computation of u and v no savings are possible. We cannot save any reductions in the computation of $A = u^2 Z_2 - v^3 - 2v^2 X_1 Z_2$ because: We need v^3 reduced anyway

Table 2. Costs of Group Operations on EC and HEC

		Doubling		Addition			
	operation	costs	operation	costs		operation	costs
EC	$2\mathcal{A}=\mathcal{A}$	I, 2m, 2s, 4R	$\mathcal{A}+\mathcal{A}=\mathcal{A}$	I, 2m, 1s, 3R			
	$2\mathcal{P}=\mathcal{P}$	7m, 5s, 10R	$\mathcal{P}+\mathcal{P}=\mathcal{P}$	12m, 2s, 13R		$\mathcal{A}+\mathcal{P}=\mathcal{P}$	9m, 2s, 10R
	$2\mathcal{J}=\mathcal{J}$	4m, 6s, 8R	$\mathcal{J}+\mathcal{J}=\mathcal{J}$	12m, 4s, 16R		$\mathcal{A}+\mathcal{J}=\mathcal{J}$	8m, 3s, 11R
	$2\mathcal{J}^c=\mathcal{J}^c$	5m, 6s, 9R	$\mathcal{J}^c+\mathcal{J}^c=\mathcal{J}^c$	11m, 3s, 14R		$\mathcal{A}+\mathcal{J}^c=\mathcal{J}^c$	8m, 3s, 11R
	$2\mathcal{J}^m=\mathcal{J}^m$	4m, 4s, 8R	$\mathcal{J}^m+\mathcal{J}^m=\mathcal{J}^m$	13m, 6s, 19R		$\mathcal{A}+\mathcal{J}^m=\mathcal{J}^m$	9m, 5s, 14R
g=2	$2\mathcal{A}=\mathcal{A}$	I, 22m, 5s, 22R	$\mathcal{A}+\mathcal{A}=\mathcal{A}$	I, 22m, 3s, 18R			
	$2\mathcal{P}=\mathcal{P}$	38m, 6s, 38R	$\mathcal{P}+\mathcal{P}=\mathcal{P}$	45m, 5s, 42R		$\mathcal{A}+\mathcal{P}=\mathcal{P}$	40m, 3s, 33R
	$2\mathcal{N}=\mathcal{N}$	34m, 7s, 37R	$\mathcal{N}+\mathcal{N}=\mathcal{N}$	47m, 7s, 50R		$\mathcal{A}+\mathcal{N}=\mathcal{N}$	36m, 5s, 37R
g=3	$2\mathcal{A}=\mathcal{A}$	I, 71(m/s), 57R	$\mathcal{A}+\mathcal{A}=\mathcal{A}$	I, 76(m/s), 55R			

for Z_3, A must be available also in reduced form to compute X_3, and from $v^2 X_1 Z_2$ we subtract A in the computation of Y_3; It is then easy to see that here no gain is obtained by delaying reduction. But Y_3 can be computed by first multiplying u by $v^2 X_1 Z_2 - A$, then v^3 by $Y_1 Z_2$, adding these two products and reducing the sum. Hence, one REDC can be saved in the addition formula.

For affine coordinates, no REDCs can be saved. Additions in $\mathcal{P}$ allow saving of 1 REDC, even if one of the two points is in $\mathcal{A}$. With no other addition formula we can save reductions. For all doublings we can save 2 REDCs, except for the doubling in $\mathcal{J}^m$, where no savings can be done due to the differences in the formulae depending on the introduction of $a_4 Z^4$.

In Table 2, we write the operation counts of the implemented operations. Results for genus 2 and 3 curves are given, too. The shorthand $\mathcal{C}_1 + \mathcal{C}_2 = \mathcal{C}_3$ means that two points in the coordinate systems $\mathcal{C}_1$ and $\mathcal{C}_2$ are added and the result is given in $\mathcal{C}_3$, where any of the $\mathcal{C}_i$ can be one of the applicable coordinate systems. Doubling a point in $\mathcal{C}_1$ with result in $\mathcal{C}_2$ is denoted by $2\mathcal{C}_1 = \mathcal{C}_2$. The number of REDCs is given separately from the multiplications and squarings.

Hyperelliptic Curves. An excellent, low brow, introduction to hyperelliptic curves is given in [28], including proofs of the facts used below.

A hyperelliptic curve $\mathcal{C}$ of genus g over a finite field $\mathbb{F}_q$ of odd characteristic is defined by a Weierstrass equation $y^2 = f(x)$, where f is a monic, square-free polynomial of degree $2g + 1$. In general, the points on $\mathcal{C}$ do *not* form a group. Instead, the *ideal class group* is used, which is isomorphic to the Jacobian variety of $\mathcal{C}$. Its elements are represented by pairs of polynomials and [7] showed how to compute with group elements in this form. A generic ideal class is represented by a pair of polynomials $U(x) = x^g + \sum_{i=0}^{d-1} U_i x^i$, $V(x) = \sum_{i=0}^{d-1} V_i x^i \in \mathbb{F}_q[x]$ such that for each root ξ of $U(x)$, $(\xi, V(\xi))$ is a point on $\mathcal{C}$ (equivalently, $U(x)$ divides $V(x)^2 - f(x)$). The *affine coordinates* are the $2g$-tuple $[U_{g-1}, \ldots, U_1, U_0, V_{g-1}, \ldots, V_1, V_0]$.

Genus 2. For genus 2 there are two more coordinate systems besides affine ($\mathcal{A}$): in *projective coordinates* ($\mathcal{P}$) [30]: a quintuple $[U_1, U_0, V_1, V_0, Z]$ corresponds to the ideal class represented by $[x^2 + U_1/Z\,x + U_0/Z, V_1/Z\,x + V_0/Z]$; with Lange's *new* co-ordinates $(\mathcal{N})$ [24], the sextuple $[U_1, U_0, V_1, V_0, Z_1, Z_2]$ corresponds to the ideal class $[x^2 + U_1/Z_1^2\,x + U_0/Z_1^2, V_1/Z_1^3 Z_2\,x + V_0/Z_1^3 Z_2]$. The system $\mathcal{N}$ is important in scalar multiplications since it has the fastest doubling. We refer to [24] for the formulae.

Table 3. Addition in genus 2, $\deg u_1 = \deg u_2 = 2$

INPUT:	$[u_1, v_1], [u_2, v_2]$, with $\deg u_1 = \deg u_2 = 2$, and $f = x^5 + f_3 x^3 + f_2 x^2 + f_1 x + f_0$	
OUTPUT:	$[u_3, v_3] = [u_1, v_1] + [u_2, v_2]$	
NOTATION:	$u_i = x^2 + u_{i1}x + u_{i0}$ and $v_i = v_{i1}x + v_{i0}$	

Step	Expression	Cost
1	compute resultant r of u_1, u_2:	1S, 3M
	$z_1 = u_{11} - u_{21}, z_2 = u_{20} - u_{10}, z_3 = u_{11}z_1 + z_2;$	
	$r = z_2 z_3 + z_1^2 u_{10};$	
2	compute almost inverse of u_2 modulo u_1 ($\imath = \imath_1 x + \imath_0 = r/u_2 \bmod u_1$):	-
	$\imath_1 = z_1, \imath_0 = z_3;$	
3	compute $s' = rs \equiv (v_1 - v_2)\imath \bmod u_1$:	5M
	$w_0 = v_{10} - v_{20}, w_1 = v_{11} - v_{21}, w_2 = \imath_0 w_0, w_3 = \imath_1 w_1;$	
	$s_1' = (\imath_0 + \imath_1)(w_0 + w_1) - w_2 - w_3(1 + u_{11}), s_0' = w_2 - u_{10}w_3;$	
	If $s_1 = 0$ handle exceptional case (e.g. with Cantor's algorithm)	
4	compute $s'' = x + s_0/s_1 = x + s_0'/s_1'$ and s_1:	I, 2S, 5M
	$w_1 = (rs_1')^{-1}(= 1/r^2 s_1), w_2 = rw_1(= 1/s_1'), w_3 = s_1'^2 w_1(= s_1);$	
	$w_4 = rw_2(= 1/s_1), w_5 = w_4^2;$	
	$s_0'' = s_0' w_2;$	
5	compute $l' = s'' u_2 = x^3 + l_2' x^2 + l_1' x + l_0'$:	2M
	$l_2' = u_{21} + s_0'', l_1' = u_{21}s_0'' + u_{20}, l_0' = u_{20}s_0''$	
6	compute $u_3 = (s(l + 2v_2) - k)/u_1$:	3M
	$u_{30} = (s_0'' - u_{11})(s_0'' - z_1) - u_{10} + l_1' + (2v_{21})w_4 + (2u_{21} + z_1)w_5;$	
	$u_{31} = 2s_0'' - z_1 - w_5;$	
7	compute $v_3 \equiv -(l + v_2) \bmod u_3$:	4M
	$w_1 = l_2' - u_{31}, w_2 = u_{31}w_1 + u_{30} - l_1', v_{31} = w_2 w_3 - v_{21};$	
	$w_2 = u_{30}w_1 - l_0', v_{30} = w_2 w_3 - v_{20};$	
total		I, 3S, 22M

We now see in an example – the addition formula in affine coordinates – how lazy and incomplete reductions are used in practice. Table 3 is derived from results in [24], but restricted to the odd characteristic case. The detailed breakdown of the REDCs we can save follows:

1. In Step 1 we can save one REDC in the computation of r, since we do not need the reduced value of $z_2 z_3$ and $z_1^2 u_{10}$ anywhere else.
2. In Step 3 we do not reduce $w_2 = \imath_0 w_0$, since it is used in the computation of s_1' and s_0', which are sums of products of two elements. So only 3 REDCs are required to implement Step 3: for w_3 and for the final results of s_1' and s_0'. This is a saving of two REDCs.
3. In Step 5, it would be desirable to leave the coefficients l_1' and l_0' of l' unreduced, since they are used in the following two steps only in additions with other products of two elements. But $l_1' = u_{21}s_0'' + u_{20}$ is a problem: we cannot add reduced and unreduced

quantities (see Remark 1). We circumvent this by computing the unreduced products $L_1 = u_{21}s_0''$ (in place of ℓ_1') and $L_0 = u_{20}s_0''$. Two REDCs are saved.

4. In Step 6, it is $u_{30} = (s_0'' - u_{11})(s_0'' - z_1) + L_1 + 2v_{21}w_4 + (2u_{21} + z_1)w_5 + z_2$. We need only one REDC to compute the (reduced) sum of the first four products: Note that, at this point, L_1 is already known and we already counted the saving of one REDC associated to it. So, we save a total of two REDCs.

Summarizing, for one addition in affine coordinates in the most common case, we need 12 Muls, 13 MulNoREDCs and 6 REDCs. Thus, we save 7 REDCs.

We implemented addition and doubling in all coordinate systems. To speed up scalar multiplication, we also implemented addition in the cases where one of the two group elements to be added is given in $\mathcal{A}$ and the second summand and the result are both given either in $\mathcal{P}$ or $\mathcal{N}$.

In Table 2 we write the operation counts of the implemented operations. The table contains also the counts for EC and genus 3 curves (see the next paragraph). The number of modular reductions is always significantly smaller than the number of multiplications.

Genus 3. Affine coordinates are the only coordinate system currently available for genus 3 curves. The formulae in [32,33] contain some errors in odd characteristic. We took the formulae of [40] – which are for general curves of the form $y^2 + h(x)y = f(x)$, and have been implemented only in even characteristic with $h(x) = 1$ – and simplified them for the case of odd characteristic, $h(x) = 0$, and vanishing second most significant coefficient of $f(x)$. A pleasant aspect of these formulae is that a large proportion of modular reductions can be saved: at least 21 in the addition and 14 in the doubling (see Table 2).

2.4 Scalar Multiplication

There are many methods for computing a scalar multiplication in a generic group, which can be used for EC and HEC. See [15] for a survey.

A simple method for computing $s \cdot D$ for an integer s and a ideal class D is based on the binary representation of s. If $s = \sum_{i=0}^{n-1} s_i 2^i$ where each $s_i = 0$ or 1, then $n \cdot D$ can be computed as

$$sD = 2(\, 2(\cdots 2(\, 2(s_{n-1}D) + s_{n-2}D) + \cdots) + s_1 D) + s_0 D \ . \qquad (2)$$

This requires $n - 1$ doublings and on average $n/2 - 1$ additions on the curve (the first addition is replaced by an assignment).

On EC and HEC, adding and subtracting an element have the same cost. Hence one can use the *non adjacent form* (NAF) [34], which is an expansion $s = \sum_{i=0}^{n} s_i 2^i$ with $s_i \in \{0, \pm 1\}$ and $s_i s_{i+1} = 0$. This leads to a method needing n doublings and on average $n/3 - 1$ additions or subtractions.

A generalization of the NAF uses "sliding windows": The wNAF [37,8] of the integer s is a representation $s = \sum_{j=0}^{n} s_j 2^j$ where the integers s_j satisfy the following two conditions: (i) either $s_j = 0$ or s_j is odd and $|s_j| \leqslant 2^w$; (ii) of any $w + 1$ consecutive coefficients $s_{j+w}, \ldots, s_j$ at most one is nonzero. The 1NAF coincides with the NAF.

The wNAF has average density $1/(w + 2)$. To compute a scalar multiplication based on the wNAF one first precomputes the ideal classes $D, 3D, \ldots, (2^w - 1)D$, and then performs a double-and-add step like (2). A left-to-right recoding with the same density as the wNAF can be found in [4].

3   Results, Comparisons, and Conclusions

Table 4 reports the timings of our implementation. Since nuMONGO provides support only for moduli up to 256 bits, EC are tested only on fields up to that size. For genus 2 curves on a 256 bit field, a group up to 513 bits is possible: We choose this group size as a limit also for the genus 3 curves.

All benchmarks were performed on a 1 GHz AMD Athlon (Model 4) PC, under the Linux operating system (kernel version 2.4). The compilers used were the GNU C Compiler (gcc), versions 2.95.3 and 3.3.1 and all the performance considerations made in § 2.1 apply.

All groups have prime or almost prime order. The elliptic curves up to 256 bits have been found by point counting on random curves, the larger ones as well as the genus 2 and 3 curves have been constructed with the CM method.

For each combination of curve type, coordinate system and group size, we averaged the timings of several thousands scalar multiplications with random scalars, using three different recodings of the scalar: the binary representation, the NAF, and the wNAF. For the wNAF we report only the best timing and the corresponding value of w. We always keep the base ideal class *and* its multiples in affine coordinates, since adding an affine point to a point in *any* coordinate system other than affine is faster than adding two points in that coordinate system. The timings always include the precomputations.

In Table 5 we provide timings for ecc and hec using gmp and the double-and-add scalar multiplication based on the unsigned binary representation. We also provide in Table 6 timings with nuMONGO but without lazy and incomplete reduction. For comparison with our timings, Lange [23] reported timings of 8.232 and 9.121 milliseconds for genus 2 curves with group order $\approx 2^{160}$ and 2^{180} respectively on a gmp-based implementation of affine coordinates on a 1.5 GHz Pentium 4 PC. In [23] the double-and-add algorithm based on the unsigned binary representation is used. In [35], a timing of 98 milliseconds for a genus 3 curve of about 180 bits ($p \approx 2^{60}$) on an Alpha 21164A CPU running at 600MHz is reported. The speed of these two CPUs is close to that of the machine we used for our tests.

A summary of the results follows:
1. Using a specialized software library one can get a speed-up by a factor of 3 to 4.5 for EC with respect to a traditional implementation. The speed-up for genus 2 and 3 curves is up to 8.
2. Lazy and incomplete reduction bring a speed-up from 3% to 10%.
3. For EC, the performance of the systems $\mathcal{J}$ and $\mathcal{J}^m$ is almost identical. The reason lies in the fact that with $\mathcal{J}^m$ no modular reductions can be saved.
4. HEC are still slower than EC, but the gap has been narrowed.
   a) Affine coordinates for genus 2 HEC are significantly faster than those for EC. Those for genus 3 are faster from 144 bits upwards.

Table 4. Comparison of running times, in msec (1 GHz AMD Athlon PC)

curve	coord.	scalar mult.	Bitlength of group order (approximate)							
			128	144	160	192	224	256	320	512
ec	$\mathcal{A}$	binary	1.671	2.521	3.074	5.385	8.536	12.619		
		NAF	1.488	2.252	2.701	4.809	7.596	11.315		
		wNAF	1.363 $(w=4)$	2.205 $(w=3)$	2.489 $(w=4)$	4.335 $(w=4)$	6.841 $(w=4)$	10.099 $(w=4)$		
	$\mathcal{P}$	binary	0.643	0.94	1.152	1.879	3.22	4.243		
		NAF	0.575	0.841	1.017	1.685	2.881	3.747		
		wNAF	0.551 $(w=3)$	0.808 $(w=3)$	0.982 $(w=3)$	1.591 $(w=3)$	2.711 $(w=4)$	3.523 $(w=4)$		
	$\mathcal{J}$	binary	0.584	0.856	1.05	1.702	2.912	3.876		
		NAF	0.517	0.776	0.907	1.499	2.558	3.325		
		wNAF	0.492 $(w=3)$	0.713 $(w=3)$	0.864 $(w=3)$	1.397 $(w=3)$	2.357 $(w=3)$	3.086 $(w=4)$		
	$\mathcal{J}^c$	binary	0.614	0.901	1.109	1.812	3.081	3.995		
		NAF	0.546	0.802	0.965	1.6	2.727	3.583		
		wNAF	0.517 $(w=3)$	0.756 $(w=3)$	0.922 $(w=3)$	1.499 $(w=3)$	2.527 $(w=3)$	3.275 $(w=3)$		
	$\mathcal{J}^m$	binary	0.607	0.872	1.076	1.782	3.005	3.945		
		NAF	0.512	0.748	0.906	1.515	2.592	3.35		
		wNAF	0.474 $(w=3)$	0.684 $(w=3)$	0.838 $(w=3)$	1.395 $(w=3)$	2.296 $(w=3)$	3.048 $(w=3)$		
hec g=2	$\mathcal{A}$	binary	0.888	1.614	1.899	2.546	4.612	5.514	10.409	39.673
		NAF	0.797	1.449	1.706	2.265	4.139	4.952	9.298	35.430
		wNAF	0.73 $(w=4)$	1.421 $(w=4)$	1.558 $(w=4)$	2.053 $(w=4)$	3.73 $(w=4)$	4.464 $(w=4)$	8.343 $(w=4)$	31.246 $(w=5)$
	$\mathcal{P}$	binary	0.839	1.473	1.642	2.102	3.996	4.712	8.653	30.564
		NAF	0.755	1.325	1.48	1.901	3.588	4.203	7.758	27.359
		wNAF	0.703 $(w=4)$	1.211 $(w=4)$	1.352 $(w=4)$	1.742 $(w=4)$	3.256 $(w=4)$	3.842 $(w=4)$	6.998 $(w=4)$	24.451 $(w=5)$
	$\mathcal{N}$	binary	0.844	1.395	1.564	2.038	3.777	4.413	8.265	29.11
		NAF	0.746	1.247	1.391	1.778	3.357	4.002	7.329	25.816
		wNAF	0.675 $(w=4)$	1.14 $(w=4)$	1.262 $(w=4)$	1.623 $(w=4)$	3.02 $(w=3)$	3.575 $(w=4)$	6.53 $(w=4)$	22.73 $(w=4)$
hec g=3	$\mathcal{A}$	binary	1.896	1.984	2.992	3.597	5.39	6.001	12.66	42.907
		NAF	1.64	1.744	2.538	3.085	4.82	5.39	11.24	38.326
		wNAF	1.424 $(w=4)$	1.528 $(w=4)$	2.077 $(w=5)$	2.584 $(w=5)$	4.33 $(w=4)$	4.86 $(w=5)$	9.92 $(w=4)$	34.117 $(w=4)$

Table 5. Timings with gmp, in msec (1 GHz AMD Athlon PC)

ec	160	192	256
$\mathcal{A}$	5.468	8.305	15.354
$\mathcal{P}$	4.306	5.845	9.16
$\mathcal{J}$	3.775	5.4	8.878
$\mathcal{J}^c$	4.029	5.75	9.67
$\mathcal{J}^m$	3.75	5.182	9.075

hec		160	192	256	320	512
g=2	$\mathcal{A}$	9.292	12.082	18.873	29.5	72.09
	$\mathcal{P}$	12.15	14.961	23.442	32.212	81.586
	$\mathcal{N}$	11.349	13.278	20.4	28.93	74.389
g=3	$\mathcal{A}$	19.799	22.452	40.39	59.691	129.541

Table 6. Timings with nuMONGO without lazy and incomplete reduction, in msec (1 GHz AMD Athlon PC)

ec	160	192	256
$\mathcal{A}$	3.074	5.385	12.619
$\mathcal{P}$	1.227	2.041	4.541
$\mathcal{J}$	1.109	1.829	4.069
$\mathcal{J}^c$	1.176	1.939	4.292
$\mathcal{J}^m$	1.076	1.782	3.945

hec		160	192	256	320	512
	$\mathcal{A}$	2.234	2.708	5.788	11.112	41.691
g=2	$\mathcal{P}$	2.02	2.352	4.894	9.415	33.23
	$\mathcal{N}$	1.831	2.113	4.494	8.731	30.653
g=3	$\mathcal{A}$	4.469	5.184	6.52	13.54	47.372

  b) Comparing the best coordinate systems and scalar multiplication algorithms for genus 2 HEC and EC, we see that:
     (i) For 192 bit, resp. 256 bit groups, EC is only 14%, resp. 15% faster than HEC. In fact, consider the best timings for EC and HEC with genus 2 with 192 bits: $(1.623 - 1.395)/1.623 = 0.1405 \approx 14\%$.
     (ii) For other group sizes the difference is often around 50%.
  c) Genus 3 curves are slower than genus 2 ones. With gmp the difference is 80% to 100% for 160 to 512 bit groups, but using nuMONGO the gap is often as small as 50%.
5. Using nuMONGO we can successfully eliminate most of the overheads, thus proving the soundness of our approach.
  a) In the gmp-based implementation, the timings with different coordinate systems are closer to each other than with nuMONGO because of the big amount of time lost in the overheads. For HEC we have the paradoxical result that $\mathcal{P}$ and $\mathcal{N}$ are slower than $\mathcal{A}$, because they require more function calls for each group operation than $\mathcal{A}$. Therefore, with standard libraries the overheads can dominate the running time.
  b) For affine coordinates the most expensive part of the operation is the field inversion, hence the speed-up given by nuMONGO is not big, and is close to that in Table 1 for the inversion alone.
6. If the *field* size for a given group is not close to a multiple of the machine word size b, there is a relative drop in performance with respect to other groups where the field size is almost a multiple of b. For example, a 160-bit group can be given by a genus 2 curve over a 80-bit field, but then 96-bit arithmetic must be used on a 32-bit CPU. Similarly, with 224-bit groups, a genus 2 HEC is penalized by the 112-bit field arithmetic. For 144-bit groups, genus 3 curves can exploit 48-bit arithmetic, which has been made faster by suitable implementation tricks (an approach which did not work for 80 and 112 bit fields), hence the gap to genus 2 is only 50%.

We conclude that the performance of hyperelliptic curves over prime fields is satisfactory enough to be considered as a valid alternative to elliptic curves, especially when large point groups are desired, and the bit length of the characteristic is close to (but smaller than) a multiple of the machine word length.

In software implementations not only should we employ a custom software library, as done for elliptic curves in [6], but for a further speed-up the use of lazy and incomplete reduction is recommended. Development of new explicit formulae should take into account the possibility of delaying modular reductions.

Acknowledgemts. The author thanks Gerhard Frey for his constant support. Tanja Lange greatly influenced this paper at several levels, theoretical and practical, considerably improving its quality. The author acknowledges feedback, support and material from Christophe Doche, Pierrick Gaudry, Johnny Großschädl, Christof Paar, Jean-Jacques Quisquater, Jan Pelzl, Nicolas Thériault and Thomas Wollinger. Thanks also to the anonymous referees for several useful suggestions.

References

1. AMD Corporation. *AMD-K6-2 Processor Data Sheet.* http://www.amd.com/us-en/assets/content_type/white_papers_and_tech_docs/21850.pdf
2. R.M. Avanzi. *Countermeasures against differential power analysis for hyperelliptic curve cryptosystems.* Proc. CHES 2003. LNCS 2779, 366–381. Springer, 2003.
3. R.M. Avanzi and P.M. Mihăilescu. *Generic Efficient Arithmetic Algorithms for PAFFs (Processor Adequate Finite Fields) and Related Algebraic Structures.* Proc. SAC 2003. LNCS 3006, 320–334. Springer 2004.
4. R.M. Avanzi. *A note on the sliding window integer recoding and its left-to-right analogue.* Submitted.
5. A. Bosselaers, R. Govaerts and J. Vandewalle. *Comparison of three modular reduction functions.* Proc. Crypto '93. LNCS 773, 175-186. Springer, 1994.
6. M.K. Brown, D. Hankerson, J, Lopez and A. Menezes. *Software implementation of the NIST elliptic curves over prime fields.* Proc. CT-RSA 2001. LNCS 2020, 250–265. Springer, 2001.
7. D. Cantor. *Computing in the Jacobian of a Hyperelliptic Curve.* Math. Comp. **48** (1987), 95–101.
8. H. Cohen, A. Miyaji and T. Ono. *Efficient elliptic curve exponentiation.* Proc. ICICS 1997, LNCS 1334, 282–290. Springer, 1997.
9. H. Cohen, A. Miyaji and T. Ono. *Efficient Elliptic Curve Exponentiation Using Mixed Coordinates,* Proc. ASIACRYPT 1998. LNCS 1514, 51–65. Springer, 1998.
10. P.G. Comba. *Exponentiation cryptosystems on the IBM PC.* IBM Systems Journal, **29** (Oct. 1990), 526–538.
11. S.R. Dussé and B.S. Kaliski. *A cryptographic library for the Motorola DSP56000.* Proc. EUROCRYPT '90. LNCS 473, 230–244. Springer, 1991.
12. P. Gaudry, *An algorithm for solving the discrete log problem on hyperelliptic curves.* Proc. EUROCRYPT 2000. LNCS 1807, 19–34. Springer, 2000.
13. P. Gaudry and E. Schost. *Construction of Secure Random Curves of Genus 2 over Prime Fields.* Proc. EUROCRYPT 2004. LNCS 3027, 239–256. Springer, 2004.
14. M. Gonda, K. Matsuo, K. Aoki, J. Chao, and S. Tsuji. *Improvements of addition algorithm on genus 3 hyperelliptic curves and their implementations.* Proc. SCIS 2004, 995–1000.
15. D.M. Gordon. *A survey of fast exponentiation methods.* J. of Algorithms **27** (1998), 129–146.
16. T. Grandlund. *GMP. A software library for arbitrary precision integers.* Available from: http://www.swox.com/gmp/
17. R. Harley. *Fast Arithmetic on Genus Two Curves.* Available at http://cristal.inria.fr/~harley/hyper/
18. T. Jebelean. *A Generalization of the Binary GCD Algorithm.* Proc. ISSAC 1993, 111–116.
19. B.S. Kaliski Jr.. *The Montgomery inverse and its applications.* IEEE Transactions on Computers, 44(8), 1064–1065, August 1995.
20. A. Karatsuba and Y. Ofman. Multiplication of Multidigit Numbers on Automata, *Soviet Physics - Doklady,* **7** (1963), 595–596.
21. N. Koblitz. *Hyperelliptic Cryptosystems.* J. of Cryptology **1** (1989), 139–150.

22. U. Krieger. `signature.c`: *Anwendung hyperelliptischer Kurven in der Kryptographie*. M.S. Thesis, Mathematik und Informatik, Universität Essen, Fachbereich 6, Essen, Germany.

23. T. Lange. *Efficient Arithmetic on Genus 2 Hyperelliptic Curves over Finite Fields via Explicit Formulae*. Cryptology ePrint Archive, Report 2002/121, 2002. `http://eprint.iacr.org/`

24. T. Lange. *Formulae for Arithmetic on Genus 2 Hyperelliptic Curves*. To appear in: J. AAECC.

25. A.K. Lenstra and E.R. Verheul. *Selecting Cryptographic Key Sizes*. J. of Cryptology **14** (2001), 255–293.

26. R. Lercier. *Algorithmique des courbes elliptiques dans les corps finis*. These. Available from `http://www.medicis.polytechnique.fr/~lercier/`

27. C.H. Lim, H.S. Hwang. *Fast implementation of Elliptic Curve Arithmetic in $GF(p^m)$*. Proc. PKC 2000, LNCS 1751, 405–421. Springer 2000.

28. A. Menezes, Y.-H. Wu and R. Zuccherato. *An Elementary Introduction to Hyperelliptic Curves*. In N. Koblitz, *Algebraic aspects of cryptography*. Springer, 1998.

29. J.-F. Mestre. *Construction des courbes de genre 2 a partir de leurs modules*. Progr. Math. **94** (1991), 313–334.

30. Y. Miyamoto, H. Doi, K. Matsuo, J. Chao, and S. Tsuji. *A Fast Addition Algorithm of Genus Two Hyperelliptic Curve*. Proc. SCIS 2002, IEICE Japan, 497–502, 2002. In Japanese.

31. P.L. Montgomery. *Modular multiplication without trial division*. Math. Comp. **44** (1985), 519–521.

32. J. Pelzl. *Fast Hyperelliptic Curve Cryptosystems for Embedded Processors*. Master's Thesis. Dept. of Elec. Eng. and Infor. Sci., Ruhr-University of Bochum, 2002.

33. J. Pelzl, T. Wollinger, J. Guajardo, J. and C. Paar. *Hyperelliptic Curve Cryptosystems: Closing the Performance Gap to Elliptic Curves*. CHES 2003, LNCS 2779, 351–365. Springer, 2003.

34. G.W. Reitwiesner. *Binary arithmetic*. Advances in Computers **1** (1960), 231–308.

35. Y. Sakai, and K. Sakurai. *On the Practical Performance of Hyperelliptic Curve Cryptosystems in Software Implementation*. IEICE-Tran. Fund. Elec., Comm. and Comp. Sci. Vol. E83-A No.4., 692–703.

36. N.P. Smart. *On the Performance of Hyperelliptic Cryptosystems*. Proc. EUROCRYPT '99, LNCS 1592, 165–175. Springer, 1999.

37. J.A. Solinas. *An improved algorithm for arithmetic on a family of elliptic curves*. Proc. CRYPTO '97, LNCS 1294, 357–371. Springer, 1997.

38. N. Thériault. *Index calculus attack for hyperelliptic curves of small genus*. Proc. Asiacrypt 2003. LNCS 2894, 75–92. Springer, 2003.

39. A. Weng. *Konstruktion kryptographisch geeigneter Kurven mit komplexer Multiplikation*. PhD thesis, Universität Gesamthochschule Essen, 2001.

40. T. Wollinger, J. Pelzl, V. Wittelsberger, C. Paar, G. Saldamli, and Ç.K. Koç. *Elliptic & Hyperelliptic Curves on Embedded μP*. Special issue on Embedded Systems and Security of the ACM Transactions in Embedded Computing Systems.

41. T. Wollinger. *Engineering Aspects of Hyperelliptic Curves*. Ph.D. Thesis. Dept. of Elec. Eng. and Infor. Sci., Ruhr-University of Bochum. July 2004.

A Collision-Attack on AES

Combining Side Channel- and Differential-Attack

Kai Schramm, Gregor Leander, Patrick Felke, and Christof Paar

Horst Görtz Institute for IT Security
Ruhr-Universität Bochum, Germany
Universitätsstrasse 150
44780 Bochum, Germany
{schramm, cpaar}@crypto.rub.de,
{leander, felke}@itsc.rub.de,
www.crypto.rub.de

Abstract. Recently a new class of collision attacks which was originally suggested by Hans Dobbertin has been introduced. These attacks use side channel analysis to detect internal collisions and are generally not restricted to a particular cryptographic algorithm. As an example, a collision attack against DES was proposed which combines internal collisions with side channel information leakage. It had not been obvious, however, how this attack applies to non-Feistel ciphers with bijective S-boxes such as the Advanced Encryption Standard (AES). This contribution takes the same basic ideas and develops new optimized attacks against AES. Our major finding is that the new combined analytical and side channel approach reduces the attack effort compared to all other known side channel attacks. We develop several versions and refinements of the attack. First we show that key dependent collisions can be caused in the output bytes of the mix column transformation in the first round. By taking advantage of the birthday paradox, it is possible to cause a collision in an output with as little as 20 measurements. If a SPA leak is present from which collisions can be determined with certainty, then each collision will reveal at least 8 bits of the secret key. Furthermore, in an optimized attack, it is possible to cause collisions in all four output bytes of the mix column transformation with an average of only 31 measurements, which results in knowledge of all 32 key bits. Finally, if collisions are caused in all four columns of the AES in parallel, it is possible to determine the entire 128-bit key with only 40 measurements, which a is a distinct improvement compared to DPA and other side channel attacks.

Keywords: AES, side channel attacks, internal collisions, birthday paradox.

1 Introduction

An internal collision occurs, if a function within a cryptographic algorithm processes different input arguments, but returns an equal output argument. A typical example of subfunctions where internal collisions may occur are non-injective mappings, e.g., the S-boxes of DES, which map 6 to 4 bits. Moreover, partial

M. Joye and J.-J. Quisquater (Eds.): CHES 2004, LNCS 3156, pp. 163–175, 2004.

collisions may also appear at the output of injective and non-injective transformations, e.g. in 3 bytes (24 bits) of a 4 byte (32 bit) output value. In the case of AES we will show that key dependent collisions can occur in one of the output bytes of the mix column transformation. We show that these internal collisions can be detected by power analysis techniques, therefore collision attacks should be regarded as a sub-category of Simple Power Analysis (SPA). The term internal collision implies itself that the collision cannot be detected at the output of the algorithm. In cooperation with Hans Dobbertin it was shown in [SWP03], that cross-correlation of power traces (or possibly EM radiation traces) makes it possible to detect internal collisions which provide information about the secret key. Furthermore, in [Nov03, Cla04] it is even claimed that internal collisions can be used to reverse-engineer substitution blocks of secret ciphers, such as unknown implementations of the A3/A8 GSM algorithm. Implementations which solely use countermeasures such as random wait states or dummy cycles will most probably succumb to internal collision attacks, since cross-correlation of power traces with variable time offsets will defeat these countermeasures. Also, in [Wie03] it was shown that the software countermeasure known as the duplication method [GP99] may not succeed against internal collisions. Another advantage of collision attacks over side channel attacks such as Simple Power Analysis (SPA) and Differential Power Analysis (DPA) [KJJ99, KJJ98] is the fact that an internal collision will usually affect a sequence of instructions whereas SPA and DPA usually evaluate the power trace at a particular instance of time. For example, in the case of DES a collision in the output of the non-linear function f_k in round one will affect almost the entire second round. Detecting collisions by examining a sequence of instructions may be advantageous in terms of measurement costs. On the other hand, it must be noted that DPA based attacks against AES have the advantage of being known plaintext attacks whereas our proposed collision attack is a chosen plaintext attack.

The rest of this publication is organized as follows: in Section 2 the collision attack originally proposed in [SWP03] is applied against the AES. It is shown that partial collisions can occur in a single output byte of the mix column transformation and that these collisions depend on the secret key. In Section 3, an optimization of this attack is presented. It uses precomputed tables of a total size of 540 MB and on average yields 32 key bits with 31 encryptions (measurements). If the attack is applied in parallel to all four columns, 128 key bits can be determined with only 40 encryptions (measurements). In Section 4, we give information about our PC simulated attacks and practical attacks against a 8051 based microcontroller running AES in assembly. Finally, in Section 5, we summarize our results and give some conclusions.

2   Collisions in AES

2.1   Collisions in the Mix Column Transformation

In this section, we first briefly review the mix column transformation in AES. Then, we show how key dependent collisions can be caused in a single output byte of the mix column transformation.

The mix column transformation is linear and bijective. It maps a four-byte column to a four-byte column. Its main purpose is diffusion. Throughout this paper we follow the notation used in [DR02]. The mathematical background of the mix column transformation is as follows: all computations take place in $GF(2^8)$, represented by polynomials over $GF(2)$ modulo $m(x) = x^8 + x^4 + x^3 + x + 1$. Columns are interpreted as polynomials over $GF(2^8)$ and multiplied modulo $m(y) = y^4 + 1$. The input polynomial is multiplied with the fixed polynomial

$$c(y) = 03 \cdot y^3 + 01 \cdot y^2 + 01 \cdot y + 02$$

where 01, 02 and 03 refer to the $GF(2^8)$ elements 1, x and $x+1$, respectively. If we refer to the input column as $a(y)$ and to the output column as $b(y)$, the mix column transformation can be stated as

$$b(y) = a(y) \times c(y) \mod y^4 + 1$$

This specific multiplication with the fixed polynomial $c(y)$ can also be written as a matrix multiplication

$$\begin{pmatrix} b_{00} \\ b_{10} \\ b_{20} \\ b_{30} \end{pmatrix} = \begin{pmatrix} 02\ 03\ 01\ 01 \\ 01\ 02\ 03\ 01 \\ 01\ 01\ 02\ 03 \\ 03\ 01\ 01\ 02 \end{pmatrix} \times \begin{pmatrix} a_{00} \\ a_{10} \\ a_{20} \\ a_{30} \end{pmatrix}$$

If we look at the first output byte b_{00}, it is given by[1]

$$b_{00} = 02 \cdot a_{00} + 03 \cdot a_{10} + 01 \cdot a_{20} + 01 \cdot a_{30}$$

If we focus on the first round, we can substitute a_{00}, a_{10}, a_{20} and a_{30} with $S(p_{00} + k_{00}), S(p_{11} + k_{11}), S(p_{22} + k_{22})$ and $S(p_{33} + k_{33})$[2]. The output byte b_{00} can then be written as

$$b_{00} = 02 \cdot S(p_{00} + k_{00}) + 03 \cdot S(p_{11} + k_{11}) + 01 \cdot S(p_{22} + k_{22}) + 01 \cdot S(p_{33} + k_{33})$$

The main idea of this attack is to find two different plaintext pairs with the same output byte b_{00}. We are only considering plaintexts with $p_{00} = p_{11} = 0$ and $p_{22} = p_{33}$. If two plaintexts with $p_{22} = p_{33} = \delta$ and $p'_{22} = p'_{33} = \epsilon \neq \delta$ result in an equal output byte b_{00}, the following equation is satisfied:

$$S(\delta + k_{22}) + S(\delta + k_{33}) = S(\epsilon + k_{22}) + S(\epsilon + k_{33})$$

Suppose that an adversary has the necessary experience and measurement instrumentation to detect this collision in b_{00} (or any other output byte of the mix column transformation) with side channel analysis. First, he sets the two plaintext bytes p_{22} and p_{33} to a random value $\delta = p_{22} = p_{33}$. As next, he encrypts the corresponding plaintext, measures the power trace and stores it on his

---

[1] The symbol + denotes an addition modulo 2, i.e. the binary exclusive-or operation.
[2] These are the diagonal elements of the plaintext and initial round key matrix due to the prior shift row transformation.

computer. He then keeps generating new random values $\epsilon = p'_{22} = p'_{33}$ unequal to previously generated values of δ, ϵ, and so on. He encrypt each new plaintext, measures and stores the corresponding power trace and cross-correlates it with all previously stored power traces until he detects a collision in output byte b_{00}. Once a collision has been found the task is to deduce information about k_{22} and k_{33}.

2.2   An Analysis of the Collision Function

To simplify the notation, we denote k_{00} (or k_{11}, k_{22}, k_{33}) simply by k_0 (or k_1, k_2, k_3) and output byte b_{00} by b_0. As described above, we are interested in values (δ, ϵ), such that for an unknown key the following equation is satisfied:

$$S(k_2 + \delta) + S(k_3 + \delta) + S(k_2 + \epsilon) + S(k_3 + \epsilon) = 0$$

Set

$$\mathcal{L}_{(a,b)} = \{(x, y) \in \mathbb{F}_{2^8} \times \mathbb{F}_{2^8} \mid S(a + x) + S(b + x) + S(a + y) + S(b + y) = 0\}$$

The interpretation of this set is twofold. Given a key pair (k_2, k_3), the set $\mathcal{L}_{(k_2,k_3)}$ is the set of all pairs (δ, ϵ), which will lead to a collision in b_0. On the other hand, due to symmetry, the set $\mathcal{L}_{(\delta,\epsilon)}$ contains all possible key pairs, for which (δ, ϵ) will lead to a collision in byte b_0.

Note that if we measure a collision for δ and ϵ, the key (k_2, k_3) cannot be uniquely determined. This is due to the following properties of the set $\mathcal{L}_{(a,b)}$:

$$\forall\, x \in \mathbb{F}_{2^8} \quad (x, x) \in \mathcal{L}_{(a,b)}$$
$$(x, y) \in \mathcal{L}_{(a,b)} \Rightarrow (y, x) \in \mathcal{L}_{(a,b)}$$
$$(x, y), (y, c) \in \mathcal{L}_{(a,b)} \Rightarrow (x, c) \in \mathcal{L}_{(a,b)}$$
$$(x, y) \in \mathcal{L}_{(a,b)} \Rightarrow (x, y + a + b) \in \mathcal{L}_{(a,b)}$$

Equations (1) to (3) establish an equivalence relation on $\mathbb{F}_{2^8}$. More explicitly, if $(k_2, k_3) \in \mathcal{L}_{(\delta,\epsilon)}$, it follows that

$$(k_2 + \delta + \epsilon, k_3) \in \mathcal{L}_{(\delta,\epsilon)} \tag{1}$$
$$(k_2, k_3 + \delta + \epsilon) \in \mathcal{L}_{(\delta,\epsilon)} \tag{2}$$
$$(k_2 + \delta + \epsilon, k_3 + \delta + \epsilon) \in \mathcal{L}_{(\delta,\epsilon)} \tag{3}$$
$$(k_3, k_2) \in \mathcal{L}_{(\delta,\epsilon)} \tag{4}$$
$$(k_3 + \delta + \epsilon, k_2) \in \mathcal{L}_{(\delta,\epsilon)} \tag{5}$$
$$(k_3, k_2 + \delta + \epsilon) \in \mathcal{L}_{(\delta,\epsilon)} \tag{6}$$
$$(k_3 + \delta + \epsilon, k_2 + \delta + \epsilon) \in \mathcal{L}_{(\delta,\epsilon)} \tag{7}$$

and thus, we cannot hope to determine k_2 and k_3 completely given one collision. Let $(\delta, \epsilon) \in \mathcal{L}_{(k_2,k_3)}$ where we always assume that $\epsilon \neq \delta$. We have to discuss several cases:

case 1: If $k_2 = k_3$ then $\mathcal{L}_{(k_2,k_3)} = \mathbb{F}_{2^8} \times \mathbb{F}_{2^8}$, every choice of (δ, ϵ), i.e., every measurement will lead to a collision.

case 2: If $k_2 \neq k_3$ and if we furthermore assume that $\delta, \epsilon \notin \{k_2, k_3\}$ we obtain

$$0 = S(k_2 + \delta) + S(k_3 + \delta) + S(k_2 + \epsilon) + S(k_3 + \epsilon).$$

By expressing $S(x)$ as $L(x^{-1})$ and applying L^{-1} (where L is the affine transformation of the S-box) we conclude

$$0 = \frac{1}{k_2 + \delta} + \frac{1}{k_3 + \delta} + \frac{1}{k_2 + \epsilon} + \frac{1}{k_3 + \epsilon}$$

which finally yields

$$k_2 + k_3 = \delta + \epsilon.$$

case 3: If $k_2 = \delta$ and $k_3 = \epsilon$ or $k_3 = \delta$ and $k_2 = \epsilon$, we also conclude that $k_2 + k_3 = \delta + \epsilon$.

case 4: This case occurs if either $k_2 \in \{\delta, \epsilon\}$ or $k_3 \in \{\delta, \epsilon\}$. If $k_2 \in \{\delta, \epsilon\}$, we compute

$$p(k_3) = \frac{k_3^2}{(\delta + \epsilon)^2} + \frac{k_3}{\delta + \epsilon} + \frac{\delta\epsilon}{(\delta + \epsilon)^2} + 1 = 0 \tag{8}$$

This can be further simplified to

$$p(k_3) = \left(\frac{k_3 + \delta}{\delta + \epsilon}\right)^2 + \frac{k_3 + \delta}{\delta + \epsilon} + 1 = 0 \tag{9}$$

which shows that

$$\alpha = \frac{k_3 + \delta}{\delta + \epsilon} \in \mathbb{F}_4^* \backslash \{1\}$$

An analysis of the case $k_3 \in \{\delta, \epsilon\}$ yields a similar result. Combining both cases, we deduce the following possibilities for (k_2, k_3)

$$k_2 = \delta \ \text{ and } \ k_3 = \alpha(\delta + \epsilon) + \delta \tag{10}$$
$$k_2 = \epsilon \ \text{ and } \ k_3 = \alpha(\delta + \epsilon) + \delta \tag{11}$$
$$k_2 = \delta \ \text{ and } \ k_3 = \alpha(\delta + \epsilon) + \epsilon \tag{12}$$
$$k_2 = \epsilon \ \text{ and } \ k_3 = \alpha(\delta + \epsilon) + \epsilon \tag{13}$$
$$k_3 = \delta \ \text{ and } \ k_2 = \alpha(\delta + \epsilon) + \delta \tag{14}$$
$$k_3 = \epsilon \ \text{ and } \ k_2 = \alpha(\delta + \epsilon) + \delta \tag{15}$$
$$k_3 = \delta \ \text{ and } \ k_2 = \alpha(\delta + \epsilon) + \epsilon \tag{16}$$
$$k_3 = \epsilon \ \text{ and } \ k_2 = \alpha(\delta + \epsilon) + \epsilon \tag{17}$$

where $\alpha \in \mathbb{F}_4^* \backslash \{1\}$. In the case of the AES S-box, α can be chosen as $\alpha(x) = BC = x^7 + x^5 + x^4 + x^3 + x^2$. Note that solutions (10) to (16) correspond exactly to the seven additional possibilities (1) to (7).

Let us assume we detect a collision for a particular $(\delta, \epsilon) \in \mathcal{L}_{(k_2,k_3)}$. In order to deduce information about k_2 and k_3 we have to decide which case we deal with. We do not have to distinguish case two and case three, as the information we deduce about k_2 and k_3 is the same in both cases.

To distinguish case one, two or three from case four we use the following idea. Given a collision (δ, ϵ), we construct a new pair (δ', ϵ'), which will not lead to a collision if and only if (δ, ϵ) corresponds to case four. For this we need

Lemma 1. *Let*

$$
\begin{aligned}
\mathcal{L}_4 = \{&(k_2, \alpha(k_2 + k_3) + k_2), (k_2, \alpha(k_2 + k_3) + k_3),\\
&(k_3, \alpha(k_2 + k_3) + k_2), (k_3, \alpha(k_2 + k_3) + k_3)\\
&(\alpha(k_2 + k_3) + k_2, k_2), (\alpha(k_2 + k_3) + k_3, k_2),\\
&(\alpha(k_2 + k_3) + k_2, k_3), (\alpha(k_2 + k_3) + k_3, k_3)\}.
\end{aligned}
$$

Given an element $(\delta, \epsilon) \in \mathcal{L}_{(k_2,k_3)}$ the pair (δ', ϵ') with

$$
\delta' \in \mathbb{F}_{2^8} \setminus \{\delta, \epsilon, \alpha(\delta + \epsilon) + \delta, \alpha(\delta + \epsilon) + \epsilon\}
$$

and

$$
\epsilon' = \delta' + \delta + \epsilon
$$

is in $\mathcal{L}_{(k_2,k_3)}$ if and only if

$$
k_2 = k_3
$$

or

$$
(\delta, \epsilon) \notin \mathcal{L}_4
$$

i.e. if and only if (δ, ϵ) does not correspond to case four.

Proof.

"$\Leftarrow$:". If $k_2 = k_3$, the set $\mathcal{L}_{(k_2,k_3)} = \mathbb{F}_{2^8} \times \mathbb{F}_{2^8}$, so in particular $(\delta', \epsilon') \in \mathcal{L}_{(k_2,k_3)}$. If on the other hand $(\delta, \epsilon) \notin \mathcal{L}_4$, we see that $\forall \delta' \in \mathbb{F}_{2^8}$, the pair $(\delta', \delta' + \delta + \epsilon) \in \mathcal{L}_{(k_2,k_3)}$.

"$\Rightarrow$:"Assume $k_2 \neq k_3$ and $(\delta, \epsilon) \in \mathcal{L}_4$. W.l.o.g. let $\delta = k_2$ and $\epsilon = \alpha(k_2 + k_3) + k_2)$. If $(\delta', \epsilon') \in \mathcal{L}_{(k_2,k_3)}$ we get

$$
\frac{1}{k_2 + \delta'} + \frac{1}{k_2 + \epsilon'} + \frac{1}{k_3 + \delta'} + \frac{1}{k_3 + \epsilon'} = 0
$$

If we substitute $k_3 = \alpha(\delta + \epsilon) + \epsilon$ and $\epsilon' = \delta + \epsilon + \delta'$, we conclude

$$
\frac{1}{\delta + \delta'} + \frac{1}{\delta + \epsilon'} + \frac{1}{\alpha(\delta + \epsilon) + \epsilon + \delta'} + \frac{1}{\alpha(\delta + \epsilon) + \epsilon + \epsilon'} = 0
$$

and due to the choice of δ' we finally get

$$
\delta + \epsilon = \alpha(\delta + \epsilon)
$$

a contradiction.   □

Thus, with the pair (δ', ϵ') as constructed in the theorem, we can decide, if (δ, ϵ) corresponds to case four or not.

Now we are in a situation where we have to distinguish case one from cases two and three. If $k_2 \neq k_3$ we see that

$$D_{k_2, k_3} := \{a + b \mid (a, b) \in \mathcal{L}_{(k_2, k_3)}\}$$

contains only the values $k_2 + k_3$ in cases two and three and $\alpha(k_2 + k_3)$ and $(\alpha + 1)(k_2 + k_3)$ in case four. As a conclusion, we are able to exactly determine in which case we are in order to determine information about (k_2, k_3). In case one if $k_2 = k_3$ then $D_{k_2, k_3} = \mathbb{F}_{2^8}$. Thus if we are given a collision (δ, ϵ), we choose new values δ'' such that $\delta'' + \epsilon \notin \{\delta + \epsilon, \alpha(\delta + \epsilon), (\alpha + 1)(\delta + \epsilon)\}$. As argued above, such a pair (δ'', ϵ) will lead to a collision iff $k_1 = k_2$.

2.3   Probability Analysis of Collisions in a Single Output Byte

The probability that a collision occurs after n measurements is given by

$$P(n) = 1 - \prod_{i=0}^{n-1} \left(1 - \frac{i}{256}\right)$$

Table 1 lists various probabilities of a collision for a different number of measurements.

Table 1. Probability of a collision after n measurements

n	$P(n)$
1	0
10	0.1631
20	0.5332
30	0.8294
40	0.9599
50	0.9941

As a result, due to the birthday paradox an average of only 20 measurements are required in order to detect a collision in a single output byte of the mix column transformation.

3   Optimization of the Attack

In the last section, we described collisions which occur in a single output byte of the mix column transformation. This attack can be optimized by equally varying all four plaintext bytes which enter the mix column transformation while still focussing on collisions in one of the four output bytes, i.e., we now try to cause collisions with two pairs of plaintexts of the form $\delta = p_{00} = p_{10} = p_{20} = p_{30}$ and $\epsilon = p'_{00} = p'_{10} = p'_{20} = p'_{30}$. Moreover, we still look for collisions in a single output byte of the mix column transformation, however we observe all four outputs for collisions.

For example, a collision occurs in the first output byte of the mix column transformation whenever the following equation is fulfilled

$$C(\delta, \epsilon, k_0, k_1, k_2, k_3) = 02S(k_0 + \delta) + 03S(k_1 + \delta) + S(k_2 + \delta) + S(k_3 + \delta)$$
$$+ 02S(k_0 + \epsilon) + 03S(k_1 + \epsilon) + S(k_2 + \epsilon) + S(k_3 + \epsilon)$$
$$= 0$$

We denote, for a known pair (δ, ϵ), the set of all solutions by

$$\mathcal{C}_{\delta,\epsilon} := \{(k_0, k_1, k_2, k_3) | C(\delta, \epsilon, k_0, k_1, k_2, k_3) = 0\}$$

Again, suppose that an adversary has the necessary equipment to detect a collision in any of the output bytes $b_{00}, \ldots, b_{30}$ with side channel analysis. In order to cause collisions in the outputs of the first mix column transformation, he sets the four plaintext bytes p_{00}, p_{11}, p_{22} and p_{33} to a random value $\delta = p_{00} = p_{11} = p_{22} = p_{33}$. As next, he encrypts the corresponding plaintext, measures the power trace and stores it on his computer. He then keeps generating new random values $\epsilon = p'_{00} = p'_{11} = p'_{22} = p'_{33}$ unequal to previously generated values of δ, ϵ, and so on. He encrypts each new plaintext, measures and stores the corresponding power trace and cross-correlates it with all previously stored power traces until he detects a collision in the observed output byte $b_{00}, \ldots, b_{30}$. Once a collision has been found the task is to deduce information about (k_0, k_1, k_2, k_3).

This equation can be solved by analysis or by using precomputed look-up tables which contain the solutions (k_0, k_1, k_2, k_3) for particular (δ, ϵ). However, this equation is much more complex than the one introduced in the previous section and an analog description is not trivial. An alternative solution to this problem is to create the sets $\mathcal{C}_{\delta,\epsilon}$ for every pair (δ, ϵ) by generating all possible values for (k_0, k_1, k_2, k_3) and checking $C(\delta, \epsilon, k_0, k_1, k_2, k_3) = 0$ for all pairs (δ, ϵ).

In our simulations we found that the resulting sets are approximately equal in size and on average contain $16,776,889 \approx 2^{24}$ keys, which corresponds to a size of 67 megabytes ($\approx 2^{26}$ bytes) per set. Multiplying this with the number of possible (δ, ϵ) sets, all sets together would require about $2,000$ gigabytes which is only possible with major efforts and distributed storage available. Reducing the amount of required disk space and still being able to compute all the necessary information is the purpose of the next section.

Moreover, it must be pointed out that there exist certain keys (k_0, k_1, k_2, k_3) for which no pair (δ, ϵ) will result in a collision. To our knowledge, there only exist three classes of keys (x, x, x, x), (x, x, x, y) and (x, x, y, y) which will not result in collisions for any pair (δ, ϵ). If the key (k_0, k_1, k_2, k_3) is an element of the key class (x, x, x, x), i.e. all four key bytes are equal, no collisions will occur in any of the four Mix Column output bytes for any pair (δ, ϵ) due to the overall required bijectivity of the Mix Column transform. The probability that this case occurs is $P = 2^8/2^{32} = 2^{-24}$. If the key (k_0, k_1, k_2, k_3) is an element of the key class (x, x, y, x) or (x, x, x, y), no collision will occur in the Mix Column output byte b_0. If the key (k_0, k_1, k_2, k_3) is an element of the key class (x, y, x, x) or (x, x, y, x), no collision will occur in the Mix Column output byte b_1. If the key (k_0, k_1, k_2, k_3) is an element of the key class (y, x, x, x) or (x, y, x, x), no collision will occur in the Mix Column output byte b_2. If the key (k_0, k_1, k_2, k_3) is an element of the key class (x, x, x, x) or (y, x, x, x), no collision will occur in the Mix Column output byte b_3. The probability that any of these cases occurs is $P = \frac{1}{256} \cdot \frac{1}{256} \cdot \frac{1}{256} \cdot \frac{255}{256} \approx 2^{-24}$. Our simulations showed that these are the only exceptional keys which will not result in collisions b_0, b_1, b_2 or b_3.

3.1   Reducing the Storage Requirements

First, note that the sets $\mathcal{C}_{\delta,\epsilon}$ also contain all the keys which will cause collisions in the output bytes b_1, b_2 and b_3. Since the entries in the mix column matrix are bytewise rotated to the right in each row, the stored 32-bit keys in the sets $\mathcal{C}_{\delta,\epsilon}$ must be cyclically shifted to the right by one, two or three bytes, as well, in order to cause collisions in b_1, b_2 and b_3.

Moreover, the amount of space can be further reduced by taking advantage of two different observations. First, we find some dependencies among the elements in a given set $\mathcal{C}_{\delta,\epsilon}$ and second we derive a relationship between two sets $\mathcal{C}_{\delta,\epsilon}$ and $\mathcal{C}_{\delta',\epsilon'}$.

The first approach uses an argument similar to an argument used in Section 2. If for a fixed pair (δ, ϵ) a key (k_0, k_1, k_2, k_3) is in $\mathcal{C}_{\delta,\epsilon}$, then the following elements are also in $\mathcal{C}_{\delta,\epsilon}$:

$$(k_0, k_1, k_2, k_3) \in \mathcal{C}_{\delta,\epsilon}$$
$$\Rightarrow$$

$$(k_0, k_1, k_3, k_2) \in \mathcal{C}_{\delta,\epsilon} \tag{18}$$
$$(k_0 + \delta + \epsilon, k_1, k_2, k_3) \in \mathcal{C}_{\delta,\epsilon} \tag{19}$$
$$(k_0, k_1 + \delta + \epsilon, k_2, k_3) \in \mathcal{C}_{\delta,\epsilon} \tag{20}$$
$$(k_0, k_1, k_2 + \delta + \epsilon, k_3) \in \mathcal{C}_{\delta,\epsilon} \tag{21}$$
$$(k_0, k_1, k_2, k_3 + \delta + \epsilon) \in \mathcal{C}_{\delta,\epsilon} \tag{22}$$

Combining these changes, we find 32 different elements in $\mathcal{C}_{\delta,\epsilon}$, given that $k_2 \neq k_3$ and $\delta + \epsilon \neq 0$. The case $\delta + \epsilon = 0$ is à priori excluded. If $k_2 = k_3$, we still find 16 different elements in $\mathcal{C}_{\delta,\epsilon}$. For the purpose of storing the sets $\mathcal{C}_{\delta,\epsilon}$, this shows that it is enough to save one out of 32 (resp. 16) elements in the $\mathcal{C}_{\delta,\epsilon}$ tables. This results in a reduction of required disk space by a factor of $(16+255*32)/256 \approx 32$. The second approach to save storage space is based on the following observation: an element (k_0, k_1, k_2, k_3) is in $\mathcal{C}_{\delta,\epsilon}$, if and only if $(k_0 + a, k_1 + a, k_2 + a, k_3 + a) \in \mathcal{C}_{\delta+a,\epsilon+a}$. Thus, every set $\mathcal{C}_{\delta,\epsilon}$ can be easily computed from the set $\mathcal{C}_{\delta+\epsilon,0}$. This shows that it is enough to store for all $\delta_0 \in \mathbb{F}_{2^8}$ the set $\mathcal{C}_{\delta_0,0}$.

Combining these two approaches reduces the required disk space by a factor of approx. $128 * 32 = 2^{12}$, and hence we only need approximately 540 megabytes which is no problem on today's PC. As a matter of fact, the sets $\mathcal{C}_{\delta+\epsilon,0}$ will fit on a regular CD-ROM.

3.2   Probability Analysis of the Optimized Attack

We analyze the functions, which map a value δ to an output b_i for a fixed key (k_0, k_1, k_2, k_3) as independent random functions from $\mathbb{F}_{2^8}$ to $\mathbb{F}_{2^8}$ in rows one to four. We want to determine the expected number of measurements until at least one collision has occurred in every output byte $b_0, \cdots, b_3$.
As stated in Section 2.3, the probability that after n measurements at least one collision occurs in a single output byte $b_0, \cdots, b_3$ is given by

$$P(n) = 1 - \prod_{i=0}^{n-1} \left(1 - \frac{i}{256}\right)$$

For $n = 20$, $P(20) = 0.5332 \geq 1/2$, which means that on average 20 measurements are required in order to detect a collision. In the optimized attack, we want to determine the number of required measurements such that at least one collision occurs in all the values $b_0, \cdots, b_3$ with a probability greater than $1/2$. Therefore, we have to compute the minimum value n such that $P(n) \geq (1/2)^{1/4}$. As a result, we obtain $n = 31$, thus after an average of 31 measurements collisions will be detected in all four rows of the mix column transformation.
Every collision (δ, ϵ) will yield possible key candidates (k_0, k_1, k_2, k_3), which can be looked up in the stored tables $C_{\delta+\epsilon,0}$. Our thorough simulations show that every new collision will decrease the intersection of all key candidates by approximately 8 bit. As a result, we are able to determine the entire 32-bit key (k_0, k_1, k_2, k_3) after collisions have been detected in all four output bytes $b_0, \cdots, b_3$.
Furthermore, it is possible to apply the optimized attack in parallel against all four columns. If we do not only consider the values $b_0, \cdots, b_3$, but also the output bytes $b_4, \cdots, b_{15}$ of the remaining columns, we have to compute the minimal value n such that $P(n) \geq (1/2)^{1/16}$. As a result, we get $n = 40$, thus after an average of 40 measurements at least one collision will be detected in each of the 16 outputs $b_0, \cdots, b_{15}$. These values are verified by our simulations. Thus, on average we only need 40 measurements to determine the whole 128-bit key.

4   Simulation and Practical Attack

As a proof of concept, the AES collision attack was simulated on a Pentium 2.4 GHz PC and results were averaged over 10,000 random keys. As stated above, whenever a collision occurs, all possible key candidates can be derived from the sets $C_{\delta+\epsilon,0}$ and every further collision will provide an additional set of key candidates. The intersection of all sets of key candidates must then contain the real key. As shown in table 2, our simulations made clear that the number of key candidates in the intersection decreases by approximately 8 bit with each new collision.
In order to check the practicability of the attack, an 8051 based microcontroller running an assembly implementation of AES without countermeasures was successfully compromised using the proposed collision attack. In our experiments,

Table 2. Average no. of key candidates after one or more collisions have occured.

no. of collisions in b_0, b_1, b_2 and b_3	0	1	2	3	4
no. of key candidates	2^{32}	16,777,114	65492	256.6	1.065

the microcontroller was running at a clock frequency of 12 MHz. At this frequency it takes about 3.017 ms to encrypt a 128-bit plaintext with a 128-bit key[3]. A host PC sends chosen plaintexts to the microcontroller and thus triggers new encryptions. In order to measure the power consumption of the microcontroller a small shunt resistance ($R_s = 39\Omega$) was put in series between the ground pad of the microcontroller and the ground connection of the power supply. Moreover, we replaced the original voltage source of the microcontroller with a low-noise voltage source to minimize noise superimposed by the source.

A digital oscilloscope was used to sample the voltage over the shunt resistance. We focused on collisions $S(k_{22}) + S(k_{33}) = S(\delta + k_{22}) + S(\delta + k_{33})$ in output byte b_{00} of the mix column transformation in the first round. Our main interest was to find out which measurement costs (sampling frequency and no. of averagings per encryption) are required to detect such a collision. Within the 8051 AES implementation the following assembly instructions in round two are directly affected by a collision in byte b_{00}:

```
mov     a, 30h       ;(1) Read round 1 mix column output byte b_00
xrl     a, 40h       ;(1) X-Or b_00 with round 2 key byte k_00
movc    a, @a+dptr   ;(2) S-box lookup
mov     30h, a       ;(1) Write back the S-box output value
```

The number of machine cycles per instruction is given in parentheses in the remarks following the assembly instructions. Since the microcontroller is clocked at 12 MHz which corresponds to a machine cycle length of 1 μs, this instruction sequence lasts about 5 μs. We began our experiments at a sampling rate of 500 MHz and one single measurement per encyption, i.e. no averaging of power traces was applied. In order to examine collisions, plaintext bytes $p_{22} = p_{33} = \delta$ were varied from $\delta = 1...255$ and compared with the reference trace at $p_{22} = p_{33} = 0$ by applying the least-squares method:

$$R[\delta] = \left(\sum_{t=t_0}^{t_0+N-1} (p[t,0] - p[t,\delta])^2 \right)^{-1} \tag{23}$$

At a sampling rate of 500 MHz the number of sampling points N is 2500. Figure 1 shows the deviation $R[\delta]$ of power traces with $\delta = 1...255$ from the reference trace with $\delta = 0$. Our AES implementation used the key bytes $k_{22} = 21$ and $k_{33} = 60$,

---

[3] using on-the-fly key scheduling

therefore we expected a distinct peak at $\delta = k_{22} \oplus k_{33} = 41$ as shown in Figure 1. It is interesting to note that no averaging of power traces was applied, therefore, it would be possible to break the entire 128-bit key with only 40 measurements[4].

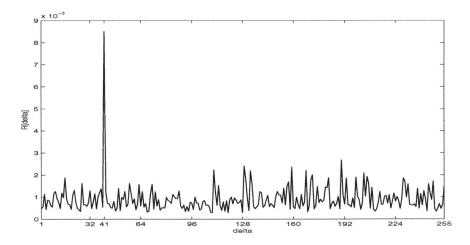

Fig. 1. Deviation of power traces with $\delta = 1...255$ from the reference trace with $\delta = 0$.

We also investigated other signal analysis methods such as computation of the normalized Pearson correlation factor [MS00] and continous wavelet analysis in order to detect internal collisions. As a result, we concluded that computation of the Pearson correlation factor does only seem to be an approriate method when focussing on very particular instances of time within a machine cycle, e.g. when bits on the data or address bus are switched. We achieved very good collision detection using wavelet analysis, however, when compared with the least-squares method, its computational costs are much higher. We will further introduce wavelet analysis in the field of simple power analysis and related reverse-engineering in the future, since it is far beyond the scope of this paper.

5   Results and Conclusions

We proposed two new variants of the collision attack which use side channel analysis to detect internal collisions in AES. Typical methods to recognize internal collisions are computation of square differences, cross-correlation of power consumption curves or application of more advanced methods used in signal analysis theory, such as wavelet analysis. We showed that partial collisions can be detected in the output bytes of the mix column transformation in the first round of AES and each collision typically provides 8 bits of the secret key.

---

[4] provided that the attacker knows the instances of time when mix column outputs are processed in round two

When compared with Differential Power Analysis (DPA) our proposed collision attack has the advantage of requiring less power trace measurements. However, DPA has the advantage of being a known plaintext attack whereas the collision attack is a chosen plaintext attack. A DPA against AES which yields the correct key hypothesis typically requires between 100 and 1,000 measurements depending on the presence of superimposed noise. Our collision attack on the other hand takes advantage of the birthday paradox. As a result, we are able to determine the entire 128-bit key with only 40 measurements.

Acknowledgements. We would like to thank Markus Bockes for pointing out that there exist certain keys which will not result in a collision in a particular Mix Column single output byte when the optimzed collision attack is applied.

References

[Cla04]   C. Clavier. Side Channel Analysis for Reverse Engineering (SCARE). http://eprint.iacr.org/2004/049/, 2004. Cryptology ePrint Archive: Report 2004/049.

[DR02]   J. Daemen and V. Rijmen. *The Design of Rijndael*. Springer-Verlag, Berlin, Germany, 2002.

[GP99]   L. Goubin and J. Patarin. DES and differential power analysis: the duplication method. In Ç. K. Koç and C. Paar, editors, *Cryptographic Hardware and Embedded Systems — CHES 1999*, volume LNCS 1717, pages 158–172. Springer-Verlag, 1999.

[KJJ98]   P. Kocher, J. Jaffe, and B. Jun. Introduction to Differential Power Analysis and Related Attacks. http://www.cryptography.com/dpa/technical, 1998. Manuscript, Cryptography Research, Inc.

[KJJ99]   P. Kocher, J. Jaffe, and B. Jun. Differential Power Analysis. In *Advances in Cryptology — CRYPTO '99*, volume LNCS 1666, pages 388–397. Springer-Verlag, 1999.

[MS00]   R. Mayer-Sommer. Smartly Analyzing the Simplicity and the Power of Simple Power Analysis on Smart Cards. In Ç. K. Koç and C. Paar, editors, *Cryptographic Hardware and Embedded Systems — CHES 2000*, volume LNCS 1965, pages 78 – 92. Springer-Verlag, 2000.

[Nov03]   R. Novak. Side-Channel Attack on Substitution Blocks. In *ACNS 2003*, volume LNCS 2846, pages 307–318. Springer-Verlag, 2003.

[SWP03]   K. Schramm, T. Wollinger, and C. Paar. A New Class of Collision Attacks and its Application to DES. In Thomas Johansson, editor, *Fast Software Encryption — FSE '03*, volume LNCS 2887, pages 206 – 222. Springer-Verlag, February 2003.

[Wie03]   A. Wiemers. Partial Collision Search by Side Channel Analysis. Presentation at the Workshop: Smartcards and Side Channel Attacks, January 2003. Horst Goertz Institute, Bochum, Germany.

Enhancing Collision Attacks

Hervé Ledig, Frédéric Muller, and Frédéric Valette

DCSSI Crypto Lab 51, Boulevard de Latour-Maubourg
75700 Paris 07 SP France
{Frederic.Muller,Frederic.Valette}@sgdn.pm.gouv.fr

Abstract. Side Channel Attacks (SCA) have received a huge interest in the last 5 years. These new methods consider non-cryptographic sources of information (like timing or power consumption) in addition to traditional techniques. Consequently block ciphers must now resist a variety of SCAs, among which figures the class of "collision attacks". This recent technique combines side channel information with tools originally developed for block cipher or hash function cryptanalysis, like differential cryptanalysis for instance.
In this paper, we propose techniques to enhance collision attacks. First we describe a general framework for collision attacks against Feistel ciphers that extends and improves on previous results specifically obtained against DES. Then, we describe an improved method to attack DES using "almost collisions". Indeed we observed that taking into account internal states which are abnormally similar results in more efficient attacks. Some experimental results obtained against a DES implementation are finally presented.

1 Introduction

The idea of using side channel information to break cryptosystems implemented on a tamper-resistant device (typically think of this device as a smart-card) appeared in 1996 following the initial work by Kocher [6,7]. This new class of attacks is generally referred to as Side Channel Attacks (SCA) and has received a huge interest since then. Some techniques are based on analyzing the power consumption of the cryptographic device, like Simple Power Analysis (SPA) or Differential Power Analysis (DPA) [7]. Others are based on analyzing errors during the execution of a cryptographic computation on the device, like Differential Fault Analysis (DFA) [3,4]. These techniques may be applied without distinction to public or secret key cryptosystems. Recently a large variety of attacks and countermeasures has been proposed. However the field is now fairly well understood and naive attacks are unlikely to work against devices implementing recent countermeasures.

Therefore new directions for more sophisticated attacks are being investigated, like Higher-Order DPA for instance [9]. Many new attacks combine "traditional" cryptanalysis techniques (coming from block cipher or hash function cryptanalysis for instance) with the use of side channel information. A good example was given in 2003 by Schramm, Wollinger and Paar [12]. They proposed a

M. Joye and J.-J. Quisquater (Eds.): CHES 2004, LNCS 3156, pp. 176–190, 2004.

Collision Attack (CA) against DES [10] based on techniques from classical "collision attacks" against hash functions. Their attack is based on the observation that an internal collision on 3 adjacent S-boxes during a DES computation can be caused with a reasonable probability. They also gave experimental evidences that such collisions could be detected using the power consumption curves of a microcontroller. It is also interesting to notice that this technique has a close link with differential attacks against DES. Independently another CA was proposed by Wiemers [13]. It is more efficient than Schramm *et.al.*'s attack and is dedicated against DES as well. Unfortunately it has not been published so far.

The difference between DPA and CA lies in the underlying assumptions and mostly on the time scale of the analysis. Both attacks consider the correlation between some intermediate data and the corresponding power consumption curve. However, compared to usual DPA, CA focuses on larger variables (typically the input of the Feistel round function) at a larger time scale (a long sequence of instructions is analyzed). Initially CA have been applied against DES but applications have been reported recently against AES [11] and even in the field of public key cryptosystems [5]. These attacks present a particular interest because they are likely to resist against countermeasures devised specifically against DPA. Since they consider a larger time scale, countermeasures operating only at a local level might not be sufficient.

In this paper, we propose a more generic and more efficient CA. Rather than limiting our analysis to collisions, we also take into account "almost collisions", *i.e.* internal states which are extremely similar. Such events result in almost identical sequences of instructions. We choose sparse input differences that either vanish or remain sparse during several rounds. Thus we use techniques coming from differential cryptanalysis against block ciphers [2]. We show that Feistel ciphers are particularly weak regarding these new attacks.

In the Section 2, we describe a basic and generic collision attack on the second round of Feistel ciphers (with application to DES). Then, we propose an improved attack using "almost collisions" occurring in the following rounds of encryption. Finally, we present experimental results obtained with DES implemented in software on a smart-card.

2   Collision Attacks Against Feistel Ciphers

Two CA against DES have been proposed recently. In [12], it is described how to obtain and detect collisions on 3 adjacent S-boxes in the first round of DES. It is also suggested that the same method could be applied to other Feistel ciphers. Actually this attack is nice but not optimal. In [13], another CA dedicated against DES, more efficient, is briefly presented. In this section we describe a generic framework for CA against Feistel ciphers. Our description is an improvement and a generalization of these previous works.

A Feistel cipher is an iterated block cipher of size $2n$ bits where the internal state is split in two halves (L, R). The round function F operates on n bits and the next state (L', R') is computed by :

$$L' = R'$$
$$R' = L \oplus F(R)$$

For most Feistel ciphers, the round function F has 3 layers

- the addition of a subkey K.
- a non-linear layer denoted NL (*e.g.* built with several S-boxes)
- a linear application denoted $\mathcal{L}$

CAMELLIA [1] and DES [10] are examples of such a construction (we can omit the expansion in DES for the moment).

The model. We assume that an attacker has access to the power consumption of a cryptographic device where some Feistel cipher is implemented without specific countermeasures. In addition, we suppose that this attacker chooses the plaintext introduced.

Although he is not able to tell from power consumption curves the values manipulated during the computation, the attacker is generally able to tell when a collision occurs. Indeed a collision usually results in two identical sequences of instructions. Hence the power consumptions curves are likely to be very similar. This assumption is reasonable as long as the corresponding computation takes many clock cycles and depends greatly on the value of the operand. For instance, we assume that a collision on the inputs of the round function F can be detected. This assumption has already been verified experimentally in [11,12,13]. In Section 4, we describe our own experimental results against DES implemented on a smart-card. These results comfort the validness of the previous assumption.

The attack. The general idea can be stated as follows : introduce chosen differences in each branch of the Feistel that will vanish in the input of the second round function. Obviously these methods use many original ideas from differential cryptanalysis [2]. For instance, a classical result, in the case of DES, is the existence of differences on 3 adjacent S-boxes which give the same output. This idea was exploited by Schramm *et. al.* in [12].

We call δ_R the difference introduced in the right branch of the Feistel (respectively δ_L in the left branch) and Δ the output difference of the first round function. The goal in this attack is to cancel out differences on the input R_1 of the second round function. Thus we want $\Delta = \delta_L$. If this happens, we hope to detect collisions by looking at the power consumption during the second round. This scenario is summarized in Figure 1

The attack described in [12] is based on the extreme case $\Delta = \delta_L = 0$. This approach is successful in the case of DES. However, most recent Feistel ciphers use bijective round functions (although it is not a requirement of the Feistel structure) so differential trails of the form

$$\delta_R \xrightarrow{F} \Delta = 0$$

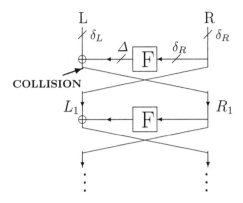

Fig. 1. Scenario of the basic collision attack

do not exist. Actually even in the case of DES this approach is not extremely efficient since about 140 messages are needed in average to obtain one collision. A more efficient approach (also used in [13]) is to introduce a low-weight difference δ_R such that only one S-box is active[1] and to cancel out this difference using δ_L. This method applies to a generic Feistel cipher, as represented in Figure 2 (where dashed areas represent differences).

We call δ_{int} the intermediate difference between layers $\mathcal{L}$ and NL. This difference is clearly limited to one S-box. Thus δ_{int} takes only 2^r different values where r is the output dimension of the S-box. We call $\delta_{int}(1), \ldots, \delta_{int}(2^r)$ these values. Looking at the coordinate on each S-box, we can write equivalently, for all i

$$\delta_{int}(i) = (i, 0, \ldots, 0)$$

Although Δ it is not necessarily limited to one S-box, it can take only 2^r values since

$$\Delta = \mathcal{L}(\delta_{int})$$

Now, the attacker tries to eliminate Δ by playing with δ_L. To that purpose, he picks a sparse δ_R which activates only one S-box and introduces the corresponding plaintexts in the block cipher :

- $P_i = (L \oplus \mathcal{L}(i, 0, \ldots, 0), R)$ for $i = 1 \ldots 2^r$
- $P'_i = (L \oplus \mathcal{L}(i, 0, \ldots, 0), R \oplus \delta_R)$ for $i = 1 \ldots 2^r$

This sums up to 2^{r+1} chosen plaintexts. Between two plaintexts P_i and P'_j, the difference in the output of the first round function is of the form

$$\Delta = \mathcal{L}(x, 0 \ldots, 0)$$

---

[1] In the context of differential cryptanalysis, "active" generally means that at least one input bit differs

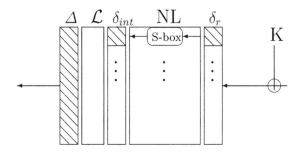

Fig. 2. The differential trail

for some value x depending only on K, R and δ_R (and not on i, j). Besides, if $i \oplus j = x$, there is a collision on R_1 because differences coming from the left branch and right branch cancel out

$$\delta_L = \mathcal{L}(i, 0, \dots, 0) \oplus \mathcal{L}(j, 0, \dots, 0)$$
$$= \mathcal{L}(i \oplus j, 0, \dots, 0)$$
$$\Delta = \mathcal{L}(x, 0, \dots, 0)$$

Analysis. We built a set of 2^{r+1} plaintexts among which 2^r pairs $(P_i, P'_{i \oplus x})$ yield a collision on the input of the second round function. This method is much more efficient than the attack described in [12] (see the summary Table 1). In fact it is almost optimal since all available plaintexts can be useful to detect collisions.

Table 1. Summary of collision attacks

Attack	Specificity	Active S-boxes	Block ciphers	Plaintexts/Coll.
Schramm *et. al.* [12]	$\delta_L = 0$	3	DES	140
Wiemers [13]	-	1	DES	32
this paper (basic)	-	1	any Feistel	2^r
this paper (improved)	-	1	any Feistel	$2^{1+r/2}$
this paper	-	1	DES	8

The result of observing **any** of these 2^r collisions is to leak x (which gives a simple condition on a few bits from the subkey K). Since one collision is sufficient, a simple improvement is to reduce the number of plaintexts. Indeed the attacker can encrypt only the $2^{\frac{r}{2}}$ plaintexts P_i such that

$$i = \underbrace{0 \cdots 0}_{\frac{r}{2} \text{ bits}} * \cdots *$$

and the $2^{\frac{r}{2}}$ plaintexts P_j such that

$$j = * \cdots * \underbrace{0 \cdots 0}_{\frac{r}{2} \text{ bits}}$$

Here the XOR difference $i \oplus j$ spans the 2^r possible values, which guarantees that the value x we are looking for is reached once. Thus we can build a set reduced to

$$2^{\frac{r}{2}} + 2^{\frac{r}{2}} = 2^{1 + \frac{r}{2}}$$

messages that yields exactly one collision. If this collision is detected, the attack succeeds. How to recover the full secret key depends highly on the key schedule, but this attack can be iterated on all S-boxes, then on the following rounds once the first subkey is entirely leaked. Furthermore, since r is typically small (from 4 to 8 bits), the number of required messages is usually reasonably small.

The case of DES. Applying this generic attack to DES is straightforward. The only difference between DES and a "generic" cipher is the expansion function which has no effect on the attack. As a direct application we can build a set of $2^r = 32$ messages (since $r = 4$ bits is the output size of the DES S-boxes). Among these messages we expect 16 collisions in the second round function. As we mentioned previously, only $2 \cdot \sqrt{16} = 8$ messages are sufficient in order to guarantee the existence of a single collision.

Each collision provides a simple condition on key bits (it is a differential condition on a S-box, equivalent to the knowledge of 4 key bits). So, roughly 14 collisions are needed to expose the full key. This corresponds naively to $14 \times 8 = 112$ messages. In case less messages are available, a trade-off with exhaustive search is also possible. This result is among the most efficient side channel attacks against DES.

Similar results could be obtained for other Feistel ciphers, including CAMEL-LIA [1] and MISTY1 [8], both selected by the European NESSIE project.

3   An Improvement Based on "Almost-Collisions"

The previous attack exploits only power consumption curves corresponding to the second round by detecting internal collisions. In our experiments with DES, we observed that curves corresponding to the following rounds are also full of information. Indeed internal states are often very similar because of the particular form of the plaintexts. Such events - that we call "almost collisions" - are almost as easy to detect as actual collisions. In this section, we describe improved attacks based on "almost collisions".

3.1   Motivation

In the model of Section 2, we supposed that internal collisions could be detected directly from power consumption curves. Hence we gave corresponding estimates for the number of messages required. However in a practical setting, it often turns out that observations are not as good as expected. For instance, countermeasures may focus on the first rounds which are known to be critical in many attacks. Sometimes the measurements obtained are also noisy for practical reasons. Hence it often turns out that observations contain a larger amount of background noise than expected. The number of messages required for an attack is accordingly increased since the noise is generally eliminated by averaging more curves.

Another possible source of problem is that collisions are not always as easy to detect as expected. Indeed even when a collision does not occur at the end of round 1, the inputs of round 2 might still be almost identical if the diffusion of the cipher is slow. We call such a situation an **almost collision**. This notion can just be seen as a shortcut for "differences with a low hamming weight and few active S-boxes".

From a practical point of view, it is well-known that electric consumption is often correlated with the hamming weight or the hamming distance (*i.e.* the numbers of bits flipped between the previous state and the actual state). This property is often used for Simple Power Analysis or Differential Power Analysis [7]. Therefore, almost collisions are likely to result in similar power consumption curves since they correspond to differences with low hamming weight. Practical results of Section 4 illustrate that this assumption is correct. The consequent problem is that distinguishing a collision from an almost collision at round 2 is not an easy to task. To improve this analysis, we wish to take into account all available information. In particular, power consumption of the third and fourth round should be considered. Since plaintexts introduced are extremely similar, these rounds do not correspond to just random computations. Indeed, internal states can remain abnormally similar during several rounds (*i.e.* they differ only on a small number of bits). So almost collisions may be helpful if we consider the rounds number 3 or 4 of encryption. In fact, the number of active bits and S-boxes at these rounds furnish good indicators of the presence of a collision at round 2. Actually they turn out to be even more reliable than the round 2 curves themselves. In the next sections we analyze these indicators.

3.2   Differential Properties of Rounds 3 and 4

Basically the attacker compares two encryptions corresponding to plaintexts P_i and P'_j using notations of Section 2. His goal is to distinguish efficiently between two situations

- a collision at round 2 (*i.e.* $i \oplus j = x$)
- no collision at round 2 (*i.e.* $i \oplus j \neq x$)

For round number t, we call Δ_t the difference on the inputs of the round function F. Similarly, L_t and R_t denote the left and right branch of the Feistel structure at the end of round t for the plaintext P_i (that we write (L_0, R_0) by convention). Like in Section 2, the input difference is written (δ_L, δ_R). In case of a collision, differences on the first rounds of encryption can be expressed as follows :

Table 2. Difference propagation after a collision

Round t	Encryption of P_i	Encryption of P'_j	Difference Δ_t
1	(L_0, R_0)	$(L_0 \oplus \delta_L\ ,\ R_0 \oplus \delta_R\ )$	δ_R
2	(L_1, R_1)	$(L_1 \oplus \delta_R\ ,\ R_1\qquad\ )$	0
3	(L_2, R_2)	$(L_2\qquad\ ,\ R_2 \oplus \delta_R\ )$	δ_R
4	(L_3, R_3)	$(L_3 \oplus \delta_R\ ,\ R_3 \oplus \Delta_4\ )$	Δ_4

Thus, differences on round 2, 3 and 4 can be expressed as

$$\Delta_2 = 0$$
$$\Delta_3 = \delta_R$$
$$\Delta_4 = F(R_2) \oplus F(R_2 \oplus \delta_R)$$

Since δ_R has only one active S-box, both Δ_3 and Δ_4 correspond to "almost collisions" where the hamming weight is low and few S-boxes are active. In opposition, when no collision occurs, differences are more complex :

Table 3. Difference propagation without collision

Round	Encryption of P_i	Encryption of P'_j	Difference Δ_t
1	(L_0, R_0)	$(L_0 \oplus \delta_L\ ,\ R_0 \oplus \delta_R\ )$	δ_R
2	(L_1, R_1)	$(L_1 \oplus \delta_R\ ,\ R_1 \oplus \Delta_2\ )$	Δ_2
3	(L_2, R_2)	$(L_2 \oplus \Delta_2\ ,\ R_2 \oplus \Delta_3\ )$	Δ_3
4	(L_3, R_3)	$(L_3 \oplus \Delta_3\ ,\ R_3 \oplus \Delta_4\ )$	Δ_4

Differences on round 2, 3 and 4 can be expressed as

$$\Delta_2 = F(R_0) \oplus F(R_0 \oplus \delta_R)$$
$$\Delta_3 = F(R_1) \oplus F(R_1 \oplus \Delta_2)$$
$$\Delta_4 = F(R_2) \oplus F(R_2 \oplus \Delta_3)$$

Here, Δ_2 is quite sparse since δ_R has only one active S-box. However, the hamming weight of Δ_3 and Δ_4 can be much higher due to the diffusion properties of the block cipher. In the next section, we give estimates of these indicators in the case of DES.

3.3   Estimating the Indicators for DES

Our focus now is to evaluate the hamming weight and the number of active S-boxes of Δ_2, Δ_3 and Δ_4, in two distinct cases (depending on an eventual collision at round 2). These indicators depend on the diffusion properties of DES and the differential properties of its S-boxes.

We call N_i the number of active bits in Δ_i and n_i the corresponding number of active S-boxes. First we give expected values using simple heuristic arguments. Then we give average values obtained experimentally.

Theoretical estimates. First, we suppose that a collision occurs at round 2. Thus we know that $\Delta_2 = 0$ and $\Delta_3 = \delta_R$ (which has only one active S-box). Hence

$$N_2 = 0 \qquad n_2 = 0$$
$$N_3 = 1 \text{ or } 2 \qquad n_3 = 1$$

Since Δ_4 is the image of input difference δ_R by the round function, its hamming weight is in the range from 1 to 4 with average value $N_4 = 2.5$. Besides each bit in DES internal state is involved in 1.5 S-boxes in average, so we expect

$$n_4 = 2.5 \times 1.5 = 3.75$$

When no collision is observed at round 2, a similar analysis can be conducted. The differential trail is of the form

$$\delta_R \xrightarrow{F} \Delta_2 \xrightarrow{F} \Delta_3 \xrightarrow{F} \Delta_4$$

Thus the expected values are

$$N_2 = 2.5$$
$$n_2 = 2.5 \times 1.5 = 3.75$$
$$N_3 = 3.75 \times 2.5 = 9.375$$

At this point, all S-boxes are likely to be active in the inputs of round 3. So we expect n_3 and n_4 close to 8 and N_4 close to 16.

Practical estimates. We obtained practical results for DES by performing a statistical simulation on a PC. Our basic experiment is to pick a random δ_R which only one active S-box, and a random plaintext P. We compute the first 4 rounds of encryption of P and $P \oplus (0, \delta_R)$ and observe the average values of indicators. After 10 millions experiments, we obtained the results described in Table 4.

Actually these results are even slightly better than the expected values. In rounds 3 and 4 we clearly observe an important difference between the two cases "collision at round 2" and "no collision at round 2".

3.4   Analysis

From Table 4 we observe that the difference on the indicators is actually much more significant in round 4 than in round 2. For instance, looking at the number of active bits in round 2, the difference we try to detect is between 0 bits (when

Table 4. Average value of the indicators for DES

Round	Collision	No Collision
2	$N_2 = 0$	$N_2 = 2.349$
	$n_2 = 0$	$n_2 = 3.534$
3	$N_3 = 1.333$	$N_3 = 9.009$
	$n_3 = 1$	$n_3 = 6.968$
4	$N_4 = 2.358$	$N_4 = 15.150$
	$n_4 = 3.551$	$n_4 = 7.817$

a collision occurs) and an average 2.349 bits (in the other case). The difference is quite small, so power consumption curves are likely to remain quite similar in both cases. However, looking at round 4, there are about 2.358 active bits in one case against 15.150 in the other. This difference is much more significant and thus easier to detect.

Our analysis is comforted by the results obtained in Section 4. In the case of DES, rounds 3 and 4 are better indicators of a collision than the round 2 itself. This is due to the slow diffusion of DES : when no collision happens at round 2 $(i \oplus j \neq x)$, the difference remains quite sparse mostly because the linear layer is just a permutation of bits.

If this permutation was replaced by a linear application with better diffusion (the Mix-Column function of AES for instance) or if we considered a Feistel cipher with good diffusion (like CAMELLIA), the analysis would be different. Collisions would be easier to distinguish using the round 2 or 3, but more difficult using round 4 because of the full diffusion reached in both cases. This is summarized in Table 5.

Table 5. Efficiency of collision detection

Round	Slow diffusion (DES)	Good diffusion (CAMELLIA)
2	difficult	easy
3	easy	easy
4	easy	difficult

To conclude, we described a thiner analysis of collision attacks using differential properties, mostly by taking into account "almost collisions". We showed that better indicators can be found to detect collisions. These improvements are extremely helpful when realizing a concrete side channel attack as we demonstrate in Section 4. We think such methods may also be helpful to defeat countermeasures which focus on protecting the second round of encryption.

4   Experimental Results

In order to verify the previous analysis we implemented a CA against DES implemented in software on a smart-card. This smart-card used classical hardware countermeasures :

- variable internal clock
- electric noise (random peaks of power)

We managed to detect collisions despite these countermeasures. The trickiest part was to get rid of the "random" peaks of power. Fortunately these peaks were not truly random (they were strongly correlated with the external clock) and were eliminated by analyzing several samples for the same encryption (*i.e.* 5 samples, but even 2 samples could be sufficient in practice). We took into account only the smallest power consumption among these samples, in order to eliminate the peaks of "over-consumption". After this preliminary work, we applied our analysis to **the full power trace of each round** (the rounds are very easy to distinguish). More precisely, we were able to identify which portions are really meaningful inside each round (namely where are located the S-box computations, etc . . .) but did not exploit it. Indeed we want to point out that collisions can be detected very simply and very efficiently.

4.1   The Attack Setting

In order to actually mount the attack, we need to introduce an appropriate set of plaintexts and detect at least one collision at round 2. As described in Section 1, 8 messages are sufficient to guarantee a collision. However we used here the full set of 32 messages described in Section 2. This simplifies the attack since we can process more data. Concretely our attack algorithm is the following

- Guess the value of x.
- For each x, identify the 16 pairs of plaintexts that should give a collision.
- For each pair of plaintexts, compute the difference Δ_{power} of power consumption curves [2].
- Average these 16 differences.

The correct value of x should yield the smallest average difference. The result obtained for round 2 are summarized in Table 6. The unit of this average value has little significance. Hence we just picked as a reference the minimal value and expressed the others as a ratio regarding this minimum.

Actually large portions of the curves are useless for this analysis (for various reasons their power consumption depends little on the arguments) and behave just like noise in practice.

---

[2] Our curves contain of course only a finite number of points corresponding to the electric consumption at instants t_i. The difference of consumption between two curves C and C' is by convention

$$\Delta_{power} = \sum_i (C(t_i) - C'(t_i))^2$$

Table 6. Average differences (correct value is $x = 11$)

Value of x	Average difference	Value of x	Average difference
0	134.26%	8	132.11%
1	121.50%	9	109.11%
2	121.86%	10	118.59%
3	113.57%	11	100%
4	140.38%	12	130.60%
5	131.55%	13	114.81%
6	131.73%	14	125.39%
7	120.70%	15	110.79%

4.2   Using Almost Collisions

In this section we implement the attack based on almost collision. Thus we analyze power consumption curves at rounds 3 and 4. After a collision at round 2, these curves remain quite similar, as predicted. This yields excellent results in Table 7, even better than those obtained with round 2. It comforts the assumption that almost collisions can be used as an efficient indicator.

Table 7. Average differences (correct value is $x = 11$)

Value of x	Average diff. for round 3	Average diff. for round 4	Value of x	Average diff. for round 3	Average diff. for round 4
0	156.26%	146.01%	8	153.38%	154.61%
1	143.45%	146.86%	9	132.05%	143.50%
2	134.32%	136.17%	10	126.01%	131.80%
3	125.03%	136.99%	11	100%	100%
4	160.36%	148.64%	12	150.70%	143.59%
5	149.98%	136.95%	13	139.99%	146.65%
6	144.10%	143.79%	14	134.46%	129.78%
7	133.34%	140.02%	15	121.11%	131.44%

To illustrate this attack, we represented a significant portion of round 4 for 3 plaintexts, among which 2 correspond to an almost collision (see Figure 3). The 2 corresponding curves are in average closer to each other than the third one. However some portions (like the right half of Figure 3) are more significant than the others (the left part of Figure 3 is very noisy).

At a larger scale, it is funny to notice that the useful portions of curves are positioned differently depending on the significant indicator. For instance the best indicator at round 3 is the number of active S-boxes (see Table 4) while, at round 4, the best indicator is the number of active bits. Our experiments have

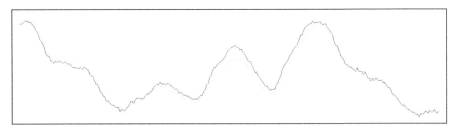

Fig. 3. Three curves corresponding to round 4

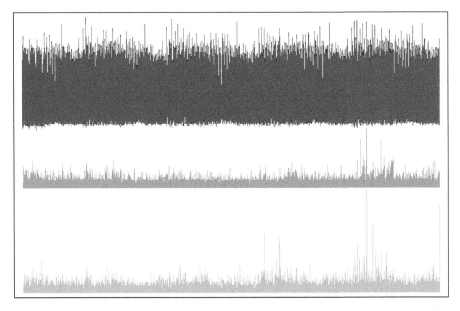

Fig. 4. The whole power consumption curves (round 1 to 4) and the corresponding differences

shown that these indicators reflect to different portions of each round (roughly, the beginning of round for active bits and the end of round for active S-boxes).

We have represented in Figure 4, the whole computation for the same plaintexts than those of Figure 3. In addition to the power consumption curves (represented on top but they are not very speaking), we represented a "wrong" difference (in the middle) and the "good" difference (at the bottom). This "good" difference corresponds to the almost collision. One observes that the average value of theses two additional curves increases along the computation. This is simply due to the diffusion of the input difference. Besides, the "good" difference curve has larger peaks than the "wrong" one, especially for rounds 3 and 4. Hence these rounds prove to be better indicators of a collision than the round 2 itself.

4.3 Summary

We have demonstrated that a thin analysis of the smart-card behavior at rounds 3 and 4 can lead to improved attacks, even when really few messages are available or a large amount of background noise. The remarkable thing with such attacks is that the curves for each round have been handled as a whole. Nevertheless an important bias (resulting from a collision at round 2) can be observed experimentally.

Therefore countermeasures limited to a local protection are unlikely to work against such "large-scale" attacks. Besides protecting only the first or second round with ad-hoc countermeasures is not sufficient. CA may exploit information up to round 4 or 5 depending on the diffusion speed. Countermeasures should modify the execution deeply. For instance, methods based on splitting or masking are the most likely to protect against CA. However their resistance against advanced versions of CA should be further investigated.

5 Conclusion

We described new methods for enhancing collision attacks. First we proposed a generic collision attack against Feistel ciphers which requires fewer messages than previous results and can be applied in many cases. Secondly, we suggested to improve collision attacks by considering several rounds of encryption instead of restricting the analysis to the first two rounds (as it is done by most side channel attacks). Indeed we showed that almost collisions - *i.e.* abnormally similar internal states - may appear in the collision attack scenario. They furnish better indicators than those used by previous attacks. Our experiments against DES implemented on a smart-card confirm our theoretical analysis.

Acknowledgments. We would like to thank Andreas Wiemers for some helpful discussions. We also thank Rémy Daudigny and the members of the LSC laboratory for helping us in the experimental work and capturing the power traces.

References

1. K. Aoki, T. Ichikawa, M. Kanda, M. Matsui, S. Moriai, J. Nakajima, and T. Tokita. Camellia: A 128-Bit Block Cipher Suitable for Multiple Platforms - Design and Analysis. In E. Tavares, editor, *Selected Areas in Cryptography – 2000*, volume 2012 of *Lectures Notes in Computer Science*, pages 39–56. Springer, 2001.

2. E. Biham and A. Shamir. Differential Cryptanalysis of DES-like Cryptosystems. In A. Menezes and S. Vanstone, editors, *Advances in Cryptology – Crypto'90*, volume 537 of *Lectures Notes in Computer Science*, pages 2–21. Springer, 1990.
3. E. Biham and A. Shamir. Differential Fault Analysis of Secret Key Cryptosystems. In B. Kaliski, editor, *Advances in Cryptology – Crypto'97*, volume 1294 of *Lectures Notes in Computer Science*, pages 513–525. Springer, 1997.
4. D. Boneh, R. DeMillo, and R. Lipton. On the Importance of Checking Cryptographic Protocols for Faults (Extended Abstract). In W. Fumy, editor, *Advances in Cryptology – Eurocrypt'97*, volume 1233 of *Lectures Notes in Computer Science*, pages 37–51. Springer, 1997.
5. P-A. Fouque and F. Valette. The Doubling Attack – Why Upwards is Better than Downwards. In C. Walter, Ç. Koç, and C. Paar, editors, *Cryptographic Hardware and Embedded Systems (CHES) – 2003*, volume 2779 of *Lectures Notes in Computer Science*, pages 269–280. Springer, 2003.
6. P. Kocher. Timing Attacks on Implementations of Diffie-Hellman, RSA, DSS, and Others Systems. In N. Koblitz, editor, *Advances in Cryptology – Crypto'96*, volume 1109 of *Lectures Notes in Computer Science*, pages 104–113. Springer, 1996.
7. P. Kocher, J. Jaffe, and B. Jun. Differential Power Analysis. In M. Wiener, editor, *Advances in Cryptology – Crypto'99*, volume 1666 of *Lectures Notes in Computer Science*, pages 388–397. Springer, 1999.
8. M. Matsui. New Block Encryption Algorithm MISTY. In E. Biham, editor, *Fast Software Encryption – 1997*, volume 1267 of *Lectures Notes in Computer Science*, pages 54–68. Springer, 1997.
9. T. Messerges. Using Second-Order Power Analysis to Attack DPA Resistant software. In Ç. Koç and C. Paar, editors, *Cryptographic Hardware and Embedded Systems (CHES) – 2000*, volume 1965 of *Lectures Notes in Computer Science*, pages 238–251. Springer, 2000.
10. NIST FIPS PUB 46-3. *Data Encryption Standard*, 1977.
11. K. Schramm, G. Leander, P. Felke, and C. Paar. A Collision-Attack on AES Combining Side Channel And Differential-Attack. 2003. Submitted for Publication.
12. K. Schramm, T. Wollinger, and C. Paar. A New Class of Collision Attacks and its Application to DES. In T. Johansson, editor, *Fast Software Encryption – 2003*, volume 2887 of *Lectures Notes in Computer Science*. Springer, 2003.
13. A. Wiemers. Partial collision search by side channel analysis, 2003. Presentation at the Workshop : Smartcards and Side Channel Attacks.

Simple Power Analysis of Unified Code
for ECC Double and Add

Colin D. Walter

Comodo Research Laboratory
10 Hey Street, Bradford, BD7 1DQ, UK
Colin.Walter@comodogroup.com

Abstract. Classical formulae for point additions and point doublings on elliptic curves differ. This can make a side channel attack possible on a single ECC point multiplication by using simple power analysis (SPA) to observe the different times for the component point operations. Under the usual binary exponentiation algorithm, the deduced presence or absence of a point addition indicates a 1 or 0 respectively in the secret key, thus revealing the key in its entirety.

Several authors have produced unified code for these operations in order to avoid this weakness. Although timing differences are thereby eliminated from this code level, it is shown that SPA attacks may still be possible on selected single point multiplications if there is sufficient side channel leakage at lower levels. Here a conditional subtraction in Montgomery modular multiplication (MMM) is assumed to give such leakage, but other modular multipliers may be equally susceptible to attack.

The techniques are applicable to a *single* decryption or signature even under prior blinding of both the input text and the secret key. This means that one should use a constant time implementation of MMM even if the secret key is blinded or replaced every time, and *all* side channel leakage should be minimised, whatever multiplier is used.

Keywords: Side channel leakage, simple power analysis, SPA, elliptic curve cryptography, ECC, unified code, Montgomery modular multiplication.

"To ensure that the data carrier consumes the same amount of current whether the requested operation is authorized or unauthorized, a bit is stored in the memory in either event." [Abstract, US Patent 4211919, "Portable data carrier including a microprocessor", filed 28 Aug 1978.]

"No one sews a patch of unshrunk cloth on an old garment, for the patch will pull away from the garment, making the tear worse." [Matt 9:16, The Bible (New International Version)]

1 Introduction

Side channel leakage of secret key information from cryptographic devices has been known publicly for a number of years [1]. In elliptic curve cryptography

M. Joye and J.-J. Quisquater (Eds.): CHES 2004, LNCS 3156, pp. 191–204, 2004.

(ECC) [9,13], techniques to reduce this leakage include the use of unified code for point additions and point doublings [3,7,8,12]. When properly implemented, this should eliminate the ability to distinguish the two operations by timing measurements on an appropriate side channel such as power variation [10,11].

However, for a point doubling some of the arguments are inevitably repeated unless extra precautions are taken. This means that doublings might be separated from additions simply by observing when identical operands, identical arithmetic computations, or identical results are likely to have occurred[1]. This might be done using timing, current or EMR variation [4,5,6,10,11,15]. The generality of such an attack shows that it may be unwise to attempt to patch up old (i.e. leaky) hardware using new, leak-resistant software counter-measures.

Here, to make the details concrete and quantifiable, this is considered for a specific choice of the algorithms and form of side channel leakage, namely: i) point multiplication using the standard square-and-multiply exponentiation algorithm, together with ii) the version of unified code presented by Brier and Joye [3] and their suggested implementation, iii) field multiplication using a version of Montgomery modular multiplication (MMM) [14] which includes a conditional subtraction and iv) a cryptographic device in which every such subtraction can be observed on some side channel or combination of side channels. It is shown that this association leaks sufficiently for it to be computationally possible to deduce some keys for standard elliptic curves over the smaller fields *even* if they are used just once. The choice of Montgomery, while perhaps not natural for the EC-DSA prime fields, has the benefit of being very well studied, so that the required probabilities are known. Almost *any* other leaky modular multiplier could be substituted.

One of the standard, recommended, EC-DSA elliptic curves is chosen for illustration, namely P-192 [2]. Some theoretical analysis shows that there are some input texts which are weaker than average in terms of the number of additions which can be positively identified as not being doublings. Increasing the sample size yields still weaker cases. Experimental results confirm the theory very strongly, showing indeed that there are even weaker instances where the secret key can be recovered without significant computational resources.

The discussion overturns several potential misconceptions. First, unified code on its own is not a panacea against simple power analysis. It protects *only one* aspect of the implementation. Secondly, the three standard blinding techniques helpfully listed by Coron [4] can provide *no* protection at all gainst some attacks. And thirdly, modular multiplication can leak sufficient data for a successful attack even when a key is used *just once*, such as in the Digital Signature Algorithm (DSA) [2]. Previously, MMM was only known to leak so severely if the same, unblinded key was used repeatedly.

In conclusion, even with modern leak-resistant algorithms, field multiplication should clearly be implemented in a time independent manner and, indeed,

---

[1] For example, for both the redundant-operation-enhanced formulae of [7] and the Hessian form in [8], doubling reveals itself if field squares can be detected. Further, the Jacobi form in [12] suffers from essentially the same potential weakness as is explored here for the Weierstraß form in [3], namely repeated evaluation of identical field products.

although the case is not detailed here, in a manner which has a low probability of emitting enough side channel leakage to distinguish successfully between identical and non-identical pairs of multiplications.

2   The Unified Point Addition/Doubling Formula of Brier and Joye

Brier and Joye [3] provide formulae which unify the classical formulae for point addition and point doubling on the Weierstraß form of an elliptic curve. They describe a number of cases, including the use of either affine or projective coordinates.

In their point addition formula for affine coordinates, there is no longer a denominator which becomes zero for point doubling. So a separate formula is not needed. Although there *is* still a denominator which may be zero, this special case is no longer associated with point doubling, but with the sum being the exceptional point $\mathcal{O}$ at infinity. So the formula breaks the previously strong connection between bit values of the secret key and sub-sequences of arithmetic operations.

Assume projective coordinates are used for the representation of points $P = (x, y, z)$ on the Weierstraß form of an elliptic curve

$$y^2 z = x^3 + axz^2 + bz^3$$

where the field characteristic is not 2 or 3. Then, for points $P_i = (x_i, y_i, z_i)$, $1 \leq i \leq 3$, the point addition $P_3 = P_1 + P_2$ is achieved by Brier and Joye using:

$$
\begin{aligned}
x_3 &= 2fw \\
y_3 &= r(g - 2w) - l^2 \\
z_3 &= 2f^3
\end{aligned}
\tag{1}
$$

where

$$
\begin{aligned}
u_1 &= x_1 z_2, & u_2 &= x_2 z_1, & t &= u_1 + u_2; \\
s_1 &= y_1 z_2, & s_2 &= y_2 z_1, & m &= s_1 + s_2; \\
z &= z_1 z_2, & f &= zm, & l &= mf, & g &= tl; \\
r &= t^2 - u_1 u_2 + az^2, & w &= r^2 - g.
\end{aligned}
\tag{2}
$$

This involves eighteen field multiplications, of which one is by the constant a, five are in the equations (1) and thirteen in the equations (2). Without loss of generality, it is assumed that the implementation under attack computes the coordinates of P_3 by taking each of these last equations (2) and calculating the right sides in the order presented before calculating those for (1).

3   The Point Multiplication Algorithm

We assume point multiplication is done using the standard *square-and-multiply* (or *double-and-add*) exponentiation method of Fig. 1. There are two main properties of this algorithm which are used here. First, each bit 1 in the key generates a point doubling followed by a point addition, but a bit 0 in the key generates a

Input: **P**, $k = (k_{N-1}....k_1 k_0)_2$ with $k_{N-1} = 1$
Output: **Q** $= k$**P**

Q $\leftarrow$ **P** ;
For $i \leftarrow N{-}2$ downto 0 do
Begin
    Q $\leftarrow 2$**Q** ;
    If $k_i \neq 0$ then **Q** $\leftarrow$ **Q** $+$ **P** ;
End

Fig. 1. Left-to-Right Binary "Double-and-Add" Algorithm.

point doubling which is followed by another point doubling. Hence, it is easy to translate from a sequence of adds and doubles obtained through a side channel into a sequence of bits which reveals the secret key. Secondly, the initial input **P** is an argument in every point addition. Although this may save some data manipulation, it occasionally produces the bias in each point addition which is exploited here. Choosing instead the right-to-left version of binary exponentiation or m-ary exponentiation ($m > 2$) would probably render the attack here computationally infeasible.

4   Notation and Montgomery Multiplication

For simplicity, we assume the main side channel leakage is from an implementation of field multiplication using Montgomery Modular Multiplication (MMM) [14] in which there is an observable, final, conditional subtraction. However, it must be emphasised that this choice is only for convenience in evaluating the probabilities. A similar attack could be mounted against any modular multiplier exhibiting data-dependent side-channel leakage.

Suppose the elliptic curve is defined over the Galois field $GF(P) = \mathbb{F}_P \cong \mathbb{Z}/P\mathbb{Z}$ and elements of this prime field are represented as long integers modulo P written to base r with digits in lowercase. Thus, for example, $A = \sum_{i=0}^{n-1} a_i r^i \in \mathbb{F}_P$. Suppose R ($\geq P$) is the upper bound we wish to have on the inputs and outputs for MMM. Then we assume the version of MMM given in Fig. 2.

Input: A and B such that $A, B < R \leq r^n$ and P prime to r.
Output: C such that $C \equiv ABr^{-n} \bmod P$ and $C < R$

C $\leftarrow$ 0 ;
For i $\leftarrow$ 0 to n-1 do
Begin
    q_i $\leftarrow$ $-(c_0{+}a_i b_0)p_0^{-1}$ mod r ;
    C $\leftarrow$ (C+a_iB+q_iP) div r ;
End ;
{ Invariant: $Cr^n \equiv A{\times}B \bmod P$ and $ABr^{-n} \leq C < P{+}ABr^{-n}$}
If C $\geq$ R then C $\leftarrow$ C-P ;

Fig. 2. Montgomery's Modular Multiplication Algorithm (MMM).

The invariant after the loop is easy to establish, and, if desired, the digits q_i could be formed into a quotient Q giving the multiple of P which has been subtracted. The post-condition $C < R$ then holds providing n and R satisfy the right properties, namely that the maximum possible value for C is less than $R+P$, i.e. $P+R^2r^{-n} \leq R+P$, which is just the stated pre-condition $R \leq r^n$. This post-condition enables output from one execution of MMM to be fed into another instance of it.

The usual values for R to take are r^n or P. The former gives a cheap test in the conditional statement, whereas the latter yields the least non-negative residue as output. Decreasing R or increasing n reduces the frequency of the final subtraction and so reduces the leakage from the timing side channel. In fact, the subtraction ceases to occur if $P+R^2r^{-n} \leq R$, i.e. if $P \leq R(1-Rr^{-n})$ [18]. As this requires $P < R < r^n$, we would take R as a power of 2 to make the condition easy to evaluate – say $R = \frac{1}{2}r^n$ – and demand that n be large enough – say $P < \frac{1}{4}r^n$. Indeed, this choice for R permits the maximum possible value of P to give no final subtraction for a given n. Hence, for a given maximum value of P, it is possible to deduce values for n and R which will always prevent the final subtraction occurring.

Where side channel attacks are possible, the final, conditional subtraction should be protected from timing variation by performing the subtraction in all cases if it can occur at all and then selecting the new or old value of C as appropriate. Eliminating the need for the final subtraction may lead to less side channel leakage, but an extra loop iteration may be the result of choosing n sufficiently large for this to happen.

Because, unlike RSA, the ECC-related equations (2) involve field additions or subtractions between some field multiplications, here it is most convenient to take $R = P$. Then, as noted, the final subtraction will occur occasionally. Observe from the post-loop invariant that its occurrence is independent of the order of inputs. So changing the input order is not a counter-measure to any attack on the final subtraction.

5   The Probability of a Conditional Subtraction

To estimate the probability of the extra subtraction of P in MMM, observe that P is large and so one can switch from discrete to continuous methods. For all practical purposes, inputs to MMM are uniformly distributed modulo P. Thus, if the random variable X represents a typical input to MMM, its probability density function f is given by $f(x) = P^{-1}$ on the interval $[0, P]$, and $f(x) = 0$ otherwise. Furthermore, outputs are also effectively uniformly distributed modulo P. So the probability of the extra subtraction for random inputs can be deduced from the invariant formula after the loop in MMM [18]. Derivations of this probability are given in [16,17,19] for various contexts[2]. In the case of squaring X, the probability is $p_S = prob(X^2r^{-n}+Z > P)$ where Z is uniform on $[0, P]$. Hence

---

[2] Taking R equal to a power of 2 leads to some interesting non-uniform distributions which are illustrated graphically in [17].

$$p_S = \int_0^P P^{-1} f(x) x^2 r^{-n} \, dx = \tfrac{1}{3} P r^{-n} \tag{3}$$

In the case of multiplying two independent, random residues X and Y, the probability of the conditional subtraction is $p_M = prob(XY r^{-n} + Z > P)$ for equi-distributed Z, namely

$$p_M = \int_0^P \int_0^P P^{-1} f(x) f(y) xy r^{-n} \, dy \, dx = \tfrac{1}{4} P r^{-n} \tag{4}$$

However, for the standard exponentiation algorithm of Fig. 1, the point doublings require field multiplications by a fixed constant, namely a coordinate of the initial (plaintext) point $\mathbf{P}$. If p_C is the probability of the final subtraction when multiplying a random input X by a constant C, then $p_C = prob(CX r^{-n} + Z > P)$ so that

$$p_C = \int_0^P P^{-1} f(x) C x r^{-n} \, dx = \tfrac{1}{2} C r^{-n} \tag{5}$$

The different coefficients of r^{-n} in these three equations enable the different operations to be distinguished by their subtraction frequencies when a number of exponentiations occur with the same secret key k [19,16]. Here cases will be selected where C has the most extreme values in order to force final subtraction behaviour that proves two products have different inputs.

6   Side Channel Leakage

In addition to the assumptions about the algorithms used, in this instance of the attack, it is supposed that *every* occurrence of the conditional subtraction in MMM can be observed. With good monitoring equipment and a lack of other hardware counter-measures, successive data loading cycles can be observed and hence the operations timed, thereby enabling the occurrences to be deduced.

Previous authors have described in detail how timing and power attacks can be performed [10,11,5,15,6]. In fact, all we require here is a reasonable probability of determining whether or not two given instances of modular multiplication have the same pair of inputs. This might be done equally well by power or EMR analysis rather than by timing – the power consumption curves may be sufficiently characteristic of the inputs for this to be possible [20]. Furthermore, this property of distinguishability may occur for any modular multiplier, implying that the attack described here is not restricted only to Montgomery multipliers.

7   Distinguishing Doublings from Additions

To provide outline theoretical justification for the later experimental results, in this section a particular single signing or decryption is selected from a randomly generated set of samples. This selection has properties which increase the number of point operations that can be definitely determined as additions or doublings from knowledge of the conditional subtractions. Consequently, for this choice there is a reduction in the computational effort to traverse the space of possible keys and recover the key used.

Brier and Joye [3] provide an algorithm for computing $P_3 = P_1 + P_2$ by imposing a suitable ordering on equations (2). In the case of the point doubling operation with $P_1 = P_2 = (x, y, z)$, the arithmetic of (2) specialises to:

$$
\begin{aligned}
u &\leftarrow x * z; & u &\leftarrow x * z; & t &\leftarrow u + u; \\
s &\leftarrow y * z; & s &\leftarrow y * z; & m &\leftarrow s + s; \\
z &\leftarrow z * z; & f &\leftarrow z * m; & l &\leftarrow m * f; & g &\leftarrow t * l; \\
r &\leftarrow t^2 - u^2 + a * z^2; & w &\leftarrow r^2 - g;
\end{aligned}
\tag{6}
$$

Here the first two applications of MMM are identical, as are the second two. So both pairs exhibit identical behaviour with respect to the occurrence of the final conditional subtraction. It is the repeated or different behaviour within the pairs which creates the handle for an attack. If the recorded behaviour is different at these points, the curve operation *must* be a point addition.

From a sample of signatures or decryptions, the attacker starts by selecting the case which has the smallest number of undetermined operations. The initial, naïve way to do this is just to count the total number of operations, and subtract the number of those for which the computations of either u_1 and s_1, or u_2 and s_2, or both, involve differences regarding the final subtraction.

Point additions involve the initial input $\mathbf{P} = P_1 = (x_1, y_1, z_1)$ where the natural variation in random (or randomized) coordinates means that occasionally x_1 and y_1 will both be small (i.e. close to 0) and z_1 will be large (i.e. close to P). By equation (5), this means the computations of u_1 and s_1 in (2) will be *less* likely than average to include the additional subtraction, while the computations of u_2 and s_2 will be *more* likely than average to include the additional subtraction. For such initial $\mathbf{P}$, this enhances the likelihood of different behaviour with respect to subtractions in these pairs of multiplications, thus increasing the number of point operations which can be definitely determined to be additions rather than doublings.

Such a point is used below to develop some theory[3]. But, in fact, with the selection criterion above and others developed later, the attacker is actually likely to choose a case which is *much* more amenable to an attack than that where $\mathbf{P}$ has such extreme coordinates.

Suppose the sample size is 512. This is a reasonably practical number of samples to obtain. In one eighth of cases, x_1 will lie in the interval $[0, \frac{1}{8}P]$ and have an average value of $\frac{1}{16}P$. So, from $512 = 8^3$ cases we can expect one instance where the initial input is

---

[3] A case with small x_1, small y_1 and large z_1 is almost always obtained by choosing the side channel trace which maximises the average number σ of differences per operation:

$$
\sigma = \frac{\sum_{op} \{\delta_{op}(u_1, u_2) + \delta_{op}(s_1, s_2)\}}{\#\text{operations}}
$$

where $\delta_{op}(x_1, x_2)$ is 1 or 0 depending on whether or not the products x_1 and x_2 differ with respect to the occurrence of a final subtraction in operation op of a complete point multiplication.

$$\mathbf{P}_0 \approx (\tfrac{1}{16}P, \tfrac{1}{16}P, \tfrac{15}{16}P) \tag{7}$$

$\mathbf{P}_0$ is always an input, say $\mathbf{P}_1$, to each point addition. It is constant over the set of all point additions of the associated signing or decryption. The other input, $\mathbf{P}_2$, for these point additions is, for all practical purposes, a point with random coordinates. Hence (5) is the formula to apply.

For each of the example EC-DSA curves [2] over a field of odd characteristic P, the field order is a generalized Mersenne prime. For example, P-192 uses $P = 2^{192} - 2^{64} - 1$. Consequently, P is very close to a large power of 2 and, in MMM, r^n will certainly be taken equal to that power of 2 (except perhaps for P-521). So $r^n = 2^{192}$ for P-192. Therefore, the ratio Pr^{-n} will be essentially 1 for most EC-DSA curves used in practice.

Using $\mathbf{P}_0$ and this value for Pr^{-n} in (5), $u_1 \leftarrow x_1 \times z_2$ incurs a final subtraction with probability approximately $p_{small} = \frac{1}{32}$, and the same holds for the computation of s_1. Similarly, $u_2 \leftarrow x_2 \times z_1$ incurs a final subtraction with probability approximately $p_{large} = \frac{15}{32}$, and the same holds for the computation of s_2. As the different inputs are independent, the probability p_{diff} of u_1 incurring a subtraction but not u_2, or *vice versa*, is

$$p_{diff} = p_{small} \times \overline{p_{large}} + \overline{p_{small}} \times p_{large} = \tfrac{241}{512} \approx \tfrac{1}{2}$$

There is the same probability of distinguishing between s_1 and s_2 in this way.

As the outputs from the loop of MMM are uniformly distributed over an interval of length P, the subtractions for the four products are all independent of each other even though some share a common input. So the probability p_{add} of proving that a point addition occurs as a result of observing differences in subtractions for at least one of the pairs is[4]

$$p_{add} = \overline{(\overline{p_{diff}})^2} = \tfrac{188703}{262144} \approx \tfrac{3}{4} \tag{8}$$

In a similar way, one can obtain the probabilities p_{A00}, p_{A02}, p_{A20} and p_{A22} of a point addition displaying, respectively, no subtractions, no subtractions for two multiplications then two subtractions, two subtractions then no subtractions, and four subtractions. These are the cases where the subtractions leave it ambiguous as to whether the operation is a point addition or a point doubling. For the fixed input $\mathbf{P}_0$ given in (7) and a random input $\mathbf{P}_2$,

$$
\begin{aligned}
p_{A00} &= \overline{p_{small}} \times \overline{p_{large}} \times \overline{p_{small}} \times \overline{p_{large}} = \tfrac{277729}{1048576} \\
p_{A02} &= \overline{p_{small}} \times \overline{p_{large}} \times p_{small} \times p_{large} = \tfrac{7905}{1048576} \\
p_{A20} &= p_{small} \times p_{large} \times \overline{p_{small}} \times \overline{p_{large}} = \tfrac{7905}{1048576} \\
p_{A22} &= p_{small} \times p_{large} \times p_{small} \times p_{large} = \tfrac{225}{1048576}
\end{aligned}
\tag{9}
$$

In the case of a (random) doubling, the field multiplications of interest have two independent random inputs and so, by (4), the corresponding probabilities are:

---

[4] The accuracy here and later is absurd, but it should enable readers to understand and check the calculations more easily.

$$p_{D00} = \overline{p_M} \times \overline{p_M} = \tfrac{9}{16}$$
$$p_{D02} = \overline{p_M} \times p_M = \tfrac{3}{16}$$
$$p_{D20} = p_M \times \overline{p_M} = \tfrac{3}{16}$$
$$p_{D22} = p_M \times p_M = \tfrac{1}{16}$$

(10)

These last probabilities sum to 1 because it is not possible for the multiplications within a pair to behave differently.

By (8), about three quarters of the additions are determined immediately. On average, this leaves about $26\tfrac{3}{4}$ additions unrecognised for P-192 (30 if the sample size is reduced to only 64). In fact, simulations below in Table 2 show that the attacker, with a better selection criterion, has a mere $19\tfrac{1}{4}$ additions unrecognised for the same sample size of 512.

For undetermined cases, the number of final subtractions can still be used to make a probabilistic decision between an add or a double. Suppose an operation is known to be a point addition with probability π_A and a point doubling with probability $\pi_D = \overline{\pi_A}$, and the subtractions do not distinguish the operation as an addition. Using the same notation as above for counting subtractions, the probabilities of a point addition in the various cases can be deduced from (9) and (10) as:

$$p_{add|00} = \frac{\pi_A \frac{277729}{293764}}{\pi_A \frac{277729}{293764} + \pi_D \frac{9}{16}} \approx \frac{\pi_A}{\pi_A + \pi_D \frac{9}{16}}$$
$$p_{add|02} = p_{add|20} = \frac{\pi_A \frac{7905}{293764}}{\pi_A \frac{7905}{293764} + \pi_D \frac{3}{16}} \approx 0$$
$$p_{add|22} = \frac{\pi_A \frac{225}{293764}}{\pi_A \frac{225}{293764} + \pi_D \frac{1}{16}} \approx 0$$

(11)

Consequently, no subtractions are most likely in such a situation, and the bias to one or other depends on the context, such as neighbouring operations, which might influence the value of π_A. In the unlikely event of two or four subtractions, the attacker would be unfortunate if more than one or two such operations were not doublings: on average he expects only $26\tfrac{3}{4} \times \frac{7905+7905+225}{277729+7905+7905+225} \approx \tfrac{3}{2}$ such operations for P-192.

8   Reconstructing the Secret Key

This section covers both the deduction of unclear key bits from the overall structure of the point operations, and a search of the subspace of keys which are consistent with that structure and with previously determined operations.

Again, for this section, numerical examples apply to the standard P-192 curve defined in FIPS 186-2 [2] for EC-DSA. This has the advantage of a short key length. The methods apply in exactly the same way to other curves, but it will become evident that larger fields require more computational effort.

From Fig. 1, the structure of point operations during signing or decryption can be viewed as a string S over the alphabet $\{A, D\}$ in which the first character of S is 'D' (a double), each 'A' (an add) is preceded by a 'D', and there are a known, fixed number of occurrences of 'D', namely $N-1$ where N is the number of bits in the key k. On average, there will be $\tfrac{1}{2}(N-1)$ 'A's, but for each case this can be established exactly by taking the total number of operations (the length of S) and subtracting the number of doublings.

By (8), a substantial number of the 'A's are known. Each known 'A' determines its neighbours as 'D' on either side (*see* Table 1). Some occurrences of 'D' are determined by two 'A's. The probability of this for an interior 'D' is $(\frac{1}{2}p_{add})^2$. Neglecting differences caused by end conditions (such as the last 'A' is, or is not, followed by a 'D' and the initial 'D' is known), the total number of determined operations is, on average, about

$$\tfrac{3}{2}(N-1)p_{add} - (N-2)(\tfrac{1}{2}p_{add})^2 \qquad (12)$$

For the on-going P-192 example, about $68\frac{3}{4}$ additions are determined from the subtractions and so, by (12), around 181.6 operations in total. This leaves about $26\frac{3}{4}$ 'A's to allocate among approximately $286.5-181.6 = 104.9$ unknown positions – approximately $\binom{104.9}{26.75} \approx 2^{82}$ choices. However, these choices cannot be made freely.

Two thirds of the string S is accurately determined as above. This leaves a number of short substrings to be guessed. These are restricted to patterns which do not have consecutive 'A's. For our parameter choices, the number of these substrings decreases exponentially with their length. So, most frequently, the unknown substrings are of length 1. They can be either 'A' or 'D'. Each possibility can occur. However, substrings of length 2 are constrained to 'AD', 'DA' or 'DD', and those of length 3 to only 'ADA', 'ADD', 'DAD', 'DDA' or 'DDD'. So only $\frac{3}{4}$ of choices are possible for length 2 substrings, only $\frac{5}{8}$ for length 3, and one half or less for longer substrings. (The numerators go up in a Fibonacci sequence: 2, 3, 5, 8, 13,...; and the denominators in powers of two.)

In the P-192 example, about 7 substrings of length 2 occur, 4 of length 3, and 7 of longer lengths. So fewer than $(\frac{3}{4})^7(\frac{5}{8})^4(\frac{1}{2})^7$ of the 2^{82} choices, and, more precisely, only roughly one in $2^{15.6}$, satisfies the constraint of preceding each 'A' by a 'D' (*see* Table 2). The search space is therefore reduced to under 2^{67}.

In allocating the 'A's, we can also note that 'D' is much more likely in some cases, and 'A' perhaps in others. For example, by (10), $\frac{7}{16}$ of doubles will exhibit 2 or 4 subtractions, but, by (11), very few operations with this behaviour could be additions. In the example, about $\frac{7}{16}(191-(2\times68\frac{3}{4}-24.6)) \approx 34$ doubles can be so identified with high probability and on average it is only necessary to try up to 2 of them as doubles. Thus, in estimating the computational effort, the $\binom{104}{26.75}$ can be replaced by $\binom{34}{2}\binom{70}{24.75} \approx 2^{71}$. With the substring constraints, this now reduces the search space to below 2^{56}.

Suppose each key in the search space is checked by applying it once in a point multiplication – some 286.5 point operations, each containing 18 field multiplications. With 32-bit arithmetic, MMM requires $6\times(1+6\times2) = 78$ native machine multiplications. Thus, about 2^{19} MULs are required per key, giving a time complexity of $O(2^{75})$ machine multiplications to break one member of the sample of 512 P-192 signings/decryptions. This is probably not yet computationally feasibility at $O(2^{18})$ Pentium® IV years, although it could be distributed easily over a number of machines. However, ...

Table 1. Example Deductions of Operation Types

Key	1 1 1 1 1 1 1 100 100 100 100 1 1 100 1 1 1 1 10 1 10 1 1 1 1 1 1
Pt Op^n	DADADADADADADADDDADDDADDDADDDADADADDDADADADADADADDDADADDDADADADADADA
u_1 sub^n	0101100000010101000011001100010101010001010000001000101000001100
u_2 sub^n	0100100101000001010011001000000010001000000000000000000111000011101
s_1 sub^n	0000101111000010001110010100001111000000010001100010000100000
s_2 sub^n	0100101011010110001110010100011010000101100111001110011000110001
Diff^{nce}	Y Y Y Y Y Y Y Y Y Y Y Y Y Y Y Y Y Y Y Y
Known	YYYYY*YYYYYYYYY*YYY*****YYY*YYYYYYY*YYYYYYYYY**YYYYYYYY***YYY*YY

9   Worked Examples

This section provides more detail for a typical P-192 attack and assesses the impact of changing various parameters. In particular, the attacker invariably chooses very much better examples than those of the previous section, showing that the attack is, in fact, already feasible. Sequences of conditional subtractions were simulated using equations (3)–(5) and continuous mathematics on randomly generated keys k and inputs P. Different sized samples were generated and one member selected to:

> *minimize the number of point operations which were not distinguishable as additions by virtue of the conditional subtractions, nor distinguishable as doublings by adjacency to a known addition.*

Table 1 shows the initial few bits, point operations, conditional subtractions and deductions for a typical example selected using this criterion. There is one column for each point add (A) or double (D). The penultimate row records differences (marked Y) within the first or the second pair of subtractions. These are all adds and the final row extends this to include the doubles on either side of a known add. The attacker computes this for each signature, and chooses the one with the fewest unknowns (marked *) in the last line.

Table 2 shows how the average number of undetermined operations in the selected sequence varies according to the sample size from which it is taken. The most significant benefit from larger samples is the decrease in the total number of indeterminate operations. The undetermined point additions, α in number, must be chosen from the undetermined operations, τ in number. The number of such combinations is given lower in the table. The longer substrings of unknown operations have more pattern restrictions. The average factor by which this cuts the search space is given in the penultimate line, and the last line presents the resultant overall order of the search space. The computational effort is this multiplied by the work involved in verifying a single key.

The figures make it clear that the criterion just given for selecting the side channel trace is hugely more powerful than if an extremal initial point $\mathbf{P}$ were used. For the sample size of 512, there is a reduction in workload by a factor of 2^{38}. This means that the computational effort is reduced to $O(2^{36.6})$ native multiplications, i.e. about a minute on a Pentium IV processor running at 2^{32}

Table 2. Average Numbers of Operations in the selected Point Multiplication.

P-192 Sample Size	32	64	128	256	512	1024
Total Ops	292.5	293.7	294.8	295.9	296.9	297.9
Unknown Ops (τ)	54.4	49.2	44.4	40.0	36.2	32.7
Unknown Adds (α)	22.4	21.4	20.4	19.9	19.2	18.7
Unknown 1-strings	11.2	11.5	11.7	11.7	11.9	12.2
Unknown 2-strings	7.1	7.1	7.1	7.2	7.2	7.0
Unknown 3-strings	4.6	4.5	4.5	4.5	4.4	4.1
Unknown 4-strings	3.0	2.9	2.8	2.7	2.6	2.6
Unknown 5-strings	1.9	1.8	1.8	1.7	1.6	1.4
Longer unknown strings	3.5	3.1	2.8	2.6	2.4	2.4
Combinations $\frac{\tau}{\alpha}$	2^{50}	$2^{45.5}$	$2^{41.1}$	$2^{37.0}$	$2^{33.2}$	$2^{29.4}$
Substring restrictions	2^{19}	2^{18}	2^{17}	$2^{16.2}$	$2^{15.6}$	$2^{15.0}$
Search Space Order	2^{31}	$2^{27.5}$	$2^{24.1}$	$2^{20.8}$	$2^{17.6}$	$2^{14.4}$

Table 3. Search Space Sizes for Different Key Lengths (Sample of 512).

Key Length	192	224	256	384	521
Total Ops	296.9	345.7	394.2	588.4	795.7
Unknown Ops (τ)	36.2	45.9	55.7	96.3	141.6
Unknown Adds (α)	19.2	23.0	26.6	41.5	57.9
Combinations $\frac{\tau}{\alpha}$	$2^{33.2}$	$2^{42.8}$	$2^{52.4}$	$2^{91.4}$	$2^{134.3}$
Substring restrictions	$2^{15.6}$	$2^{18.8}$	$2^{22.0}$	$2^{35.4}$	$2^{50.1}$
Search Space Order	$2^{17.6}$	$2^{24.0}$	$2^{30.4}$	$2^{56.0}$	$2^{84.2}$

cycles per second. This is certainly feasible for any back street attacker with access to suitable monitoring equipment, not just for government organisations. Indeed, less than a week of computing reveals 1 in 32 keys.

The table also shows that twice as many keys can be extracted from a given sample for about 10 times the effort – the easiest keys are found first, after which they become steadily more difficult to find.

Finally, in Table 3 a comparison is made of the search spaces for the other recommended EC-DSA curve sizes[5]. It would appear that it is still computationally feasible to attack some keys over fields as large as that of P-256.

---

[5] Here Pr^{-n} is assumed to be essentially 1. However, 521-bit numbers cannot be partitioned into words of equal length without loss. So, for P-521, Pr^{-n} may not be close to 1. This would result in many fewer final subtractions and so more unknown operations than tabulated.

10 Conclusion

The clear conclusion is that, on its own, unified code for point operations provides insufficient security in some standard implementations of ECC which employ arithmetic hardware that is subject to side channel leakage. In particular, we demonstrated the feasibility of attacking hardware that uses a time-varying implementation of Montgomery modular multiplication with the Brier-Joye formulae for point addition [3].

Several easy counter-measures would defeat the attack. For example, it should be possible to re-code the point evaluation to avoid repeated field operations when a doubling occurs. The formulae of [7] and [8] avoid the problem, but have field squares precisely when a doubling occurs – leaky hardware might still reveal this. Alternatively, picking any other exponentiation algorithm than the standard binary one may reduce or entirely eliminate the bias given in some decryptions as a result of re-using an extremal input in every point addition. Thus, using m-ary exponentiation with $m > 2$ would reduce the frequency of weak cases as well as introducing ambiguities about which point addition is being performed. Certainly, using a more leak-resistant multiplier would improve matters.

However, the three standard counter-measures listed by Coron [4] are insufficient here; they may make no difference or even make the attack more feasible. Key blinding only helps if more than one decryption is required for key recovery. Only one decryption was used here, but if side channel leakage is weak then several decryptions with the same key could help to distinguish additions from doublings with enough certainty for it to be computationally feasible to search the key space. So this counter-measure might ameliorate the situation, although not solve it. Message blinding only helps against chosen ciphertext attacks, but that was not required here. Indeed, the third counter-measure of randomizing the input point coordinates may help the attack to succeed by guaranteeing a uniform distribution of coordinate values which will contain the necessary examples of attackable extremal points.

Previously it was uncertain that time variation was a serious threat except when unblinded keys were used at least several hundred times in an embedded cryptographic device [19]. Now it is clear that constant time modular multiplication is essential for security even when secret keys are always blinded.

References

1. *Portable data carrier including a microprocessor*, Patent no. 4211919 (Abstract), US Patent and Trademark Office, July 8, 1980.
2. *Digital Signature Standard (DSS)*, FIPS PUB 186-2 (Appendix 6), U.S. National Institute of Standards and Technology, 27 Jan 2000.
3. E. Brier & M. Joye, *Weierstraß Elliptic Curves and Side-Channel Attacks*, Public Key Cryptography (Proc. PKC 2002), D. Naccache & P. Paillier (editors), LNCS **2274**, Springer-Verlag, 2002, pp. 335–345.
4. J.-S. Coron, *Resistance against Differential Power Analysis for Elliptic Curve Cryptosystems*, Cryptographic Hardware and Embedded Systems (Proc. CHES 99), C. Paar & Ç. Koç (editors), LNCS **1717**, Springer-Verlag, 1999, pp. 292–302.

5. J.-F. Dhem, F. Koeune, P.-A. Leroux, P. Mestré, J.-J. Quisquater & J.-L. Willems, *A practical implementation of the Timing Attack*, Proc. CARDIS 1998, J.-J. Quisquater & B. Schneier (editors), LNCS **1820**, Springer-Verlag, 2000, pp. 175–190.

6. K. Gandolfi, C. Mourtel & F. Olivier, *Electromagnetic Analysis: Concrete Results*, Cryptographic Hardware and Embedded Systems – CHES 2001, Ç. Koç, D. Naccache & C. Paar (editors), LNCS **2162**, Springer-Verlag, 2001, pp. 251–261.

7. C. Gebotys & R. Gebotys, *Secure Elliptic Curve Implementations: An Analysis of Resistance to Power-Attacks in a DSP Processor*, Cryptographic Hardware and Embedded Systems – CHES 2002, B. Kaliski, Ç. Koç & C. Paar (editors), LNCS **2523**, Springer-Verlag, 2003, pp. 114–128.

8. M. Joye & J.-J. Quisquater, *Hessian Elliptic Curves and Side Channel Attacks*, Cryptographic Hardware and Embedded Systems – CHES 2001, Ç. Koç, D. Naccache & C. Paar (editors), LNCS **2162**, Springer-Verlag, 2001, pp. 402–410.

9. N. Koblitz, *Elliptic Curve Cryptosystems*, Mathematics of Computation **48**, 1987, pp. 203–209.

10. P. Kocher, *Timing attack on implementations of Diffie-Hellman, RSA, DSS, and other systems*, Advances in Cryptology – CRYPTO '96, N. Koblitz (editor), LNCS **1109**, Springer-Verlag, 1996, pp. 104–113.

11. P. Kocher, J. Jaffe & B. Jun, *Differential Power Analysis*, Advances in Cryptology – CRYPTO '99, M. Wiener (editor), LNCS **1666**, Springer-Verlag, 1999, pp. 388–397.

12. P.-Y. Liardet & N. P. Smart, *Preventing SPA/DPA in ECC Systems using the Jacobi Form*, Cryptographic Hardware and Embedded Systems – CHES 2001, Ç. Koç, D. Naccache & C. Paar (editors), LNCS **2162**, Springer-Verlag, 2001, pp. 391–401.

13. V. Miller, *Use of Elliptic Curves in Cryptography*, Advances in Cryptology – CRYPTO '85, H. C. Williams (editor), LNCS **218**, Springer-Verlag, 1986, pp. 417–426.

14. P. L. Montgomery, *Modular Multiplication without Trial Division*, Mathematics of Computation **44**, no. 170, 1985, pp. 519–521.

15. J.-J. Quisquater & D. Samyde, *ElectroMagnetic Analysis (EMA): Measures and Counter-Measures for Smart Cards*, Smart Card Programming and Security (Proc. e-Smart 2001), I. Attali & T. Jensen (editors), LNCS **2140**, Springer-Verlag, 2001, pp. 200–210.

16. W. Schindler, *A Combined Timing and Power Attack*, Public Key Cryptography (Proc. PKC 2002), P. Paillier & D. Naccache (editors), LNCS **2274**, Springer-Verlag, 2002, pp. 263–279.

17. W. Schindler & C. D. Walter, *More detail for a Combined Timing and Power Attack against Implementations of RSA*, Cryptography and Coding, K.G. Paterson (editor), LNCS **2898**, Springer-Verlag, 2003, pp. 245–263.

18. C. D. Walter, *Precise Bounds for Montgomery Modular Multiplication and Some Potentially Insecure RSA Moduli*, Topics in Cryptology – CT-RSA 2002, B. Preneel (editor), LNCS **2271**, Springer-Verlag, 2002, pp. 30–39.

19. C. D. Walter & S. Thompson, *Distinguishing Exponent Digits by Observing Modular Subtractions*, Topics in Cryptology – CT-RSA 2001, D. Naccache (editor), LNCS **2020**, Springer-Verlag, 2001, pp. 192–207.

20. C. D. Walter, *Sliding Windows succumbs to Big Mac Attack*, Cryptographic Hardware and Embedded Systems – CHES 2001, Ç. Koç, D. Naccache & C. Paar (editors), LNCS **2162**, Springer-Verlag, 2001, pp. 286–299.

DPA on n-Bit Sized Boolean and Arithmetic Operations and Its Application to IDEA, RC6, and the HMAC-Construction

Kerstin Lemke, Kai Schramm, and Christof Paar

Communication Security Group (COSY)
Department of Electrical Engineering and Information Sciences
Ruhr-Universität Bochum, Germany
{lemke, schramm, cpaar}@crypto.rub.de

Abstract. Differential Power Analysis (DPA) has turned out to be an efficient method to attack the implementations of cryptographic algorithms and has been well studied for ciphers that incorporate a nonlinear substitution box as e.g. in DES. Other product ciphers and message authentication codes are based on the mixing of different algebraic groups and do not use look-up tables. Among these are IDEA, the AES finalist RC6 and HMAC-constructions such as HMAC-SHA-1 and HMAC-RIPEMD-160. These algorithms restrict the use of the selection function to the Hamming weight and Hamming distance of intermediate data as the addresses used do not depend on cryptographic keys. Because of the linearity of the primitive operations secondary DPA signals arise. This article gives a deeper analysis of the characteristics of DPA results obtained on the basic group operations XOR, addition modulo 2^n and modular multiplication using multi-bit selection functions. The results shown are based both on simulation and experimental data. Experimental results are included for an AVR ATM163 microcontroller which demonstrate the application of DPA to an IDEA implementation.

Keywords: DPA, Boolean and arithmetic operations, IDEA, RC6, HMAC-construction.

1 Introduction

Since 1998 ([2]) it is known that Simple Power Analysis (SPA) and Differential Power Analysis (DPA) can be applied to extract cryptographic keys by measuring the power dissipation of the cryptographic module during the processing. Early investigations on SPA/DPA against symmetric ciphers have been done on the DES Feistel scheme. For the AES candidates the key whitening process was studied using bitwise key hypotheses ([1]). Algorithms that are based on the mixing of different algebraic groups as IDEA and RC6 are theoretically treated in [1] and [6], but not deeply studied in practice, yet.

Software countermeasures to secure cryptographic algorithms with arithmetic and boolean operations turn out to be costly for the conversion algorithm from

M. Joye and J.-J. Quisquater (Eds.): CHES 2004, LNCS 3156, pp. 205–219, 2004.

arithmetic to boolean masking ([9], [10]). In constrained environments these performance costs might not be acceptable for iterated product ciphers, so DPA remains an issue.

This paper aims to give a deeper analysis of DPA scenarios against product ciphers based on arithmetic and boolean operations. Therefore, the expected DPA signals are studied for primitive operations as XOR, addition modulo 2^n and modular multiplication using multi-bit selection functions. For these algorithms, multi-bit selection functions offer an improved trade-off between the number of key hypotheses and the number of DPA calculations regarding to single-bit selection functions. Moreover, the use of single-bit selection functions can require detailed information on the implementation ([1]), which is not as critical for multi-bit selection functions.

Experimental results are given using an implementation of IDEA on an ATM163 micro-controller which is based on the Harvard architecture. To the knowledge of the authors, detailed DPA methods against IDEA and related algorithms as well as concrete results have not previously been published, though it is generally agreed that DPA should be successful.

2   Differential Power Analysis

Differential Power Analysis (DPA) was first introduced by Kocher et al.([2]) and turned out to be a very efficient side channel attack that makes use of a statistical analysis of the power consumption during the execution of a cryptographic algorithm. DPA needs the knowledge of either the plaintext or the ciphertext as a pre-condition.

Power Analysis exploits the dependency of the power consumed by the hardware on the value of intermediate data and addresses used. The attacker knows or assumes a model for this dependency. Two types of leakage have been confirmed which are caused by the Hamming weight and by the Hamming distance of data ([4], [3]). The Hamming weight model is applied best if a pre-charged bus is used. The Hamming distance model considers the dynamic dissipation due to the number of gates that change the state during a transition.

The choice of the key hypotheses and the selection functions depends on the cryptographic algorithm and the implementation to be attacked. In case of DES and AES the preferred selection functions focus on S-box look-ups. Both the address of the S-box table look-up (which is the S-box input), if implemented in software, and the S-box output can leak information. In case of DES, a selection function targeting one S-box access makes use of 6-bit key hypotheses. In case of the AES there are 8-bit key hypotheses. The selection function can be set up on 1-bit or on multiple-bits of intermediate data.

DPA identifies the correct key value by statistical methods for hypothesis testing. An attacker does not need to know details of the implementation as DPA points itself to the relevant points in time. Suitable tests are the 'Distance-of -Means' test, the student's T-Test and the correlation method ([5]).

Algorithms that do not incorporate small S-box tables and use algebraic functions restrict the use of the selection function to the Hamming weight and Hamming distance of intermediate data, since the addresses used do not depend on cryptographic key material. Whereas S-box tables are sufficiently non-linear and have uniform distributions of output values for all key values, this is in general not the case for algebraic constructions. Due to their linearity, secondary DPA peaks occur at related but wrong key hypotheses.

Difficulties evolve if the Hamming distance corresponding to transition counts is the dominant source for power leakage. In this case the selection function should be adapted to the implementation and eventually even restricted to a certain time frame. In case of microcontrollers based on the von-Neumann architecture (shared data/address bus), the Hamming distance to an additional unknown reference variable might be incorporated for the optimisation of DPA results ([8]). In case of an Harvard architecture, the correlation signals depend on the concrete sequence of instructions and registers used by the implementation.

3 DPA Correlation Signals Using n-Bit Sized Basic Operations

Each operation that is considered below is carried out between a known n-bit variable X and a secret n-bit variable K. As the assumption for DPA, X is known and follows the uniform distribution while K is a secret, constant value.

K and X can be represented as the concatenation of k-bit ($k \leq n$) blocks: $K = K_{n/k-1}|K_{n/k-2}|...|K_1|K_0$ and accordingly $X = X_{n/k-1}|X_{n/k-2}|...|X_1|X_0$. A common choice is $k = 8$. We define:

$$K_j = (K \bmod 2^{(j+1)*k}) \operatorname{div}(2^{j*k}) \tag{1}$$

$$X_j = (X \bmod 2^{(j+1)*k}) \operatorname{div}(2^{j*k}) \tag{2}$$

where $j \in \{0, ..., n/k - 1\}$. In the following, the index j is the block number of a n-bit sized variable.

The key hypotheses are set up on each value of K_j. There are 2^k key hypotheses H_{ji}, namely for each j

$$H_{ji} \text{ is } \{K_j = i\} \tag{3}$$

where $i \in \{0, ..., 2^k - 1\}$. From now on, the index i is the key hypothesis for a certain value K_j.

The selection function is defined by the Hamming weight W of an intermediate k-bit-wise result $f(X, j, i)$. $f(X, j, i)$ can be a primitive operation $X_j * i$, wherein $*$ marks the actual operation used.

$$d(X, j, i) = W(f(X, j, i)) - \overline{W(f(X, j, i))} \tag{4}$$

$\overline{W(f(X, j, i))}$ is the mean value of the Hamming weight for the function $f(X, j, i)$ using a summation of all possible input values X. Group operations that are bijective and show a uniform distribution of the resulting values lead to the mean $\overline{W(f(X, j, i))} = k/2$.

If the power leakage is dominated by the Hamming distance the selection function is modified to

$$d(X, j, i) = W(Z_j \oplus (f(X, j, i))) - \overline{W(f(X, j, i))} \tag{5}$$

where Z_j is an additional data item (which can be either constant or random, known or secret) that is in conjunction with the predecessor or successor, the secret intermediate value to be attacked. If Z_j is zero, the Hamming weight model is revealed as a special case of the Hamming distance model. The application of the Hamming weight model can lead to erroneous results, e.g. if $*$ is the XOR operation and Z_j is a constant nonzero value, DPA will point to $(Z_j \oplus K_j)$ as the correct key value. Note, that in the case where Z_j is a random secret value, (first order) DPA will fail. Generally, the Hamming distance model requires a more detailed analysis of the implementation than the Hamming weight model.

If the selection function $d(X, j, i)$ is zero for certain values of X, these single measurements are neglected for DPA; otherwise they are weighted according to the result of the selection function. This multi-bit approach is different to [3] who suggested to use only measurements with the extreme results of $d(X, j, i)$, namely $k/2$ and $-k/2$, which, however, results in highly increased measurement costs. Using our method, only $\binom{k}{k/2}$ single measurements are discarded.

DPA tests for significant statistical power differences between the distributions of single measurements with positive and negative values of $d(X, j, i)$. According to [3] we assume that the data dependent power difference $\Delta P(X, t) = P(X, t) - \overline{P(X, t)}$ is proportional to the Hamming weight of processed data. This power difference $\Delta P(X, t)$ is the signal to be detected.

The DPA results presented here were produced by using the correlation method as follows:

$$c(t, j, i) = \frac{\sum_m d(X_m, j, i)\, \Delta P(X_m, t)}{\sqrt{\sum_m d(X_m, j, i)^2}\sqrt{\sum_m \Delta P(X_m, t)^2}} \tag{6}$$

The number m runs through all single measurements. The correlation coefficient $c(t, j, i)$ will be near zero if the selection function $d(X, j, i)$ and $\Delta P(X, t)$ are uncorrelated. In case of a strong correlation $c(t, j, i)$ approaches 1 or -1 at some points in time.

The following subsections exclusively deal with the generally applicable assumption of the Hamming weight model. The selection functions are to be modified if the Hamming distance is the major source of correlation signals.

3.1   Boolean Operation XOR

XOR is the most important boolean operation that is used in cryptographic algorithms. The selection function used is
$$d(X, j, i) = W(X_j \oplus i) - k/2$$

The correlation coefficient between $d(X, j, i)$ and the power consumption $\Delta P(X, t)$ reaches the maximum if i equals K_j and the minimum if i is $\neg K_j$. The absolute value of the correlation coefficient for both cases is the same. If the power consumption increases with the Hamming weight (which is the normal case), the correct key hypothesis has a positive correlation coefficient; otherwise the correlation coefficient is negative. If the attacker does not know the sign of the linear dependency, a small brute-force analysis has to be applied. Besides the correct value and its bitwise inverted value, less significant correlation coefficients occur at other key hypotheses that differ only by 1-3 bits regarding the correct key hypothesis or the bitwise inverted key hypothesis. Key hypotheses that differ by 4 bits are uncorrelated. The number of key hypotheses that differ by m bits regarding a certain correct key hypothesis is given by $\binom{k}{m}$.

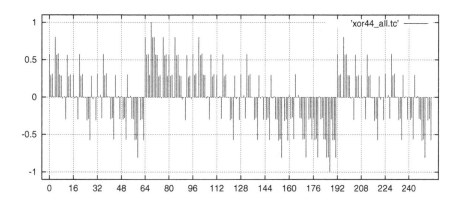

Fig. 1. Correlation coefficient (y-axis) versus all key hypotheses (x-axis) for a XOR operation in case the key hypothesis 68 (0x44) is correct. The results were obtained using simulation data.

Other binary operations such as OR, AND, NOR, NAND, do not form a group operation on the set $\mathbb{Z}_n$. A corresponding k-bit selection function leads to the fact that $W(f(X, j, i))$ is dependent on the key hypothesis as the number of single measurements that yield a certain Hamming weight is determined by the number of bits set to 1.

3.2   Addition Modulo 2^n

Addition and XOR operation are related primitive operations with the difference that the carry propagates between the bit positions.

The selection function uses the addition modulo 2^n which is denoted by the symbol $\boxplus$. For the case $j = 0$ the selection function is
$$d(X, 0, i) = W(X_0 \boxplus i) - k/2.$$

In case of $j > 0$ the carry of all previous additions has to be incorporated as $C(X_0, K_0, ..., X_{j-1}, K_{j-1}) \in \{0, 1\}$. This results in
$$d(X, j, i) = W(X_j \boxplus i \boxplus C(X_0, K_0, ..., X_{j-1}, K_{j-1})) - k/2$$

In contrast to boolean operations there is a preferred direction for DPA starting from the least significant block $j = 0$ to incorporate the carry. The

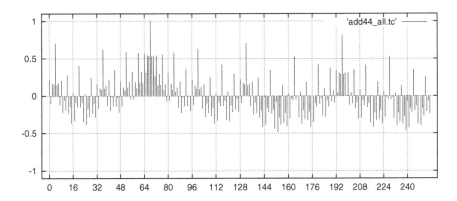

Fig. 2. Correlation coefficient versus all key hypotheses in case of an Addition modulo 2^n with the correct key hypothesis 68 (0x44). The results were obtained using simulation data.

correlation coefficient between $d(X, j, i)$ and the power consumption $\Delta P(X, t)$ reaches the maximum if i equals K_j.

Besides the correct value less significant correlation coefficients occur at related hypotheses. The ranking of these hypotheses is $\{K_j, K_j \pm 2^{k-1}, K_j \pm 2^{k-2}, ...\}$ and can be explained by the carry propagation. The result of the selection function using $K_j \pm 2^{k-1}$ differs for all possible values of X_j only by 1-bit with respect to the correct Hamming weight assuming that not all more significant bits of K are set to 1. The two hypotheses $K_j \pm 2^{k-2}$ lead for $2^k/2$ values to a 1-bit difference, for $2^k/4$ values to a zero-bit difference, but for $2^k/4$ values the Hamming weight differs by 2-bits. If the hypotheses differ only at the least significant bit position with respect to the correct key value, the carry propagation leads to a maximal mismatch of the prediction at the transition values 0 and $2^k - 1$.

3.3 Modular Multiplication

The set $\mathbb{Z}_n^* = \{a \in \mathbb{Z}_n | gcd(a, n) = 1\}$ forms a group with the operation multiplication modulo n, whereas the set $\mathbb{Z}_n$ is not a group.

For IDEA a modified multiplication modulo $n = 2^{16} + 1$ is relevant which is denoted by $\odot$. The number of key hypotheses (2^{16}) for DPA is computationally costly, but still feasible using standard equipment. This algebraic operation can be interpreted as a large S-box though it is not implemented as a look-up table. The selection function is

$$d(X, j, i) = W((X \odot i)_j) - k/2.$$

The simulation results in Figure 3 show that some signals occur at related hypotheses. We observed related hypotheses which are given by four sequences $K_{1,m}, K_{2,m}, K_{3,m}$ and $K_{4,m}$ ($m \in \{0, 1, 2, 3, ...\}$), namely

1. $K_{1,m} = 2^m K \bmod n,$
2. $K_{2,m} = 2^m (n - K) \bmod n,$
3. the following recursive sequence of divisors starting with $K_{3,0} = K$:

   if $K_{3,m}$ is even, then $K_{3,m+1} = \frac{K_{3,m}}{2}$;

   otherwise, $K_{3,m+1} = \frac{(n - K_{3,m})}{2}$.
4. $K_{4,m} = (n - K_{3,m})$

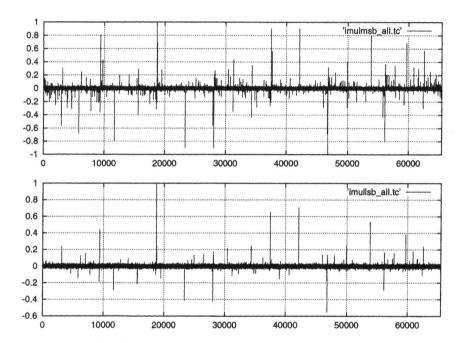

Fig. 3. Correlation coefficient versus all key hypotheses in case the key hypothesis 18737 (0x4931) is correct. The results were obtained using simulation data. The selection function used was at the most significant byte (upper picture) and at the least significant byte (lower picture).

To give an example regarding Figure 3: let the correct key value be 0x4931. Then the related key hypotheses are

1. $K_1 = \{$0x4931, 0x9262, 0x24C3, 0x4986, 0x930C,$\dots\}$
2. $K_2 = \{$0xB6D0, 0x6D9F, 0xDB3E, 0xB67B, 0x6CF5,$\dots\}$
3. $K_3 = \{$0x4931, 0x5B68, 0x2DB4, 0x16DA, 0x0B6D,$\dots\}$
4. $K_4 = \{$0xB6D0, 0xA499, 0xD24D, 0xE927, 0xF494,$\dots\}$

In case of an 8-bit hardware architecture, both the least significant byte and the most significant byte of the intermediate result can be used for DPA. The correct key value is more highlighted at the least significant byte of the selection function.

As the number of key hypotheses is increased to 2^{16}, DPA against an unknown implementation of IDEA's modified multiplication is much more time-consuming compared to DES or AES. A two-stage approach is desirable that first localizes the relevant points in time and afterwards applies DPA using all key hypotheses. The selection function at the most significant byte can be used for this purpose. For instance, a test based on all hypotheses showed that more than 99,9 % of them are detected at the first stage DPA step using 2^{14} key hypotheses. For this test we assumed that secondary correlation signals can be detected for $m < 5$ for all four sequences. Further improvements are likely to succeed.

4   Application to IDEA, RC6, and the HMAC-Construction

4.1   IDEA

IDEA uses three 16-bit group operations as there are XOR ($\oplus$), addition modulo 2^{16} ($\boxplus$) and the multiplication modulo $2^{16} + 1$ ($\odot$) which treats the all-zero subblock as 2^{16} ([11], [16]). The IDEA encryption is reprinted below.

```
for r:=0 to 8 {
```
$$X_1 = X_1 \odot K_1^{(r)}; X_4 = X_4 \odot K_4^{(r)}; X_2 = X_2 \boxplus K_2^{(r)}; X_3 = X_3 \boxplus K_3^{(r)};$$
$$t_0 = K_5^{(r)} \odot (X_1 \oplus X_3);$$
$$t_1 = K_6^{(r)} \odot (t_0 \boxplus (X_2 \oplus X_4));$$
$$t_2 = t_0 \boxplus t_1;$$
$$X_1 = X_1 \oplus t_1; X_4 = X_4 \oplus t_2; a = X_2 \oplus t_2; X_2 = X_3 \oplus t_1; X_3 = a;$$
```
}
```
$$Y_1 = X_1 \odot K_1^{(9)}; Y_4 = X_4 \odot K_4^{(9)}; Y_2 = X_3 \boxplus K_2^{(9)}; Y_3 = X_2 \boxplus K_3^{(9)};$$

X_1, X_2, X_3 and X_4 are the four 16-bit input words, and Y_1, Y_2, Y_3 and Y_4 are the four 16-bit output words. $K_1^{(r)}$ to $K_6^{(r)}$ are the 16-bit subkey values entering round r of IDEA. Due to the key schedule, the first eight 16-bit subkeys directly give the original IDEA key.

The selection functions used are set up on the operations $\boxplus$ and $\odot$. DPA against the subkey values $K_1^{(r)}$, $K_4^{(r)}$, $K_5^{(r)}$ and $K_6^{(r)}$ uses the operation $\odot$ for the selection function; DPA against the subkey values $K_2^{(r)}$ and $K_3^{(r)}$ uses the operation $\boxplus$.

The operation $\oplus$ can also serve as an additional selection function that reduces remaining candidates of previous results.

4.2   RC6

The design of RC6 makes use of simple primitive operations (integer addition modulo 2^w, integer multiplication modulo 2^w , bitwise exclusive-or and key-dependent bit rotations).

RC6-w/r/b ([12]) works on four w-bit registers A, B, C and D which contain the plaintext and the corresponding ciphertext. The number of rounds is given by r and b denotes the number of key bytes. The key schedule of RC6 yields $2r + 4$ w-bit subkeys $S[i]$, with $i \in \{0, 1, ..., 2r + 3\}$. The RC6-w/r/b encryption is reprinted below.

```
B = B + S[0];
D = D + S[1];
for i:=1 to r {
        t = (B × (2B + 1)) ≪ lg w;
        u = (D × (2D + 1)) ≪ lg w;
        A = ((A ⊕ t) ≪ u) + S[2i];
        C = ((C ⊕ u) ≪ t) + S[2i+1];
        (A, B, C, D) = (B, C, D, A);
}
A = A + S[2r + 2];
C = C + S[2r + 3];
```

Key addition is carried out using the addition modulo 2^w. The first keys to be attacked are $S[0]$ and $S[1]$ using the known values B and D. During each iteration, A, B, C, D, t and u are known if all previous subkeys are already compromised by DPA. The key hypotheses are set up on $S[2i]$ and $S[2i + 1]$. The selection function is always the addition modulo 2^w. Signals are expected in the subsequent iteration wherein this intermediate value acts as partial multiplicator. Due to the complex key schedule all r rounds of RC6-w/r/b have to be attacked by DPA iteratively.

4.3   HMAC-Construction

The specification of the HMAC construction can be found in [13] and [14]. The HMAC makes use of a secure hash function H, as e.g. RIPEMD-160 and SHA-1. Let $Text$ be the input message to be secured for message authentication and let K be the secret key used. Further, two fixed strings $ipad$ and $opad$ are defined. The HMAC is a nested construction that uses two calls to the hash function H.

$$HMAC(Text, K) = H(K \oplus opad, H(K \oplus ipad, Text)) \qquad (7)$$

As the first block for each call to H is a constant value that depends only on K in efficient implementations these two values can be precalculated and stored instead of K. Let the two secret values for the inner and outer hash function be defined as follows:

$$K_i = H(K \oplus ipad) \qquad (8)$$

and

$$K_o = H(K \oplus opad) \qquad (9)$$

In the HMAC-Construction these initialisation vectors IV are the secret values K_i and K_o to be attacked by DPA.

DPA is applied against the first iterations of the inner hash function of the HMAC and after the disclosure of K_i afterwards against the first iterations of the outer hash function. The preferred choice is to start DPA at the first iteration of the hash function which is assumed in the following considerations.

The selection functions depend on the hash function used. The concrete procedure is given only for RIPEMD-160; the approach for SHA-1 is similar.

HMAC-RIPEMD-160. In [15] RIPEMD-160 is specified including a pseudo code in Annex A that is reprinted below for the main loop of iterations.

```
for j:=0 to 79{
        T = rol_{s(j)} (A + f(j,B,C,D) + X[r(j)] + K(j)) + E;
        A:= E; E:=D; D:= rol_{10}(C); C:= B; B:=T;
        T = rol_{s'(j)} (A' + f(79-j,B',C',D') + X[r'(j)] + K'(j)) + E';
        A':= E'; E':=D'; D':= rol_{10}(C'); C':= B'; B':=T';
}
```

The secret IV is splitted into the five 32-bit words A, B, C, D and E as well as A', B', C', D' and E' before this main loop. X is the message. For each iteration j, $s(j)$ and $s'(j)$ give the number of left shifts and $r(j)$ and $r(j')$ are the number of the message block. The addition $+$ is modulo 2^{32}.

Herein, we focus on the calculation of the five 32-bit words A, B, C, D, and E and skip the similar parallel processing part. For the first 16 iterations, $r(j)$ equals j and the compression function f is $f(x,y,z) = x \oplus y \oplus z$.

The selection functions are applied at successive intermediate results d_1 to d_5 that occur during the processing of the first three iterations. The intermediate results at d_1, d_2, and d_4 are revealed by an addition modulo 2^{32}, d_3 and d_5 are obtained by a XOR operation. The key value to be attacked at each selection function is included in brackets '[' and ']'. An additional subindex is used which denotes the current iteration number.

Intermediate results at the first iteration:
$$d_1 = [A_0 + (B_0 \oplus C_0 \oplus D_0)] + X_0$$
$$d_2 = T_0 = rol_{11}(A_0 + (B_0 \oplus C_0 \oplus D_0) + X_0) + [E_0]$$

Intermediate results at the second iteration:
$$d_3 = B_1 \oplus [C_1 \oplus D_1] = T_0 \oplus [(B_0 \oplus rol_{10}(C_0))]$$
$$d_4 = T_1 = rol_{14}(A_1 + (B_1 \oplus C_1 \oplus D_1) + X_1) + [E_1] =$$
$$rol_{14}(E_0 + (T_0 \oplus (B_0 \oplus rol_{10}(C_0)) + X_1) + [D_0]$$

Intermediate results at the third iteration:
$$d_5 = B_2 \oplus C_2 \oplus [D_2] = T_1 \oplus (B_1 \oplus [rol_{10}(C_1)]) = T_1 \oplus (T_0 \oplus [rol_{10}(B_0)])$$

If DPA is successful, the results of all selection functions can be combined to reveal A_0, B_0, C_0, D_0 and E_0 which is the IV.

5   Experimental Results of an IDEA Implementation

For the experimental testing IDEA was chosen as it uses three algebraic groups. The IDEA implementation was carried out in Assembly on an 8051 microcontroller (CISC, von-Neumann architecture) and on an 8-bit ATM163 AVR microcontroller (RISC, Harvard architecture). It was assured that both implementations have a constant execution time to exclude broad correlation signals based on timing displacements. The implementations did not include software countermeasures to counteract DPA.

In both tests the DPA characteristics of the simulation results were confirmed using the Hamming weight model. For the 8051 microcontroller we obtained nearly perfect DPA signals. The experimental results are presented in more detail for the ATM163 AVR microcontroller which turned out to be the more difficult analysis.

At a previous characterisation step of the ATM163 the following properties were determined:

- The outstanding DPA signals are caused by Hamming distances of data that is subsequently transferred on the internal bus.
- Correlation signals on the input data to an operation can be revealed with sufficient clarity using the Hamming weight model whereas correlation signals on the output data of an operation are difficult to prove.

Consequently, the Hamming weight model is expected to be successful at the points in time that process the output data of previous operations as the input values.

An additional result is that care has to be taken at the load sequence when alternating key data with known input/output data at subsequent instructions at an AVR core. If known data and secret data are moved one after the other from the SRAM to the working registers using the *ldd* instruction, nearly perfect correlation signals are revealed using the 8-bit XOR selection function. Note, that this observation was also made if two *ldd* instructions are seperated by some arithmetic instructions. An appropriate countermeasure would be to encapsulate the transfer of secret key data by the load of internal, random data.

For the experimental analysis, 5000 single measurements were accumulated at a sampling rate of 200 MHz using a standard DPA measurement set-up. The IDEA key used was in hexadecimal notation:
    '7E 24 95 E1 E5 0C 86 CE 8C C3 1B 80 C0 65 B2 AF'

Addition modulo 2^{16}: Generally, if not superposed by strong correlation signals on the input data, the correct key values are revealed by DPA using 8-bit selection functions for the modular addition. The particular points in time that show correlation signals on the input data can be independently identified by correlation signals on the input data of IDEA.

The experimental DPA characteristics do not always correspond to the expected ones (see Fig. 4). The deviations can be explained by the superposing of signals, especially by leakage of the input data. The analysis on the primary origin of each signal obtained turns out to be a difficult task on the ATM163.

The following is the actual code sequence of the modular addition:

```
ldd r0,Z+2 ; 1st addition: load subkey bytes from SRAM
ldd r1,Z+3
add r5,r1 ; addition with input bytes
adc r4,r0
ldd r0,Z+4 ; 2nd addition: load subkey bytes from SRAM
ldd r1,Z+5
add r21,r1 ; addition with input bytes
adc r20,r0
```

The *add* instruction turns out to be extremely vulnerable against the 8-bit XOR selection function if certain registers are used. In the current example, the instruction *add r5, r1* yields significant DPA signals using the 8-bit XOR selection function at the least significant key byte (see Fig. 5). However, this strong dependency was not confirmed at the instruction *add r21, r1*.

Multiplication modulo $2^{16}+1$: The points in time that yield high signals are identified using the advantage, that the key is known. DPA yielded clear correlation signals for the least and most significant byte of the selection function at all relevant positions in time (see Fig. 6). The experimental DPA characteristics are consistent with the expected ones.

As result, the Hamming weight selection function was sucessfully applied, even in presence of a hardware platform that leaks for the most part differential signals.

6   Conclusions

This contribution provides an analysis of DPA signals that are revealed in n-bit sized primitive operations such as XOR, addition modulo 2^n and modular multiplication. The characteristics of the DPA results differ for these basic operations and can support the analysis of an unknown implementation.

The theoretical approach to apply DPA in ciphers and message authentication based on primitive operations is included, as are the specific examples of IDEA, RC6 and the HMAC-Construction.

Experimentally, both an IDEA implementation on an 8051 microcontroller and on an AVR ATM163 microcontroller were evaluated. The Hamming weight model was successfully applied at the primitive operations for both architectures and the expected DPA characteristics were confirmed.

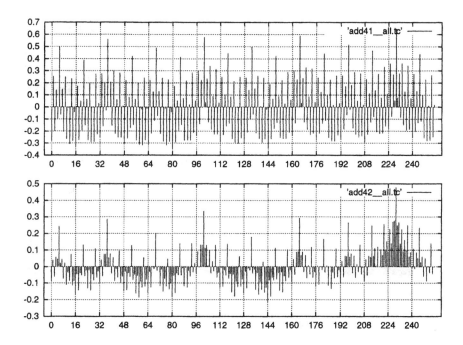

Fig. 4. Correlation coefficient versus all key hypotheses using the ADD selection function at two different points in time. The correct key value 229 (0xE5) for the most significant byte of K_3 is revealed, but only the characteristic in the lower plot points to a pure signal. During the time of the upper plot (negative) correlation signals on the input data are also proven.

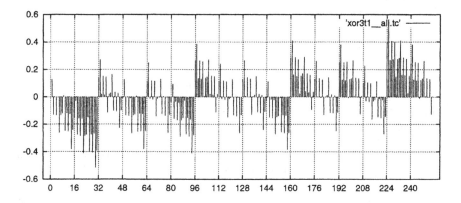

Fig. 5. Correlation coefficient versus all key hypotheses using the XOR selection function at the ldd instruction $ldd\ r1, Z + 3$. The correct key value 225 (0xE1) for the least significant byte of K_2 is revealed.

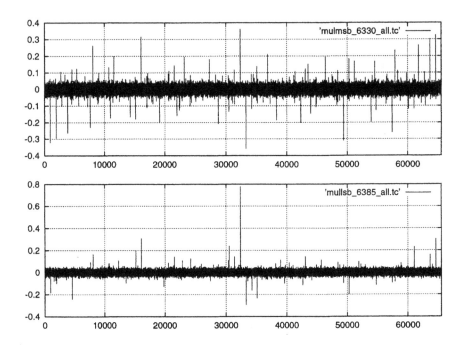

Fig. 6. Correlation coefficient versus all key hypotheses at two points in time. The key value K_1=32292 (0x7E24) is confirmed. The selection function used was at the most significant byte (upper plot) and at the least significant byte (lower plot).

Acknowledgements. The authors thank Gregor Leander and Jonathan Hammell for the valuable comments which improved this paper.

References

1. S. Chari, C. Jutla, J. R. Rao, P. Rohatgi, *A Cautionary Note Regarding Evaluation of AES Candidates on Smart-Cards*, Proceedings of the second AES conference, pp. 135-150, 1999
2. P. Kocher, J. Jaffe, B. Jun, *Differential Power Analysis*, Advances in Cryptology — Crypto '99 Proceedings, LNCS 1666, pages 388-397, Springer, 1999
3. T. Messerges, E. Dabbish, R. Sloan, *Investigation of Power Analysis Attacks on Smartcards*, USENIX Workshop on Smartcard Techonolgy, USENIX Association, 1999, pp. 151-161
4. R. Mayer-Sommer, *Smartly Analyzing the Simplicity and the Power of Simple Power Analysis on Smartcards*, Cryptographic Hardware and Embedded Systems — CHES 2000, LNCS 1965, pages 78-92, Springer, 2000
5. M. Aigner, E. Oswald, *Power Analysis Tutorial*, available at http://www.iaik.tu-graz.ac.at/aboutus/people/oswald/papers/dpa_tutorial.pdf

6. E. Oswald, B. Preneel, *A Theoretical Evaluation of some NESSIE Candidates regarding their Susceptibility towards Power Analysis Attacks*, October 4, 2002, available at http://www.cosic.esat.kuleuven.ac.be/nessie/reports/phase2/kulwp5-022-1.pdf

7. J. Kelsey, B. Schneier, D. Wagner, C. Hall, *Side Channel Cryptanalysis of Product Ciphers*, Journal of Computer Security, v. 8, n. 2-3, 2000, pp. 141-158.

8. E. Brier, C. Clavier, F. Olivier, *Optimal Statistical Power Analysis*, IACR Cryptology ePrint Archive, Report 2003/152, available at: http://eprint.iacr.org/2003/152.pdf

9. L. Goubin, *A Sound Method for Switching between Boolean and Arithmetic Masking*, Cryptographic Hardware and Embedded Systems — CHES 2001, LNCS 2162, pages 3-15, Springer, 2001

10. J.-S. Coron, A. Tchulkine, *A New Algorithm for Switching from Arithmetic to Boolean Masking*, Cryptographic Hardware and Embedded Systems — CHES 2003, LNCS 2779, pages 89-97, Springer, 2003

11. X. Lai, J. L. Massey, *Markov Ciphers and Differential Cryptanalysis*, Advances in Cryptology — Eurocrypt '91, LNCS 547, pages 17-38, Springer, 1991

12. R. L. Rivest, M. J. B. Robshaw, R. Sidney, X. L. Yin, *The $RC6^{TM}$ Block Cipher*, Version 1.1, August 20, 1998

13. M. Bellare, R. Canetti, H. Krawczyk, *Message Authentication using Hash Functions — The HMAC Construction*, RSA Laboratories' CryptoBytes, Vol. 2, No. 1, 1996

14. M. Bellare, R. Canetti, H. Krawczyk, *Keying Hash Functions for Message Authentication*, Advances in Cryptology — Crypto '96 Proceedings, LNCS 1109, N. Koblitz ed, Springer, 1996

15. H. Dobbertin, A. Bosselaers, B. Preneel, *RIPEMD-160: A Strengthened Version of RIPEMD*, Fast Software Encryption, Cambridge Workshop, LNCS 1039, pages 71-82, Springer, 1996, corrected version available at http://www.esat.kuleuven.ac.be/~cosicart/pdf/AB-9601/AB-9601.pdf

16. A. Menezes, P. van Oorschot, S. Vanstone, *Handbook of Applied Cryptography*, CRC Press, 1996

17. *ATmega163 ATmega163L, 8-bit AVR Microcontroller with 16K Bytes In-System Programmable Flash*, Rev. 1142E-AVR-02/03, Atmel, available at www.atmel.com

Side-Channel Attacks in ECC:
A General Technique for Varying the
Parametrization of the Elliptic Curve

Loren D. Olson

Dept. of Mathematics and Statistics
University of Tromsø
N-9037 Tromsø, Norway

Abstract. Side-channel attacks in elliptic curve cryptography occur with the unintentional leakage of information during processing. A critical operation is that of computing nP where n is a positive integer and P is a point on the elliptic curve E. Implementations of the binary algorithm may reveal whether $P + Q$ is computed for $P \neq Q$ or $P = Q$ as the case may be. Several methods of dealing with this problem have been suggested. Here we describe a general technique for producing a large number of different representations of the points on E in characteristic $p \geq 5$, all having a uniform implementation of $P + Q$. The parametrization may be changed for each computation of nP at essentially no cost. It is applicable to all elliptic curves in characteristic $p \geq 5$, and thus may be used with all curves included in present and future standards for $p \geq 5$.

Keywords: Elliptic curves, ECC, cryptography, side-channel attacks, weighted projective curves, uniform addition formula.

1   Introduction

Side-channel attacks in elliptic curve cryptography (ECC) have received considerable attention. They take advantage of information unintentionally leaked from a supposedly tamper-resistant device. Such information is often obtained via measurements of power consumption or timing. In ECC, a fundamental operation is the computation of nP where n is an integer and P is a point on the elliptic curve E at hand. A naive implementation of the binary algorithm for this computation may reveal whether $P + Q$ is computed for $P \neq Q$ or $P = Q$ (doubling). One method of defense against this attack is to find a parametrization of the points on the elliptic curve E such that the implementation of the group law does not reveal any information in this regard. Several authors have suggested specific parametrizations, notably Liardet and Smart ([1]) with the intersection of two quadric surfaces, Joye and Quisquater ([2]) with a Hessian model, and Billet and Joye ([3]) with the Jacobi quartic. The latter provided a great deal of the motivation for the present work.

M. Joye and J.-J. Quisquater (Eds.): CHES 2004, LNCS 3156, pp. 220–229, 2004.

We discuss a general technique for producing a large number of different representations of the points on an elliptic curve and its group law all having a uniform computation of $P + Q$. This gives rise to a corresponding variation in the implementation of ECC to avoid certain side-channel attacks. Concretely, given an elliptic curve E with identity element e and any point $M \neq e$ on it, we may attach to the pair (E, M) a weighted projective quartic curve C_M which is isomorphic to E. On this curve C_M, we will be able to compute $P+Q$ in a uniform fashion. The point M and thus the curve C_M may be changed at virtually no cost, so that a new parametrization may be chosen for each computation of nP.

2   The General Technique

In this section we present the mathematics of our technique. Let k be a field of characteristic different from 2 and 3. Consider an elliptic curve $E \subseteq \mathbb{P}^2$ defined by the homogeneous equation

$$Y^2Z = X^3 + a_4XZ^2 + a_6Z^3 \tag{1}$$

with identity element $e = (0, 1, 0)$. Let $M \neq e$ be a k-rational point on E with coordinates $M = (\alpha, \beta, 1)$. Define constants $c_i \in k$ as follows

$$
\begin{aligned}
c_2 &= -(3\alpha/2) \\
c_3 &= -\beta \\
c_4 &= -(4a_4 + 3\alpha^2)/16
\end{aligned}
\tag{2}
$$

Let D_M be the affine quartic curve defined by

$$
\begin{aligned}
W^2 = R(S) &= S^4 + c_2S^2 + c_3S + c_4 \\
&= S^4 - (3\alpha/2)S^2 - \beta S - (4a_4 + 3\alpha^2)/16
\end{aligned}
\tag{3}
$$

This will be the affine part of the curve we wish to associate to the elliptic curve E and the point $M \neq e$.

Conversely, consider a quartic plane curve given by the affine equation

$$W^2 = R(S) = S^4 + c_2S^2 + c_3S + c_4 \tag{4}$$

with $c_i \in k$ such that $R(S)$ has no multiple roots. Define

$$
\begin{aligned}
a_4 &= -[(c_2^2/3) + 4c_4] \\
a_6 &= [2(c_2/3)^3 - 8(c_2c_4/3) + c_3^2] \\
\alpha &= -2c_2/3 \\
\beta &= -c_3
\end{aligned}
\tag{5}
$$

Then the equation

$$Y^2Z = X^3 + a_4XZ^2 + a_6Z^3 \tag{6}$$

defines an elliptic curve E together with a point $M \neq e$ on E with coordinates $M = (\alpha, \beta, 1)$. There is an isomorphism between $E - \{M, e\}$ and D_M given by

$$
\begin{aligned}
S &= (Y + \beta)/2(X - \alpha) \\
W &= (X/2) + (\alpha/4) - (Y + \beta)^2/4(X - \alpha)^2 \\
X &= 2W + 2S^2 - (\alpha/2) \\
Y &= 4SW + 4S^3 - 3\alpha S - \beta
\end{aligned}
\tag{7}
$$

These formulas are classical and may be found, for example, in Fricke ([5]); here they are slightly modified to conform with the standard notation for the Weierstrass equation.

If we homogenize equation (4) by introducing a variable T to obtain

$$W^2T^2 = S^4 + c_2S^2T^2 + c_3ST^3 + c_4T^4 \tag{8}$$

this equation will define a projective quartic curve in $\mathbb{P}^2$. This curve has a singular point at infinity and is not very convenient for our purposes. However, a slight variant of this will prove highly useful, as we shall now see.

A very helpful and unifying concept in studying elliptic curves, parametrizations with quartic curves, and various choices of coordinates is that of weighted projective spaces. A good reference for an introduction to the subject is Reid ([4]).

Definition 1. *Let $n \geq 1$ and $d_0, \dots, d_n \geq 1$ be positive integers. Weighted projective space $\mathbb{P} = \mathbb{P}(d_0, \dots, d_n)$ consists of all equivalence classes of $n+1$-tuples $(x_0, \dots, x_n)$ where not all x_i are zero and $(x_0, \dots, x_n) \sim (\lambda^{d_0}x_0, \dots, \lambda^{d_n}x_n)$ for $\lambda \in k^*$. We refer to $(d_0, \dots, d_n)$ as the* weight system.

This concept then encompasses the standard definition of projective space $\mathbb{P}^n$ with all $d_i = 1$ and provides a natural context for Jacobian coordinates, Chudnovsky coordinates, López-Dahab coordinates, etc. We may speak of weighted homogeneous polynomials and weighted projective varieties.

Remark 1. Throughout the remainder of this article *weighted* will refer to the weight system $(1, 1, 2)$ and $\mathbb{P} = \mathbb{P}(1, 1, 2)$. We denote the coordinate system in $\mathbb{P}$ by (S, T, W).

Returning to the material at hand, the weighted homogeneous equation

$$W^2 = S^4 + c_2S^2T^2 + c_3ST^3 + c_4T^4 \tag{9}$$

now defines a weighted quartic projective curve C_M in $\mathbb{P} = \mathbb{P}(1, 1, 2)$. The affine part where $T \neq 0$ is just D_M. C_M contains the two points $(1, 0, 1)$ and $(1, 0, -1)$ in addition. C_M is non-singular and is an elliptic curve with $(1, 0, 1)$ as identity element. E is isomorphic to C_M where the isomorphism on D_M is described previously and $e \leftrightarrow (1, 0, 1)$ and $M \leftrightarrow (1, 0, -1)$. We also note the following: If $\beta \neq 0$, then $-M = (\alpha, -\beta) \leftrightarrow (-(3\alpha^2 + 4)/4\beta, 1, (3\alpha/4) - ((3\alpha^2 + 4)/4\beta)^2))$.

3   The Group Law on C_M

We shall now make explicit the group law on C_M, and show that the addition of two points on C_M may be given by formulas independent of whether the two points are equal or not. Let $\phi : E \to C_M$ be the isomorphism given above. We shall compute using coordinates in the two weighted projective spaces $\mathbb{P}^2 = \mathbb{P}(1,1,1)$ and $\mathbb{P}(1,1,2)$, which are the respective ambient spaces for E and C_M. First, let $Q = (s,1,w)$ be a k-rational point with $Q \in C_M - \{(1,0,1), \pm(1,0,-1)\}$ and let $-Q = (\bar{s},1,\bar{w})$. Then $\bar{s} = -s - (c_3/(2w + s^2 + c_2))$ and $\bar{w} = w + s^2 - \bar{s}^2$. Let $P_i = (x_i, y_i, 1)$ be k-rational points on $E - \{M, e\}$ corresponding to points $Q_i = (s_i, 1, w_i)$ on $D_M - \{(1,0,1),(1,0,-1)\}$ via ϕ, i.e. $\phi(P_i) = Q_i$. Assume $P_1 \neq -P_2$ and that $P_1 + P_2 = P_3$, so that $Q_1 + Q_2 = Q_3$. We wish to compute the coordinates of Q_3 in terms of the coordinates of Q_1 and Q_2. We will utilize ϕ as well as the classical formulas for computing P_3 to achieve this. They are given by

$$
\begin{aligned}
x_3 &= \lambda^2 - x_1 - x_2 \\
y_3 &= \lambda(x_1 - x_3) - y_1 \\
&= \lambda(x_2 - x_3) - y_2 \\
2y_3 &= \lambda(x_1 + x_2 - 2x_3) - (y_1 + y_2)
\end{aligned}
\tag{10}
$$

where

$$
\lambda = \begin{cases} (y_2 - y_1)/(x_2 - x_1) & \text{for } P_1 \neq P_2 \\ (3x_1^2 + a_4)/2y_1 & \text{for } P_1 = P_2 \end{cases}
$$

Brier and Joye ([6]) have previously consolidated these two formulas into one single formula for λ, thus providing a uniform implementation of the computation of $P + Q$ for elliptic curves in Weierstrass form. We briefly recall their computation in the case of $char(k) \geq 5$ as follows:

$$
\begin{aligned}
y_2^2 &= x_2^3 + a_4 x_2 + a_6 \\
y_1^2 &= x_1^3 + a_4 x_1 + a_6 \\
y_2^2 - y_1^2 &= (x_2^3 - x_1^3) + a_4(x_2 - x_1)
\end{aligned}
$$

Thus for $P_1 \neq P_2$,

$$
\begin{aligned}
(y_2 + y_1)\lambda &= (y_2^2 - y_1^2)/(x_2 - x_1) \\
&= (x_2^2 + x_1 x_2 + x_1^2) + a_4
\end{aligned}
$$

and

$$
\lambda = [(x_2^2 + x_1 x_2 + x_1^2) + a_4]/(y_2 + y_1)
\tag{11}
$$

On the other hand, if $P_1 = P_2$, then this formula for λ reduces to $\lambda = (3x_1^2 + a_4)/2y$ which is precisely the formula given above in the original definition of λ.

In our case, we are interested in computing Q_3 in terms of the coordinates of Q_1 and Q_2. We begin by computing the quantity $\tau = (w_2 - w_1)/(s_2 - s_1)$. In a fashion similar to the above, we have

$$w_2^2 = s_2^4 + c_2 s_2^2 + c_3 s_2 + c_4$$
$$w_1^2 = s_1^4 + c_2 s_1^2 + c_3 s_1 + c_4$$
$$w_2^2 - w_1^2 = (s_2^4 - s_1^4) + c_2(s_2^2 - s_1^2) + c_3(s_2 - s_1)$$
$$(w_2^2 - w_1^2)/(s_2 - s_1) = (s_2^2 + s_1^2 + c_2)(s_2 + s_1) + c_3$$
$$(w_2 + w_1)\tau = (s_2^2 + s_1^2 + c_2)(s_2 + s_1) + c_3$$

Finally, this yields

$$\tau = [(s_2^2 + s_1^2 + c_2)(s_2 + s_1) + c_3]/(w_2 + w_1) \tag{12}$$

We now compute λ in terms of the coordinates of Q_1 and Q_2 as follows:

$$
\begin{aligned}
\lambda &= \frac{y_2 - y_1}{x_2 - x_1} \\
&= \frac{[4s_2 w_2 + 4s_2^3 - 3\alpha s_2 - \beta] - [4s_1 w_1 + 4s_1^3 - 3\alpha s_1 - \beta]}{[2w_2 + 2s_2^2 - (\alpha/2)] - [2w_1 + 2s_1^2 - (\alpha/2)]} \\
&= \frac{[4s_2 w_2 - 4s_1 w_1] + [(4s_2^3 - 4s_1^3) - 3\alpha(s_2 - s_1)]}{2(w_2 - w_1) + 2(s_2^2 - s_1^2)]} \\
&= \frac{[4s_2 w_2 - 4s_1 w_2 + 4s_1 w_2 - 4s_1 w_1] + [(4s_2^3 - 4s_1^3) - 3\alpha(s_2 - s_1)]}{2(w_2 - w_1) + 2(s_2^2 - s_1^2)]} \\
&= \frac{4w_2(s_2 - s_1) + 4s_1(w_2 - w_1) + 4(s_2^2 + s_1 s_2 + s_1^2)(s_2 - s_1) - 3\alpha(s_2 - s_1)}{2(w_2 - w_1) + 2(s_2 + s_1)(s_2 - s_1)]} \\
&= \frac{4w_2 + 4s_1\tau + 4(s_2^2 + s_1 s_2 + s_1^2) - 3\alpha}{2\tau + 2(s_2 + s_1)} \\
&= \frac{4w_2 + 4s_1\tau + 4(s_2^2 + s_1 s_2 + s_1^2) + 2c_2}{2\tau + 2(s_2 + s_1)} \\
&= \frac{2w_2 + 2s_1\tau + 2(s_2^2 + s_1 s_2 + s_1^2) + c_2}{\tau + (s_2 + s_1)} \tag{13}
\end{aligned}
$$

By the symmetry of Q_1 and Q_2, we obtain

$$\lambda = \frac{(w_1 + w_2) + (s_1 + s_2)\tau + 2(s_2^2 + s_1 s_2 + s_1^2) + c_2}{\tau + (s_2 + s_1)} \tag{14}$$

If we now assume that $Q_1 = Q_2$ (i.e. $P_1 = P_2$) and evaluate the above expressions for τ and λ, we obtain

$$
\begin{aligned}
\tau &= \frac{(2s_1^2 + c_2)(2s_1) + c_3}{2w_1} \\
&= \frac{(2s_1^2 - (3\alpha/2))(2s_1) - \beta}{2w_1} \\
&= \frac{4s_1^3 - 3\alpha s_1 - \beta}{2w_1}
\end{aligned}
\tag{15}
$$

Furthermore,

$$
\begin{aligned}
\lambda &= \frac{(4w_1 + 12s_1^2 - 3\alpha) + 4s_1\tau}{4s_1 + 2\tau} \\
&= \frac{(8w_1^2 + 24s_1^2 w_1 - 6\alpha w_1) + 4s_1(2w_1\tau)}{2(4s_1 w_1 + 2w_1\tau)} \\
&= \frac{(8w_1^2 + 24s_1^2 w_1 - 6\alpha w_1) + 4s_1(4s_1^3 - 3\alpha s_1 - \beta)}{2(4s_1 w_1 + 4s_1^3 - 3\alpha s_1 - \beta)} \\
&= \frac{8w_1^2 + 24s_1^2 w_1 - 6\alpha w_1 + 16s_1^4 - 12\alpha s_1^2 - 4\beta s_1}{2y_1} \\
&= \frac{12w_1^2 + 24s_1^2 w_1 + 12s_1^4 - 6\alpha w_1 - 6\alpha s_1^2 + (3\alpha^2/4) + a_4}{2y_1} \\
&= \frac{3[2w_1 + 2s_1^2 - (\alpha/2)]^2 + a_4}{2y_1} \\
&= \frac{3x_1^2 + a_4}{2y_1}
\end{aligned}
\tag{16}
$$

This is exactly the original formula for λ in the case $Q_1 = Q_2$ (i.e. $P_1 = P_2$). Hence (14) gives us a single uniform formula for λ in terms of Q_1 and Q_2 analogous to Brier and Joye ([6]) in the Weierstrass case. We shall use formula (14) in the calculation of the coordinates of $Q_3 = Q_1 + Q_2$.

Let $Q_i = (S_i, T_i, W_i) = (s_i, 1, w_i)$, so that $s_i = S_i/T_i$ and $w_i = W_i/T_i^2$. We have $Q_3 = (s_3, 1, w_3) = ((y_3 + \beta)/2(x_3 - \alpha), 1, (x_3/2) + (\alpha/4) - (y_3 + \beta)^2/4(x_3 - \alpha)^2) = ((y_3 + \beta), 2(x_3 - \alpha), (2x_3 + \alpha)(x_3 - \alpha)^2 - (y_3 + \beta)^2)$. Let

$$
G = w_1 + w_2 + s_1^2 + s_2^2
$$
$$
H = 2s_1 w_1 + 2s_1^3 + 2s_2 w_2 + 2s_2^3 + c_2(s_1 + s_2) + 2c_3
\tag{17}
$$

Then $x_1 + x_2 + \alpha = 2G$ and we have

$$2(y_3 + \beta) = \lambda(x_1 + x_2 - 2x_3) - (y_1 + y_2) - 2c_3 \tag{18}$$
$$= \lambda(-2\lambda^2 + 6G + 2c_2) - [4s_1w_1 + 4s_1^3 + 4s_2w_2 + 4s_2^3$$
$$+ 2c_2(s_1 + s_2) + 4c_3]$$
$$= \lambda(-2\lambda^2 + 6G + 2c_2) - 2H$$

Thus

$$\lambda = \frac{(w_1 + w_2)(G + c_2)}{(s_1 + s_2)(G + c_2) + c_3} + (s_1 + s_2)$$
$$x_3 - \alpha = \lambda^2 - 2G$$
$$2x_3 + \alpha = 2(\lambda^2 - 2G - c_2) \tag{19}$$
$$y_3 + \beta = \lambda(-\lambda^2 + 3G + c_2) - H$$

Putting all this together, we can now state the group law on the weighted quartic C_M formally.

Proposition 1. *Let C_M be the elliptic curve given by the weighted quartic curve $W^2 = S^4 + c_2S^2T^2 + c_3ST^3 + c_4T^4$ in $\mathbb{P}(1,1,2)$. Let $Q_1 = (s_1, 1, t_1)$ and $Q_2 = (s_2, 1, t_2)$ be k-rational points in $C_M - \{(1,0,1),(1,0,-1)\}$ such that $Q_1 \neq -Q_2, -Q_2 + (1,0,-1)$. Let $Q_1 + Q_2 = Q_3$. Then $Q_3 = (\lambda(-\lambda^2 + 3G + c_2) - H, 2(\lambda^2 - 2G), 2(\lambda^2 - 2G - c_2)(\lambda^2 - 2G)^2 - (\lambda(-\lambda^2 + 3G + c_2) - H)^2)$.*

We note that the proposition accomplishes two objectives:
a.) it gives a uniform description of the group law on the weighted quartic C_M, i.e. the addition formula is independent of whether $Q_1 = Q_2$ or not.
b.) the group law is given entirely in terms of the coefficients of the equation for C_M and the coordinates of the Q_i's, making no explicit reference to the curve E and the point M which we had as our starting point. While this is not used in the sequel, it may prove to be of some independent interest.

To make the group law more accessible and to evaluate its usefulness, we provide an algorithm for its computation in the next section.

4   An Algorithm for the Group Law

We will now give an explicit algorithm for the computation of Q_3 in terms of weighted projective coordinates and count the number of multiplications involved. We define quantities e_i and N_j for $i, j = 1, 2, \ldots$ in terms of the c_i's, S_i's, T_i's, and W_i's. The operations used to obtain the e_i will consist of addition/subtraction and multiplication by integer constants ≤ 4. The operation involved in the computation of the N_j will be a single multiplication. This will enable us to keep track of the number of multiplications involved in a convenient fashion. Define

$$N_1 = T_1^2 \qquad\qquad N_2 = T_2^2$$
$$N_3 = T_1 T_2 \qquad\qquad N_4 = S_1 T_2$$
$$N_5 = S_2 T_1 \qquad\qquad N_6 = W_1 N_2$$
$$N_7 = W_2 N_1 \qquad\qquad N_8 = N_3^2$$
$$N_9 = N_3 N_8 \qquad\qquad N_{10} = N_4^2$$
$$N_{11} = N_5^2 \qquad\qquad N_{12} = c_2 N_8$$
$$N_{13} = c_3 N_9 \qquad\qquad e_1 = N_4 + N_5$$
$$e_2 = N_6 + N_7 \qquad\qquad e_3 = e_2 + N_{10} + N_{11} + N_{12}$$
$$e_4 = e_3 + N_{13} \qquad\qquad N_{14} = e_1 e_3 + N_{13}$$
$$e_5 = N_{13} + N_{14} \qquad\qquad N_{15} = e_2 e_3$$
$$N_{16} = e_1 N_{14} \qquad\qquad e_6 = N_{15} + N_{16} \qquad (20)$$
$$e_7 = N_6 + N_{10} \qquad\qquad e_8 = N_7 + N_{11}$$
$$N_{17} = N_4 e_7 \qquad\qquad N_{18} = N_5 e_8$$
$$N_{19} = N_{12} e_1 \qquad\qquad e_9 = 2N_{17} + 2N_{18} + N_{19} + 2N_{13}$$
$$e_{10} = N_6 + N_7 + N_{10} + N_{11} \qquad N_{20} = e_6^2$$
$$N_{21} = N_{14}^2 \qquad\qquad N_{22} = e_{10} N_{21}$$
$$N_{23} = N_{12} N_{21} \qquad\qquad e_{11} = -N_{20} + 3N_{22} + N_{23}$$
$$N_{24} = e_6 e_{11} \qquad\qquad e_{12} = N_{20} - 2N_{22}$$
$$N_{25} = N_3 e_{12} \qquad\qquad N_{26} = N_{25}^2$$
$$e_{13} = 2N_{25} - 2N_{23} \qquad\qquad N_{27} = e_{13} N_{26}$$
$$N_{28} = e_{16}^2 \qquad\qquad e_{14} = N_{27} - N_{28}$$
$$N_{29} = N_{25} N_{14} \qquad\qquad e_{15} = 2N_{29}$$
$$N_{30} = e_9 N_{14} \qquad\qquad N_{31} = N_{30} N_{21}$$
$$e_{16} = N_{24} - N_{31}$$

Some computation yields the following useful formulas

$$T_1 T_2 \lambda = e_6 / N_{14}$$
$$(T_1 T_2)^3 H = e_9 \qquad (21)$$
$$(T_1 T_2)^2 G = e_{10}$$

From Proposition 1 and these formulas, we have that $Q_3 = (\lambda(-\lambda^2 + 3G + c_2) - H, 2(\lambda^2 - 2G), 2(\lambda^2 - 2G - c_2)(\lambda^2 - 2G)^2 - (\lambda(-\lambda^2 + 3G + c_2) - H)^2) = ((T_1 T_2)^3)(\lambda(-\lambda^2 + 3G + c_2) - H), 2(T_1 T_2)^3)(\lambda^2 - 2G), (T_1 T_2)^6)[2(\lambda^2 - 2G - c_2)(\lambda^2 - 2G)^2 - (\lambda(-\lambda^2 + 3G + c_2) - H)^2]) = (e_{16}/N_{14}^3, 2N_{25}/N_{14}^2, e_{14}/N_{14}^6) = (e_{16}, 2N_{25} N_{14}, e_{14}) = (e_{16}, e_{15}, e_{14})$.

From this we see that the algorithm sketched above requires 31 multiplications including all necessary multiplications by the c_i's. In contrast, the algorithm given in Brier and Joye ([6]) for elliptic curves in Weierstrass form requires 17 multiplications plus 1 multiplication with a constant from the equation.

5   Applications to Side-Channel Attacks

In the previous sections, we showed how to attach to any elliptic curve E and any k-rational point $M \neq e$ on E an isomorphic elliptic curve C_M which is given as a weighted quartic projective curve.

The first advantage of this representation is that the addition $P + Q$ of two points may be expressed by formulas independent of whether or not P and Q are different. This uniformity defends against SPA.

Standard techniques of defending against DPA involve either using projective coordinates or changing the representation of the elliptic curve. The method outlined offers both of these features. The addition may be carried out with projective coordinates as indicated above.

Another advantage is that this representation is available for all elliptic curves. Thus, it may be applied to all curves included in present and future standards.

Each elliptic curve admits of a large number of such representations, which can be changed at virtually no cost.

6   Examples

A crucial point with this approach is that we may choose *any* point $M \neq e$ on E to obtain a new parametrization. Some applications may not mandate this and it is of some interest to examine certain special examples. We begin by looking at the work of Billet and Joye ([3]) which sparked our interest to begin with.

Example 1. (Billett-Joye). An important example of our construction is to be found in the Jacobi model of Billett and Joye ([3]) and its application to side-channel attacks. They begin with an elliptic curve E defined by the affine Weierstrass equation

$$Y^2 = X^3 + aX + b \tag{22}$$

and a k-rational point $M = (\theta, 0)$ of order 2. Applying the procedure outlined above, we obtain the curve

$$W^2 = S^4 - (3\theta/2)S^2 - (4a + 3\theta^2)/16 \tag{23}$$
$$= S^4 - 2\delta S^2 + \epsilon$$

where $\delta = 3\theta/4$ and $\epsilon = -(4a + 3\theta^2)/16$. A simple change of variables then gives the equation

$$y^2 = \epsilon x^4 - 2\delta x^2 + 1 \tag{24}$$

used by Billet and Joye.

Example 2. A situation which leads to a particularly simple quartic is the use of a point $M = (\alpha, \beta) = (0, \beta)$ where the X-coordinate of M is 0. This yields the quartic

$$W^2 = R(S) = S^4 - \beta S - a_4/4 \tag{25}$$

References

1. Liardet, P.-V., Smart, N.B.: *Preventing SPA/DPA in ECC Systems Using the Jacobi Form*. In: Ç.K. Koç, D. Naccache, and C Paar, editors, Cryptographic Hardware and Embedded Systems – CHES 2001, Volume 2162 of Lecture Notes in Computer Science, pages 391-401. Springer-Verlag, 2001.
2. Joye, M., Quisquater, J.-J.: *Hessian Elliptic Curves and Side-Channel Attacks*. In: Ç.K. Koç, D. Naccache, and C Paar, editors, Cryptographic Hardware and Embedded Systems – CHES 2001, Volume 2162 of Lecture Notes in Computer Science, pages 402-410. Springer-Verlag, 2001.
3. Billet, O., Joye, M.: *The Jacobi Model of an Elliptic Curve and Side-Channel Analysis*. In: Fossorier, M.,Høholdt, T.,Poli, A., editors, Applied Algebra, Algebraic Algorithms and Error-Correcting Codes, Volume 2643 of Lecture Notes in Computer Science, pages 34-42, Springer-Verlag, 2003.
4. Reid, M. *Graded rings and varieties in weighted projective space*. Manuscript, M. Reid's Web page (www.maths.warwick.ac.uk/~miles/surf/more/grad.pdf), Jan. 2002.
5. Fricke, R. *Die elliptische Funktionen und ihre Anwendungen*, B.G. Teubner, 1922.
6. Brier, É., Joye, M.: *Weierstraß Elliptic Curves and Side-Channel Attacks*. In: Naccache, D and Paillier, P., editors, Public Key Cryptography 2002, Volume 2274 of Lecture Notes in Computer Science, pages 335-345. Springer-Verlag, 2002.

Switching Blindings with a View Towards IDEA

Olaf Neiße and Jürgen Pulkus

Giesecke & Devrient, Department of Cryptology, Prinzregentenstr. 159,
81677 Munich, Germany

Abstract. Cryptographic algorithms implemented on smart-cards must be protected against side-channel attacks. Some encryption schemes and hash functions like IDEA, RC6, MD5, SHA-1 alternate various arithmetic and boolean operations, each of them requiring a different kind of blinding. Hence the maskings have to be changed frequently. How to switch reasonably between standard arithmetic masking and boolean masking was shown in [2], [3], [5] and [9].

In this paper we propose more space-efficient table-based conversion methods. Furthermore, we deal with some non-standard arithmetic operations, namely arithmetic modulo $2^k + 1$ for some $k \in \mathbb{N}$ and a special multiplication used by IDEA.

Keywords: DPA, IDEA, MD5, Masking Techniques, RC6, SHA-1.

1 Introduction

Running cryptographic algorithms on systems vulnerable to side-channel attacks (e.g., on smart-cards), implementation issues become crucial and non-trivial. By side-channel information we mean all information a physical system leaks into the environment, like computation time, power consumption, electromagnetic emissions. In the literature a variety of attacks is known that exploit side-channels to gain sensitive information like secret keys. Attacks based on statistical examinations, such as Differential Power Analysis (DPA) [6], Differential Electromagnetic Analysis (DEMA) [1],[11] and higher-order DPA, force special protection and therefore special and careful implementations. One way to counteract this problem is to randomly split sensitive data into at least two shares such that computations can be carried out by manipulating only the shares, never reconstructing the original data. In case of two shares we call the two parts *masked data* and *mask*.

Some encryption schemes like IDEA [7], TWOFISH [4] or RC6 [12] and some hash functions like MD5, SHA-1 (see [8]) or SHA-2 [10] use the concept of "incompatible mixed group operations" to achieve the desired confusion and diffusion. The most frequent group structures employed by the designers are the boolean operation $\mathbf{Xor}_L$ (addition on $(\mathbb{Z}/2\mathbb{Z})^L$) and the standard arithmetic operation $\mathbf{Add}_{2^L}$ (addition on $\mathbb{Z}/2^L\mathbb{Z}$) for some integer L, mainly $L = 8, 16, 32$ or 64. But non-standard arithmetic operations like multiplication $\mathbf{Mult}_{2^L+1}$ on $\mathbb{Z}/(2^L + 1)\mathbb{Z}$ are used as well. The masking has to be adapted to these group

M. Joye and J.-J. Quisquater (Eds.): CHES 2004, LNCS 3156, pp. 230–239, 2004.

structures. If such group operations are mixed in a scheme, one has to convert the masking. Methods for switching masks between boolean and standard arithmetic are presented in [2], [3], [5] and [9]. Unlike the conversion from $\mathbf{Xor}_L$ to $\mathbf{Add}_{2^L}$ (using the very efficient method proposed by Goubin [5]) the contrary direction still waits for a time- and space-efficient method.

In Section 3 we present Algorithm 3.2 which transforms $\mathbf{Add}_{2^L}$-maskings into $\mathbf{Xor}_L$-maskings using a compressed table. In comparison to the method proposed by Coron and Tchulkine in [3] our algorithm requires only half the memory for tables. In Section 4 we explain how to use our table to enable switching from $\mathbf{Add}_{2^L}$-maskings to $\mathbf{Add}_{2^L+1}$-maskings and conversely. As an application we show in Sect. 5 how to implement the block cipher IDEA [7] efficiently and securely.

2   Notation

Since several kinds of operations with varying length or modulus have to be mixed in our investigation, we use the following notation: For $l \in \mathbb{N}$ let

$V(l)$	set of bit sequences of length l	
	also viewed as set of integral numbers $\{0, \ldots, 2^l - 1\}$.	
$x \oplus_l y$	infix-notation for bitwise exclusive or	$(x, y \in V(l))$
$x +_l y$	infix-notation for addition modulo l	$(x, y \in \{0, \ldots, l-1\})$
$\mathbf{Sub}_l(x, y)$	prefix-notation for subtraction modulo l	$(x, y \in \{0, \ldots, l-1\})$
$x -_l y$	infix-notation for subtraction modulo l	$(x, y \in \{0, \ldots, l-1\})$
$x \cdot_l y$	infix-notation for multiplication modulo l	$(x, y \in \{0, \ldots, l-1\})$
-0	bit sequence $(0, 0, \ldots, 0)$	
-1	bit sequence $(1, 1, \ldots, 1)$	
$\overline{x}$	1-complement of x	$(x \in V(l))$
$(x \mid y)$	concatenation of the bit sequences	
$x \gg 1$	logical shift right by 1: $(x_{l-1}, x_{l-2}, \ldots, x_0) \mapsto (0, x_{l-1}, \ldots, x_1)$	
$\mathbb{1}_<(x, y)$	comparison function $\mathbb{1}_<(x, y) = \begin{cases} 1 & \text{if } x < y \\ 0 & \text{else} \end{cases}$	$(x, y \in \mathbb{Z})$

3   From $\mathbf{Add}_{2^L}$ to $\mathbf{Xor}_L$

Throughout the paper we start with some sensitive data $d \in V(L)$ (with $L \in \mathbb{N}$, mainly $L = 8, 16, 32$) given by a mask x and the masked data y using one type of masking. Our goal is always to switch blinding so that d is then represented by a new mask u and masked data v with respect to another masking. For this we use randomized tables of size $m = 2^l$, where l is a small divisor of L, e.g. $(L, l) = (32, 8), (16, 8)$ or $(16, 4)$. An additional random bit z will be needed to make the calculation DPA-resistant. For variables we signal a certain dependency on z by a tilde. Setting $M = 2^L$ and $k = L/l$, the elements of $V(L)$ are viewed as the k-digit m-ary numbers from 0 to $M - 1$.

Now suppose that d is represented using a standard arithmetic masking. We describe algorithms that perform the conversion into a boolean masking of d:

Input: $(x, y) \in V(L)^2$ such that $y -_{2^L} x = d$

           $u \in V(L)$

Output: $v \in V(L)$ such that $u \oplus_L v = d$

The easiest DPA-resistant algorithm precomputes, depending on x and u, one big table $S : V(L) \to V(L)$ which contains for every value $y \in V(L)$ the corresponding value $v \in V(L)$. The conversion is done by a simple table-lookup. This is fast during the computation; however, for L large this algorithm is not practical because generating the table S needs too much time and space. We overcome this problem by working with such a table S only virtually – i.e. the entries of S are calculated using smaller tables T and C.

The basic idea is similar to the approach presented by Coron and Tchulkine in [3, 3.2]: one precomputes a small randomized table $T : V(l) \to V(l)$ which turns an $+_m$-masked digit for some input-falsifier r into an $\oplus_l$-masked digit for an output-falsifier s. With the help of this table, the result is calculated iteratively digit by digit from the lowest to the highest. More precisely, the digits d_j of $d = (d_k| \dots |d_1)$ are calculated in the additively masked form $d_j +_m r$, and then plugged into the table T to switch securely into the $\oplus_l$-blinding $d_j \oplus_l s$ with falsifier s. So one needs to find the masked digits $d_j +_m r$ using x, y and r. Let $a := (r| \dots |r)$ and $g := x -_M a$. Then $y -_M g = (d_k| \dots |d_1) +_M (r| \dots |r) = (d_k + r + c_{k-1} - c_k m| \dots |d_2 + r + c_1 - c_2 m|d_1 + r - c_1 m)$ for some carry bits $c_j \in \{0, 1\}$. In order to correct the j-th digit of $d + a$ to $d_j +_m r$, one needs to determine the carry bit c_{j-1}, which equals 1 in d_{j-1} out of m cases and therefore is susceptible to DPA. Hence a carry bit table providing the information, if the addition $d_j + r$ yields a carry mod m or not, has to be randomized.

Coron and Tchulkine propose in [3, Algorithm 4] to work with a random mask $\gamma \in V(l)$ and the table $\mathbf{C} : V(l) \to V(l)$, $\mathbf{C}[i] = \mathbb{1}_<(i, r) +_m \gamma$.

Our solution works with the much smaller bit-table $C : V(l) \to \{0, 1\}$, $C[i] = \mathbb{1}_<(i, r)$. We do not randomize the carry bit table directly, instead we blind the carry bit information during the conversion itself by a single random bit z (described below).

Furthermore, the operations $\mathbf{Add}_{2^l}$ and $\mathbf{Xor}_l$ coincide on the least significant bit (LSB). Hence we can spare the LSB of each entry $T[i]$ and replace it by the carry bit $C[i]$. This enables us to store $T[i]$ and $C[i]$ in one table, whereas Coron and Tchulkine needed twice the space.

This explains our precomputation:

ALGORITHM 3.1: PRECOMPUTATION FOR $\mathbf{Add}_{2^L} \to \mathbf{Xor}_L$

(a) Generate uniformly distributed random values $r \in V(l)$, $s \in V(l-1)$
(b) For $i = 0$ to $m - 1$ do
(c) $T[i] = \mathbf{Xor}_{l-1}(\mathbf{Sub}_m(i, r) \gg 1, s)$
(d) $C[i] = \mathbb{1}_<(i, r)$

Our switching algorithm 3.2 uses the following fact: the addition $\overline{d}_j + r$ contributes in $m - d_j - 1$ out of m cases a carry bit $= 1$, balancing out the d_j cases when the carry bit is 1 for $d_j + r$. Therefore we work with d_j or its one-complements, depending on a randomly chosen bit z.

For a variable w, let $\tilde{w}$ denote w if $z = 0$, and $\overline{w}$ if $z = 1$, so $\tilde{w} := \mathbf{Xor}(w, -z)$. The computations are based on the following observation: For $p, q \in V(L)$ let $w = p +_M q$. Then

$$\tilde{w} = \tilde{p} +_M \tilde{q} +_M z. \qquad (*)$$

Especially, $\tilde{y} = \tilde{d} +_M \tilde{x} +_M z$. Solving for $\tilde{d}$ and adding a on both sides gives $\tilde{d} +_M a = \tilde{y} -_M (\tilde{x} -_M a) -_M z$, which is in case $z = 0$ just what we wanted to calculate above. In case $z = 1$ we do the same calculation, but the role of d is taken by its complement $\overline{d}$ with two consequences: each additively masked digit plugged into the table yields the complement of the result of the case $z = 0$. This can be corrected easily. And, instead of reading the carry c_j of the addition $d_j + r$ from the carry table, we read the carry of the addition $\overline{d}_j + r$.

ALGORITHM 3.2: $\mathbf{Add}_{2^L} \to \mathbf{Xor}_L$

---

(1) Generate a random bit $z \in \{0, 1\}$
(2) Create $\tilde{s} = (s|r_0) \oplus_l -z$ with $r_0 =$ the LSB of r
(3) Calculate $g = \mathbf{Sub}_M(\mathbf{Xor}_L(x, -z), (r|\ldots|r))$; let $g = (g_k|\ldots|g_1)$ with $g_j \in V(l)$
(4) Calculate $h = \mathbf{Xor}_L((\tilde{s}|\ldots|\tilde{s}), u)$; let $h = (h_k|\ldots|h_1)$ with $h_j \in V(l)$
(5) Set $f = \tilde{y} = y \oplus_L -z$
(6) Initialize $c = z$
(7) For $j = 1$ to k do
(8)   Subtract $f = \mathbf{Sub}_{2^{(k-j)l}}(f, c)$
(9)   Subtract $f = \mathbf{Sub}_{2^{(k-j)l}}(f, g_j)$; let $f_j = f \bmod m$
(10)   Look up $o = T[f_j]$, $c = C[f_j]$
(11)   Calculate $v_j = h_j \oplus_l (o|c')$ with c' the LSB of f
(12)   Redefine $f = f \gg l$
(13) Let $v = (v_k|\ldots|v_1)$

Although the steps look rather complicated, they mostly describe elementary operations on a processor.[1] Steps (3) and (4) are precalculations supporting the mask changes in Steps (8), (9) and (11) from x and $\tilde{s}$ to $\tilde{r}$ and u, respectively. They could also be part of the loop. All intermediate variables and all carry bits

---

[1] Steps (8) and (9) could even be done at the same time by a subtraction with carry, but then the change of the carry bit would not be independent of the data d, which might cause troubles on certain platforms.

in (8)-(11), as well as all changes of these values are independent of d, whence this algorithm turns out to be DPA-resistant. Indeed, all values depending on d for $z = 0$ are calculated in the case $z = 1$ using the complement of d.

The algorithm can be varied in many ways: instead of starting with a mask x and a masked value $y = d +_M x$ one can also work with two shares x and $y = d -_M x$. For this, one just has to replace some subtractions by additions. Or, one can calculate in the loop instead of $d + a$ the value $d - a$. For this, one has to modify the tables by using additions instead of subtractions.

For practical implementations on a chip card one might use either one table of size 256 bytes or sixteen tables of size 16 nibbles each. In the latter case one can generate all tables with pairwise different input and output randomizations (in random order) and then use different tables in each round of the loop. As for all possible input randomizations there is a table available in RAM, one can choose in Step (3) instead of $(r|\ldots|r)$ an arbitrary value. For example one can make g to zero, such that the subtraction in Step (9) in the loop can be skipped.

4   From $\mathbf{Add_{2^L}}$ to $\mathbf{Add_{2^L+1}}$ and Back

In this section we deal with the question how to switch between standard arithmetic masking modulo 2^L and additive maskings modulo $2^L + 1$ without leaking any information about the data. Our solution is based on the following fact:

Proposition 4.1. *Let $M \in \mathbb{N}$.*
i) *For $a, d \in \{0, 1, \ldots, M - 1\}$ let $b = \mathbf{Add}_M(d, a)$ and $c = \mathbb{1}_<(b, a)$.*
    Then $\mathbf{Add}_{M+1}(d, a) = \mathbf{Sub}_{M+1}(b, c)$.
ii) *For $a, d \in \{0, 1, \ldots, M\}$ let $b = \mathbf{Add}_{M+1}(d, a)$ and $c = \mathbb{1}_<(b, a)$.*
    Then $\mathbf{Add}_M(d, a) = \mathbf{Add}_M(b, c)$.

Proof. We first examine the case $c = 0$, that is $b \geq a$ and therefore $b = d + a$. Both conclusions are obvious except if $a + d = b = M$, where in fact $b +_M c = 0 +_M 0 = 0 = d +_M a$. The case $c = 1$ follows immediately from $d + a = M + b = (M + 1) + (b - 1)$ for i) and $d + a = (M + 1) + b = M + (b + 1)$ for ii).   □

So we just have to add respectively subtract the carry bit c. As before, this bit is correlated to the sensitive data d and therefore has to be randomized.

Starting from an additive mask modulo 2^L, the carry bit can be determined employing the same ideas we have seen in Algorithm 3.2: for masks a of the special form $(r|\ldots|r)$, the carry bit $c = \mathbb{1}_<(d, a)$ equals the bit c_k in $d +_M a = (d_k + r + c_{k-1} - c_k m|\ldots|d_2 + r + c_1 - c_2 m|d_1 + r - c_1 m)$. In Algorithm 3.2, Step (10) for $j = k$ yields c, masked with the chosen bit z. Hence we adapt Algorithm 3.2 to our new problem such that $\mathbf{Sub}_{M+1}(b, c)$ is computed without leaking information.

Starting from an additive mask modulo $2^L + 1$, additional to the ideas of Sect. 3 more ideas are needed, since the special value 2^L has to be treated differently. However, since 2^m is not a divisor of $2^L + 1$, not all intermediate values are totally independent of d. Few values show weak dependency which should not leak side channel information in practice.

Both conversion algorithms employ the unmasked carry bit table C:

ALGORITHM 4.2: PRECOMPUTATION $\mathbf{Add}_M \leftrightarrow \mathbf{Add}_{M+1}$

(a) Generate a random value $r \in V(l)$

(b) For $i = 1$ to m do

(c) $C[i] = \mathbb{1}_<(i, r)$

Before going into details of the algorithms, we give an analogue of the formula
$(*)$ for calculations modulo $2^L + 1$. We use the notation

$$\widetilde{x} = \mathbf{Sub}_{M+1}(\mathbf{Xor}_L((x_k|\ldots|x_1), -z), x_{k+1} \oplus z) = \begin{cases} x & \text{if } z = 0 \\ -3 -_{M+1} x & \text{if } z = 1 \end{cases}$$

where, as usual, $x = (x_{k+1}|x_k|\ldots|x_1)$ with $x_{k+1} \in \{0,1\}$ and $x_j \in V(l)$ for
$x \in \{0,\ldots,M\}$. For $x \in V(L)$ and $z = 1$ this is the usual one-complement.

Let $w = x +_{M+1} y$. Then an easy calculation shows:

$$\widetilde{w} = \widetilde{x} +_{M+1} \widetilde{y} +_{M+1} 3 \cdot z. \qquad (**)$$

This formula is helpful in verifying the correctness of our algorithms. Another
fact one should keep in mind is: instead of adding two elements of $V(L)$ modulo
$M + 1$ one can add them modulo M, if the occuring carry is later subtracted
modulo $M + 1$. For subtraction the carry has accordingly to be added modulo
$M + 1$.

Subsequently we propose our conversion Algorithm 4.3 for the transformation
$\mathbf{Add}_M \to \mathbf{Add}_{M+1}$:

Input: $(x, y) \in V(L) \times V(L)$ such that $y -_M x = d$
           $u \in \{0, 1, \ldots, M\} \subset V(L+1)$

Output: $v \in V(L+1)$ such that $v -_{M+1} u = d$

As mentioned above, we modify Algorithm 3.2 for our purpose. Clearly Steps
(2), (4), (11), (13) and the first half of (10) in 3.2 can be skipped. The new steps
will be explained below.

ALGORITHM 4.3: $\mathbf{Add}_M \to \mathbf{Add}_{M+1}$

---

(1) Generate a random bit $z \in \{0,1\}$

(2) Calculate $g = \mathbf{Sub}_M(\mathbf{Xor}_L(x, -z), (r|\ldots|r))$; let $g = (g_k|\ldots|g_1)$ with $g_j \in V(l)$

(3) Set $\widetilde{u} = \mathbf{Sub}_{M+1}(\mathbf{Xor}_L((u_k|\ldots|u_1), -z), u_{k+1} \oplus_1 z)$

(4) Initialize $v = \mathbf{Sub}_{M+1}(\widetilde{u}, (r|\ldots|r))$

(5) Set $f = \widetilde{y} = \mathbf{Xor}_L(y, -z)$

(6) Initialize $c = z$

(7) For $j = 1$ to k do

(8)   Subtract $f = \mathbf{Sub}_{2^{(k-j)l}}(f, c)$

(9)   Subtract $f = \mathbf{Sub}_{2^{(k-j)l}}(f, g_j)$; let $f_j = f \bmod m$

(10) $v = \mathbf{Add}_{M+1}(v, c << (l \cdot j))$

(11) $v = \mathbf{Add}_{M+1}(v, f_j << (l \cdot j))$

(12)   Look up $c = C[f_j]$
(13)   Redefine $f = f \gg l$
(14) $v = \mathbf{Sub}_{M+1}(v, c)$
(15) $v = \mathbf{Add}_{M+1}(v, z)$
(16) $v = \mathbf{Sub}_{M+1}(\mathbf{Xor}_L((v_k| \ldots |v_1), -z), v_{k+1} \oplus_1 z)$ with $v = (v_{k+1}|v_k| \ldots |v_1)$

During the loop of 4.3, we have to determine the digits $\tilde{d}_j +_m r$ (namely f_j in Step (9)) to obtain the intermediate carry bits c_j and the required carry bit $c = c_k$ (Step (12)). Therefore we have to exchange $y = d +_M x$ for $b = d +_M a$ (Steps (8) and (9)), where $a = (r| \ldots |r)$ denotes the concatenation of k copies of r. Moreover, the masked data $v = d +_{M+1} u = (d +_M a) -_{M+1} c -_{M+1} a$ is calculated in Steps (4), (10), (11), (14) and (15). These calculation have to be balanced via the two cases $z = 0$ and $z = 1$:

(z=0) $v = d + u = d + a + u - a \overset{4.1}{=} b - c + u - a \bmod M + 1$

(z=1) $v = \overline{d} + u = (M - 1) - d - a + u + a \overset{4.1}{=} c - b + u + a - 2 \bmod M + 1$

From these equations one sees that what has to be added to u to get v in the case $z = 0$ has to be subtracted in the case $z = 1$ and vice versa. The simplest solution is to invert u at the beginning and at the end of the calculation if $z = 1$. That is done in Steps (3) and (16) using $(**)$.

Clearly, the digits $\tilde{d}_j + r$ give no information about d, and the carry bits are balanced for the same reason as they are in 3.2 . Additionally, all those values are combined independently with u. So all variables are independent of the sensitive data d. Hence our algorithm does not leak any side-channel information.

Although Algorithm 4.3 looks rather complicated, our method works fast, since most calculations decribe basic operations on a processor and the carry bits occur automatically within those calculations.

In the same manner we also deal with the converse $\mathbf{Add}_{M+1} \rightarrow \mathbf{Add}_M$:

Input: $x, y \in \{0, 1, \ldots, M\}$ such that $y -_{M+1} x = d$, $d \in V(L)$
            $u \in V(L)$
Output: $v \in V(L)$ such that $v -_M u = d$.

The Algorithm 4.4 looks very similar to Algorithm 4.3 since we use the same technique to obtain the carry bit c in a blinded way. A difficult part of the Algorithm 4.4 is how to calculate the digits $d_j +_m r$ using $b = d +_{M+1} a$ ($a = (r| \ldots |r)$) from below in the case $b = M$ without having to correct the result at the end, because this correction term would give vulnerable information about d.

This difficulty we solve by comparing $(f_k| \ldots |f_1)$ and $(g_k| \ldots |g_1)$, where $f = (f_{k+1}|f_k| \ldots |f_1) := y +_{M+1} 1$ resp. its complement, and $g = (g_{k+1}|g_k| \ldots |g_1) := \tilde{x} -_{M+1} a$. This information is not totally, but well enough balanced – at least in the interesting case $L = 16$ and $l = 4$ or $l = 8$ – such that it should not provide sufficient information for an effective DPA-attack.

ALGORITHM 4.4: $\mathbf{Add}_{M+1} \to \mathbf{Add}_M$

---

(1) Generate a random bit $z \in \{0,1\}$

(2) Calculate $\widetilde{x} = \mathbf{Sub}_{M+1}(\mathbf{Xor}_L((x_k|\ldots|x_1), -z), x_{k+1} \oplus_1 z)$

(3) Calculate $g = \mathbf{Sub}_{M+1}(\widetilde{x}, (r|\ldots|r))$
   let $g = (g_{k+1}|\ldots|g_1)$ with $g_{k+1} \in \{0,1\}$ and $g_j \in V(l)$

(4) Adjust $y = \mathbf{Sub}_{M+1}(y, 1)$

(5) Calculate $f = \widetilde{y} = \mathbf{Sub}_{M+1}(\mathbf{Xor}_L((y_k|\ldots|y_1), -z), y_{k+1} \oplus_1 z)$
   let $f = (f_{k+1}|\ldots|f_1)$ with $f_{k+1} \in \{0,1\}$ and $f_j \in V(l)$

(6) Determine $c' = \mathbb{1}_<((f_k|\ldots|f_1), (g_k|\ldots|g_1))$

(7) Calculate $\widetilde{u} = \mathbf{Xor}_L(u, -z)$

(8) Initialize $v = \widetilde{u} -_M (r|\ldots|r)$

(9) $v = v -_M 1 +_M z +_M (f_k|\ldots|f_1) -_M f_{k+1} -_M (g_k|\ldots|g_1) +_M g_{k+1} +_M c'$

(10) Initialize $c = f_{k+1}$

(11) For $j = 1$ to k do

(12)   Subtract $f = \mathbf{Sub}_{2^{(k-j)l}}(f, g_j)$; let $f_j = f \bmod m$

(13)   Set $c_{\text{Aux}} = \mathbb{1}_<(f_j, c)$, subtract $f_j = \mathbf{Sub}_m(f_j, c)$ and set $c = c_{\text{Aux}}$

(14)   Look up and redefine $c = c \oplus C[f_j]$

(15)   Redefine $\widetilde{f} = \widetilde{f} >> l$

(16) Calculate $v = \mathbf{Add}_M(v, c)$

(17) $v = \mathbf{Xor}_L(v, -z)$

The basic equations read as follows:

$$(z=0) \quad v = u + d = u + d + a - a \overset{4.2}{=} u + b + c - a \mod M$$

$$(z=1) \quad v = u + \widetilde{d} = u + (-3 -_{M+1} d) - a + a \text{ and}$$

$$u - d - a + a \overset{4.2}{=} u - b - c + a \mod M$$

So, for $z = 1$, we invert u at the beginning and at the end of the calculations. Moreover, we have to transform $u + (-3 -_{M+1} d) - a + u + a$ to $u - d - a + a$, which explains those tricky calculations.

Instead of manipulating the masked data $v = d + u$ inside the loop (see Steps (10) and (11) of Algorithm 4.3), we suggest to exchange masks outside the loop in Steps (8) and (9) of Algorithm 4.3. The more complicate calculation is due to the arithmetic mod $M + 1$.

As for Algorithm 4.3, all steps of Algorithm 4.4 can easily be realised on a processor. Inside the loop, we need just two subtractions and one table lookup.

5   Application to IDEA

One of the algorithms using the principle of "mixed group operations" is the block cipher IDEA (International Data Encryption Algorithm, see [7]). Besides the boolean and standard arithmetic on $L = 16$ bits, the designers employ an operation $\odot$ based on the multiplication modulo $2^L + 1$. Since $2^{16} + 1$ is a prime number, multiplication on $\mathbb{Z}/(2^{16} + 1)\mathbb{Z}$ yields a cryptographically good operation on the set $\{1, 2, 3, \ldots, M = 2^{16}\}$. Identifying the value $0 \in V(L)$ with 2^{16} this defines the third operation $\odot$ on $V(16)$:

$$d \odot d' = \mathbf{I}^{-1}(\mathbf{I}(d) \cdot_{2^{16}+1} \mathbf{I}(d')) \text{ with } \mathbf{I}(0) = 2^{16} \text{ and } \mathbf{I}(d) = d \text{ else.}$$

IDEA has a block size of 64 bit. It iterates eight rounds followed by an output transformation. Each round takes as input 64 bits, given by four values $X_1, \ldots, X_4 \in V(16)$, and six key values (obtained by some key scheduling) $K_1, \ldots, K_6 \in V(16)$. Combining the three operations $\oplus = \oplus_{16}$, $+ = +_{2^{16}}$ and $\odot$ on $V(16)$ the output $Y_1, Y_2, Y_3, Y_4 \in V(16)$ of each round is calculated as follows:

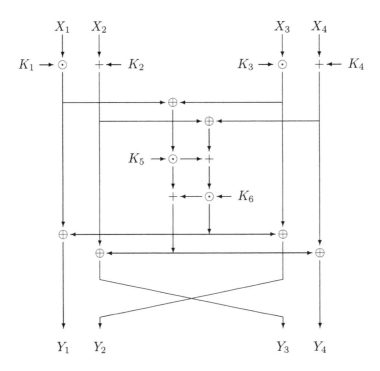

The data of all three operation have to be blinded. For $\oplus$ and $+$ we use the boolean and standard arithmetic masking, respectively. As a blinding for the $\odot$-operation we recommend arithmetic blinding modulo $M+1 = 2^{16}+1$; a sensitive data $d \in V(L)$ is given by a mask $x \in \{0, 1, \ldots, 2^{16}\}$ and the masked data $y = \mathbf{I}(d) +_{M+1} x$. Then it is clear how to calculate $\mathbf{I}(d \cdot d') = \mathbf{I}(d) \cdot_{M+1} \mathbf{I}(d')$ using addition and multiplication modulo $M+1$. So we just have to develop a method to switch maskings between this kind of blinding and the arithmetic masking modulo M. As it turns out, this is an application of the methods presented in Sect. 4. This is based on the observation

$$\mathbf{I}(d) = (d -_M 1) +_{M+1} 1 \qquad \text{for } d \in V(L) .$$

Suppose we have $x, y \in V(L)$ with $y = d +_M x$, and $u \in \{0, 1, \ldots, M\}$. Then $(y -_M 1, x)$ represents $d -_M 1$. We use the algorithms of Sect. 4 to obtain the

"$+_{M+1}$"-masking (u, v) of $d -_M 1$, that is $v = (d -_M 1) +_{M+1} u$. Finally $v +_{M+1} 1 = \mathbf{I}(d) +_{M+1} u$. So $v = \mathbf{I}(d) +_{M+1} u$ can be computed easily without leaking any information about d.

Conversely, let (u, v) represent $\mathbf{I}(d)$ for some sensitive data $d \in V(L)$. Then we apply the algorithm $\mathbf{Add}_{M+1} \to \mathbf{Add}_M$ on $(u, v -_{M+1} 1)$ and some mask $x \in V(L)$ to receive $y \in V(L)$ such that $y = d -_L 1 +_L x$, i.e $y +_M 1 = d +_L x$ is the masked value of d with mask x. Indeed, $v -_{M+1} 1 = (d -_M 1) +_{M+1} u$. This shows how to convert some "$\odot$"-masking into a blinding for standard arithmetic.

6   Conclusion

Motivated by the task of a DPA-resistant implementation of IDEA and other encryption schemes using mixed group operations, we presented algorithms to switch the mask between blindings of boolean, standard arithmetic and some non-standard arihmetic operations. Our methods are based on small randomized tables with an additional random bit deciding the computation mode.

References

1. R. Anderson, M. Kuhn: *Soft Tempest: Hidden Data Transmission Using Electromagnetic Emanations.* Proc. of Information Hiding (1998).
2. J.-S. Coron, L. Goubin: *On Boolean and Arithmetic Masking against Differential Power Analysis.* CHES 2000, LNCS **1965** pp. 231–237.
3. J.-S. Coron, A. Tchulkine: *A New Algorithm for Switching from Arithmetic to Boolean Masking.* CHES 2003, LNCS **2779** pp. 89–97.
4. N. Ferguson, C. Hall, J. Kelsey, B. Schneier, D. Wagner, D. Whiting: *Twofish: A 128-Bit Block Cipher.*
5. L. Goubin: *A Sound Method for Switching between Boolean and Arithmetic Masking.* CHES 2001, LNCS **2162** pp. 3–15.
6. P. Kocher, J. Jaffe, B. Jun: *Differential Power Analysis.* Advances in Cryptology – CRYPTO 1999, Proceedings, LNCS **1666**, pp. 388-397.
7. X. Lai, J.L. Massey: *A Proposal for a New Block Encryption Standard.* Advances in Cryptology – EUROCRYPT 1990, Proceedings, LNCS **473**, pp. 389-404.
8. A.J. Menezes, P.C. van Oorschot, S.A. Vanstone: *Handbook of Applied Cryptography.* CRC, (1996).
9. T.S. Messerges: *Securing the AES Finalists Against Power Analysis Attacks.* FSE 2000, LNCS **1978** (Springer).
10. NIST: *FIPS 180-2: Secure Hash Standard.* August 2001.
11. J.-J. Quisquater, D. Samyde: *A new tool for non-intrusive analysis of Smart Cards based on electro-magnetic emmisions: the SEMA and DEMA methods.* Eurocrypt rump session, Bruges, Belgium, May 2000.
12. R.L. Rivest, M.J.B. Robshaw, R. Sidney, Y.L. Yin: *The RC6 Block Cipher.*

Fault Analysis of Stream Ciphers

Jonathan J. Hoch and Adi Shamir

Department of Computer Science and Applied Mathematics,
The Weizmann Institute of Science, Israel

Abstract. A fault attack is a powerful cryptanalytic tool which can be applied to many types of cryptosystems which are not vulnerable to direct attacks. The research literature contains many examples of fault attacks on public key cryptosystems and block ciphers, but surprisingly we could not find any systematic study of the applicability of fault attacks to stream ciphers. Our goal in this paper is to develop general techniques which can be used to attack the standard constructions of stream ciphers based on LFSR's, as well as more specialized techniques which can be used against specific stream ciphers such as RC4, LILI-128 and SOBER-t32. While most of the schemes can be successfully attacked, we point out several interesting open problems such as an attack on FSM filtered constructions and the analysis of high Hamming weight faults in LFSR's.

Keywords: Stream cipher, LFSR, fault attack, Lili-128, SOBER-t32, RC4.

1 Introduction

1.1 Background

Attacks against cryptosystems can be divided into two classes, direct attacks and indirect attacks. Direct attacks include attacks against the algorithmic nature of the cryptosystem regardless of its implementation. Indirect attacks make use of the physical implementation of the cryptosystem and include a large variety of techniques which either give the attacker some 'inside information' on the cryptosystem (such as power or timing analysis) or some kind of influence on the cryptosystem's internal state such as ionizing radiation flipping random bits in the device's internal memory. Fault analysis is based on a careful study of the effect of such faults (which can affect either the code or the data) on the ciphertext, in order to derive (partial) information about either the key or the internal state of the cryptosystem. Recently Anderson in [1] discovered an extremely low-tech, low-cost technique which allows an attacker with physical access to the cryptoprocessor (especially when implemented on a smartcard) to cause faults at very specific locations. This discovery transfers the ability to perform fault attacks to one's backyard making this kind of attack a major threat to smartcard issuers and users. Fault analysis was first used in 1996 by Boneh, Demillo, and Lipton in [2] to attack number theoretic public key cryptosystems

M. Joye and J.-J. Quisquater (Eds.): CHES 2004, LNCS 3156, pp. 240–253, 2004.

such as RSA (by using a faulty CRT computation to factor the modulus n), and later by Biham and Shamir in [3] to attack product block ciphers such as DES (by using a high-probability differential fault attack on the last few rounds). While these techniques were generalized and applied to other public key and block ciphers in many subsequent papers, there are almost no published results on the applicability of fault attacks to stream ciphers, which requires different types of attacks and analytic tools. A notable exception is the re-synchronization attack of [9] which deals with a similar situation although in their model the changes (which correspond to our faults) are known. Our goal in this paper is to fill this void by embarking on a systematic study of all the standard techniques used to construct stream ciphers, and by analyzing their vulnerability to various types of fault attacks.

1.2   Our Results

We have succeeded in attacking a wide variety of stream ciphers. We first concentrated on attacking constructions based on LFSRs. With the exception of FSM filtered constructions we were able to attack almost any synthetic construction which appeared in the literature. The linearity of the LFSR is at the heart of all of these attacks. Although we have found a couple of attacks against very specific FSM filtered constructions, it would be interesting to find attacks against more general constructions. These results are covered in Section 2, where we present a comprehensive attack strategy against non-linearly filtered LFSRs as well as attacks against other LFSR based constructions. In section 3 we present fault attacks against LILI-128 and Sober (two LFSR based NESSIE candidates) and against RC4. The attack against RC4 applies random faults to the S-table after the initialization to recover the internal state by analyzing the first output byte of RC4 after initialization. All the attacks were analyzed theoretically and verified experimentally, in order to gain better understanding of their actual complexity and success rate. Due to space limitations we omit from this paper results which are harder to describe or require a longer introduction, such as a new DFA-like fault attack on the stream cipher Scream[5]. These results will be included in the full version of this paper.

1.3   The Attack Model

The basic attack model used in this paper assumes that the attacker can apply some bit flipping faults to either the RAM or the internal registers of the cryptographic device, but that he has only partial control over (and knowledge of) their number, location and timing. In addition, he can reset the cryptographic device to its original state and then apply another randomly chosen fault to the same device. In general, there is a tradeoff between the amount of control he has and the number of faults needed to recover the key. This model tries to reflect a situation in which the attacker is in possession of the physical device, and the faults are transient rather than permanent.

2   LFSR Based Stream Ciphers

2.1   Introduction

A very common component in stream ciphers is the Linear Feedback Shift Register (LFSR). LFSR's have provably long cycles and good statistical properties, but due to their inherent linearity LFSRs do not generate good output streams by themselves. Hence, LFSRs are typically used in conjunction with some non-linear component. There are three general constructions for implementing a stream cipher based on LFSRs:

- Filter the output of the LFSR(s) through a non-linear function.
- Have the clocking of one LFSR controlled by the output sequence of another LFSR.
- Filter the output of the LFSR(s) through a finite state machine.

In this section we develop several types of fault attacks against such generic constructions. We denote the length of the LFSR by n, the XOR of the original and faulted value of the LFSR at the time the fault was introduced by Δ, and the number of flipped bits (i.e., the Hamming weight of Δ) by k.

2.2   Attacks on Non-linearly Filtered LFSR Based Stream Ciphers

Let $(x_1, x_2, ..., x_n)$ be the internal state of the LFSR where $x_i \in \{0,1\}$. A non-linear filter applied to a LFSR is a boolean function $f(x_{i_1}, x_{i_2}, .., x_{i_t})$ whose inputs are a subset of the LFSR's internal state bits (typically, $n \le 128$ and $t \le 12$). More generally the inputs to the function may come from several LFSRs. Each output bit is produced either by evaluating f on the current state, or by using a lookup table of pre-computed values of f. The LFSR is then clocked and f is evaluated again on the resulting state to generate the next output bit. Existing attacks against this construction include the algebraic attack [12] which is generally infeasible when t is not extremely small and the re-synchronization attack [9] which shares a similar setting with our attack.

   Now assume that the attacker has the power to cause low Hamming weight faults in the LFSR's internal state bits. The attack will proceed as follows:

1. Cause a fault and produce the resulting output stream
2. Guess the fault
3. Check the guess, if incorrect guess again
4. Repeat 1-3 $O(t)$ times
5. Solve a system of linear equations in the original state bits

   We need to show how to check the correctness of a guess and then how to construct the system of linear equations. Notice that due to the linearity of the LFSR clocking operation L, if we know the initial difference Δ due to the fault then at any time i the difference will be $L^i(\Delta)$. To verify a guess for Δ we predict the future differences in the t input bits to f. Whenever this difference is 0 we expect to see an output difference of 0. If our guess was incorrect, then for half of these occasions we will see a non-zero output difference. So on average after 2^{t+1} output bits we expect to reject incorrect guesses.

This identification procedure leaves room for optimization by a preprocessing stage in which the for each possible non-zero difference location, all inconsistent faults are pre-computed. This Enables us to simultaneously reject all faults inconsistent with the observed differences. This can greatly reduce the time complexity of the attack; the details of this approach are not presented here due to space limitations.

Now let us concentrate on a single output bit. For each faulted stream the attacker observes the difference in the output bit and can compute the input difference to f. We collect pairs of input/output differences corresponding to the same output bit location. Given about t pairs we can narrow down by exhaustive search the possible input bits to one possibility. By determining these bits we get linear equations in terms of the initial state bits. Using the same faulted output streams we can also compute the input differences for other output bits collecting more linear equations. Once we collect enough ($\theta(n)$) equations we can solve the set of equations and determine the initial LFSR state.

We can sometimes improve the amount of data needed for the attack by analyzing the structure of f. Define $A = \{\Delta \mid Pr[f(x) \oplus f(x \oplus \Delta) = 0] > \frac{1}{2} + \epsilon\}$. After guessing Δ, the initial difference, we compute as before the differences $\Delta_n = L^n(\Delta)$ at any future time. When $\Delta_n \in A$ we know that with probability at least $\frac{1}{2} + \epsilon$ the difference in the output of f will be 0. I.e, the average of the difference over the output bits for which $\Delta_n \in A$ should be $\frac{1}{2} + \epsilon$. If our guess of Δ was incorrect then we expect to see an average of $\frac{1}{2}$. Thus after seeing about $O(\epsilon^2 \frac{|A|}{2^n})$ we should be able to tell with high probability whether our guess of Δ was correct. Analysis of f will show us the optimal ϵ and whether we achieve an advantage over the previous strategy.

If the Hamming weight of the faults is very low then we can apply another strategy to reduce the amount of data required by guessing and verifying m faults simultaneously. This will increase the time complexity by a factor of $\binom{n}{k}^{m-1}$, but we can now check our guess by comparing the relative difference in the input of f for each pair of the $m+1$ streams. This gives us a probability of approximately $2^{-t}\binom{m+1}{2}$ of having a zero relative difference, thus reducing the amount of data required by a factor of $\binom{m+1}{2}$.

So far we assumed that the function f is known, but we can apply a fault attack even if f is unknown. First notice that in order to verify a guessed fault in the simple variation we did not need to know f. So we can carry out steps 1-4 even when the non-linear function f is unknown or key-dependent.

Definition 1. *Let $D(i)$ be the set of input-output difference pairs resulting from the faults at position i in the output stream.*

Definition 2. *A 0-order linear structure of f is n-bit vector γ s.t. for all X $f(X) = f(X \oplus \gamma)$*

Proposition 1. *The 0-order linear structures of f form a vector space.*

Now if for two positions i and j $D(i) = D(j)$ and $|D(i)| = 2^t$ then either the un-faulted inputs X, Y to f at positions i and j were the same or $X \oplus Y$ is a 0-order linear structure of f. Analysis of $D(i)$ can give us the linear structures of f in time $O(t2^t)$ using the Walsh-Hadamard transform of f [9], [11]. In either case, we get linear equations in the original state variables. After recovering the LFSR state we can easily recover f. Even if $D(i) \bigcap D(j) < 2^t$ we can still conclude with high probability that $X = Y$ (or $X \oplus Y$ is a 0-order linear structure) if the intersection is large enough. Experimental results show that for a random 10-bit boolean function f, about 300 faults were sufficient to successfully carry out the attack.

Another improvement can be made to the total amount of data required by comparing the new faults against the already identified ones. For example, after the first fault has been identified we compare the next fault against the original data and the first faulted stream. When 2^t faults are required this will reduce the total amount of data to $O(t2^t)$ instead of $O(2^{2t})$.

The only property of the LFSR which we used for these attacks is that we can compute future differences based on the initial fault. Thus the attacks generalize directly to a construction composed of several LFSRs connected to the same non-linear filter, providing that the total Hamming weight of the faults in all the registers is low. However, we were unable to find any fault attacks utilizing faults with high (and thus un-guessable) Hamming weight.

2.3   Attacks on Clock Controlled LFSR Based Stream Ciphers

The basic clock controlled LFSR construction is composed of two components: the clock LFSR and the data LFSR. The output stream is a subsequence of the output of the data LFSR which is determined by the clock LFSR. For example, when the clock LFSR output bit is 0 clock the data LFSR once and output its bit, and when the clock LFSR bit is 1 clock the data LFSR twice and output its bit. Unless specified otherwise, all attacks in this section will refer to this construction.

Other variations include considering more than one bit of the clock LFSR to control the clocking of the data LFSR (E.g., in LILI-128 two bits of the clock LFSR are used to decide whether to clock the data LFSR one to four times). The last variation considered here is the shrinking generator [6] in which the output bits of the clock LFSR decide whether or not the current data LFSR output bit will be sent to the output stream, and thus there is no fixed upper bound on the time difference between consecutive output bits. Existing attacks against clock controlled constructions include correlation attacks [10], algebraic attacks [12] and re-synchronization attacks [10].

Throughout this section we will use the term *data stream* to indicate the sequence produced by the data LFSR $\{d_i\}_{i=1}^\infty$ as opposed to the *output stream* denoted $S = \{S_i\}_{i=1}^\infty$ which is the sequence of output bits produced by the device. The control sequence produced by the clock LFSR will be denoted $\{c_i\}_{i=1}^\infty$, and we define $pos_S(i)$ to be the position of the ith bit of the output stream S in the data stream.

A phase shift in the data register. A phase shift is a fault in which one of the components is clocked while the other is not. Once the phase shift takes place the device continues operating as usual. In a clock controlled construction a phase shift in the data LFSR can give us information about the clock register. Denote by S the non-faulted output stream and by $\hat{S}$ the faulted output stream. Notice that for every bit i after the fault $pos_{\hat{S}}(i) = pos_S(i) + 1$ since the data register was clocked one extra time. So the attacker looks for i s.t. $\hat{S}_i \neq S_{i+1}$, this implies that at the ith location the data register was clocked twice. Thus we can recover a bit of the clock LFSR state (which corresponds to a linear equation in the original state) each time we have such an occurrence.

110101001001010 - clock register
00101011010101010100101010 - data register
110100100101001 - output stream

01010110101010100101010 - data register after phase shift
000101101100011 - output stream

110100100101001 - original output stream
001011011000110 - faulted output stream
Each bit in the original sequence is compared with the bit to its left in the faulted sequence. When a difference is observed the clock register must have been 1.

```
*1***1**1**1*1*  - Partial data recovered by comparing the two sequences.
110101001001010  - The actual clock register.
```

Fig. 1. An example of a Phase Shift Attack

We need about twice the length of the clock register to recover the whole state since the probability of such an occurrence is $\frac{1}{2}$. After recovering the clock LFSR's state we can easily recover the data LFSR's since we now know the position of each output bit in the data stream.

It is left as an easy exercise to show that this attack can be adapted to deal with phase shift faults in the shrinking generator and the stop & go generator.

Faults in the clock register. For simplicity of description we assume that the attacker can apply random single bit faults to the clocking LFSR at a chosen point in the execution. The full attack, which is too technical to describe here, can be carried out even if the timing of the fault is not exactly known and it affects a small number of bits. The first stage of the attack will be to produce the n possible separate faulted output streams by applying a single bit fault at the same timing (at different locations) to the clocking register. We will designate the stream resulting from a fault in the ith location by S^i, S^i_j being the jth bit of S^i (counting from the timing of the fault). Let us observe S^i_j for a fixed j s.t. $j < n$. This condition assures that the feedback of the clock register has not affected the output stream yet as a result of the fault. I.e., the only changes are a result of the single bit change at the ith location. If $i \geq j$ then the fault will not have enough time to affect S_j^i and $S_j^i = S_j$. However, if $i < j$ then similar to the phase shift example, $|pos_{S^i}(j) - pos_S(j)| = 1$. If $c_i = 1$ then we will get $pos_{S^i}(j) - pos_S(j) = -1$ (we have clocked the data LFSR one time less) and $pos_{S^i}(j) - pos_S(j) = 1$ if $c_i = 0$. Now assume that for all i S_j^i is the same. This implies that both neighbors of the original bit in the data stream are identical to the bit itself.

...$0\hat{0}0$... - the original data stream where the $\hat{*}$ was chosen for the output
...$\hat{0}00$... - the original data with faulted clocking
...$00\hat{0}$... - the original data with faulted clocking

The only other case in which this could happen is if the first j bits of the clock register were identical, since then we only see one of the neighbors. By choosing j large enough we can neglect this possibility. If we see $j - 1$ streams which are identical in the jth bit but different from the original j^{th} bit then the data stream must have looked as follows:

...$1\hat{0}1$... - the original data stream where the $\hat{*}$ was chosen for the output

In this case we know that both neighbors of the bit in the data stream were equal. If the next output bit in the actual stream was different from the neighbors, then the data register must have been clocked twice.

...$0\hat{0}0\hat{1}$... - the $\hat{*}$ bits were chosen for the output
...$1\hat{0}1\hat{0}$... - the $\hat{*}$ bits were chosen for the output

In this case we have recovered a bit of the clock LFSR or more generally a linear equation in the original LFSR state. By analyzing similar structures we show that there is a probability of at least $\frac{6}{32}$ of this situation occurring. Hence we can get about $\frac{3n}{16}$ linear equations. We now repeat the attack and collect another batch of faulted streams with the timing of the faults changed. After repeating this procedure ~ 10 times we will have collected an over-determined set of equations which we can solve for the clocking LFSR's original state. After recovering the clock LFSR we can easily solve for the data LFSR. The attack requires about $10n$ faults and for each fault a little more than n bits (for unique identification of the streams). This attack is also applicable to the decimating and stop & go generators since the effect of a single bit fault in the control LFSR is also locally identical to a phase shift in the data LFSR.

Faults in the data register. The next attack will focus on the data LFSR, but before we give a description of the attack we will show a general algorithm for recovering the clock register given the data register.

For a clock controlled construction $pos(i) = \Sigma_{j=1}^i c_j$ is the position of the ith bit of the output stream in the data stream. The input to the algorithm will be the sequence $\{d_i\}$ and we will identify $pos(i)$ for various i. Notice that each value of $pos(i)$ gives us a linear equation in the original state of the LFSR, since each of the c_i's can be represented as a linear combination of the original state bits and $pos(i)$ is a linear combination of the c_i's. Once we have collected enough values we can solve the set of equations for the initial state of the clock LFSR. The algorithm works by keeping a list of all possible values of $pos(i)$ for each output bit of the device. This is done by simple elimination: check for each existing position in the list whether it is possible to receive the actual output with one of the possible values of c_i. Now if we find an i such that the list of candidates for $pos(i)$ is a single value we know the corresponding $pos(i)$. Experimental results show that given a random initial state for LFSRs of size 128 bits, the algorithm finds the original state after seeing a few hundred bits, finding a linear equation every 5 or 6 bits. If the output sequence was not produced from $\{d_i\}$ then the algorithm finds an inconsistency in the output stream (the size of the list shrinks to zero) after at most a few tens of bits. This behavior can also be studied analytically. Let x_i and y_i be the minimal and maximal candidate values for $pos(i)$ respectively. Assuming y_i is not the real value for $pos(i)$ let us calculate the expectation of $y_{i+1} - y_i$. This expectation is bounded from above by $\frac{5}{4}$, since there is a probability of $\frac{1}{2}$ that the maximum grows by 2 and a probability of $\frac{1}{4}$ that the maximum grows by 1. On the other hand the expectation of $x_{i+1} - x_i$ is bounded from below by $\frac{1}{2} + \frac{2}{4} + \frac{3}{8} = \frac{11}{8}$ so the expectation of the change to the size of the list of possibilities for $pos(i)$ is negative. I.e., the size of the list is expected to shrink unless one of the endpoints is the true position. This implies that the average size of the list is constant and thus the running time is linear. Now our attack will proceed as follows:

1. Generate a non-faulted output stream of length $10n$
2. Re-initialize the device, and cause a low Hamming weight fault in the data register
3. Generate a new (faulted) stream of length $10n$
4. Guess the fault and verify by running the above algorithm with the calculated difference in the data stream and the output stream difference
5. Repeat until the guess is consistent with the output stream
6. Recover the data register state from the actual output and the known clocking register

Since the clocking register was not affected, the difference in the output stream is equivalent to a device with the same clocking and with the data register initialized to the fault difference. Since given a guess of the initial state of the data register, the attacker can calculate the difference at any future point, we can apply the algorithm for recovery of the clock register. For incorrect guesses of the fault, the algorithm will find the inconsistency and for the correct guess the algorithm will find the initial state of the clock register.

2.4 Attacks on Finite State Machine Filtered LFSR Based Stream Ciphers

In this section we will show some attacks on a basic FSM filtered LFSR construction. The FSM contains some memory whose initial content is determined by the key. Each time the LFSR is clocked, the LFSR output bit is inserted into a specific address determined by a subset of the LFSR's state, and the bit previously occupying that memory location is sent to the output. The number of memory bits will be denoted by M and thus there are $\log M$ address bits. The leading attacks against general FSM filtered LFSR constructions are algebraic attacks [12], but these attacks are only feasible against very specific constructions.

Randomizing the LFSR. Assume that the attacker has perfect control over the timing of the fault, and that he can cause a fault which uniformly randomizes the LFSR bits used to address the FSM. The first output bit after the fault has been applied will be uniformly distributed over the bits currently stored in the FSM. By repeating the fault at the same point in time we can recover the number of ones currently stored in the FSM. If we do the same at a different point in time we can, by examining the actual output stream, recover the total number of ones entering the FSM. This gives us a linear equation in the initial LFSR state. By collecting enough equations we can solve for the initial state.

Faults in the FSM. If a random fault is applied to the current contents of the FSM the output stream will have differences at the timings when the LFSR points to the faulted bits' addresses. We start by giving some intuition about the attack. Assume that the LFSR points to the same address at two consecutive clockings. If the fault in the FSM happened at this location before these points in time, only the first occurrence of this location in the output stream will be faulted. When examining the second occurrence no matter what fault occurred in the FSM the bit will not be faulted as long as the timing of the fault was before the first occurrence. When we notice a case like this we know that the address is the same in the two consecutive timings, this gives us linear relations on the bits of the LFSR. By collecting enough relations we can derive the LFSR state. More generally, let p be the probability of a single bit in the FSM being affected by the fault and let us assume that the timing of the fault is uniformly distributed over an interval $[t_1, t_2]$ of length T. The probability of a difference in bit t between the faulted and non-faulted streams is $\frac{t-t_1}{t_2-t_1} p$ provided that this is the first occurrence of the address. If the most recent occurrence of the same address before time t is at time t_0 then the probability is $\frac{t-t_0}{t_2-t_1}$. So by estimating this probability within $\frac{1}{2(t_2-t_1)}$ we can tell when the address bits were the same at two different timings t_0 and t. This gives us $\log M$ linear equations in the original LFSR bits. We repeat this $\frac{n}{\log M}$ times and recover the initial state of the LFSR from the resulting set of linear equations

3   Fault Attacks on Actual Stream Ciphers

3.1   A Fault Attack on LILI-128

In this section we will bring some of the techniques presented into action in a fault attack against LILI-128 [4], one of the NESSIE candidates. For existing attacks on this stream cipher see [12] and [13].

LILI-128 is composed of two LFSRs: $LFSR_c$, which is 39 bits long, and $LFSR_d$, which is 89 bits long (with a total of 128 bits of internal state). Both have primitive feedback polynomials. For each keystream bit:

- The keystream bit is produced by applying a nonlinear function f_d to 10 of the bits in $LFSR_d$.
- $LFSR_c$ is clocked once. Two bits from $LFSR_c$ determine an integer c in the range $\{1, 2, 3, 4\}$.
- $LFSR_d$ is clocked c times.

The keystream generator is initialized simply by loading the 128 bits of key into the registers. Keys that cause either register to be initialized with all zeroes are considered invalid. The exact function f_d used, which bits are taken as inputs and the feedback polynomials of the LFSRs are irrelevant to the attack.

The first stage of the attack is to apply a random one bit fault to the data register. Repeat this until 89 (the length of $LFSR_d$) distinct streams are observed. Now repeat the same with the construction clocked once before applying the faults. Notice that some of the streams produced will be the same as in the first batch. This is due to the fact that applying the fault and then shifting the LFSR is equivalent to shifting the LFSR and then performing the fault, provided the fault did not affect the feedback. By counting how many streams are repeated one can deduce how many times $LFSR_d$ was clocked, which provides two bits of $LFSR_c$. Thus after repeating the experiment about 20 times we can recover the full $LFSR_c$ state. Once this state is known we can use the algorithm presented in section 1.2 to recover the state of $LFSR_d$. Notice that no further faults are necessary and the data collected in the previous stage can be reused. A tradeoff between the number of faults used and the length of the attack can be achieved by stopping after part of the state has been recovered and guessing the rest.

3.2   A Fault Attack on SOBER-t32

SOBER-t32 [7] is another NESSIE candidate with a LFSR based design. SOBER is composed of a LFSR, a non linear filter (NLF) and a form of irregular decimation called *stuttering*. The LFSR works over the field $GF(2^{32})$, and produces a stream of 32-bit words $L_1, L_2, \dots$ called the L-stream. The internal state of the LFSR will be denoted $\sigma_i = (s_i, s_{i+1}, \dots, s_{i+16})$, and σ_0 will denote the initial state. The L-stream is fed through the NLF to produce 32-bit words $N_1, N_2, \dots$ called the N-stream, $N_i = NLF(\sigma_i)$. The stuttering decimates the N-stream as follows: the first N-word N_1 is the first stutter control word SCW. The SCW is partitioned into 16 pairs of bits, each pair of bits is read in order and accordingly one of four actions is performed:

1. Clock the LFSR once but do not output anything.
2. Clock the LFSR once, output the current N-word xored with $0x6996C53A$ and clock the LFSR again (without producing more output).
3. Clock the LFSR twice and then output the current N-word.

4. Clock the LFSR once and then output the current N-word xored with $0x96693AC5$.

When all the bits of the SCW have been read, the LFSR is clocked and the output of the NLF becomes the next SCW. The NLF is defined as $NLF(\sigma_i) = ((f(s_i + s_{i+16}) + s_{i+1} + s_{i+6} \oplus Konst) + s_{i+13}$ where f is some non linear function whose exact definition is not relevant to the attack. The key determines σ_0 and $Konst$. Existing attacks against SOBER-t32 can be found in [14]and [15].

The attack will proceed in two stages. The aim of the first stage is to strip away the stuttering and recover the full N-stream, i.e., the output after the NLF. The aim if the second stage is to recover the original state of the LFSR based on the faults seen in the N-stream.

Stripping the Stuttering. To achieve this goal we assume that we can apply random single bit faults to the output of the N-stream. If we damage a word which is not a stutter control word, then depending on whether the word appeared in the original stuttered output we will see either a single bit difference in the faulted output stream or no change at all. If we fault a stutter control word, then we will see a significant difference in the output stream. However, we know that both streams originated from the same N-stream hence we can use them to reconstruct the original N-stream. To check whether two output words originated from the same N-word we simply check if their xor is in the set $\{0, 0x6996C53A, 0x96693AC5\}$, and the probability of a wrong identification is negligible since we are matching 32-bit words. We know that in each stream the order of the words is the same so with enough faults we can fully reconstruct the N-stream. Since the probability of a N-word being sent to the output is slightly below $\frac{2}{3}$ (remember that $\frac{1}{17}$ of the N-words are used as SCWs) it is enough to cause ~ 10 faults in the SCW to ensure that we reconstruct a significant part of the N-stream. Since the probability of causing a fault in a SCW is $\frac{1}{17}$, we can carry out this stage of the attack with less than 200 faults.

Recovering the LFSR State. Now we will use faults to the LFSR to retrieve its original state. Assume for now that the fault occurred in σ_{13} where σ is the current state of the LFSR. Let us denote the timing of the fault by i, i.e., we faulted σ_{i+13}. Notice that we have not assumed control over the timing of the fault, only over the location of the fault within the LFSR. We observe the first nonzero difference in the output stream which results from our fault. If N_t was sent to the output then the observed difference with respect to subtraction mod 2^{32} will be $\sigma_{i+13} - \hat{\sigma}_{i+13} = \pm 2^j$ where $\hat{\sigma}_{i+13}$ represents the faulted version and j is the bit faulted. If N_i was not sent to the output then the first observed difference is very unlikely to be of the above form. The sign of the difference will give us the original bit in the jth position (we are exploiting here the nonlinearity of $+$ with respect to $\oplus$). Notice that until now we have not used the fact that we know the N-stream. Since we know the position of the current output word in the N-stream we know the exact place of the bit recovered in the L-stream and hence have a linear equation in the original bits of the equivalent $GF(2)$ LFSR. By repeatedly applying faults we can recover enough linear equations and reconstruct the initial state. Notice that what actually remains to be shown is how to identify faults whose first effect on the N-stream is when the fault is in σ_{13}. But as we have shown before, such faults have a unique signature (an output difference of $\pm 2^j$) which allows us to identify them. Some care must be taken as to not confuse them with faults in σ_1 or σ_6, this can be done by rejecting candidates for which the output difference (in the N-stream) is a single bit. After reconstructing the LFSR state we can find $Konst$ from the equation for the NLF, the observed N-stream and the calculated L-stream.

In the full description of SOBER-t32, there is also a key-loading procedure which mixes the secret key and session key to initialize $Konst$ and σ_0. A similar fault attack can be applied to recover the secret key from the session key and the initial state.

3.3   An Attack on RC4

RC4 is a stream cipher designed by Ron Rivest in 1987. Its source code was kept as a trade secret until an alleged version was posted to the Cyberpunks mailing list [8]. RC4 consists of a key scheduling which initializes the permutation S, initialization and a generation loop. The key schedule will not be of interest for our attack. The most successful attacks against RC4 are guess and determine [8] but even these are prohibitively time consuming (more than 2^{700} time).

Initialization:
    $i = 0$
    $j = 0$
Generation Loop:
    $i = i + 1$
    $j = j + S[i]$
    Swap S[i] and S[j]
    Output S[S[i]+S[j]]

Fig. 2. Pseudo-code for RC4

Our attack will proceed in three stages:

1. Apply a fault to the S table and generate a long stream (repeat many times)
2. Analyze the resulting streams and generate equations in the original entries of S
3. Solve these equations to reconstruct S.

We assume that the attacker can fault a single entry of the S table immediately after the key-scheduling. Our first observation is that the attacker can recognize which value was faulted. I.e., if $S[x] = a$ and the fault changed its value to b then we will identify both a and b (but not x). This can be done by observing the frequency of each symbol in the output stream. If a was changed to b then a will never appear in the output stream, while b will appear with double frequency. Thus we need a stream of length about 10,000 bytes to reliably identify a and b. Our next mission is to identify faults in $S[1]$. This is done by looking at the first output byte. If this byte changed as a result of the fault then one of three cases must hold:

1. $S[1]$ was faulted
2. $S[S[1]]$ was faulted
3. $S[S[1] + S[S[1]]]$ was faulted

We know what the original value of $S[S[1] + S[S[1]]]$ was so we can check if the fault affected this cell (by identifying a and b). If we fault $S[1]$ and can identify the fault, i.e. $S[1]$ changed from a to b, then we know two things. First the original value of $S[1]$ was a and second, $S[b + S[b]] = c$ where c is the actual observed output in the faulted stream. So our first issue is how to recognize faults. If case 2 holds then with high probability the second output byte $S[S[2] + S[S[1] + S[2]]]$ will not be faulted. If the first case holds then the second output byte will always be faulted.

Now that we have identified a fault that affected $S[1]$ and changed its value from a to b we know two things: $S[1] = a$ and $S[b + S[b]] = c$ where c is the first output byte of the faulted stream. For each fault in $S[1]$ we get an equation, and after collecting many such equations we start utilizing our knowledge of $S[1]$ to deduce other values is S. For example, if $S[1] = 17$ then the equation $S[1 + S[1]] = 7$ will give us the value of $S[18] = 7$. We deduce as many values as possible from the given equations. If at the end we have not recovered $S[S[1]]$ then we guess its value. From our knowledge (guess) of $S[S[1]]$ we can carry out an analysis of the second output byte and recover more equations, this time of the form $S[b + S[b + S[1]]] = d$ (where d is the second output byte). Empirical results show that at this stage we recover on average 240 entries of S, and this is more than enough to deduce the rest from the observed non-faulted stream. We can easily reject incorrect guesses of $S[S[1]]$ by either noticing an inconsistency in the equations we collect or by recovering S and comparing the output stream to the observed one.

4   Summary of Results

The complexity of the attacks described in the previous sections are summarized in the table below. For the synthetic constructions an asymptotic analysis was done while for LILI-128, RC4 and SOBER-t32, the analysis was done for the recommended parameters of the ciphers. The parameters n,t,T,k and M are as defined in the relevant subsection. For the sake of simplicity the results for the clocking constructions assume that the length of the clocking LFSR is the same as the length of the data LFSR. Note that there are many possible tradeoffs between the various parameters, and the table describes only one of the potential combinations in each case.

5   Summary

We have shown that fault attacks are an extremely powerful technique for attacking stream ciphers. We demonstrated their applicability to a wide variety of

Attack	#Faults	Data	Time	Space
Filtered LFSRs (known filter)	t	$t2^t$	$\binom{n}{k}2^t + n^3$	$t2^t + n^2$
Filtered LFSRs (unknown filter)	2^t	$t2^t$	$\binom{n}{k}t2^t + n^3$	$t2^t + n^2$
Clock controlled (faults in clock register)	n	n^2	n^3	n^2
Clock controlled (faults in data register)	1	n	$\binom{n}{k}n + n^3$	n^2
FSM filtered LFSR (totally randomized)	nM^2	nM^2	$nM^2 + n^3$	n^2
FSM filtered LFSR (faults in FSM)	$T^2\frac{n}{\log M}$	$T^3\frac{n}{\log M}$	n^3	$T^3\frac{n}{\log M} + n^2$
LILI-128	10K	1M	2^{25}	1M
SOBER-t32	1K	100K	2^{30}	100K
RC4	2^{16}	2^{26}	2^{26}	2^{16}

Fig. 3. Summary of out results

synthetic and actual schemes, and identified several interesting open problems. Further work on this subject could include practical attacks on smart card implementations of stream ciphers, and finding attacks on more general classes of stream ciphers which are not based on LFSR's or arrays of updated values.

References

1. Ross Anderson *Optical Fault Induction*, June 2002
2. Boneh, Demillo, and Lipton *On the Importance of Checking Cryptographic Prtocols for Faults*, September 1996
3. Biham, Shamir *A New Cryptanalytic Attack on DES: Differential Fault Analysis*, October 1996
4. E. Dawson A. Clark J. Golic W. Millan L. Penna L. Simpson *The LILI-128 Keystream Generator*, November 2000.
5. Shai Halevi, Don Coppersmith & Charanjit Jutla *Scream an efficient stream cipher*, June 2002
6. Coppersmith, Krawczyk & Y. Mansour *The Shrinking Generator*, Proceedings of Crypto'93, pp.22–39, Springer-Verlag, 1993
7. Philip Hawks & Gregory G. Rose *Primitive Specification and Supporting Documentation for SOBER-t32 Submission to NESSIE*, June 2003.
8. Itsik Mantin & Adi Shamir *A Practical Attack on Broadcast RC4*, FSE 2001
9. Jovan Dj. Golic & Guglielmo Morgari *On the Resynchronization Attack*, FSE 2003
10. Jovan Dj. Golic & Guglielmo Morgari *Correlation Analysis of the Alternating Step Generator*, Designs, Codes and Cryptography, 31, 51–74, 2004
11. S. Dubuc, *Characterization of linear structures*, Designs, Codes and Cryptography, vol. 22, pp. 33-45, 2001
12. Nicolas Courtois and Willi Meier, *Algebraic Attacks on Stream Ciphers with Linear Feedback*, Eurocrypt 2003
13. Steve Babbage, *Cryptanalysis of LILI-128*, Proceedings of the 2nd NESSIE Workshop, 2001
14. Steve Babbage, Christophe De Cannière, Joseph Lano, Bart Preneel, Joos Vandewalle, *Cryptanalysis of SOBER-t32*, FSE 2003
15. Joo Yeon Cho and Josef Pieprzyk, *Algebraic Attacks on SOBER-t32 and SOBER-128*, FSE 2004

A Differential Fault Attack Against Early Rounds of (Triple-)DES

Ludger Hemme

Giesecke & Devrient GmbH
Prinzregentenstr. 159, 81677 Munich, Germany
ludger.hemme@de.gi-de.com

Abstract. Previously proposed differential fault analysis (DFA) techniques against iterated block ciphers mostly exploit computational errors in the last few rounds of the cipher to extract the secret key. In this paper we describe a DFA attack that exploits computational errors in early rounds of a Feistel cipher. The principle of the attack is to force collisions by inducing faults in intermediate results of the cipher. We put this attack into practice against DES implemented on a smart card and extracted the full round key of the first round within a few hours by inducing one bit errors in the second and third round, respectively.

1 Introduction

In 1997 Biham and Shamir [4] proposed the so called Differential Fault Analysis (DFA) and applied it to secret key cryptosystems such as DES. Their attack exploits computational errors induced during the last few rounds of DES to extract the secret key of the last round. At least since the results of Anderson and Skorobogatov [2] the application of this attack to tamper resistant devices such as smart cards is a real threat: By exposing a chip to a laser beam or even the focused light from a flash lamp it is possible to induce the kinds of errors that are needed by the attack to succeed. Therefore in addition to possibly existing hardware countermeasures it is advisable to implement also adequate software countermeasures like verifying the correctness of an encryption by a subsequent encryption or decryption. To optimize performance, one might think of reducing these countermeasures to the critical last few rounds or, in case of Triple-DES, for example, to the last DES operation. This, however, can lead to a lack of security, as we will show in this paper. We will present a DFA attack against early rounds of a Feistel cipher and show that it is not sufficient to protect only the last few rounds against inducing computational errors. Since the attack targets at the first few rounds of the cipher (more exactly rounds 2,3,...) it is advisable to protect also these rounds.

The attack requires a chosen plaintext situation. The attacker must be able to choose various plaintexts and to encrypt them with the secret key that he wants to compromise. Associated with smart cards this might be a realistic scenario. By inducing a fault during the encryption of a plaintext P the attacker tries

M. Joye and J.-J. Quisquater (Eds.): CHES 2004, LNCS 3156, pp. 254–267, 2004.

to get a collision with another plaintext $\widetilde{P}$, meaning that the faulty ciphertext belonging to P equals the correct ciphertext belonging to $\widetilde{P}$. This is in some sense a reversion of the original DFA attack of Biham and Shamir [4]. The problem, however, is to find the pairs of colliding plaintexts in an efficient way. To solve this problem we make use of the concept of characteristics introduced by Biham and Shamir [3]. Once having found a pair of colliding plaintexts one can apply methods of differential cryptanalysis to gain some information about the first round key. Other pairs will provide further information until at last the full round key of the first round will be recovered.

In the following we will first provide some notations and definitions and then describe in detail the principle of the attack against a Feistel cipher. Finally we will describe the application of the attack on DES and Triple-DES, respectively.

2 Notations and Definitions

Definition 1. *A Feistel cipher of block length $2n$ with r rounds $(n, r \in \mathbb{N})$ is a function $F_K : \mathrm{GF}(2)^{2n} \longrightarrow \mathrm{GF}(2)^{2n}$ with a key $K = (K_1, \ldots, K_r)$ consisting of r round keys $K_i \in \mathrm{GF}(2)^m$ of length $m \in \mathbb{N}$, which maps a plaintext $P = (P^L, P^R) \in \mathrm{GF}(2)^n \times \mathrm{GF}(2)^n$ to the corresponding ciphertext $C = (C^L, C^R) = F_K(P)$ in the following way:*

1. *$L_0 := P^L, R_0 := P^R$*
2. *For $i = 1, \ldots, r$*
   $(L_i, R_i) := (R_{i-1}, L_{i-1} \oplus f(R_{i-1}, K_i))$,
   where the round function $f : \mathrm{GF}(2)^n \times \mathrm{GF}(2)^m \longrightarrow \mathrm{GF}(2)^n$ is any mapping and $\oplus$ is the ordinary componentwise addition over $\mathrm{GF}(2)$.
3. *$C^L := R_r, C^R := L_r$*

Traditionally, the round keys $(K_1, K_2, \ldots, K_r)$ are computed by a key schedule algorithm on input a master key, but in Definition 1 also the case of independent round keys is included. Figure 1 shows the Feistel scheme as a flowchart.

The attack described in Sect. 3 deals with inducing errors during the encryption of plaintexts. Hence we introduce a notation for the faulty encryption of a plaintext P. Let F_K be a Feistel cipher of block length $2n$ with r rounds and let $k \in \{1, \ldots, r\}$, $\varepsilon \in \mathrm{GF}(2)^n$. Then $F_K^{(k,\varepsilon)} : \mathrm{GF}(2)^{2n} \to \mathrm{GF}(2)^{2n}$ denotes the mapping which maps P to $F_K^{(k,\varepsilon)}(P)$ by applying the encryption algorithm F_K to P, whereby the output Y_k of the round function f in the k-th round is replaced with $Y_k \oplus \varepsilon$.

In the following we will have to deal with pairs of plaintexts, ciphertexts and intermediate results and with their differences with regard to $\oplus$, the so called XOR-differences. So for a pair of plaintexts $(P, \widetilde{P})$ and a Feistel cipher F_K we denote the XOR-differences occurring during the calculation of $F_K(P)$ and $F_K(\widetilde{P})$ in the following way:

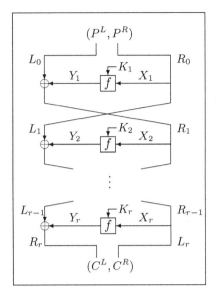

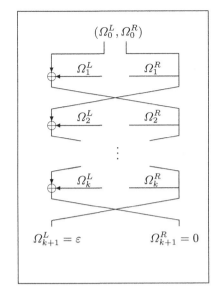

Fig. 1. Feistel scheme   **Fig. 2.** A k-round ε-characteristic

$\Delta P := P \oplus \widetilde{P}$ plaintext difference

$\Delta C := C \oplus \widetilde{C}$ ciphertext difference

$\Delta L_i := L_i \oplus \widetilde{L}_i,$

$\Delta R_i := R_i \oplus \widetilde{R}_i$ differences of the intermediate results in the i-th round

Besides we denote the inputs of the round function f in the i-th round by $X_i, \widetilde{X}_i$, respectively, and its outputs by $Y_i, \widetilde{Y}_i$, respectively (see Fig. 1). The corresponding XOR-differences are denoted the same way as above:

$\Delta X_i := X_i \oplus \widetilde{X}_i$ input difference of the round function f in the i-th round

$\Delta Y_i := Y_i \oplus \widetilde{Y}_i$ output difference of the round function f in the i-th round

In this paper we will be mainly interested in differences between intermediate results occurring during the faulty encryption of P and the correct encryption of $\widetilde{P}$, more exactly during the calculation of $F_K^{(k,\varepsilon)}(P)$ and $F_K(\widetilde{P})$. For the sake of simplicity we denote also these differences with the above defined symbols. Though the exact meaning of the symbols should always be clear from the context.

Definition 2. *A k-round characteristic with respect to a Feistel cipher of block length $2n$ with r rounds $(k, n, r \in \mathbb{N}, k \leq r)$ is a tuple $\Omega = (\Omega_0, \Omega_1, \ldots, \Omega_{k+1})$, where the $\Omega_i = (\Omega_i^L, \Omega_i^R) \in GF(2)^n \times GF(2)^n$ satisfy the following conditions:*

i) $\Omega_1^R = \Omega_0^R,$

ii) $\Omega_2^R = \Omega_0^L \oplus \Omega_1^L,$

iii) $\Omega_{k+1}^L = \Omega_k^R$,

iv) $\Omega_{i+1}^R = \Omega_i^L \oplus \Omega_{i-1}^R \ \forall \, i \in \{2, 3, \ldots, k\}$.

For $\varepsilon \in \mathrm{GF}(2)^n$ *a* k-*round characteristic* Ω *is called a* k-*round* ε-*characteristic if* $(\Omega_{k+1}^L, \Omega_{k+1}^R) = (\varepsilon, 0)$.

Definition 3. *A right pair with respect to a* k-*round characteristic* $\Omega = (\Omega_0, \Omega_1, \ldots, \Omega_{k+1})$ *and with respect to a key* K *of the associated Feistel cipher* F_K *is a pair of plaintexts* $(P, \widetilde{P})$ *satisfying the following conditions:*

i) $\Delta P = \Omega_0$,

ii) $(\Delta Y_i, \Delta X_i) = (\Omega_i^L, \Omega_i^R) \ \forall \, i \in \{1, \ldots, k\}$,

where $\Delta Y_i, \Delta X_i$ *are the above defined differences at the encryption by* F_K.

Definition 4. *The probability* $p_{\Omega,K}$ *of a characteristic* $\Omega = (\Omega_0, \Omega_1, \ldots, \Omega_{k+1})$ *with respect to a key* K *of the associated Feistel cipher is the probability that a random pair of plaintexts* $(P, \widetilde{P})$ *satisfying* $\Delta P = \Omega_0$ *is a right pair with respect to* Ω *and* K.

3 Description of the Attack Against a Feistel Cipher

Let F_K be a Feistel cipher of block length $2n$ with r rounds, where K is the secret key that we would like to compromise. To carry out the attack the following preconditions must be fulfilled:

i) *Chosen plaintext scenario:* It is possible to encrypt arbitrarily chosen plaintexts with the secret key and to check the corresponding ciphertexts for pairwise equality. In particular, if the computed ciphertexts are returned to the attacker as result, this check is trivially possible.

ii) *Fault model:* It is possible to induce errors during computation of $F_K(P)$, more exactly to replace the output Y_k of the round function f in the k-th round ($k \geq 2$) with $Y_k \oplus \varepsilon$, where $\varepsilon \in E$ is a not necessarily known element of the a priori chosen subset $E \subseteq \mathrm{GF}(2)^n$. In the notation of Sect. 2 this means that it is possible to 'compute' $F_K^{(k,\varepsilon)}(P)$ for some $\varepsilon \in E$. Considering E as a probability space we denote by $\mathrm{prob}(\varepsilon)$ the probability that the induced error is ε.

By executing the following algorithm we will now try to get a pair of plaintexts $(P, \widetilde{P})$, where for the encryption by F_K the difference ΔY_1 at the output of the round function f in the first round is known. In the following we will call a triple $(P, \widetilde{P}, \Delta Y_1)$ consisting of a pair of plaintexts $(P, \widetilde{P})$ and the corresponding output difference ΔY_1 of the round function f 'a useful pair'.

Algorithm 1

> *INPUT* · *error round $k \geq 2$*
> · *error set $E \subseteq GF(2)^n$*
> · *index set $\hat{E} \subseteq E$*
> · *for each $\varepsilon \in \hat{E}$ a $(k-1)$-round ε-characteristic*
> $\Omega_\varepsilon = (\Omega_{\varepsilon,0}, \Omega_{\varepsilon,1}, \ldots, \Omega_{\varepsilon,k})$

1. *Choose a random plaintext $P \in GF(2)^{2n}$ and 'compute' $F_K^{(k,\varepsilon)}(P)$ for some random $\varepsilon \in E$;*
2. *For every $\hat{\varepsilon} \in \hat{E}$*
   a) *Set $\widetilde{P} := P \oplus \Omega_{\hat{\varepsilon},0}$ and compute $F_K(\widetilde{P})$;*
   b) *If $F_K(\widetilde{P}) = F_K^{(k,\varepsilon)}(P)$ then output the triple $(P, \widetilde{P}, \Omega_{\hat{\varepsilon},1}^L)$;*

The following proposition shows why we may expect that Algorithm 1 will output useful pairs after a certain number of runs.

Proposition 1. *The probability that one pass of Algorithm 1 outputs at least one useful pair is at least $\sum_{\varepsilon \in \hat{E}} \mathrm{prob}(\varepsilon) p_{\Omega_\varepsilon, K}$, where the $p_{\Omega_\varepsilon, K}$ are the probabilities of the characteristics Ω_ε with respect to the secret key K.*

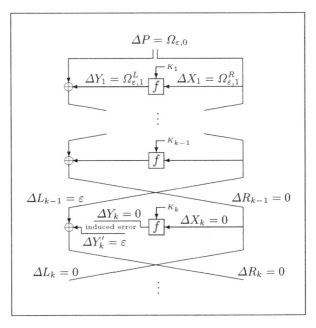

Fig. 3. $(P, \widetilde{P})$ is a right pair with respect to Ω_ε and K

Proof. Let $P \in \mathrm{GF}(2)^{2n}$ and $\varepsilon \in \mathrm{GF}(2)^n$ be the plaintext and the induced fault, respectively, from step 1 of Algorithm 1. Assume that $\varepsilon \in \hat{E}$. So during one pass of Algorithm 1, in one of the steps 2a the plaintext $\widetilde{P} \in \mathrm{GF}(2)^{2n}$ is defined, such that $\Delta P = \Omega_{\varepsilon,0}$. With probability $p_{\Omega_\varepsilon,K}$ the pair $(P, \widetilde{P})$ is a right pair with respect to Ω_ε and the secret key K. If this is the case (see Fig. 3), then in particular $\Delta Y_1 = \Omega_{\varepsilon,1}^L$, $\Delta L_{k-1} = \varepsilon$ and $\Delta R_{k-1} = 0$. In the k-th round of the encryption of P the output Y_k of the round function f is replaced by $Y_k' := Y_k \oplus \varepsilon$. At the end of the k-th round we have $\Delta L_k = \Delta R_{k-1} = 0$ and $\Delta R_k = \Delta L_{k-1} \oplus \Delta Y_k \oplus \varepsilon = \varepsilon \oplus \varepsilon = 0$, since $\Delta Y_k = f(R_{k-1}, K) \oplus f(\widetilde{R}_{k-1}, K) = 0$ due to $\Delta R_{k-1} = 0$. This implies that $F_K^{(k,\varepsilon)}(P) \oplus F_K(\widetilde{P}) = 0$ and the triple $(P, \widetilde{P}, \Omega_{\varepsilon,1}^L)$, which is a useful pair due to $\Delta Y_1 = \Omega_{\varepsilon,1}^L$, is output by Algorithm 1. Since in step 1 the error $\varepsilon \in \hat{E}$ occurs with probability $\mathrm{prob}(\varepsilon)$, the probability that one pass of Algorithm 1 outputs at least one useful pair is at least $\sum_{\varepsilon \in \hat{E}} \mathrm{prob}(\varepsilon) p_{\Omega_\varepsilon,K}$. $\square$

To get a high output rate of Algorithm 1 the probabilities of the used characteristics should be as high as possible. The existence of a $(k-1)$-round ε-characteristic $\Omega = (\Omega_0, \Omega_1, \ldots, \Omega_k)$ of probability $p_{\Omega,K} > 0$ for any $\varepsilon \in \mathrm{GF}(2)^n$ is ensured by the following consideration: Due to the invertibility of the Feistel structure there is a pair of plaintexts $(P, \widetilde{P})$ such that $L_{k-1} = \varepsilon$ and $R_{k-1} = \widetilde{L}_{k-1} = \widetilde{R}_{k-1} = 0$ (for the encryption by F_K). For the choice $\Omega_0 := \Delta P$, $\Omega_k := (\varepsilon, 0)$ and $\Omega_i := (\Delta Y_i, \Delta X_i)$, $i \in \{1, \ldots, k-1\}$, the tuple $\Omega = (\Omega_0, \Omega_1, \ldots, \Omega_k)$ is a $(k-1)$-round ε-characteristic and $(P, \widetilde{P})$ is a right pair with respect to Ω and K.

Although the existence of appropriate characteristics is ensured, it is a problem to find some without knowing the key K. However, depending on the round function of the considered Feistel cipher, it may be possible to define a probability of characteristics that is independent of the key K and still a good approximation for the probability of Definition 4. In case of DES, for example, we can use a definition of Biham and Shamir [3] that helps us to calculate characteristics of high probability.

Another problem we have to take into consideration is that Algorithm 1 might output pairs which are erroneously regarded as useful pairs. We denote by p_{err} the probability that a triple $(P, \widetilde{P}, \Omega_{\varepsilon,1}^L)$ output by Algorithm 1 is not a useful pair. The following proposition says that we don't have to worry if the induced error occurs in the second round of the cipher.

Proposition 2. *Let* $(P, \widetilde{P}, \Omega_{\hat{\varepsilon},1}^L)$ *be a triple output by Algorithm 1 with error round* $k = 2$. *Then* $(P, \widetilde{P}, \Omega_{\hat{\varepsilon},1}^L)$ *is a useful pair.*

Proof. Let ε be the error occurred in step 1 of Algorithm 1. Since $(P, \widetilde{P}, \Omega_{\hat{\varepsilon},1}^L)$ was output by Algorithm 1, we have $\Delta C = F_K^{(2,\varepsilon)}(P) \oplus F_K(\widetilde{P}) = 0$. Due to the structure of the Feistel cipher this implies $\Delta R_1 = 0$. By the choice of $\widetilde{P}$ we have $\Delta P^L = P^L \oplus \widetilde{P}^L = \Omega_{\hat{\varepsilon},0}^L = \Omega_{\hat{\varepsilon},2}^R \oplus \Omega_{\hat{\varepsilon},1}^L = \Omega_{\hat{\varepsilon},1}^L$, where $\Omega_{\hat{\varepsilon}} = (\Omega_{\hat{\varepsilon},0}, \Omega_{\hat{\varepsilon},1}, \Omega_{\hat{\varepsilon},2})$ is the characteristic used by Algorithm 1 to define $\widetilde{P}$. Thus the difference at the output of the round function f in the first round is $\Delta Y_1 = \Delta R_1 \oplus \Delta P^L = 0 \oplus \Omega^L_{\hat{\varepsilon},1} = \Omega^L_{\hat{\varepsilon},1}$ and $(P, \widetilde{P}, \Omega^L_{\hat{\varepsilon},1})$ is a useful pair. $\qquad\qquad\square$

Once having found useful pairs we can exploit them by means of differential cryptanalysis to get some information about the round key K_1 of the first round. So let $(P, \widetilde{P}, \Delta Y_1)$ be a useful pair. Then we test for each candidate $\hat{K}_1 \in \mathrm{GF}(2)^m$ of the round key K_1 if it satisfies

$$f(P^R, \hat{K}_1) \oplus f(\widetilde{P}^R, \hat{K}_1) = \Delta Y_1. \qquad (1)$$

If this is the case we increment a counter for this candidate. After having processed several useful pairs, the candidate with the highest counter is taken to be the value of K_1. The success of this method depends on the signal to noise ratio S/N which is the expected number of times the right key is counted over the expected number of times a randomly picked wrong key is counted. For $S/N > 1$ the method succeeds and the number of needed pairs decreases with increasing S/N. If $S/N = 1$ the method does not succeed.

In our case the pairs to be analysed are output by Algorithm 1. For every useful pair the right key is counted and in addition several wrong keys, which we suppose to be uniformly distributed. With probability p_{err} an output pair is not a useful pair. In this case there are counted several keys, which we suppose again to be uniformly distributed. This time it is not guaranteed that the right key is counted but it can happen. Let γ be the average number of counted keys per pair and Q be the number of key candidates. Then the signal to noise ratio is

$$S/N = \frac{(1 - p_{\mathrm{err}}) + p_{\mathrm{err}} \cdot \gamma/Q}{\gamma/Q} = \frac{(1 - p_{\mathrm{err}}) \cdot Q}{\gamma} + p_{\mathrm{err}}. \qquad (2)$$

In the worst case we have $p_{\mathrm{err}} = 1$ and no output pair is a useful pair. The signal to noise ratio is then $S/N = 1$ and the attack fails. If however p_{err} is small, then $S/N \approx Q/\gamma$.

As a consequence of these considerations a characteristic $\Omega = (\Omega_0, \Omega_1, \ldots, \Omega_k)$ used in Algorithm 1 should satisfy the condition $\Omega^R_0 \neq 0$. Assume this is not the case. Then every useful pair output by Algorithm 1 using Ω has the form $(P, \widetilde{P}, 0)$, where $\Delta P^R = \Omega^R_0 = 0$. Thus (1) is obviously satisfied for all key candidates $\hat{K}_1 \in \mathrm{GF}(2)^m$ and Ω does not contribute to compromise the key.

Before discussing the application of the attack on DES we give a slightly generalised version of Algorithm 1 that provides higher flexibility and thus better possibilities of optimizing the attack. In Algorithm 1 for each possible error $\varepsilon \in E$ there is used at most one characteristic. According to Proposition 1 the probability of this characteristic should be as high as possible to ensure a high output rate of useful pairs. In general, however, for some errors $\varepsilon \in E$ there might be only ε-characteristics of relatively low probability, whereas for some other errors there are even several ε-characteristics of relatively high probability. Algorithm 2 takes this situation into account. At least in the case of DES this generalised algorithm yields slightly better results than Algorithm 1 as we will see in Sect. 4.

Algorithm 2

> *INPUT* · *error round $k \geq 2$*
> · *error set $E \subseteq GF(2)^n$*
> · *for each $\varepsilon \in E$ a set $\mathcal{C}_\varepsilon$ of $(k-1)$-round ε-characteristics*

1. *Choose a random plaintext $P \in GF(2)^{2n}$ and 'compute' $F_K^{(k,\varepsilon)}(P)$ for some random $\varepsilon \in E$;*
2. *For every $\hat{\varepsilon} \in E$, for every $\Omega = (\Omega_0, \Omega_1, \ldots, \Omega_k) \in \mathcal{C}_{\hat{\varepsilon}}$*
   a) *Set $\tilde{P} := P \oplus \Omega_0$ and compute $F_K(\tilde{P})$;*
   b) *If $F_K(\tilde{P}) = F_K^{(k,\varepsilon)}(P)$ then output the triple $(P, \tilde{P}, \Omega_1^L)$;*

A lower bound for the output probability of Algorithm 2 is given by Proposition 3. The proof is in principle the same as for Proposition 1.

Proposition 3. *The probability that one pass of Algorithm 2 outputs at least one useful pair is at least $\sum_{\varepsilon \in E} \sum_{\Omega \in \mathcal{C}_\varepsilon} \mathrm{prob}(\varepsilon) p_{\Omega,K}$, where the $p_{\Omega,K}$ are the probabilities of the characteristics Ω with respect to the secret key K.*

Again we can be sure that an output triple is a useful pair, if the error is induced in the second round.

Proposition 4. *Let $(P, \tilde{P}, \Omega_1^L)$ be a triple output by Algorithm 2 with error round $k = 2$. Then $(P, \tilde{P}, \Omega_1^L)$ is a useful pair.*

The proof is exactly the same as for Proposition 2.

4 Application of the Attack on (Triple-)DES

Now we will show how the attack described above can be applied to the Data Encryption Standard (DES) [7]. Here we refer to 'DES' as a Feistel cipher of block length 64 with 16 rounds that has additional bit permutations at the beginning and at the end. Throughout this section we ignore the existence of these permutations. We can do this by the following convention. Whenever we use the word 'plaintext' ('ciphertext') we imagine that this is the already permuted actual plaintext (ciphertext). The round function f consists of the E-expansion, the addition of the 48 bit round key, the S-box transformations and the P-permutation. For details refer to [7].

From the principle of the attack it is clear that Triple-DES can be attacked in exactly the same way as DES, meaning that the determination of the first round key is equal for both ciphers. Thus, in the following, whenever we write 'DES' one may also read 'Triple-DES' instead.

To carry out Algorithm 1 and Algorithm 2, respectively, we first have to choose an appropriate error set $E \subseteq GF(2)^n$. Generally the choice depends on the implementation of DES, on the hardware platform and on the equipment used for inducing the faults. The more information an attacker has about the kind of faults he is able to induce, the more selective he can choose the set E. For the beginning we choose E to be the set $E_{\text{onebit}} := \{\varepsilon \in \text{GF}(2)^{32}; \text{hammingweight}(\varepsilon) = 1\}$ of all one bit faults. So our goal is to induce a one bit error in the output of the round function f. This could be done, for example, by inducing a bit flip in the register containing this intermediate result [2]. But this is not the only way to reach the goal. Another possibility is to disturb the program flow during the calculation of the P-permutation, the S-box transformations or even the E-expansion or the addition of the round key [1]. Assume, for example, that at one point of the DES calculation we are able to prevent the correct reading of an S-box table entry, so that a random value instead of the correct 4 bit result is returned. Then with probability $1/4$ there will be a one bit error in the output of the S-box transformations and thus in the output of the round function f. Such a 'random' S-box output can also be forced indirectly, for example by inducing an appropriate error during the E-expansion or the addition of the round key.

Once having chosen the set E, we have to choose the error round number $k \geq 2$ and to calculate $(k-1)$-round ε-characteristics Ω of high probability $p_{\Omega,K}$. Unfortunately we cannot calculate $p_{\Omega,K}$ of a given characteristic Ω because we do not know the secret key K. Though for the case of DES, Biham and Shamir [3] defined a probability p_{Ω} of a characteristic Ω that is independent of the secret key K and a good approximation for the probability $p_{\Omega,K}$ of Definition 4.

Definition 5. *Let $\Omega = (\Omega_0, \Omega_1, \ldots, \Omega_{k+1})$ be a k-round characteristic with respect to DES.*
The probability $p_{\Omega}^{(i)}$ of round i of Ω is the fraction

$$p_{\Omega}^{(i)} := 2^{-32 \cdot 48} \cdot |\{(x,y) \in \text{GF}(2)^{32} \times \text{GF}(2)^{48} \,;\, f(x,y) \oplus f(x \oplus \Omega_i^R, y) = \Omega_i^L\}|$$

of all input pairs $x, x \oplus \Omega_i^R$ of f, 'encrypted' by all round keys y, for which the output difference equals Ω_i^L.
The probability p_{Ω} of the characteristic Ω is the product

$$p_{\Omega} := \prod_{i=1}^{k} p_{\Omega}^{(i)}$$

of the probabilities of all rounds.

With this definition it is possible to calculate the best $(k-1)$-round ε-characteristics $\Omega_{\varepsilon} = (\Omega_{\varepsilon,0}, \Omega_{\varepsilon,1}, \ldots, \Omega_{\varepsilon,k})$ for all $\varepsilon \in E$. Here 'the best' means those with the highest probability $p_{\Omega_{\varepsilon}}$. For the calculation we implemented the search algorithm of Matsui [6], slightly modified due to the side condition for Ω_{ε}. The results of the calculation for the one bit fault model $E = E_{\text{onebit}}$ are listed in the appendix, where tables 4 to 6 show the best $(k-1)$-round ε-characteristics for all $\varepsilon \in E_{\text{onebit}}$ and for $k = 2, 3, 4$. Note that all these ε-characteristics satisfy $\Omega_{\varepsilon,1}^R \neq 0$ and thus can be used to recover the first round key. A brief overview of the corresponding probabilities is given in Table 1.

We implemented Algorithm 1 and Algorithm 2 on a PC and simulated the attack against DES for the following fault model. *It is possible to flip a single*

Table 1. Probabilities of the best $(k-1)$-round ε-characteristics for $\varepsilon \in E_{\text{onebit}}$

$k-1$	$\dfrac{1}{32} \sum\limits_{\varepsilon \in E_{\text{onebit}}} p_{\Omega_\varepsilon}$	$\max\limits_{\varepsilon \in E_{\text{onebit}}} p_{\Omega_\varepsilon}$	$\min\limits_{\varepsilon \in E_{\text{onebit}}} p_{\Omega_\varepsilon}$
1	0.111	0.250	0.016
2	$1.78 \cdot 10^{-3}$	$7.32 \cdot 10^{-3}$	$3.13 \cdot 10^{-6}$
3	$1.38 \cdot 10^{-6}$	$4.89 \cdot 10^{-6}$	$1.43 \cdot 10^{-9}$

random bit (uniformly distributed) of the output of the round function f in the k-th round. That means that the error set E is the set E_{onebit} of the 32 possible one bit faults and $\text{prob}(\varepsilon) = 1/32$ for all $\varepsilon \in E$. For the analysis of the found pairs we use a counting scheme that counts over 6 bit subkeys (corresponding to the 6 bit S-box inputs) of the first round key. Let us assume that the probability p_{err} of an output triple being not a useful pair is negligible. For error round $k = 2$ this is guaranteed by Proposition 2 and Proposition 4, respectively. According to (2) for the signal to noise ratio of this counting scheme we have

$$S/N \approx \frac{Q}{\gamma} \geq \frac{2^6}{16} = 4,$$

where the upper bound 16 for the counted keys per pair is given by the difference distribution tables of DES [3]. The ratio S/N is high enough for the attack to succeed with a reasonable amount of useful pairs. Table 2 shows some results of the simulation using Algorithm 1 for the error rounds $k = 2, 3, 4$. For various numbers of runs of Algorithm 1 and various numbers $|\hat{E}|$ of used characteristics it is stated how many faulty and how many correct encryptions were calculated, how many useful pairs were found and how many bits of information about the key were extracted. The numbers of found pairs and key bits are averaged over the number of performed simulations, which can be found in the last column. Note that for each single simulation the secret key to be compromised was randomly chosen. Finally Table 2 shows for each case the expected minimum number of useful pairs, calculated using Proposition 1. The characteristics used for the simulation were chosen in the following way. Assume the number of used characteristics given by Table 2 being N. Then the used characteristics are the N most probable characteristics of the appropriate table in the appendix.

Table 3 shows some results of the simulation using Algorithm 2. The used characteristics were chosen in the following way. For errors $\varepsilon \in E$, for which there exist ε-characteristics Ω_ε of relatively high probability, we chose various ε-characteristics, whereas for other errors $\varepsilon \in E$ we did not choose any ε-characteristic due to the low probabilities. Furthermore the choice was made taking care that the number of different values of $\Omega_{\varepsilon,1}^R$ is as high as possible. The reason for that is a better distribution of the wrong subkey values counted during the differential analysis, resulting in a higher signal to noise ratio of the counting scheme. The results in Table 3 show that the number of induced errors required

Table 2. Simulation on PC (Algorithm 1, fault model $E = E_{\text{onebit}}$)

k	faulty + correct DES-calculations		charac-teristics	found pairs	expected pairs	extracted key bits	simu-lations
2	100 +	1600	16	9.16	9.18	17.46	10000
	500 +	8000	16	45.95	45.90	41.03	10000
	500 +	16000	32	55.43	55.53	46.74	10000
	1000 +	32000	32	110.92	111.05	47.94	10000
	1500 +	48000	32	166.46	166.58	48.00	10000
3	$5 \cdot 10^3 + 4.0 \cdot 10^4$		8	6.20	6.26	17.65	1000
	$1 \cdot 10^4 + 1.6 \cdot 10^5$		16	17.67	17.64	36.36	1000
	$5 \cdot 10^4 + 8.0 \cdot 10^5$		16	88.88	88.19	45.59	1000
	$5 \cdot 10^5 + 1.6 \cdot 10^7$		32	888.11	889.24	47.86	1000
	$1 \cdot 10^6 + 3.2 \cdot 10^7$		32	1779.18	1778.48	48.00	1000
4	$5 \cdot 10^6 + 7.0 \cdot 10^7$		14	6.25	6.57	34.52	100
	$1 \cdot 10^7 + 1.4 \cdot 10^8$		14	13.40	13.15	42.42	100
	$5 \cdot 10^7 + 1.0 \cdot 10^9$		20	67.25	68.55	47.30	20

Table 3. Simulation on PC (Algorithm 2, fault model $E = E_{\text{onebit}}$)

k	faulty + correct DES-calculations		charac-teristics	found pairs	expected pairs	extracted key bits	simu-lations
2	10 +	990	99	3.96	3.96	10.55	10000
	200 +	12800	64	58.62	58.59	45.84	10000
	400 +	40000	100	94.21	94.17	48.00	10000
3	100 +	28100	281	2.09	2.17	10.23	1000
	500 +	140500	281	11.07	10.87	31.25	1000
	1000 +	160000	160	12.67	12.62	36.18	1000
	2000 +	278000	139	15.67	15.70	41.34	1000
	5000 +	555000	111	26.42	26.57	46.83	1000
	10000 +	1110000	111	53.42	53.14	47.95	1000
4	$1 \cdot 10^5 + 1.62 \cdot 10^7$		162	1.56	1.35	13.82	100
	$5 \cdot 10^5 + 8.10 \cdot 10^7$		162	6.52	6.72	36.21	100
	$1 \cdot 10^6 + 1.62 \cdot 10^8$		162	13.96	13.44	45.78	100
	$5 \cdot 10^6 + 8.10 \cdot 10^8$		162	66.68	67.20	48.00	100

for extracting a certain amount of key bits is lower than for Algorithm 1. This gain, however, is diminished by the higher amount of correct DES-calculations resulting from the higher number of used characteristics. Apart from this one can see that for error rounds $k = 3, 4$ the total amount of DES-calculations required for extracting many key bits is slightly less than for using Algorithm 1.

Now let us consider another fault model. Assume that during the DES calculation we are able to disturb the access to the S-box tables in a way that instead of the correct S-box entry a random 4 bit value is read. Hence we consider the error sets $E_i := \{\pi(x) \in \text{GF}(2)^{32}; x = (x_1, \ldots, x_8) \in \text{GF}(2)^{4 \cdot 8} \wedge x_j = 0 \text{ for } j \neq i\}$ of all the errors that arise from a random fault in the output of S-box S_i $(i = 1, \ldots, 8)$, where π denotes the P-Permutation of the DES round function. The calculation of the best ε-characteristics for all $\varepsilon \in \bigcup_{i=1}^{8} E_i$ showed that the probabilities for $\varepsilon \in \bigcup_{i=1}^{8} E_i \setminus E_{\mathrm{onebit}}$ are much smaller than for $\varepsilon \in E_{\mathrm{onebit}}$. Hence it is reasonable also for this fault model to use ε-characteristics for $\varepsilon \in E_{\mathrm{onebit}}$ only.

To test the attack in a real life situation, we implemented DES on a smart card and induced computational errors during calculation of the S-boxes by exposing the chip to a laser beam. For the determination of the correct timing we exploited information obtained by measuring the power consumption of the chip. The distribution of the induced 1-, 2-, 3- and 4-bit faults showed that we managed it to approximately realise the just considered fault model. Of course not every shot induced an error in the desired S-box output and finally we reached average probabilities between 13% and 17% for generating a 1-bit error in the output of a certain S-box by one shot. After these preliminary examinations we carried out the attack against the smart card by applying Algorithm 1 for the inputs $k = 2$, $E = E_i$ and $\hat{E} = E_i \cap E_{\mathrm{onebit}}$ $(i = 1, 5, 6, 7)$, using the characteristics from Table 4. In other words we induced errors in the outputs of the S-boxes 1,5,6 and 7 in the second round and looked for useful pairs using four characteristics in each of the four cases. In total we carried out 13000 passes of Algorithm 1, i.e. 13000 faulty and 52000 correct DES calculations, and found 187 useful pairs that revealed the full round key of the first round. As one DES calculation took about 0.1 seconds, including the time for communication between smart card and terminal, the attack took about two hours.

Next we attacked the third DES round on the same smart card by disturbing the S-boxes 1,4 and 8 in the same manner as described above. This time we found in total 263 pairs by $6.9 \cdot 10^5$ runs of Algorithm 1, meaning an effort of $6.9 \cdot 10^5$ faulty and $2.76 \cdot 10^6$ correct DES calculations or 96 hours runtime, respectively. Again the found pairs compromised the full round key of the first round.

5   Conclusion

In this paper we introduced a DFA attack on early rounds of a Feistel cipher showing that it is not sufficient to protect only the last few rounds of the cipher against inducing computational errors. By carrying out the attack against DES implemented on a smart card we proved that the attack is not only of theoretical nature but a real threat in practice. An evident question is if the principle of the attack can also be applied to a non-Feistel cipher, for example to the AES. The answer is yes. In case of AES, for example, it is possible to combine the attack of Dusart et al. [5] with our principle to force collisions by inducing computational errors in early rounds of the cipher. The problem is that the probabilities of characteristics or differentials, respectively, for AES are much smaller than for DES. So even by using counting schemes over four key bytes, as Piret and Quisquater [8] did to optimise the attack in [5], the amount of AES calculations required to extract the secret key is quite large at the moment, but our investigations are still in progress.

References

1. R. Anderson and M. Kuhn. Low Cost Attacks on Tamper Resistant Devices. In *IWSP: 5th International Workshop of Security Protocols*, volume 1361 of *Lecture Notes in Computer Science*, pages 125–136. Springer, 1997.
2. R. Anderson and S. Skorobogatov. Optical Fault Induction Attacks. In *Cryptographic Hardware and Embedded Systmes - CHES 2002*, volume 2523 of *Lecture Notes in Computer Science*. Springer, 2002.
3. E. Biham and A. Shamir. Differential cryptanalysis of DES-like cryptosystems. *Journal of Cryptology*, 4(1):3–72, 1991.
4. E. Biham and A. Shamir. Differential Fault Analysis of Secret Key Cryptosystems. *Lecture Notes in Computer Science*, 1294:513–525, 1997.
5. P. Dusart, G. Letourneux, and O. Vivolo. Differential Fault Analysis on A.E.S. Available at http://eprint.iacr.org/, 2003/010, 2003.
6. M. Matsui. On Correlation Between the Order of S-boxes and the Strength of DES. *Lecture Notes in Computer Science*, 950:366–375, 1995.
7. NIST FIPS PUB 46-3. *Data Encryption Standard (DES)*. U.S. Department of Commerce, 1999.
8. G. Piret and J.J. Quisquater. A Differential Fault Attack Technique against SPN Structures, with Application to the AES and KHAZAD. In *Cryptographic Hardware and Embedded Systmes - CHES 2003*, volume 2779 of *Lecture Notes in Computer Science*. Springer, 2003.

A   Tables of Characteristics

The following tables show the best 1-, 2- and 3-round ε-characteristics Ω_ε of DES for all $\varepsilon \in E_{\mathrm{onebit}}$. The components of the characteristics are listed in hexadecimal notation. Components not given in the tables can be calculated according to Definition 2.

Table 4. Best 1-round ε-characteristics of DES for $\varepsilon \in E_{\mathrm{onebit}}$

ε	$\Omega_{\varepsilon,0}^{L}$	p_{Ω_ε}	ε	$\Omega_{\varepsilon,0}^{L}$	p_{Ω_ε}
80 00 00 00	00 00 8A 22	0.0546875	00 00 80 00	A0 04 10 80	0.046875
40 00 00 00	00 00 02 02	0.1875	00 00 40 00	00 04 00 80	0.15625
20 00 00 00	00 00 80 02	0.15625	00 00 20 00	00 04 00 80	0.15625
10 00 00 00	00 88 80 10	0.041015625	00 00 10 00	30 24 00 08	0.0244140625
08 00 00 00	40 80 02 10	0.029296875	00 00 08 00	01 24 20 08	0.03515625
04 00 00 00	40 08 00 00	0.25	00 00 04 00	00 20 00 08	0.25
02 00 00 00	40 00 40 10	0.21875	00 00 02 00	10 20 20 00	0.15625
01 00 00 00	44 09 01 10	0.046875	00 00 01 00	02 00 24 08	0.0341796875
00 80 00 00	04 09 41 00	0.0478515625	00 00 00 80	12 00 24 09	0.0390625
00 40 00 00	04 00 00 04	0.15625	00 00 00 40	00 00 04 01	0.1875
00 20 00 00	04 00 01 00	0.1875	00 00 00 20	02 00 04 01	0.1875
00 10 00 00	80 40 11 04	0.03515625	00 00 00 10	02 12 0C 01	0.0546875
00 08 00 00	04 40 11 00	0.041015625	00 00 00 08	02 12 0C 20	0.041015625
00 04 00 00	80 00 10 00	0.125	00 00 00 04	08 02 08 20	0.1875
00 02 00 00	00 40 10 00	0.1875	00 00 00 02	00 02 08 20	0.1875
00 01 00 00	A0 40 00 80	0.015625	00 00 00 01	00 00 88 22	0.029296875

Table 5. Best 2-round ε-characteristics of DES for $\varepsilon \in E_{\text{onebit}}$

ε	$\Omega^L_{\varepsilon,0}$	$\Omega^R_{\varepsilon,0}$	p_{Ω_ε}
80 00 00 00	10 02 38 A0	00 02 8A 02	1.760199666e − 5
40 00 00 00	50 22 28 20	00 00 02 02	5.493164063e − 3
20 00 00 00	30 22 28 20	00 00 02 02	2.746582031e − 3
10 00 00 00	02 36 2C 81	00 00 42 12	1.564621925e − 5
08 00 00 00	1A 32 2E 03	40 00 02 12	1.173466444e − 5
04 00 00 00	00 40 13 02	40 08 00 00	1.922607422e − 3
02 00 00 00	06 40 13 02	40 08 00 00	1.201629639e − 3
01 00 00 00	A2 54 0C A1	00 01 40 14	3.129243851e − 6
00 80 00 00	E5 CC 01 80	04 09 40 00	4.380941391e − 5
00 40 00 00	48 4A 08 20	04 00 00 04	7.32421875e − 3
00 20 00 00	48 2A 08 20	04 00 00 04	2.9296875e − 3
00 10 00 00	28 16 08 20	00 00 11 44	3.755092621e − 5
00 08 00 00	44 00 20 0C	04 40 01 40	3.650784492e − 5
00 04 00 00	04 04 04 05	00 40 00 40	3.662109375e − 3
00 02 00 00	00 02 8E 23	80 00 00 40	1.922607422e − 3
00 01 00 00	12 01 A8 28	A0 00 00 C0	1.907348633e − 5
00 00 80 00	52 08 A0 1C	01 40 00 C0	5.722045898e − 5
00 00 40 00	80 00 D0 02	20 04 00 00	2.44140625e − 3
00 00 20 00	80 00 B0 02	20 04 00 00	1.220703125e − 3
00 00 10 00	04 80 D2 06	31 20 00 00	7.724761963e − 5
00 00 08 00	C4 0C 18 94	01 24 20 00	1.609325409e − 5
00 00 04 00	04 04 05 80	00 20 20 00	2.746582031e − 3
00 00 02 00	04 04 03 80	00 20 20 00	3.662109375e − 3
00 00 01 00	04 A0 80 08	12 20 04 00	1.87754631e − 5
00 00 00 80	84 65 10 0C	00 30 24 00	1.609325409e − 5
00 00 00 40	40 20 40 58	02 00 04 00	6.8359375e − 3
00 00 00 20	40 20 40 38	02 00 04 00	6.8359375e − 3
00 00 00 10	C0 80 43 04	0A 12 00 00	1.086294651e − 5
00 00 00 08	40 40 DA 38	0A 02 00 01	2.011656761e − 5
00 00 00 04	02 40 14 05	00 02 00 20	2.197265625e − 3
00 00 00 02	02 40 14 03	00 02 00 20	3.295898438e − 3
00 00 00 01	90 00 30 81	00 02 8A 00	7.152557373e − 5

Table 6. Best 3-round ε-characteristics of DES for $\varepsilon \in E_{\text{onebit}}$

ε	$\Omega^L_{\varepsilon,0}$	$\Omega^R_{\varepsilon,0}$	$\Omega^R_{\varepsilon,2}$	p_{Ω_ε}
80 00 00 00	04 03 8A 00	00 60 00 00	00 02 8A 00	6.034970284e − 7
40 00 00 00	46 88 C5 01	58 20 00 20	00 00 02 02	4.526227713e − 6
20 00 00 00	46 08 45 03	38 20 00 20	00 00 02 02	1.885928214e − 6
10 00 00 00	00 00 03 16	03 34 00 00	00 00 42 12	4.400499165e − 8
08 00 00 00	40 80 83 06	13 34 00 00	40 00 42 12	4.813045962e − 9
04 00 00 00	50 08 8A 02	80 00 03 42	40 08 00 00	2.695305739e − 6
02 00 00 00	50 08 CA 12	86 00 03 42	40 08 00 00	3.684988314e − 7
01 00 00 00	04 88 C2 06	30 20 00 00	00 00 41 14	1.432454155e − 9
00 80 00 00	42 14 0D 94	00 00 20 0A	40 00 01 14	8.952838471e − 9
00 40 00 00	C4 C0 92 56	48 4A 00 00	04 00 00 04	4.190951586e − 6
00 20 00 00	C0 C1 92 56	48 2A 00 00	04 00 00 04	1.676380634e − 6
00 10 00 00	84 C0 83 04	60 1C 00 00	04 00 11 40	1.426087692e − 7
00 08 00 00	66 58 0D C0	04 00 60 0C	04 40 01 40	3.655742375e − 8
00 04 00 00	88 62 58 78	06 04 04 04	00 40 00 40	3.129243851e − 6
00 02 00 00	C6 29 25 51	02 80 06 20	80 00 00 40	4.125467967e − 7
00 01 00 00	B2 64 04 00	00 00 1B 60	A0 44 00 00	8.381903172e − 9
00 00 80 00	23 72 0C 69	40 00 04 17	21 40 00 40	6.446043699e − 9
00 00 40 00	A0 04 14 89	00 00 D2 40	20 04 00 00	2.682209015e − 6
00 00 20 00	A0 00 14 09	00 00 B2 40	20 04 00 00	1.173466444e − 6
00 00 10 00	A1 00 10 88	00 00 D0 00	31 20 00 00	1.676380634e − 7
00 00 08 00	B0 04 30 08	00 00 C8 00	31 20 00 00	2.514570951e − 8
00 00 04 00	40 08 A0 0B	24 00 05 80	00 20 20 00	2.514570951e − 6
00 00 02 00	40 28 80 0B	24 00 03 80	00 20 20 00	2.793967724e − 6
00 00 01 00	10 30 09 00	04 A0 00 0A	12 20 04 00	1.403805072e − 8
00 00 00 80	90 00 34 00	00 06 00 20	12 00 20 01	3.274180926e − 8
00 00 00 40	04 51 10 21	00 28 00 58	02 00 04 00	4.889443517e − 6
00 00 00 20	04 41 14 21	00 28 00 38	02 00 04 00	4.889443517e − 6
00 00 00 10	1A 12 08 20	00 00 03 46	0A 12 00 00	2.900719664e − 8
00 00 00 08	1A 10 08 20	00 00 03 5E	0A 12 00 00	1.178705133e − 8
00 00 00 04	08 22 8C 29	80 00 04 45	00 02 00 20	2.011656761e − 6
00 00 00 02	00 22 8C 09	80 00 04 43	00 02 00 20	3.017485142e − 6
00 00 00 01	04 01 80 00	A0 60 00 01	00 02 8A 00	1.005828381e − 7

An Offset-Compensated Oscillator-Based Random Bit Source for Security Applications

Holger Bock, Marco Bucci, and Raimondo Luzzi

Infineon Technologies Austria AG
Babenbergerstrasse 10, A-8020 Graz (AUSTRIA)
{holger.bock,bucci.external,raimondo.luzzi}@infineon.com

Abstract. In this paper, a new, patent pending, architecture for a jitter-based random bit source which is cost-effective and suitable for applications in cryptography, is presented. The source is designed to be robust against parameter variations and attacks aimed to force its output. It also features an auto-test which allows to detect faults and to estimate the source entropy. The proposed design is an enhancement of the oscillator-based architecture where a compensation loop is added to maximize the statistical quality of the output sequence, especially in presence of low-jittered oscillators. As a consequence, a fully-digital implementation, without any amplified noise source, can be adopted for the proposed generator. From an analysis of the known techniques for random number generation, the proposed architecture is derived and implementation details are also reported.

Keywords: Random bit source, random numbers, ring oscillators, jitter, entropy.

1 Introduction

A random bit generator (RBG) is a system whose output consists of fully unpredictable (i.e. statistically independent and unbiased) bits. In security applications, the unpredictability of the output also implies that it must not be possible for any attacker to observe and manipulate the generator.

An RBG basically differs from a pseudo-random generator because the complete knowledge of the generator structure and of whatever previously generated sequence does not result in any knowledge of any following bit. In other terms, the entropy of an n-bit output sequence should be ideally equal to n. On the contrary, the entropy of a n-bit output sequence from a pseudo-random generator cannot exceed the entropy of its seed, whatever n is. While pseudo-random generators are suitable in those applications where just a flat statistic is needed [1], random number generators are required in security applications, where unpredictability is a requirement.

A true random bit generator has necessarily to be based on some kind of non-deterministic phenomena that could act as the source of the system randomness.

M. Joye and J.-J. Quisquater (Eds.): CHES 2004, LNCS 3156, pp. 268–281, 2004.

Electronic noises and time jitter are usually the only stochastic phenomena that are suitable in integrated implementations.

When designing an RBG for a chipcard IC, a wide spectrum of implementation issues has to be considered and fulfilled. Due to cost reasons and mechanical stress requirements, the silicon area is a limited resource in chipcard microcontrollers (a typical area is $5 - 10mm^2$ for a 8/16-bit card) and, at the same time, there is the demand to integrate non-volatile memory blocks of ever-increasing size. As a consequence, the silicon area for integrating the CPU core and its peripheral devices (including the RBG macro-cell) has to be minimized. Furthermore, no external components can be used due to packaging constraints and security reasons: any externally accessible circuit node seriously affects the chip tamper resistance [2].

To avoid complex power management policies, power consumption is another stringent constraint, especially in a chipcard IC which is designed to be used also in hand-held equipment such as mobile phones. A related issue is the chip resistance to power analysis attacks [3]: for example, when the RBG is employed in a key generation process, a current consumption waveform highly correlated to the RBG's output bit stream can be exploited by an attacker to infer the generated secret values.

Few noise-based RBG's are reported in the technical literature due to the classified nature of most researches in this field; however, four different techniques for generating random streams are widely exploited: direct amplification of a noise source [4,5,6], jittered oscillator sampling [7,8,9,10], discrete-time chaotic maps [11,12] and metastable circuits [13,14].

Hardware RBG's can feature a very high throughput, but the random sources commonly used present several statistic defects, due to physical limitations (bandwidth limitation, fabrication tolerances, aging and temperature drifts), implementation issues, deterministic disturbances, and external attacks aimed at manipulation. Substrate and power supply interference are a major concern since their power levels can be higher than the random noise level if proper design techniques are not employed. To address this problem and since different techniques feature different advantages, in [15], a truly RBG which adopts a mixing of three mentioned RBG methods is presented. A source quite resistant to deterministic disturbances is achieved even if, due to the mixing of different techniques, it is difficult to perform a rigorous statistical analysis of the system.

As a more effective solution, the post-processing of the raw bit stream from the source with a carefully designed compressing algorithm can be employed. A lower speed bit stream with increased statistical quality is generated from a high speed near-random input stream by 'distilling' its entropy. In [16], an adaptive decorrelating algorithm is reported which dynamically modifies its compression ratio according to the statistical properties of the input sequence and can reveal failures and external attacks.

This paper presents a new architecture for a jitter-based random source which is an enhancement of a standard oscillator-based generator where a feedback compensation is added in order to maximize the statistical quality of the output sequence, especially in presence of low jittered oscillators. At the same time, the proposed generator is not affected by the frequency beating between the sampled and sampling oscillator which, enhancing the pseudo-random behavior of the sequence, makes difficult detecting a lack of randomness condition. As a further advantage, the presented RBG is suitable to be implemented as a fully-digital standard-cell based circuit, with a substantial reduction in terms of design time, power and area requirements with respect to other designs where a significant analog part is present.

In Section 2, a comparison between an amplification-based and an oscillator-based RBG is carried out which allows to establish an equivalence between the two techniques and leads to the definition of the new architecture proposed in this paper as an optimal solution for an integrated noise-based RBG. Circuit details for a standard-cell implementation of the presented architecture are reported in Section 3.

2   Random Bit Source Design

A raw random bit source is a system that generates a sequence X by sampling and quantizing an analog non-deterministic value S. Two quantization modes represent the most common cases: a *sign*-mode and a *mod* 2-mode. The quality of the output sequence X and the robustness of the random bit source depend on both the quality of the source S and the quantization procedure.

A simple model for the source S can help to clarify the effect of some parameters and issues that are typical in the implementation of a random bit source. The source S is modeled as the sum of a random component $a \cdot R$, its mean value m and a deterministic signal D:

$$S = a \cdot R + m + D \tag{1}$$

where, the factor a represents the intrinsic amplitude of the noise source and a possible amplification, being the actual random source modeled by R as a normalized random process. Of course, due to the physical limitations of the source, R is a bandwidth limited process. As a consequence, the output bits $x[i]$ will show some correlation depending of the sampling rate and their reciprocal position. The mean value m represents the mutual offset error that typically exists between the source and the quantization device. In this model it is modeled by a constant but, actually, it can slowly drift depending on environmental conditions. Finally, the signal D takes into account for every deterministic signal that is superimposed on the random process R. It can consist of disturbances from the surrounding environment, from other components of the device in which the generator is embedded or from an attacker aimed to force the source. In the last case, the amplitude of D could be even greater than the random contribution $a \cdot R$.

The operation of the *sign* and the *mod* 2 quantization modes on a source S are depicted in Figure 1. In this example, R is a normalized Gaussian distribution, $a = 0.5$ and $\frac{m+d[i]}{a} = 0.6$. The x-axis is normalized to a and is divided in 0 and 1 zones to show how the source distribution P_S is partitioned between 0 and 1 samples. The $mod\,2$ quantization results in alternated 0 and 1 bands as shown in Figure 1(b). Of course, in actual implementations, these bands could be asymmetric and this issue must be taken into account as a possible cause of offset on the sequence X.

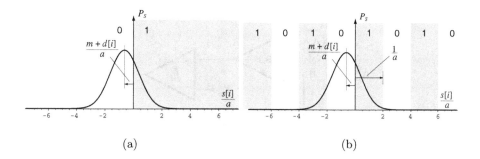

(a)   (b)

Fig. 1. Source quantization modes: (a) sign-mode ($x[i] = sign(s)$), (b) mod 2-mode ($x[i] = \lfloor s \rfloor\, mod\, 2$).

From Figure 1 it follows that, the quantity $\frac{m+d[i]}{a}$ acts as an instantaneous offset which is superimposed on the distribution of the process R. In principle, in order to reduce this offset, it is possible to reduce $m + d[i]$ as well as to increase a. Unfortunately, in practice, increasing the noise amplification, the factor a increases, but m and D increase too. As a general rule, increasing the noise amplification also results in a reduction of the process R bandwidth, due to the fact that, for a generic amplifying circuit, the gain-bandwidth product is roughly constant.

The comparison between Figure 1(a) and 1(b) makes also evident some relevant advantages of the $mod\,2$ quantization. In particular, while the $sign$ quantization can be saturated, the $mod\,2$ mode is not affected by that. As an important consequence, as long as a is large enough, an attacker cannot control the source by injecting a properly chosen D signal. Furthermore, the effective offset error cannot be greater that the distance to the bound of the next quantization band (i.e. half of the band width). This means that the factor a can be increased without taking care of the resulting increasing of m and D. In practice, a can be increased without the need to implement a wide range offset compensation or even without any offset compensation at all. Basically, the $mod\,2$ quantization limits the effect of m and D, making it negligible in case a is large enough. This results in a more robust design both with respect to electrical variances and possible attacks.

As to the entropy source S, in integrated implementations, it usually consists on some kind of electronic or phase noise. Basically, the primary sources are electronic noise contributions, since phase noise is a consequence of electronic noise.

Among electronic noise sources, both the thermal noise in a resistor and the pn-junction shot noise offer the advantage of being white noises with a Gaussian distribution whose intensity depends on physical quantities easy to keep under control. This make possible the implementation of sources characterized by a simple statistical model instead of an empirical and technological-dependent one.

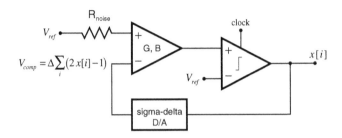

Fig. 2. Amplification-based RBG.

Figures 2, 3 and 4 show three very common solutions for the implementation of a raw random bit source. The scheme depicted in Figure 2 is perhaps the straightest solution: an explicit thermal noise source is amplified and then quantized and sampled. The noise source consists of the resistor R_{noise}, the clocked comparator performs the sampling and the quantization of the amplified noise and the sigma-delta D/A converter compensates the offset due to the amplifier and the comparator. This kind of source can have a very high throughput. In practice, the only limitation is due to the bandwidth B of the noise amplifier since, as the sampling frequency increases, so does the correlation among samples. An interesting feature of this source is that, as long as the noise source is not disturbed by an interfering signal, most of the possible faults can be revealed by simply counting the transitions in the output sequence X. Basically, this is due to the fact that each bit generation restarts from the same state. As a consequence, a lack of entropy is expected to result in a lack of transitions in the generated sequence. Actually, the offset compensation, the status of the clocked comparator and the bandwidth limitation of the noise amplifier make the source not completely "stateless". Nevertheless, the source is "by construction" not capable to deceive even a simple transition test. As a result, this source can be easily tested in real time against faults.

Notice that the offset compensation is a critical issue in this design. A lower precision in the offset zeroing results in the need of a higher noise amplification. On the other hand, a higher noise amplification results in a higher offset on the comparator input and, moreover, in a reduction of the amplifier bandwidth. Definitely, since the noise source has a very low amplitude, the offset compensation must feature both a high dynamic and a high precision.

The accuracy of the offset compensation also impacts the output bias since every error generated in the feedback loop will result in a bias error on X. In principle, the feedback loop could be implemented by a sigma-delta D/A converter as well as by an integrator. Nevertheless, if an integrator is used, errors can arise due to the offset of the integrator and its reference voltage as well as to any possible asymmetry in the waveform of the X signal. On the contrary, the sigma-delta DAC feedbacks X as a digital signal, independently of its analog features (i.e. its waveform). In this latter case, the feedback loop balances the system in such a way that, in the steady state, it holds:

$$P\{x[i] = 0\}/P\{x[i] = 1\} = \Delta_-/\Delta_+ \qquad (2)$$

where Δ_- and Δ_+ are the amplitudes of the down and up steps of the sigma-delta DAC.

Due to the low level of the noise source, this circuit is also sensitive to internal or external interfering signals. Since the *sign*-mode is used, an interfering signal D could actually force the source. On the whole, this design can implement a good quality source but an accurate design is required and its robustness against attacks is low.

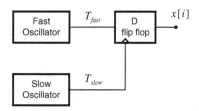

Fig. 3. Oscillator-based RBG.

Sources based on jittered oscillators have, in general, a simpler and more robust implementation. In Figure 3 a basic scheme is depicted: a slow oscillator T_{slow} samples a fast oscillator T_{fast}. The D flip-flop performs the *mod* 2 sampling of the phase difference between the two oscillators. Width and symmetry of the quantization bands depend on the frequency and duty cycle of the fast oscillator.

This scheme has an intrinsic periodic behavior due to the phase shifting, i.e. the beating, that always occurs if T_{slow}/T_{fast} is not an integer. In Figure 1(b), this beating can be seen as a deterministic component D that produces a continuous drift between the S distribution and the quantization bands. Of course, since the *mod* 2 quantization is used, this beating effect is negligible if the phase noise is large with respect to half the period of the fast oscillator. More in general, the *mod* 2 quantization makes this design robust against any kind of phase signals that could be superimposed on the phase noise.

The achievable throughput depends on the fast oscillator frequency and on the mutual phase noise between the two oscillators. In facts, once the fast oscillator frequency is maximized (i.e. the quantization bands are as narrow as possible), the sampling period T_{slow} must be long enough in order to accumulate a sufficient jitter between two subsequent samples. Notice that in this scheme there is not an explicit noise source. The oscillators can be implemented in different ways and, in general, the statistical model is not known a priori, being determined by several technological and implementation factors. Anyhow, if a better noise characterization is requested, a possible solution is to embed an explicit electronic noise source in one of the oscillators. In [10] a random bit source is presented where a thermal noise source is embedded in a triangular wave oscillator. As a result, the oscillator features a phase noise with a distribution that is directly derived from the thermal noise.

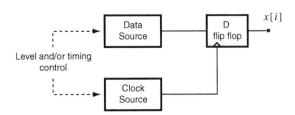

Fig. 4. Metastability-based RBG.

Random sources based on flip-flop metastability also exploit electronic and phase noise. Flip-flop metastability occurs when the data and clock signals are very close to the switching threshold or when they switch very close in time one to each other [14]. In these conditions, a small variation in level or in phase results is a different output value from the flip-flop. Actually, this source can be seen as a degeneration of the previous schemes. Depending whether the metastability is produced by setting a critical input level or a critical input phase, the working principle is very similar to that in Figure 2 or Figure 3 respectively.

In this kind of source, the main implementation issue is the level or phase control of the inputs. In facts, since there is not an explicit electronic or phase noise source, nor any noise amplification mechanism, a very precise control is required in order to force a metastability condition.

To summarize, the oscillator-based scheme has the simplest and most robust implementation. On the other hand, due to the beating effect, the randomness source cannot be tested by a simple transition test. Moreover, if the oscillators are implemented by means of digital ring oscillators, the achievable jitter is very low thus resulting in a very low speed or poor quality generator.

The architecture proposed in this work is depicted in Figure 5. In essence, this scheme merges the direct amplification and the oscillator-based techniques. It features the simple implementation of an oscillator-based RBG but it can be seen as a direct amplification scheme where the electronic noise is replaced by time jitter and the *sign* quantization is replaced by the *mod* 2 one. A comparison between Figure 2 and Figure 5 can clarify the analogies.

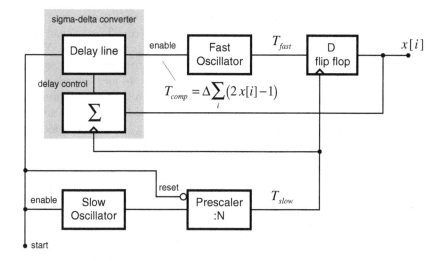

Fig. 5. The RBG proposed in this work.

In the proposed scheme, the oscillators are re-synchronized before each bit generation. As a results, the periodical behavior typical of the oscillator-based sources is suppressed and each bit generation restarts from the same state as in a direct-amplification source. The T_{slow} prescaler actually implements a noise amplification mechanism since, scaling down the oscillator frequency, the accumulation period for the jitter increases. The analogy between the "jitter amplifier" (i.e. the prescaler) and the noise amplifier in Figure 2 is very close: in both cases, a higher noise amplification costs in term of bandwidth. In fact, in Figure 5, noise amplification is obtained by reducing the sampling frequency. In a similar way, in Figure 2, as the gain G increases, the amplifier bandwidth B decreases and, to maintain the same correlation among samples, the sampling frequency must be reduced.

The delay line performs a time offset compensation that is similar to the voltage offset compensation implemented by the D/A converter in Figure 2. A T_{comp} delay is generated in such a way the slow oscillator samples the fast one on its edges. Therefore, the random bit $x[i]$ is, actually, the least significant bit of the ratio between the period T_{slow} of the slow oscillator and period of the fast one T_{fast}:

$$x[i] = \left\lfloor \frac{T_{slow}[i]/2 - T_{comp}[i]}{T_{fast}/2} \right\rfloor \bmod 2 \tag{3}$$

where T_{comp} makes sure the *floor* function works around one of its discontinuities. This quantization mode combines the offset compensation of the direct-amplification scheme with the *mod 2*-mode of the oscillator-based architecture. As a result, the required jitter can be reduced by increasing the precision Δ of the offset compensation (Figure 6). Basically, the device can operate with a minimal jitter intensity of about $\Delta/2$, while, without the offset compensation, the required jitter is about $T_{fast}/2$. Therefore, the ratio $\alpha = T_{fast}/\Delta$ can be seen as equivalent to a jitter amplification and represents the gain obtained by this design. Since the $mod\, 2$ quantization is adopted, the source cannot be saturated and cannot be easily forced by means of external signals. In fact, in order to force the source, an attacker should control the phase between the two oscillators with a precision better than $T_{fast}/4$. Basically, the $mod\, 2$-mode makes the device robust with respect to large T_{slow} variations, while the T_{comp} compensation makes the device robust with respect to T_{slow}/T_{fast} variations.

As a further advantage of the proposed architecture, the T_{comp} feedback suppresses the effect of several source asymmetries that could be difficult to control. Asymmetries in the waveform of the fast oscillator (e.g. an unbalanced duty cycle) as well as asymmetries in setup and hold times of the sampling flip-flop are automatically compensated. Finally, it can be noticed that, if the offset compensation is very precise, the device degenerates in a metastability-based source due to the feedback loop that forces the sampling flip-flop to operate in a metastable state.

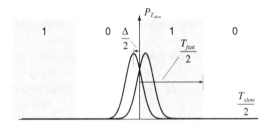

Fig. 6. Offset compensated $mod\, 2$ quantization.

3   Circuit Details

A fully digital implementation on a $90nm$ CMOS standard-cell library has been adopted for the design and simulation of the proposed RBG and a detailed block scheme is depicted in Figure 7. Both oscillators are implemented as ring oscillators. The fast one is designed for the maximal frequency which allows a saturated waveform. Really, this is not strictly required since an amplitude as large as needed for the sampling flip-flop toggling is enough. Nevertheless, even under this conservative constraint, a nominal value of about $250ps$ is expected for T_{fast}. Note that an attacker aimed to force the source will need a precision better than $T_{fast}/4 = 75ps$ (Figure 6).

The main threat for a oscillator-based RBG is the mutual synchronization between the two oscillators. That could occur because of a direct coupling or because of a coupling between the oscillators and some other signal (e.g. the system clock) [17]. In both cases, the mutual jitter between T_{slow} and T_{fast} will be

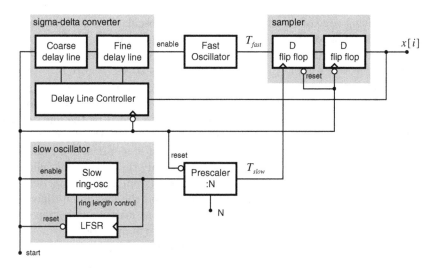

Fig. 7. Detailed block scheme for the proposed RBG.

low whatever pre-scaling factor N is employed. In order to address this synchronization issue, the slow oscillator is implemented as a spread spectrum oscillator by means of a ring oscillator whose length is controlled by a linear feedback shift register (LFSR). Note that the frequency spreading does not produce any artificial pseudo-randomness on the output sequence X. Actually, since the LFSR is reset before the generation of each bit, it produces every time the same sequence. Therefore, after the prescaler, variations on T_{slow} are due to the intrinsic oscillator jitter and no pseudo-random modulation is visible. A mean value of about $5ns$ is adopted for T_{slow} and the pre-scaling factor N will be chosen according to the available jitter. Different trade-offs between statistical quality and speed could be adopted depending on the post-processing compressing ratio [16].

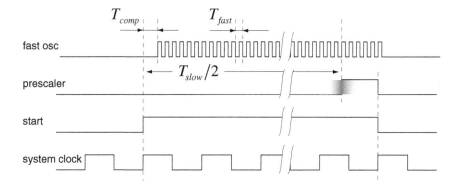

Fig. 8. Waveforms of the main signals.

On the raising edge of the *start* signal, the slow oscillator is enabled whereas the fast one is enabled after a delay T_{comp} which is adjusted by the feedback loop in Figure 7 according to the mean value of the output stream, thus forcing the slow oscillator to sample the fast one close to its edges (Figure 8).

As shown in Figure 7, the delay T_{comp} is implemented with a two stages adjustable delay line where the coarse grained line fixes the dynamic of the time offset compensation whereas its precision is determined by the fine grained line, thus obtaining a high dynamic and high precision without an excessive area requirement. Each delay line consists of a string of identical delay elements (Figure 9) and, thanks to the $mod\,2$ quantization, only the differential delays are relevant for the system operation. In particular, a maximum differential delay for the coarse line greater than $\pm T_{fast}/2$ is required and the maximum differential delay of the fine line must be long enough to cover at least a single step of the coarse line. These constraints assure the correct system operation.

According to a post-layout simulation, the fine grained delay line is expected to have a precision of $10ps$ which results in a gain factor $\alpha > 25$. Given that there are no constraints on the absolute delays, differential delays can be fined controlled by exploiting slight differences in signal propagation paths (Figure 9(b)), thus obtaining such a high precision. Moreover, since the delay cells are identical, a full-custom layout can guarantee the same parasitics on each cell. Notice that the connection between cells is not critical because it does not affect the differential delay. Regarding the symmetry between the sigma-delta DAC increasing and decreasing steps (Δ_+, Δ_- in (2)), it is guaranteed by construction since each increasing/decreasing delay step is obtained by adding/removing the same delay element.

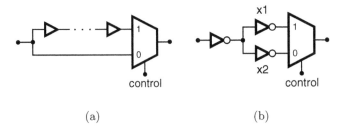

(a)   (b)

Fig. 9. Implementation of the coarse (a) and fine (b) differential delay elements. The fine delay cell exploits the differential delay between two inverters having different drive strength (x1 and x2). Since the inverters are driven in parallel, inputs signals are aligned while, on the output, the stronger inverter (x2) switches faster.

On the falling edge of the *start* signal, both oscillators are stopped, the sampling flip-flop is reset and the sampled bit is saved in the output flip-flop. The sampling flip-flop reset is required to remove the dependency that, in a real flip-flop, exists between its input thresholds and timings, and its logic state. Such dependency, and in general every state variables in the system, can generate a pseudo-random evolution which prevents the detection of a lack of entropy condition.

Disturbances coming from the system clock are typically very intense and can heavily influence the oscillators. Therefore, a further implicit state variable results from the phase shift between the start of a new bit generation and the system clock. In order to clear this state dependence too, the start signal is synchronized with the system clock (Figure 8) in such a way clock disturbances are the same during each bit generation and their effects are compensated by the feedback loop.

4   Fault Detection and Entropy Evaluation

An important feature of the presented source is the possibility to check its operation in real time. This feature can be exploited to detect faults as well as to adapt the post-processing compression ratio depending on the estimation of the source entropy. Basically, a source is as easier to check as much as it cannot deceive tests by means of pseudo-random behaviors. On the other hand, the ability of a system to behave pseudo-randomly is limited by the state space in which its free evolution can take place. As a consequence, a source having a very small state space can be checked even by means of a very simple test.

In the presented scheme several measures are adopted to suppress explicit or implicit state variables, hence, a lack of jitter condition can be immediately recognized since, in absence of jitter, the device has a straightforward deterministic model. Actually, if the jitter is not sufficient, the device produces the periodic sequence "...010101..." that results from the delay feedback loop. The other potential deterministic behaviors can arise because of a transient or a fault status of the feedback. In this case, the constant sequences "...000000..." or "...111111..." are expected. As a consequence, the following transition counting has been adopted in the proposed source:

$$N_{trans} = \sum_i x[i] \oplus x[i-2]. \tag{4}$$

In fact, for a maximal entropy sequence, this counter is expected to return half the number of the generated symbols, whereas, for the discussed deterministic sequences, it does not increase at all. It is also noticeable that N_{trans} is equally sensitive to both symbol and transition biasing. Actually, N_{trans} is an indicator of how much the source differs from its deterministic model, i.e. an estimator of its entropy. Therefore, it allows to choose a suitable pre-scaling factor as well as to detect faults and to perform an adaptive post-processing depending on the quality of the source [16]. As an example, in order to produce a 32 bit random block, the post-processing compression can be carried on until $N_{trans} = 64$. As a result, the compressing ratio will be about 4 if the source features a large jitter and will increase automatically in a low jitter condition.

5   Conclusions

A new, patent pending, architecture for an integrated random bit source has been presented which is low demanding in terms of area and power consumption and suitable for security applications. The proposed generator is an enhancement of the oscillator-based architecture but, at the same time, it presents the advantages of a direct amplification-based RBG, thus resulting in a reliable and robust solution for high quality random bit generation. The source also features a tuning and a real-time test of its statistical quality. A standard-cell based implementation, without any amplified noise source, can be adopted for the proposed generator and implementation details have been also discussed.

Future work will involve the experimental verification of the presented architecture and the obtained results will be reported in a following paper.

References

1. B. Schneier, *Applied Cryptography*, second ed., New York, John Wiley & Sons, 1996.
2. D. Naccache and D. M'Raibi, *Cryptographic Smart Cards*, IEEE Micro, vol. 16, no. 3, pp. 14-24, June 1996.
3. P. Kocher, J. Jaffe, and B. Jun, *Differential Power Analysis*, Advances in Cryptology (Crypto '99), M. Wiener, ed., pp. 388-397, 1999.
4. W.T. Holman, J.A. Connelly, and A.B. Downlatabadi, *An Integrated Analog/Digital Random Noise Source*, IEEE Trans. Circuits and Systems I, vol. 44, no. 6, pp. 521-528, June 1997.
5. V. Bagini and M. Bucci, *A Design of Reliable True Random Number Generator for Cryptographic Applications*, Proc. 1st Workshop Cryptographic Hardware and Embedded Systems (CHES '99), Heidelberg, Germany, Springer-Verlag, 1999, vol. 1717, pp. 204-218.
6. M. Bucci, L. Germani, R. Luzzi, P. Tommasino, A. Trifiletti, and M. Varanonuovo, *A High-Speed IC Random-Number Source for SmartCard Microcontrollers*, IEEE Trans. Circuits and Systems I, vol. 50, no. 11, pp. 1373-1380, Nov. 2003.
7. M. Dicht and N. Janssen, *A High Quality Physical Random Number Generator*, Proc. Sophia Antipolis Forum Microelectronics (SAME 2000), pp. 48-53, 2000.
8. B. Jun and P. Kocher, *The Intel Random Number Generator*, Cryptographic Research Inc., white paper prepared for Intel Corp., Apr. 1999, http://www.cryptography.com/resources/white papers/IntelRNG.pdf.
9. C.S. Petrie and J.A. Connelly, *Modeling and Simulation of Oscillator-Based Random Number Generators*, Proc. IEEE Int'l Symp. Circuits and Systems (ISCAS '96), vol. 4, pp. 324-327, 1996.
10. M. Bucci, L. Germani, R. Luzzi, A. Trifiletti, and M. Varanonuovo, *A High-Speed Oscillator-Based Truly Random Number Source for Cryptographic Applications*, IEEE Trans. Computers, vol. 52, no. 4, pp. 403-409, April 2003.
11. T. Stojanovski and L. Kocarev, *Chaos-Based Random Number Generators - Part I: Analysis*, IEEE Trans. Circuits and Systems I, vol. 48, no. 3, pp. 281-288, Mar. 2001.
12. T. Stojanovski, J. Pihl, and L. Kocarev, *Chaos-Based Random Number Generators - Part II: Practical Realization*, IEEE Trans. Circuits and Systems I, vol. 48, no. 3, pp. 382-385, Mar. 2001.

13. M.J. Bellido, A.J. Acosta, et al., *A Simple Binary Random Number Generator: new approaches for CMOS VLSI*, Proc. 35th Midwest Symposium on Circuits and Systems, Aug. 1992.
14. M. Epstein, Laszlo Hars, R. Krasinski, M. Rosner, and H. Zheng, *Design and Implementation of a True Random Number Generator Based on Digital Circuit Artifacts*, Proc. 5th Workshop Cryptographic Hardware and Embedded Systems (CHES '03), Heidelberg, Germany, Springer-Verlag, 2003, vol. 2779, pp. 152-165.
15. C.S. Petrie and J.A. Connelly, *A Noise-Based IC Random Number Generator for Applications in Cryptography*, IEEE Trans. Circuits and Systems I, vol. 47, no. 5, pp. 615-621, May 2000.
16. E. Trichina, M. Bucci, D. De Seta, and R. Luzzi, *Supplementary Cryptographic Hardware for Smart Cards*, IEEE Micro, vol. 21, no. 6, pp. 26-35, Nov./Dec. 2001.
17. T. Pialis and K. Phang, *Analysis of Timing Jitter in Ring Oscillators Due to Power Supply Noise*, Proc. IEEE Int. Symp. Circuits and Systems (ISCAS 2003), vol. 1, pp. 685-688, May 2003.

Improving the Security of Dual-Rail Circuits

Danil Sokolov, Julian Murphy, Alex Bystrov, and Alex Yakovlev

School of Electrical, Electronic and Computer Engineering
University of Newcastle, Newcastle upon Tyne, UK
{danil.sokolov,j.p.murphy,a.bystrov,alex.yakovlev}@ncl.ac.uk

Abstract. Dual-rail encoding, return-to-spacer protocol and hazard-free logic can be used to resist differential power analysis attacks by making the power consumption independent of processed data. Standard dual-rail logic uses a protocol with a single spacer, e.g. all-zeroes, which gives rise to power balancing problems. We address these problems by incorporating two spacers; the spacers alternate between adjacent clock cycles. This guarantees that all gates switch in each clock cycle regardless of the transmitted data values. To generate these dual-rail circuits an automated tool has been developed. It is capable of converting synchronous netlists into dual-rail circuits and it is interfaced to industry CAD tools. Dual-rail and single-rail benchmarks based upon the Advanced Encryption Standard (AES) have been simulated and compared in order to evaluate the method.

1 Introduction

Secure applications such as smart cards require measures to resist Differential Power Analysis (DPA). Dual-rail encoding provides a method to enhance the security properties of a system making DPA more difficult. As an example, in the design described in [1] the processor can execute special secure instructions. These instructions are implemented as dual-rail circuits, whose switching activity is meant to be independent from data. Whilst alternatives exist at the software level to balance power, the need at the hardware level is also mandatory. Special types of CMOS logic elements have been proposed in [2], but this low-level approach requires changing gate libraries and hence is costly for a standard cell or FPGA user. As a solution, using balanced data encoding such as dual-rail or together with self-timed design techniques has been proposed in [3,4].

The clock signal is typically used as a reference in power analysis techniques. System "desynchronisation" as in [3,5] can help hide the clock signal. To mask the operation of a block of logic is a much more complex task which could demand very expensive changes to the entire design flow. A cheaper desynchronisation method to rebuild individual blocks within the same synchronous infrastructure so, that their power signatures become independent from the mode of operation and from the data processed. This method is used in [5], where synchronous pipelines are transformed into asynchronous circuits using dual-rail coding.

These desynchronisation methods represent a combination of two aspects of security: reference signal hiding and balancing of data encoding w.r.t. switching activity. In this paper we separate these aspects, concentrating on data encoding only.

Our idea is to replace blocks in existing architectures dominated by synchronous single-threaded CPU cores and their slow buses, having no pipelining or concurrency,

M. Joye and J.-J. Quisquater (Eds.): CHES 2004, LNCS 3156, pp. 282–297, 2004.

with secure and hazard free dual-rail circuits. Using the standard dual-rail protocol with a single spacer still has certain balancing problems due to the asymmetry between logic gates within a dual-rail gate. In this paper we address and solve these problems by using a new protocol with two spacers alternating in time; leading to all gates switching within every clock cycle. This is the first contribution of the paper.

The other idea is to stay as close to the standard industry design flow as possible. Our method is applied via an automated tool to a clocked single-rail netlist obtained by standard RTL synthesis tools from a behavioural specification. Such circuits have an architecture depicted in Figure 1(a). The result is also a netlist which can be simulated and passed to the back-end design tools. Furthermore, all DFT (Design For Testability) features incorporated at the logic synthesis stage are preserved in our approach.

The resultant dual-rail circuit can be built in either of two architectures: *self-timed dual-rail* or *clocked dual-rail*, Figure 1(b, c) respectively.

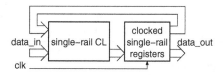

(a) Single-rail architecture (standard RTL design)

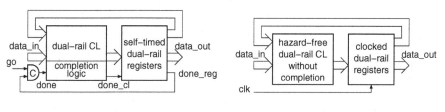

(b) Self-timed dual-rail architecture   (c) Clocked dual-rail architecture

Fig. 1. Design architectures

Self-timed dual-rail circuits do not have a clock and their registers are controlled by a completion signal formed in the completion detection logic. Being asynchronous, these circuits should exhibit better throughput, but they suffer from a significant size overhead due to additional logic from completion detection.

Clocked dual-rail circuits do not have completion detection logic and rely on the assumption that the hazard-free dual-rail combinational logic switches by the end of the clock period. In our method this assumption is easy to meet, because the delay characteristics of the dual-rail circuit are inherited from single-rail prototype.

While the method and the tool support both dual-rail architectures, in this paper we concentrate on the latter one. The security aspects of system level, memory elements, buses, etc. also do not belong to the focus of the paper. We are looking at security of logic circuits only.

The rest of the paper is organised as follows. Firstly the theory of applying dual-rail coding to synchronous circuits using a single spacer and two spacers is described, then the operation of the tool is discussed. The AES benchmark results and potential improvements follow and finally the conclusions are presented.

2   Method

2.1   Single Spacer Dual-Rail

Dual-rail code uses two rails with only two valid signal combinations $\{01, 10\}$, which encode values 0 and 1 respectively. Dual-rail code is widely used to represent data in self-timed circuits [6,7], where a specific protocol of switching helps to avoid hazards. The protocol allows only transitions from all-zeroes $\{00\}$, which is a non-code word, to a *code word* and back to all-zeroes as shown in Figure 2(a); this means the switching is monotonic. The all-zeroes state is used to indicate the absence of data, which separates one code word from another. Such a state is often called a *spacer*.

An approach for automatic converting single-rail circuits to dual-rail, using the above signalling protocol, that is easy to incorporate in the standard RTL-based design flow has been described in [5]. Within this approach, called Null-Convention Logic [8] one can follow one of two major implementation strategies for logic: one is with full completion detection through the dual-rail signals (NCL-D) and the other with separate completion detection (NCL-X). The former one is more conservative with respect to delay dependence while the latter one is less delay-insensitive but more area and speed efficient. For example, an AND gate is implemented in NCL-D and NCL-X as shown in Figure 2(b,c) respectively. NCL methods of circuit construction exploit the fact that the negation operation in dual-rail corresponds to swapping the rails. Such dual-rail circuits do not have negative gates (internal negative gates, for example in XOR elements, are also converted into positive gates), hence they are race-free under any single transition.

If the design objective is only power balancing (as in our case), one can abandon the completion detection channels, relying on timing assumptions as in standard synchronous designs; thus saving a considerable amount of area and power. This approach was followed in [9], considering the circuit in a clocked environment, where such timing assumptions were deemed quite reasonable to avoid any hazards in the combinational logic. Hence, in the clocked environment the dual-rail logic for an AND gate is simply a pair of AND and OR gates as shown in Figure 2(d).

The above implementation techniques certainly help to balance switching activity at the level of dual-rail nodes. Assuming that the power consumed by one rail in a pair is the same as in the other rail, the overall power consumption is invariant to the data bits propagating through the dual-rail circuit. However, the physical realisation of the rails at the gate level is not symmetric, and experiments with these dual-rail implementations show that power source current leaks the data values.

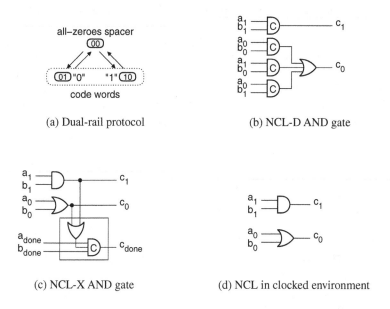

(a) Dual-rail protocol

(b) NCL-D AND gate

(c) NCL-X AND gate

(d) NCL in clocked environment

Fig. 2. Single spacer dual-rail

For example, in the structure in Figure 2(d) we compare the gate switching profiles when computing two different binary sequences of values c for corresponding input sequences on a and b. The first sequence is $a = 0000$, $b = 1111$, $c = 0000$, and the second sequence is $a = 1111$, $b = 1111$, $c = 1111$. The switching profile of these sequences at the level of gates is different: in the first sequence there are eight firings of OR gate and in the second there eight firings of AND (note that we counted both *spacer→code word* and *code word→spacer* phases).

While there could be ways of balancing power consumption between individual gates in dual-rail pairs by means of modifications at the transistor level, adjusting loads and changing transistor sizes, etc., all such measures are costly. The standard logic library requires finding a more economic solution. We do not consider randomisation techniques in this paper as they can be applied independently, and possibly in conjunction with our method.

Synchronous flip-flops are built to be power efficient, so if they switch to the same value (data input remains the same within several clocks) then nothing changes at the output. The absence of the output transition saves power, but in the same time it makes the power consumption data dependent. In order to avoid this, we make flip-flops operate in the return-to-spacer protocol as in Figure 2(a). The solution in Figure 3(a) uses the master-slave scheme, writing to the master is controlled by the positive edge of the clock and writing to the slave is controlled by the negative edge. At the same time the high value of the clock enforces slave outputs into zero (output spacer as in Figure 2(a)) and

the low clock value enforces master outputs into one (a similar spacer for the logic with
active zero).

This circuit operates as explained in Figure 3(b). Both master and slave latches have
their respective reset and enable inputs (active zero for the master). The delay between
removing the reset signal and disabling writing for each latch (hold time) is formed by
the couple of buffers in the clock circuit. Buffers between master and slave are needed
to delay *m_code-set* value until *s_En-*. The advantage of this implementation is the use
of a single cross-coupled latch in each stage for a couple of input data signals.

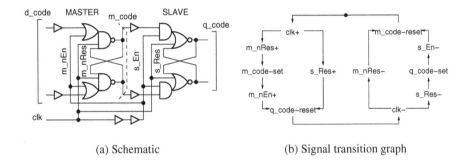

(a) Schematic   (b) Signal transition graph

Fig. 3. Single spacer dual-rail flip-flop

2.2   Dual Spacer Dual-Rail

In order to balance the power signature we propose to use two spacers (i.e. two
spacer states, $\{00\}$ for *all-zeroes spacer* and $\{11\}$ for *all-ones spacer*), resulting in
a dual spacer protocol as shown in Figure 4. It defines the switching as follows:
spacer→code word→spacer→code word. The polarity of the spacer can be arbitrary
and possibly random as in Figure 4(a). A possible refinement for this protocol is the
alternating spacer protocol shown in Figure 4(b). The advantage of the latter is that all
bits are switched in each cycle of operation, thus opening a possibility for perfect energy
balancing between cycles of operation.

As opposed to single spacer dual-rail, where in each cycle a particular rail is switched
up and down (i.e. the same gate always switches), in the alternating spacer protocol both
rails are switched from *all-zeroes spacer* to *all-ones spacer* and back. The intermediate
states in this switching are *code words*. In the scope of the entire logic circuit, this means
that for every computation cycle we always fire all gates forming the dual-rail pairs.
In [10] we introduce two security characteristics of a circuit w.r.t. DPA attacks: *imbalance*
and *exposure time*. By imbalance we mean the variation in power consumption when
processing different data values. Exposure time is the time during which the imbalance
is exhibited. Our experiments show that the worst case imbalance in a dual-rail circuits

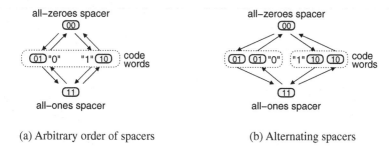

(a) Arbitrary order of spacers   (b) Alternating spacers

Fig. 4. Dual-spacer dual-rail protocol

under a realistic load is 2.1%. The worst case exposure time depends on the spacer protocol. It is up to the whole time of circuit operation if the single spacer protocol is used. By using of the alternating spacer protocol the exposure time is reduced to less than one clock cycle, which makes the circuit more resistant to DPA.

The new alternating spacer discipline cannot be directly applied to the implementation techniques shown in Figure 2(b,c). Those, both in the logic rails as well as in completion detection assume the fact that for each pair of rails, the $\{11\}$ combination never occurs. In fact the use of *all-ones spacer* would upset the speed-independent implementation in Figure 2(b), because the outputs of the second layer elements would not be acknowledged during *code word→all-ones spacer* transition. The completion detection for those gates can of course be ensured by using an additional three-input C-element, but this extra overhead would make this implementation technique much less elegant because of the additional acknowledgement signal channel. In the single spacer structure, due to the principle of orthogonality (one-hot) between min-terms $a_0 \cdot b_0$, $a_1 \cdot b_0$ and $a_0 \cdot b_1$, only one C-element in the rail c_0 fires per cycle.

If some parts of a dual-rail circuit operate using the single spacer and the others the alternating spacer protocol, then spacer converters should be used. The alternating-to-single spacer converter shown in Figure 5(a) is transparent to *code words* and enforces *all-zeroes spacer* on the output if the input is all-ones or all-zeroes.

The implementation of a single-to-alternating spacer converter, Figure 5(b), uses a toggle to decide which spacer to inject all-ones or all-zeroes. The toggle can be constructed out of two latches as shown in Figure 5(c). It operates in the following way: $x+ \rightarrow x1+ \rightarrow x- \rightarrow x2+ \rightarrow x+ \rightarrow x1- \rightarrow x- \rightarrow x2-$, i.e. $x1$ changes on positive edge of x, and $x2$ switches on its negative edge. The frequency of $x1$ and $x2$ is half the frequency of x.

The alternation of spacers in time is enforced by flip-flops. The alternating spacer flip-flop can be built combining a single spacer dual-rail flip-flop with a single spacer to alternating spacer converter. The power consumption of the single spacer dual-rail flip-flop is data independent due to the symmetry of its rails. The rails of the spacer converter are also symmetric, which makes the power consumption of the resultant alternating spacer flip-flop data independent. The optimised version of such a flip-flop

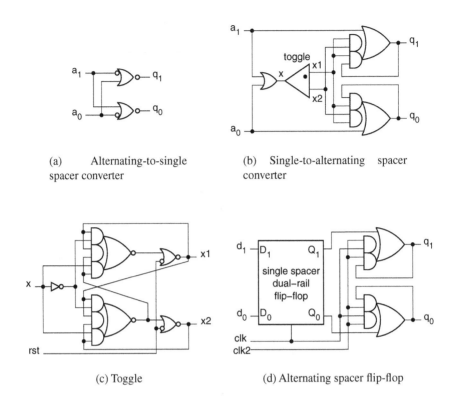

(a)   Alternating-to-single
spacer converter

(b)   Single-to-alternating   spacer
converter

(c) Toggle

(d) Alternating spacer flip-flop

Fig. 5. Alternating spacer converters

(toggle is moved outside) is depicted in Figure 5(d). This implementation uses $clk2$ signal to decide which spacer to inject on the positive phase of clk. The signal $clk2$ changes on the negative edge of the clock and is formed by a toggle (one for the whole circuit) whose input is clk. The timing assumption for $clk2$ is that it changes after the output of single spacer flip-flop. Both, the slave latch of the single spacer flip-flop and the toggle which generates $clk2$ signal, are triggered by the negative edge of clk. The depth of logic in the toggle is greater than in the slave latch of the flip-flop. At the same time $clk2$ goes to all flip-flops of the circuit and requires buffering, which also delays it. This justifies our timing assumption.

It should be mentioned that the inputs of the dual-rail circuit must also support the alternating spacer protocol. Moreover, the same spacer should appear each cycle on the inputs of a dual-rail gate. That means the spacer protocol on the circuit inputs and flip-flop outputs must be synchronised in the reset phase.

2.3   Negative Gate Optimisation

In CMOS a positive gate is usually constructed out of a negative gate and an inverter. That is why the total area overhead in dual-rail logic is more than twofold comparing to single-rail. Use of positive gates is not only a disadvantage for the size of dual-rail circuit, but also for the length of the critical path. Our method for negative gate optimisation [9] is described in this section.

If the *all-zeroes spacer* of the dual-rail code is applied to a layer of negative gates (NAND, NOR, AND-NOR, OR-NAND), then the output will be *all-ones spacer*. The opposite is also true: *all-ones spacer* is converted into *all-zeroes spacer*. The polarity of signals within *code words* remains the same if the output rails are swapped.

The spacer alternation between odd and even layers of combinational logic can be used for *negative gate optimisation* of dual-rail circuits. The optimised circuit uses either *all-ones spacer* or *all-zeroes spacer* in different stages (the spacer changes between the layers of logic) as captured in Figure 6.

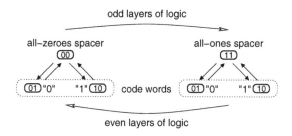

Fig. 6. Spacer polarity after logic optimisation

In order to optimise a dual-rail circuit for negative gates the following transformations should be applied. First, all gates of positive dual-rail logic are replaced by negative gates. Then, the output rails of those gates are swapped. Finally, *spacer polarity converters* are placed at the wires that connect the layers of logic of the same parity (odd-to-odd or even-to-even).

Consider negative gate optimisation using a simple example shown in Figure 7(a). Dotted lines in the single-rail circuit indicate signals which will be mapped into the dual-rail with the *all-ones spacer*. The bar on the wire is the location of a spacer polarity converter. The circuit in Figure 7(b) is obtained by replacing gates by their dual-rail versions. These gates are built from traditional positive dual-rail gates by adding signal inversion to their outputs and swapping the output rails (the latter is needed to preserve the polarity of signals in the output code words). The operation of negation is implemented by a rail swapping and does not require any logic gates. The spacer polarity converter is implemented as a pair of inverters having their outputs crossed in order to preserve the polarity of signals in the output code words. It is possible to combine such an optimisation with the alternation of spacers in time.

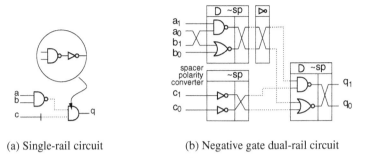

(a) Single-rail circuit   (b) Negative gate dual-rail circuit

Fig. 7. Constructing negative gate dual-rail circuit

This section presented the application of dual-rail coding to the building of secure circuits, whose power consumption is independent of the data they process. An extension of the dual-rail protocol was presented, namely *dual spacer in time* (alternating spacer protocol). This aims at power balancing by switching all gates in each cycle of circuit operation. The negative gate optimisation was applied to the circuits implementing such a protocol.

3   Tool Description

The described conversion procedure of single-rail into dual-rail circuit has been implemented as a software tool named the "Verimap design kit". It successfully interfaces to the Cadence CAD tools. It takes as input a structural Verilog netlist file, created by Cadence Ambit (or another logic synthesis tool), and converts it into dual-rail netlist. The resulting netlist can then be processed by Cadence or other EDA tools.

The structure of our Verimap design kit is displayed in Figure 8. The main parts are the tool itself and two libraries. The *library of gate prototypes* contains the description of gates used in the input netlist. It facilitates the structural analysis of the input netlist. The *library of transformation rules* defines: complementary gates needed for construction of the dual-rail logic, the polarity of gate inputs and outputs and specifies if the corresponding dual-rail gate requires completion signal

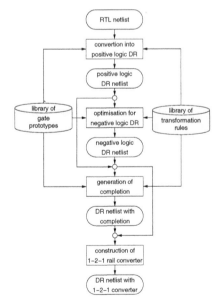

Fig. 8. Verimap design kit

(for asynchronous design only) and if it inverts the spacer. If a predefined dual-rail implementation of a gate is found in the library the tool uses it, otherwise an implementation is built automatically using the rules.

The main function of the tool is conversion of single-rail RTL netlist into dual-rail netlist of either of two architectures: self-timed and clocked, Figure 1(b, c) respectively. It is done in four stages. First, a single-rail circuit is converted into positive logic dual-rail. Second, the positive dual-rail gates are replaced by negative dual-rail gates and the spacer polarity inverters are inserted. Then, the completion signal is generated (asynchronous design only). Finally, a wrapper module connecting the dual-rail circuit to the single-rail environment is added (optional).

Apart from generating netlists, Verimap tool reports statistics for the original and resultant circuits: estimated area of combinational logic and flip-flops, number of negative gates and transistors, number of wires.

The tool also generates a behavioural Verilog file assisting the power analysis of the original and resultant circuits. Being included into simulation testbench these Verilog counts the number of switching events in each wire of the circuits.

4   Benchmark Results and Future Improvements

This section summarises the experiments performed to characterise the proposed method in terms of security, size and power consumption. Two AES designs were used: *Open core AES* and *AES with computable sbox* (for details see Appendix A). For each design a single-rail AES circuit was synthesised from RTL specification by using Cadence Ambit v4.0 tool and AMS-0.35μ library. Our Verimap tool was applied to the netlist generated by Ambit and the dual-rail netlist was produced. The dual-rail circuits were optimised for negative gates and used alternating spacer dual-rail protocol. Both, single-rail and dual-rail designs were analysed for static delays (SDF delay annotation) and simulated in Verilog-XL v3.10. By keeping to the RTL design flow the netlists can be directly used in the back-end design tools of Cadence.

The statistics for the parts of AES, namely *ciphers* and *sboxes,* are shown in Table 1, Table 2 and Table 3.

The purpose of the first experiment was to evaluate the correlation between data and switching activity of the circuits. Switching activity is the number of switching events in the circuit within one clock cycle. Table 1 presents the minimum, average and maximum switching activity for the sboxes and ciphers. These values were obtained by simulating the circuits with a number of input vectors: 10,000 random input vectors for sboxes and 284 standard AES testbench vectors for ciphers.

The experiment shows a significant difference between the min/average/max switching activity values for the single-rail sbox benchmarks. The minimum value is zero, and the maximum values are up to 48% higher than the average values. At the same time, switching activity for the dual-rail circuits is constant. In the single-rail switching activity varies significantly depending on data and clearly they exhibit zero switching activity if the input data does not change. In addition many switching events in single-rail circuits are caused by hazards and the single-rail sbox benchmarks are no exception. Here the hazards caused up to 80% of data dependent switching events. The number of switching

Table 1. Switching activity

benchmark name		switching activity (hazards)		
		min	avg	max
sbox (open core)	single-rail	0 (0)	162 (33)	277 (124)
	dual-rail	1,180	1,180	1,180
	overhead	∞	628%	326%
sbox (comp.)	single-rail	0 (0)	525 (345)	936 (746)
	dual-rail	868	868	868
	overhead	∞	65%	-17%
cipher (open core)	single-rail	0	9,147	13,236
	dual-rail	41,285	41,285	41,285
	overhead	∞	351%	211%
cipher (comp.)	single-rail	0 (0)	3,810 (2,013)	6,140 (3,682)
	dual-rail	13,055	13,055	13,055
	overhead	∞	242%	112%

events in dual-rail combinational logic is constant for any input data and is equal to the number of wires. It shows that all gates are switching in each clock cycle, thus making power consumption data independent (described in detail in Section 2.2).

The single and dual-rail implementations of the AES ciphers were simulated and compared against combinational logic blocks (sboxes). Switching activity in the open core dual-rail cipher is 351% higher than in the single-rail cipher and 255% higher for the AES design with computed sboxes. These values are greater than the results for the corresponding sboxes. The increased difference can be explained by the nature of computations in complex circuits. They execute in bursts defined by their algorithms. Under a burst the switching is similar to our experiments with combinational circuits. However, between the bursts the situation is significantly different: a single-rail circuit is inactive and a dual-rail circuit continues to 'burn power' by switching between code words and spacers.

A possible way to address this issue is to implement *clock gating*. This, however, should be different from the conventional clock gating technique. It is important to make it data independent. At this stage we do not see a feasible way of implementing this at the netlist level. Most likely it will require analysis of behavioural specifications. We view this idea as a subject of future work.

In order to compare the security features of single spacer and alternating spacer circuits, the AES design with computable sboxes was also converted into single spacer dual-rail. Both, single spacer and alternating spacer dual-rail implementations were simulated with 284 input vectors from the standard AES testbench in the encryption and decryption modes. The switching activities of "1" and "0" rails were recorded separately. Table 2 shows the worst case difference in switching activity between "1" and "0" rails. The imbalance between the number of switching events in the rail_1 and rail_0 is calculated as $disbalance = \frac{|rail\_1 - rail\_0|}{rail\_1 + rail\_0} \cdot 100\%$. While the total switching activity is the same in both implementations, the single spacer implementation exhibits

Table 2. Switching activity in dual-rail rails

benchmark name		switching activity	
		single spacer	alternating spacer
cipher	rail_1	8,388	6,505
(encryption)	rail_0	4,622	6,505
	disbalance	29%	0%
cipher	rail_1	8,572	6,505
(decryption)	rail_0	4,438	6,505
	disbalance	32%	0%

significant differences in the number of switching events on the complementary rails. As the complementary gates within a dual-rail gate have different power consumptions, the power signature of the single spacer dual-rail circuit becomes dependent on the processed data. Alternating spacer dual-rail circuits do not suffer from this leakage because all gates are switching in every clock cycle.

Table 3. Circuit size

benchmark name		negative gate count (comb. logic)	transistor count (comb. logic)	wire count	estimated area	
					comb. logic	flip-flops
sbox	single-rail	655	3,180	482	44,593	0
(open	dual-rail	1,523	6,672	1,180	101,364	0
core)	overhead	133%	110%	145%	127%	0
sbox	single-rail	634	2,362	400	32,975	0
(comp.)	dual-rail	1,164	4,628	868	68,603	0
	overhead	84%	96%	117%	108%	0
cipher	single-rail	12,752	68,184	9,980	873,175	142,370
(open	dual-rail	26,396	139,828	24,367	1,925,190	466,870
core)	overhead	107%	105%	144%	120%	228%
cipher	single-rail	10,372	50,344	5,936	580,046	118,678
(comp.)	dual-rail	19,510	95,066	13,055	1,237,260	462,021
	overhead	88%	89%	120%	113%	289%

The cost of improved security features is the increase in the number of gates, wires and area, see Table 3.

The benchmarks indicate only 84-88% overhead in gate numbers (a positive gate is counted as a pair of a negative gate and an inverter) for AES design with computable sboxes. This is less than 100% due to the negative gate optimisation. For Open core design the overhead is more than 100% due to the structure of its sbox module. During the negative logic optimisation of Open core sbox more inverters were inserted into not-critical path (as components of spacer inverters) than removed from the critical path.

The number of wires is increased by 117-145%. Wires are duplicated in a dual-rail circuit and then spacer converters are added, further increasing the number of wires.

The estimated area of the benchmarks combinational logic indicates a 102%-127% overhead. A significant area increase for flip-flops (228%-289%) can be explained by using dual-rail flip-flops constructed out of standard logic gates. This can be improved by transistor level optimisation of the flip-flops.

It is clear that in the AES designs there are opportunities to minimise power consumption as not all logic is necessarily being used all the time. Industry synthesis tools can identify sleep mode logic and use this information to annotate places in the netlist which could be committed to sleep mode logic later in the design flow. This low power optimisation could be utilised in our dual-rail circuitry, one approach would be to put a spacer on the input to the identified sleep mode logic and holding this there for the clock cycles whilst it is not used. By doing so the switching is now zero, thus saving power. This technique would not reveal data as the sleep mode logic is in a "meaningless" spacer state. By using the synthesis tool to identify the sleep mode logic we are adhering to the RTL design flow and our conversion tool could use the annotated netlist to apply the optimisation to dual-rail circuits; note the committal stage of the sleep mode logic would need to be different to what the synthesis tools would do (simple AND gates using a control signal). Presently this has not been implemented in the tool but investigated using schematic entry with simple examples which gave promising results. This needs to be investigated further together with the clock gating idea.

5   Conclusions

We have presented a technique for improving resistance to DPA attacks at the hardware level by power balancing in a deterministic way. The power consumption within each cycle of operation is constant. Our technique uses two spacers alternating in time within the dual-rail logic framework. It is very cheap yet effective and is supported by software tools that interface to standard RTL design flow tools used by most ASIC designers. The idea of using two spacers is deemed particularly efficient for dual-rail logic, where the Hamming distance between each spacer and a valid combination is the same. While it can still be used without too much overhead in optimally balanced k-of-n codes (e.g. 3-of-6) it would be much less efficient in other popular codes such as 1-of-4 [11].

The AES benchmarks indicate that we have fully eliminated the dependency which existed between data and switching activity in the dual-rail circuits. The price to pay for the improved security features is the increased average switching activity and area overheads.

Acknowledgements.   We are grateful to A.Koelmans, A.Kondratyev, S.Moore, A.Taubin for useful comments. EPSRC supports this work via GR/R16754 (BESST), GR/S81421 (SCREEN)

References

1. H.Saputra, N.Vijaykrishnan, M.Kandemir, M.J.Irwin, R.Brooks, S.Kim, W.Zhang: "Masking the energy behaviour of DES Encryption". Proc. DATE'03, Munich, Germany, March 2003.
2. K.Tiri, M.Akmal, I.Verbauwhede: "A Dynamic and Differential CMOS Logic with Signal Independent Power Consumption to Withstand Differential Power Analysis on Smart Cards". Proc. ESSCIRC 2002.
3. S.Moore, R.Anderson, P.Cunningham, R.Mullins, G.Taylor: "Improving smart card security using self-timed circuits". ASYNC'02, 2002, pp. 211–218.
4. Z.Yu, S.Furber, L.Plana: "An investigation into the security of self-timed circuits". Proc. of ASYNC'03, Vancouver, May 2003, IEEE CS Press, pp. 206–215.
5. A.Kondratyev, K.Lwin: "Design of asynchronous circuits using synchronous CAD tools". Proc. DAC'02, New Orleans, USA, 2002, pp. 107–117.
6. V.Varshavsky (editor): "Self-timed control of concurrent processes" Kluwer, 1990 (Russian edition 1986).
7. I.David, R.Ginosar, M.Yoeli: "An efficient implementation of boolean functions as self-timed circuits". *IEEE Trans. on Computers*, 1992, 41(1), pp. 2–11.
8. K.Fant, S.Brandt: "Null Convention Logic: a complete and consistent logic for asynchronous digital circuit synthesis". Proc. Int. Conf. Application-Specific Systems, Architectures and Processors (ASAP'96), IEEE CS Press, Los Alamos, Calif., 1996, pp. 261–273.
9. A.Bystrov, D.Sokolov, A.Yakovlev, A.Koelmans: "Balancing Power Signature in Secure Systems". 14th UK Asynchronous Forum, Newcastle, June 2003.
10. D.Sokolov, J.Murphy, A.Bystrov, A.Yakovlev: "Improving the security of dual-rail circuits", Technical report, Microelectronic System Design Group, School of EECE, University of Newcastle upon Tyne, April 2004, http://www.staff.ncl.ac.uk/i.g.clark/async/tech-reports/NCL-EECE-MSD-TR-2004-101.pdf
11. W.Bainbridge, S.Furber: "Delay insensitive system-on-chip interconnect using 1-of-4 data encoding". In Proc. ASYNC'01, March 2001.
12. S.Mangard, M.Aigner, S.Dominikus: "A Highly Regular and Scalable AES Hardware Architecture". IEEE Trans. On Computers, 2003, 52(4), pp. 483–491
13. J.Daemen, V. Rijmen: "The Design of Rijndael". Springer-Verlag, 2002
14. National Institute Of Standards and Technology: "Federal Information Processing Standard 197, The Advanced Encryption Standard (AES)".
http://csrc.nist.gov/publications/fips/fips197/fips197.pdf, 2001.
15. R.Usselmann: "Advanced Encryption Standard / Rijndael IP Core". http://www.asic.ws/.
16. J.Wolkerstorfer, E.Oswald, M.Lamberger: "An ASIC implementation of AES S-Boxes", Topics in Cryptology RSA'02, Proc. RSA Conf. 2002, Feb 2002.

A   Advanced Encryption Standard

The symmetric block cipher Rijndael [13] was standardised by NIST as the Advanced Encryption Standard (AES) [14] in November 2001 as the successor to DES. The algorithm is a block cipher that encrypts/decrypts blocks of 128, 192, or 256 bits, and uses symmetric keys of 128, 192 or 256 bits. It consists of a sequence of four primitive functions, SubBytes, ShiftRows, MixColumns and AddRoundKey called a round. A round is executed 10, 12 or 14 times depending on the key and plain text lengths. Before the rounds are executed the AddRoundKey function is applied for initialisation plus the last round omits the MixColumns operation. A new key is derived for each round from the previous key.

For decryption the procedure is reversed and inverse versions of the aforementioned functions are applied, excluding AddRoundKey, this has no inverse.

A detailed explanation of each function can be found in [12,13]. For clarity the SubBytes function performs a non linear transformation using byte substitution tables (Sboxes), each Sbox is a multiplicative inversion in GF(256) followed by an affine transformation.

Both designs were synthesised from a RTL Verilog specification using the Cadence Ambit v4.0 tool and AMS-0.35μ library. A brief description of the two architectures follows.

A.1   Open Core AES Architecture

This design operates on 128 bits and has two separate 'sub-cores' one for encryption and the other for decryption; they share the same type of key generation module [15] and initial permutation module, however separate instances exist inside each sub-core. The core is shown in Figure 9; each sub core has 16 inverse/S-boxes inside the round permutation module. The initial permutation modules simply perform the AddRoundKey function and the round permutation modules loops internally to perform the 10 rounds and the final permutation module performs the last round. For this yields a complete encryption in 12 clock cycles. The decryption core consists of 16 inverse S-boxes these differ from the S-boxes used for encryption. The key reversal buffer stores keys for all the rounds and these are presented to the round permutation module each round in reverse order. Using this principle a complete decryption can be performed in 12 clock cycles. It must be highlighted that since the keys are used in reverse order - the initial key must be first expanded 10 times to get the last key, taking 10 extra clock cycles. In this design the Inv/SubBytes transformations (sboxes) are hardwired instead of being computed on the fly or stored in a ROM. This can be seen as simply a large decoder. The sub-cores both have 128 pins for plain/cipher text and 128 pins for the key and miscellaneous control pins and logic.

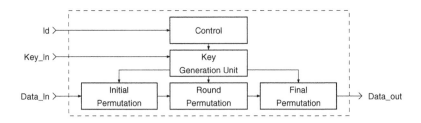

Fig. 9. Open core AES

A.2   AES with Computed Sboxes Architecture

This architecture combines encryption and decryption into one core working on 128 bits. The designs' basis is taken from [12], it was chosen due to its structure namely: it is highly regular (this keeps the layout small), it has short balanced combinational paths, hardware reuse for encryption and decryption which yields a small area and finally it has a 32 pin interface for the data (128 pin for the key) and shared computed sboxes.

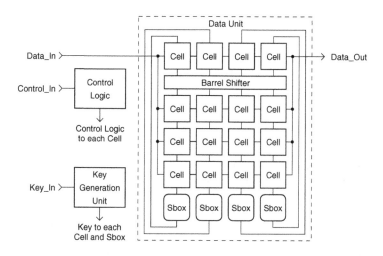

Fig. 10. AES with computed sboxes

The design consists of a key generation unit, control logic and a data unit incorporating 16 data cells, 4 sboxes (these perform the sbox and inverse sbox unlike the open core design) and a barrel shifter. The core is displayed in Figure 10, since the core does both encryption and decryption the diagram summarises both.

The data unit can perform any of the AES round functions and uses the key provided by the key unit for the AddRoundKey function. A single data cell comprises of a register, a GF(256) multiplier [12], a bank of XOR gates, and an input selection multiplexer. Additional multiplexers are included to enable the required function to be selected.

The Sboxes are able to perform either the Sbox transformation or the inverse Sbox transformation taking two clock cycles to compute a result due to a two-stage pipeline. Whilst the Sboxes are not used by the data unit (the MixColumns operation) the key generation unit takes advantage of this to generate the next key. The Sbox is computed by reducing the computation to GF(16) and GF(16) arithmetic and then applying the affine transformation as illustrated in [16].

Since the design has a 32 pin interface for the data, four clock cycles are required to clock the plain text, or cipher text into the data unit, and the same number to retrieve the data. After loading, the round functions are selected by the control logic. In total 60 clock cycles are needed for a complete encryption or decryption. As with the other design the input key needs to be expanded to the last key value before any rounds can take place; this takes an extra 20 clock cycles due to the pipelined Sbox. The total number of cycles for encryption or decryption could be reduced to 30 by using 16 sboxes at the expense of more area.

A New Attack with Side Channel Leakage During Exponent Recoding Computations

Yasuyuki Sakai[1] and Kouichi Sakurai[2]

[1] Mitsubishi Electric Corporation,
5-1-1 Ofuna, Kamakura, Kanagawa 247-8501, Japan
ysakai@iss.isl.melco.co.jp
[2] Kyushu University,
6-10-1 Hakozaki, Higashi-ku, Fukuoka 812-8581, Japan
sakurai@csce.kyushu-u.ac.jp

Abstract. In this paper we propose a new side channel attack, where exponent recodings for public key cryptosystems such as RSA and ECDSA are considered. The known side channel attacks and countermeasures for public key cryptosystems were against the main stage (square and multiply stage) of the modular exponentiation (or the point multiplication on an elliptic curve). We have many algorithms which achieve fast computation of exponentiations. When we compute an exponentiation, the exponent recoding has to be carried out before the main stage. There are some exponent recoding algorithms including conditional branches, in which instructions depend on the given exponent value. Consequently exponent recoding can constitute an information channel, providing the attacker with valuable information on the secret exponent. In this paper we show new algorithms of attack on exponent recoding. The proposed algorithms can recover the secret exponent, when the width-w NAF [9] and the unsigned/signed fractional window representation [5] are used.

Keywords: Side channel attack, exponent recoding, RSA cryptosystems, elliptic curve cryptosystems.

1 Introduction

Smart cards are one of the major application fields of cryptographic algorithms, and may contain sensitive data, such as RSA private key. Some implementations of cryptographic algorithms often leak *"side channel information."* Side channel information includes power consumption, electromagnetic fields and timing to process. Side channel attacks, which use side channel information leaked from real implementation of cryptographic algorithms, were first introduced by Kocher, Jaffe and Jun [2,3]. Side channel attacks can be often much more powerful than mathematical cryptanalysis. Thus, many papers on side channel cryptanalysis have been published.

RSA based cryptosystems and elliptic curve based cryptosystems require computation of the modular exponentiation (or the point multiplication on an

M. Joye and J.-J. Quisquater (Eds.): CHES 2004, LNCS 3156, pp. 298–311, 2004.

elliptic curve). The computational performance of cryptographic protocols with public key cryptosystems strongly depends on the efficiency of the modular exponentiation procedure. Therefore, it is very attractive to provide algorithms that allow efficient implementation. One approach to reducing the computational complexity of the modular exponentiation is to replace the binary representation of the given exponent with a representation which has fewer non-zero terms. Transforming an exponent from one representation to another is called *"exponent recoding."*

Since the concept of the side channel attacks was firstly proposed by Kocher, Jaffe and Jun [2,3], various methods of attacks and countermeasures have been proposed. For example related to public key cryptosystems, Coron proposed three concepts of countermeasures for differential power analysis (DPA) on elliptic curve cryptosystems [1]: 1) randomization of the secret exponent, 2) blinding the point, 3) randomized projective coordinates. Side channel information leaked from cryptographic devices may provide much information about the operations that take place and involved parameters. Known power analysis in the literature were related to modular exponentiation (or elliptic point multiplication).

If we carefully observe the exponentiation procedure, we can find one more stage in which instructions depend on the secret exponent. Some efficient modular exponentiations have to perform the exponent recoding in advance, then the main stage (square and multiply stage) of the modular exponentiation is computed. Since the exponent recoding may be executed with conditional branches depending on the secret exponent value, the computation of the exponent recoding can constitute an information channel which provides valuable information for the attacker. In this paper, we discuss side channel information leaked from cryptographic devices during exponent recoding computation. We will show methods of attacks on the exponent recoding for width-w NAF [9] and signed/unsigned fractional window representation [5].

The rest of this paper is organized as follows. Section 2 will give a brief description of exponent recoding algorithms. In Section 3, information leakage during exponent recoding will be discussed. Section 4 gives algorithms of attacks on the exponent recodings. Finally, Section 5 gives our conclusion.

2   Exponent Recoding

In this section we will give a brief description of exponent recodings. In some efficient modular exponentiations, an exponent recoding has to be performed in advance, then the main stage (square and multiply stage) of the modular exponentiation is computed. In the exponent recoding stage, the binary representation of the given exponent is replaced by a representation which has fewer non-zero terms. We will examine three methods of exponent recoding: width-w NAF [9] and signed/unsigned fractional window representation [5].

2.1 NAF

The signed binary representation, which is also referred to as non-adjacent form (NAF), is a *"sparse"* signed binary representation of an integer. An algorithm of recoding to NAF is given in Algorithm 1 [8]. Step 3 and 4 of Algorithm 1 can be carried out with a table which contains all possible inputs to i-th iteration of Step 3 and 4 and the corresponding outputs. Algorithm 2 also generates NAF, and is equivalent to Algorithm 1.

The average density achieved by NAF is $1/3$ for exponent $d \to \infty$.

Algorithm 1 Exponent recoding for NAF

Input   a non-negative t-bit integer $d = (d_{t-1} \cdots d_0)_2$
Output $b = (b_t \cdots b_0)$, where $b_i \in \{-1, 0, 1\}$ and $b_i b_{i+1} = 0$ for all i
1. $c_0 \leftarrow 0, d_{t+1} \leftarrow 0, d_t \leftarrow 0$
2. for i from 0 to t do
3. $c_{i+1} \leftarrow \lfloor (c_i + d_i + d_{i+1})/2 \rfloor$
4. $b_i \leftarrow c_i + d_i - 2c_{i+1}$
5. end for
6. Return $b = (b_t \cdots b_0)$

Algorithm 2 Exponent recoding for NAF: a variant

Input   a non-negative t-bit integer $d = (d_{t-1} \cdots d_0)_2$
Output $b = (b_t \cdots b_0)$, where $b_i \in \{-1, 0, 1\}$ and $b_i b_{i+1} = 0$ for all i
1. $b = (s_t \cdots s_0 d_0)_2 \leftarrow 3d$
2. $b \leftarrow b - 2d$ ($b_i = s_i - d_{i+1}$ with $0 - 1 = \tilde{1}$, where $\tilde{1}$ denotes $- 1$)
3. Return $b = (b_t \cdots b_0)$

2.2 Width-w NAF

Width-w NAF, proposed by independently Solinas [9] and Cohen, can be viewed as a generalization of NAF. The case $w = 2$ is that of the ordinary NAF. Algorithm 3 is a typical implementation of the exponent recoding for width-w NAF representation.

The average density achieved by width-w NAF is $1/(w + 1)$ for exponent $d \to \infty$.

Algorithm 3 Exponent recoding for the width-w NAF

Input   a non-negative t-bit integer d, an integer $w \geq 2$
Output $b = (b_t \cdots b_0)$, where $b_i \in \{0, \pm 1, \pm 3, \cdots, \pm(2^{w-1} - 1)\}$ and among any
         w consecutive b_is, at most one is nonzero.

1. $c \leftarrow d$, $i \leftarrow 0$
2. while $c > 0$ do
3.   if c odd then
4. $b_i \leftarrow c \bmod 2^w$
5.   if $b_i \geq 2^{w-1}$ then
6. $b_i \leftarrow b_i - 2^w$
7.   end if
8. $c \leftarrow c - b_i$
9.   else
10. $b_i \leftarrow 0$
11.   end if
12. $c \leftarrow \lfloor c/2 \rfloor$, $i \leftarrow i + 1$
13. end while
14. Return $b = (b_t \cdots b_0)$

2.3 Fractional Window

In small devices, the choice of w for exponentiation using the width-w NAF may be dictated by memory limitations. Möller proposed a *fractional window* technique [5], which can be viewed as a generalization of the sliding window and width-w approach. The fractional window exponentiation has better flexibility of the table size. See [5] for details.

The fractional window method of exponentiation has two variants. One is the signed version, where negative digits are allowed. The other is the unsigned variant of the fractional window method for the case that only non-negative digits are permissible. The recoding methods for unsigned fractional window representation and signed fractional window representation are described in Algorithm 4 and 5, respectively.

Let $w \geq 2$ be an integer and m an odd integer such that $1 \leq m \leq 2^w - 3$. The average density of signed fractional window representations with parameters w and m is

$$\frac{1}{w + \frac{m+1}{2^w} + 2}$$

for $d \rightarrow \infty$ [5]. The average density of unsigned fractional window representations with parameters w and m is

$$\frac{1}{w + \frac{m+1}{2^w} + 1}$$

for $d \rightarrow \infty$ [5].

Algorithm 4 Exponent recoding for the unsigned fractional window representation

---

Input   a non-negative integer d, an integer $w \geq 2$, an odd integer m, $1 \leq m \leq 2^w - 3$

Output $b = (b_{i-1} \cdots b_0)$, $b_i \in \{0, 1, 3, \cdots, 2^w + m\}$

1. $c \leftarrow d, i \leftarrow 0$
2. while $c > 0$ do
3.   if c odd then
4. $b_i \leftarrow c \bmod 2^{w+1}$
5.   if $2^w + m < b_i$ then
6. $b_i \leftarrow b_i - 2^w$
7.   end if
8. $c \leftarrow c - b_i$
9.   else
10. $b_i \leftarrow 0$
11.   end if
12. $c \leftarrow \lfloor c/2 \rfloor, i \leftarrow i + 1$
13. end while
14. Return $b = (b_{i-1} \cdots b_0)$

Algorithm 5 Exponent recoding for the signed fractional window representation

---

Input   a non negative integer d, an integer $w \geq 2$, an odd integer m, $1 \leq m \leq 2^w - 3$

Output $b = (b_{i-1} \cdots b_0)$, $b_i \in \{0, \pm 1, \pm 3, \cdots, \pm(2^w + m)\}$

1. $c \leftarrow d, i \leftarrow 0$
2. while $c > 0$ do
3.   if c odd then
4. $b_i \leftarrow c \bmod 2^{w+2}$
5.   if $2^w + m < b_i < 3 \cdot 2^w - m$ then
6. $b_i \leftarrow b_i - 2^{w+1}$
7.   else if $3 \cdot 2^w - m \leq b_i < 2^{w+2}$ then
8. $b_i \leftarrow b_i - 2^{w+2}$
9.   end if
10. $c \leftarrow c - b_i$
11.   else
12. $b_i \leftarrow 0$
13.   end if
14. $c \leftarrow \lfloor c/2 \rfloor, i \leftarrow i + 1$
15. end while
16. Return $b = (b_{i-1} \cdots b_0)$

---

3   Information Leakage During Exponent Recoding

As we have seen in Section 2, exponent recodings of Algorithms 3, 4 and 5 have conditional branches during the computation.

While the effects of the conditional branch might be difficult to identify from direct observations of a device's power consumption, the statistical operations used in DPA are able to reliably identify extraordinarily small differences in power consumption [4]. In this section we will discuss the information leaked from cryptographic devices during the exponent recodings.

3.1   The Model of the Attacker

We assume the model of the attacker as follows.

- The attacker has access to a device which calculates exponent recoding.
- The attacker has knowledge about the implementation, i.e., he knows the algorithm, including the parameter w and m, of the exponent recoding implemented on the device.
- The attacker can distinguish the conditional branch in Algorithm 3, 4 and 5 by monitoring power consumption during the computation of the exponent recoding.

The goal of the attacker is:

- Recovering the secret exponent.

3.2   Leakage During Exponent Recoding

Width-w NAF recoding (Algorithm 3) has two conditional branches, Step 3 and 5, in the main loop. If the symbol in the window of width-w is odd, Step 4 through 8 should be performed. Else if the symbol is even, Step 10 should be performed. When the symbol is odd, inner conditional branch will be evaluated, then if the symbol $b_i \geq 2^{w-1}$, b_i has to be subtracted by 2^w. Consequently the execution path of width-w recoding branches into three cases. In the execution path, subtraction instruction have to be performed depending on the exponent value.

We define a "$\mathcal{SN}$-sequence" as follows.

- At the i-th loop of the main loop, if the subtraction instruction is performed two times, we call the observed power consumption $\mathcal{SSN}$.
- If the subtraction instruction is performed one time, we call the observed power consumption $\mathcal{SN}$.
- If no subtraction instruction is performed, we call the observed power consumption $\mathcal{N}$.

$\mathcal{SN}$-sequence is a series of $\mathcal{SSN}$, $\mathcal{SN}$ and $\mathcal{N}$ observed during the computation of the exponent recoding:

$$\mathcal{SN}\text{-sequence} := \{\mathcal{SSN}, \mathcal{SN}, \mathcal{N}\}^*$$

The attacker can obtain $\mathcal{SN}$-sequences by monitoring power consumption. A $\mathcal{SN}$-sequence is the side channel information leaked from cryptographic devices.

As in the case of width-w NAF recoding, both the unsigned/signed fractional recoding (Algorithm 4, 5) have conditional branches depending on the exponent value. Hence the attacker can observe $\mathcal{SN}$-sequences during the computation of the recoding.

It is straight forward to implement the basic NAF recoding without conditional branches as described in Algorithm 1 with a look-up table. Algorithm 2 is also a secure implementation of NAF recoding.

4   The Attacks

In this section we describe new attacks on exponent recodings for width-w NAF and signed/unsigned fractional window representation given in Section 2. The attacker tries to recover the secret exponent from observed $\mathcal{SN}$-sequences. We assume that exponent recodings are implemented by Algorithm 3, 4 and 5.

4.1   Basic Strategy

As we have already mentioned, execution of width-w recoding has three branches. For a given exponent, the $\mathcal{SN}$-sequence is uniquely determined. For example, when width-3 NAF recoding is implemented by Algorithm 3, $\mathcal{SN}$-value ($\in \{\mathcal{SSN}, \mathcal{SN}, \mathcal{N}\}$) in each i-th loop will be as the following Table 1.

Table 1. Relation between data in the window and resulting $\mathcal{SN}$-value: width-3 NAF

data in the window	mapped digit b_i	$\mathcal{SN}$-value
$0 = (000)_2$	0	$\mathcal{N}$
$1 = (001)_2$	1	$\mathcal{SN}$
$2 = (010)_2$	0	$\mathcal{N}$
$3 = (011)_2$	3	$\mathcal{SN}$
$4 = (100)_2$	0	$\mathcal{N}$
$5 = (101)_2$	-3	$\mathcal{SSN}$
$6 = (110)_2$	0	$\mathcal{N}$
$7 = (111)_2$	-1	$\mathcal{SSN}$

Basically an attack can be constructed based on Table 1. However, there exist a difficulty in guessing the secret exponent value from given $\mathcal{SN}$-sequence. While the $\mathcal{SN}$-sequence is uniquely determined from the given exponent, the converse is not true. When $\mathcal{SN}$ is observed, the data in the window should be $(001)_2$ or

$(011)_2$. Therefore the attacker can decide the LSB and MSB in the window, but the middle bit can not be guessed uniquely. The same situation happens when $\mathcal{SSN}$ is observed.

The second difficulty is the "*carry.*" When the data in the window is odd and greater than 2^{w-1}, mapped digit b_i has to be subtracted by 2^w, then the resulting b_i (Step 6) will have negative value. The following subtraction instruction (Step 8) should be addition and a carry will always occur. Consequently, at the next $(i+1)$-th loop, the temporary exponent c will has a different bit-pattern from the originally given exponent d. For example, assume $45 = (101101)_2$ is the given exponent d and width-3 NAF recoding is performed. At the first loop, mapped digit b_i should be -3 (Step 6). Then at Step 8, the temporary exponent c should be $48 = (110000)_2$. Since the carry occurs, at the later loop, observed $\mathcal{SN}$-value can not be a direct information of the exponent value.

We have to construct attacks in consideration of above two observations.

4.2   An Attack on Width-w NAF Recoding

We show an attack on width-w NAF recoding. The algorithm of the attack is based on the following observations.

- In the case of $\mathcal{SSN}$, a carry occurs at Step 8.
- In the case of $\mathcal{SSN}$ and all the passed values after previously observed $\mathcal{SSN}$ were $\mathcal{N}$s, i.e., sub-sequence is $(\mathcal{SSN},\mathcal{N},\mathcal{N},\cdots,\mathcal{N},\mathcal{SSN})$, the carry was transmitted to the current $\mathcal{SSN}$.
- In the case of $\mathcal{SSN}$ and if a carry is transmitted, the attacker should guess $d_i = 0$. Otherwise if a carry is not transmitted, the attacker should guess $d_i = 1$.
- In the case of $\mathcal{SSN}$, the attacker should guess $d_{i+w-1} = 1$.
- In the case of $\mathcal{N}$ and a carry is transmitted, the attacker should guess $d_i = 1$. Otherwise if a carry is not transmitted, the attacker should guess $d_i = 0$.
- In the case of $\mathcal{SN}$, the attacker should guess d_i as the same strategies as in the case of $\mathcal{SSN}$.
- In the case of $\mathcal{SN}$ and the length of the rest bits to be guessed is smaller than the window width w, the attacker should guess $d_{t-1} = 1$ by definition such that MSB of d is always "1".
- In the case of $\mathcal{SN}$, the transmission of a carry stops at this place.

The attack is described in Algorithm 6. The symbol "*state*" is used for the consideration of a carry. If the data of the middle in the window can not be guessed uniquely, the symbol "*unknown*" is used.

Algorithm 6 An attack on width-w NAF recoding

Input $\mathcal{SN}$-sequence $(v_0, v_1, \cdots)$, where $v_i \in \{\mathcal{SSN}, \mathcal{SN}, \mathcal{N}\}$, an integer $w \geq 2$, $t =$bitlength of d

Output   an exponent $d = (d_{t-1} \cdots d_0)_2$

```
 1.  i ← 0
 2.  state ← 0
 3.  while i < t do
 4.     if v_i = SSN then
 5.         if state = 1 then d_i ← 0
 6.         else if state = 0 then d_i ← 1
 7.         for j from i + 1 to i + w − 2 do d_i ← "unknown"
 8.         d_{i+w−1} ← 1
 9.         i ← i + w
10.         state ← 1
11.     else if v_i = SN then
12.         if i + w − 1 > t
13.             if state = 1 then d_i ← 0
14.             else if state = 0 then d_i ← 1
15.             for j from i + 1 to t − 2 do d_i ← "unknown"
16.             d_{t−1} ← 1
17.             i ← t
18.         else
19.             if state = 1 then d_i ← 0
20.             else if state = 0 then d_i ← 1
21.             for j from i + 1 to i + w − 2 do d_i ← "unknown"
22.             d_{i+w−1} ← 0
23.             i ← i + w
24.         end if
25.         state ← 0
26.     else if v_i = N then
27.         if state = 1 then d_i ← 1
28.         else if state = 0 then d_i ← 0
29.         i ← i + 1
30.     end if
31.  end while
32.  Return d = (d_{t−1} ··· d_0)_2
```

We can evaluate that how many bits can be recovered from observed $\mathcal{SN}$-sequences in the case of the width-w NAF recoding.

Theorem 1. *Assume that width-w NAF recoding is implemented by Algorithm 3 and that $\mathcal{SN}$-sequence can be observed during the recoding. The ratio of successfully recovered bits can be evaluated by $3/(w + 1)$ for $t \to \infty$.*

Proof. It is easy to prove from the fact that the density of width-w NAF recoding is $1/(w + 1)$ for $t \to \infty$.   □

4.3   An Attack on Unsigned Fractional Window Recoding

We show an attack on the unsigned fractional window recoding. Similar strategies as in the width-w recoding case can be applied. Data dependent subtraction instructions have to be carried out at Step 6 and 8 of Algorithm 4. Therefore, the attacker can observe $\mathcal{SN}$-sequence during the recoding. The difference on the strategies from the case of width-w NAF is that even when the subtraction instruction at Step 8 is carried out, no carry occur.

The attack is shown in Algorithm 7.

Remark 1. Even if the case of "*unknown*", the probability of "0" or "1" may not be equal in some cases depending on the parameter m. In such a case we can modify the attack with weighted probability of guessed value. In appendix A relations between successive unknown bits are described.

Algorithm 7 An attack on unsigned fractional window recoding

Input $\mathcal{SN}$-sequence $(v_0, v_1, \cdots)$, $v_i \in \{\mathcal{SSN}, \mathcal{SN}, \mathcal{N}\}$, an integer $w \geq 2$, an
   odd integer m, $1 \leq m \leq 2^w - 3$, $t =$bitlength of d
Output   an exponent $d = (d_{t-1} \cdots d_0)_2$
1. $i \leftarrow 0$
2.   while $i < t$ do
3.   if $v_i = \mathcal{SSN}$ then
4. $d_i \leftarrow 1$
5.   for j from $i+1$ to $i+w-1$ do $d_i \leftarrow$ "*unknown*"
6. $i \leftarrow i + w$
7.   else if $v_i = \mathcal{SN}$ then
8. $d_i \leftarrow 1$
9.   if $i + w + 1 > t$
10.   for j from $i+1$ to $t-2$ do $d_i \leftarrow$ "*unknown*"
11. $d_{t-1} \leftarrow 1$
12. $i \leftarrow t$
13.   else
14.   for j from $i+1$ to $i+w$ do $d_i \leftarrow$ "*unknown*"
15. $i \leftarrow i + w + 1$
16.   end if
17.   else if $v_i = \mathcal{N}$ then
18. $d_i \leftarrow 0$
19. $i \leftarrow i + 1$
20.   end if
21. end while
22. Return $d = (d_{t-1} \cdots d_0)_2$

4.4   An Attack on Signed Fractional Window Recoding

An attack on the signed fractional window recoding is shown in Algorithm 8. The similar strategies as width-w recoding can be applied, but handling of the transmission of a carry should be more complicated. Only when $w+1$ continuous $\mathcal{N}$s are observed after $\mathcal{SSN}$, a carry may be transmitted to $\mathcal{SN}$ or $\mathcal{SSN}$. The variable c in Algorithm 8 is used to store the number of continuous $\mathcal{N}$.

Algorithm 8 An attack on signed fractional window recoding

Input $\mathcal{SN}$-sequence $(v_0, v_1, \cdots)$, $v_i \in \{\mathcal{SSN}, \mathcal{SN}, \mathcal{N}\}$, an integer $w \geq 2$ an odd integer m, $1 \leq m \leq 2^w - 3$, $t =$bitlength of d

Output an exponent $d = (d_{t-1} \cdots d_0)_2$

1. $i \leftarrow 0$
2. $state \leftarrow 0$
3. $c \leftarrow 0$
4.   while $i < t$ do
5.   if $v_i = \mathcal{SSN}$ then
6.   if $c \geq w + 1$ and $state = 1$ then $d_i \leftarrow 0$
7.   else if $c = w$ and $state = 1$ then $d_i \leftarrow$ "unknown"
8.   else $d_i \leftarrow 1$
9.   for j from $i + 1$ to $i + w$ do $d_i \leftarrow$ "unknown"
10. $i \leftarrow i + w + 1$
11. $c \leftarrow w$
12. $state \leftarrow 1$
13.   else if $v_i = \mathcal{SN}$ then
14.   if $c \geq w + 1$ and $state = 1$ then $d_i \leftarrow 0$
15.   else if $c = w$ and $state = 1$ then $d_i \leftarrow$ "unknown"
16.   else $d_i \leftarrow 1$
17.   if $i + w + 1 > t$
18.   for j from $i + 1$ to $t - 2$ do $d_i \leftarrow$ "unknown"
19. $d_{t-1} \leftarrow 1$
20. $i \leftarrow t$
21.   else
22.   for j from $i + 1$ to $i + w$ do $d_i \leftarrow$ "unknown"
23. $d_{i+w+1} \leftarrow 0$
24. $i \leftarrow i + w + 2$
25.   end if
26. $c \leftarrow w$
27. $state \leftarrow 0$
28.   else if $v_i = \mathcal{N}$ then
29.   if $state = 1$ then $d_i \leftarrow 1$
30.   else if $state = 0$ then $d_i \leftarrow 0$
31. $c \leftarrow c + 1$
32. $i \leftarrow i + 1$
33.   end if
34. end while
35. Return $d = (d_{t-1} \cdots d_0)_2$

4.5   Experimental Results

We carried out experiments by a simulation on the attacks described in the previous sections as follows.

1. randomly generate 10,000 exponents d, which have 160-bit, 512-bit or 1024-bit.
2. implement algorithms for exponent recodings described in Algorithms 3, 4 and 5 in S/W written in C-language.
3. generate $\mathcal{SN}$-sequences using this S/W.
4. using the $\mathcal{SN}$-sequences, we guess the secret exponent d by Algorithm 6, 7 and 8.
5. count the successfully recovered bits ($=$ number of recovered bits / bitlength of exponent d)

The results are given in Table 2. The experiments were carried out with 160-bit, 512-bit and 1024-bit exponents. Almost the same percentages were obtained in each case.

The window width w were examined from 2 through 5. In the fractional window expansion the parameter m were examined from 1 through the upper bound, i.e. $2^w - 3$. The intermediate ($2 \leq m \leq 2^w - 4$) are omitted because of the space limitation. The successfully recovered bits decrease in larger w, because as we have already mentioned, the bits of the middle in the window can not be guessed uniquely. In the fractional window expansion the successfully recovered bits increase in larger m. Examples of the three proposed attacks with small exponents are illustrated in Appendix B.

Remark 2. No guessing errors occur in the attacks. Only "*unknown*" bits can be un-recovered bits.

Table 2. Successfully recovered bits (%) (= number of recovered bits / bitlength of exponent d): Experimental results

w	m	width-w NAF	unsigned fract.	signed fract.
2	—	100	—	—
	1	—	50.5	50.3
3	—	75.1	—	—
	1	—	38.9	36.3
	5	—	40.0	46.0
4	—	60.2	—	—
	1	—	31.3	28.3
	13	—	33.7	41.4
5	—	50.3	—	—
	1	—	26.2	23.5
	29	—	29.1	37.1

5   Concluding Remarks

We have shown that unless the exponent recoding is carefully implemented, RSA and elliptic curve based cryptosystems are vulnerable to power analysis. We have introduced new side channel attacks on exponent recoding.

While the effects of a single transistor switching would be normally be impossible to identify from direct observations of a device's power consumption [4], the statistical operations are able to reliably identify extraordinarily small differences in power consumption.

Okeya and Takagi proposed efficient counter measures for side channel attacks [6,7]. The exponent recodings given in [6,7] are based on width-w NAF or fractional window. Therefore, it may be possible to construct attacks on the recodings.

References

1. J.-S. Coron, "Resistance against differential power analysis for elliptic curve cryptosystems," CHES'99, LNCS 1717, pp.292–302, Springer-Verlag, 1999.
2. P.C. Kocher, "Timing attacks on implementations of Diffie-Hellman, RSA, DSS, and other systems," Advances in Cryptology – CRYPTO'96, LNCS 1109, pp.104–113, Springer-Verlag, 1996.
3. P.C. Kocher, J. Jaffe, and B. Jun, "Differential power analysis," Advances in Cryptology – CRYPTO'99, LNCS 1666, pp.388–397, Springer-Verlag, 1999.
4. P.C. Kocher, J. Jaffe, and B. Jun, "Introduction to differential power analysis and related attacks," Cryptography Research, http://www.cryptography.com
5. B. Möller, "Improved techniques for fast exponentiation," ICISC 2002, LNCS 2587, pp.298–312, Springer-Verlag, 2002.
6. K. Okeya, T. Takagi, "The width-w NAF method provides small memory and fast elliptic scalar multiplications secure against side channel attacks," CT-RSA 2003, LNCS 2612, pp.328–342, Springer-Verlag, 2003.
7. K. Okeya, T. Takagi, "A more flexible countermeasure against side channel attacks using window method," CHES 2003, LNCS 2779, pp.397–410, Springer-Verlag, 2003.
8. G.W. Reitwiesner, "Binary arithmetic," Advances in Computers, vol.1, pp.231–308, 1960.
9. J.A. Solinas, "Efficient arithmetic on Koblitz curve," Designs, Codes and Cryptography, vol.87, pp.195–249. Kluwer Academic Publishers, 2000.

A   Relation Between Unknown Bits

In this appendix we show relations between unknown bits. If several unknown bits occur in succession, some unknown bits can be "0" or "1" with high probability. Table 3 shows the probability that unknown bits can be "0" or "1" in the case of the unsigned fractional window recoding with the parameter $w = 3$ and $m = 1$.

Table 3. Observed $\mathcal{SN}$-values and unknown bits: unsigned fractional window recoding with $w = 3$, $m = 1$

observed $\mathcal{SN}$-value	$\mathcal{SN}$	$\mathcal{SSN}$
candidates of the	0 0 0 1	1 0 1 1
secret exponent	0 0 1 1	1 1 0 1
in the window	0 1 0 1	1 1 1 1
	0 1 1 1	
	1 0 0 1	
recovered bits ("x" denotes the unknown)	x x x 1	1 x x 1
probability that x=0	$\frac{4}{5}$ $\frac{3}{5}$ $\frac{3}{5}$	$\frac{1}{3}$ $\frac{1}{3}$

B Examples of the Attacks

In this appendix we illustrate small examples of the three attacks. In examples below, given randomly generated 32-bit exponents, recoded representations and expected $\mathcal{SN}$-sequences are described. The attacker can recover the exponents from the observed $\mathcal{SN}$-sequences as shown below. The symbol "x" in the recovered bits denotes the *"unknown"* bit.

width-3 NAF

```
      exponent:  1 1 1 0 0 0 0 1 1 1 1 0 1 0 1 0 1 1 1 0 1 1 0 1 0 1 1 0 0 1 1
       recoded: 1 0 0 -1 0 0 0 1 0 0 0 0 0 -3 0 0 3 0 0 0 0 -1 0 0 0 -3 0 0 3 0 0 0 3
SN-sequence: 1 0 0 0 1 0 0 2 0 0 0 2 0 0 0 1 0 0 2 0 0 0 0 1 0 0 0 2 0 0 1
     recovered:  1 x 1 0 0 x 0 1 x 1 1 0 x 0 1 0 1 x 1 1 x 1 1 0 1 0 x 1 0 0 x 1
```

unsigned fractional window with w = 3, m = 1

```
      exponent: 1 0 1 1 1 0 0 0 1 1 1 1 0 0 0 0 1 0 1 1 1 0 1 0 1 0 0 0 0 1 1 1
       recoded: 1 0 0 0 7 0 0 0 1 0 0 7 0 0 0 0 1 0 0 0 7 0 0 0 5 0 0 0 0 0 0 7
SN-sequence: 1 0 0 0 1 0 0 0 1 0 0 2 0 0 0 0 1 0 0 0 1 0 0 0 1 0 0 0 0 0 0 1
     recovered: 1 x x x 1 x x x 1 x x 1 0 x x x 1 x x x 1 x x x 1 0 0 0 x x x 1
```

signed fractional window with w = 3, m = 1

```
      exponent: 1 0 0 1 1 0 1 1 0 0 1 1 1 1 1 0 1 0 0 1 1 0 1 0 0 0 1 0 0 1 0 0
       recoded: 1 0 0 0 0 7 0 0 0 -3 0 0 0 0 -1 0 0 0 5 0 0 0 -3 0 0 0 0 0 0 9 0 0
SN-sequence: 1 0 0 0 0 1 0 0 0 2 0 0 0 0 2 0 0 0 2 0 0 0 2 0 0 0 0 0 0 1 0 0
     recovered: 1 0 x x x x x x x 0 1 x x x x x x x x x x x 1 0 0 0 x x x 1 0 0
```

Defeating Countermeasures Based on Randomized BSD Representations

Pierre-Alain Fouque[1], Frédéric Muller[2], Guillaume Poupard[2], and Frédéric Valette[2]

[1] École normale supérieure, Département d'informatique
45 rue d'Ulm 75230 Paris Cedex 05 France
`Pierre-Alain.Fouque@ens.fr`
[2] DCSSI Crypto Lab 51, Boulevard de Latour-Maubourg
75700 Paris 07 SP France
{`Frederic.Muller,Guillaume.Poupard,Frederic.Valette`}`@sgdn.pm.gouv.fr`

Abstract. The recent development of side channel attacks has lead implementers to use increasingly sophisticated countermeasures in critical operations such as modular exponentiation, or scalar multiplication on elliptic curves. A new class of countermeasures is based on inserting random decisions when choosing one representation of the secret scalar out of a large set of representations of the same value. For instance, this is the case of countermeasures proposed by Oswald and Aigner, or Ha and Moon, both based on randomized Binary Signed Digit (BSD) representations. Their advantage is to offer excellent speed performances. However, the first countermeasure and a simplified version of the second one were already broken using Markov chain analysis.

In this paper, we take a different approach to break the full version of Ha-Moon's countermeasure using a novel technique based on detecting local collisions in the intermediate states of computation. We also show that randomized BSD representations present some fundamental problems and thus recommend not to use them as a protection against side-channel attacks.

1 Introduction

Modular exponentiation or scalar multiplication are used by most popular public key cryptosystems like RSA [22] or DSA [4]. However, data manipulated during these computations should generally be kept secret, since any leakage of information (even only a few bits of secret information) might be useful to an attacker. For example, during the generation of an RSA signature by a cryptographic device, the secret exponent is used to transform an input related to the message into a digital signature via modular exponentiation.

Timings and power attacks, first introduced by Kocher [11,12] are now well studied and various countermeasures have been proposed. These attacks represent a real threat when considering operations that involve secret data and require a long computation time. In general, naive implementations leak information about the secret key.

M. Joye and J.-J. Quisquater (Eds.): CHES 2004, LNCS 3156, pp. 312–327, 2004.

In [2], Coron has shown that several countermeasures are possible to prevent this type of leakage. In the context of Elliptic Curve Cryptosystems (ECC), he proposed different techniques based on blinding the critical data manipulated. An alternative approach is to randomize the number and the sequence of steps in the multiplication algorithm itself. In this type of countermeasure the usual scalar multiplication algorithm on ECC is replaced by a randomized addition-subtraction chain. From a general perspective, the idea is to allow additional symbols in the secret scalar representation. When using the set of digits $\{0, 1, -1\}$, we generally speak of Binary Signed Digit (BSD) representation. Then the multiplication algorithm picks at random a valid representation of the secret scalar. Actually several algorithms of this class have been proposed in the recent years [7,13,20], many of which have been broken quickly [16,26,27]. In this paper, we present a new side channel attack against randomized exponentiation countermeasures. We believe this result enlightens fundamental defects in these constructions.

Basically our attack scenario is that an attacker has physical access to a cryptographic device and tries to find the private key used by the device. He first obtains different encryptions of a fixed message. Since the scalar representation is randomized, the cryptographic device performs a different computation each time. However, we will show that collisions occur frequently at each step of computation. They can be detected using power consumption curves and reveal critical information concerning the private key. Our attack does not depend much on which public key encryption scheme is actually used, so we focus on the case of ECCs. Furthermore, the Ha-Moon's countermeasure [7], proposed at CHES'02, was designed originally for ECCs. It is straightforward to apply our ideas to RSA-based encryption schemes and even to signature schemes based on RSA with a deterministic padding (i.e. without randomization) such as PKCS#1 v1.5 [23]. Indeed all we need is the ability to send the same input several times to the cryptographic device.

In this paper, we first recall the classical binary scalar multiplication on elliptic curves. Then, we briefly describe different types of side channel attacks such as Simple Power Analysis (SPA) and Differential Power Analysis (DPA) but also the attack of Messerges, Dabbish and Sloan [14] in order to motivate common countermeasures. Next, we describe the principles of countermeasures using a randomized BSD representation through the example of [7]. In the last two sections, we expose some major weaknesses in this family of algorithms and describe a new collision-based attack against the full Ha-Moon's countermeasure.

2   Binary Scalar Multiplication Algorithms

In classical cryptosystems based on the RSA or on the discrete logarithm problem, the main operation is modular exponentiation. In the elliptic curve setting, the corresponding operation is the scalar multiplication. From an algorithmic point of view, those two operations are very similar; the only difference is the underlying group structure. In this paper, we consider operations over a generic group with additive notations. We do not use additional properties of this group. The consequence is an immediate application to the elliptic curve setting but it should be clear that all what we state can be easily transposed to modular exponentiation.

Scalar multiplication is usually performed using the "double-and-add" method that computes $k \times P$ from a point P, using the binary representation of the scalar $k = \sum_{i=0}^{n-1} k_i 2^i$:

$$k \times P = \sum_{i=0}^{n-1} k_i \times \left(2^i \times P\right)$$

This method is obviously analog to the "square-and-multiply" method for modular exponentiation. The resulting algorithm is described in Figure 1, where $\mathcal{O}$ is the point at infinity.

Input: a point P, an n-bit integer $k = \sum_{i=0}^{n-1} k_i 2^i$
Output: $k \times P$
$Q = \mathcal{O}$
for i from $n-1$ down to 0
    $Q = 2Q$
    if $(k_i == 1)$ then $Q = Q + P$
return Q

Fig. 1. Naive "double-and-add" scalar multiplication algorithm

3   Power Analysis Attacks

It is well known that the naive double-and-add algorithm is subject to the power attacks introduced by Kocher *et al* [12]. More precisely, they introduced two types of power attacks : Simple Power Analysis (SPA) and Differential Power Analysis (DPA).

3.1   Simple Power Analysis

The first type of attack consists in observing the power consumption in order to guess which instruction is executed. For example, in the previous algorithm, one can easily recover the exponent $k = \sum_{i=0}^{n-1} k_i 2^i$, provided the doubling instruction can be distinguished from the point addition. To avoid this attack, the basic "double-and-add always" algorithm is usually modified using so-called "dummy" instructions (see Figure 2).

Although this new algorithm is immune to SPA, a more sophisticated treatment of power consumption measures still enables the recovery of the secret scalar k.

Input: a point P, an n-bit integer $k = \blacksquare \sum_{i=0}^{n-1} k_i 2^i$
Output: $k \times P$
$Q[0] = \mathcal{O}$
for i from $n - 1$ down to 0
    $Q[0] = 2Q[0]$
    $Q[1] = Q[0] + P$
    $Q[0] = Q[k_i]$
return $Q[0]$

Fig. 2. Double-and-add always algorithm resistant against SPA

3.2 Differential Power Analysis

DPA uses power consumption to retrieve information on the operand of the instruction. More precisely, it no longer focuses on which instruction is executed but on the Hamming weight of the operands used by the instruction. Such attacks have been described, in the elliptic curve setting, in [2,17].

This technique can also be used in a different way. Messerges, Dabbish and Sloan introduced "Multiple Exponent Single Data" attack [14]. Note that, for our purpose, a better name would be "Multiple Scalar Single Data". We first assume that we have two identical devices available with the same implementation of the algorithm of Figure 2, one with an unknown scalar k and another one for which the scalar e can be chosen and modified. In order to discover the value of k, using correlation between power consumption and operand value, we can apply the following algorithm. We guess the bit k_{n-1} of k which is first used in the double-and-add algorithm and we set e_{n-1} to this guessed value. Then, we compare the power consumption of the two devices doing the scalar multiplication of the same message. If the consumption is similar during the first two steps of the inner loop, it means that we have guessed the correct bit k_{n-1}. Otherwise, if the consumption differs in the second step, it means that the values are different and that we have guessed the wrong bit. So, after this measure, we know the most significant bit of k. Then, we can improve our knowledge on k by iterating this attack to find all bits as it is illustrated in the algorithm of Figure 3.

This kind of attack is well known and some classical countermeasures are often implemented (see [2,9]).

4 Countermeasures Using a Randomized Scalar Representation

In the case of scalar multiplication on ECC, the most popular countermeasures against DPA are those proposed by Coron [2]. They include randomizing the secret scalar, blinding the point and using randomized projective coordinates. New directions for attacking these countermeasures have recently been proposed [5, 6] but none of them works when all protections proposed by Coron are applied

```
for i from 0 to n − 1
    e_i = 0
for i from 0 to n − 1
    e_{n−1−i} = 1
    choose P randomly
    double-and-add(P,k) on device 1
    double-and-add(P,e) on device 2
    if no correlation at step (i + 1) e_{n−1−i} = 0
return e
```

Fig. 3. MESD attack to find secret scalar k

simultaneously. It remains to be investigated if Coron's countermeasures can be defeated in the general case.

An alternative to Coron's countermeasures is to randomize the multiplication algorithm itself by introducing some random decisions. Two recent propositions [7,20] use a randomized addition-subtraction chain, which is equivalent to represent the scalar with the alternative set of digits $\{0, 1, -1\}$. Both of them claim excellent performances in terms of speed, so they appear to be very attractive.

However, these countermeasures alone do not protect against SPA. This was illustrated recently by several new attacks [16,18,19]. They result from the assumption that distinguishing between the point addition (or subtraction) and the doubling instruction is possible. At CHES'03, a unified framework for such attacks, called the Hidden Markov Model attacks was proposed by Karlof and Wagner [10]. Hence randomized representation techniques are useful to counteract DPA attack but need to be strengthened in order to resist SPA.

A possible enhancement is to use special elliptic curves where the point addition (or subtraction) and the doubling instruction require exactly the same field operations [1,8,13]. Another approach is to transform these algorithms into "double-and-add-always" algorithms. Basically, this corresponds to the SPA countermeasure proposed by Coron [2]. The Ha and Moon's paper [7] actually proposes a SPA-immune algorithm using this technique. This strengthened version still remains to be broken. In the next sections, we focus on this algorithm and show how to break it using a completely different approach to the Markov model. More generally we expose some important defects in this class of countermeasures.

4.1 The Ha-Moon Countermeasure

It is well known that any positive integer k can be represented as a finite sum of the form $k = \sum d_i \times 2^i$ where d_i is in a suitable fixed set of digits. When $d_i \in \{0, 1\}$, we obtain the usual binary representation of k. Another possible choice is to use the set of digits $\{0, 1, -1\}$ then we speak of Binary Signed Digit (BSD) representation. Such a representation of k is clearly no longer unique.

However, there exists a unique representation where no two consecutive d_i's are non-zero, i.e. $d_i d_{i+1} = 0$ for all $i \geq 0$. This representation is called the "Non Adjacent Form" (NAF).

The Ha-Moon countermeasure [7] uses concepts from the NAF recoding algorithm to pick at random a representation from a scalar of initial length n bits. Actually there exist many ways to build a representation of the form

$$k = \sum_{i=0}^{n-1} d_i \times 2^i$$

where $d_i \in \{0, 1, -1\}$. Indeed this system includes the binary representation, thus all positive integers $k \leq 2^n - 1$ are included along with their opposites. But there are 3^n possible combinations, so the representation is clearly redundant. The proposed countermeasure picks one of these representations using an auxiliary random source. This randomization is described in Section 4.2. During the process, it may increase the number of digits of k from n to $n + 1$.

Once a new representation of k has been chosen, the new digits are used in the multiplication algorithm. With the usual methods, only doubling and addition are mixed. Now, subtractions are also mixed into the algorithm. This idea of mixing addition and subtraction in elliptic curve computations has been known since a long time [15]. The full SPA-immune countermeasure with "double-and-add always" algorithm becomes :

Input: a point P, an integer $k = \sum_{i=0}^{n} d_i 2^i$
Output: $k \times P$
$Q[0] = \mathcal{O}$
$P[1] = P$, $P[-1] = -P$ and $P[0] = P$
for i from n down to 0
    $Q[0] = 2Q[0]$
    $Q[1] = Q[0] + P[d_i]$
    $Q[-1] = Q[1]$
    $Q[0] = Q[d_i]$
return $Q[0]$

Fig. 4. NAF based Multiplication Algorithm

4.2 The Randomization Algorithm

The technique used to generate digits $d_i \in \{0, 1, -1\}$ is very efficient since it uses a simple table and increases the length of the scalar by at most one digit. It is very similar to the technique used to transform a binary representation into a NAF representation, referred to as NAF recoding algorithm. An analysis of this algorithm is given in [3]. For the purpose of our attack, we will describe it using the following notations :

A random value called $R = \sum_{i=0}^{i=n-1} r_i \times 2^i$ is generated and auxiliary carry bits, called c_i, are used (c_0 is set to 0). The digits d_i are then computed using the following table (taken from [7]).

Input				Output	
k_{i+1}	k_i	c_i	r_i	c_{i+1}	d_i
0	0	0	0	0	0
0	0	0	1	0	0
0	0	1	0	0	1
0	0	1	1	1	-1
0	1	0	0	0	1
0	1	0	1	1	-1
0	1	1	0	1	0
0	1	1	1	1	0
1	0	0	0	0	0
1	0	0	1	0	0
1	0	1	0	1	-1
1	0	1	1	0	1
1	1	0	0	1	-1
1	1	0	1	0	1
1	1	1	0	1	0
1	1	1	1	1	0

For instance, for a scalar of length $n = 9$ bits, $k = 111011110_2 = 478$ and with $r = 110101001_2$ we obtain, $c = 1110111100_2$ and $d = 100\bar{1}1000\bar{1}0_2$ where $\bar{1} = -1$ by definition. We call a the sum of k and $\frac{k}{2} \oplus r$, and $\sum_{i=0}^{i=n} a_i \times 2^i$ its binary representation. Consequently,

$$k + \left(\frac{k}{2} \oplus r\right) = a = \sum_{i=0}^{n} a_i \times 2^i$$

The c_i's can be seen as the carry bits in this addition. Then, by definition of the bits d_i's in the previous table,

$$d_i = a_i - (k_{i+1} \oplus r_i)$$

for $0 \leq i \leq n$. Therefore, the following relation holds

$$\sum_{i=0}^{n} d_i \times 2^i = a - (k/2 \oplus r) = k$$

which shows that we actually compute an alternative representation of k.

5   Weaknesses in Randomized Representations

In this section, we describe how to attack the Ha-Moon full countermeasure. Our attack takes advantage of inherent weaknesses in the randomized BSD representation. Moreover, it might also be applied to any countermeasure based on a similar principle.

5.1   Collision Attacks

Side channel attacks based on collision detection have been recently applied with success to block ciphers [24] and to public key cryptosystems [5]. Although it might be difficult in practice to detect which computation is done by the cryptographic device, it is usually much easier to detect internal data collisions. For instance, by analyzing the power consumption of a smart card, an adversary may be able to tell when the same sequence of instructions is executed by the card. More precisely, if the card computes $2 \times A$ and $2 \times B$, the attacker is not able to tell the value of A nor B, but he is able to check if $A = B$. Such an assumption is reasonable as long as the computation takes many clock cycles and depends greatly on the value of the operand. A stronger variant of this assumption has been validated by Schramm *et al.* in [24]. Indeed, they are able to detect collisions during one DES round computation which is arguably more difficult than detecting collisions during a doubling operation. If the noise is negligible, a simple comparison of the power consumption curves is sufficient to detect a collision.

We now focus on the randomized BSD representation and show how to obtain internal data collisions using the randomization algorithm described previously.

5.2   Intermediate States in the Multiplication Algorithm

The randomization algorithm proposed in [7] apparently generates a large number of alternative representations of the number k. Since n bits of randomness are used, we may indeed expect to obtain up to 2^n different sequences of digits d_i for each k. However, as we have seen before, there are only 3^{n+1} representations with $(n + 1)$ digits d_i which must correspond to 2^n possible values of k. Consequently, there are on average $\simeq \left(\frac{3}{2}\right)^n$ representations per value of k, and not 2^n randomized representations. Moreover, at each step of the multiplication algorithm, the internal state may only take a reduced number of values. For sake of simplicity, we suppose in the following that computations are made upwards, while the algorithm initially proposed is downwards (see Figure 4). It should be clear that both directions yield similar properties. In the upward direction, after t steps, the value of $Q[0]$ corresponds to

$$Q[0] = \left(\sum_{i=0}^{t-1} d_i \times 2^i\right) \times P = D_t \times P$$

where $D_t = \sum_{i=0}^{i=t-1} d_i \times 2^i$ denotes the partial sum of the digits d_i and it is clear that $D_{n+1} = k$. At each step, the internal value D_t must also be compatible with $(k \bmod 2^t)$. Indeed, when we reach the most significant bit, we obtain the right value of k, except for a term of correction of the form $d_n \times 2^n$. More generally, it is easy to verify that

$$D_t = k \bmod 2^t - \varepsilon_t \times 2^t$$

where $\varepsilon_t = 0$ or 1. This can be directly seen from the relations of Section 4.2. Indeed, at step number t,

$$D_t = ((k + (k/2 \oplus r)) \bmod 2^t) - ((k/2 \oplus r) \bmod 2^t)$$

Therefore, after t steps of computation, although there are 2^t possible sequences of random bits, only 2 intermediate values - say V_t and V_t' - are possible, depending on ε_t. This is true independently of the direction of the computation . If we do it upwards, these values are $V_t = (k \bmod 2^t) \times P$ and $V_t' = ((k \bmod 2^t) - 2^t) \times P$ respectively. Furthermore, in Figure 5, we have represented the full computation of a NAF representation on a small integer using a customized scale. The two curves correspond to the two sequences of possible states V_t and V_t' for $0 \le t \le n$. At each step, the arrows represent the possible transitions. Horizontal segments represent the case $d_i = 0$, while upwards and downwards segments respectively represent the cases $d_i = 1$ and $d_i = -1$. Here, we use the value $k = 10011110101_2$. The upper and lower curve respectively correspond to the representations 010011110101_2 and $10\bar{1}\bar{1}0000\bar{1}0\bar{1}\bar{1}_2$.

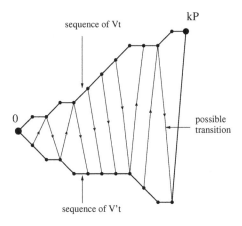

Fig. 5. A full NAF computation

However only a few state transitions are possible at each step. Indeed,

$$d_t \times 2^t = D_{t+1} - D_t$$
$$= k_t \times 2^t + \varepsilon_t \times 2^t - \varepsilon_{t+1} \times 2^{t+1}$$

Hence, $d_t = k_t + \varepsilon_t - 2 \times \varepsilon_{t+1}$. It is easy to see that when k_t is fixed, there is a unique solution for each value of d_t

k_t	d_t	ε_t	ε_{t+1}
0	0	0	0
0	1	1	0
0	-1	1	1
1	0	1	0
1	1	0	0
1	-1	0	1

Thus, to each value of d_t corresponds a unique transition from one internal state to another at the corresponding step of computation. For instance, in the case of the upwards algorithm, this table of transitions is given in figure 6. A similar property holds in the downwards direction.

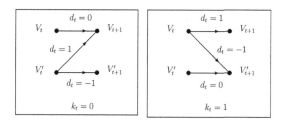

Fig. 6. State transitions

5.3   Fundamental Weaknesses in the BSD Representation

Generally, although the number of valid randomized BSD representation for any given scalar is huge, only 3 situations are possible locally, at each step of the multiplication. If we analyze things more carefully, we notice that the arguments given previously hold independently of the randomization algorithm used to build an alternative representation of k. Indeed, after step t, the difference from the current intermediate value to the "real" intermediate value (the one that should be obtained with the usual multiplication algorithm) has to be $\pm 2^t$, otherwise it is impossible to correct this error at the following stages of computation (indeed they correspond to powers of 2 greater than 2^t). Thus, independently of the randomization algorithm, any given input scalar k yields a small limited number of local behaviors of the multiplication algorithm.

As we argued previously, it is possible to detect when collisions occur in the intermediate steps of computations by looking at the power consumption curves. Over a set of measurements, 3 groups ($d_t = 0, d_t = 1, d_t = -1$) will be distinguished at each step t according to collisions on these power consumption curves. Each group corresponds to a value of d_t, but an attacker cannot tell which group corresponds to which value.

6   The Attack

In the last section, weaknesses of the BSD representation have been investigated. We suppose that no additional countermeasure is added, thus an attacker can repeat the same computation with a different randomization each time. This provides him with a set of measurements. Depending on local behaviors, groups can be built at each step of computation. In fact, when considering only one step, the transitions do not provide any useful information on the secret scalar. However, when considering two consecutive state transitions, we show that the case $k_t = k_{t+1}$ and the case $k_t \neq k_{t+1}$ can be distinguished.

6.1   Two Cases: Consecutive Key Bits That Are Equal and Different

First, let us consider the case where $k_t = k_{t+1} = 0$ (similar observations hold when $k_t = k_{t+1} = 1$). Let $p_t(x)$ denote the probability that $d_t = x$ for $x = 0, 1, -1$

$$p_t(x) = Prob\,[d_t = x]$$

The transition function is represented in Figure 6. In addition, it is easy to see from the randomization table of Section 4.2 that when two state transitions are possible (corresponding to $d_t = \pm 1$), both occur with probability $\frac{1}{2}$. For example, in the case $k_t = k_{t+1} = 0$, when considering two consecutive state transitions, it is possible to derive the following relations :

$$p_{t+1}(0) = p_t(0) + p_t(1), \quad p_{t+1}(1) = \frac{1}{2} \times p_t(-1), \quad p_{t+1}(-1) = \frac{1}{2} \times p_t(-1)$$

Therefore, the cardinality of the group of collisions corresponding to $d_t = 0$ will grow very quickly when consecutive key bits are equal to 0. Actually, exactly the same property holds when they are equal to 1. More precisely, when we start from any probabilities at step t and two consecutive bits of the secret key are the same, we can even guarantee that

$$p_{t+1}(0) \geq \frac{1}{2}$$

Indeed, we have seen that $p_t(1) = p_t(-1)$. Besides, $p_t(1) + p_t(-1) + p_t(0) = 1$, thus

$$p_t(-1) \leq \frac{1}{2}$$

and

$$p_{t+1}(0) = 1 - p_{t+1}(1) - p_{t+1}(-1) = 1 - p_t(-1) \geq \frac{1}{2}$$

On the other hand, when two consecutive bits of secret key are different, the probabilities tend to average. If we suppose $k_t = 0$ and $k_{t+1} = 1$, then

$$p_{t+1}(0) = p_t(-1)$$

$$p_{t+1}(1) = \frac{1}{2} \times (p_t(0) + p_t(1))$$

$$p_{t+1}(-1) = \frac{1}{2} \times (p_t(0) + p_t(1))$$

Using similar arguments as in the previous case, it is straightforward to verify that all 3 probabilities fulfill

$$p_{t+1}(x) \le \frac{1}{2}$$

for $x = 0, 1, -1$. To summarize, we have two very distinct situations. When two consecutive key bits are equal, one of the transitions will be by far over-represented inside our group of measurements. It is guaranteed that this will happen with probability $\ge 50\%$. In contrary, when two consecutive bits differ, the probability of the 3 transitions tend to average and none can be $> 50\%$. Thus, we have two cases which are very easy to distinguish : $k_t = k_{t+1}$ and $k_t \ne k_{t+1}$.

The limit case is when the distribution of d_t is of the form $(\frac{1}{2}, \frac{1}{2}, 0)$. In this particular situation, it is difficult to distinguish $k_t = k_{t+1}$ from $k_t \ne k_{t+1}$ since both will yield distributions of the form $(\frac{1}{2}, \frac{1}{4}, \frac{1}{4})$ at the next step.

6.2 An Efficient Key Recovery Technique

As we have seen, it is easy in the general case to determine whether $k_t = k_{t+1}$ or $k_t \ne k_{t+1}$ by observing the distributions of d_t and d_{t+1}. Roughly, using 100 measurement curves appears to be sufficient to recover this information. However, we have a problem when the distribution at step i is close to $(\frac{1}{2}, \frac{1}{2}, 0)$. Typically, this happens just after a long run of 0's or 1's. Then, the distribution at the previous step was of the form $(1, 0, 0)$. When the long run ends, we can detect it easily because the distribution changes to $(\frac{1}{2}, \frac{1}{2}, 0)$. But the next step is very tricky, since distributions will be the same whatever the next secret key bit may be.

If the run is not too long - say t consecutive bits - there is a small bias at the tricky step, say $\varepsilon \simeq 2^{-t}$ between both distributions. Thus they can be distinguished if the number of available curves is about $M \simeq 2^{2t}$. In practice, if $n = 160$ bits, there will be few runs of more than $t = 5$ consecutive equal bits. We picked randomly 10^6 values of k and we obtained an average of 4.91 such long runs. Therefore, it is not a problem to guess the "tricky" bits in these cases. For shorter runs (of length $\le t$), we can recover secret key bits after about $2^{2t} \simeq 1000$ requests to the cryptographic device.

Moreover, our algorithm is quite resistant to errors of measurement. Indeed, if this probability of error is not too high, we can basically apply the same statistical arguments, using an increased number of message. In situations were the bias ε is smaller than the probability of error in the measurements, it may become impossible to distinguish the two cases $k_t = k_{t+1}$ and $k_t \ne k_{t+1}$. However, as we argued previously, this happens quite rarely and it is not a problem to guess a few additional bits of secret key.

6.3 Practical Simulation

We have implemented a simulation of our attack. Using numbers of length $n = 160$ bits, we have fixed threshold values corresponding to the previous analysis.

For different values of the number of messages M, we have applied our technique. Results are summarized in the following table (sequences have been truncated to 40 bits in order to fit). The terminology of symbols is the following

- = represents the case $k_t = k_{t+1}$
- # represents the case $k_t \neq k_{t+1}$
- ! represents the case when our algorithm has made an error
- ? represents the case when our algorithm has been unable to make a decision

M	n	Secret key	Errors	Unknowns
		0010100100011101011111101111010011001011 ...		
10	160	=#!#?=#?==#????##=====#!===#?#=#??=###? ...	8	46
		Average over 1000 keys	10.7	43.6
100	160	=#?#?=##==#?=#?#?=====#?===#?#=#?#=##?? ...	0	33
		Average over 1000 keys	1.5	32.4
1000	160	=#?##=##==#==####=====#?===###=#=#=###= ...	0	7
		Average over 1000 keys	0.5	8.8

Then we repeated the same experience, but we introduced errors of measurement. Supposing a 10% rate of errors, we obtain the following table

M	n	Secret key	Errors	Unknowns
		0110010011001110101001100111010001000001 ...		
10	160	#=#=#??#??=#==##????#??=#=!#?#?=##====# ...	14	47
		Average over 1000 keys	20.9	48.0
100	160	#?#?##=#?#?#?=###?#=#?#=#?=###?=#?====# ...	5	38
		Average over 1000 keys	5.6	35.7
1000	160	#!#=##=#?#=#==#####=#=#=#==###==##====# ...	1	10
		Average over 1000 keys	2.6	10.9

One sees that our algorithm is quite efficient. In practice, 100 queries are sufficient to reduce the entropy of the secret key to about 40 bits. Using 1000 messages, only 10 bits remain unknown. Errors of decision are not problematic, since we can usually detect which positions are likely to cause such errors. Recovering the secret bits that remain unknown can be done in different ways. The simpler technique is an exhaustive search, which is not a problem if the entropy is of 40 bits. An improved strategy would be the "baby step-giant step" technique, which would lower the complexity to 2^{20}, but would also require a memory of size 2^{20}. It is still an open problem to avoid this memory complexity, for instance using a lambda-method [21,25] when the missing bits are disseminated.

6.4 Link with Markov Model Cryptanalysis

Recently, a new framework for attacking randomized multiplication algorithm has been proposed [10]. This technique is called Hidden Markov Model Cryptanalysis (HMMC). The idea is that randomized computations realized by a cryptographic device can be represented by a probabilistic finite state machine (which might also support inputs), with known probabilities of transition. The attacker has no direct access to the state of the machine, however each state corresponds to an output to which the attacker has access. This output can be seen as the side channel information. The cryptanalysis problem is to infer the most likely secret key from this partial information about the sequence of state. Applications have been proposed to variants of the "double-and-add" algorithm using randomization, like [20]. In this case, the partial information is the sequence of doubling instructions and additions performed during the computation.

However, this technique does not work on the full randomized BSD countermeasure proposed in [7], since it uses a "double-and-add-always" algorithm. Therefore, the usual attack based on distinguishing additions from doubling instructions does not work here. Although there exists a clear state transition function, no obvious state-related output can be observed through side channel.

Our contribution here is a new attack that can still be viewed in the framework of HMMC. Indeed, in our case, the probabilistic finite state machine contains the 3 probabilities corresponding to $d_i = 0$, 1, and -1 in an unknown order. What we observe corresponds to an experimental distribution resulting from multiple measurements. We have shown that it was possible to infer the sequence of states and the bits of secret key from this observation.

7   Conclusion

A new powerful attack against algorithms using a randomized BSD representation has been presented. It is based on detecting and exploiting internal collisions. We have taken the example of Ha-Moon countermeasure and demonstrated how to break their full SPA-immune algorithm, by comparing power consumption curves for the same message and different randomizations. This is the first attack against the full Ha-Moon countermeasure proposed at CHES'02. However it works only in situations where the messages are not randomized.

More generally we have pointed out the lack of entropy in these BSD representations. Indeed, at each step of computation, only a small number of states are possible which results in collisions on intermediate values. Any reasonable countermeasure based on randomizing the multiplication algorithm should guarantee locally a large number of possible internal states and a large number of possible transitions from each state. Randomized BSD representations do not satisfy this constraint, which is a fundamental weakness.

References

1. E. Brier and M. Joye. Weierstrass Elliptic Curves and Side-Channel Attacks. In *Public Key Cryptography – 2002*, LNCS 2274, pages 335–345. Springer, 2002.
2. J-S. Coron. Resistance Against Differential Power Analysis for Elliptic Curve Cryptosystems. In *Cryptographic Hardware and Embedded Systems (CHES) – 1999*, LNCS 1717, pages 292–302. Springer, 1999.
3. N. Ebeid and A. Hasan. Analysis of DPA Countermeasures Based on Randomizing the Binary Algorithm. Technical Report CORR 2003-14, 2003.
   http://www.cacr.math.uwaterloo.ca/techreports/2003/corr2003-14.ps.

4. FIPS PUB 186-2. Digital Signature Standard (DSS), 2000.
5. P-A. Fouque and F. Valette. The Doubling Attack – Why Upwards is Better than Downwards. In *Cryptographic Hardware and Embedded Systems (CHES) – 2003*, LNCS 2779, pages 269–280. Springer, 2003.
6. L. Goubin. A Refined Power-Analysis Attack on Elliptic Curve Cryptosystems. In *Public Key Cryptography – 2003*, LNCS 2567, pages 199–210. Springer, 2003.
7. J. Ha and S. Moon. Randomized signed-scalar Multiplication of ECC to resist Power Attacks. In *Cryptographic Hardware and Embedded Systems (CHES) – 2002*, LNCS 2523, pages 551–563. Springer, 2002.
8. M. Joye and J.-J. Quisquater. Hessian Elliptic Curves and Side-Channel Attacks. In *Cryptographic Hardware and Embedded Systems (CHES) – 2001*, LNCS 2162, pages 402–410. Springer, 2001.
9. M. Joye and C. Tymen. Compact Encoding of Non-adjacent Forms with Applications to Elliptic Curve Cryptography. In *Public Key Cryptography*, LNCS 1992, pages 353–364. Springer, 2001.
10. C. Karlof and D. Wagner. Hidden Markov Model Cryptanalysis. In *Cryptographic Hardware and Embedded Systems (CHES) – 2003*, LNCS 2779, pages 17–34. Springer, 2003.
11. P. Kocher. Timing Attacks on Implementations of Diffie-Hellman, RSA, DSS, and Others Systems. In *Advances in Cryptology – Crypto'96*, LNCS 1109, pages 104–113. Springer, 1996.
12. P. Kocher, J. Jaffe, and B. Jun. Differential Power Analysis. In *Advances in Cryptology – Crypto'99*, LNCS 1666, pages 388–397. Springer, 1999.
13. P.-Y. Liardet and N. Smart. Preventing SPA/DPA in ECC Systems Using the Jacobi Form. In *Cryptographic Hardware and Embedded Systems (CHES) – 2001*, LNCS 2162, pages 391–401. Springer, 2001.
14. T. Messerges, E. Dabbish, and R. Sloan. Power Analysis Attacks of Modular Exponentiation in Smartcards. In *Cryptographic Hardware and Embedded Systems (CHES) – 1999*, LNCS 1717, pages 144–157. Springer, 1999.
15. F. Morain and J. Olivos. Speeding up the Computation on an Elliptic Curve using Addition-Substraction Chains. In *Inform. Theory Appl.*, 24:531–543, 1990.
16. K. Okeya and D.-G. Han. Side Channel Attack on Ha-Moon's Countermeasure of Randomized Signed Scalar Multiplication. In *Advances in Cryptology – INDOCRYPT'03*. To appear.
17. K. Okeya and K. Sakurai. Power Analysis Attacks and Algorithmic Approaches to their Countermeasures for Koblitz curve Cryptosystems. In *Advances in Cryptology – INDOCRYPT'00*, LNCS 1965, pages 93–108. Springer, 2000.
18. K. Okeya and K. Sakurai. On Insecurity of the Side Channel Attack Countermeasure using Addition-Substraction Chains under Distinguishability Between Addition and Doubling. In *Australasian Conference on Information Security and Privacy - ACISP'02*, LNCS 2384, pages 420–435. Springer, 2002.
19. E. Oswald. Enhancing Simple Power-Analysis Attacks on Elliptic Curves Cryptosystems. In *Cryptographic Hardware and Embedded Systems (CHES) – 2002*, LNCS 2523, pages 83–97. Springer, 2002.
20. E. Oswald and K. Aigner. Randomized Addition-substraction Chains as a Countermeasure against Power Attacks. In *Cryptographic Hardware and Embedded Systems (CHES) – 2001*, LNCS 2162, pages 39–50. Springer, 2001.
21. J. M. Pollard. Monte Carlo Methods for Index Computation (mod p). *Mathematics of Computation*, 32(143):918–924, July 1978.

22. R. Rivest, A. Shamir, and L. Adleman. A method for obtaining digital signatures and public-key cryptosystems. In *Communications of the ACM*, 21(2):120–126, 1978.
23. RSA Laboratories. PKCS #1 v1.5 : RSA Encryption Standard, 1993. Available at `http://www.rsalabs.com/pkcs/pkcs-1`.
24. K. Schramm, T. Wollinger, and C. Paar. A New Class of Collision Attacks and its Application to DES. In *Fast Software Encryption – 2003*, LNCS 2887. Springer, 2003.
25. P. C. van Oorschot and M. J. Wiener. On Diffie-Hellman Key Agreement with Short Exponents. In *Eurocrypt '96*, LNCS 1070, pages 332–343. Springer, 1996.
26. C. Walter. Breaking the Liardet-Smart Randomized Exponentiation Algorithm. In *CARDIS 2002*, 2002. Available at `http://www.usenix.org/`.
27. C. Walter. Issues of Security with the Oswald-Aigner Exponentiation Algorithm. In *CT-RSA 2004*, LNCS 2964, pages 208–221. Springer, 2004.

Pipelined Computation of Scalar Multiplication in Elliptic Curve Cryptosystems

Pradeep Kumar Mishra

Cryptographic Research Group
Indian Statistical Institute
203 B T Road, Kolkata - 700108, INDIA
pradeep_t@isical.ac.in

Abstract. In the current work we propose a pipelining scheme for implementing Elliptic Curve Cryptosystems (ECC). The scalar multiplication is the dominant operation in ECC. It is computed by a series of point additions and doublings. The pipelining scheme is based on a key observation: to start the subsequent operation one need not wait until the current one exits. The next operation can begin while a part of the current operation is still being processed. To our knowledge, this is the first attempt to compute the scalar multiplication in such a pipelined method. Also, the proposed scheme can be made resistant to side-channel attacks (SCA). Our scheme compares favourably to all SCA resistant sequential and parallel methods.

Keywords: Elliptic curve cryptosystems, pipelining, scalar multiplication, Jacobian coordinates.

1 Introduction

Elliptic Curve Cryptosystems (ECC) were first proposed independently by Koblitz [16] and Miller [21] in 1985. The cryptosystem is based on the additive group of points on an elliptic curve over a finite field. It derives its security from the hardness of the elliptic curve discrete logarithm problem (ECDLP). For a carefully chosen curve over a suitable underlying field there is no subexponential time algorithm to solve ECDLP. This fact enables ECC to provide a high level of security with much smaller keys than RSA and primitives based on discrete logarithm problems on finite fields. However, this security does not come for free. The group operation in ECC is more complex than that of finite field based cryptosystems. This provides a strong motivation for the cryptographic community to work on ECC to make them more efficient.

The fundamental operation in ECC is scalar multiplication, namely, given an integer m and an elliptic curve point P, the computation of mP. It is computed by a series of doubling (DBL) and addition (ADD) operation of the point P, depending upon the bit sequence representing d. A plethora of methods have been proposed to perform the scalar multiplication in a secure and efficient way. For an excellent review see [10]. The performance of all these methods is dependent

M. Joye and J.-J. Quisquater (Eds.): CHES 2004, LNCS 3156, pp. 328–342, 2004.

on the efficiency of the elliptic curve group operations: DBL and ADD. In the current work we will refer to them as EC-operations. EC-operations in affine coordinates involve inversion, which is a very costly operation particularly over prime fields. To avoid inversion various co-ordinate systems have been proposed in literature. In this work we will use Jacobian coordinates.

In the current work we describe a very general technique to compute the scalar multiplication. It can be applied to any scalar multiplication method that only uses doubling and addition (or subtraction), with or without precomputations.

The computation of scalar multiplication proceeds in a series of EC-operations. A key observation is that these operations can be computed in a pipeline, so that the subsequent operation need not wait till the current one exits. The ADD and DBL algorithms have their own set of inputs. These algorithms can be divided into parts some of which can be executed with only a part of the input. So one part of the algorithm can begin execution as soon as the corresponding part of the inputs is available to it. Thus two or more EC-operations can be executed in a pipeline.

In the current work we propose a two stage pipeline. At any point of time there will be at most two operations in the pipeline in a "Producer-Consumer Relation". The one which enters the pipeline earlier will be producing outputs which will be consumed by the second operation as inputs. As soon as the producer process exits the pipeline the subsequent EC-operation will enter the pipeline as the consumer process. The earlier consumer would be producing outputs now which will be consumed by the newer process.

Any processor capable of handling ECC must have capabilities (in hardware or software) for executing field arithmetic. It must have modules for field element addition, subtraction, multiplication and inversion. In computing the scalar multiplication using a co-ordinate system other than affine coordinates, only one field inversion is necessary. So the most important operations are addition and multiplication. In the pipelined architecture we need a multiplier and an adder for each of the pipe stages. The adder can be shared by the pipe stages as the addition operation is much cheaper in comparison to multiplication. Note that in this work, *we will consider a squaring as a multiplication*. However, this is not true in general.

Our method will also require slightly more memory. As two EC-operations will be computed simultaneously in two pipe stages more memory will be required for processing. This extra memory requirement is discussed in details in Section 5.

In [17], [18], Paul Kocher et al. proposed Side-channel attacks (SCA), which are considered to be the most potential threat against mobile devices and ECC. Many countermeasures against SCA have been proposed in literature. Almost all of them involve some computational overhead to resist SCA. One of the latest methods proposed in [3] involves the least amount of computational overhead to get rid of simple power analysis attacks (SPA). The authors divide each EC-operation into *atomic blocks* which are indistinguishable from the side-channel.

So, in this model the computation of scalar multiplication is a sequence of indistinguishable atomic blocks. We use a variant of this method to resist SPA. To resist DPA many standard methods can be incorporated to it.

In this work we have used the computation time of an atomic block as a unit of time. One atomic block has one multiplication, two additions and one negation. As computation time of an addition is quite small in comparison to that of a multiplication, computation time of an atomic block is approximately that of a finite field multiplication. A point addition (mixed coordinates) takes 11 atomic blocks and a doubling takes 10 atomic blocks. So they can be computed in 10 and 11 units of time respectively. In our pipelining scheme an EC-operation can be computed in 6 units of time. This leads to a significant improvement in performance (see Section 5). Furthermore, our scheme can be combined with windowing methods to obtain even faster scalar multiplication.

2   Background

In this section we briefly discuss the current state of affairs in ECC and side-channel attacks.

2.1   Elliptic Curve Preliminaries

There exists an extensive literature on elliptic curve cryptography. Here we only mention the results that we need, without proof. We refer the reader to [10] for details. In the current work we will concentrate on curves over large prime fields only. Over a finite field F_q, $q = p^r$ of odd characteristic $p > 3$, an elliptic curve has an equation of the form $y^2 = x^3 + ax + b$ where $a, b \in F_q$ and $4a^3 + 27b^2 \neq 0$. An elliptic curve point is represented using a pair of finite field elements. The group operations in affine coordinates involve finite field inversion, which is a very costly operations, particularly over prime fields [9]. To avoid these inversions, various co-ordinate systems like, projective, Jacobian, modified Jacobian, Chudnovsky-Jacobian have been proposed in literature [6]. We present our work in Jacobian coordinates, which are extensively used in implementations. In Jacobian coordinates, $(X : Y : Z)$ represents the point $(X/Z^2, Y/Z^3)$ on the curve.

The scalar multiplication is generally computed using a left-to-right binary algorithm.

Binary Algorithm (left-to-right) for scalar multiplication
Input: An integer $m = m_{n-1}2^{n-1} + \cdots + m_0, m_{n-1} \neq 0$ and a point P
Output: mP.
1. $P_0 = P$
2. for $i = 0$ to $n - 2$;
3. $P_{i+1} = \text{DBL}(P_i)$;
4.   if $m_{n-2-i} = 1$
5. $P_{i+1} = \text{ADD}(P_{i+1}, P)$;
6. Return (P_{n-1})

The ADD operation in Jacobian coordinates is much cheaper if the Z-coordinate of one point is 1. This operation is called mixed addition [6]. In implementations of scalar multiplication, the addition operation in Step 5 is generally a mixed addition.

The algorithm needs $n - 1$ point doublings and on the average $n/2$ additions to compute the scalar multiplication. As computing the additive inverse of a given point is almost for free, addition and subtraction in the elliptic curve group have almost the same complexity. To reduce the complexity the *Non-adjacent form* (NAF) representation of the scalar multiplier has been proposed. In NAF, the coefficients of the representation belong to the set $\{0, 1, -1\}$ and no two consecutive coefficients are non-zero. The number of non-zero terms in NAF representation is on the average $n/3$. Thus if the scalar multiplier is represented in NAF, the average number of point additions in the scalar multiplication algorithm reduces to $n/3$. To further reduce the number of additions the w-NAF representations have been proposed (see [22] [5]). With a precomputed table of size 2^{w-1} points, the number of additions comes down to $n/(w + 1)$. The complexity of scalar multiplication is thus dependent on the efficiency of point addition and doubling. We discuss the ADD and DBL algorithm in Jacobian coordinates below.

If two points $P(X, Y, Z)$ and $P_i(X_i, Y_i, Z_i)$ are in Jacobian coordinates, then the double of P_i i.e. $2P_i = P_{i+1}(X_{i+1}, Y_{i+1}, Z_{i+1})$ is computed as:

$X_{i+1} = M^2 - 2S, Y_{i+1} = M(S - X_{i+1}) - 8Y_i^4$ and $Z_{i+1} = 2Y_i Z_i,$

where $M = 3X_i^2 + aZ_i^4$ and $S = 4X_i Y_i^2$.

The sum $P + P_i = P_{i+1}(X_{i+1}, Y_{i+1}, Z_{i+1})$ is computed as:

$X_{i+1} = W^3 - 2U_1 W^2 + R^2, Y_{i+1} = -S_1 W^2 + R(U_1 W^2 - X_{i+1}), Z_{i+1} = ZZ_i W,$

where $U_1 = XZ_i^2, U_2 = X_i Z^2, S_1 = YZ_i^3, S_2 = Y_i Z^3, W = U_1 - U_2, R = S_1 - S_2$.

Let $[a], [m]$ and $[s]$ denote the time required for one addition, multiplication and squaring in the underlying field respectively. Then, ADD has complexity $7[a] + 12[m] + 4[s]$ and DBL has complexity $11[a] + 4[m] + 6[s]$. In the current work, we do not distinguish between a multiplication and a squaring and neglect additions. So, roughly, we can say ADD involves 16 multiplications and DBL involves 10 multiplications. Mixed addition is quite cheaper, requiring only 11 multiplications.

2.2   Side-Channel Attacks and Side-Channel Atomicity

Side-channel attacks (SCA) are one of the most dangerous threat to ECC-implementations. Discovered by Paul Kocher et al. [17], [18] SCA reveals the secret information by sampling and analyzing the side-channel information like timing, power consumption and EM radiation traces. ECC is very suitable for mobile and hand held devices, which are used in hostile outdoor environments. Hence an implementation must be side-channel resistant. SCA's which use power consumption traces of the computation are called power attacks. Power attacks subsumes timing attacks [11]. They can be divided into simple power attacks

(SPA) and differential power attacks (DPA). Simple power attacks use information from one observation to break the secret. Differential power attacks use data from several observations and reveal the secret information by statistically analyzing them. Power analysis can be performed with very inexpensive equipments, hence the threat is real. Several countermeasures have been proposed in

Table 1. DBL Algorithm in Atomic Blocks

DBL Algorithm
Input: $P_i(X_i, Y_i, Z_i)$
Input: $P_i = (X_i, Y_i, Z_i)$
Output: $2P_i = (X_{i+1}, Y_{i+1}, Z_{i+1})$

Δ_1	$R_1 = T_8 \times T_8$ (Z_i^2) * * * *	Δ_6	$R_4 = T_7 \times T_7$ (Y_i^2) $R_2 = R_4 + R_4$ $(2Y_i^2)$ $R_2 = R_4 + R_4$ $(2Y_i^2)$ * *
Δ_2	$R_1 = R_1 \times R_1$ (Z_i^4) * * *	Δ_7	$R_4 = T_6 \times R_2$ $(2X_i Y_i^2)$ $R_4 = R_4 + R_4$ (S) $R_4 = -R_4$ $(-S)$ $R_5 = R_4 + R_4$ $(-2S)$
Δ_3	$R_1 = a \times R_1$ (aZ_i^4) * * *	Δ_8	$R_3 = R_1 \times R_1$ (M^2) $T_6 = R_3 + R_5$ (X_{i+1}) * $R_4 = T_6 + R_4$ $(X_{i+1} - S)$
Δ_4	$R_2 = T_6 \times T_6$ (X_i^2) $R_3 = R_2 + R_2(2X_i^2)$ * $R_2 = R_3 + R_2$ $(3X_i^2)$	Δ_9	$R_2 = R_2 \times R_2$ $(4Y_i^4)$ $R_2 = R_2 + R_2(8Y_i^4)$ * *
Δ_5	$T_8 = T_7 \times T_8$ $(Y_i Z_i)$ $T_8 = T_8 + T_8$ $(\underline{Z_{i+1}})$ * $R_1 = R_1 + R_2$ (M)	Δ_{10}	$T_7 = R_1 \times R_4$ $(M(X_{i+1} - S))$ $T_7 = T_7 + R_2$ $(-Y_{i+1})$ $T_7 = -T_7$ $(\underline{Y_{i+1}})$ *

literature to guard ECC against SPA and DPA (see [2], [7], [11], [15], [4] for example). Almost all of them need some computational overhead for the immunization. *Side-Channel Atomicity* recently proposed in [3] involves nearly no overhead. There, the authors split the EC-operations into *atomic blocks*, which are indistinguishable from each other by means of side-channel analysis. Hence, if an implementation does not leak out any data regarding which operation being performed, the side-channel information becomes uniform. In order to immunize our computations against SPA, we choose this countermeasure with some modifications. Our division of the EC-operations into atomic blocks will be different than the one given in [3]. This is to facilitate our pipelining scheme.

To immunize ECC from DPA, many countermeasures have been proposed. Most of them involve randomization of the processed data, such as the representation of the point or of the curve or of the scalar. We do not discuss the these issues at length here. The interested reader can refer to Ciet's Thesis [4] for a comprehensive treatment. We just observe that almost all schemes can be adapted to our method to make it DPA resistant.

3   Dividing EC-Operations into Atomic Blocks

We divide each EC-operation into atomic blocks. Following [3], each block contains one multiplication and two additions. Subtraction is treated as a negation followed by an addition. To accommodate subtractions we include one negation in each atomic block. The atomic blocks are presented in Table 1 and Table 2. Our ADD and DBL algorithms are designed, keeping in mind scalar multiplication algorithm. In the binary algorithm, described in Section 2.1 whenever an addition is carried out, one input is fixed i.e. P. So we may assume that like DBL, algorithm ADD has also one input P_i. Also, we can keep the point P in affine coordinates and gain efficiency by using mixed addition algorithm. Note that in Table 1 and Table 2, we have assumed that the EC-operations always get their inputs (X_i, Y_i, Z_i) at three specific locations T_6, T_7, T_8 respectively. Also, the EC-operation write back their outputs as these are computed to these locations only. The coordinates of the point $P = (X, Y, 1)$, which is an argument to all addition operations are also stored in two specific locations $T_x = X, T_y = Y$. Also, the curve parameter a needs to be stored. These six locations are public in the sense that any EC-operations in any of the two pipe stages can use them. One more location is required for the dummy operations. Both operations in the pipeline will share this location. Besides while two EC-operations being computed in the pipeline, each of them will have some locations (five each) private to them to store their intermediate variables. Thus the method requires 17 locations for the computation.

In Table 2 we provide the mixed addition algorithm in atomic blocks. Mixed addition requires 11 multiplications and doublings involves 10. So, adding one dummy multiplication to the DBL and some additions and negations to ADD/DBL, we can use whole of them as atomic blocks. However in that case we have to use these EC-operations as atomic units of computation. So, one operation has to be completed before the other begins. We do not adopt this approach as our aim in this work is to break the EC-operations into parts such that a part of one can start execution while a part of another is still in the pipeline.

3.1   An Analysis of ADD and DBL

Let us analyze the ADD and DBL algorithms presented in the Table 1 and Table 2. To DBL, there are three inputs, namely, X_i, Y_i, Z_i. It computes the double of the input point. Let us look at the various atomic blocks more closely.

We make the following observations on DBL:

- The atomic blocks $\Delta_1, \Delta_2, \Delta_3$ can be computed with the input Z_i only.
- Input X_i is needed by DBL at block Δ_4 and thereafter.
- The block Δ_5 needs the input Y_i as well. But Δ_5 produces the output Z_{i+1}. So, the next EC-operation can begin after DBL completes Δ_5.
- The atomic block Δ_8 produces the output X_{i+1}.
- Δ_{10} produces the output Y_{i+1} and the process terminates.

Table 2. ADD Algorithm in Atomic Blocks

ADD Algorithm
Input: $P = (T_x, T_y), P_i = (X_i, Y_i, Z_i)$
Output: $P + P_i = (X_{i+1}, Y_{i+1}, Z_{i+1})$.

Γ_1	$R_1 = T_8 \times T_8 \ (Z_i^2)$ * * *	Γ_7	$R_2 = R_2 \times R_4 \ (-U_1 W^2)$ $R_5 = R_2 + R_2 \ (-2U_1 W^2)$ * *
Γ_2	$R_2 = T_x \times R_1 \ (U_1)$ * $R_2 = -R_2 \ (-U_1)$ *	Γ_8	$R_1 = R_4 \times R_1 \ (W^3)$ $R_1 = R_1 + R_5 \ (W^3 - 2U_1 W^2)$ $R_3 = -R_3 \ (-S_1)$ $R_5 = R_3 + T_7 \ (S_2 - S_1 = -R)$
Γ_3	$R_3 = T_y \times T_8 \ (YZ_i)$ * * *	Γ_9	$T_6 = R_5 \times R_5 \ (R^2)$ $T_6 = T_6 + R_1 \ (\underline{X_{i+1}})$ $R_2 = T_6 + R_2 \ (X_{i+1} - U_1 W^2)$
Γ_4	$R_3 = R_3 \times R_1 \ (S_1)$ $R_1 = R_2 + T_6 \ (-W)$ $R_1 = -R_1 \ (W)$ *	Γ_{10}	$R_2 = R_5 \times R_2 \ (-R(X_{i+1} - U_1 W^2))$ * *
Γ_5	$T_8 = R_1 \times T_8 \ (\underline{Z_{i+1}})$ * * *	Γ_{11}	$T_7 = R_3 \times R_4 \ (-S_1 W^2)$ $T_7 = T_7 + R_2 \ (\underline{Y_{i+1}})$ * *
Γ_6	$R_4 = R_1 \times R_1 \ (W^2)$ * * *		

If instead a subtraction should be performed (add the negative $(-T_x, T_y)$), incorporate $R_2 = -T_x$ in Γ_1 and replace the first step of Γ_2 by $R_2 = R_2 \times R_1$.

We have similar observations on ADD:

- The atomic blocks $\Gamma_1, \Gamma_2, \Gamma_3$ can be computed with the input Z_i only.
- Input X_i is needed by ADD at block Γ_4 and thereafter.

- Γ_5 produces the output Z_{i+1}. So, the next EC-operation can begin after ADD completes Γ_5.
- The input Y_i is not required till the atomic block Γ_8.
- Γ_9 produces the output X_{i+1} and Γ_{11} produces Y_{i+1} and the process terminates.

The most interesting part of this division into atomic blocks is that both EC-operations perfectly match in a producer-consumer relation. In most situations as we will see in the next section, as soon as an output is produced by the producer process the consumer process consumes it. In some situations when the consumer process requires the input before it is produced by the producer, the consumer process has to wait an atomic block. However, such situations will not arise much frequently, hence it does not affect the efficiency much.

4   Pipelining the Scalar Multiplication Algorithm in ECC

In this section we describe our pipelining scheme – a two stage one, each stage executing an EC-operation in parallel. In the following discussion we assume that the EC-operation executing in pipe stage 1 gets its inputs when it needs. Later we will see, it is not always true. However such cases will not occur very frequently.

In the computation of the scalar multiplication, an DBL is always followed by an ADD or DBL, but an ADD is always followed by an DBL. So in the proposed pipeline we always see a pattern like DBL(producer)-DBL(consumer) or DBL(producer)-ADD(consumer) or ADD(producer)-DBL(consumer). This is true even if the scalar is represented in NAF or w-NAF and makes the sequence DBL-DBL more frequent.

Let us see how these EC-operations play their parts in this producer-consumer relation. We show this in the Table 3. The atomic blocks Γ_i's belong to an ADD and Δ_j's belong to DBL. Besides we have given a superscript to each of them to denote which EC-operation has entered the pipeline earlier. In the following description we will refer to pipe stage 1 and pipe stage 2 as PS1 and PS2 respectively. Also, in this discussion *our unit of time is time taken to execute one atomic block*. In the next three subsections we will discuss how EC-operations coupled with each other behave in the pipeline.

4.1   DBL-DBL Scenario

Let us first consider the DBL-DBL scenario. It is presented in Columns 2 and 3 of Table 3.

- Let us assume that the first DBL (say, $DBL^{(i)}$) and enters PS1 at time $k+1$.
- At time $k+5$, $DBL^{(i)}$ produces its first output (Z_{i+1}) and enters PS2. The second doubling $DBL^{(i+1)}$ enters the stage PS1.
- At time $k+8$, $DBL^{(i)}$ produces its second output. $DBL^{(i+1)}$ completes its 3rd atomic block $\Delta_3^{(i+1)}$ at the same time.

Table 3. EC-operations in the pipeline

Time	DBL-DBL		DBL-ADD		ADD-DBL	
	PS1	PS2	PS1	PS2	PS1	PS2
k	$\vdots$	$\vdots$	$\vdots$	$\vdots$	$\vdots$	$\vdots$
$k+1$	$\Delta_1^{(i)}$	-	$\Delta_1^{(i)}$	-	$\Gamma_1^{(i)}$	-
$k+2$	$\Delta_2^{(i)}$	-	$\Delta_2^{(i)}$	-	$\Gamma_2^{(i)}$	-
$k+3$	$\Delta_3^{(i)}$	-	$\Delta_3^{(i)}$	-	$\Gamma_3^{(i)}$	-
$k+4$	$\Delta_4^{(i)}$	-	$\Delta_4^{(i)}$	-	$\Gamma_4^{(i)}$	-
$k+5$	$\Delta_5^{(i)}$	-	$\Delta_5^{(i)}$	-	$\Gamma_5^{(i)}$	-
$k+6$	$\Delta_1^{(i+1)}$	$\Delta_6^{(i)}$	$\Gamma_1^{(i+1)}$	$\Delta_6^{(i)}$	$\Delta_1^{(i+1)}$	$\Gamma_6^{(i)}$
$k+7$	$\Delta_2^{(i+1)}$	$\Delta_7^{(i)}$	$\Gamma_2^{(i+1)}$	$\Delta_7^{(i)}$	$\Delta_2^{(i+1)}$	$\Gamma_7^{(i)}$
$k+8$	$\Delta_3^{(i+1)}$	$\Delta_8^{(i)}$	$\Gamma_3^{(i+1)}$	$\Delta_8^{(i)}$	$\Delta_3^{(i+1)}$	$\Gamma_8^{(i)}$
$k+9$	$\Delta_4^{(i+1)}$	$\Delta_9^{(i)}$	$\Gamma_4^{(i+1)}$	$\Delta_9^{(i)}$	*	$\Gamma_9^{(i)}$
$k+10$	*	$\Delta_{10}^{(i)}$	$\Gamma_5^{(i+1)}$	$\Delta_{10}^{(i)}$	$\Delta_4^{(i+1)}$	$\Gamma_{10}^{(i)}$
$k+11$	$\Delta_5^{(i+1)}$	*	$\Gamma_6^{(i+1)}$	*	*	$\Gamma_{11}^{(i)}$
$k+12$	$\vdots$	$\Delta_6^{(i+1)}$	$\vdots$	$\Gamma_7^{(i+1)}$	$\Delta_5^{(i+1)}$	*

- At time $k+9$ DBL$^{(i)}$ computes $\Delta_9^{(i)}$ and DBL$^{(i+1)}$ computes $\Delta_4^{(i+1)}$. Note that DBL$^{(i+1)}$ requires its second input i.e. X_i in this block, which is available to it. It was computed by DBL$^{(i)}$ in the previous atomic block.
- During time $k+10$, DBL$^{(i)}$ computes $\Delta_{10}^{(i+1)}$ and computes its third output (Y_{i+1}). DBL$^{(i+1)}$ should compute $\Delta_5^{(i)}$. But it needs its third input which is being computed at this time only. Hence it waits. DBL$^{(i)}$ terminates at the end of time $k+10$.
- DBL$^{(i+1)}$ computes $\Delta_5^{(i)}$, produces its first output and moves to PS2 in the next time unit. Although the other pipe stage is vacant now it can not be utilized as DBL$^{(i+1)}$ has not yet produced its first output.

Note that in this scenario, when two DBL's enter the pipeline one by one, two pipeline stages remain idle (one at time $k+10$ and another at time $k+11$) during the computations. We have marked them by '*' in the table. If the attacker using the side-channel information can detect this he may be able to conclude that two doubling were being computed now. To keep the adversary at bay we can compute two dummy blocks at these times. That will also implement the wait for the other process.

One can easily convince oneself that these choices are optimal. The computation of Z_{i+1} requires Y_i which is only provided in the final stage of the previous doubling. Hence, a wait stage cannot be avoided.

4.2 DBL-ADD Scenario

Let us consider the situation when an DBL is followed by an ADD. This scenario is described in Columns 4 and 5 of Table 3. Unlike the previous discussion we will refer to the operations as ADD and DBL only, without any superscript. Note that the DBL has entered the pipeline first and ADD later. Suppose the DBL starts at time $k + 1$. We can see that:

- At time $k + 5$, DBL computes block $\Delta_5^{(i)}$, its first output Z_{i+1} and then it enters PS2 at the next time unit.
- At time $k + 6$, the ADD enters at PS1, uses the output Z_{i+1} of DBL.
- At time $k + 8$, the DBL completes its block $\Delta_8^{(i)}$ and produces the output X_{i+1}.
- At time $k+9$, ADD computes $\Gamma_4^{(i+1)}$. It needs its second input (X_{i+1}), which is produced by the DBL in the previous time interval.
- At time $k + 10$, the DBL computes its last atomic block and provides its third output. The ADD computes $\Gamma_5^{(i+1)}$. The last output computed by the DBL is required by the ADD two time units later.

In this scenario the coupling of operations is perfect. No pipeline stages are wasted. Note however, that this sequence is always followed by a doubling. That sequence is discussed in the next paragraph.

4.3 ADD-DBL Scenario

The scenario, when an ADD is followed by an DBL has been presented in Columns 6 and 7 of Table 3. For sake of brevity we are not going for an analysis of it. One can see that here the combination of the EC-operations involves three wait stages at times $k + 9$, $k + 11$ and $k + 12$. Still this is the optimal way of performing this sequence and it fits perfectly after the DBL-ADD sequence discussed above. In DBL-ADD-DBL the addition finishes 12 steps after entering PS1 and at the same time the following doubling can enter PS2. These observations also guarantee that 6 atomic blocks are necessary for computation of each EC-operation (see Section 5), except for the first and the last ones. This requirement of 6 atomic blocks is exact and not just asymptotic.

5 Implementation and Results

In this section we will discuss the issues related to the implementation of the scheme. Also, we will demonstrate the speed-up that can be achieved in an implementation.

Hardware Requirement: As the proposed scheme processes two EC-operation simultaneously, we will require more hardware support than is generally required for ECC. To implement the pipe stages we will require a multiplier and an adder for each of the pipe stages. As addition is a much cheaper operation than multiplication one adder can be shared between the pipe stages. We do not need separate (multiplicative) inverter for each pipe stage. In fact, we need only an inversion after completing all the EC-operations. So one inverter would suffice. Thus, in comparison to a sequential computation we need only one more multiplier to implement the proposed scheme.

Memory Requirement: In general ADD requires 7 locations and DBL requires 6 locations in memory in sequential execution, where one EC-operation is executed at a time. So in a sequential implementation the whole scalar multiplication can be computed using 7 locations for the EC-operations. The proposed scheme requires 17 memory locations i.e. 10 extra memory locations. From the space this corresponds to 5 precomputed points, however our scheme needs active registers and not only storage. For a fair comparison we will later compare our algorithm to a sequential one with 8 precomputed points.

Synchronization: As we have said there are seven locations where some values will be stored during whole process of computation. So, if two processes working at two stages of the pipeline wish to access these values simultaneously, conflict may arise. Particularly, if one process is trying to read and the other is trying to write the same location at the same time, then it will lead to a very serious problem. The input values X, Y and a are static and no attempt is made to write on these locations. Checking the above tables one can observe that the atomic blocks are arranged in a manner that no conflicts occur.

Resistance Against SCA: As the technique uses side-channel atomicity, it is secure against simple power analysis under the assumption (cf. [3,4]) that dummy operations cannot be detected and that squarings and multiplications are indistinguishable from the side channel. Note that the Hamming weight of the scalar is leaked; we come back on this later. To resist DPA Joye-Tymen's curve randomization [15] can be easily adopted into the scheme. It will require two more storage locations. As the scheme uses affine representation of the point, it is does not adapt directly to Coron's point randomization [7]. However, note that after the first doubling, the output point is no more affine. Hence it can be randomized. Also this later randomization does not compromise the security because, the first EC-operation is always a doubling.

A second option is to do the preprocessing step $T_6 = T_x \times Z^2, T_7 = T_y \times Z^3, T_8 = Z$, for some randomly chosen Z. This requires 4 multiplications and the input to the first doubling is no longer affine; hence, the costs are higher than in the first proposal. Both ways there is absolutely no problem in the scheme to adapt to scalar randomizations.

Performance: We discuss the performance of the scheme in depth. There are two multipliers, one for each of the pipe stages. The multiplications in the atomic blocks being executed in the pipe stages are computed in parallel. As said earlier, the scheme can be made resistant against DPA, using various randomization techniques. That will require some routine computations. In the discussion below we neglect these routine computations. Also, we will neglect the routine computation required at the end to convert the result from the Jacobian to affine coordinates.

To compute mP, if m has hamming weight h and length n one has to compute $n - 1$ DBL and h ADD. An DBL operation requires 10 atomic blocks and an ADD requires 11 atomic blocks to complete. In a sequential execution that will consume $10(n - 1) + 11h$ units of time.

In the binary algorithm with the scalar multiplier m expressed in binary, $h = n/2$ on average. So, the computation of the scalar multiplication requires $10(n - 1) + 11(n/2) = 15.5n - 10$ atomic blocks. That is, one has to compute about 15.5 atomic blocks per bit on the average. If m is represented in 160 bits, i.e. $n = 160$, the scalar multiplication can be carried out by executing 2470 atomic blocks or in 2470 units of time.

In NAF representation of the multiplier, $h = n/3$ on average. So the computation time is $10(n - 1) + 11 \times n/3$ time units. That is one has to compute about $13.6n$ atomic blocks or 13.6 atomic blocks per bit of the multiplier. If m is expressed in NAF and $n = 160$, the computation requires to execute 2177 atomic blocks. That is the computation takes 2177 units of time.

The binary methods with or without NAF representation use less memory than our methods. For sake of fairness let us compare the performance of our method with with the method using w-NAF (see [22]). The method requires storing of 2^{w-1} points and $n-1$ doublings and $1/(w+1)$ additions on the average. For a scalar of 160 bits with $w = 5$, the method in a sequential execution requires to store 16 points and computes the scalar multiplication in 1893 units of time.

Example:

In Table 4, we have exhibited the computation process for a small scalar multiplier $38 = 100110$. To compute $38P$, one has to carry out EC-operations as DBL, DBL, DBL, ADD, DBL, ADD, DBL. Note that this multiplier encompasses all possibilities, i.e. DBL-DBL, DBL-ADD and ADD-DBL. The computation takes 46 units of time. In the table we have shown how the computation progresses. Each atomic block has been assigned a superscript to denote the serial number of the EC-operation to which it belongs. Also some atomic blocks are prefixed or suffixed by (X) or (Y) or (Z). A suffix indicates that at that atomic block the EC-operation outputs the corresponding value. A prefix indicates that at the specified atomic block the EC-operation consumes that input. Also, a '#' sign in the time column indicates that an EC-operation exits the pipeline at that time. A '*' in a pipe stage indicates a dummy atomic block has to be computed there. A '-' indicates no computation.

As we can check from the table, in the pipelining scheme, the first EC-operation which is usually an DBL, completes in 10 time units. In fact, as we take the base point in affine coordinates, first three blocks are not necesssary and it needs only 7 blocks. If we use Coron's randomization here 5 more blocks are required for that. After that an EC-operation (be it an DBL or an ADD) completes in every 6 units of time. Let m be represented by n bits with hamming weight h. Then the scalar multiplication will involve $h + n - 1$ EC-operations ($n - 1$ doublings and h additions). The first doubling will take 7 units of time and the other $n + h - 2$ will be computed in 6 units of time in the pipelining scheme. So it will take $7 + 6(n + h - 2) + 5 = 6(n + h)$ units of time. For a scalar

Table 4. An Example of the Pipelining

Time	PS1	PS2	Time	PS1	PS2
1	$(Z)\Delta_1^{(1)}$	-	24	$\Delta_2^{(5)}$	$\Gamma_7^{(4)}$
2	$\Delta_2^{(1)}$	-	25	$\Delta_3^{(5)}$	$(Y)\Gamma_8^{(4)}$
3	$\Delta_3^{(1)}$	-	26	*	$\Gamma_9^{(4)}(X)$
4	$(X)\Delta_4^{(1)}$	-	27	$(X)\Delta_4^{(5)}$	$\Gamma_{10}^{(4)}$
5	$(Y)\Delta_5^{(1)}(Z)$	-	28#	*	$\Gamma_{11}^{(4)}(Y)$
6	$(Z)\Delta_1^{(2)}$	$\Delta_6^{(1)}$	29	$(Y)\Delta_5^{(5)}(Z)$	*
7	$\Delta_2^{(2)}$	$\Delta_7^{(1)}$	30	$(Z)\Gamma_1^{(6)}$	$\Delta_6^{(5)}$
8	$\Delta_3^{(2)}$	$\Delta_8^{(1)}(X)$	31	$\Gamma_2^{(6)}$	$\Delta_7^{(5)}$
9	$(X)\Delta_4^{(2)}$	$\Delta_9^{(1)}$	32	$\Gamma_3^{(6)}$	$\Delta_8^{(5)}(X)$
10#	*	$\Delta_{10}^{(1)}(Y)$	33	$(X)\Gamma_4^{(6)}$	$\Delta_9^{(5)}$
11	$(Y)\Delta_5^{(2)}(Z)$	*	34#	$\Gamma_5^{(6)}(Z)$	$\Delta_{10}^{(5)}(Y)$
12	$(Z)\Delta_1^{(3)}$	$\Delta_6^{(2)}$	35	$(Z)\Delta_1^{(7)}$	$\Gamma_6^{(6)}$
13	$\Delta_2^{(3)}$	$\Delta_7^{(2)}$	36	$\Delta_2^{(7)}$	$\Gamma_7^{(6)}$
14	$\Delta_3^{(3)}$	$\Delta_8^{(2)}(X)$	37	$\Delta_3^{(7)}$	$(Y)\Gamma_8^{(6)}$
15	$(X)\Delta_4^{(3)}$	$\Delta_9^{(2)}$	38	*	$\Gamma_9^{(6)}(X)$
16#	*	$\Delta_{10}^{(2)}(Y)$	39	$(X)\Delta_4^{(7)}$	$\Gamma_{10}^{(6)}$
17	$(Y)\Delta_5^{(3)}(Z)$	*	40#	*	$\Gamma_{11}^{(6)}(Y)$
18	$(Z)\Gamma_1^{(4)}$	$\Delta_6^{(3)}$	41	$(Y)\Delta_5^{(7)}(Z)$	*
19	$\Gamma_2^{(4)}$	$\Delta_7^{(3)}$	42	-	$\Delta_6^{(7)}$
20	$\Gamma_3^{(4)}$	$\Delta_8^{(3)}(X)$	43	-	$\Delta_7^{(7)}$
21	$(X)\Gamma_4^{(4)}$	$\Delta_9^{(3)}$	44	-	$\Delta_8^{(7)}(X)$
22#	$\Gamma_5^{(4)}(Z)$	$\Delta_{10}^{(3)}(Y)$	45	-	$\Delta_9^{(7)}$
23	$(Z)\Delta_1^{(5)}$	$\Gamma_6^{(4)}$	46#	-	$\Delta_{10}^{(7)}(Y)$

Table 5. Comparison of Performance for $n = 160$

Algorithm	Binary	NAF	w-NAF ($w = 4$)
Sequential	2477	2177	1893
Pipelined	1438	1278	1152

multiplier of length n bits represented in binary form, $h = n/2$ on average. Thus the pipelining scheme will require $6(n + n/2) = 9n$ units of time on the average. For $n = 160$ the proposed scheme will take 1440 units of time to compute the scalar multiplication.

If the scalar multiplier is expressed in NAF, then $h = n/3$ on the average. Hence time requirement will be $8n$ time-units. This implies, for $n = 160$ the time required is 1280. In either case it is a speed-up of around 41 percent.

Note that in both cases described above our method is better than even sequential w-NAF method. If w-NAF is used in pipelining scheme with those extra storage, then for $w = 4$, the scalar multiplication can be computed in 1152 units of time. We have summarized this discussion in the Table 5.

Comparison with Parallel Implementations

Parallelised computation of scalar multiplication on ECC was described for the first time by Koyama and Tsuruoka in [19]. A special hardware was used to carry out the computation in their proposal. We compare our scheme with some of the recent proposals which are claimed to be SCA resistant. The scheme proposed in [8], uses a parallelized encapsulated-add-and-double algorithm using Montgomery arithmetic. This algorithm uses two multipliers and takes $10[m]$ computations per bit of the scalar. Our algorithm as shown previously with NAF representation of the scalar takes only $8[m]$ computation per bit. The storage requirements are similar. Furthermore, we can obtain additional speed-up by allowing precomputations. In [1], the authors have proposed efficient algorithms for computing the scalar multiplication with SIMD (*Single Instruction Multiple data*). Similar and more efficient algorithms are also proposed in [12]. In [12] the authors have given two proposals. The first proposal, like our scheme, does not use precomputations and takes $1629[m]$ to compute the scalar multiplication. They have taken $[s] = 0.8[m]$ and the cost includes all routine calculation including the cost of Joye-Tymen's countermeasure for DPA. In contrast, pipelining requires only $1319[m]$ (all inclusive). Their second proposal uses precomputed points, applies signed window expansions of the scalar and is quite efficient. However, in a later work with Möller, the same authors (see [11]) remark that using a precomputed table in affine coordinates is not secure against *fixed table attacks*, a differential power attack. Even in Jacobian coordinates while using a fixed precomputed table, the values in the table should always be randomized before use.

Acknowledgment. The author is thankful to Dr. T. Lange, Prof. D. Hankerson and Dr. P. Sarkar for reading the manuscript of the paper and giving some constructive comments. Particularly, he is greatly indebted to Dr. Lange, who made several suggestions for improvement of the paper.

References

1. K. Aoki, F. Hoshino, T. Kobayashi and H. Oguro. *Elliptic Curve Arithmetic Using SIMD*, In ISC, 2001, LNCS 2200, pp. 235-247, Springer-Verlag, 2001
2. E. Briér and M. Joye. *Weierstrass Elliptic Curves and Side-Channel Attacks*. In PKC 2002, LNCS 2274, pages 335-345, Springer-Verlag,2002.
3. B. Chevallier-Mames, M. Ciet and M. Joye. *Low-cost Solutions for Preventing Simple Side-Channel Analysis: Side-Channel Atomicity*, IEEE Trans. on Computers, 53(6):760-768, 2004.
4. M. Ciet. *Aspects of Fast and Secure Arithmetics for Elliptic Curve Cryptography*, Ph. D. Thesis, Louvain-la-Neuve, Belgique.
5. C. Cohen. Analysis of the flexible window powering algorithm, To appear *J. Cryptology*, 2004.

6. H. Cohen, A. Miyaji, and T. Ono. *Efficient Elliptic Curve Exponentiation Using Mixed coordinates*, In ASIACRYPT'98, LNCS 1514, pp. 51-65, Springer-Verlag, 1998.

7. J. -S. Coron. *Resistance against Differential Power Analysis for Elliptic Curve Cryptosystems*, In *CHES 1999*, pages 292-302.

8. W. Fischer, C. Giraud, E. W. Knudsen, J. -P. Seifert. *Parallel Scalar Multiplication on General Elliptic Curves over $\mathbf{F}_p$ hedged against Non-Differential Side-Channel Attacks*, Available at IACR eprint Archive, Technical Report No 2002/007, http://www.iacr.org.

9. K. Fong and D. Hankerson and J. López and A. Menezes. *Field inversion and point halving revisited*, Technical Report, CORR 2003-18, Department of Combinatorics and Optimization, University of Waterloo, Canada, 2003.

10. D. Hankerson, A. Menezes and S. Vanstone. *Guide to Elliptic Curve Cryptography*, Springer-Verlag, 2004.

11. T. Izu, B. Möller and T. Takagi. Improved Elliptic Curve Multiplication Methods Resistant Against Side Channel Attacks, Proceedings of Indocrypt 2002, LNCS 2551, pp 296-313, Springer-Verlag.

12. T. Izu and T. Takagi. Fast Elliptic Curve Multiplications with SIMD operation, ICICS 2002, LNCS, pp 217-230, Springer-Verlag.

13. T. Izu and T. Takagi. A Fast Parallel Elliptic Curve Multiplication Resistant against Side Channel Attacks, ICICS 2002, LNCS, pp 217-230, Springer-Verlag.

14. T. Izu and T. Takagi. Improved Elliptic Curve Multiplication Methods Resistant against Side Channel Attacks, INDOCRYPT 2002, LNCS, pp , Springer-Verlag.

15. M. Joye and C. Tymen. *Protection against differential attacks for elliptic curve cryptography*, CHES 2001, LNCS 2162, pp 402-410, Springer-Verlag.

16. N. Koblitz. *Elliptic Curve Cryptosystems*, Mathematics of Computations, 48:203-209, 1987.

17. P. Kocher. *Timing Attacks on Implementations of Diffie-Hellman, RSA, DSS and Other Systems*, CRYPTO'96, LNCS 1109, pp. 104-113, Springer-Verlag, 1996.

18. P. Kocher, J. Jaffe and B, Jun. *Differential Power Analysis,* CRYPTO'99, LNCS 1666, pp. 388-397, Springer-Verlag, 1999.

19. K. Koyama, Y. Tsuruoka. *Speeding up elliptic Curve Cryptosystems Using a Signed Binary Windows Method*, In CRYPTO'92, LNCS 740, pp 345-357, Springer-Verlag, 1992.

20. A. J. Menezes, P. C. van Oorschot and S. A. Vanstone. *Handbook of Applied Cryptography*. CRC Press, 1997.

21. V. S. Miller. *Use of Elliptic Curves in Cryptography*, CRYPTO'85, LNCS 218, pp. 417-426, Springer-Verlag, 1985.

22. J. Solinas. *Efficient arithmetic on Koblitz curves*, in Designs, Codes and Cryptography, 19:195-249, 2000.

Efficient Countermeasures Against RPA, DPA, and SPA*

Hideyo Mamiya, Atsuko Miyaji, and Hiroaki Morimoto**

Japan Advanced Institute of Science and Technology
{hmamiya, miyaji,h-morimo}@jaist.ac.jp

Abstract. In the execution on a smart card, side channel attacks such as simple power analysis (SPA) and the differential power analysis (DPA) have become serious threat [15]. Side channel attacks monitor power consumption and even exploit the leakage information related to power consumption to reveal bits of a secret key d although d is hidden inside a smart card. Almost public key cryptosystems including RSA, DLP-based cryptosystems, and elliptic curve cryptosystems execute an exponentiation algorithm with a secret-key exponent, and they thus suffer from both SPA and DPA. Recently, in the case of elliptic curve cryptosystems, DPA is improved to the Refined Power Analysis (RPA), which exploits a special point with a zero value and reveals a secret key [10]. RPA is further generalized to Zero-value Point Attack (ZPA) [2]. Both RPA and ZPA utilizes a special feature of elliptic curves that happens to have a special point or a register used in addition and doubling formulae with a zero value and that the power consumption of 0 is distinguishable from that of an non-zero element. To make the matters worse, some previous efficient countermeasures are neither resistant against RPA nor ZPA. Although a countermeasure to RPA is proposed, this is not universal countermeasure, gives each different method to each type of elliptic curves, and is still vulnerable against ZPA [30]. The possible countermeasures are ES [3] and the improved version [4]. This paper focuses on countermeasures against RPA, ZPA, DPA and SPA. We show a novel countermeasure resistant against RPA, ZPA, SPA and DPA without any pre-computed table. We also generalize the countermeasure to present more efficient algorithm with a pre-computed table.

Keywords: Elliptic curve exponentiation, ZPA, RPA, DPA, SPA.

1 Introduction

Koblitz [14] and Miller [20] proposed a method by which public key cryptosystems can be constructed on the group of points of an elliptic curve over a finite field. If elliptic curve cryptosystems satisfy both MOV-conditions [19] and

---

* This work is partially supported by National Institute of Information and Communications Technology (NICT).

** The author is currently with Hitachi Systems & Services, Ltd.

M. Joye and J.-J. Quisquater (Eds.): CHES 2004, LNCS 3156, pp. 343–356, 2004.

FR-conditions [7], and avoid p-divisible elliptic curves over $\mathbb{F}_{p^r}$ [31,1,29], then the only known attacks are the Pollard ρ−method [26] and the Pohlig-Hellman method [25]. Hence with current knowledge, we can construct elliptic curve cryptosystems over a smaller definition field than the discrete-logarithm-problem (DLP)-based cryptosystems like the ElGamal cryptosystems [9] or the DSA [8] and RSA cryptosystems [27]. Elliptic curve cryptosystems with a 160-bit key are thus believed to have the same security as both the ElGamal cryptosystems and RSA with a 1,024-bit key. This is why elliptic curve cryptosystems have been attractive in smart card applications, whose memory storage and CPU power is very limited. Elliptic curve cryptosystems execute an exponentiation algorithm of dP for a secret key d and a publicly known P as a cryptographic primitive. Thus, the efficiency of elliptic curve cryptosystems on a smart card depends on the implementation of exponentiation.

In the execution on a smart card, side channel attacks such as the simple power analysis (SPA) and the differential power analysis (DPA) have become serious threat. Side channel attacks, first introduced in [15,16], monitor power consumption and even exploit the leakage information related to power consumption to reveal bits of a secret key d although d is hidden inside a smart card. Thus, it is a serious issue that the implementation should be resistant against SPA and DPA, and many countermeasures have been proposed in [3,4,13,16, 21,22,24]. We may note here that almost public key cryptosystems including RSA and DLP-based cryptosystems also execute an exponentiation algorithm with a secret-key exponent, and, thus, they also suffer from both SPA and DPA in the same way as elliptic curve cryptosystems. However, recently, in the case of elliptic curve cryptosystems, DPA is further improved to the Refined Power Analysis (RPA) by [10], which exploits a special point with a zero value and reveals a secret key. An elliptic curve happens to have a special point $(0, y)$ or $(x, 0)$, which can be controlled by an adversary because the order of basepoint is usually known. RPA utilizes such a feature that the power consumption of 0 is distinguishable from that of an non-zero element. Although elliptic curve cryptosystems are vulnerable to RPA, RPA are not applied to RSA or DLP-based cryptosystems because they don't have such a special zero element. Furthermore, RPA is generalized to Zero-value Point Attack (ZPA) by [2]. ZPA makes use of any zero-value register used in addition formulae. ZPA utilizes a special feature of elliptic curves that addition and doubling formulae need a lot of each different operations stored in auxiliary registers, one of which happens to become 0. To make the matters worse, some previous efficient countermeasures of the randomized-projective-coordinate method (RPC)[6] or the randomized-curve method (RC)[13] are neither resistant against RPA nor ZPA. Because, a special point $(0, y)$ or $(x, 0)$ has still a zero value even if it is converted into $(0, ry, r)$ or $(rx, 0, r)$ by using RPC or RC. A countermeasure to RPA is proposed in [30], but this is not a universal countermeasure, gives each different method to each type of elliptic curves, and is still vulnerable against ZPA. The only possible countermeasure is the exponent-splitting method (ES) in [3,4], which splits an exponent and computes $dP = rP + (d - r)P = \lfloor d/r \rfloor rP + (d \bmod r)P$ by using a random number r. ES computes dP by the same cost as the add-and-double-always algorithm with an extra point for computation.

This paper focuses on countermeasures against both RPA and ZPA, which are also resistant against both SPA and DPA. Our countermeasure makes use of a random initial point R, computes $dP + R$, subtracts R, and gets dP. By using a random initial point at each execution of exponentiation, any point or any register used in addition formulae changes at each execution. Thus, it is resistant against DPA, RPA, and ZPA. In order to be secure against SPA, we have to compute $dP + R$ in such a way that it does not have any branch instruction dependent on the data being processed. The easiest way would be to compute $dP + R$ in the add-and-double-always method[6]. However, it does not work so straightforwardly if we execute it from MSB as we will see below. Our remarkable idea lies in the computation method of $dP + R$ that uses the binary expansion from MSB and not LSB and is resistant against SPA. The binary expansion from MSB has an advantage over that from LSB in that it is more easily generalized to a sophisticated method with a pre-computed table like the window method[18] or the extended binary method [32]. Let us remark that the computation of $dP + R$ based on the binary expansion from LSB is realized in the straightforward way: change an initial value $\mathcal{O}$ to R in the binary expansion from LSB as follows [12]:

$$dP + R = R + d_0 P + d_1 2P + d_2 2(2P) + \cdots + d_{n-1} 2(2^{n-2})P$$

with the binary expansion of $d = (d_{n-1}, \cdots, d_0)_2$. We can easily change the algorithm to the add-and-double-always method. However, the computation of $dP + R$ based on the binary expansion from MSB (see Algorithm 1) is not straightforward: if we change an initial value $\mathcal{O}$ to R in the binary expansion from MSB, then it computes $2^{n-1}R + dP$, and we thus have to subtract $2^{n-1}R$ to get dP. Apparently, it needs more work than the straightforward way of binary expansion from LSB.

In this paper, we first show the basic computation method of $dP + R$ that uses the binary expansion from MSB and is resistant against SPA. This is called BRIP in this paper. Next we apply the extended binary method[32] and present more efficient computation method of $dP + R$ with a pre-computed table, which is still resistant against SPA. This is called EBRIP in this paper. EBRIP is a rather flexible algorithm that can reduce the total computation amount by increasing the size of a pre-computed table. BRIP can get dP in the computation of approximately 24.0 M in each bit without using a pre-computed table, where M shows the computation amount of 1 modular multiplication on the definition field. EBRIP can get dP in the computation of approximately 12.9 M in each bit with using a pre-computed table of 16 points. Compared with the previous RPA-, ZPA-, and SPA-resistant method ES, the computation amount of BRIP is the same as that of ES without an extra point for computation and the computation amount of EBRIP can be reduced to only 54 % of that of ES.

This paper is organized as follows. Section 2 summarizes some facts of elliptic curves like coordinate systems and reviews power analysis of SPA, DPA,

RPA, and ZPA together with some known countermeasures. Section 3 presents our new countermeasures, the basic countermeasure (BRIP) and the generalized countermeasure with a pre-computed table (EBRIP). Section 4 presents the performance of our strategy compared with the previous RPA-, ZPA-, and SPA-resistant countermeasure.

2 Preliminary

This section summarizes some facts of elliptic curves like coordinate systems and reviews power analysis of SPA, DPA, RPA, and ZPA together with some known countermeasures.

2.1 Elliptic Curve

Let $\mathbb{F}_p$ be a finite field, where $p > 3$ is a prime. The Weierstrass form of an elliptic curve over $\mathbb{F}_p$ is described as

$$E/\mathbb{F}_p : y^2 = x^3 + ax + b \quad (a, b \in \mathbb{F}_p, 4a^3 + 27b^2 \neq 0).$$

The set of all points $P = (x, y)$ satisfying E, together with the point of infinity $\mathcal{O}$, is denoted by $E(\mathbb{F}_p)$, which forms an abelian group. Let $P_1 = (x_1, y_1)$ and $P_2 = (x_2, y_2)$ be two points on $E(\mathbb{F}_p)$ and $P_3 = P_1 + P_2 = (x_3, y_3)$ be the sum. Then the addition formulae in affine coordinate are given as follows [5].

•**Addition formulae in affine coordinate**$(P \neq \pm Q)$

$$x_3 = \lambda^2 - x_1 - x_2, \quad y_3 = \lambda(x_1 - x_3) - y_1,$$

where $\lambda = (y_2 - y_1)/(x_2 - x_1)$.

•**Doubling formulae in affine coordinate**$(P = \pm Q)$

$$x_3 = \lambda^2 - 2x_1, \quad y_3 = \lambda(x_1 - x_3) - y_1,$$

where $\lambda = (3x_1^2 + a)/(2y_1)$.

Let us denote the computation time of an addition (resp. a doubling) in the affine coordinate by $t(\mathcal{A}+\mathcal{A})$ (resp. $t(2\mathcal{A})$) and represent multiplication (resp. inverse, resp. squaring) in $\mathbb{F}_p$ by M (resp. I, resp. S). Then we see that $t(\mathcal{A} + \mathcal{A}) = I + 2M + S$ and $t(2\mathcal{A}) = I + 2M + 2S$. Both addition and doubling formulae need one inversion over $\mathbb{F}_p$, which is much more expensive than multiplication over $\mathbb{F}_p$. Therefore, we transform affine coordinate (x, y) into other coordinates, where the inversion is free. We give the addition and doubling formulae with Jacobian coordinate, which are widely used.

In the Jacobian coordinates [5], we set $x = X/Z^2$ and $y = Y/Z^3$, giving the equation

$$E_{\mathcal{J}} : Y^2 = X^3 + aXZ^4 + bZ^6.$$

Then, two points (X, Y, Z) and (r^2X, r^3Y, rZ) for some $r \in \mathbb{F}_p^*$ are recognized as the same point. The point at infinity is represented with $(1, 1, 0)$. Let $P_1 = (X_1, Y_1, Z_1), P_2 = (X_2, Y_2, Z_2)$, and $P_3 = P_1 + P_2 = (X_3, Y_3, Z_3)$. The doubling and addition formulae can be represented as follows.

- **Addition formulae in Jacobian coordinate$(P \neq \pm Q)$**

$$X_3 = -H^3 - 2U_1H^2 + R^2,$$
$$Y_3 = -S_1H^3 + R(U_1H^2 - X_3),$$
$$Z_3 = Z_1Z_2H,$$

where $U_1 = X_1Z_2^2$, $U_2 = X_2Z_1^2$, $S_1 = Y_1Z_2^3$, $S_2 = Y_2Z_1^3$, $H = U_2 - U_1$, and $R = S_2 - S_1$.

- **Doubling formulae in Jacobian coordinate$(P = \pm Q)$**

$$X_3 = T, \; Y_3 = -8Y_1^4 + M(S - T), \; Z_3 = 2Y_1Z_1,$$

where $S = 4X_1Y_1^2$, $M = 3X_1^2 + aZ_1^4$, and $T = -2S + M^2$.

The computation times in the Jacobian coordinate are $t(\mathcal{J} + \mathcal{J}) = 12M + 4S$ and $t(2\mathcal{J}) = 4M + 6S$, where $\mathcal{J}$ means Jacobian coordinates.

Elliptic curve cryptosystems often execute the elliptic curve exponentiation of $dP = P + P + \cdots + P$, where $P \in E(\mathbb{F}_p)$ and d is an n-bit integer. The simple method to compute dP is a so-called binary algorithm. Algorithm 1 shows the binary algorithm to compute dP from MSB, where the binary expansion of d is $d = (d_{n-1}, \cdots, d_0)$. Average computing complexity of Algorithm 1 is $nD + n/2A$, where A and D denotes the computation amount of addition and doubling, respectively. When we compute dP from LSB, we have to keep another point 2^iP instead of $T_1 = P$ but can apply the iterated doubling formulae in Jacobian coorinate [11], which computes 2^kP for $k \geq 1$ by $4kM + (4k+2)S$. However, the binary algorithm from LSB is not easily generalized to a sophiticated method with a pre-computed table.

Algorithm 1 (Binary algorithm (MSB))
Input: d, P
Output: dP
1. $T_0 = \prime, T_1 = P$.
2. for $i = n - 2$ to 0
       $T_0 = 2T_0$
       if $d_i = 1$ then $T_0 = T_0 + T_1$
3. output T_0.

2.2 Power Analysis

There are two types of power analysis, the simple power analysis (SPA) and the differential power analysis (DPA), which are described in [15,16]. In the case of elliptic curve and also hyper elliptic curve, DPA is further improved to use a special point with a zero value, which is called the Refined Power Analysis (RPA) [10]. RPA is generalized to the Zero-value Point Analysis (ZPA) [2]. In this paper, DPA, RPA, and ZPA are called DPA variants generically.

Simple Power Analysis. SPA makes use of such an instruction performed during an exponentiation algorithm that depends on the data being processed. Apparently, Algorithm 1 has a branch instruction conditioned by a secret exponent d, and thus it reveals the secret d. In order to be resistant against SPA, any branch instruction of exponentiation algorithm should be eliminated. There are mainly two types of countermeasures: the fixed procedure method [6] and the indistinguishable method [3]. The fixed procedure method deletes any branch instruction conditioned by a secret exponent d like add-and-double-always method [6], Montgomery-ladder method [23], and window-based method [18]. Add-and-double-always method is described in Algorithm 2. The indistinguishable method conceals all branch instructions of exponentiation algorithm by using indistinguishable addition and doubling operations, in which dummy operations are inserted.

Algorithm 2 (Add-and-double-always algorithm)
Input: d, P
Output: dP
1. $T_0 = P$ and $T_2 = P$.
2. for $i = n - 2$ to 0
        $T_0 = 2T_0$. $T_1 = T_0 + T_2$.
        if $d_i = 0$ then $T_0 = T_0$.
        else $T_0 = T_1$.
3. output T_0.

Differential Power Analysis. DPA uses correlation between power consumption and specific key-dependent bits. Algorithm 2 reveals d_{n-2} by computing the correlation between power consumption and any specific bit of the binary representation of 4P. In order to be resistant against DPA, power consumption should be changed at each new execution of the exponentiation. There are mainly 3 types of countermeasures, the randomized-projective-coordinate method (RPC) [6], the randomized curve method (RC)[13], and the exponent splitting (ES) [3,4]. RPC uses the Jacobian or Projective coordinate to randomize a point $P = (x, y)$ into $(r^2 x, r^3 y, r)$ or (rx, ry, r) for a random number $r \in \mathbb{F}_p^*$, respectively. RC maps an elliptic curve into an isomorphic elliptic curve by using an isomorphism map of (x, y) to $(c^2 x, c^3 y)$ for $c \in \mathbb{F}_p^*$. However, all these two methods are vulnerable against RPA and ZPA, which will be described in Section 2.2. The only method secure against RPA and ZPA is ES, which splits an exponent and computes $dP = rP + (d - r)P$ for a randomly integer r.

Refined Power Analysis and Zero-value Point Attack. DPA is specialized to reveal a secret key d by using a special elliptic-curve point with a zero value, which is defined as $(x, 0)$ or $(0, y)$. These special points of $(x, 0)$ and $(0, y)$ still have a zero value like $(rx, 0, r)$ and $(0, ry, r)$ even if it is converted into the projective coordinate, respectively. This is why special points can not be randomized by RPC or RC, and an adversary can thus make use of a zero value in the execution of exponentiation. A countermeasure to RPA are proposed in [30], but this is not a universal countermeasure, gives each different method to each type of elliptic curves, and is still vulnerable against ZPA, described below.

RPA is generalized to ZPA by [2], which makes use of any zero-value register in addition formulae, which is not randomized by RPC or RC. The addition and doubling formulae have a lot of each different operations stored in auxiliary registers, one of which may become zero. ZPA uses the difference in any zero value register between addition and doubling.

We may note that ES can resist both RPA and ZPA because an attacker cannot handle an elliptic curve point in such a way that any special point with zero-value value can appear during an execution of exponentiation algorithm.

3 Efficient Countermeasures Against SPA and DPA Variants

In this section, we propose a new countermeasure against all DPA variants.

3.1 Our Basic Countermeasure

Here we show our basic countermeasure, called BRIP. Our method uses a random initial point (RIP) R, computes $dP + R$, and subtracts R to get dP. By using a random initial point at each execution of exponentiation, any point or any register used in addition formulae changes at each execution. Thus, it is resistant against DPA, RPA, and ZPA. In order to be secure against SPA, we have to compute $dP + R$ in such a way that it does not have any branch instruction dependent on the data being processed. Our remarkable idea lies in a sophisticated combination to compute $dP + R$ from MSB by the same complexity as Algorithm 2: first let 1 express $1 = (1\overline{11}\cdots\overline{11})_2$ and apply the extended binary method [17] to compute

$$(1\underbrace{\overline{11}\cdots\overline{11}}_{n})_2 R + (\underbrace{d_{n-1}d_{n-1}\cdots d_1 d_0}_{n})_2 P.$$

Algorithm 3 shows our idea in detail. We get dP by computing $dP + R$ and subtracting R. BRIP makes all variables $T_0, T_1,$ and T_2 dependent on a random point R, and thus let all variables of each addition and doubling differ at each execution.

Algorithm 3 (Binary Expansion with RIP (BRIP))
Input: d, P
Output: dP
1. $R =$ randompoint()
2. $T_0 = R, T_1 = -R, T_2 = P - R$
3. for $i = n - 1$ to 0
    $T_0 = 2T_0$

```
    if d_i = 0 then T_0 = T_0 + T_1
    else  T_0 = T_0 + T_2
4. output T_0 + T_1
```

We discuss the security, the computation amount, and the memory amount. BRIP lets the power-consumption pattern be fixed regardless of the bit pattern of a secret key d, and thus it is resistant against SPA. The resistance against DPA depends on the method of generating a random initial point R. The simplest way to generate R is to generate the x-coordinate randomly and compute the corresponding y-coordinate if exists. It should require much work. The cheaper way is to keep one point R_0 and convert R_0 into a randomized point R by RPC [12]. If R is chosen randomly by some ways mentioned above, BRIP can be resistant against DPA, RPA, and ZPA, since any special point or zero-value register can not appear during each execution. The computation amount required for Algorithm 3 is $nD + nA$, which is the same as Algorithm 2. The number of variables necessary for computation is only 3.

3.2   Our Generalized Countermeasure

Our basic countermeasure BRIP can be generalized to a faster method with a pre-computed table since BRIP makes use of the binary expansion from MSB. We may note that the binary expansion from LSB can not be easily generalized to a faster method with a pre-computed table.

As for methods of using a pre-computed table, there are mainly two methods: the window method [18] and the extended binary method [17,32]. The extended binary method is originally used to compute two exponentiations $aP + bQ$, which is applied to compute one exponentiation as follows [32]. Let $d = \sum_{i=0}^{n-1} d_i 2^i$ and n be even.

1. Divide d into two components of $d = b \parallel a$, where $b = (d_{n-1} \cdots d_{\frac{n}{2}})_2$ and $a = (d_{\frac{n}{2}-1} \cdots d_0)_2$.
2. Compute $Q = 2^{\frac{n}{2}} P$.
3. Set a pre-computed table $\{P, Q, P + Q\}$.
4. Compute $aP + bQ$ in the extended binary method by using the pre-computed table.

The detailed algorithm is shown in Algorithm 4.

Algorithm 4 (Extended-binary algorithm with 2 divisions)
Input: d, P
Output: dP
1. Set $d = b \parallel a$, $b = (b_{\frac{n}{2}-1} \cdots b_0)_2 = (d_{n-1} \cdots d_{\frac{n}{2}})_2$, and $a = (a_{\frac{n}{2}-1} \cdots a_0)_2 = (d_{\frac{n}{2}-1} \cdots d_0)_2$.
2. $T_1 = P$, $T_2 = 2^{\frac{n}{2}} P$, $T_3 = T_1 + T_2$, and $T_0 = \mathcal{O}$.
3. for $i = \frac{n}{2} - 1$ to 0
       $T_0 = 2T_0$.

```
if (a_i, b_i) = (1,0) then T_0 = T_0 + T_1.
elseif (a_i, b_i) = (0,1) then T_0 = T_0 + T_2.
elseif (a_i, b_i) = (1,1) then T_0 = T_0 + T_3.
```
4. output T_0.

Going back to the countermeasure using a pre-computed table, it is necessary for both the extended binary and window methods to make power-consumption pattern same in order to be resistant against SPA. In the case of the window method, some SPA-resistant methods are proposed in [21,22,24]. However, all of these are not resistant against RPA or ZPA even if they are combined with the methods of RC and RPC. In the case of the extended binary method, up to the present, any SPA-resistant method has not been proposed.

Our generalized method is both SPA and DPA-variant resistant, which is able to reduce the computation amount with a pre-computed table. Our sophisticated idea lies in the length of representation of $1 = (1\overline{1}\overline{1}\cdots\overline{1}\overline{1})_2$, which is adjusted to be applied on any bit length of d and output the same executed pattern, while holding down the additional compuation and memory amount. As a result, our method is SPA-resistant naturally. In the following, two algorithms based on the extended-binary and the window methods are described. The extended-binary-based method is more efficient than window-based method although extended-binary method usually does not work on a single exponentiation as efficient as the window method.

Our extended-binary-based method with RIP. Let us show our extended-binary-based method with RIP, which is called EBRIP for short.

1. Choose a random point R.
2. Let the number of divisions be t.
3. Adjust n to be the least common multiple n' of t and n by setting 0 to MSB of d $(n' < n + t)$, where

$$d' = 0\cdots 0\, d_{n-1}\cdots d_0.$$

4. Divide d' into t components $(\frac{n'}{t} = k)$ of $d' = \alpha_{t-1} \| \cdots \| \alpha_1 \| \alpha_0$, that is,

$$
\begin{aligned}
\alpha_{t-1} &= \quad 0 \quad \cdots d_{(t-1)k} \\
&\;\;\vdots \\
\alpha_1 &= \quad d_{2k-1} \cdots d_k \\
\alpha_0 &= \quad d_{k-1} \quad \cdots d_0 \\
1 &= 1\overline{1} \quad \cdots \overline{1}
\end{aligned}
$$

5. Compute $P_i = 2^{ki}P$ for $i = 1$ to $t - 1$. (Set $P_0 = P$).
6. Compute a pre-computed table $T_t = \{\sum_{i=0}^{t-1} a_i P_i - R\ (a_i \in \{0,1\})\}$, which consists of 2^t points.
7. Compute $\alpha_0 P_0 + \cdots + \alpha_{t-1}P_{t-1} + 1R$ in the way of the extended binary method.

Algorithm 5 shows the case of $t = 2$ and an even n for simplicity. Let us discuss the resistance, computation amount, and memory amount. As for SPA, the power-consumption pattern is not changed for any initial point R and any secret key d thanks to the expansion of 1, and EBRIP is thus secure against SPA. We may note one remarkable point that the length of expansion of 1 is not fixed to n but adjusted to $\lceil \frac{n}{t} \rceil + 1(< n)$. As a result, it realizes more efficient computation than the window-based method. Moreover, under the assumption that an initial point R is completely random, EBRIP is secure against DPA, RPA, and ZPA, as we mentioned in Section 3.1. As for the computation amount, EBRIP consists of these parts: compute base points $P_1, \cdots, P_{t-1}$, a pre-computed table T_t, and the main routine. The computation amount for base points, T_t, or main routine is $\frac{(t-1)n'}{t}D$, $2^t A$, or $\frac{n'}{t}D + \frac{n'}{t}A$, respectively. Thus, the total computation amount is $n'D + \frac{n'}{t}A + 2^t A$. On the other hand, the number of points in T_t is 2^t, which includes a random point R. EBRIP needs one more point of variable to execute. Thus, the necessary memory is $2^t + 1$ in total.

Algorithm 5 (EBRIP (2 divisions))
```
Input: d, P
Output: dP
1. R =randompoint().
1. Set d = b ∥ a, b = (b_{n/2 −1} ··· b_0)_2 = (d_{n−1} ··· d_{n/2})_2, and
   a = (a_{n/2 −1} ··· a_0)_2 = (d_{n/2 −1} ··· d_0)_2.
2. T_4 = P, T_3 = 2^{n/2} P, T_0 = R, T_1 = −R, T_2 = T_1 + T_4, T_3 = T_1 + T_3 and
   T_4 = T_3 + T_4.
3. for i = n/2 − 1 to 0
        T_0 = 2T_0.
        if (a_i, b_i) = (0,0) then T_0 = T_0 + T_1.
        elseif (a_i, b_i) = (1,0) then T_0 = T_0 + T_2.
        elseif (a_i, b_i) = (0,1) then T_0 = T_0 + T_3.
        else then T_0 = T_0 + T_4.
4. output T_0 + T_1.
```

Our window-based method with RIP. Our window-based method with RIP is summarized as follow, which is is called WBRIP for short.

1. Choose a random point R.
2. Set the width of window to be w.
3. Adjust n to be the least common multiple n' of w and n by setting 0 to MSB $(n' < n + w)$ of d, where

$$d' = 0 \cdots 0\, d_{n-1} \cdots d_0.$$

4. Compute $R' = -(2^w - 1)R$.
5. Set a pre-computed table $T_w = \{R', P + R', 2P + R', 3P + R', \cdots, (2^w - 2)P + R', (2^w - 1)P + R'\}$, where the number of points in T_w is 2^w.

6. Compute $(\underbrace{0\cdots 0\, d_{n-1}\cdots d_0}_{n'})_2 P + (1\underbrace{\overline{11}\cdots \overline{11}}_{n'})_2 R$ in the way of window method by using T_w.

Let us discuss the security, the computation amount, and the memory amount. Power-consumption pattern is not changed for any random R and any secret key d thanks to the expansion of 1. This is why WBRIP is resistant against SPA. This means that WBRIP is secure against SPA without any additional modification on the window method seen in [21,22,24]. Furthermore, under the assumption that an initial point R is completely random, our method is resistant against DPA, RPA, and ZPA. Next we investigate the computation amount of WBRIP. WBRIP consists of three parts: compute an intermediate point R', a pre-computed table T_w, and main routine. The computation amount of R', a pre-computed table T_w, or main routine is $wD + A$, $(2^w - 1)A$, or $\frac{n'}{w}A + n'D$, respectively. Therefore, the total computation amount is $n'D + \frac{n'}{w}A + 2^w A + wD$, where $n' < n + w$. It is not as efficient as the extended-binary-based method since the length of expansion of 1 is fixed to n' to reduce the number of points in T_w, which is the same as that in T_t for $t = w$. If we change the length of expansion of 1 to a shorter length like n, then T_w must include other points and thus the size of T_w becomes larger. Finally we discuss the memory amount necessary to execute WBRIP. The number of points in T_w is 2^w, which includes a random point R. Additional one variable is necessary for computation. Thus, the necessary memory is $2^w + 1$ points in total.

As a result, compared with EBRIP, WBRIP needs more computation amount with the same memory amount.

4   Performance

From the point of view of computation and memory amount, we compare our countermeasures BRIP and EBRIP with the previous method ES [4], which are resistant against SPA and DPA variants. The previous SPA-resistant window methods[21,22,24] are not resistant against RPA or ZPA even if they are combined combined with RC or RPC as we mentioned before. Thus, these SPA-resistant window methods have to be combined with ES to be resistant both RPA and ZPA. As a result, the computation and memory amount would be less efficient than WBRIP, which is not so efficient as EBRIP. Table 1 shows the comparison, where M or S shows the computation amount of modular multiplication or modular square on the definition field, respectively. We assume that $S = 0.8M$ as usual. In all cases of BRIP, EBRIP, and ES, the Jacobian coordinate is the most efficient, and thus we use the Jacobian coordinate to compute the total number of modular multiplications. Table 1 shows two types of computation amount. One gives the computation amount in the case of 160-bit definition field. The other gives the average computation amount in each bit, which does not depend on the size of definition field. In order to discuss the efficiency generally, the average computation amount in each bit is useful.

We note that EBRIP can fully make use of the technique of m-repeated elliptic curve doublings [11] although it computes from MSB. Because pre-computation of base points requires m-repeated elliptic curve doublings.

BRIP can compute dP in the computation amount of $160D + 160A$ with 3 points. The computation amount in each bit is $24.0M$, which is the same as that of ES. EBRIP with $t = 2$ can compute dP in the computation amount of $160D + 84A$ with 5 points. The computation amount in each bit is $16.0M$, which is reduced to only 66% of ES. EBRIP with $t = 4$ can execute dP in the computation amount of $160D+56A$ with 17 points. In this case, the computation amount in each bit is $12.9M$, which is reduced to only 54% of ES. Note that $t = 4$ is the fastest when the size of definition filed $\mathbb{F}_p$ is 160.

Table 1. Comparison of countermeasures

	memory amount (#points, #scalar)	computation amount[†] #D + #A	#M + #S	computation amount in each bit
ES [4]	(4, 2)	160D+160A	$2856M + 1600S(3840M)$	$16M + 10S(24.0M)$
BRIP	(3, 0)	160D+160A	$2856M + 1600S(3840M)$	$16M + 10S(24.0M)$
EBRIP($t = 2$)	(5, 0)	160D+84A	$1648M + 1140S(2560M)$	$10.3M + 7.1S(16.0M)$
EBRIP($t = 3$)	(9, 0)	162D+62A	$1392M + 1008S(2198M)$	$8.7M + 6.3S(13.7M)$
EBRIP($t = 4$)	(17, 0)	160D+56A	$1312M + 948S(2069M)$	$8.2M + 5.9S(12.9M)$

[†] This shows the computation amount in the case of 160-bit definition field.

5   Concluding Remarks

In this paper, we have presented countermeasures of BRIP and EBRIP that are resistant against RPA, ZPA, DPA, and SPA. Our countermeasure BRIP does not require any pre-computed table and can get dP in the computation of approximately 24.0 M in each bit. EBRIP with $t = 4$ can get dP in the computation of approximately 12.9 M in each bit with using a pre-computed table and one more point of 17 points in total. Both RPA and ZPA are easily applied to the hyper elliptic curve cryptosystems because a divisor in a hyper elliptic curve consists of more than two parts, some of which would happen to become 0. Our countermeasure improves the addition-chain itself and not use a specific feature of an elliptic curve such as a coordinate system. Therefore, BRIP and EBRIP can also be generalized to deal with hyper elliptic curve cryptosystem. We will describe BRIP and EBRIP on a hyper elliptic curves and discuss the efficiency in our final paper.

References

1. K. Araki and T. Satoh "Fermat quotients and the polynomial time discrete log algorithm for anomalous elliptic curves", *Commentarii Math. Univ. St. Pauli.*, vol. **47** (1998), 81–92.

2. T. Akishita and T. Takagi, "Zero-value Point Attacks on Elliptic Curve Cryptosystem", ISC2003, Lecture Notes in Computer Science, **2851**(2003), Springer-Verlag, 218–233.

3. C. Clavier and M. Joye, "Universal exponentiation algorithm - A first step towards provable SPA-resistance –", CHES2001, Lecture Notes in Computer Science, **2162**(2001), Springer-Verlag, 300–308.

4. M. Ciet and M. Joye, "(Virtually) Free randomization technique for elliptic curve cryptography", ICICS2003, Lecture Notes in Computer Science, **2836**(2003), Springer-Verlag, 348–359.

5. H. Cohen, A. Miyaji and T. Ono, "Efficient elliptic curve exponentiation using mixed coordinates", *Advances in Cryptology-Proceedings of ASIACRYPT'98*, Lecture Notes in Computer Science, **1514**(1998), Springer-Verlag, 51-65.

6. J. Coron, "Resistance against differential power analysis for elliptic curve cryptosystem", CHES'99, Lecture Notes in Computer Science, **1717**(1999), Springer-Verlag, 292–302.

7. G. Frey and H. G. Rück, "A remark concerning m-divisibility and the discrete logarithm in the divisor class group of curves", *Mathematics of computation*, **62**(1994), 865-874.

8. "Proposed federal information processing standard for digital signature standard (DSS)", *Federal Register*, **56** No. 169, 30 Aug 1991, 42980–42982.

9. T. ElGamal, "A public key cryptosystem and a signature scheme based on discrete logarithms", *IEEE Trans. Inform. Theory*, **IT-31** (1985), 469–472.

10. L. Goubin, "A Refined Power-Analysis Attack on Elliptic Curve Cryptosystems", PKC2003, Lecture Notes in Computer Science, **2567**(2003), Springer-Verlag, 199–210.

11. K. Itoh, M. Takenaka, N. Torii, S. Temma, and Y. Kurihara, "Fast implementation of public-key cryptography on DSP TMS320C6201", CHES'99, Lecture Notes in Computer Science, **1717**(1999), Springer-Verlag, 61–72.

12. K. Itoh, T. Izu, and M. Takenaka, "Efficient countermeasures against power analysis for elliptic curve cryptosystems", SCIS2004, 2004 (previous version). The final version will be appeared in the proceedings of CARDIS 2004.

13. M. Joye and C. Tymen, "Protections against Differential Analysis for Elliptic Curve Cryptosystem", CHES2001, Lecture Notes in Computer Science, **2162**(2001), Springer-Verlag, 377–390.

14. N. Koblitz, "Elliptic curve cryptosystems", *Mathematics of Computation*, **48** (1987), 203–209.

15. C. Kocher, "Timing attacks on Implementations of Diffie-Hellman, RSA, DSS, and other system", CRYPTO'96, Lecture Notes in Computer Science, **1109**(1996), Springer-Verlag, 104–113.

16. C. Kocher, J. Jaffe, and B. Jun, "Differential power analysis", Crypto'99, Lecture Notes in Computer Science, **1666**(1999), Springer-Verlag, 388-397.

17. D. E. Knuth, *The Art of Computer Programming*, Vol. 2: Seminumerical Algorithms, 2nd ed., Addison-Wesley, 1981.

18. K. Koyama and Y. Tsuruoka, "Speeding up elliptic cryptosystems by using a signed binary window method", *Advances in Cryptology-Proceedings of Crypto'92*, Lecture Notes in Computer Science, **740** (1993), Springer-Verlag, 345–357.

19. A. Menezes, T. Okamoto and S. Vanstone, "Reducing elliptic curve logarithms to logarithms in a finite field", *Proceedings of the 22nd Annual ACM Symposium on the Theory of Computing* (1991), 80–89.

20. V. S. Miller, "Use of elliptic curves in cryptography", *Advances in Cryptology-Proceedings of Crypto'85*, Lecture Notes in Computer Science, **218** (1986), Springer-Verlag, 417–426.

21. B. Möller, "Securing Elliptic Curve Point Multiplication against Side-Channel Attacks", ISC2001, Lecture Notes in Computer Science, **2200**(2001), Springer-Verlag, 324–334.

22. B. Möller, "Parallelizable Elliptic Curve Point Multiplication Method with Resistance against Side-Channel Attacks", ISC2002, Lecture Notes in Computer Science, **2433**(2002), Springer-Verlag, 402–413.

23. P. L. Montgomery, "Speeding the Pollard and elliptic curve methods for factorization", *Mathematics of Computation*, **48**(1987), 243-264.

24. K. Okeya and T. Takagi, "The Width-w NAF Method Provides Small Memory and Fast Elliptic Scalar Multiplications Secure against Side Channel Attacks", CT-RSA2003, Lecture Notes in Computer Science, **2612**(2003), Springer-Verlag, 328–342.

25. S. C. Pohlig and M. E. Hellman, "An improved algorithm for computing logarithms over $GF(p)$ and its cryptographic significance", *IEEE Trans. Inf. Theory*, **IT-24** (1978), 106–110.

26. J. Pollard, "Monte Carlo methods for index computation (mod p)", *Mathematics of Computation*, **32** (1978), 918–924.

27. R. Rivest, A. Shamir and L. Adleman, "A method for obtaining digital signatures and public-key cryptosystems", *Communications of the ACM*, **21** No. 2 (1978), 120–126.

28. Roberto M. Avanzi, "On multi-exponentiation in cryptography", Cryptology ePrint Archive, Report 2002/154, http://eprint.iacr.org/2002/154/ , 2002.

29. N. P. Smart "The discrete logarithm problem on elliptic curves of trace one", to appear in J. Cryptology.

30. N. P. Smart "An Analysys of Goubin's Refined Power Analysis Attack", CHES2003, Lecture Notes in Computer Science, **2779**(2003), Springer-Verlag, 281–290.

31. I. A. Semaev "Evaluation of discrete logarithms in a group of p-torsion points of an elliptic curve in characteristic p", *Mathematics of computation*, **67** (1998), 353-356.

32. J. A. Solinas, "Low-Weight Binary Representation for Pairs of Integers", Centre for Applied Cryptographic Research, University of Waterloo, Combinatorics and Optimization Reseach Report CORR 2001-41, 2001.

Strong Authentication for RFID Systems Using the AES Algorithm*

Martin Feldhofer, Sandra Dominikus, and Johannes Wolkerstorfer

Institute for Applied Information Processing and Communications,
Graz University of Technology, Inffeldgasse 16a, 8010 Graz, Austria
{Martin.Feldhofer, Sandra.Dominikus,
Johannes.Wolkerstorfer}@iaik.tugraz.at

Abstract. Radio frequency identification (RFID) is an emerging technology which brings enormous productivity benefits in applications where objects have to be identified automatically. This paper presents issues concerning security and privacy of RFID systems which are heavily discussed in public. In contrast to the RFID community, which claims that cryptographic components are too costly for RFID tags, we describe a solution using strong symmetric authentication which is suitable for today's requirements regarding low power consumption and low die-size. We introduce an authentication protocol which serves as a proof of concept for authenticating an RFID tag to a reader device using the Advanced Encryption Standard (AES) as cryptographic primitive. The main part of this work is a novel approach of an AES hardware implementation which encrypts a 128-bit block of data within 1000 clock cycles and has a power consumption below 9 μA on a 0.35 μm CMOS process.

Keywords: Radio frequency identification (RFID), symmetric challenge-response, Advanced Encryption Standard (AES), low-power design.

1 Introduction

Radio frequency identification (RFID) systems are used for the automatic retrieval of data about goods, persons, or animals, more generally speaking: an object. The object is equipped with a small circuit, called RFID tag, and the information stored on the medium can be automatically retrieved by a reader device. This property can be used in industrial applications for tracking of goods or in access systems. RFID systems do not require line-of-sight and work contactless. Data and energy are transmitted via radio frequency.

Each RFID system consists of a tag, which is attached to the object to identify, and a reader which is able to retrieve data from the tag. The reader may as well be able to write data to the tag's memory. Additionally, to implement an application on data received from the tags, a host is used (see figure 1).

---

* This work origins from the Austrian Government funded project *ART* established under the embedded system program FIT-IT.

M. Joye and J.-J. Quisquater (Eds.): CHES 2004, LNCS 3156, pp. 357–370, 2004.

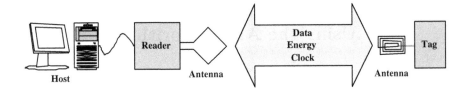

Fig. 1. Structure of an RFID system

Host commands are converted into reader requests and broadcasted via radio frequency. If a tag is inside the reader's field, it sends a response. Tag responses can be processed by the host corresponding to the current application.

In this paper we concentrate on passive tags. This means that they receive their energy from the reader field. The field's intensity is limited by national and international regulations, so the power consumption of the tag as well underlies limitations. For this reason power-aware designing of the tag circuitry is necessary. Less power consumption also leads to longer reader ranges where tags can work with the available energy. More technical details about RFID systems (coupling mechanisms, data rates, data coding, modulation, frequency...) can be found in [4] and in RFID standards [7,3].

RFID technology offers convincing benefits in many sectors. Industry and retailers save money by enhanced automation of fabrication and warehousing. Consumers can also take advantage from goods being able to communicate with their environment (e.g. washing machine communicates with clothes, milk packs communicate with refrigerator). Other applications for RFID systems are access control, animal tracking, proof of origin of goods, toll systems, car immobilization, and so on. There are even approaches to secure money with RFID tags [8]. So it looks like RFID will be a very popular technology in the near future.

Because of this popularity, people began to think about security and privacy issues concerning this technology. The public opinion was awakened by the "discovery" of consumer tracking: the ability of RFID readers to identify RFID tags in their environment could be used to track the movements of a consumer, who just bought an article equipped with an RFID tag. Another security concern is the forgery of tags, when RFID tags are used for access control, theft or loss control, or for proof of origin. The third security issue to be mentioned is the unauthorized access to tag's memory contents. If sensible data are stored in the memory, this is a serious security problem.

Enhanced security always comes along with extra costs. Although the industry claims low-cost tags, sooner or later the security issue has to be faced in order to make RFID an everyday technology. In this paper we propose the implementation of an authentication method for RFID systems using strong cryptography. The Advanced Encryption Standard (AES) is used as cryptographic primitive, because it is standardized and considered to be secure. We propose an authentication protocol and how it can be integrated into existing standards. Furthermore, we present a low-power implementation of the AES which is suitable for RFID tags in terms of power consumption and die size.

2   Security Considerations for RFID Systems

RFID systems are susceptible to security attacks: as they work non-line-of-sight and contactless, an attacker can work remote and passive attacks will not be noticed. Some of the main concerns are (unwanted) consumer tracking, tag forgery and the unauthorized access to the tag's memory content. These security risks have to be dealt with in order to gain a broad user acceptance.

2.1   Related Work

Some publications already deal with security aspects for RFID systems. Juels, Rivest, and Szydlo [9] propose so called "blocker tags" to protect consumers from tracking. One tag simulates a broad range of ID numbers, so a reader cannot identify it uniquely and tracking is circumvented. This was an approach to secure low-price tags which cost less than US$ 0.05.

Weis addresses the security and privacy issue of RFID systems in his master thesis [17] and in another publication together with Sarma, Rivest, and Engels [18]. He also deals with low-cost tags for industrial applications. He suggests a hash-lock mechanism as access control and a randomized version of it to deal with consumer tracking. He also presents some other concepts to enhance security in RFID tags. The assumptions made about the environment, for example that eavesdroppers cannot monitor signals from the tag, make the proposals sometimes not generally applicable.

Sarma, Weis, and Engels [15] also mention the problem of consumer tracking and recommend erasing the ID number of a tag at the point of sale as countermeasure. They also address the protection of tag contents and introduce the concept of access control through mutual authentication of tag and reader.

Juels and Pappu make a proposal how to secure banknotes with RFID tags [8]. They want to reach various security goals, some of them are consumer privacy, forgery resistance, and fraud detection. They propose a system which satisfies the requirements for all of the four main actors: the central bank, the merchants, the executive, and the consumer. The proposal in this publication is an RFID system using asymmetric cryptography combined with some methods which require physical access to the tag.

Finally, the "RFID Handbook" [4] deals with data security of RFID systems by using authentication mechanisms. This is also the topic of our paper. We propose using strong cryptographic algorithms to perform authentication.

2.2   Authentication

Authentication means that an object proves its claimed identity to its communication partner. This technique can solve all of the former mentioned security problems. Consumer tracking can be avoided, if tags only communicate their identity to authenticated readers. An unauthorized reader cannot get any information about tags which are currently in its field. The authentication of the reader to the tags also solves the unauthorized-access problem. Only authorized readers can read from or write to the tag's memory. Authentication of a tag means that the tag proves its identity to the reader. A forged tag cannot convince the reader of its authenticity, so forgery of tags can be circumvented.

Menezes, Oorschot, and Vanstone [12] differentiate between three authentication methods: password systems (weak authentication), challenge-response authentication (strong authentication), and customized and zero-knowledge authentication. Password systems offer a weak level of security and zero-knowledge techniques are often related to "strong" mathematical problems which are very costly in calculation and implementation. So we aim for the second type, the challenge-response techniques, which are broadly used.

There are asymmetric and symmetric challenge-response techniques. The disadvantage of asymmetric authentication methods is that they are very time consuming and costly to implement in hardware. So, they are not the first choice for RFID systems. There were attempts to design resource-saving asymmetric authentication algorithms. NTRU [5] has been proposed for RFID system implementations, but it was shown to have some security weaknesses [2,11].

Symmetric methods work with one shared secret key. Authentication is done by proofing the possession of this secret key. The problem when using symmetric authentication methods is the key distribution and key management. Every update of the key has to be communicated to all participants. The compromising of only one device holding the key affects the whole system. This problems and some solutions were addressed in [12].

Symmetric authentication can be performed with encryption algorithms or can be based on keyed hash functions. Various reasons made the AES algorithm our favorite to use for the proposed authentication protocol. This encryption algorithm was chosen 2001 as encryption standard [13] and is considered to be highly secure. Furthermore, it is well suited for hardware implementations.

Protocols for symmetric challenge-response techniques based on encryption are defined in the ISO/IEC 9798-2 standard [6]. Unilateral authentication work as follows: there are two partners A and B. Both possess the same private key K. B sends a random number r_B to A. A encrypts the random number with the shared key K and sends it back to B. B proofs the result and can verify the identity (in other words the possession of K) of A.

$$A \leftarrow B: \qquad r_B \tag{1}$$
$$A \rightarrow B: \qquad E_K(r_B) \tag{2}$$

The mutual authentication protocol works similarly. B sends a random number to A. A encrypts r_B and a self-generated random number r_A with the shared key K and sends it to B. B decrypts the message and can proof if r_B is correct and gets r_A. B changes the sequence of the random numbers encrypts it with K and sends it to A. A proofs the result and verifies the identity of B.

$$A \leftarrow B: \qquad r_B \tag{3}$$
$$A \rightarrow B: \qquad E_K(r_A, r_B) \tag{4}$$
$$A \leftarrow B: \qquad E_K(r_B, r_A) \tag{5}$$

In order to minimize the power consumption and die size of the circuit, we decided to design our circuit for AES encryption only. By using modified protocols one-way authentication as well as mutual authentication can be performed, even if no AES decryption is available. Mutual authentication protocols require an additional random number generator, so they are more costly to implement.

2.3   Application Examples

Due to the key management problem, symmetric authentication methods are more suitable for closed systems. In closed systems each component can be controlled by one central instance. All devices can get their keys and key updates easily from the central control instance. In open systems, where the components can join the system unsolicited and no central control instance is available, key distribution and management is more difficult.

In airport luggage tracking systems each controlled bag can be equipped with an RFID tag and can be tracked throughout the whole airport. All assigned tag numbers are stored in a central server. In that way automated cargo and baggage transportation systems as well as security applications are possible (access control, checking if the holder of the bag is in the same plane as the luggage, etc.). Tag forgery and unauthorized access to the tag's memory should be avoided. Luggage tracking should also only be possible for authorized readers.

During transportation, RFID systems can be used to track and route goods on their way from the factory to the retailer. Here, theft and loss of goods can be rapidly detected, but the substitution with forged goods can only be avoided by using tag authentication mechanisms. Authentication of the reader could be used to prohibit unauthorized persons from spying the content of cargo. Tag memory can be used to record environmental incidents (for example, the disruption of the cold chain when transporting food). In this case, memory access must be secured by using reader authentication to prevent unauthorized memory manipulation.

Another application are car immobilizers, where symmetric authentication is already in use. In general, these implementations use proprietary encryption algorithms, which are optimized for the specific application. The security of these algorithms cannot be evaluated. Using AES would add some extra security. As a final example, for proof of origin of goods authentication is essential. In the next section we propose a method to integrate an one-way authentication protocol into existing RFID standards.

3   Security Protocol Design

In a security-enhanced RFID system, the level of security does not only rely upon the strength of the used cryptographic algorithms. The used protocols play a decisive role whether an attacker can successfully break into a system or not. Even if we use strong cryptographic algorithms, we need to ensure that the protocol is also secure. The protocol presented in this section allows the authentication of an RFID tag to a reader using the Advanced Encryption Standard (AES) [13] as the cryptographic primitive. In RFID systems, the limited computing power and low-power constraints of the tags require special considerations concerning

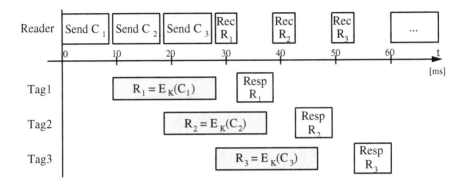

Fig. 2. Interleaved challenge-response protocol in RFID systems.

the used protocols. In addition to the available bandwidth for data transmission, attention should be paid to the compatibility to existing standards like the ISO/IEC 18000 [7] or the Electronic Product Code (EPC) [3].

The protocol is based on the unilateral authentication mechanism using random numbers presented in section 2. Integrating the presented challenge-response authentication protocol into the ISO/IEC 18000 [7] standard requires some additional considerations. In addition to the mandatory commands, which all tags must implement, custom commands can be specified. The two commands, integrated for authentication, are sending a challenge to the tag and requesting the encrypted value. These commands extend the existing standard although the basic functionality remains unchanged. Due to the low-power restrictions, the internal clock frequency of the RFID tag must be divided from 13.56 MHz to 100 kHz. The applied standard demands that a response must follow 320 μs after a request. Otherwise, the tag has to stay quiet. This available time of 32 clock cycles at a frequency of 100 kHz is not enough for encrypting a challenge using the AES algorithm.

The solution to this problem is to modify the protocol as shown in figure 2. The challenges and the responses to the tags are interleaved to each other. Normally, there are a lot of RFID tags to be authenticated in the environment of a reader. After retrieving all unique IDs of the tags using the inventory request and the anti-collision sequence, the reader sends a challenge C_1 to *Tag1*. This tag immediately starts the encryption of the challenge without sending any response. In the meanwhile, the reader sends further challenges to the tags *Tag2* and *Tag3*. They also start encrypting their challenges after reception. After finishing the encryption of $E_K(C_1)$, *Tag1* waits for the request to send the encrypted value R_1 back to the reader. When the reader has sent the three challenges, it sends a request for receiving the response from *Tag1*. The received value R_1 is verified by encrypting the challenge C_1 and comparing the result with the received value. The two other unanswered challenges are received using the same method. Then the reader starts from the beginning authenticating all other tags in the environment. This protocol was evaluated using high level models of the

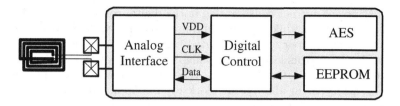

Fig. 3. Architecture of an RFID tag.

RFID communication channel and is a proof of concept for future research on authentication protocols in RFID systems.

This interleaving challenge-response protocol has the advantage that each tag has at least 18 ms (1800 clock cycles at a clock frequency of 100 kHz) time for encryption. A maximum of 50 tags can be authenticated per second. If there are only few tags in the range of a reader, the reader can decide to make breaks of at least 18 ms instead of sending interleaved requests.

4   RFID Tag Architecture

The architecture of a security-enhanced RFID tag is sketched in figure 3. It consists of four parts: analog frontend, digital controller, EEPROM, and AES module. The analog frontend is responsible for the power supply of the tag which is transmitted from the reader to the tag. Other tasks of the analog frontend are the modulation and demodulation of data and the clock recovery from the carrier frequency. The digital control unit is a finite state machine that handles communication with the reader, implements the anti-collision mechanism, and executes the commands in the protocol. Furthermore, it allows read and write access to the EEPROM and the AES module. The EEPROM stores tag-specific data like the unique ID and the cryptographic key. These data must be retained when the power supply is lost. The security-enhanced RFID tag calculates strong cryptographic authentication with an AES module which is designed for low-power requirements and low die-size restrictions. The requirements concerning power consumption and chip area and a description of the AES module are presented in the following sections.

4.1   Requirements for RFID Tag Design

In order to achieve a significant economic benefit from using RFID systems, tags will need to be priced under US\$ 0.10 [15] for simple identification tags and a little bit higher for security-enhanced tags. Additionally to the aspect of low cost, the environmental conditions play a decisive role because contactless identification must work within a distance of a few meters. The limiting factors thereby are the available power supply for the tag and the signal strength for modulation and demodulation. The available power consumption for the digital part of the RFID tag (digital controller and AES module) is amounting to 20 μA.

Estimating the current consumption of the digital controller to 5 μA, 15 μA remain for the AES module which should not exceed a chip area of 5,000 gates. Additionally, the number of authenticated tags per second is about 50. As presented in chapter 3, this leads to an available time slot of 18 ms for encrypting a 128-bit block of data. Our proposed AES architecture, which is presented in section 4.2, encrypts in about 1000 clock cycles. As a consequence, the clock frequency of the AES module can be reduced under 100 kHz. This allows to reach the ambitious power consumption goal.

4.2   AES Architecture

The Advanced Encryption Standard (AES) is a symmetric encryption algorithm which was selected in 2001 by the National Institute of Standards and Technology (NIST) as the Federal Information Processing Standard FIPS-197 [13]. It operates on blocks of data, the so called State, that have a fixed size of 128 bits. The State is organized as a matrix of four rows and four columns of bytes. The defined key lengths are 128 bits, 192 bits, or 256 bits. Our implementation uses a fixed key size of 128 bits. As most symmetric ciphers, AES encrypts an input block by applying the same round function. The ten round function iterations alter the State by applying non-linear, linear, and key-dependent transformations. Each transforms the 128-bit State into a modified 128-bit State. Every byte of the State matrix is affected by these transformations:

1. **SubBytes** substitutes each byte of the State. This operation is non-linear. It is often implemented as a table look-up. Sometimes the SubBytes transformation is called S-Box operation.
2. **ShiftRows** rotates each row of the State by an offset. The actual value of the offset equals the row index, e.g. the first row is not rotated at all; the last row is rotated three bytes to the left.
3. **MixColumns** transforms columns of the State. It is a multiplication by a constant polynomial in an extension field of $GF(2^8)$.
4. **AddRoundKey** combines the 128-bit State with a 128-bit round key by adding corresponding bits *mod* 2. This transformation corresponds to a XOR-operation of the State and the round key.

The calculation of the 128-bit round keys works by applying the KeySchedule function. The first round key is equal to the cipher key. The computation of all other round keys is based on the S-Box functionality and the Rcon operation.

AES is a flexible algorithm for hardware implementations. A large number of architectures are possible to cover the full range of applications. AES hardware implementations can be tailored for low die-size demands in embedded systems or can be optimized for high throughput in server applications. This flexibility of the AES algorithm was intended by its creators. They paid attention that the algorithm can be implemented on systems with different bus sizes. Efficient implementations are possible on 8-bit, 32-bit, 64-bit, and 128-bit platforms.

Although many AES hardware architectures have been proposed, none of the reported architectures meets the requirements of an AES module for RFID tags regarding low die-size and low power-consumption requirements. Nearly all of these architectures have GBit throughput rates as optimization goal. This is contrarious to our needs where throughput is not of concern. Only a few published AES architectures do not optimize throughput at any cost. To name some: [14,1] are FPGA implementations and [10,16] are ASIC implementations of AES which care about hardware efficiency. All these implementations do not unroll the AES rounds for sake of silicon size. The more S-Boxes are used, the less clock cycles are needed for encryption. The encryption-only AES processor of I. Verbauwhede et al. [16] is a 128-bit architecture that utilizes 32 S-Boxes. It is able to calculate one AES round in a single clock cycle. The compact 32-bit AES architecture of S. Mangard et al. in [10] is confident with four S-Boxes and takes eight cycles for one round. The FGPA implementations of N. Pramstaller et al. [14] and P. Chodowiec et al. [1] are 32-bit architectures too. They also use four S-Boxes. Four S-Boxes suit a 32-bit architecture as each S-Box substitutes 8 bits. The MixColumns operation and the ShiftRows operation are 32-bit operations too because they transform either four columns bytes or four row bytes of the AES State. The AddRoundKey operation (128-bit XOR) can also be split-up into 32-bit operations.

Implementing the AES algorithm as a 32-bit architecture allows to quarter the hardware resources compared to an 128-bit architecture [10,1]. This comes at the expense of quadrupling the time for an AES encryption. The lower amount of hardware resources has a positive side effect on the power consumption: a quarter of hardware resources consumes only a quarter of power. This is an important feature for wireless devices where the average power consumption is an even more important quality aspect than the overall energy needed to encrypt one block. The overall energy consumption of a 32-bit architecture might be worse than for 128-bit architectures. But RFID tags offer neither the silicon space nor is the electromagnetic field strong enough to power an 128-bit datapath.

The power requirements for RFID tags are even too restrictive to allow the operation of a 32-bit AES implementation. Therefore, we decided to implement the AES algorithm as an 8-bit architecture instead of a 32-bit architecture. This novel approach for a hardware implementation of the AES algorithm is motivated by two reasons. First, an 8-bit architecture allows to decrease the number of S-Boxes from four to one to save silicon resources. Second, 8-bit operations consume significantly less power than 32-bit operations do. A penalty of an 8-bit architecture is the increased number of clock cycles for encryption. In RFID authentication applications an encryption lasting for 1000 cycles does not deteriorate the authentication throughput when several tags are authenticated concurrently (see section 3).

The architecture of the proposed 8-bit AES module is depicted in figure 4. It is presumably the smallest hardware implementation of the AES algorithm. The module consists basically of three parts: a controller, RAM, and a datapath. The controller communicates with other modules on the tag to exchange data and it sequences the ten rounds of an AES encryption. Therefore, it addresses the RAM accordingly and generates control signals for the datapath. The RAM stores the 128-bit State and an 128-bit round key. These 256 bits are organized as 32 bytes to suit the intended 8-bit architecture. 32 bytes are the smallest pos-

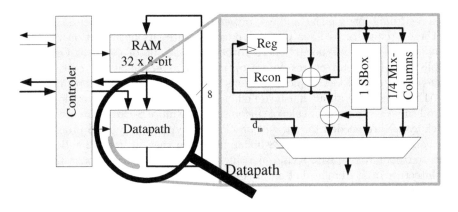

Fig. 4. Architecture of the AES module.

sible memory configuration for AES. The memory is single ported to ease silicon implementation. Modified States and calculated round keys overwrite previous values. As no spare memory is present for storing intermediate values, the controller has to assure that no State byte nor a key byte is overwritten if it is needed again during encryption. The RAM implementation is register based. It makes use of clock gating to minimize power consumption. The datapath of the AES module contains combinational logic to calculate the AES transformations *SubBytes*, *MixColumns*, and *AddRoundKey* (see figure 4). The *ShiftRows* transformation is implemented by the controller. During the execution of SubBytes the controller addresses the RAM such that the ShiftRows operation is executed.

The biggest part of the AES datapath is the S-Box which is used for the SubBytes operation. There are several options for implementing an AES S-Box. The most obvious option is a 256×8-bit ROM to implement the 8-bit table lookup. Unfortunately, ROMs do not have good properties regarding low-power design. A more appropriate option is to calculate the substitution values using combinational logic as presented in [19]. We adapted the proposed combinational S-Box by omitting the decryption circuitry to suit our encryption-only AES. One feature of this S-Box is that it can be pipelined by inserting register stages. The S-Box makes use of one pipeline stage. This shortens the critical path of the S-Box to seven XOR gates and lowers glitching probability. Moreover, the pipeline register is used as intermediate storage for a pipelined SubBytes operation: during the substitution of one byte, the next byte is read from the memory. The substituted byte is written to the current read address. By choosing the read addresses properly this procedure combines efficiently the SubBytes and the ShiftRows operation. ShiftRows degrades to mere addressing.

Another innovative solution is the calculation of the MixColumns operation. We achieved to build a submodule which calculates only one fourth of the MixColumns operation. By accessing the submodule four times a complete Mix-Columns operation for one column of the State is executed. The MixColumns operation for one column is shown in equation 6. The equation reveals that all output bytes q_i of MixColumns are calculated by the same function—just the order of the input column bytes a_i differs.

$$q(x) = a(x) \cdot c(x) = \bmod \ n(x) \tag{6}$$

$$q_0 = (a_0 \otimes \{02\}) \oplus (a_3 \otimes \{01\}) \oplus (a_2 \otimes \{01\}) \oplus (a_1 \otimes \{03\})$$
$$q_1 = (a_1 \otimes \{02\}) \oplus (a_0 \otimes \{01\}) \oplus (a_3 \otimes \{01\}) \oplus (a_2 \otimes \{03\})$$
$$q_2 = (a_2 \otimes \{02\}) \oplus (a_1 \otimes \{01\}) \oplus (a_0 \otimes \{01\}) \oplus (a_3 \otimes \{03\})$$
$$q_3 = (a_3 \otimes \{02\}) \oplus (a_2 \otimes \{01\}) \oplus (a_1 \otimes \{01\}) \oplus (a_0 \otimes \{03\}).$$

We used this property to reduce the MixColumns circuitry to one fourth of its original size. The resulting circuit can calculate one output byte in one clock cycle. The $\frac{1}{4}$-MixColumns circuit contains, besides the combinational circuit to calculate q_i, three 8-bit registers to store three input column bytes a_i. These registers have to be filled before the first output q_i can be calculated. The fourth input a_i is taken directly from the RAM. Consequent output values are calculated by shifting the RAM output value to the registers and selecting the next value from RAM. The processing of one column takes seven clock cycles. A complete MixColumns operation to transform the entire State takes 28 clock cycles. The critical path of the MixColumns circuit is even shorter than the S-Box.

Remaining components of the datapath are the submodule Rcon, some XOR gates and an 8-bit register. Rcon is a simple circuit needed for key schedule. The XOR gates are needed for round key generation and are used to combine the State with the round key during the AddRoundKey transformation. The 8-bit register is needed during key schedule for storing intermediate results.

An encryption of a plaintext block works as follows. Before encryption is started the plaintext block has to be loaded into the RAM of the AES module. In the RFID tag application, the plaintext block is the 128-bit challenge which was received from the reader. The communication between the reader and tag is byte-oriented which fits nicely into the 8-bit architecture of the AES module: every received byte can be stored in the AES module. No intermediate memory is necessary. The cryptographic key is obtained in a similar way from the tag's EEPROM. Now the AES algorithm can be executed. It starts with a modification of the State by an AddRoundKey operation using the unaltered cipher key. Ten AES rounds follow by applying the transformations SubBytes, ShiftRows, MixColumns, and AddRoundKey. Only the last round lacks the MixColumns operation. Roundkeys are calculated just in time. This is usually called on-the-fly key schedule. The round key is derived from its predecessor by using the S-Box, the Rcon, and the XOR functionality of the datapath.

5   Results

The implementation of the datapath of our AES-128 encryption design has a current consumption of 8.15 μA on a 0.35 μm CMOS process. It operates at a frequency of 100 kHz and needs 1,016 clock cycles for encryption of an 128-bit data block. The required hardware complexity is estimated to be 3,595 gate equivalents (GEs). All presented results come from simulations on transistor level. The complexity of each component is listed in table 1. Table 2 presents a comparison of our approach with the 32-bit implementation of S. Mangard et al. [10] and the 128-bit encryption-only AES processor of I. Verbauwhede et al. [16]. It can be seen that only our solution achieves the high demands for integrating cryptographic components into RFID tags. These requirements are the low power consumption and low die-size while conforming the requirements concerning encryption speed.

Table 1. Components and their complexity of the AES module.

Module/ Component	μA @100kHz	GE	Clock cycles
S-Box	0.67	395	280
MixColumns	0.41	252	288
AddRoundKey	0.53	90	144
KeySchedule	0.92	161	304
RAM	4.64	2,337	
Controller	0.98	360	
Total	**8.15**	**3,595**	**1,016**

Table 2. Comparison based on energy consumption, gate count, and clock cycles.

AES-128 Encryption	μA @100kHz	GE	Clock cycles
This work	8.15	3,628	992
Mangard [10]	47.24	10,799	64
Verbauwhede [16]	307	173K	10

6   Conclusions and Future Research

This paper presented a security-enhanced RFID system which allows the strong cryptographic authentication. With this security-enhanced RFID systems, we pave the way for new security-demanding applications and for the everyday usage of RFID technology. A symmetric challenge-response authentication protocol was proposed which was integrated into the existing ISO/IEC 18000 standard. We showed an architecture for a low-power and low die-size implementation of the AES algorithm. The AES implementation has a chip area of 3,595 gates and has a current consumption of 8.15 μA at a frequency of 100 kHz. The encryption of 128 bits requires about 1000 clock cycles.

Future work will consist in the examination of advanced authentication protocols for one-way and mutual authentication. Other authentication methods (e.g. asymmetric techniques) should be analyzed for the suitability for RFID systems and circuits can be found for this purpose. In this way, the application range for RFID systems will be pushed further.

References

1. P. Chodowiec and K. Gaj. Very Compact FPGA Implementation of the AES Algorithm. In C. D. Walter, Çetin Kaya Koç, and C. Paar, editors, *Cryptographic Hardware and Embedded Systems - CHES 2003, 5th International Workshop, Cologne, Germany, September 8-10, 2003, Proceedings*, volume 2779 of *Lecture Notes in Computer Science*, pages 319–333. Springer, 2003.
2. W. Diffie and M. Hellman. Cryptanalysis of the NTRU Signature Scheme (NSS). In *ASIACRYPT: International Conference on the Theory and Application of Cryptology*, volume 2248 of *Lecture Notes in Computer Science*. Springer, June 2001.
3. EPCglobal. 13.56 MHz ISM Band Class 1 Radio Frequency (RF) Identification Tag Interface Specification. http://www.epcglobalinc.org/, February 2003.
4. K. Finkenzeller. *RFID-Handbook*. Carl Hanser Verlag München, 2nd edition, April 2003.
5. J. Hoffstein, J. Pipher, and J. H. Silverman. NTRU: A Ring-Based Public Key Cryptosystem. In *Algorithmic Number Theory, Third International Symposium, ANTS-III, Portland, Oregon, USA, June 21-25, 1998, Proceedings*, volume 1423 of *Lecture Notes in Computer Science*, pages 267–288. Springer, 1998.
6. International Organization for Standardization. *ISO/IEC 9798-2: Information Technology - Security techniques — Entity Authentication Mechanisms Part 2: Entity authentication using symmetric techniques*. ISO/IEC, 1993.
7. International Organization for Standardization. ISO/IEC 18000-3. Information Technology AIDC Techniques — RFID for Item Management, March 2003.
8. A. Juels and R. Pappu. Squealing Euros: Privacy protection in RFID-enabled banknotes. In *Financial Cryptography, 7th International Conference, FC 2003, Guadeloupe, French West Indies, January 27-30, 2003, Revised Papers*, volume 2742 of *Lecture Notes in Computer Science*, pages 103–121. Springer, 2003.
9. A. Juels, R. L. Rivest, and M. Szydlo. The Blocker Tag: Selective Blocking of RFID Tags for Consumer Privacy. In *Proceedings of the 10th ACM Conference on Computer and Communication Security*, pages 103–111. ACM Press, 2003.
10. S. Mangard, M. Aigner, and S. Dominikus. A Highly Regular and Scalable AES Hardware Architecture. *IEEE Transactions on Computers*, 52(4):483–491, April 2003.
11. A. May. Cryptanalysis of NTRU. preprint, (unpublished), February 1999.
12. A. J. Menezes, P. C. van Oorschot, and S. A. Vanstone. *Handbook of Applied Cryptography*. CRC Press, 1997. Available online at
http://www.cacr.math.uwaterloo.ca/hac/.
13. National Institute of Standards and Technology (NIST). FIPS-197: Advanced Encryption Standard, November 2001. Available online at
http://www.itl.nist.gov/fipspubs/.
14. N. Pramstaller and J. Wolkerstorfer. An Efficient AES Implementation for Reconfigurable Devices. In *Austrochip 2003, Linz, Austria, October 1st, 2003, Proceedings*, pages 5–8, 2003.
15. S. E. Sarma, S. A. Weis, and D. W. Engels. RFID Systems and Security and Privacy Implications. In *Cryptographic Hardware and Embedded Systems - CHES 2002, 4th International Workshop, Redwood Shores, CA, USA, August 13-15, 2002, Revised Papers*, volume 2523 of *Lecture Notes in Computer Science*, pages 454–470. Springer, 2002.
16. I. Verbauwhede, P. Schaumont, and H. Kuo. Design and Performance Testing of a 2.29 Gb/s Rijndael Processor. *IEEE Journal of Solid-State Circuits*, pages 569–572, March 2003.

17. S. A. Weis. Security and Privacy in Radio-Frequency Identification Devices. Master's thesis, Massachusetts Institute of Technology, Cambridge, MA 02139, May 2003.

18. S. A. Weis, S. E. Sarma, R. L. Rivest, and D. W. Engels. Security and Privacy Aspects of Low-Cost Radio Frequency Identification Systems. In *Security in Pervasive Computing, 1st Annual Conference on Security in Pervasive Computing, Boppard, Germany, March 12-14, 2003, Revised Papers*, volume 2802 of *Lecture Notes in Computer Science*, pages 201–212. Springer, 2004.

19. J. Wolkerstorfer, E. Oswald, and M. Lamberger. An ASIC implementation of the AES SBoxes. In *Topics in Cryptology - CT-RSA 2002, The Cryptographer's Track at the RSA Conference, 2002, San Jose, CA, USA, February 18-22, 2002*, volume 2271 of *Lecture Notes in Computer Science*, pages 67–78. Springer, 2002.

TTS: High-Speed Signatures on a Low-Cost Smart Card

Bo-Yin Yang[1], Jiun-Ming Chen[2], and Yen-Hung Chen[3]

[1] Mathematics Department, Tamkang University, Tamsui, Taiwan, by@moscito.org
[2] Chinese Data Security Inc. & National Taiwan University, jmchen@math.ntu.edu.tw
[3] Comp. Sci. & Info. Eng., Nat'l Taiwan U., Taipei, Taiwan, r92014@csie.ntu.edu.tw

Abstract. TTS is a genre of multivariate digital signature schemes first proposed in 2002. Its public map is composed of two affine maps sandwiching a *Tame Map*, which is a map invertible through serial substitution and solving linear equations. We implement the signing and key generation operations for a TTS instance with 20-byte hashes and 28-byte signatures, on popular extant microcontroller cores compatible to the Intel 8051. Our tests demonstrates that TTS can be even faster than SFLASH^{v2}, which is known for its celerity. The sample scheme TTS$(20, 28)$ is fast enough for practical deployment on a low-end 8051-based embedded device. A really low-end part like a stock Intel 8051AH running at 3.57 MHz can sign in just 170ms. A better 8051-compatible chip will take a lot less time.

Security requirements today demand on-card key generation, and the big public keys of a multivariate PKC create a storage problem. TTS is unusual in that public keys can be synthesized on-card at a decent pace for block-by-block output, using some minimal information kept on-card. Since this does not take much more time than the I/O needed to transmit the public key to a reader, we can avoid holding the entire public key in the limited memory of a smart card. We show that this to be a gain for multivariate PKC's with relatively few terms per central equation. The literature is not rich in this kind of detailed description of an implementation of a signature scheme — capable of fast on-card public key generation, on a low-cost smart card without a co-processor, and at NESSIE-approved security levels.

We look into other theory issues like safeguarding against side-channel attacks, and using unusual techniques for linear algebra under serious space restrictions, which may help implementations of other multivariate PKC's such as SFLASH.

Keywords: Multivariate public-key cryptosystem, finite field, smart card, 8051.

1   Introduction

For most adopters of Public-Key Infrastructure, the quarter-century-old RSA still remains the public-key cryptosystem of choice. We see that all is not perfect:

> RSA is too slow to be used on a smart card and this keeps the security achieved by smart card solutions insufficient: unable to implement a real public key signature. ... N. Courtois *et al* ([1], 2003).

This must be taken in context as a historical perspective: Acceptable signing speed on smart cards with reasonably long RSA keys has become feasible around the turn of the millennium, especially with special-purpose hardware co-processors.

M. Joye and J.-J. Quisquater (Eds.): CHES 2004, LNCS 3156, pp. 371–385, 2004.

However, cost of deployment is still an obstacle, and there is clearly room for improvement: Chips must get even faster and cheaper, or the algorithms need revamping.

Traditionally, Public-Key Infrastructure (PKI) implementers stick to well-established Public-Key Cryptosystems (PKC) based on RSA, occasionally ECC. However these are comparatively slow, so cryptologists sought faster alternatives, among which are the "multivariate PKC", cryptosystems that use substitution into quadratic polynomials as a public map. The currently best known scheme of this type is SFLASH^{v2} ([15]), a derivative ([14]) of the prototype C^* ([9], broken in 1995 by [12]). Multivariate cryptosystems (more literature on the extended family: [3,5,7,8]) are usually conceded to be faster than RSA and other traditional alternatives with a large algebraic structure. Unfortunately, the only such scheme to get a mention in the recently announced NESSIE final recommendations ([11]) is SFLASH^{v2}, and only grudgingly:

... not recommended for general use but this signature scheme is very efficient on low cost smart cards, where the size of the public key is not a constraint.

Granted NESSIE was more concerned about SFLASH's untried security than size of its public keys, but still this rather sells SFLASH^{v2} and other multivariate PKC's short.

We aim to provide another example of how a multivariate PKC can provide superior performance for less. Our sample scheme, unlike the C^{*-}-derived SFLASH^{v2}, is a digital signature scheme from the different family of TTS ([2,17]). Techniques shown here are applicable to other multivariate PKC's, however. Our test results on 8051-compatible microcontrollers are tabulated along with data published by the NESSIE project ([11]) and other recent sources (e.g. [1]). It showcases TTS well:

Table 1. 8051-compatible results for various digital signature schemes (* = with co-processor)

Scheme	Platform (T number)	Clock	Pr. Key	Code	RAM	Signature
TTS $(20, 28)$	Intel 8032AH (12)	3.57 MHz	1.4 kB	1.4 kB	128 B	144 ms
	Intel 8051AH (12)			1.6 kB		170 ms
	Winbond W77E58 (4)					64 ms
ESIGN	Intel 8051AH (12)		336 B	3.0 kB	800 B	12.0 s
SFLASH^{v2}			2.4 kB	3.3 kB	344 B	1.07 s
	Infineon SLE66 (2)	10 MHz				59 ms
RSA-PSS (1024 bits)			320 B	N/A	≥ 1kB	many s
	NEC μPD789828*(12)	40 MHz				100 ms
		5 MHz				230 ms
RSA-2048	Infineon SLE66*(2)		640 B			1.1 s
ECDSA-191		10 MHz	24 B			180 ms
NTRU-Sign	Philips 8051 (6)	16 MHz	100 B	5 kB	N/A	160 ms

Special Note: 8051-compatible parts running at the same nominal clock frequency have widely divergent speeds on the same program. On every 8051-compatible part, a majority of common instructions execute in the same amount of time, which is called the *instruction cycle* for this part. Every instruction executes in an integral number of instruction cycles. The ratio of one instruction cycle to one clock cycle is called the "T number". So a Siemens-Infineon SLE66 is up to six and usually 4-5 times faster than a 8051 at the same clock rate. Some platforms also have extras goodies including cryptographic co-processors, so some care is needed in interpreting the tabulated results.

Sometimes $TTS(20, 28)$ need to hash just once while ESIGN or $SFLASH^{v2}$, repeated hashes must be taken. Without worrying about details, all told $TTS(20, 28)$ is 6 times faster on the same resources than $SFLASH^{v2}$, which in turn was noted for being faster without a coprocessor than the traditional alternatives with a coprocessor.

This paper details an implementation of $TTS(20, 28)$ on an 8051 compatible microcontroller. Sec. 2 describes the mathematics. Sec. 3 summarizes the 8051 platform (with a more complete review provided in Appendix A). Sec. 4 and in particular Secs. 4.4–4.6 give the innards of the algorithm. Sec. 5 discusses technical issues, including side-channel attack concerns. Some unusual maneuvers in linear algebra help to manage the large amounts of data efficiently during key generation on RAM-poor smart cards. We also explain why TTS can sign *and* generate keys quickly and efficiently. The real-time on-card public key generation capability ameliorates a problem affecting most multivariates *even when the keys are not stored on-card*, i.e., the large public key makes on-card key generation frequently infeasible and key management difficult (cf. [16]).

2 Principles of TTS and Our Sample Scheme $TTS(20, 28)$

In a multivariate PKC, usually the public map is a composition $V = \phi_3 \circ \phi_2 \circ \phi_1$ with both $\phi_1 : \mathbf{w} \mapsto \mathbf{x} = \mathsf{M}_1\mathbf{w} + \mathbf{c}_1$ and $\phi_3 : \mathbf{y} \mapsto \mathbf{z} = \mathsf{M}_3\mathbf{y} + \mathbf{c}_3$ being affine and invertible. All arithmetic is done over a finite field (the *base field*) which in TTS is $K = \mathrm{GF}(2^8)$.

A digital signature scheme is considered to be in the TTS family ([2]) if ϕ_2 is a **tame map**, a polynomial map *with relatively few terms in the equations, easily invertible through serial substitution or solution of linear equations, but without a low degree explicit inverse*. Tame maps extend the concept of *Tame Transformations* from algebraic geometry ([10]), and may be said to combine the traits of triangular constructs (introduced to cryptography in [5], cf. also [6,17]) and Oil-and-Vinegar ([7,8]).

We refer the reader to [2] for some background, and [17] for a topical assessment of TTS. We will use for illustration the TTS instance exhibited in [17] with the following central map $\phi_2 : \mathbf{x} = (x_0, x_1, \ldots, x_{27}) \mapsto \mathbf{y} = (y_8, y_9, \ldots, y_{27})$:

$$y_i = x_i + \textstyle\sum_{j=1}^{7} p_{ij}x_jx_{8+(i+j \bmod 9)}, \; i = 8 \cdots 16;$$

$$\begin{aligned} y_{17} = x_{17} &+ p_{17,1}x_1x_6 + p_{17,2}x_2x_5 + p_{17,3}x_3x_4 \\ &+ p_{17,4}x_9x_{16} + p_{17,5}x_{10}x_{15} + p_{17,6}x_{11}x_{14} + p_{17,7}x_{12}x_{13}; \end{aligned}$$

$$\begin{aligned} y_{18} = x_{18} &+ p_{18,1}x_2x_7 + p_{18,2}x_3x_6 + p_{18,3}x_4x_5 \\ &+ p_{18,4}x_{10}x_{17} + p_{18,5}x_{11}x_{16} + p_{18,6}x_{12}x_{15} + p_{18,7}x_{13}x_{14}; \end{aligned}$$

$$\begin{aligned} y_i = x_i &+ p_{i,0}x_{i-11}x_{i-9} + \textstyle\sum_{j=19}^{i} p_{i,j-18} \, x_{2(i-j)} \, x_j \\ &+ \textstyle\sum_{j=i+1}^{27} p_{i,j-18} \, x_{i-j+19} \, x_j, \; i = 19 \cdots 27. \end{aligned}$$

This central map works with 20-byte hashes and 28-byte signatures, and the corresponding TTS instance will be henceforth called $TTS(20, 28)$.

To Generate Keys: Assign non-zero random values in $K = \mathrm{GF}(2^8)$ to parameters p_{ij}; generate random nonsingular matrices $\mathsf{M}_1 \in K^{28 \times 28}$ and $\mathsf{M}_3 \in K^{20 \times 20}$ (usually via LU decomposition) and vector $\mathbf{c}_1 \in K^{28}$. Compose $V = \phi_3 \circ \phi_2 \circ \phi_1$; assign $\mathbf{c}_3 \in K^{20}$ so that V has no constant part. Save quadratic and linear coefficients of V as public key (8680 bytes). Find M_1^{-1}, M_3^{-1}; save them with $\mathbf{c}_1$, $\mathbf{c}_3$, and the parameters p_{ij} as the private key (1399 bytes).

To Sign: From the message M, first take its digest $\mathbf{z} = H(M) \in K^{20}$, then compute $\mathbf{y} = \mathsf{M}_3^{-1}(\mathbf{z} - \mathbf{c}_3)$, then compute a possible $\mathbf{x} \in \phi_2^{-1}(\mathbf{y})$ as follows:

1. Randomly assign $x_1, \ldots, x_7$ and try to solve for x_8 to x_{16} in the first 9 equations. Since the determinant (for any $x_2 \cdots x_7$) of this system is a degree-9 polynomial in x_1, there can only be at most 9 choices of x_1 out of 256 to make the first system degenerate. Keep trying until we find a solution.
2. Solve serially for x_{17} and x_{18} using the next two equations (y_{17} and y_{18}).
3. Assign a random x_0 and try to solve for x_{19} through x_{27} from the last 9 equations. Again, at most 9 values of x_0 can make the determinant of the system zero. So keep trying new values of x_0 until a solution is found.

Our desired signature is $\mathbf{w} = \mathsf{M}_1^{-1}(\mathbf{x} - \mathbf{c}_1)$. Release $(M, \mathbf{w})$.

To Verify: On receiving $(M, \mathbf{w})$, compute $\mathbf{z} = H(M)$ and match with $V(\mathbf{w})$.

3   Summary of the 8051 Hardware Platform

The reader may find the details of the key-generation and signing processes (particularly those of Sec. 4.5) tedious, but all the contortions are necessitated by the fact that EEPROM memory cannot be reliably read from soon after it is written to. This is not uncommon in the embedded realm. This section provides an executive summary for those unfamiliar with the 8051 chip. Those who are already familiar with the 8051 can skip the rest of this section. Those interested in such things can please refer to the appendix.

Memory: The 8051 has 128 bytes of fast directly-addressable RAM on-board, called **data**. Some **data** locations are used as architectural stack and registers including the important registers R0 and R1. The rest hold important system and user data.

Most extant 8051-compatibles have 128 bytes more fast RAM onboard, only addressable indirectly through the registers R0 and R1. As the **data** can also be accessed this way, all 256 bytes are together called **idata**. In theory the 8051 can address 64kB of immutable memory (**code**) and 64kB of off-board RAM or EEPROM (**xdata**), both indirectly using the DPTR register. The **code** cannot be written to and can be accessed with an offset for table lookups. In practice usually all external memory are accessed identically. Accessing **code** and **xdata** takes twice as much time as **data** and **idata** besides being harder to set up for.

EEPROM and flash memory are accessed just like RAM except that *one must wait, usually for a few milliseconds, before accessing a recently written EEPROM location*. A write followed too soon by another access results in an error.

ALU: The Arithmetic-Logic Unit has many specialized registers (the most important being the accumulator A and the Data Pointer DPTR) and instructions. There is an integer multiply and divide, and instruction to increment – but not decrement – DPTR, so large arrays are best accessed in increasing order. Each instructions execute serially in a fixed number of **instruction cycles** (cf. paragraph after Tab. 1).

Resources: I/O is through specialized latches, and *communication to a computer or other device must be done through a reader unit, often attached to a PC on a USB port. The access is serial and slow say 1 kB/s*. Hardware random-number generation can be added cheaply to most cards. Cheap smart cards today have 4 kB or more in ROM and EEPROM, and a little RAM – sometimes 256B, frequently 0.5kB, sometimes 1 kB. 1.5kB or more RAM is mostly available in heavyweight cards.

4   Actual Performance and Implementation Details

We recompiled portable C code for TTS$(20, 28)$ (cf. [17]), with C51, a popular embedded compiler. A few routines were rewritten in assembly. Test results from standard development kits are given in Sec. 4.2 and implementation details in Sec. 4.4–4.6.

4.1   Hardware Resource Requirements

As mentioned in Appendix A.3, a low-end card can either just sign or do both key generation and signing. We list our requirements in RAM (**data**, **idata** and external RAM or **xdata**, see Appendix A.1), EEPROM, total ROM, etc.:

To Sign: 128 bytes of RAM (19 bytes of **data** for state, 109 more bytes in **data/idata** or **xdata** for temporary storage), 1.3kB of EEPROM for private keys, 1.6kB of further **code** space (0.8kB of program, 0.8kB of tables). For controllers with 256 bytes of on-board RAM (**idata**), it is an option to keep all the data for the Gaussian elimination in the **idata**, which means shorter code (no need to move things between **idata** and **xdata**) at 1.4kB (0.2kB less) and at least a 12% speed up. Since we must have some RAM to put the matrix for the elimination stage, a plain-vanilla Intel 8051 will be assumed to have least 128 bytes of **xdata** RAM storage.

Both To Sign and To Generate Keys: There are two choices:

- On EEPROM-poor cards, we do not store the entire public key. During setup only the private key and some critical intermediate data are generated and stored in EEPROM, enough that chunks of the public key can be computed and output on-the-fly as requested. This requires 2.7 kB of EEPROM (1399B in the private key plus 1212B in intermediate data, plus some left-over wasted space) plus 4.2 kB more **code** space (in ROM or EEPROM) is required. There is 3.8 kB in the program for both key generation and signing, 0.4 kB in subsidiary I/O, including 0.8kB for tables as above.
- We can compute and store the entire public key for later retrieval. This takes 11.3kB of EEPROM space, plus 4.2 kB more ROM or EEPROM **code** space.

In both cases we need 128 bytes in **data**, **idata** or **xdata** storage. If we need block-writes to EEPROM or do block-outputs from the smart card, we will also need 128 more bytes of RAM for buffer. When we can afford to usually we do the entire Gaussian elimination from **idata**. PC access provided through USB-port device.

4.2   Performance Data and Brief Description of Programs

The signing portion of the program is straightforward and can be implemented straight out of Sec. 2. *On average, signing takes about 170ms on a 3.57MHz stock Intel 8051AH (a really low-end part).* Every other part is faster than the 8051AH. The same code running on a 3.57MHz ("4T") WinBond W77E58 only takes 64ms.

For reference, of the 170ms average time taken by the signing operation on the Intel 8031/32 at 3.57MHz is divided as follows: The ϕ_3 portion takes 34ms, ϕ_2 71ms, and ϕ_1 65ms. On a Winbond W77E58, the times are 13ms, 27ms, 24ms respectively. *Using 10MHz parts, the speedup is almost linear. The W77E58 takes about 23ms to sign and the Intel 8032AH takes 61ms — 51ms if we run the entire elimination from* **idata***.*

Once we get to 16MHz or faster clocks, some instructions require extra *instruction cycles* to execute, and I/O times start to dominate, so the scaling is a lot less than linear.

The process for key generation is a lot more complicated and slower than signing. When the smart card is initialized, we must first generate M_1, M_1^{-1}, M_3, M_3^{-1} via LU decomposition, store to EEPROM, then generate $(p_{ij})_{8 \le i \le 27}$ and c_1, compute c_3 and store everything in EEPROM along the way. Note that $c_3 = M_3\,(\phi_2(c_1))$ and hence:

$$(c_3)_k = \sum_{\ell=n-m}^{n-1} \left[(M_3)_{k,(\ell-n+m)} \left((c_1)_\ell + \sum_{p\,x_\alpha x_\beta \text{ in } y_\ell} p\,(c_1)_\alpha (c_1)_\beta \right) \right]. \quad (1)$$

The sum is over each term $p\,x_\alpha x_\beta$ in the equation for y_ℓ. We may end the setup process here, and the generated information is enough to compute the coefficients of the public key polynomials, 20 at a time. In this mode, the card awaits an appropriate outside input before signing or computing and emitting the public key in small chunks on-the-fly.

Setting up on an Intel 8032AH at 3.57MHz (computing the private key and intermediate data) takes 7.7 seconds, including a little error checking. The process takes 3.6 seconds on a 3.57MHz Winbond W77E58.

The rest of public-key generation is to compute for each (i, j) the coefficients of $w_i w_j$ or w_i^2 or w_i in z_k for every k at once. To show that this is possible, we will follow Imai and Matsumoto ([9]) and divide the coefficients involved in each public key polynomial into linear, square, and crossterm portions as follows:

$$z_k = \sum_i P_{ik} w_i + \sum_i Q_{ik} w_i^2 + \sum_{i>j} R_{ijk} w_i w_j. \quad (2)$$

The coefficients $(P_{ik}, Q_{ik}, R_{ijk})$ are related to M_1, M_3, c_1, and the parameters $(p_{ij})_{8 \le i \le 27}$ as follows, where each sum is over the terms $p\,x_\alpha x_\beta$ in the equation for y_ℓ:

$$P_{ik} = \sum_{\ell=n-m}^{n-1} \left[(M_3)_{k,(\ell-n+m)} \left((M_1)_{\ell i} + \sum_{p\,x_\alpha x_\beta \text{ in } y_\ell} p\,((M_1)_{\alpha i}(c_1)_\beta + (c_1)_\alpha (M_1)_{\beta i}) \right) \right] (3)$$

$$Q_{ik} = \sum_{\ell=n-m}^{n-1} \left[(M_3)_{k,(\ell-n+m)} \left(\sum_{p\,x_\alpha x_\beta \text{ in } y_\ell} p\,(M_1)_{\alpha i}(M_1)_{\beta i} \right) \right] \quad (4)$$

$$R_{ijk} = \sum_{\ell=n-m}^{n-1} \left[(M_3)_{k,(\ell-n+m)} \left(\sum_{p\,x_\alpha x_\beta \text{ in } y_\ell} p\,((M_1)_{\alpha i}(M_1)_{\beta j} + (M_1)_{\alpha j}(M_1)_{\beta i}) \right) \right] (5)$$

Here $m = 20$, $n = 28$. For a smart card equipped with a lot of EEPROM or flash, we need not compute and emit the public key piecemeal. It is possible to compute everything right there and write everything to EEPROM, to be read at a later time.

A 3.57MHz Intel 8051 or 8032AH averages about 150ms to generate a 20-byte block of the public key from the intermediate data and signal that it is ready to send. On a 3.57MHz Winbond W77E58 with sufficient storage, generating the entire public key takes 33 seconds. It takes some 15 seconds to transmit everything from card to PC.

4.3   Finite Field Arithmetic and Other Details

As in any other multivariate PKC, we need to represent each element of $GF(2^8)$ as an integer between 0 and 255 (an unsigned char). We choose the "Standard" representation used by AES ([4]), but we could choose any encoding as long as addition can be represented as a bitwise xor.

A standard way of implementing finite field multiplication is to choose a fixed primitive element[1] $g \in GF(2^8)$ and store logarithm and exponential look-up tables in base g, intending to multiply non-zero x and y as $xy = g^{(\log_g x + \log_g y) \bmod 255}$. We will do a lot of manipulations of data in *log-form*, which means we represent the zero of the field $GF(2^8)$ by the byte 0, and any other field element a by the unique positive integer $x \leq 255$ that satisfies $a = g^x$. *Note: 1 is represented as g^{255}, not g^0.*

In implementing the signing portion of the algorithm, we need the following data in ROM: 256-byte log-table in base g; 512-byte table of exponentiation $(x \mapsto g^x)$, this can be shortened to 256 bytes at a roughly 15% speed penalty.

The private key comprises the matrices $(M_1^T)^{-1}$ and $(M_3^T)^{-1}$, parameters (p_{ij}) of the central map, and the vectors c_1, c_3. We store everything except the vectors c_1 and c_3 in $\log_g$-form, and the matrices column-first (as indicated by the transposed notation).

The intermediate key-generation data are M_1^T, M_3^T (in column-first, $\log_g$-form), and a componentwise log of c_1. The public key consists of coefficients (P_{ik}), (Q_{ik}), $(R_{ijk})_{i>j}$, with each block arranged in order of increasing i, j, then k.

4.4   The Signing Process

The actual signing program operates on a 20-byte array z in **idata** in three stages, corresponding to ϕ_1^{-1}, ϕ_2^{-1}, and ϕ_3^{-1}. Due to the amount of array access in the Gaussian elimination, ϕ_2^{-1} takes most of the time. If we put the entire system matrix in **idata** we can save at least 10 percent upwards of running time, but most often we forego that and do it mostly from **xdata** due to memory resource problems.

1. Do $(\phi_3)^{-1}$, which is essentially a matrix multiplication, as follows:
    a) Zero out a 20-byte area y and replace z by z', the componentwise log of $c_3 + z$;
    b) looping over $i = 19, 18 \cdots 0$ and do the following loop if $z_i' \neq 0$:
    c) Looping over $j = 19 \cdots 0$, when $(M_3)_{ji} \neq 0$, add (xor) $g^{(z_i' + \log_g (M_3)_{ji}) \bmod 255}$ into y_{j+8}. **Note:** M_3 is stored in log-form and transposed so that it can be accessed sequentially, and we can compute $(R + A)$ mod 255 in only two instructions: add A,R (add register R to the accumulator A) then adc A,#0 (add the carry from the last add into accumulator).
    The inner loop of this routine reads coefficients off a table, multiplies to a variable, then adds them to different components of a vector (cf. also Sec. 5.3).
2. Do $(\phi_2)^{-1}$, which is performed as follows:
    a) For $i = 1 \cdots 7$, generate randomly and save (in an **idata** array) $\log_g x_i$, again with the proviso that 0 represents 0, not 1 which is represented by 255.
    b) Establish in a 90-byte block BA (in **xdata** or **idata**) of RAM the first linear system to be solved for $x_8, \ldots, x_{16}$ by doing the following for $i = 8 \cdots 16$:
       i. The constant of each equation location $(BA[10(i-8)+9])$ is filled with y_i.

---

[1] We chose as g the canonical generator of the AES field representation.

    ii. Looping over $j = 1..7$, insert into the location corresponding to the coefficient of $x_{(i+j\,(\mathrm{mod}\ 9))+8}$ (location $\mathtt{BA}[10(i-8)+(i+j\,(\mathrm{mod}\ 9))]$).

    iii. $\mathtt{xor\ BA}[10(i-8)+(i+1\,(\mathrm{mod}\ 9))]$ with 1.

    iv. Let $\mathtt{BA}[10(i-8)+(i+8\,(\mathrm{mod}\ 9))] = \mathtt{BA}[10(i-8)+(i+9\,(\mathrm{mod}\ 9))] = 0$.

 c) Run elimination on 9 variables to get $x_8, \ldots, x_{16}$, then find x_{17} and x_{18} by solving for them in the next two equations (all x_i will be stored in log-form).

 d) Establish another system of equations in $\mathtt{BA}$ by looping over $i = 19 \cdots 27$:

    i. Insert $y_i + p_{i0}x_{i-11}x_{i-9}$ as the constant term (location $\mathtt{BA}[10(i-19)+9]$).

    ii. Looping over $j = 0 \cdots i - 19$, let $\mathtt{BA}[10(i-19)+j] = p_{i,j+1}x_{2(i-j-19)}$.

    iii. Looping over $j = i - 19 \cdots 8$, let $\mathtt{BA}[10(i-19)+j] = p_{i,j+1}x_{i-j}$.

    iv. $\mathtt{xor\ BA}[10(i-8)+(i+1\,(\mathrm{mod}\ 9))]$ with 1.

 e) Run elimination on 9 variables to obtain $x_{19}, \ldots, x_{27}$ (again in log-form).

3. Do $(\phi_1)^{-1}$, another matrix multiplication like $(\phi_3)^{-1}$, with different parameters.

4.5   Key Generation, First Half: Generating M_1, M_3, and Their Inverses

The following routine computes and stores M_1^T, $(M_1^T)^{-1}$, M_3^T, $(M_3^T)^{-1}$, (p_{ij}) for $8 \leq i \leq 18$, $1 \leq j \leq 6$ and $19 \leq i \leq 27$, $0 \leq j \leq 9$, c_1, $\log_g c_1$, and c_3. Total EEPROM space required is 2768 bytes, with 1399 bytes in private keys $((M_1^T)^{-1}, (M_3^T)^{-1}$, the (p_{ij}), c_1, $c_3)$ and 1212 bytes of intermediate data to be used to produce the public keys. There are 157 bytes used and erased. No more RAM than the 256 bytes of **idata** is needed; in fact, only 128 bytes are necessary if a write buffer is not needed. Of course, extra RAM helps. Recall that matrices M_1, M_1^{-1}, M_3, M_3^{-1} are stored transposed and in log-form (cf. Sec. 4.3) for convenience.

1. Generate matrices M_1 and $(M_1)^{-1}$ via LU decomposition.

 a) Generate and write to EEPROM entries (in log-form) of the diagonal matrix D_1 (28 non-zero bytes), the lower triangular matrix L_1 ($28 \times 27/2 = 378$ bytes, also in log-form), and the upper triangular matrix U_1 (same as above), and do so in the area from the 1569th to 2352th bytes from the beginning (hence, leaving the first 1568 bytes empty). The entries of L and U are generated in an unusual format. We line L up column-first, but U will be in *column-first but reverse order*, i.e.: $L_{10}, L_{20}, \ldots, L_{n-1,0}, L_{21}, \ldots, L_{n-1,1}, \ldots, L_{n-1,n-2}$ and $U_{n-2,n-1}, \ldots, U_{0,n-1}, U_{n-3,n-2}, \ldots, U_{0,n-2}, \ldots, U_{23}, U_{13}, U_{12}$.

 b) Invert D_1, L_1, U_1 and write to EEPROM (in the first 784 bytes). Inverting D_1 is easy. We invert L_1 into L_1^{-1} (stored in the same format) as follows:

    i. Repeat (ii.–v.) over $i = 1, 2, \ldots, n - 1$:

    ii. Read $[(L_1)_{i,i-1}, \ldots, (L_1)_{n-1,i-1}]$ from **xdata** into $[z_i, \ldots, z_n]$ in **idata**.

    iii. For each $j = i, \ldots, n - 1$ where $z_j \neq 0$, replace z_j by $(\log_g z_j)$ and do:

    iv. For each $k = j + 1, \ldots, n - 1$ such that $L_{kj} \neq 0$, add $g^{m+L_{kj}}$ to z_k.

    v. Now $[z_i, \ldots, z_n]$ is the column $[\log_g(L_1^{-1})_{i,i-1}, \ldots, \log_g(L_1^{-1})_{n-1,i-1}]$. Write to EEPROM, or (for parts with special EEPROM/flash writing rules) copy to a 128-byte buffer and block-write only if the buffer is full.

    The same subroutine can invert U_1 into U_1^{-1} in the same inverted column order.

 c) Compute $M_1^{-1} = U_1^{-1}D_1^{-1}L_1^{-1}$ and write to EEPROM in the next 784 bytes:

    i. Read $[\log_g((D_1^{-1})_{jj})]$ into array $[d_j]$ in **idata**; repeat (ii.–v.) for $i < n$.

  ii. Zero out z_0 to z_{i-1} (array $z_0, \ldots, z_{n-1}$ is in **idata**); let $z_i = d_j$; for $i+1 \leq j \leq n-1$ let $z_j = \left(d_j + \log_g(L_1^{-1})_{ji}\right)$ mod 255. Note (cf. 1b) that $\log(L_1^{-1})_{ji}$ was stored serially.

  iii. Looping over $j = i, i+1, \ldots, n-1$, do the following:

  iv. For $k = 0, \ldots, j-1$, add $g^{(z_j + \log_g(U_1^{-1})_{kj}) \bmod 255}$ into z_k. Note that U_1^{-1} is in reverse order. After the k-loop, replace z_j by g^{z_j}.

  v. Now (end of j-loop) the $[z_j]$ array holds the i-th column of M_1. Take the componentwise log, then write appropriately into EEPROM (cf. 1b).

  Note that we used n instead of 28 because the same routines are used for M_3.

 d) Erase the first 784 bytes, the memory block used for D_1^{-1}, L_1^{-1}, U_1^{-1}.

 e) Compute (and write out to the freshly erased block of 784 bytes) $\mathsf{M}_1 = L_1 D_1 U_1$.

  i. Read $[\log_g((D_1)_{jj})]$ into array $[d_j]$ in **idata**; repeat (ii.–v.) for $i < n$.

  ii. Read $\left(\log_g(U_1)_{ji} + d_j\right)$ mod 255 to z_j (in **idata**) for $j = 0 \cdots i - 1$.

  iii. Let $z_i = d_i$. For $j = 0 \cdots i$, let $y_i = g^{z_i}$, and zero out $y_{i+1}, \ldots, y_{n-1}$.

  iv. Looping over $0 \leq j \leq i, j \leq k < n$, add $g^{(z_k + \log_g(L_1)_{kj}) \bmod 255}$ into y_k.

  v. The $(\log y_k)$ is the i-th column of $\log_g \mathsf{M}_1$, write to EEPROM.

 f) Erase the 784-byte EEPROM block used for D_1, L_1, U_1.

We should conclude with 1568 bytes of data and 784 freshly erased bytes.

2. Generate M_3 and $(\mathsf{M}_3)^{-1}$ as above, reusing the memory from Step 1. We should have written 800 bytes of data and have 400 recently erased bytes.

3. Generate and store (p_{ij}) for $8 \leq i \leq 18$, $1 \leq j \leq 7$ and $19 \leq i \leq 27$, $0 \leq j \leq 9$ (167 bytes), reusing the memory from Step 2.

4. Generate $\mathbf{c}_1$ (28 bytes) and store in space left from Step 2. Compute $\mathbf{c}_3$ (20 bytes):

 a) Storing (in **idata**) in the arrays $\mathbf{c}$ and $\mathbf{y}$ the componentwise log of $\mathbf{c}_1$.

 b) Reading from the parameter table, compute $\phi_2(\mathbf{c}_1)$ by looping over all indices $i = 8 \cdots 27$, adding each cross-term into the appropriate y_i.

 c) Write the $\log(\mathbf{c}_1)_i$ to EEPROM. Take the logs of y_i; jump to the multiplication routine in Sec. 4.2. The result $(\mathbf{c}_3)$ is written to EEPROM. We are done.

4.6 Key Generation, Second Half: Computing and Outputting the Public Key

After the process of Sec. 4.5, we can generate the public key in units of 20 bytes (see Sec. 4.2). Generating the public key takes a long time, but the routine itself is simpler:

Generating R_{ijk}: It is more convenient to compute first the coefficients of $w_i w_j$ in y_k:

1. Read in the i-th and j-th columns of $\log_g \mathsf{M}_1$ and place in the arrays $\mathbf{c}$ and $\mathbf{c}'$.
2. Zero out the array $\mathbf{z}$ and loop over each cross-term $p\, x_\alpha x_\beta$ in the equation for y_i (reading off parameter table) thusly:
3. Compute $p\, [(\mathsf{M}_1)_{\alpha i}(\mathsf{M}_1)_{\beta j} + (\mathsf{M}_1)_{\alpha j}(\mathsf{M}_1)_{\beta i}]$ via $\log_g \left(g^{c_\alpha + c'_\beta} + g^{c'_\alpha + c_\beta}\right)$, adding $\log_g p$ (read off the parameter table) and exponentiating. Add to z_i.
4. We now have the coefficient of $x_i x_j$ in y_k. Take the logs and multiply by M_3 and jump to the matrix multiplication routine (Sec. 4.2) to get R_{ijk} for each k.

Generating P_{ik}: As above, except for initializing the array $\mathbf{z}$ to $[(\mathsf{M}_1)_{ki}]_{k=8\cdots27}$ instead of zeroing out $\mathbf{z}$, and reading in $\mathbf{c}_1$ and the i-th column of M_1 instead of the i-th and j-th columns of M_1.

Generating Q_{ik}: Like the above, but we only need to read a single column of the M_1, and it is faster because there is one fewer add and one fewer multiply in Eq. 4.

After each block of 20 is produced, write it to EEPROM or accumulate for buffered output as needed. Our test code outputs every 6 blocks to get max throughput.

5   Discussions and Conclusion

We discuss some issues germane to our study including side channel attack considerations, optimization, and possible changes to the scheme to suit smart cards better.

5.1   Why Does TTS Have Faster Key Generation?

The state-of-the-art in key generation for multivariate PKC's is probably the kind of procedures as given by C. Wolf ([16]). At least, we can find no better, and he managed to save 30% of running time from previous algorithms. However Wolf states, and it seems commonly agreed to, that computations of the public polynomial using interpolation for large field multivariates, i.e. HFE ([13]) or C^*-derivatives where the private map really operates on some googol-sized field, take time proportional to n^6. A cursory look at Eqs. 3–5 will reveal that the number of multiplications in key generation is about n^4 (really m^2n^2) times the average number of terms in an equation in ϕ_2, hence $O(n^4)$. So we expect key generation in TTS to run at about a few hundred times the speed that SFLASH might need if they use the same dimensions.

Timings given in [2,17] support this hypothesis. We do not claim to be anywhere close to as good 8051 programmers as the authors of [1], but the factor of n^4 vs. n^6 gives an edge that makes on-card key generation passably quick as opposed to snail-like. In general, a multivariate PKC can be called *tame-like* ([17]) if its central map has relatively few terms per equation and has a fast inverse. Sec. 4.6 and Eqs. 3–5 demonstrate tame-like-ness are useful for a smart card.

5.2   Side Channel Attack Considerations

In [1], the authors discuss defending against a possible differential-power attacks. The structure of SFLASH^{v2} is somewhat simpler, but we can take similar precautions against DPA probes to those in [1]. The steps for a DPA-safe signing are:

1. Start out with hash value $\mathbf{z}$. Take a random vector $\mathbf{z}' \in K^m$. Compute $\mathbf{z}'' = \mathbf{z} + \mathbf{z}'$.
2. Compute $\mathbf{y}' = (\mathsf{M}_3)^{-1}(\mathbf{z}' - \mathbf{c}_3)$ and $\mathbf{y}'' = (\mathsf{M}_3)^{-1}\mathbf{z}''$. We see that $\mathbf{y} = \mathbf{y}' + \mathbf{y}''$.
3. Take random bytes x_i', x_i'' for $i = 0 \cdots 7$. Loop until the systems are solvable.
4. Construct linear systems as in Sec. 4.4, except that we use twice as large a RAM buffer, put in two systems: One filled in using the x_i' and y_i', one with the x_i'' and y_i''. Note: Step 2(b)iii of Sec. 4.4 only needs to be performed on one of the matrices.
5. Run a "conjoined Gaussian" with the two matrices. A key operation is division by the sum of the two coefficients at the pivot position. If they are $c_{ii}' \neq c_{ii}''$, then we can achieve division by the pivot coefficient $(c_{ii}' + c_{ii}'')$ through dividing successively with c_{ii}' and then by $(1 + c_{ii}''/c_{ii}')$. For 9×9 matrices, this means slightly less than triple the number of multiplications and is time-consuming, but we eventually come down to $(x_8' \cdots x_{16}', x_8'' \cdots x_{16}'')$, where $x_i' + x_i'' = x_i$.
6. For $i = 17$ and 18, do the following so that $x_i = x_i' + x_i''$.

$$x_i' = y_i' + \sum_{px_\alpha x_\beta \text{ in } y_i} p \cdot (x_\alpha' x_\beta' + x_\alpha'' x_\beta''); \quad x_i'' = y_i'' + \sum_{px_\alpha x_\beta \text{ in } y_i} p \cdot (x_\alpha'' x_\beta' + x_\alpha' x_\beta''). \quad (6)$$

7. Similarly for $i = 19 \cdots 27$ we do the "conjoined Gaussian". We have found $\mathbf{x}'$ and $\mathbf{x}''$ that sum to the $\mathbf{x}$ of Sec. 2 at about one-quarter speed.
8. Compute $\mathbf{w}' = (\mathsf{M}_1)^{-1}\mathbf{x}'$ and $\mathbf{w}'' = (\mathsf{M}_1)^{-1}(\mathbf{x}'' - \mathbf{c}_1)$. Output $\mathbf{w} = \mathbf{w}' + \mathbf{w}''$.

Since $\mathrm{TTS}(20, 28)$, like SFLASH^{v2} uses each byte of the entire key continuously, it should be as safe as SFLASH^{v2} under the same attacks. The signing code expands to about 3.2 kB, and the speed is between a third and a quarter of what it was (still ok). This is obviously not optimal programming and we should be able to optimize it better.

5.3 Optimization Concerns

Since we are only doing proof-of-concept work we used C51-compiled code with only a few key routines hand-coded 8051 assembly. This is not the optimal performance available from our hardware, but is a lot better than using just C51, and saves many man-hours compared to doing assembly from the ground up. We feel that we are not giving up much in the way of performance because this is common practice in software design. A local expert on the 8051 offered his opinion that we might be able to improve it by a factor of two in pure assembly. However, the quaint, quirky 8051 architecture severely restricts our options. There is only so much possible with our limited resources, especially the single pointer into **xdata**. Some notes on optimization possibilities:

- Of particularly note is the idiosyncratic ways the arrays were arranged in memory. *We do not have hard proofs but believe that this arrangement is already correctly optimized under the circumstances.*
- If the μC has access to 1.5kB of **xdata** RAM, all the temporary data can stay in RAM and we need not erase from EEPROM at all during key generation. Even 1 kB RAM would make life easier.
- The `movx A,@Ri` command that use the output latch P0 for the high byte of the address line and the register R0 or R1 for the low byte is seldom used, because I/O lines from the outside often get in the way, changing the value of the latch when it shouldn't. With custom solutions, it is possible to have programs up to 20% faster by using these specialized commands.
- An $n \mapsto \log_g(1 + g^n)$ table can help. Let this table be E. When computing R_{ijk} (Sec. 4.6), we need to do $\left[\log_g\left(g^{c_\alpha + c'_\beta} + g^{c'_\alpha + c_\beta}\right) + \log_g p\right]$ mod 255. Instead, we can save lookups via $\left[(c_\alpha + c'_\beta) + \mathrm{E}[c'_\alpha + c_\beta - (c_\alpha + c'_\beta)] + \log_g p\right]$ mod 255.
- We never really rewrote our programs for parts with dual DPTR's. With proper utilization, this is said to increase the speed by some 25% for array-heavy code.
- With the base field $K = \mathrm{GF}(2^7)$, the signing can run with the exponential table in **idata** (did the designer of SFLASH think of this?). More extremely, with $K = \mathrm{GF}(2^6)$, both the log and the exponential table can fit into the **idata**. We can change to a $(\mathrm{GF}(2^7))^{28} \mapsto (\mathrm{GF}(2^7))^{36}$ version of TTS for speed if key size and extra RAM storage is not a problem. Preliminary tests show that it is about 13% faster.

5.4 Conclusion

We believe that our test result shows the TTS family of multivariate signature schemes in general and $\mathrm{TTS}(20, 28)$ in particular to be very speedy. Not only is it fast, but it also consumes little enough resources that it definitely merits further attention as an on-card solution. The family of schemes has great potential for use in low-cost smart cards, especially those without a cryptographic coprocessor.

We note that TTS$(20, 28)$ by current estimates should be at least as secure as RSA-1024, and TTS$(24, 32)$ at least as secure to RSA-1536 (cf. [17]). Even if this estimate is slightly off, the speed of the implementations should still make TTS quite useful for smart cards. Furthermore, TTS is clearly an extensible system and we did an implementation for the following central map ([17])

$$y_i = x_i + \sum_{j=1}^{7} p_{ij} x_j x_{8+(i+j+1 \bmod 10)}, \ i = 8 \cdots 17;$$

$$y_i = x_i + p_{i1} x_{i-17} x_{i-14} + p_{i2} x_{i-16} x_{i-15} + p_{i3} x_{i-10} x_{i-1} + p_{i4} x_{i-9} x_{i-2}$$
$$+ p_{i5} x_{i-8} x_{i-3} + p_{i6} x_{i-7} x_{i-4} + p_{i7} x_{i-6} x_{i-5}, \ i = 18 \cdots 21;$$

$$y_i = x_i + p_{i,0} x_{i-10} x_{i-14} + \sum_{j=22}^{i} p_{i,j-21} \ x_{2(i-j)} \ x_j$$
$$+ \sum_{j=i+1}^{31} p_{i,j-21} \ x_{i-j+21} \ x_j, \ i = 22 \cdots 31.$$

This scheme has $m = 24$ (192-bit hashes) and $n = 32$. We tabulate our new test results with the old. Again, only the $i8032$AH code ran the elimination entirely in **idata**.

As we observed in Sec. 5.3, we expect to improve on our work still. All in all, we think that we have shown TTS and similar variants are worth more attention.

Table 2. Summary for TTS on a 8051

Scheme	Controller	PrivKey Length	Signing Time	Signing Code	Keygen Time	Keygen Code	Extra EEPROM	Setup Time
TTS$(20, 28)$	$i8032$AH	1399 B	144ms	1.5 kB	78.5 s	4.2 kB	1.2 kB	7.7s
	$i8051$AH		170ms	1.6kB				
	W77E58		60ms		38.3 s			3.6s
TTS$(24, 32)$	$i8032$AH	1534 B	191ms	1.5 kB	134 s		1.6kB	11.7s
	$i8051$AH		227ms	1.6kB				
	W77E58		85ms		65.2 s			5.4s

Acknowledgments. We thank Messrs. Po-Yi Huang and Sam Tsai of Solutioninside Inc. for technical assistance, and to Messrs. Bo-Yuan Peng and Hsu-Cheng Tsai of National Taiwan University for commentary and discussion. We thank the anonymous referees for their suggestions and constructive criticism. The first author would also like to thank his beloved Ping.

References

1. M. Akkar, N. Courtois, R. Duteuil, and L. Goubin, *A Fast and Secure Implementation of SFLASH*, PKC 2003, LNCS v. 2567, pp. 267–278.

2. J.-M. Chen and B.-Y. Yang, *A More Secure and Efficacious TTS Scheme*, ICISC '03, LNCS v. 2971, pp. 320-338; full version at http://eprint.iacr.org/2003/160.

3. D. Coppersmith, J. Stern, and S. Vaudenay, *The Security of the Birational Permutation Signature Schemes*, Journal of Cryptology, 10(3), 1997, pp. 207–221.

4. J. Daemen and V. Rijmen, *The Design of Rijndael, AES - The Advanced Encryption Standard*. Springer-Verlag, 2002.
5. H. Fell and W. Diffie, *Analysis of a Public Key Approach Based on Polynomial Substitution*, CRYPTO'85, LNCS v. 218, pp. 340–349.
6. L. Goubin and N. Courtois, *Cryptanalysis of the TTM Cryptosystem*, ASIACRYPT 2000, LNCS v. 1976, pp. 44–57.
7. A. Kipnis, J. Patarin, and L. Goubin, *Unbalanced Oil and Vinegar Signature Schemes*, CRYPTO'99, LNCS v. 1592, pp. 206–222.
8. A. Kipnis and A. Shamir, *Cryptanalysis of the Oil and Vinegar Signature Scheme*, CRYPTO'98, LNCS v. 1462, pp. 257–266.
9. T. Matsumoto and H. Imai, *Public Quadratic Polynomial-Tuples for Efficient Signature-Verification and Message-Encryption*, EUROCRYPT'88, LNCS v. 330, pp. 419–453.
10. T. Moh, *A Public Key System with Signature and Master Key Functions*, Communications in Algebra, 27 (1999), pp. 2207–2222.
11. The NESSIE project webpage: http://www.cryptonessie.org.
12. J. Patarin, *Cryptanalysis of the Matsumoto and Imai Public Key Scheme of Eurocrypt'88*, CRYPTO'95, LNCS v. 963, pp. 248–261.
13. J. Patarin, *Hidden Fields Equations (HFE) and Isomorphisms of Polynomials (IP): Two New Families of Asymmetric Algorithms*, EUROCRYPT'96, LNCS v. 1070, pp. 33–48.
14. J. Patarin, L. Goubin, and N. Courtois, C^*_{-+} *and HM: Variations Around Two Schemes of T. Matsumoto and H. Imai*, ASIACRYPT'98, LNCS v. 1514, pp. 35–49.
15. J. Patarin, N. Courtois, and L. Goubin, *FLASH, a Fast Multivariate Signature Algorithm*, CT-RSA 2001, LNCS v. 2020, pp. 298–307. Updated version available at [11].
16. C. Wolf, *Efficient Public Key Generation for Multivariate Cryptosystems*, preprint, available at http://eprint.iacr.org/2003/089/.
17. B.-Y. Yang and J.-M. Chen, *Rank Attacks and Defence in Tame-Like Multivariate PKC's*, see http://eprint.iacr.org/2004/061.

A   Architecture of 8051-Based Smart Cards

We summarize the specifics of our hardware platforms for implementation and testing. Some discussion about clock vs. actual execution speed can be found in Sec. 1 (following Tab. 372).

A.1   Storage Areas on an 8051-Based Smart Card

The general structure of an 8051-based 8-bit microcontroller (μC) core is the same across implementations. The chip usually has a CPU portion plus some extra memory. On a 8051-like device, we have the following different locations for data storage:

data. The 128 bytes of on-chip high-speed RAM directly addressable by the 8051 core in one instruction cycle. Sometimes referred to as "Register RAM" because in effect they are registers, like the zeroth page of the 6502 and other 8-bit CPUs. A peculiarity of the 8051 instruction set is that some **data** can be accessed bitwise as flags. This saves valuable **data** space as well as instructions.

idata. On-chip high-speed RAM that may be accessed in indirect address mode through a byte-long pointer (either of the special registers R0 or R1) in one instruction cycle. The **data** can also be accessed this way and is considered part of the **idata**. Almost every 8051-compatibles has the 128 extra bytes of **idata** for 256 bytes total.

code. ROM, not writable. May be only read indirectly through the Data Pointer (DPTR) register with a fixed latency (normally 2 instruction cycles on a cheap part) via a special movc command. An 8051-like μC can address up to 64 kB of **code** ROM.

xdata. Off-chip read-write memory, accessible only via the movx command, with indirection through either DPTR or a combination of the I/O port register P0 and either of the special register R0 and R1. Normally movx takes 2 instruction cycles, but on a high-end part there may be banks of memory with different latency, and a special register to control the access time.

One expect **xdata** to be RAM, and because the movx/movc commands both set signals lines, effectively adding an extra address line, an 8051-like part can theoretically address 64kB of ROM (**code**) and 64kB of RAM (**xdata**) for 128kB memory. However, when the μC does not use more than 64kB total, as a rule the control lines are wired together for convenience[2], and code and data are read identically. Another important point is that read-write memory can be EEPROM or flash memory as well as RAM:

- RAM for a μC is usually costly SRAM. In theory there may be as much as 64kB, but there is often only 256B, seldom more than 1kB and almost never more than 2kB. *A smart card intended for RSA or ECC work will always have at least 1 kB (usually 1.5kB), because there is a lot of data and co-processors also need memory.*
- We will use EEPROM and flash memory as synonyms like most people, although EEPROM can often be written to much faster and far more times than flash.
  A μC may have no EEPROM at all or as much as 64kB. Reading EEPROM is just like reading off-chip RAM, but completing a write into one EEPROM location takes about $50\mu s$ and erasing (resetting it into a writable state) takes much longer, about 5ms per access. Often erasure and sometimes writes must be by *lines*, which are units of access that may be 8 to 128 bytes each. Control signals from the EEPROM can be polled via I/O port latches to tell the programmer whether the EEPROM is ready for writing or successfully written. *After an EEPROM address is written to but before the requisite amount of time (some 100 instruction cycles or more) has elapsed, reading that location generates unpredictable results.*

There are several modes of writing into EEPROM/flash, and a given part normally does only one. There are 8051 parts with safeguards against loss of power and a block-write operation with a same latency of 5ms per 128-byte block, but these tend to be very expensive parts. In parts without the power-failure guard and block-writing features, EEPROM is essentially accessed like RAM, but the program needs to check manually the signal lines. If you are safety-minded, you check first, write, then keep checking the signals to make sure that it is done properly. A more cavalier designer would go about his business after the write is issued, but would presumably do some error-checking.

A.2   The 8051-Based Parts We Tested and Their Characteristics

Intel 8051AH. One of the original MCS-51 NMOS single-chip 8-bit microcontroller parts, with 32 I/O lines, 2 Timers/Counters, 5 Interrupts/2 Priority Levels, and 128 bytes on-chip RAM (i.e. no extra **idata**). It has 2 kB of on-chip ROM.

---

[2] movx also can often be faster than movc on high-end parts for a speed advantage.

Intel 8032AH. A stripped-down 8052; just like the i8051 except for having 3 Timers (Counters), 6 Interrupts/4 priority levels, no ROM and 128B more RAM on-chip.

Winbond W77E58. A more upscale CMOS part, with 36 I/O lines, 3 Timers/Counters, 12 Interrupts/2 priority levels, and 256 bytes on-chip RAM. 32kB ROM built-in. Its big pluses are: Dual Data Pointers (so that using two off-chip memory blocks is a lot faster), 1kB extra on-chip SRAM (appropriately latched for optimal movx access), and the fact that it is "4T", i.e., many frequently used instructions takes 4 clock cycles to execute, so it is up to 3 times faster at the same nominal clock.

Dual Data Pointers is a common goodie in high-end 8051-like parts. By toggling a special flag bit, the programmer can switch between two possible DPTR's, which means that the μC can quickly access two different look-up tables, among other things.

A.3   Random Number Generation and Other I/O Concerns on an 8051

For modern-day PKI applications, security concerns dictate that keys be generated on-card. The private key should stay there, never read by any human. The public key can be released off-card to a PC or other device when the appropriate commands are issued. A hardware random-number generator must be accessible on-card by the CPU for this purpose. If only signing is needed, then the RNG does not need to be all that fast, because with each signing action only around 8 bytes of entropy is needed. During key generation, it is better to have a faster RNG; it is feasible that a cryptography-grade software PRNG be used, seeded with a hardware randomness source. It would be slow, but not overly so. According to local vendors, in practice the *marginal cost of adding a hardware RNG is very low, essentially nil.*

Access to random number generation hardware is either implemented via an I/O port read or as special memory whence a random byte can always be read. Usually it is as easy as using a single movx instruction (takes about 4 instruction cycles including setup). In our tests, the sampling of a random byte is implemented as a separate "black-box" routine in assembly that returns a value after about 10 instruction cycles, because we wish to account for slower hardware RNG implementations.

For signing, it is assumed that only the hash value of a message needs to be passed into a smart card. For key generation, the smart card needs to be able to save the key to EEPROM (flash memory) or spitted out of the card in blocks of an appropriate size. In general, the smart card is wired up to transmit data only in blocks of 128 or 256 bytes (at most) at a time, and the transfer rate is about 9600 baud, which makes for an effective bandwidth of at most 1 kB/s.

XTR Implementation on Reconfigurable Hardware

Eric Peeters[1], Michael Neve[1*], and Mathieu Ciet[2]

[1] UCL Crypto Group
Place du Levant, 3
1348 Louvain-La-Neuve, Belgium.
{peeters, mneve}@dice.ucl.ac.be − http://www.dice.ucl.ac.be/crypto
[2] INNOVA CARD,
Avenue Coriandre, 13 600 La Ciotat, France.
mathieu.ciet@innova-card.com

Abstract. Recently, Lenstra and Verheul proposed an efficient cryptosystem called XTR. This system represents elements of $\mathbb{F}_{p^6}^*$ with order dividing $p^2 - p + 1$ by their trace over $\mathbb{F}_{p^2}$. Compared with the usual representation, this one achieves a ratio of three between security size and manipulated data. Consequently very promising performance compared with RSA and ECC are expected.

In this paper, we are dealing with hardware implementation of XTR, and more precisely with Field Programmable Gate Array (FPGA). The intrinsic parallelism of such a device is combined with efficient modular multiplication algorithms to obtain effective implementation(s) of XTR with respect to time and area.

We also compare our implementations with hardware implementations of RSA and ECC. This shows that XTR achieves a very high level of speed with small area requirements: an XTR exponentiation is carried out in less than 0.21 ms at a frequency beyond 150 MHz.

Keywords: Public key cryptosystem, XTR, reconfigurable hardware, efficient implementation.

1 Introduction and Basics

Nowadays more and more applications need security components. However, these requirements should not interfere with the performance, otherwise security would be disregarded. Ideally, the best solution is when security does not penalize the application. However, two ways are possible to achieve this characteristic: design efficient primitive algorithms and/or try to find fast and optimized implementations of existing algorithms.

XTR, first presented in [12], has been designed as a classical discrete logarithm (crypto)system, see also [11]. However, element representation is done in a special form that allows efficient computation and small communications. This

---

★ Supported by the FRIA Belgium fund.

system also has the advantage of very efficient parameter generations. As shown in [26], the performance of XTR is competitive with RSA in software implementations, see also [7] for a performance comparison of XTR and an alternative compression method proposed in [22]. Mainly two kinds of implementation have to be distinguished: software and hardware. The latter generally allows a very high level of performance since "dedicated" circuits are developed. Moreover it also provides designers with a large array of implementation strategies. This is particularly true for the size of multiplier, possible parallel processing, stages of pipelining, and algorithm strategies. In this paper, we propose an efficient hardware implementation of this primitive that can be used for asymmetric digital signature, key exchange and asymmetric encryption. To our knowledge this is the first hardware implementation of XTR.

In 1994, Smith and Skinner introduced the LUC public key cryptosystem [24] based on Lucas function. This is an analog to discrete logarithm over $\mathbb{F}_{p^2}^*$ with elements of order $p+1$ represented by their trace over $\mathbb{F}_p$. More recently, Gong and Harn [6] used a similar idea with elements in $\mathbb{F}_{p^3}^*$ of order p^2+p+1. Finally, Lentra and Verheul proposed XTR in [12], that represents elements of $\mathbb{F}_{p^6}^*$ with order (dividing) p^2-p+1 by their trace over $\mathbb{F}_{p^2}$. These representations induce security over the fields $\mathbb{F}_{p^i}^*$, with $i=2,3,6$ with respect to LUC, Gong-Harn or XTR cryptosystems, whereas numbers manipulated are over $\mathbb{F}_{p^2}$ for XTR or $\mathbb{F}_p$ for the others. XTR is the most efficient out of the three since it allows a reduction factor of 3 between size of security and size of manipulated numbers.

Parameter p is chosen as a prime number. Another condition for security requirements is that there exists a sufficiently large prime number q that divides p^2-p+1. Typically, p is chosen as a 160-bit integer whereas q is a 170-bit integer. With these parameters, XTR security is considered as "equivalent" to RSA security with 1024-bit modulus or an elliptic curve cryptosystem (ECC) based on 160-bit field. The parameter p is also chosen to be equivalent to 2 modulo 3. In this case, $\mathbb{F}_{p^2}$ is isomorphic to $\mathbb{F}_p[X]/(X^2+X+1)$. If α denotes the root of (X^2+X+1), then (α, α^2) is a normal basis of $\mathbb{F}_{p^2}$ over $\mathbb{F}_p$. Finally, any element of $\mathbb{F}_{p^2}$ can be represented as (x_1, x_2) with $x_1, x_2 \in \mathbb{F}_p$.

XTR operations are performed over $\mathbb{F}_{p^2}$. This is achieved by representing elements of the subgroup of $\mathbb{F}_{p^6}^*$ of order q (dividing p^2-p+1), generated by g, by their trace over $\mathbb{F}_{p^2}$. Trace over $\mathbb{F}_{p^2}$ of an element is just the sum of its conjugates. Let a be an element of $< g >$, then $\mathrm{Tr}(a) := \mathrm{Tr}_{\mathbb{F}_{p^6}/\mathbb{F}_{p^2}}(a) = a + a^{p^2} + a^{p^4}$ and $\mathrm{Tr}(a) \in \mathbb{F}_{p^2}$.

Let x and y be two elements of $\mathbb{F}_{p^2}$ represented respectively by (x_1, x_2) and (y_1, y_2), then it is shown in [12, Lem. 2.1.1] that

1. x^p is represented by (x_2, x_1) and this way computing x^p from x is obtained by permuting elements representing x,
2. x^2 is represented by $(x_2(x_2 - 2x_1), x_1(x_1 - 2x_2))$ and this way computing x^2 is done with two multiplications in $\mathbb{F}_p$,
3. $x \cdot y$ is represented by $(x_2y_2 - x_1y_1 - x_2y_1, x_1y_1 - x_1y_2 - x_2y_1)$ or by $(x_1y_1 + 2x_2y_2 - (x_1+x_2)(y_1+y_2), 2x_1y_1 + x_2y_2 - (x_1+x_2)(y_1+y_2))$ and this way

the product of two $\mathbb{F}_{p^2}$-elements is obtained through three multiplications in $\mathbb{F}_p$.

4. $x \cdot z - y \cdot z^p$ is represented by $(z_1(y_1 - x_2 - y_2) + z_2(x_2 - x_1 + y_2), z_1(x_1 - x_2 - y_1) + z_2(y_2 - x_1 + y_1))$ and this way this special operation on $\mathbb{F}_{p^2}$-elements is obtained through four multiplications in $\mathbb{F}_p$.

In the remainder of this paper, we follow the notation used in [12,13,14,15,26]. We denote $\mathrm{Tr}(g)$ by c and for any integer k, $\mathrm{Tr}(g^k)$ by c_k. The basic operation with XTR is the analog to exponentiation, *i.e.* from an integer k and a subgroup element g of $\mathbb{F}_{p^6}^*$, computing $\mathrm{Tr}(g^k)$. This is performed in an efficient way by using formulæ from [13, Cor. 2.3.3] quoted below:

1. $c_{2n} = c_n^2 - 2c_n^p$; it is obtained with two multiplications in $\mathbb{F}_p$.
2. $c_{n+2} = c \cdot c_{n+1} - c^p \cdot c_n + c_{n-1}$; it is obtained with four multiplications in $\mathbb{F}_p$.
3. $c_{2n-1} = c_{n-1} \cdot c_n - c^p \cdot c_n^p + c_{n+1}^p$; it is obtained with four multiplications in $\mathbb{F}_p$.
4. $c_{2n+1} = c_{n+1} \cdot c_n - c \cdot c_n^p + c_{n-1}^p$; it is obtained with four multiplications in $\mathbb{F}_p$.

With the previous formulæ an XTR exponentiation is carried out using Algorithm 1.1 from [13].

Algorithm 1.1 Computation of $S_n(c)$ given n and c, from [13, Algorithm 2.3.5]

INPUT: $n = \sum_{j=0}^r n_j 2^j$ and c
OUTPUT: $S_n(c) = (c_{n-1}, c_n, c_{n+1})$

if $n < 0$ then apply this algorithm to $-n$ and c, then use negative result.
if $n = 0$ then $S_0(c) \leftarrow (c^p, 3, c)$.
if $n = 1$ then $S_1(c) \leftarrow (3, c, c^2 - 2c^p)$.
if $n = 2$ then use formulæ from App. A and $S_1(c)$ to compute c_3.
else $\overline{S}_0(c) \leftarrow S_1(c)$ and $\overline{m} \leftarrow n$.
    if $\overline{m}$ is even then $\overline{m} \leftarrow \overline{m} - 1$.
    $m \leftarrow \dfrac{\overline{m} - 1}{2}$, $k = 1$,
    $\overline{S}_k(c) \leftarrow S_3(c)$ with formulæ in App. A.
    $m = \sum_{j=0}^r m_j 2^j$ with $m_j \in \{0, 1\}$ and $m_r = 1$.
    for j from $r - 1$ to 0 do
        if $m_j = 0$ then compute $\overline{S}_{2k}(c)$ from $\overline{S}_k(c)$
            (using formulæ from App. A).
        if $m_j = 1$ then compute $\overline{S}_{2k+1}(c)$ from $\overline{S}_k(c)$
            (using formulæ from App. A).
        $k \leftarrow 2k + m_j$
    if n is even then use $S_{\overline{m}}(c)$ to compute $S_{\overline{m}+1}(c)$ and $\overline{m} \leftarrow \overline{m} + 1$.
return $S_n(c) = S_{\overline{m}}(c)$

We can first remark that computing $\overline{S}_{2k}(c)$ or $\overline{S}_{2k+1}(c)$ is done exactly in the same manner. More importantly, triplet representing $\overline{S}_{2k}(c)$ and $\overline{S}_{2k+1}(c)$

can be calculated *independently*. This is one of the very useful characteristic of XTR that allows us to reach a very high speed performance in our hardware implementation.

This paper is organized as follows. Next section deals with modular product evaluation. A new algorithm, of independent interest, using a look-up table is presented together with an algorithm proposed by Koç and Hung [9]. Based on these two algorithms, Section 3 presents the main results of this paper: implementation choices and performance obtained to compute an XTR exponentiation. We also make comparison between hardware implementations of XTR and other cryptosystems like RSA and ECC. Finally, we conclude in Section 4.

2   Algorithms: Implementation Options

As already shown in Section 1.1, XTR exponentiation is done with a very uniform set of operations. Contrary to classical exponentiation where a 'square-and-multiply' algorithm is used, the only changes at each loop of XTR are the inputs. According to the bit of the exponent expressed as binary expansion, $\overline{S}_{2k}(c)$ or $\overline{S}_{2k+1}(c)$ are computed from $\overline{S}_k(c)$. Details of performed operations over $\mathbb{F}_p$ are given in Appendix A.

Costly operations are products of elements. This can be done using the Koç and Hung algorithm from [9]. An alternative is simply to use a look-up table.

2.1   Modular Multiplication in Hardware

Let A and B be two integers. The product of A and B cannot be achieved in one single step without a big loss in timing performance and in consumed hardware resources (area). Thus this product is usually obtained by iteratively accumulating partial products $a_i B$. This type of multiplier is also called *scaling accumulator* or *shift-and-add* method. One of the advantages is that only one single adder is reused for all the multiplication steps.

Unfortunately, when large numbers have to be manipulated, typically 1024-bit with RSA, the important length of the carry chain may become an issue. This is especially true when using reconfigurable hardware where the length of fast carry chains is limited to the size of columns. An alternative is the use of *redundant representations, i.e. carry-save representations*. This eliminates the carry propagation delay. The delay of a carry-save adder (CSA) is independent of the length of operands.

Many different algorithms to compute modular multiplication using the *shift-and-add* technique exist in the literature [2,4,17,21,23]. Most of them suggest interleaving the reduction step with the accumulating one in order to save hardware resources and computation time. The usual principle is to compute or estimate the quotient $Q = \lfloor U/p \rfloor$ and then subtract the required amount from the intermediate result.

2.2   Modular Multiplication Using Look-Up Table

As aforementioned, redundant representations can lead to very good timing performances. Moreover, to obtain a light hardware, we have chosen to base the multiplication on a scaling accumulator. In order to prevent the growth in length of the temporary value of the product, the addition steps are interleaved with the reduction ones.

Let p be a prime of l bits, such as $2^{l-1} < p < 2^l$. Let A and B be two integers, $0 \leq A, B < p$. Then, the modular multiplication of A and B can simply be written as

$$A.B \bmod p = \left(\sum_i (a_i.B.2^i \bmod p) \right) \bmod p$$

$$= (a_{l-1}.B.2^{l-1} \bmod p + \ldots) \bmod p$$

$$= \left(((\ldots (((a_{l-1}.B \bmod p).2 + a_{l-2}.B) \bmod p).2 \right.$$

$$\left. + \ldots) \bmod p).2 + a_0.B \right) \bmod p$$

This suggests the successive reduction of the temporary value in the case of 'left-to-right' multiplication. Our fairly simple idea is based on the following observation: reduction can be carried out using a look-up table.

If S and C denote the redundant representation, the three most significant bits (MSB) of S and C are extracted and added together. The corresponding reduced number is then chosen among the precalculated values. All the $2^{3+1} - 1 = 15$ possible cases are stored in memory. The reduced number is then added with the two MSB-free values, pre-multiplied by 2 before being re-used in the multiplication loop. The next partial product $a_i B$ is also added providing a new S and C pair of redundant representation.

The operation is repeated until all bits of A have been covered. Eventually the values are processed one last time, but without new partial product input. This extra step guarantees the sum of the redundant vectors to be lower than $2p$. After the step -1, the result then requires at most one final reduction. This can be simply proven by the observation that after step 0: $S, C < 2^{l-2}$. After the shift and the addition with the feedback of the residues: $S + C < 2^l + 2p$. Since $2^l < 2p$, the following relation holds: $S + C < 4p$. Finally, dividing the result by 2 gives $R < 2p$. Algorithm 2.1 gives a detailed description.

2.3   Modular Multiplication with Sign Estimation Technique

Another type of algorithm (more advanced) was proposed by Koç and Hung in [9]. Once again, it interleaves the reduction step with the addition of the partial product and the intermediate result is stored in redundant representation.

This algorithm is based on the following clever idea: the sign of the number represented by the carry-sum pair can be evaluated and used to add/subtract a multiple of the modulus in order to keep the intermediate result within two

---

Algorithm 2.1 Algorithm for computing modular multiplication

INPUT: $0 < A, B < p$ and $2^{l-1} < p < 2^l$
OUTPUT: $R = AB \bmod p$

$S_l := 0$, $C_l := 0$, $a_{-1} := 0$.
for i **from** $l - 1$ **to** -1 **do**
   $(S_i', C_i') := 2(S_{i+1} \bmod 2^{l-2}) + 2(C_{i+1} \bmod 2^{l-2}) + a_i B$.
   $(S_i, C_i) := S_i' + C_i' + 2(S_{i+1} \operatorname{div} 2^{l-2} + C_{i+1} \operatorname{div} 2^{l-2}).2^{l-2} \bmod p$.
$R = (S_{-1} + C_{-1})/2$.
if $R > p$ **then** $R := R - p$.
return R.

Algorithm 2.2 Algorithm from [9], computing modular multiplication

INPUT: $0 < A, B < p$ and $2^{l-1} < p < 2^l$
OUTPUT: $R = AB \bmod p$

$p' = 8p$, $S := 0$, $C := 0$
for i **from** $l - 1$ **to** -3 **do** .
  if $ES(S, C) = (+)$ **then** $(S, C) := 2S + 2C + a_i B - p'$.
  else if $ES(S, C) = (-)$ **then** $(S, C) := 2S + 2C + a_i B + p'$.
  else $(S, C) := 2S + 2C + a_i B$.
  loop invariant: $S + C \in \left[-\frac{3p'}{4}, \frac{7p'}{8} \right]$.
$R := S + C$.
if $R < 0$ **then** $R := R + p'$.
return $R/8$.

---

boundaries. This is done by $ES(S, C)$. The sign estimation requires to add the 5 MSB of the two vectors S and C.

The skeleton is given in Algorithm 2.2 and we refer the interested reader to [9] for further details.

3 Implementation Results

3.1 Methodology

After having introduced a new algorithm for modular multiplication using look-up table in the intermediate reductions and having recalled the Koç and Hung algorithm, let us now consider the subject of this paper: XTR implementation. In this section, the global approach of the design is discussed and two architectures are presented. Implementation results and performances are given as well. Particular considerations about scalability and portability conclude the section.

One of our purposes for implementing XTR architectures on reconfigurable hardware is to achieve a well-balanced trade-off between hardware size and frequency. Nevertheless, particular care has been taken to keep the architectures open to all kinds of FPGAs. This is the reason why some available features have not been used, *e.g.* internal multipliers. This way, designs can be directly synthesized, whatever the device target.

Even if our architecture is more general than an FPGA oriented implementation, we decide to adopt the classical design methodology described in [25]. The authors introduced the concept of hardware efficiency which could be represented as the ratio *Nbr. of registers / Nbr. of LUTs*. To achieve a high level of sub-pipelining, this ratio must be as close as possible to one. This was presented in the view of designing efficient implementation of symmetric ciphers but remains partially true for general designs, at least it suggests a method. And while implementing our design, we tried to use this concept to reach high clock frequency. Implementation results appear in Section 3.

As aforementioned, the 'parallel characteristic' of XTR is obvious. Indeed, each component of $\overline{S}_n(c)$, with $n = 4k$ or $4k+1$, can be computed independently. As an illustration, if we consider elliptic curve cryptosystems point addition or doubling, many dependencies exist during computation, see [1]. This issue is removed using the Montgomery ladder principle, see for an overview [8]. Moreover each element of $\mathbb{F}_{p^2}^*$ is represented as a couple. Each component of the couple is evaluated at the same time *and* independently. Then computations for the α and α^2 components are similar and can thus be executed separately. This means that $\overline{S}_n(c)$ is represented by 6 components that can be evaluated independently. A closer look shows that the computation of c_{4k+1} (and/or c_{4k+3}) is composed of two parts alike, with a final addition. Hence it is possible to process one step of the encryption at once in parallel with *eight independent* processes.

Furthermore, operations are quite similar. A generic cell can easily be derived to design a generic process unit able to perform the encryption in a sequential mode, at a lighter hardware cost. This also underlined the flexibility of design allowed by XTR.

Parallel designs are presented underneath. The general layout of both architectures is as follows. A 160-bit shift register containing n produces the MSB m on each iteration 1.1. With respect to this bit, different multiplexors forward the data to the inputs of the corresponding processing units. Each of them computes its data and returns the results to the multiplexors, for the next iterations.

The core of the process unit is the modular multiplier. It is preceded by some logic dealing with the preliminary additions and subtractions. Its result is stored in a shift-register.

3.2   Architectures of a Process Unit

The internal structures of Koç and Hung algorithm and ours are displayed in Fig. 1. Our look-up table based algorithm is centered around two CSA taking as input the partial product $a_i B$, the $(l - 2)$-bit truncated result vectors and the reduced values based on the 3 most significant bits. The originality of this method is due to the modular reduction technique. Just recall the Algorithm 2.1: the most significant bits are extracted and added together in order to keep the intermediate values in fixed boundaries. According to the initial values ($S_l = C_l = 0$), the utmost limits are $0 \leq S_i, C_i < 2^{l+1}$. The 15 possible values for

$$(S_{i+1} \text{ div } 2^{l-2} + C_{i+1} \text{ div } 2^{l-2}).2^{l-2} \bmod p \qquad (1)$$

are precalculated according to p and stored in the memory (denoted M in the figure). Both 3-bit MSB are added together in order to produce 4-bit address. The memory can thus be mapped by the use of l LUT. Throughout each iteration of the multiplication, a new partial product is inserted and the feedback values must therefore be doubled.

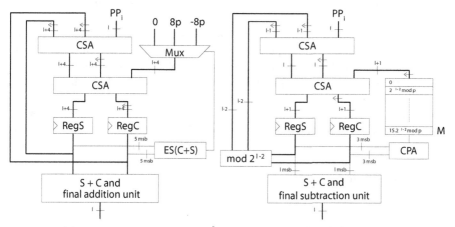

(a) Implementation of Koç and Hung algorithm and (b) of ours.

Fig. 1. The two modular multiplication algorithms.

As previously explained, one final iteration without inserting a new partial product ensures the final result to be under $2p$. After addition by a ripple carry adder (RCA), there may thus be an extra p left over. It is easily handled by the use of another RCA and a multiplexor, as suggested in [20]. The RCA uses the fast carry chain available on every FPGA. Nevertheless the carry chain for a 170-bit RCA would lengthen the critical path. They are then composed of pipelined smaller RCAs.

The implementation structure of the Koç and Hung algorithm is very similar to ours. Most of the design choices were identical for both algorithms. The main difference lies in the number of bits taken to evaluate the estimation function (*i.e.* 2×5 for Koç and Hung algorithm and 2×3 for ours). Moreover the Koç and Hung algorithm keeps the whole value intact (no truncation is applied after the registers S and C), this requires thus a bus length of $l + 4$-bit.

3.3   Discussion About Algorithms Performances

Efficiency of two implementations is always difficult to compare. The same algorithm could lead to very different performances depending on the type of device used (ASIC or FPGA) and on the technology ($0.12\mu m$ CMOS for Virtex II), on the cleverness of designers (smart trade-offs between area and latency) and finally on the options chosen for *place-and-route* (PAR).

Algorithms described above present many similarities. They require two CSAs of size $O(l)$, a module of last reduction and an estimation function feeding a look-up table. Both of them shift their feedbacked S and C pair at each iteration. Koç-Hung algorithm requires less memory than ours. However, the estimation function given by Koç-Hung takes 2×5 inputs, and our algorithm takes 2×3 inputs.

A Field Programmable Gate Array is a tool situated between hardware and software. With the increase of powerful internal features it becomes very competitive compared to ASIC. We used FPGA to implement our design. This gives an advantage to our algorithm in terms of latency (critical path) with small area increase.

Most FPGA devices use 4-input look-up tables (LUTs) to implement function generators. Four independent inputs are provided into each of the 2 function generators in a slice. Then, any boolean function of four inputs can be mapped in a LUT. So the propagation delay is independent of the function implemented. Moreover, each Virtex slice contains two multiplexers (MUXF5 and MUXF6). This allows the combination of slices to obtain higher-level logic functions (any function of 5 or 6 inputs)[1].

From these considerations, we can consider the delay of the 2 estimation functions. In our algorithm, the estimation function can be mapped as a 6-input boolean function with a propagation delay of 1 LUT. In the case of Koç-Hung algorithm a 10-input function must be implemented, so 2 stages of LUT are needed. This implies a latency of 2 LUTs.

This endows to our algorithm an advantage for an FPGA implementation but the two algorithms have very similar performances and it is difficult to evaluate the performance for Koç and Hung algorithm using another technology. Table 1 gives the synthesis result of our implementation. We can see that our algorithm can achieve a higher frequency, as expected.

Table 1. Evaluation of the performances between the two algorithms

Our Implementation	Nbr. of LUT	Nbr. of FF.	Nbr. of Slices	Freq (MHz)	Hardware Efficiency Nbr. Reg/Nbr. LUT	AT complexity (slices*cycles/freq.)
of K-H	1,402	1,230	805	189.2	0.88	7.5 e-4
of LUT	1,450	1,246	857	203.3	0.86	7.6 e-4

---

[1] In Virtex II family, up to 8 slices can be combined with similar multiplexers.

In [3], the complexity of the implementation of a binary multiplication is formally defined. This definition includes many parameters such as the technology used, the area and time required and the length of the operand. In this way, we decide to adopt an *Area-Time Complexity* and then the product *AT* as an element of comparison of the algorithms we implemented.

3.4   Performances

As far as we know, this paper is the first dealing with XTR cryptosystem implementation on reconfigurable hardware. Even if it is not fully satisfactory, we decided to compare it with the best existing implementations (as we know) of the RSA algorithm [5,16] and elliptic curve processors [18,19]. Table 2 indicates that our implementation is definitely competitive with respect to other designs for equivalent security. Note that no assumption on the form of p has been made: this freedom brings an enormous flexibility in the use of our designs.

Table 2. Evaluation of the performances between different public-key cryptosystems. (-) denotes unknown values.

Implement-ation	Technology	Nbr. of LUT	Nbr. of FF.	Nbr. of Slices	Block RAM	Freq (MHz)	Comput. Time (ms)
RSA 1024 [5]	Xilinx XC40250XV-9	-	-	27,304	0	45.6	3.1
RSA 1024 [16]	Xilinx XC2V6000	-	-	24,767	0	100.49	2.63
ECP [18] $GF(2^m)$	Xilinx XCV400E-8	3,002	1,769	-	10	76.7	0.21
ECP [19] $GF(p)$	Xilinx XCV1000E-8	11,416	5,735	-	35	40	3
XTR with K-H	**Xilinx XC2V6000-6**	**17,903**	**13,509**	**10,607**	**0**	**150**	**0.21**
XTR with LUT	**Xilinx XC2V6000-6**	**18,103**	**13,752**	**10,737**	**0**	**162.4**	**0.21**

Our designs were synthesized on a Virtex2 XC2V6000-6-FF152, which contains 33,792 Slices, 144 Select RAM Blocks, 144 18-bit x 18-bit Multipliers. The synthesis was performed with Synplify Pro 7.3 (SYNPLICITY) and automatic place-and-route (PAR) was carried out with XILINX ISE 6.1i. Moreover, concerning the timing performances, we decided to pack the input/output registers of our implementation into the input/output blocks (IOB) in order to try and reach the achievable performance.

4   Conclusion

In this article, the first implementation of the XTR (crypto)system on reconfigurable hardware (FPGA) is presented. Various implementations are discussed. Evaluation of modular products is the costly part. This can be carried out using the clever algorithm from Koç and Hung. We also propose a (competitive) alternative based on look-up table. The performances of these two algorithms seem to be in a similar gap.

The main subject of this paper is XTR implementation. The intrinsic parallelism of XTR allows us to obtain a very high level of performance with very small memory requirements. Compared with RSA exponentiation, XTR appears as a very interesting alternative in hardware: an XTR exponentiation is carried out in about 0.21 ms at frequency beyond 150 MHz.

Moreover, implementations are fully generic and have been designed for any FPGA device without using any particular feature. Portability is then another characteristic of our designs. Once again there is absolutely no constraint on p (characteristic of the field over which XTR is defined). Designs are dedicated to any p up to 170 bits and it would be obvious to oversize their length. Eventually, using special forms of p (*e.g.* Mersenne primes as used for elliptic curves) could lead to considerable improvements, to the detriment of the present generality.

We stress that porting our implementation on ASIC would also underline the very good efficiency of XTR compared with RSA or elliptic curve cryptosystems.

Acknowledgments. We are grateful to Christophe Giraud and Martijn Stam for providing us fruitful comments on the preliminary version of this paper. We would also like to thank anonymous reviewers for their useful observations.

References

1. IEEE Std 1363-2000. *IEEE Standard Specifications for Public-Key Cryptography.* IEEE Computer Society, August 29, 2000.
2. Paul Barrett. Implementing the Rivest Shamir and Adleman public key encryption algorithm on a standard digital signal processor. In A.M. Odlyzko, Ed., *Advances in Cryptology, Proc. Crypto'86*, pages 311–323, vol. 263 of *Lecture Notes in Computer Science*, Springer-Verlag, 1987.
3. Richard P. Brent and H.T. Kung. The Area-Time Complexity of Binary Multiplication. In *J.ACM*, vol. 28, 1981, pages 521–534, July 1981.
4. Ernest F. Brickell. A fast modular multiplication algorithm with application to two key cryptography. In D. Chaum, R.L. Rivest, and A.T. Sherman, Ed., *Advances in cryptology Proc. of CRYPTO '82*, pages 51–60. Plenum Press, 1983.
5. Thomas Blum and Christof Paar. High-Radix montgomery modular exponentiation on reconfigurable hardware. *IEEE Trans. on Computers*, 50(7), pages 759–764, 2001.
6. Guang Gong and Lein Harn. Public key cryptosystems based on cubic finite field extensions. In *IEEE Trans. on Inf. Theory*, Nov. 1999.

7. Robert Granger, Dan Page and Martijn Stam. A Comparison of CEILIDH and XTR. In D.A. Buell Ed. *Algorithmic Number Theory, 6th International Symposium – ANTS-VI*, pages 235–249, vol. 3076 of *Lecture Notes in Computer Science*. Springer-Verlag, 2004.

8. Marc Joye and Sung-Ming Yen. The Montgomery powering ladder. In B.S. Kaliski Jr. and Ç. K. Koç, Ed., *Cryptographic Hardware and Embedded Systems (CHES 2002)*, pages 291–302, vol. 2523 of *Lecture Notes in Computer Science*. Springer-Verlag, 2002.

9. Çetin Kaya Koç and Ching Yu Hung. A Fast Algorithm for Modular Reduction. In *IEE Proceedings - Computers and Digital Techniques*, 145(4), pages 265–271, July 1998.

10. Seongan Lim, Seungjoo Kim, Ikktwon Yie, Jaemoon Kim and Hongsub Lee. XTR Extended to $GF(p^{6m})$. In S. Vaudenay and A.M. Youssef, Ed., *Selected Areas in Cryptography – SAC 2001*, vol 2259 of *Lecture Notes in Computer Science*, pages 301–312. Springer-Verlag, 2001.

11. Arjen K. Lenstra. Using Cyclotomic Polynomials to Construct Efficient Discrete Logarithm Cryptosystems Over Finite Fields In V. Varadharajan, J. Pieprzyk, Y. Mu, Eds. *Information Security and Privacy, Second Australasian Conference – ACISP'97*, vol. 1270 of *Lecture Notes in Computer Science*, pages 127–138. Springer-Verlag, 1997.

12. Arjen K. Lenstra and Eric R. Verheul. The XTR public key system. In M. Bellare, Ed., *Advances in Cryptology – CRYPTO 2000*, vol. 1880 of *Lecture Notes in Computer Science*, pages 1–19. Springer-Verlag, 2000.

13. Arjen K. Lenstra and Eric R. Verheul. An overview of the XTR public key system. *Public Key Cryptography and Computational Number Theory Conference*, 2000.

14. Arjen K. Lenstra and Eric R. Verheul. Key improvements to XTR. In T. Okamoto, Ed., *Advances in Cryptology – ASIACRYPT 2000*, vol. 1976 of *Lecture Notes in Computer Science*, pages 220–233. Springer-Verlag, 2000.

15. Arjen K. Lenstra and Eric R. Verheul. Fast irreductibility and subgroup membership testing in XTR. In K. Kim, Ed., *Public Key Cryptography – PKC 2001*, vol. 1992 of *Lecture Notes in Computer Science*, pages 73–86. Springer-Verlag, 2001.

16. Ciaran McIvor, Máire McLoone, John McCanny, Alan Daly and William Marnane. Fast Montgomery Modular Multiplication and RSA Cryptographic Processor Architectures. *37th Asilomar Conference on Signals, Systems, and Computers*, Nov. 2003.

17. Peter L. Montgomery. Modular multiplication without trial division. *Math. Comp.*, 44(170), pages 519–521, April 1985.

18. Gerardo Orlando and Christof Paar. A High Performance Reconfigurable Elliptic Curve Processor for $GF(2m)$. In Ç.K. Koç, C. Paar, Ed., *Cryptographic Hardware and Embedded Systems (CHES 2000)*, vol. 1965 of *Lecture Notes in Computer Science*, pages 41–56, Springer-Verlag, 2001.

19. Gerardo Orlando and Christof Paar. A Scalable GF(p) Elliptic Curve Processor Architecture for Programmable Hardware. In Ç.K. Koç, D. Naccache, C. Paar, Ed., *Cryptographic Hardware and Embedded Systems (CHES 2001)*, vol. 2162 of *Lecture Notes in Computer Science*, pages 348–363, Springer-Verlag, 2001.

20. Behrooz Parhami. RNS representation with redundant residues. In Proc. of the *35th Asilomar Conf. on Signals, Systems, and Computers*, Pacific Grove, CA, pages 1651-1655, November 4-7, 2001.

21. Jean-Jacques Quisquater. Fast modular exponentiation without division. At *Rump session of EUROCRYPT '90*, May 1990.

22. Karl Rubin and Alice Silverberg. Torus-based cryptography. In D. Boneh, Ed., *Advances in Cryptology – CRYPTO 2003*, vol. 2729 of *Lecture Notes in Computer*, pages 349–365. Springer, 2003.

23. Holger Sedlak. The RSA cryptography processor. In D. Chaum and W.L. Price, Ed., *Advances in Cryptology - EUROCRYPT '87*, Amsterdam, The Netherlands, vol. 304 of *Lecture Notes in Computer Science*, pages 95–105. Springer-Verlag, 1988.

24. Peter Smith and Christopher Skinner. A public-key cryptosystem and a digital signature system based on the Lucas function analogue to discret logarithms. In J. Pieprzyck and R. Safavi-Naini, Ed., *Advances in Cryptology – ASIACRYPT '94*, vol. 917 of *Lecture Notes in Computer Science*, pages 357–364. Springer-Verlag, 1995.

25. François-Xavier Standaert, Gaël Rouvroy, Jean-Jacques Quisquater, Jean-Didier Legat. Efficient Implementation of Rijndael Encryption in Reconfigurable Hardware: Improvements and Design Tradeoffs. In C. Walter, Ed., *Cryptographic Hardware and Embedded Systems (CHES 2003)*, Volume 2779 of *Lecture Notes in Computer Science*. Springer-Verlag, September 2003.

26. Martijn Stam and Arjen K. Lenstra. Speeding up XTR. In C. Boyd, Ed., *Advances in Cryptology – ASIACRYPT 2001*, vol. 2248 of *Lecture Notes in Computer Science*, pages 125–143. Springer-Verlag, 2001.

27. Eric R. Verheul. Evidence that XTR Is More Secure then Supersingular Elliptic Curve Cryptosystems. In B. Pfitzmann, Ed., *Advances in Cryptology – EUROCRYPT 2003*, vol. 2045 of *Lecture Notes in Computer Science*, pages 195–210. Springer-Verlag, 2001.

28. Johannes Wolkerstorfer. Dual-Field Arithmetic Unit for $GF(p)$ and $GF(2^m)$. In B.S. Kaliski Jr., Ç.K. Koç, C. Paar, Ed., *Cryptographic Hardware and Embedded Systems — CHES 2002*, vol. 2523 of *Lecture Notes in Computer Science*, pages 500–514. Springer-Verlag, 2002.

A   Details of Basic XTR Operations

To compute $S_{2k} = (c_{4k}, c_{4k+1}, c_{4k+2})$ from $S_k(c_{2k}, c_{2k+1}, c_{2k+2})$, the following operations are required:

$$
\begin{aligned}
c_{4k} &= c_{2k}^2 - 2c_{2k}^p \\
&= c_{2k,2}(c_{2k,2} - 2c_{2k,1} - 2)\,\alpha + c_{2k,1}(c_{2k,1} - 2c_{2k,2} - 2)\,\alpha^2 \\
c_{4k+1} &= c_{2(2k+1)-1} = c_{2k}c_{2k+1} - c^p c_{2k+1}^p + c_{2k+2}^p \\
&= c_{2k+1,1}(c_{1,2} - c_{2k,2} - c_{1,1}) + c_{2k+1,2}(c_{2k,2} - c_{2k,1} + c_{1,1}) + c_{2k+2,2}\,\alpha \\
&\quad + c_{2k+1,1}(c_{2k,1} - c_{2k,2} + c_{1,2}) + c_{2k+1,2}(c_{1,1} - c_{2k,1} - c_{1,2}) + c_{2k+2,1}\,\alpha^2 \\
c_{4k+2} &= c_{2k+1}^2 - 2c_{2k+1}^p \\
&= c_{2k+1,2}(c_{2k+1,2} - 2c_{2k+1,1} - 2)\,\alpha + c_{2k+1,1}(c_{2k+1,1} - 2c_{2k+1,2} - 2)\,\alpha^2
\end{aligned}
$$

Computing $S_{2k+1} = (c_{4k+2}, c_{4k+3}, c_{4k+4})$ from $S_k(c_{2k}, c_{2k+1}, c_{2k+2})$, is done with the following operations:

$$c_{4k+2} = c_{2k+1}^2 - 2c_{2k+1}^p$$
$$= c_{2k+1,2}(c_{2k+1,2} - 2c_{2k+1,1} - 2)\,\alpha + c_{2k+1,1}(c_{2k+1,1} - 2c_{2k+1,2} - 2)\,\alpha^2$$

$$c_{4k+3} = c_{2(2k+1)+1} = c_{2k+2}c_{2k+1} - cc_{2k+1}^p + c_{2k}^p$$
$$= c_{2k+1,1}(c_{1,1} - c_{2k+2,2} - c_{1,2}) + c_{2k+1,2}(c_{2k+2,2} - c_{2k+2,1} + c_{1,2}) + c_{2k,2}\,\alpha$$
$$+ c_{2k+1,1}(c_{2k+2,1} - c_{2k+2,2} + c_{1,1}) + c_{2k+1,2}(c_{1,2} - c_{2k+2,1} - c_{1,1}) + c_{2k,1}\,\alpha^2$$

$$c_{4k+4} = c_{2k+2}^2 - 2c_{2k+2}^p$$
$$= c_{2k+2,2}(c_{2k+2,2} - 2c_{2k+2,1} - 2)\,\alpha + c_{2k+2,1}(c_{2k+2,1} - 2c_{2k+2,2} - 2)\,\alpha^2$$

Concurrent Error Detection Schemes for Involution Ciphers

Nikhil Joshi, Kaijie Wu, and Ramesh Karri

Department of Electrical and Computer Engineering, Polytechnic University
Brooklyn, NY 11201 USA
{njoshi01, kwu03}@utopia.poly.edu
ramesh@india.poly.edu

Abstract. Because of the rapidly shrinking dimensions in VLSI, transient and permanent faults arise and will continue to occur in the near future in increasing numbers. Since cryptographic chips are a consumer product produced in large quantities, cheap solutions for concurrent checking are needed. Concurrent Error Detection (CED) for cryptographic chips also has a great potential for detecting (deliberate) fault injection attacks where faults are injected into a cryptographic chip to break the key. In this paper we propose a low cost, low latency, time redundancy based CED technique for a class of symmetric block ciphers whose round functions are involutions. This CED technique can detect both permanent and transient faults with almost no time overhead. A function F is an involution if F(F(x))=x. The proposed CED architecture (i) exploits the involution property of the ciphers and checks if x=F(F(x)) for each of the involutional round functions to detect transient and permanent faults and (ii) uses the idle cycles in the design to achieve close to a 0% time overhead. Our preliminary ASIC synthesis experiment with the involutional cipher KHAZAD resulted in an area overhead of 23.8% and a throughput degradation of 8%. A fault injection based simulation shows that the proposed architecture detects all single-bit faults.

Keywords: Concurrent Error Detection (CED), Fault Tolerance, Involutional ciphers, KHAZAD

1 Introduction

Because of the rapidly shrinking dimensions in VLSI, faults arise and will continue to occur in the near future in increasing numbers. Faults can broadly be classified in to two categories: Transient faults that die away after sometime and permanent faults that do not die away with time but remain until they are repaired or the faulty component is replaced. The origin of these faults could be due to the internal phenomena in the system such as threshold change, shorts, opens etc. or due to external influences like electromagnetic radiation. The faults could also be deliberately injected by attackers in order to extract sensitive information stored in the system. These faults affect the memory as well as the combinational parts of a circuit and can only be detected using Concurrent Error Detection (CED). This is especially true for sensitive devices such

M. Joye and J.-J. Quisquater (Eds.): CHES 2004, LNCS 3156, pp. 400–412, 2004.

as cryptographic chips. Hence, CED for cryptographic chips is growing in importance. Since cryptographic chips are a consumer product produced in large quantities, cheap solutions for concurrent checking are needed. CED for cryptographic chips also has a great potential for detecting (deliberate) fault injection attacks where faults are injected into a cryptographic chip to break the key [1 2 3 4]. A Differential Fault Attack technique against AES and KHAZAD was discussed in [5]. It exploited the faults in bytes. It was shown that if the fault location could be chosen by the attacker, it required only 2 ciphertexts for a successful attack. CED techniques could help prevent such kind of attacks.

Until now some of the following CED methods for cryptographic algorithms are known. In [6] a CED approach for AES and other symmetric block ciphers that exploits the inverse relationship between the encryption and decryption at the algorithm level, round level and individual operation level was developed. This technique had an area overhead of 21% and a time overhead up to 61.15%. In [7] this inverse-relationship based technique was extended to AES round key generation. A drawback of this approach is that it assumes that the cipher device operates in a half-duplex mode (i.e. either encryption or decryption but not both are simultaneously active).

In [8] a parity-based method of CED for encryption algorithms was presented. The technique adds one additional parity bit per byte resulting in 16 additional bits for the 128-bit data stream. Each of the sixteen 8-bit×8-bit AES S-Boxes is modified into 8-bit×9-bit S-Boxes. In addition, this technique adds an extra parity bit per byte to the outputs of the Mix-Column operation because Mix-Column does not preserve parity of its inputs at the byte-level.

In this paper, we propose a low cost, low latency CED technique for involution-based symmetric block ciphers. Any function F is an involution if $F(F(x))=x$. An involutional symmetric block cipher is one in which each round operation of the cipher is an involution. Usually, in symmetric block ciphers, the decryption operation differs significantly from encryption. Although it is possible to implement decryption in such a way that it has the same sequence of operations as encryption, round level operations such as S-Box etc are different. With involutional ciphers, all the operations are involutions. So, it becomes possible to implement the decryption in such a way that only the round keys used are different from that for encryption. Besides the implementation benefit, an involutional structure also implies equivalent security for both encryption and decryption [9].

The CED technique we propose exploits the involution property of the round operations of this class of symmetric block ciphers and checks if $x=F(F(x))$ for each of the involutional round functions to detect the faults in the system. It offers optimum trade-off between area and time overhead, performance and fault detection latency. Further, it requires minimal modification to the encryption device and is easily applicable to all involution-based symmetric block ciphers. Traditionally, time redundancy based CED schemes cannot detect permanent faults but usually entail >100% time overhead. Although the CED scheme we propose is time redundancy based, it entails almost zero time overhead.

The paper is organized as follows. In section 2 we will recapitulate Involution-based symmetric block ciphers. In section 3 we will describe the involution based CED architecture and the error detection capability of the proposed method. To obtain the area overhead and the additional time delay, we modeled the method using VHDL and synthesized using cadence ASIC synthesis tool PKS. The results of this implementation are presented in section 4. The error detection capabilities of the proposed methods are discussed in section 5 and finally, Conclusions are reported in section 6.

2 Involutional Block Ciphers

A substitution permutation network (SPN) symmetric block cipher is composed of several rounds and each round consists of a non-linear substitution layer (S-Box), a linear diffusion layer and a layer to perform exclusive-or operation with the round key. The linear diffusion layer ensures that after a few rounds all the output bits depend on all the input bits. The nonlinear layer ensures that this dependency is of a complex and nonlinear nature. exclusive-or with the round key introduces the key material. Recently, several SPN symmetric block ciphers that are composed of involution functions have been proposed and analyzed [10,11,12,13,14]. In an involutional SPN cipher, the non-linear S-Box layer and the linear diffusion layer are involutions. An advantage of using involutional components is that the encryption data path is identical to the decryption data path. In an involutional SPN cipher, the round key generation algorithm for decryption is the inverse of the round key generation algorithm for encryption.

In this paper we will consider the 64-bit involutional SPN cipher KHAZAD[10] shown in Figure 1 as a running example. The involutional SPN cipher KHAZAD uses seven identical encryption/decryption rounds (ρ) with each encryption/decryption round composed of an involutional non-linear byte substitution γ (i.e. $\gamma(\gamma(x)) = x$), an involutional linear diffusion layer θ (i.e. $\theta(\theta(x)) = x$) and exclusive-or with key σ which is an involution as well (i.e. $\sigma(\sigma(x)) = x$).

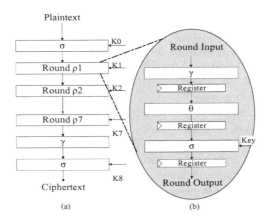

Fig. 1. (a) Khazad Cipher (b) Round Function $\rho[Key](x) = \sigma_{Key}(\theta(\gamma(x)))$

2.1 The Non-linear Substitution Function γ

The involutional non-linear substitution layer γ of KHAZAD uses eight 8x8 involutional S-Boxes, each of which is constructed from three layers of 4x4 involutional P-Boxes and Q-Boxes as shown in Figure 2. The truth tables for the P-Box and the Q-Box are given in Table 1. Observe that the P-Box and the Q- box are also involutions. We implemented the P-Box and Q-box as ROMs and the γ layer uses a total of 24 P-Boxes and 24 Q-Boxes.

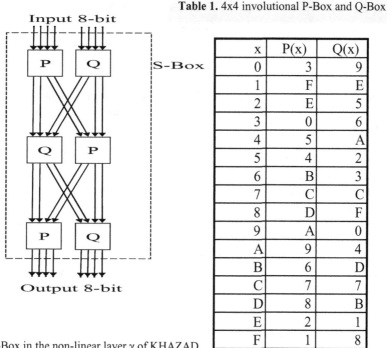

Table 1. 4x4 involutional P-Box and Q-Box

x	P(x)	Q(x)
0	3	9
1	F	E
2	E	5
3	0	6
4	5	A
5	4	2
6	B	3
7	C	C
8	D	F
9	A	0
A	9	4
B	6	D
C	7	7
D	8	B
E	2	1
F	1	8

Fig. 2. S-Box in the non-linear layer γ of KHAZAD

2.2 The Linear Diffusion Layer θ

The diffusion layer θ is a linear mapping based on the [16, 8, 9] MDS code with generator matrix GH = [I H], and H = had(01x, 03x, 04x, 05x, 06x, 08x, 0Bx, 07x)
i.e. θ (a) = b ⇔ b = a × H, where

$$
H = \begin{bmatrix}
01x & 03x & 04x & 05x & 06x & 08x & 0Bx & 07x \\
03x & 01x & 05x & 04x & 08x & 06x & 07x & 0Bx \\
04x & 05x & 01x & 03x & 0Bx & 07x & 06x & 08x \\
05x & 04x & 03x & 01x & 07x & 0Bx & 08x & 06x \\
06x & 08x & 0Bx & 07x & 01x & 03x & 04x & 05x \\
08x & 06x & 07x & 0Bx & 03x & 01x & 05x & 04x \\
0Bx & 07x & 06x & 08x & 04x & 05x & 01x & 03x \\
07x & 0Bx & 08x & 06x & 05x & 04x & 03x & 01x
\end{bmatrix}
$$

The H matrix is symmetric and unitary and therefore θ is an involution. For efficient hardware implementation the θ layer was described in [15] as follows:

$$b_0 = a_0 \oplus a_1 \oplus a_3 \oplus a_6 \oplus a_7 \oplus X(a_1 \oplus a_4 \oplus a_6 \oplus a_7) \oplus X^2(a_2 \oplus a_3 \oplus a_4 \oplus a_7) \oplus X^3(a_5 \oplus a_6)$$

$$b_1 = a_0 \oplus a_1 \oplus a_2 \oplus a_6 \oplus a_7 \oplus X(a_0 \oplus a_5 \oplus a_6 \oplus a_7) \oplus X^2(a_2 \oplus a_3 \oplus a_5 \oplus a_6) \oplus X^3(a_4 \oplus a_7)$$

$$b_2 = a_1 \oplus a_2 \oplus a_3 \oplus a_4 \oplus a_5 \oplus X(a_3 \oplus a_4 \oplus a_5 \oplus a_6) \oplus X^2(a_0 \oplus a_1 \oplus a_5 \oplus a_6) \oplus X^3(a_4 \oplus a_7)$$

$$b_3 = a_0 \oplus a_2 \oplus a_3 \oplus a_4 \oplus a_5 \oplus X(a_2 \oplus a_4 \oplus a_5 \oplus a_7) \oplus X^2(a_0 \oplus a_1 \oplus a_4 \oplus a_7) \oplus X^3(a_5 \oplus a_6)$$

$$b_4 = a_2 \oplus a_3 \oplus a_4 \oplus a_5 \oplus a_7 \oplus X(a_0 \oplus a_2 \oplus a_3 \oplus a_5) \oplus X^2(a_0 \oplus a_3 \oplus a_6 \oplus a_7) \oplus X^3(a_1 \oplus a_2)$$

$$b_5 = a_2 \oplus a_3 \oplus a_4 \oplus a_5 \oplus a_6 \oplus X(a_1 \oplus a_2 \oplus a_3 \oplus a_4) \oplus X^2(a_1 \oplus a_2 \oplus a_3 \oplus a_7) \oplus X^3(a_0 \oplus a_3)$$

$$b_6 = a_0 \oplus a_1 \oplus a_5 \oplus a_6 \oplus a_7 \oplus X(a_0 \oplus a_1 \oplus a_2 \oplus a_7) \oplus X^2(a_1 \oplus a_2 \oplus a_4 \oplus a_5) \oplus X^3(a_0 \oplus a_3)$$

$$b_7 = a_0 \oplus a_1 \oplus a_4 \oplus a_6 \oplus a_7 \oplus X(a_0 \oplus a_1 \oplus a_3 \oplus a_6) \oplus X^2(a_0 \oplus a_3 \oplus a_4 \oplus a_5) \oplus X^3(a_1 \oplus a_2)$$

where a_7-a_0 and b_7-b_0 are the eight input bytes and the eight output bytes of the diffusion layer θ.

Assuming that a(7),a(6),a(5),a(4),a(3),a(2),a(1) and a(0) are the eight bits in an input byte a, the three byte level functions $X(a)$, $X^2(a)=X(X(a))$ and $X^3(a)=X(X(X(a)))$ can be defined as follows:

$X(a(7),a(6),a(5),a(4),a(3),a(2),a(1),a(0))$

$= a(6),a(5),a(4),a(3) \oplus a(7),a(2) \oplus a(7),a(1) \oplus a(7),a(0),a(7)$

$X^2(a(7),a(6),a(5),a(4),a(3),a(2),a(1),a(0))$

$= a(5),a(4),a(3) \oplus a(7),a(2) \oplus a(7) \oplus a(6),a(1) \oplus a(7) \oplus a(6),a(0) \oplus a(6),a(7),a(6)$

$X^3(a(7),a(6),a(5),a(4),a(3),a(2),a(1),a(0))$

$= a(4),a(3) \oplus a(7),a(2) \oplus a(7) \oplus a(6),a(1) \oplus a(7) \oplus a(6) \oplus a(5),a(0) \oplus a(6) \oplus a(5),a(7) \oplus a(5),a(6),a(5)$

It can be seen that if bit a(7) is "0" then function $X(a)$ reduces to a single bit left rotate. Similarly, the function $X^2(a)$ reduces to a 2-bit left rotate when a(7) and a(6) are "0" and finally, the function $X^3(a)$ reduces to a 3-bit left rotate when a(7), a(6) and a(5) are "0".

2.3   The Exclusive-or Function σ

The key addition σ layer consists of bitwise exclusive-or of the 64-bit round-key K^r with the input to the module. Hence, σ is also an involution.

3   Concurrent Error Detection of Involution Functions

We will first describe a simple CED scheme that exploits the involution property of any involution function and then extend it to the involutional SPN cipher KHAZAD.

If a hardware module implements a function F that satisfies the involution property, faults in this module can be detected by checking if x=F(F(x)). At the beginning of operation, the input x is buffered. The output of the hardware module implementing F is fed back to the input of the module F. The result is compared to the original input x and a mismatch indicates an error. Figure 3 shows this basic idea behind CED scheme for an involutional function.

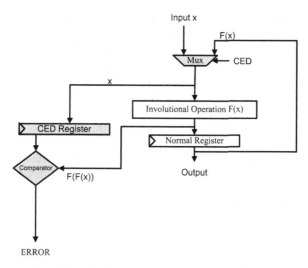

Fig. 3. CED scheme for an involution function

We will show how this CED scheme can be incorporate into a non-pipelined architecture for KHAZAD. Since symmetric block ciphers are frequently used in one of three feedback modes: Cipher Block Chaining (CBC), Output FeedBack (OFB) or Cipher Feedback (CFB), such a non-pipelined architecture is indeed reasonable. The proposed scheme works even in a non-feedback Electronic Code Book (ECB) mode to facilitate pipelining, with an appropriately modified architecture. If a pipelined architecture is implemented, the scheme can result in increased throughput at the cost of a little extra hardware compared to the non-pipelined version owing to a more complex controller. Also, ECB mode is not popularly implemented. Hence, we will consider a non-pipelined version. In the non-pipelined KHAZAD architecture, each KHAZAD round ρ takes three clock cycles to finish with round operation γ, round operation θ and round operation σ completing in clock cycles 1, 2 and 3 respectively.

3.1 CED Scheme 1

Consider a straightforward time redundancy based CED scheme (Scheme 1) wherein round operation γ is performed in clock cycles 1 and 2 on the same input x both the times. If $\gamma(x)$ obtained at the end of clock cycle 1 = $\gamma(x)$ obtained at the end of clock cycle 2 (i.e. no transient fault is detected in module γ), round operation θ is performed in clock cycles 3 and 4 on the same input $\gamma(x)$. If $\theta(\gamma(x))$ at the end of clock cycle 3 = $\theta(\gamma(x))$ at the end of clock cycle 4 (i.e. no transient fault is detected in module θ), round operation σ is performed in clock cycles 5 and 6 on the same input $\theta(\gamma(x))$. If $\sigma(\theta(\gamma(x)))$ at the end of clock cycle 5= $\sigma(\theta(\gamma(x)))$ (i.e. no transient fault is detected in module σ) one KHAZAD round ρ is successfully completed. This time redundancy based scheme can only detect transient faults and entails >100% time overhead.

3.2 CED Scheme 2

As a first modification to the above CED scheme, we propose to integrate involution based CED shown in Figure 4 into the non-pipelined KHAZAD (Scheme 2) as follows. Round operation γ is performed in clock cycle 1 on input x followed by the corresponding CED operation $\gamma(\gamma(x))$ in clock cycle 2. If x= $\gamma(\gamma(x))$ (i.e. no fault is detected in module γ), round operation θ is performed in clock cycle 3 on $\gamma(x)$ followed by the corresponding CED operation $\theta(\theta(\gamma(x)))$ in clock cycle 4. If $\gamma(x)$= $\theta(\theta(\gamma(x)))$ (i.e. no fault is detected in module θ) then round operation σ is performed in clock cycle 5 on $\theta(\gamma(x))$ followed by the corresponding CED operation $\sigma(\sigma(\theta(\gamma(x))))$ in clock cycle 6. If $\theta(\gamma(x))$= $\sigma(\sigma(\theta(\gamma(x))))$ (i.e. no fault is detected in module σ) one KHAZAD round ρ is successful. This modification can detect permanent faults in addition to the transient faults. This is because, although the same module is used twice, the data that it is operating on is different in each case. This was possible due to the involution property of the modules. The time overhead of this modified time redundancy based CED is still >100%.

3.3   CED Scheme 3

During a complete KHAZAD encryption/decryption, round operation γ is busy in clock cycles 1, 4, 7 … and idles in clock cycles 2, 3, 5, 6, 8, 9… Similarly, round operation θ is busy in clock cycles 2, 5, 8 ... and idles in clock cycles 1, 3, 4, 6, 7… Finally, round operation σ is busy in clock cycles 3, 6, 9 … and idles in clock cycles 1, 2, 4, 5, 7, 8 … The involution based CED scheme in Figure 4 can be adapted to the non-pipelined KHAZAD architecture to exploit these idle clock cycles as follows (Scheme 3): Round operation $\gamma(x)$ is performed in clock cycle 1. The corresponding CED operation for $\gamma(x)$ i.e., $\gamma(\gamma(x))$ is performed in clock cycle 2 concurrent with the round operation $\theta(\gamma(x))$. If x= $\gamma(\gamma(x))$ then no fault was detected in module γ and hence no errors are reported. The corresponding CED operation for $\theta(\gamma(x))$ i.e., $\theta(\theta(\gamma(x)))$ is performed in clock cycle 3 concurrent with round operation $\sigma(\theta(\gamma(x)))$. If $\gamma(x)$= $\theta(\theta(\gamma(x)))$ then no fault was detected in module θ. At this point, one KHAZAD round ρ is completed only in 3 clock cycles in contrast to the 6 cycles consumed by the two other schemes described above. Now, in clock cycle 4, the corresponding CED operation for $\sigma(\theta(\gamma(x)))$ i.e., $\sigma(\sigma(\theta(\gamma(x))))$ is performed concurrent with the round operation $\gamma(y)$ where y is the input to the second round of the KHAZAD encryption/decryption given by y= $\sigma(\theta(\gamma(x)))$. If $\sigma(\sigma(\theta(\gamma(x))))$= $\theta(\gamma(x))$ then no fault was detected in module σ. The comparisons between the 3 schemes are presented in Table 2.

As explained above, Scheme 3 uses idle clock cycles to re-compute the round operations on the corresponding round outputs by feeding back the output as the input. The result obtained is compared to the original input value stored in the buffer. These two values should be equal since every round operation is an involution. If they are not equal, an error is reported. As seen from Table 2, this time redundancy based CED method (Scheme 3) entails almost no time overhead because one round operation is completed per clock cycle. Another inherent advantage of the proposed CED method is that we can detect permanent faults in the system even though the faults might not affect the output, i.e. are not activated by current inputs. Consider a situation where a faulty bit is stuck- at-1 and the output at that bit was supposed to be logic '1'. Now, although the output is correct, the fault in the system will be detected because the involution will not yield the correct result. This enhances the security of the implementation since any attempts to clandestinely attack the algorithm by an external agent can be detected. This also improves the overall fault coverage as well as the error detection latency. The CED architecture for Scheme 3 is shown in Figure 4 with the hardware overhead shown by the shaded blocks in Figure 4.

Table 2. Comparison between the three CED schemes during the first six clock cycles

Clock Cycle	Time redundancy based CED		
	Scheme 1 (Basic approach) Transient faults only 100% time overhead	Scheme 2 (+involution) Transient and permanent faults 100% time overhead	Scheme 3 (+involution +idle cycles) Transient and permanent faults almost 0% time overhead
1	$\gamma(x)$ of round 1	$\gamma(x)$ of round 1	$\gamma(x)$ of round 1
2	$\gamma(x)$ of round 1+check	$\gamma(\gamma(x))$ of round 1+check	$\theta(\gamma(x))$ of round 1, $\gamma(\gamma(x))$ of round 1+check
3	$\theta(\gamma(x))$ of round 1	$\theta(\gamma(x))$ of round 1	$\sigma(\theta(\gamma(x)))$ of round 1, $\theta(\theta(\gamma(x)))$ of round 1+check
4	$\theta(\gamma(x))$ of round 1+check	$\theta(\theta(\gamma(x)))$ of round 1 +check	$\gamma(y)$* of round 2, $\sigma(\sigma(\theta(\gamma(x))))$ of round 1 +check
5	$\sigma(\theta(\gamma(x)))$ of round 1	$\sigma(\theta(\gamma(x)))$ of round 1	$\theta(\gamma(y))$ of round 2, $\gamma(\gamma(y))$ of round 2 +check
6	$\sigma(\theta(\gamma(x)))$ of round 1 +check	$\sigma(\sigma(\theta(\gamma(x))))$ of round 1 +check	$\sigma(\theta(\gamma(y)))$ of round 2, $\theta(\theta(\gamma(y)))$ of round 2 +check

* 'y' is the input to round 2

An interesting observation in the figure 4 is the requirement of a second multiplexer for the CED of the σ operation. This is due to the fact that a direct involutional operation on the σ layer yields in a fault-coverage of only 50%. The σ function is a 64-bit exclusive-or operation, and applying an involution operation on an XOR module will not enable us to detect all faults. i.e, if an exclusive-or function has a stuck-at fault at one of its output bits and a faulty output is obtained because of this fault, the result of involution would in fact, be the correct input that was applied. For example, if the input to the σ layer is 0x12345678 and the round key value is 0xABCDEF01, the normal output would be 0xB9F9B979. If there is a fault in the system such that the 2nd

LSB (Least Significant Bit) of the exclusive-or output is stuck-at-1, instead of obtaining the correct result, we obtain 0xB9F9B97B which is a faulty output. But when we perform the exclusive-or operation again on this faulty output, we get back 0x12345678. In such cases, ordinary involution based CED fails. In such cases, ordinary involution based CED fails. To solve this problem, we propose the following. The operands for all the exclusive-or operators are exchanged. So, the 64-bit exclusive-or operation is now divided into two parts, the left and the right with each part consisting of 32-bit exclusive-or   operations. Similarly the 64-bit exclusive-or   operator is also divided into two parts, the left and the right with each part consisting of 32-bit exclusive-or   operators. During the normal computation, the left part of exclusive-or   operation is allocated to the left part of exclusive-or   operator while the right part of exclusive-or   operation is allocated to the right part of exclusive-or   operator. But for the involution based CED, we interchange the operators. i.e., the right part is allocated to the left and vice-versa. Fault simulation shows the single-bit fault coverage of this scheme is 100%.

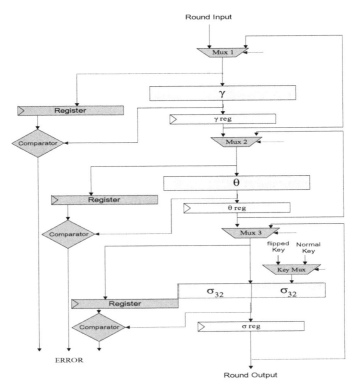

Fig. 4. KHAZAD round function ρ with CED

4   Implementation Based Validation

We implemented KHAZAD with involution based CED using IBM 0.13 micron library. The modeling of the architecture was done using VHDL, and Cadence Buildgates PKS was used to do the synthesis and place route. KHAZAD without CED datapath was also implemented using the same library and design flow. Table 3 shows the details of the overhead. The second row shows the area used by both designs. An inverter of this library takes 32 units area. The area overhead of the CED design is 23.8%. The third row shows the minimum clock period of synthesized designs. Due to the multiplexers inserted in the datapath, the clock period of CED design is 3.3%

more than the normal design. The fourth row shows that the CED design takes one more clock cycle than the normal design. This is because in the CED design, the re-computation of a round operation lags one clock cycle to the normal computation. This means that if we ignore the CED only for the σ layer in the last round, the normal architecture and the involution based CED architecture in fact take the same number of clock cycles to complete i.e., no time overhead. Finally the throughput comparison is shown in the fifth row. The throughput is calculated as the number of bits encrypted per second, i.e. the # of text / (the # of clock cycles × clock period).

Table 3. Overhead for the CED computation

	Normal	Involution based CED (scheme 3 above)	Overhead
Area	27453	34024	23.8%
Clock period	4712.69 ps	4870.99 ps	3.4%
#clock cycles	22	23	4.5%
Throughput	0.62 Gbps	0.57 Gbps	8%

5   Fault Injection Simulation

5.1   Single-Bit Faults

To check the error detection capability, we modeled our implementation using C. A stuck-at fault at a function output was injected by adding a multiplexer at the output of the function as shown in Figure 5.

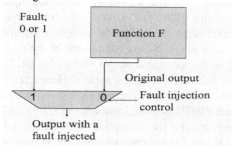

Fig. 5. Fault injection on the output of the function

By setting the fault injection control to 1, a stuck-at fault (either 0 or 1) is injected at the output of the function. Similarly, a stuck-at fault can be injected at the input of a function. Therefore, the number of connections between gates/functions gives the number of possible single-bit faults. Note that in this simulation we treat Function F as a black box and only consider the faults at inputs and outputs. If we break down the Function F into smaller components and consider the inputs and outputs of these smaller components, the number of single-bit faults is increased. In our simulation we

consider the P-Box and Q-box of an S-Box, and the exclusive-or   for the functions θ
and σ as the black box operations. The number of single-bit faults is shown in Table 4.
For example, as shown in figure 2, since an S-Box consists of three 4x4 P-Box and
three 4x4 Q-Boxes, the total number of connections of an S-Box is 4 × 3 (for P-Box)
+ 4 × 3 (for Q-Box) + 8 (the number of inputs to S-Box) = 32. Since the γ function of
KHAZAD consists of 8 S-Boxes, the total number of connections and hence the total
number of single-bit faults is 256. We ran simulations for random 1.5 million inputs,
and for every input we simulated all the possible single-bit faults, i.e. only one bit is
stuck at 1 or 0. Table 4 shows the fault coverage. The lowest level of fault injection in
the design was performed at the bit-wise exclusive-or   level. As seen from the table,
all the single-bit faults are detected.

Table 4. Fault Coverage of the Implementation

Function Module	# of possible single bit faults	# of inputs applied	Fault coverage
γ	256	1500000	100%
θ	1072	1500000	100%
σ	192	1500000	100%

5.2 Multiple-Bit Faults

The injection of random multiple bit faults into the system yielded an overall fault
coverage of approximately 99% over a random 1.5 million input test simulation run.
The reason for not achieving 100% fault coverage with multiple-bit faults is because
in some exceptionally rare cases, the fault in the system gets nullified in the case of the
γ and σ layers. Consider a single S-Box component of the non-linear γ layer. If we
have an input of 0xD5 to the S-box, the output obtained is 0x11. After involution, we
get back 0xD5, which was the original input applied. Hence, the system will not report
an error. Now, if a fault occurs in the system such that the two LSBs of the P-box are
stuck at logic 1, then after 0xD5 is passed through the S-Box, 0x71 is obtained, which
is a faulty output. Interestingly, the involution output obtained in this case is also
0xD5. Since this value is equal to the original input, the system fails to report an error.
This implies that in extremely rare cases as the one explained above, the CED method
that we propose does not yield accurate results. Problems like the one described above
do not affect the θ layer because θ is a diffusion layer and every bit in the output is
dependent on every bit in the input. Hence, on performing involution, all multiple-bit
errors are also detected, giving 100% fault coverage.

6 Conclusion

We proposed a low cost CED technique for involutional ciphers which exploits the involution property of the cipher. For the involutional cipher the proposed technique entails an additional 23.8% silicon area and degrades the throughput by less than 10%. This technique entails a 4.5% time overhead (which can be reduced to 0% if the CED is ignored only for the σ layer in the last round of encryption/decryption). The fault injection based simulation shows the proposed CED technique detects all single-bit faults and around 99% of all multiple-bit faults.

KHAZAD round key generation algorithm expands the 128-bit user key K in to nine 64-bit round keys $K^0, K^1 ..., K^8$. The round key K^r for the rth round is derived as $K^r = \rho[c^r](K^{r-1}) \oplus K^{r-2}, 0 \le r \le 8$ where, K^{-2} and K^{-1} are the most and least significant parts of the key user key K and c^r is a 64-bit constant for the rth round derived as $c^r_i = S[8r + i], 0 \le r \le 8, 0 \le i \le 7$. Since round key generation uses the KHAZAD round function ρ, the CED method proposed in this paper can be applied to detect all single-bit faults.

References

1. D. Boneh, R. DeMillo and R. Lipton, "On the importance of checking cryptographic protocols for faults", *Proceedings of Eurocrypt*, Lecture Notes in Computer Science vol 1233, Springer-Verlag, pp. 37-51, 1997
2. E. Biham and A. Shamir, "Differential Fault Analysis of Secret Key Cryptosystems", *Proceedings of Crypto*, Aug 1997
3. J. Bloemer and J.P. Seifert, "Fault based cryptanalysis of the Advanced Encryption Standard," www.iacr.org/eprint/2002/075.pdf
4. C. Giraud, "Differential Fault Analysis on AES", http://eprint.iacr.org/2003/008.ps
5. Jean-Jacques Quisquater, Gilles Piret, "A Differential Fault Attack Technique Against SPN Structures, with Application to the AES and KHAZAD,"*Fifth International Workshop on Cryptographic Hardware and Embedded Systems (CHES 2003)*, Volume 2779 of Lecture Notes in Computer Science, pages 77-88, Springer-Verlag, September 2003
6. R. Karri, K. Wu, P. Mishra and Y. Kim, "Concurrent Error Detection of Fault Based Side Channel Cryptanalysis of 128-Bit Symmetric Block Ciphers," *IEEE Transactions on CAD*, Dec 2002
7. G. Bertoni, L. Breveglieri, I. Koren and V. Piuri, "On the propagation of faults and their detection in a hardware implementation of the advanced encryption standard," *Proceedings of ASAP'02*, pp. 303-312, 2002
8. G. . Bertoni, L. Breveglieri, I. Koren, and V. Piuri, "Error Analysis and Detection Procedures for a Hardware Implementation of the Advanced Encryption Standard," *IEEE Transactions on Computers*, vol. 52, No. 4, pp. 492-505, Apr 2003
9. Joan Daemen, Vincent Rijmen, Paulo S.L.M. Barreto, "Rijndael: Beyond the AES," *Mikulášská kryptobesídka 2002 -- 3rd Czech and Slovak cryptography workshop*, Dec. 2002, Prague, Czech Republic

10. P.S.L.M. Barreto and V.Rijmen, "The KHAZAD legacy-level Block Cipher," *First open NESSIE Workshop*, Leuven, 13-14 November 2000
11. A. Biryukov, "Analysis of Involutional Ciphers: KHAZAD and ANUBIS," Proceedings of the 3rd NESSIE Workshop, Springer-Verlag pp. 45 – 53
12. J. Daemen, M.Peeters, G.Assche and V.Rijmen, "The Noekeon Block Cipher," First Open NESSIE workshop, November 2000
13. P.S.L.M. Barreto and V.Rijmen, "The ANUBIS Block Cipher," Primitive submitted to NESSIE, September 2000,available at www.cosic.esat.kuleuven.ac.be/nessie
14. F. Standaert, G. Piret, G. Rouvroy, "ICEBERG: an involutional cipher Efficient for block encryption in Reconfigurable hardware," *FSE 2004*, Springer-Verlag, February 2004
15. F. Standaert, G. Rouvroy, J. Quisquater, J.Legat, "Efficient FPGA Implementations of Block Ciphers KHAZAD and MISTY1," proceedings of the 3rd NESSIE Workshop, Munich, November, 2002

Public Key Authentication with One (Online) Single Addition

Marc Girault and David Lefranc

France Télécom R&D
42 rue des Coutures
F-14066 Caen, France
{marc.girault,david.lefranc}@francetelecom.com

Abstract. We focus on the GPS identification scheme implementation in low cost chips, i.e not equipped with a microprocessor (such as those embedded in some prepaid telephone cards or RFID tags). We present three solutions to decrease the overall number of manipulated bits during the computation of the answer by a factor two or three. All the solutions stand in the use of low Hamming weight parameters. The first one consists in building the private key as the product of low Hamming weight sub-keys. The second one suggests the choice of full size low Hamming weight private keys. Finally, the third solution corresponds to a variant of the basic GPS scheme in which large challenges with low Hamming weight are used. Whereas the first solution does not withdraw the need for a multiplier in the chip, the two other ones are ideally suited to low cost chips as they can be implemented with only one serial addition. Therefore, as a surprising result, one entity can be public key authenticated by doing one on-line addition only at the time of authentication!

Keywords: Low cost chips, GPS identification scheme, RFID tags, zero-knowledge.

1 Introduction

In 1989, C.P. Schnorr [11] presented an asymmetric identification scheme, based on *the discrete logarithm modulo a prime integer* problem, which contains three passes: the prover first sends a *commitment*, then receives a *challenge* from the verifier and finally sends an *answer* depending on both the challenge and private parameters.

One year before, J.J. Quisquater and L.C Guillou had presented the algorithm GQ [6], based on *the e-th root modulo a composite integer* problem, which also contains three passes. In both schemes, the first step consists in computing a commitment with one modular exponentiation; but, on average, the exponents used in the Schnorr scheme have a larger binary size than (the constant one) in GQ: as a consequence, computing commitments in the Schnorr scheme requires the manipulation of more bits than in GQ. Whereas the challenge steps are

M. Joye and J.-J. Quisquater (Eds.): CHES 2004, LNCS 3156, pp. 413–427, 2004.

identical, a second difference between the two schemes stands in the answer: the Schnorr one only requires one modular multiplication and one modular addition while GQ requires another (small) modular exponentiation. Thus, in this third step, the GQ answer computation manipulates more bits than the Schnorr one.

Moreover, in his article, C.P. Schnorr presented a *preprocessing* algorithm to efficiently calculate the commitments. A few years later, P. de Rooij [2] proved this solution to be insecure. However, as in most discrete-logarithm-based identification schemes, the commitment can be computed in advance, so that it does not require the exponentiation to be efficiently computed. Moreover, one can even envisage that the commitment be computed by another entity, namely a trusted third party, subsequently stored in the non-volatile memory of the chip. Thus, the Schnorr scheme, as claimed by its author, is well-designed for identification by smart cards as the computation power can be limited to the one needed to perform one modular addition and one modular multiplication.

With this scheme, C.P. Schnorr was able to efficiently use (ordinary) smart cards for authentication. But, the price of such devices still limits their wide development. Thus, chips with small computation power, typically between 500 and 2000 logical gates, called low cost chips in the following, represent a good alternative: their low price makes it usable everywhere. But, for such devices, the Schnorr scheme is no longer well-designed. Indeed, performing modular reductions and even multiplications (see subsection 2.3) are quite difficult for these devices. Then, new schemes appear, trying to modify the answer structure to decrease the computation cost.

In 1991, the GPS scheme was introduced by M. Girault in [3] and proved secure by J. Stern and G. Poupard in 1998 [10]. This scheme is quite similar to the Schnorr one except it is based on *the discrete logarithm modulo a composite integer* problem and the answer computation is easier than the Schnorr one, as it only contains one multiplication and one addition without any modular reduction.

At Financial Cryptography 2002, T. Okamoto, M. Tada and A. Miyaji presented the OTM scheme [8] based on the discrete logarithm problem; the new fact was the absence of multiplication in the answer which only contains one addition and one modular reduction. But one year later, in the same conference, J. Stern and J.P. Stern presented an efficient attack against the OTM scheme [12]. The authors presented at the same time a new scheme also based on the discrete logarithm problem; once again the main fact stood in the answer which contains no multiplication; its computation is based on a new easy operation called dovetailing (this scheme is described in appendix B).

At Information Security Conference 2002, T. Okamoto, H. Katsuno and E. Okamoto [14] presented another variant of GPS, but which does not substantially decrease the number of operations of the basic GPS scheme.

In this paper, we continue the saga of implementing cryptographic schemes in low-cost devices. We focus on the basic GPS scheme which seems to be the best designed for such a goal: the absence of modular reduction makes the optimization of the multiplication very important as most of the manipulated bits come from this operation (whereas in the Schnorr scheme, it also comes from the modular reduction). So, we first recall the GPS scheme with its computation and security properties. After recalling the baby-step giant-step algorithm in part 3, we introduce two new types of private keys: in part 4, the private key is the product of low Hamming weight numbers such that it improves the answer computation cost in comparison with the use of GPS with classical private keys, or the Stern-Stern scheme. In part 5, we present full size private keys with low Hamming weight and such that the non-zero bits are far enough from each other: a direct application is for low cost chips, as the answer computation only requires one addition so that it can be done quickly and sequentially. In part 6, we focus on the type of challenges sent to the prover. Thus, we present a variant of the classical GPS scheme in which a new set of challenges is used; we also give security proofs of such a variant. Once again, such sets make this variant of GPS ideally designed for low cost chips. With reasonable sizes of parameters, we can achieve a level of security around 32, an adequate value in many environments, by only computing one on-line addition. In a final part, we compare these three solutions with the existing schemes: the basic GPS one and the Stern-Stern one.

2   The Basic GPS Identification Scheme

2.1   The GPS Scheme

The GPS identification scheme from [3,10], such as labellized by the NESSIE project [4] in 2003, is an interactive protocol between a prover and a verifier which contains one or several rounds of three passes. It is based on the discrete logarithm modulo a composite integer problem: during a round of authentication, a user proves his knowledge of a private value s related to the public value v by the equation: $v = g^{-s} \bmod n$. More precisely, a prover holds a private key s and a public key (n,g,v) such that:

- $n = pq$ is the product of two prime integers such that factoring n is difficult (thus, different sizes of n should be used depending on the fact that n is a universal or individual public key),
- g is an element of $\mathbb{Z}_n^*$ ($\mathbb{Z}_n$ denotes the residue class ring modulo n and $\mathbb{Z}_n^*$ the multiplicative group of invertible elements in $\mathbb{Z}_n$); preferably g is of maximal order modulo n,
- $v = g^{-s} \bmod n$.

There are also four security parameters S, k, R and l defined as follows:

- $S \geq 160$ is the binary size of the private key s,
- k is the binary size of the challenges sent to the prover and determines the level of security of the scheme.
- R is the binary size of the exponents used in the commitment computation. It is typically equal to $R = S + k + 80$.
- l is the number of rounds the scheme is iterated. Theoretically, l is polynomial in the size of the security parameters; l is often chosen equal to 1.

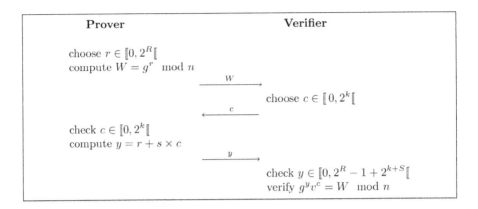

Fig. 1. The basic GPS identification scheme

2.2   Security of the Scheme

We briefly recall the security properties of the GPS scheme (more details are given in [10]).

- An honest prover is always accepted.
- It can be shown that if a dishonest prover is able to be authenticated with a probability substantially greater than 2^{-k} (the probability of guessing the value of the challenge), then this prover can be used to recover the private key. Thus, k is called the level of security of the scheme.
- Finally, it can be proved that a passive eavesdropper cannot learn information about the private key even from "many" executions of the protocol.

2.3   Answer Computation Cost

The computational cost of the answer is expressed in bit additions (assuming adding a t-bit number is equivalent to adding t times one bit). The answer y is equal to the addition of r with the result of the product $s \times c$. As the final goal is to implement such a scheme in low-cost devices, the *shift and add paradigm* seems to be an adequate implementation for the multiplication. On average, c has a Hamming weight equal to $k/2$ so that adding $s \times c$ to r with this algorithm leads on average to $k/2$ additions of a S-bit number so that the computation cost is equal to $kS/2$ bit additions.

In a low cost chip, decreasing the number of bit additions is important but it is not the essential. The essential is to make the operations as serial as possible, since (costful) RAM (Random Access Memory) is very small, read/write operations in NVM (Non-Volatile Memory) are slow, and addressing is sequential rather than random. This is why, while the first method we propose only decreases the number of bit additions, the two other ones propose to compute the answer with one large number addition, a serial operation in essence.

3   The Baby-Step Giant-Step Algorithm and Some Variants

In this section, we recall Shanks' *baby-step giant-step algorithm* [1] and some variants, which will be used in the following sections.

3.1   The Classical Algorithm

This algorithm was presented by D. Shanks in order to find discrete logarithms modulo n, where n is an integer (prime or not). Thus, given a public value $v = g^s$ mod n with s a S-bit secret number (we suppose S is an even integer), it recovers s in $\mathcal{O}(2^{S/2})$ in time and space. J.M. Pollard presented a variant [9] the running time of which is still $\mathcal{O}(2^{S/2})$, but uses very little space.

Shanks' algorithm consists in computing two lists of values: $\{g^i \bmod n \mid 0 \le i \le m-1\}$ and $\{v \times g^{-j \times m} \bmod n \mid 0 \le j \le m-1\}$ where $m = \lceil 2^{S/2} \rceil$. In the two sets, two values meet for one j_0 and one i_0 such that $s = i_0 + m \times j_0$.

The efficiency of this algorithm stands in the fact that it "cuts" the value s as an addition of two values.

3.2   Case of Low Hamming Weight Secret Exponents

In 1999, D.R. Stinson described variants in the case of low Hamming weight secret exponents [13]. Thus, given a public value $v = g^s$ mod n with s a S-bit secret number with an Hamming weight equal to t, it recovers s in $\mathcal{O}(S\binom{S/2}{t/2})$ (assuming S and t are even integers).

The algorithm uses *splitting systems*: it splits the set $[\![0, 2^S - 1]\!]$ in $S/2$ sets B_i, $0 \le i \le S/2 - 1$, such that any subset of $t/2$ values of $[\![0, 2^S - 1]\!]$ stands in a B_k. Thus, with such systems, it finds a decomposition of the t positions of the non-zero bits in two sets of $t/2$ values that stand respectively in one B_{j_0} and one B_{i_0}. Finally, an exhaustive search over all the possible sets of $t/2$ elements in each set B_j as in the classical algorithm (two lists) recovers the two $t/2$-sets corresponding to the positions of the non-zero bits.

Once again, this algorithm "cuts" the value s as an addition of two values.

3.3   Case of Secret Exponents Equal to a Product in a Group of Known Order

Let $G = \langle g \rangle$ be a group of known order N, v be a public value equal to g^s in G where s is the product of two elements respectively picked in X_1 and X_2. This variant takes advantage of the structure of s (we assume than N is larger than all the possible values s) and recovers s in $\mathcal{O}(max(\#(X_1), \#(X_2)))$.

As described by J. Hoffstein and J.H. Silverman in [7], computing the two sets $\{v^{j^{-1}} \bmod N \mid j \in X_1\}$ and $\{g^i \mid i \in X_2\}$ makes two values meet in the two sets for one j_0 and one i_0; the value s is then equal to $j_0 \times i_0 \bmod N$.

The practicality of this variant relies upon the fact that the order of the group is known, which makes possible to compute the values $j^{-1} \bmod N$.

4   Low Hamming Weight Private Sub-keys

In the second variant of the baby-step giant-step algorithm described in 3.3, note that if the order is unknown, the algorithm cannot be applied. Hence, it becomes possible to build a GPS private key as the product of smaller values, in order to optimize the computation cost of the answer, and more generally to speed up any multiplication involving the private key. A concrete solution consists in selecting private keys as equal to the product of low Hamming weight sub-keys.

The GPS scheme has this particular feature that the group generator g is of unknown order (at least to an enemy). As stated above, this can be used to optimize the computation of the answer. In the following, we make more precise the structure of the private keys that we suggest and the different properties it needs to ensure to protect this particular implementation from existing attacks.

4.1   The Structure of the Private Key

The construction of the S-bit private key s consists in choosing randomly t numbers, $s_1, s_2, \ldots, s_t$ of respective binary sizes $l_1, l_2, \ldots, l_t$ with $n_1, n_2, \ldots, n_t$ non-zero bits randomly located, such that $s = \prod_{j=t}^{1} s_j$.

A first constraint stands on such a decomposition: we impose that the s be exactly (and always) a S-bit number. Thus, we need to take into account the position of the non-zero bits and impose for each s_j, a range of bit positions, denoted by $[0, b_j]$ ($b_j < l_j$), where the n_j random bits are located such that even if all the random bits in each s_j correspond to the n_j possible most significant bits, we still obtain a S-bit value.

Finally, as in all schemes based on the discrete logarithm problem, the binary size of the private key must be at least 160 so that the classical baby-step giant-step algorithm has a complexity of around $\mathcal{O}(2^{80})$ or more.

As explained below, the goal of this approach is to optimize the computation cost of the answer $y = r + s \times c$. The trick consists in first computing $s_1 \times c$, then $s_2 \times (s_1 c)$, and going on with the other factors s_j. Thus, if c is a k-bit number, computing $s_1 \times c$ implies exactly n_1 additions of a k-bit number and the result value is a $(k + l_1)$-bit number. Then, computing $s_2 \times (s_1 c)$ implies n_2 additions of a $(k + l_1)$-bit number. If we generalize, (assuming adding a k-bit number is equivalent to adding k times one bit) we obtain as a final cost for the multiplication $\sum_{j=1}^{t} n_j \times (k + \sum_{u=1}^{j-1} l_u)$. Finally we need to add the number sc to r which requires $S + k$ bit additions. the answer computation cost is equal to $S + k + \sum_{j=1}^{t} n_j \times (k + \sum_{u=1}^{j-1} l_u)$. To optimize this computation cost equation, we need to minimize this expression considered as a function of t, l_j, n_j with still the other constraints cited above.

4.2   Other Security Aspects

Since the last variant of baby-step giant-step algorithm cannot be used, performing an exhaustive search seems to be the only way of retrieving s. So, the different factors s_j should be chosen such that the set of possible private keys is large enough: typically 2^{80} elements. It implies that: $\prod_{j=1}^{t} \binom{b_j+1}{n_j} \geq 2^{80}$.

Moreover, to prevent our construction from being vulnerable to the Stinson algorithm recalled above, we need to ensure that the Hamming weight of the private keys is not too low. This can be achieved by choosing numbers n_j such that their product is great enough (depending on the private key binary size).

4.3   Numerical Application

The number of factors t should preferably be equal to 2; in that case, the private key s is the product of s_1 of size l_1 with $n_1 + 1$ bits equal to 1 and s_2 of size l_2 with $n_2 + 1$ bits equal to 1. To avoid the Stinson attack, we also suggest that $n_1 \times n_2$ be great enough (more than 80 for example) in order to obtain a private key with a large enough Hamming weight. Finally, if we look at the computation cost equation, it becomes: $S + k + n_2 \times (k + l_1) + n_1 \times k$ which can be rewritten as $S + k \times (n_1 + n_2 + 1) + n_2 \times l_1$.

For example, a 160-bit private key s can be chosen equal to $s_2 \times s_1$ where s_2 is a 142-bit number with 16 random bits chosen among the 138 least significant ones and s_1 a 19-bit number with 5 random bits chosen among the 16 least significant ones. With such values, we obtain private keys of average Hamming weight equal to 64, which is enough to prevent from the Stinson attack (since the complexity is then around $\mathcal{O}(2^{80})$). The cost equation becomes $22 \times k + 464$.

5   Low Hamming Weight Full Size Private Keys

In this part, we focus on full size (i.e size of n) private keys which can be used in GPS. Generally, using large private keys is not recommended for low cost chips. Here we explain how to take advantage of a full size private key to obtain a very efficient answer computation. Moreover, we also suggest in appendix A a way for efficiently storing such private keys.

5.1   Description of the Private Key Structure

This approach consists in using a full size private key with a few non-zero bits which are distant enough to each other, so that multiplying a number with this key comes to concatening shifted versions of this number.

More precisely, assuming k is the binary size of the challenges sent to the prover, the non-zero bits of the private key must be separated by at least $k - 1$ zero bits. Thus, performing $s \times c$ only consists in writing disjoint blocks of bits, each block representing the binary decomposition of the challenge. So, computing the answer $y = r + s \times c$ can be performed sequentially as all the shifted challenges are disjoint. The computation is then very well suited to low cost chips.

Moreover, the computation cost of the answer is small: if we denote by t the Hamming weight of s, it consists of t additions of blocks of k bits so that the computation cost of the answer is equal to $k \times t$ bit additions.

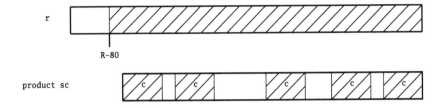

Fig. 2. A private key with a Hamming weight equal to 5

5.2   Security Aspects

We first need to obtain a key space large enough; so let us explain how to determine it for a S-bit private key with a Hamming weight equal to t and with non-zero bits separated by at least $k - 1$ zero bits.

As the $k - 1$ bits following a non-zero bit must be equal to zero, we can reduce the evaluation of such private keys cardinality to the one of private keys of size $S - (t - 1) \times (k - 1) - 1$ with a Hamming weight equal to $t - 1$ (subtracting $(t - 1) \times (k - 1)$ corresponds to the numbers of bits necessarily equal to zero and 1 corresponds to the Sth bit, equal to 1). Thus, with this reduction, the cardinality is obviously equal to the number of ways to locate $t - 1$ non-zero bits among $S - (t - 1) \times (k - 1) - 1$, which is equal to $\binom{S-(t-1)\times(k-1)-1}{t-1}$.

So let us now explain how to construct efficiently such private keys. The first step consists in finding integer value nb_{free} and t such that $\binom{nb_{free}}{t-1}$ is greater than a required key space size. Then, in a second step, depending on the level of security required denoted by k, we obtain the private key binary size, S, as follows : $S = nb_{free} + (t - 1) \times (k - 1) + 1$.

The second security point focus on the Stinson algorithm, recalled before. The complexity of the algorithm is then around $\binom{nb_{free}/2}{t/2}$. As shown in the below numerical application, this condition is generally ensured.

5.3   Numerical Application

If we use 600 free zero bits and a private key with a Hamming weight equal to 29, the key space cardinality is then equal to $\binom{600}{28} > 2^{159}$ and the complexity of the Stinson attack is then around $\binom{300}{14} > 2^{79}$. If we now want to use the private key in environments requiring at most a level of security $k = 32$, we finally obtain private keys binary size $S = 600 + 28 \times 31 + 1 = 1469$ (for $k = 16$, $S = 1021$).

6   Low Hamming Weight Challenges

In this section, we present a new way of selecting challenges, which may be of independent interest. Usually, the set of challenges is chosen as an interval of integers $[0, 2^k[$, where k is the level of security of the scheme. But it can also be defined as a set of values verifying a particular property, in order to achieve a specific goal. For example, in the following, we show how to speed up the computation of the answer in GPS scheme by defining a challenge as a sum of "sufficiently distant" powers of two (so that multiplying by the private key comes to adding several shifted and disjoint versions of the key). This is quite similar to the solution presented in the previous section, except that the roles of the private key and the challenge are swapped. But, contrary to it (and also in section 4) in which specific private keys are suggested but the protocol is not altered, the present one slightly modifies the protocol so that the security proofs must be adapted (which can be done in a straightforward manner).

6.1   Security

In most zero-knowledge interactive protocols [5], the verifier selects a random challenge in an interval of integers $[0, C[$, and it can be proven (by an "extraction" method) that, at each protocol iteration, a fake prover can answer to at most one value of the challenge. In other words, the probability of a successful masquerade is (substantially) upper bounded by $1/C$. The logarithm in base 2 of C is often reffered to as the "level of security" of the scheme, expressed in bits. For example, if this level is equal to 32 bits, an enemy will remain undetected with probability at most 2^{-32}.

   In the Schnorr scheme, the challenges are randomly picked in the interval $[0, 2^k[$, $2^{2k} < q$, where q is the order of the subgroup which is used. But they actually could be chosen in any subset of the interval $[0, q[$ of cardinality 2^k, without changing anything else in the protocol: the security proof (the so-called "soundness property") would remain valid. Note however that not any integer subset of cardinality 2^k would be convenient, since two challenges which are equal modulo q call for the same answer by the prover.

   In the GPS scheme, the situation is different in two ways. First, the size R of the exponent used in the commitment computation must grow with the maximum size of the challenge, in order to maintain the zero-knowledge property. Second, any integer subset of cardinality 2^k (with a "not too large" greatest element) can take the place of the interval $[0, 2^k[$, since the order of the subgroup is, in this case, unknown (at least to the enemy). More precisely:

Definition 1 *Let n be a modulus and g an element of $\mathbb{Z}_n^*$. Let S be an integer smaller than the order of g. The short discrete logarithm problem is to find s in $[0, S[$ given $g^s \bmod n$.*

Assumption 1 *The short discrete logarithm problem is polynomially intractable.*

Theorem 1 *(using notations of section 2). Let GPS* the variant of GPS in which the set of challenges is an integer subset of cardinality B bounded by the* *integer C. Then GPS^* is a (statistically) zero-knowledge interactive proof of knowledge of a short discrete logarithm if l, C and B are polynomial in $|n|$, lSC/R is negligible and $log(|n|) = o(l \times logB)$.*

Proof. (Hints) In the classical GPS, the challenges are randomly picked in the set $[\![0, 2^k[\![$ and the value 2^k, used during the security proofs, has two different goals. Indeed, it represents both the cardinality of the set and its upper bound. So, in order to correctly establish the security proofs of GPS*, we rely on the classical GPS proofs given in [10], by separating the two goals of 2^k.

   Completeness. Nothing is modified to the classical proof, as it only consists in the verification of the equation $g^y v^c = W \mod n$.

   Soundness. We can remark, as in the classical GPS, that the probability of impersonation is equal to $1/B^l$, so that we need $log(|n|) = o(l \times logB)$. Moreover, during the extraction, the running time is linear in l so that l must be polynomial in $|n|$. Finally, an exhaustive search over values smaller than C is required so that C must be polynomial in $|n|$.

   Statistical zero-knowledge. First, to generate valid triplets (W, c, y), and assuming that c is not randomly chosen (in the case of a dishonest verifier), we need to try B triplets in average to obtain one with a valid c. In order to obtain l valid triplets, we need on average $l \times B$ tries. So $l \times B$ must be polynomial in $|n|$. In a second part, we need to compare the distribution of a simulation and a real communication. Relying on the proof given in [10], lSC/R must be negligible.

   This approach leads to a new secure solution to speed up the multiplication in the GPS scheme, by using specific challenges. Let us now present how they are constructed.

6.2   A New Set of Challenges: The Property

The computation of the answer y in GPS requires an addition and a multiplication ($y = r + s \times c$). Whereas in the previous part we focused on the private key construction to decrease the cost of the multiplication, here we deal with the structure of the challenges. Roughly, our proposal consists in using large and low Hamming weight challenges with the non-zero bits far enough from each other.

   More precisely, if r and s are respectively R and S-bit integers, the challenge size k should be such that $R = S + k + 80$. Thus, adding the product $s \times c$ to r mainly transforms the $R - 80$ least significant bits of r.

   So, if we denote by B_s the binary representation of the private key s, the present solution consists in using challenges such that adding the product $s \times c$ to r only implies the addition of disjoint blocks B_s on the $R - 80$ bits of lowest Hamming weight of r. To obtain disjoint blocks B_s, the challenges only need to have non-zero bits separated by at least $S - 1$ zero bits. Thus, with this type of challenges, there is no longer any multiplication but only one serial addition of r with a large number composed of disjoint blocks B_s.

   Let us now consider the number of such challenges for a given R and S. Let u be the quotient of the Euclidean division of $R - 80$ by S; we can add at most u disjoint blocks representing the private key. The set $\mathcal{C}$ of challenges is:

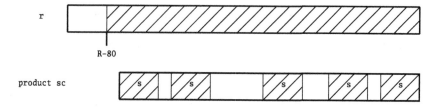

Fig. 3. A large challenge with an Hamming weight equal to 5

$$
\mathcal{C} = \left\{ \sum_{j=1}^{t} 2^{i_j} \mid \forall j \in [\![1, t-1[\![\; i_{j+1} \ge i_j + S, \; i_0 \ge 0, i_t < R - 80 - S, \; t \le u \right\}
$$

6.3   Cardinality of the Set

Let us denote by $\mathcal{N}\mathcal{B}_{R,S}(h)$ the number of challenges in $\mathcal{C}$ inducing $h \le u$ additions of blocks B_s for a S-bit private key s and commitment exponents r of size R. First, we consider in the following that the challenges size is at most $R - S - 80$ bits. As in the previous section, for a given h, $\mathcal{N}\mathcal{B}_{R,S}(h)$ is also equal to the number of ways to locate h non-zero bits among $R - 80 - S - h \times (S-1)$ since for each non-zero bit, the $S - 1$ following ones must be equal to zero. So we obtain that $\mathcal{N}\mathcal{B}_{R,S}(h) = \binom{R-80-S-h\times(S-1)}{h}$. Then, the cardinality of $\mathcal{C}$ is equal to:

$$
\sum_{h=0}^{u} \binom{R - 80 - S - h \times (S - 1)}{h}
$$

It is quite obvious that $\mathcal{N}\mathcal{B}_{R,S}(h)$ is higher for some h around u. However, in some cases, it can be more interesting to limit h to $u - 1$ or $u - 2$ as the level of security is not really modified and the computation cost can be decreased. For example, if $S = 160$ and $R = 880$, we obtain $u = 5$ and $\mathcal{N}\mathcal{B}_{880,160}(5) = 1$! Thus limiting h to 4 decreases the computation cost downto one addition of S bits.

6.4   Numerical Application

With this new type of challenges, we can achieve a level of security of around 32 if $R = 1088$ and $S = 160$ (using challenges with an Hamming weight equal to 5 and with a binary size at most equal to 850). This solution can be very efficient in environments using very little power such as low cost chips. Indeed, this solution only increases the regeneration time of the value r.

7   Comparison of the Answer Computation Costs

In this section we compare the three new solutions presented in this article with the existing efficient schemes: the GPS and the Stern-Stern schemes. We recall that these two schemes respectively lead on average to an overall number of $kS/2$ and $kS/3$ bit additions.

In the following table, S is the private key size and HW its Hamming weight.

Level of security	Existing solutions		Our solutions		
	Basic GPS S=160 HW unknown	Stern-Stern S=160 HW unknown	first solution S=160 HW around 64	second solution S=1469 HW=29	third solution S=160 HW unknown
16	1280	853	816	464	480 (380 3)
32	2560	1706	1168	928	800 (850 5)
64	5120	3413	1872		1600 (1800 10)
80	6400	4266	2224		1920 (2270 12)

Fig. 4. Number of bit additions in answer computation

To compare with the solution in which the private key is the product of low Hamming weight sub-keys, we use the numerical application given in section 4: s_2 a 142-bit number with 16 random bits and s_1 a 19-bit number with 5 random bits. The computation cost is equal to $22k + 464$.

For the second solution with full size low Hamming weight private keys, we also use the given example where s is a 1469-bit number with a Hamming weight equal to 29 (which can be used for level of security until 32).

For the last solution, which makes use of large and low Hamming weight challenges, three figures are given: the first one corresponds to the computation cost of the answer and the two last ones into brackets correspond respectively to the challenge binary size needed to obtain the target level of security and the smallest number of disjoint shifts of the private key that can be added to obtain the wanted level.

8   Conclusion

We have presented three new solutions to improve the implementation of the GPS scheme in low cost chips. Two of them use specific private keys the construction of which seems to resist to the current state of the art. The third solution lets the private key unchanged and only implies the use of particular challenges. The latter solution is as secure as the standard GPS scheme and is also the one which best improves the computational cost of the answer. The consequence of this solution is a very efficient implementation in low cost chips, so that one can be public-key authenticated by doing one on-line addition only!

References

1. H. Cohen. *A Course in Computational Algebraic Number Theory*, volume 138. Springer-Verlag, 1993.

2. P. de Rooij. On Schnorr's Preprocessing for Digital Signature Schemes. *Journal of Cryptology*, 10(1):1–16, 1997.
3. M. Girault. Self-certified public keys. In D. W. Davies, editor, *Advances in Cryptology - Eurocrypt'91*, volume 547, pages 490–497, Berlin, 1991. Springer-Verlag.
4. M. Girault, Poupard, and J. Stern. Some modes of use of the GPS identification scheme. In *3rd Nessie Conference*. Springer-Verlag, November 2002.
5. S. Goldwasser, S. Micali, and C. Rackoff. The Knowledge Complexity of Interactive Proof Systems. In *19th Annual ACM Symposium on the Theory of Computing*, pages 210–217, 1987.
6. L.C. Guillou and J.J. Quisquater. A practical zero-knowledge protocol fitted to security microprocessor minimizing both transmission and memory. In C. G. Günther, editor, *Advances in Cryptology - Eurocrypt'88*, volume 330, pages 123–128, Berlin, 1988. Springer-Verlag.
7. J. Hoffstein and J.H. Silverman. Random Small Hamming Weight Products with Applications to Cryptography. Technical report, NTRU Cryptosystems.
8. T. Okamoto, M. Tada, and A. Miyaji. An Improved Fast Signature Scheme without on-line Multiplication. In *Financial Crypto 2002*, 2002.
9. J.M. Pollard. Monte Carlo methods for index computations modulo p. *Mathematics of Computation (1978)*, 32:918–924, 1978.
10. G. Poupard and J. Stern. Security Analysis of a Practical "on the fly" Authentication and Signature Generation. In *Advances in Cryptology - Eurocrypt'98*, volume 1403, pages 422–436. Springer-Verlag, 1998.
11. C.P. Schnorr. Efficient identification and signatures for smart cards. In G. Brassard, editor, *Advances in Cryptology - Crypto'89*, volume 435, pages 239–252, Berlin, 1989. Springer-Verlag.
12. J. Stern and J.P. Stern. Cryptanalysis of the OTM signature scheme from FC'02. In *Financial Cryptography 2003*, 2003.
13. D.R. Stinson. Some baby-step giant-step algorithms for the low Hamming weight discrete logarithm problem. *Mathematics of Computation (2002)*, 71:379–391, 2002.
14. T.Okamoto, H.Katsuno, and E.Okamoto. A Fast Signature Scheme based on new on-line Computation. In *Information Security Conference'02*, number 2851, pages 111–121. Springer-Verlag, 2003.

A   Full Size Secret Key Storage

We denote by k the challenge binary size, by S the secret key binary size and by t the private key (low) Hamming weight. Moreover, we also consider that the level of security cannot be greater than k. Once the maximum level of security is determined, the private key storage directly depends on k, so that k cannot be changed after the creation of the card.

This (non unique) method consists in using private keys the non-zero bits of which are quite regularly located.

Indeed, assuming $t - 1$ divides $S - 1$ (otherwise, we can increase S), we can divide the $S-1$ bits (the Sth one is equal to 1) of the private key in $t-1$ intervals of $(S - 1)/(t - 1)$ bits, the position of the least significant bit of each interval corresponding to a multiple of $(S - 1)/(t - 1)$. In any interval of $(S - 1)/(t - 1)$, there is one block of k bits used to write the shifted challenge so that there are

$(S-1)/(t-1)-k$ free bits in the interval and as a consequence $(S-1)/(t-1)-k+1$ possible positions to write a non-zero bit in the interval. Thus, the private key can be written as:

$$s = 2^{S-1} + \sum_{i=1}^{t-1} 2^{(i-1)\frac{S-1}{t-1}+j_i}, \forall\ 1 \leq i \leq t-1,\ 0 \leq j_i \leq \frac{S-1}{t-1} - k$$

Thus, storing the private key can be reduced to the storage of the $t-1$ values j_i of constant size $log_2((S-1)/(t-1)-k+1)+1$; some values can be written with less than $log_2((S-1)/(t-1)-k+1)+1$ bits, but we would rather add zero bits to obtain the above size, so that we only need to store the value j_i without its binary size: storing s requires $(t-1)(log_2((S-1)/(t-1)-k+1)+1)$ bits.

For example, with this method, we can use a 1485 bit private key with an Hamming weight equal to 29 and in environments requiring a level of security at most equal to 32. Storing this private key leads to the storage of 28 numbers equal at most to 21 ($= 2^4 + 2^2 + 2^0$), so that $28 \times 5 = 140$ bits are necessary to store such private keys.

B   The Stern-Stern Scheme

B.1   The Scheme

Like GPS, it is based on the discrete logarithm modulo a composite integer problem. The private key is an odd s such that $1 = g^s \bmod n$ where g and n are public parameters. There are also four security parameters R, S, k and l which have the same goal and properties than in the basic GPS.

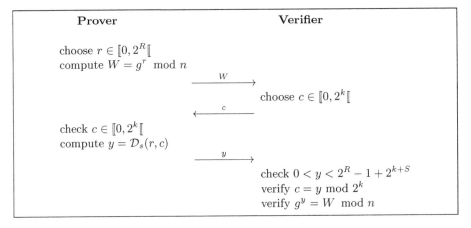

Fig. 5. The Stern-Stern scheme

B.2   The Dovetailing Operation

Let us now explain how to compute the answer practically. The operation $\mathcal{D}_s(r, c)$, called dovetailing, consists in making the k-bit number c appear as the k least significant bits of r by adding adequate shifts of s.

Notations. For any integer b, we denote by $|b|$ its binary size and by b_j, the $(j+1)^{th}$ bit of b starting from the least significant bit; thus $b = b_{|b|-1} \ldots b_1 b_0$.

First method. In a first way, the authors perform the dovetailing operation by only using s_0 (which is equal to 1 since s is odd). The answer is built progressively; the value y is first initialized with the value r. Then, we look at the bit r_0; if it is equal to c_0, then nothing is done, else we add s to r so that the wanted bit appears. We go on with the following bits. For example, if r_i is different from c_i, then we need to add an adequate shift of s, i.e $2^i \times s$, such that s_0 location coincides with the one of r_i. We follow this algorithm until r_k.

With this method, on average, $k/2$ bits over the k least significant bits of r need the addition of s, a S bit number. Thus, we obtain on average an overall number of $kS/2$ bit additions.

Second method. In a second way, the authors suggest the use of a private key the two least significant bits of which are equal to 01. Thus, they transform the value of r not only by adding, but also by subtracting some shifts of the private key. Indeed, when r_i is not equal to c_i, instead of automatically adding a shift of s, they first compute $t = 2r_{i+1} + r_i - 2c_{i+1} - c_i \bmod 4$. Depending on the value of t, they determine if it is better to add ($t = 3$) or to subtract ($t = 1$) a shift of the private key in order to obtain the wished value for r_{i+1} at the same time.

With this second method, on average, one bit over three requires one addition. The number of bit additions falls down from $k/2$ to $k/3$ so that, finally we obtain $kS/3$ bit additions.

Attacking DSA Under a Repeated Bits Assumption

P.J. Leadbitter, D. Page, and N.P. Smart

Dept. Computer Science,
University of Bristol,
Merchant Venturers Building,
Woodland Road,
Bristol, BS8 1UB,
United Kingdom.
{peterl,page,nigel}@cs.bris.ac.uk

Abstract. We discuss how to recover the private key for DSA style signature schemes if partial information about the ephemeral keys is revealed. The partial information we examine is of a second order nature that allows the attacker to know whether certain bits of the ephemeral key are equal, without actually knowing their values. Therefore, we extend the work of Howgrave-Graham, Smart, Nguyen and Shparlinski who, in contrast, examine the case where the attacker knows the actual value of such bits. We also discuss how such partial information leakage could occur in a real life scenario. Indeed, the type of leakage envisaged by our attack would appear to be feasible than that considered in the prior work.

1   Introduction

In previous work [4], Howgrave-Graham and Smart introduced a lattice based attack on DSA and EC-DSA in which they assumed that the adversary could obtain a certain number of bits of the secret ephemeral key for each message signed. By knowing only a few bits of each ephemeral key, an attacker could use their method to recover the entire secret and hence break the underlying cryptosystem. This method is related to the attacks of Bellare et. al. [1] and Bleichenbacher [2] who looked at issues related to poor generation of the random numbers which should be used in DSA/EC-DSA. Nguyen and Shparlinski [12, 13] subsequently extended the work of [4] to produce a more rigorous attack.

The concept of revealing secret information from a secure device such as a smart-card was made practical by the introduction of side-channel analysis. Specifically, on an undefended device, a simple power analysis (SPA) attack could leak a small number of bits from an exponentiation. When combined with the lattice techniques above, this leakage would result in the static private key being determined. However, defences against side-channel analysis are both increasingly well understood and frequently used in the field. Therefore the assumption that an attacker may be able to determine a specific set of bits from

M. Joye and J.-J. Quisquater (Eds.): CHES 2004, LNCS 3156, pp. 428–440, 2004.

the ephemeral secrets is less probable than when the original attacks were first published. It is far more probable that second order, seemingly innocuous information can still be recovered and used by the attacker, even if defence against first order leakage is implemented.

Consider the possibility that an attacker can determine some relation amongst the bits of the secret ephemeral key rather than their specific values. For example, if the target device were using a window method for exponentiation, by examining the data transfers across the bus it could be possible for the attacker to determine that the first window of bits is equal to the second window of bits. This would be the case whenever the same value was fetched from memory in successive iterations of the main exponentiation loop. In such a situation we would have

$$k_i = z_i + 2^t y_i + 2^{t+w} y_i + 2^{t+2w} x_i$$

where x_i, y_i and z_i are variables satisfying

$$x_i < 2^{l-t-2w}, \quad y_i < 2^w, \quad z_i < 2^t,$$

for a secret of l bits in length. We use this information to formulate a lattice reduction problem which, when solved, gives us the value of the static secret key.

In this paper, for convenience, we investigate the case where $z_i = t = 0$ so k_i is the concatenation

$$y_i \| y_i \| x_i.$$

Such a scenario requires we take on average 2^w samples before one of this form should present itself by chance. This simplification is advantageous since it allows us to keep the lattice dimension small, speeding up the lattice reduction stage of the attack. A successful attack yields the private key of the signer enabling the attacker to impersonate his victim and forge a signature of any message without the victim's consent or knowledge of his having done so. Although we focus on the applicability to DSA/EC-DSA, we note that it is possible to apply the attack to protocols with a similar signing equation such as Schnorr signatures.

We organise our work as follows. To justify our assumption that obtaining relational information about bits in the ephemeral secret, in Section 2 we start by investigating situations where such leakage could occur. We then recap on the DSA/EC-DSA algorithm and basics of lattice basis reduction in Section 3. In Section 4 we examine how one embeds the information obtained from the side channel into a lattice before reporting on some experimental results from our technique in Section 5. Finally, we present some concluding remarks in Section 6.

2   Possible Attack Scenario

Side-channel analysis is a fairly new but increasingly effective cryptanalytic method that focuses on the implementation of an algorithm rather than the specification. By observing an implementation being executed, the attacker can make correlations between the events that occur in the host processor and the data being processed. Perhaps the most famous of these types of attack involve timing [7,3] and power analysis [8]. In the former method, the attacker uses execution timings for either the whole algorithm or constituent parts to reason about the execution flow. For example, an implementation might take longer to run if a conditional branch is taken than if it is not taken. If that branch depends on a secret, key related value then being able to determine if it was taken or not can reveal said value. The later method uses the amount of power a processor uses to infer what operations and data items are being processed. A multiplication, for example, has a distinct profile within a power usage trace and will differ considerably from an addition. Furthermore, it is possible to discover the values of information being written into register or transfered across a bus since the state change in underlying logic will be different, and hence draw a different amount of power, depending on what values are used. If these values are assumed secret as part of the algorithm specification, the attacker is granted an easy and dangerous method of bypassing whatever hard mathematical problem the cryptosystem is based. There are two well accepted methods for performing power analysis attacks: simple power analysis (SPA) where only a single profile is enough to reveal information and differential power analysis (DPA) where correlation between multiple profiles is used to mount attacks that might otherwise fail in the SPA setting.

These techniques are made more dangerous by the environment in which they exist and the processing devices that are involved. Traditionally, side-channel attacks are mounted against accessible, portable processing units such as smartcards. Such devices are attractive to the attacker since they carry a potentially valuable, money or identity related payload and the physical access required for attacks is easier than in other cases. Furthermore, it has consistently been shown that a skilled engineer can mount side-channel attacks with low cost, commodity equipment essentially lowering the bar in terms of the investment required to break a given cryptosystem.

Often in side-channel attacks, directly revealing secret information is made difficult either by the inherent problems of mounting the profiling phase to collect observations of execution, or by defences employed in either hardware or software by the system designers. Such defences aim to reduce the amount of exploitable information that can be collected by the attacker. However, it has often been the case that seemingly innocuous information can still be harnessed by the attacker to their advantage thereby enabling new attacks that were not thought possible. Three such examples of new attack methods involve fixed table based implementations of elliptic curve (ECC) point multiplication [14,18]; so called address-bit DPA which uses address calculation rather than data utilisation to provide information; and cache directed analysis of block ciphers [16,17].

2.1   Table Based Exponentiation

Consider the following algorithm for computing an ECC point multiplication using the windowed, or w-ary, method.

- *Preprocessing Stage*
  - $T_i \leftarrow \mathcal{O}$.
  - For $i = 1$ upto $2^w - 1$.
    * $T_i \leftarrow T_{i-1} + P$.
- *Main Loop*
  - $Q \leftarrow \mathcal{O}$.
  - For $i = |k|/w$ downto 0.
    * For $j = 0$ upto w.
      · $Q \leftarrow 2Q$.
    * $Q \leftarrow Q + T_{k_i}$.
  - Return Q.

In order to improve upon standard methods, the algorithm precomputes a table containing small multiples of P. Using this table, we process the multiplier k in chunks of w bits in size rather than one bit at a time, by writing

$$k = \sum_{i=0}^{|k|/w} k_i 2^{iw}.$$

This acts to reduce the number of additive operations we perform and hence accelerate execution.

Although this method is attractive where memory for the precomputation can be spared, it is vulnerable to side-channel attack. If the attacker can isolate the portion of execution where the point T_{k_i} is read from memory he can compare this to known bit patterns, discover which table index is being read and thereby recover k. Even if the point in question can not be uniquely determined for some reason, equality or relations between two points, and hence values of k_i, may be established which at least lessen the workload of the attacker using further analytic methods. This vulnerability was thought to be such a problem that Möller [11], among others, formulated a defence whereby each point in the table was subject to some form of projective randomisation so that the points are no longer fixed and hence present an observer with no useful information.

2.2 Address-Bit DPA

Table based point multiplication algorithms are also attackable via address-bit DPA [5] since if one can focus on and recover the index k_i that is calculated and used to perform the load of T_{k_i}, the multiplier k is insecure. Defences against this new form of attack have been proposed [6] that mix a random value r into the index so that the access is performed as $T_{k_i \oplus r}$. If r is refreshed before each application of the point multiplication algorithm, the table accesses are permuted to some extent meaning that simply recovering the address of a given access does not reveal the corresponding part of the secret multiplier. The problem with this approach is that relationships between the permuted indices will be retained so that if $k_i = k_j$ then after application of the proposed defence, it is still true that $k_i \oplus r = k_j \oplus r$. If the attacker can recover this relational information either directly or as part of some higher-order statistical approach [10], it could perhaps be used to break the defence.

2.3   Cache-Based Cryptanalysis

Using the behaviour of the bus is one way to snoop on how the table is accessed but since it is located in memory and potentially accessed through a cache, the data dependent behaviour of said cache could also yield information. This form of attack was successfully performed against DES [16,17] whereby the attacks processed many plaintexts and collected those which took the longest to operate on. The attackers then made the correlation that longer execution time means more cache misses and that more cache misses meant a higher probability that two S-box entries were distinct. Hence, by using only conglomerate information about the total time of execution the attackers used the statistical bias in their collected sample to break the algorithm using further processing involving a workload of 2^{24} DES applications. This attack was performed on and against a desktop computer with a normal cache memory and minimal profiling tools. Clearly a similar principle applies in the point multiplication algorithm described above. Under the admittedly gross assumption that the cache is initially empty, the accesses to T_{k_i} will provoke a series of cache hits or misses depending on if the point in question has been loaded before or not. Using this information, relations about the values of k_i that provoked the table accesses can be recovered. Indeed, direct probing of the cache hits and misses might not even be required since statistical methods as described above could be used to guess the required value from a biased set of collected results.

2.4   Attack Summary

Clearly, as in most side-channel attack methods, the ability to perform a phase of profiling that yields the required information is vital to success. The rest of this paper assumes that an attacker can construct such a profiling phase and extract relational information as described. That is, we assume the attacker can recover w_i, a set of relations about w bit sized windows of k, with the following form

$$w_0 \; = \; w_1$$
$$w_1 \; \neq \; w_2$$
$$\cdots$$

This example indicates that window zero is equal to window one which in turn is not equal to window two. If $w = 4$ and we count from the least significant bit, this means bits zero to three of k are equal to bits four to seven and so on. It is imperative to note that in each case we have no idea about the actual value of the bits involved, only relations between them.

Under this assumption, we focus on lattice based mathematical techniques that could be used to exploit such information should the attacker be able to recover it, using multiple runs of DSA/EC-DSA style signature schemes. Although we should consider the effect of an algorithm under attack within context, i.e. within a system with a composite defence against a number of attack avenues, our goal is to explore the effect of neglecting to secure this sort of presumed innocuous side-channel information. As such, this work provides three main contributions: a potential side-channel attack technique, a warning to those implementing systems that may fall under attack and an advancement in lattice based analytic methods. All are useful since it is clearly important to understand new vulnerabilities, even of a potential or theoretical nature, so that they can be solved before production systems are released into the market.

3 Notation: Signature Schemes and Lattices

In this section we introduce the notations and ideas required in subsequent discussion of our attack technique. In particular we recap on DSA style signature schemes and the notion of lattice basis reduction.

3.1 DSA-Style Signature Schemes

The DSA algorithm, or equivalently EC-DSA, works in a finite abelian group G of prime order q generated by g. The private key is an integer $\alpha \in \{0, \dots, q-1\}$, and the public key is the group element $y = g^\alpha$. We assume a conversion function

$$f : G \longrightarrow \mathbb{F}_q.$$

For DSA this function is given by

$$f : \begin{cases} G < \mathbb{F}_p^* \longrightarrow & \mathbb{F}_q \\ h & \longmapsto h \pmod{q}. \end{cases}$$

Whilst for ECDSA the conversion function is given by

$$f : \begin{cases} E(\mathbb{F}_p) \longrightarrow & \mathbb{F}_q \\ P & \longmapsto x(P) \pmod{q}, \end{cases}$$

where we interpret the x coordinates of P, denoted $x(P)$, as an integer before reduction modulo q.

Signing: To sign a message m, the owner of the key α selects an ephemeral secret k and computes

$$r = f(g^k)$$

before evaluating the signing equation

$$s = (H(m) + r\alpha)/k \pmod{k}.$$

The signature on the message m is then the pair (r, s).

Verification: To verify a signature (r, s) on a message m one first computes

$$a = H(m)/s \pmod{q} \text{ and } b = r/s \pmod{q}.$$

One then checks that

$$f\left(g^a y^b\right) = f\left(g^{(H(m)+r\alpha)/s}\right)$$
$$= f\left(g^{ks/s}\right) = f(g^k)$$
$$= r.$$

3.2   Lattice Basis Reduction

We first fix a positive integer d. For our purposes a lattice is a $\mathbb{Z}$-module spanned by n-linearly independent vectors in $\mathbb{R}^d$. The spanning set $\{b_1, \ldots, b_d\}$ is called the basis of the lattice. If we let the $d \times d$ matrix B be defined by column i being equal to lattice basis vector b_i then the associated lattice L is given by the set

$$L = \{B \cdot z : z \in \mathbb{Z}^d\}.$$

Lattice bases, and hence bases matrices, are unique up to multiplication on the right by an element of $GL_d(\mathbb{Z})$. Hence the integer

$$\Delta(L) = |\det(B)|$$

is well defined and does not depend on the actual basis being considered.

Amongst all possible basis there are some which are "better" than others, however finding a "good" basis and defining what one means by "good" can be quite difficult. In 1983 Lenstra, Lenstra and Lovász [9] defined a notion of a "good" lattice basis and gave a polynomial time algorithm to reduce an arbitrary lattice basis to one which satisfied their conditions. A basis which is reduced in the sense of Lenstra, Lenstra and Lovász is called LLL-reduced. We do not give the definition and algorithm here but simply refer the reader to [9] for more details. However, we do require the following result about LLL-reduced lattice bases

Theorem 1. *If $B = \{b_1, \ldots, b_d\}$ denotes an LLL-reduced basis for the lattice L then*

1. For all $x \neq 0$ in the lattice L we have, for some constant c,

$$\|b_1\|^2 \leq c\|x\|^2.$$

   The constant c in the above statement can be taken to be 2^{d-1}.
2. We have

$$\|b_1\| \leq 2^{(d-1)/4} \Delta(L)^{1/d}.$$

The above theorem tells us that the first vector in an LLL-reduced basis is a close approximation to the smallest vector in a lattice and that the lattice size is approximately $\Delta(L)^{1/n}$. One should note that the problem of finding the smallest non-zero vector in a lattice appears to be a very hard computational problem, but that the LLL-algorithm provides an approximation in polynomial time.

4   Embedding into a Lattice Problem

Suppose we run DSA/EC-DSA repeatedly and, through the side-channel attacks mentioned previously, or otherwise, we find $n+1$ signatures where the ephemeral key k_i is of the form, for $i = 0, \ldots, n$,

$$y_i \| y_i \| x_i$$

where

$$q \approx 2^l, \ y_i < 2^w \text{ and } x_i < 2^{l-2w},$$

i.e. we have

$$k_i = x_i 2^{l-2w} + y_i(1 + 2^w)$$

where x_i and y_i are unknowns. Note that it will take on average $n2^w$ signatures to obtain all this data if ephemeral keys are chosen at random and the means of detecting whether such an ephemeral key occurs is one hundred percent accurate. From the $n + 1$ signing equations

$$s_i = (H(m_i) + r_i\alpha)k_i^{-1} \pmod{q} \text{ for } i = 0, \ldots, n,$$

we can form n equations

$$r_0 s_i k_i - r_i s_0 k_0 = r_0 H(m_i) - r_i H(m_0) \pmod{q} \text{ for } i = 1, \ldots, n,$$

by eliminating the variable α corresponding to the static private key. Substituting $k_i = x_i 2^{l-2w} + y_i(1 + 2^w)$ we have,

$$y_i = a_i + b_i x_0 + c_i x_i + d_i y_0 + \lambda_i q \text{ for } i = 1, \ldots, n,$$

for some $\lambda_i \in \mathbb{Z}$ where

$$
\begin{aligned}
a_i &= (2^w + 1)^{-1} s_i^{-1}(H(m_i) - H(m_0)r_i r_0^{-1}) \\
b_i &= 2^{l-2w}(2^w + 1)^{-1} s_i^{-1} s_0 r_i r_0^{-1} \\
c_i &= -2^{l-2w}(2^w + 1)^{-1} \\
d_i &= s_i^{-1} s_0 r_i r_0^{-1}
\end{aligned}
$$

Embedding these equations into the $d = 2n + 3$ dimensional lattice L generated by the columns of the matrix

$$
E = \begin{pmatrix}
\beta & 0 & 0 & & 0 & & 0 & & \\
0 & \gamma & 0 & & 0 & & 0 & & \\
0 & 0 & \gamma & & 0 & 0 & & & \\
\vdots & \vdots & & \ddots & & \vdots & & 0 & \\
0 & 0 & 0 & & \gamma & 0 & & & \\
0 & 0 & 0 & \ldots & 0 & \delta & 0 & \ldots & 0 \\
a_1 & b_1 & c & & 0 & d_1 & \delta q & & 0 \\
\vdots & \vdots & & \ddots & & \vdots & & \ddots & \\
a_n & b_n & 0 & & c & d_n & 0 & & \delta q
\end{pmatrix}.
$$

Then we have that $E \cdot \underline{x} = \underline{z}$ where

$$\underline{x}^t = (1, x_0, x_1, \ldots, x_n, y_0, \lambda_1, \ldots, \lambda_n),$$
$$\underline{z}^t = (\beta, \gamma x_0, \gamma x_1, \ldots, \gamma x_n, \delta y_0, \delta y_1, \ldots, \delta y_n).$$

In addition we would like the target vector $\underline{z}$ to be a short vector in the lattice. Hence, we need to choose the weights β, γ and δ in such a way as to increase the likelihood that $\underline{z}$ is indeed a short vector and hence likely to be found by lattice basis reduction. In our implementation we chose β, γ and δ to be related by $\gamma = 2^{2w-l}\beta$ and $\delta = 2^{-w}\beta$, to see why this is a good choice we need perform the following calculation.

From Theorem 1, a useful heuristic for predicting the success of such a lattice attack is to check whether our target vector z satisfies

$$\|z\| \le \Delta(L)^{1/d}.$$

It is easy to see that, for our t

$$
\begin{aligned}
\Delta(L)^2 &= \beta \gamma^{n+1} \delta^{n+1} q^n \\
&= \beta^{2n+3} 2^{(n+1)((2w-l)-w)} 2^{ln} \\
&= \beta^{2n+3} 2^{(n+1)(w-l)+ln} \\
&= \beta^{2n+3} 2^{nw+w-l}.
\end{aligned}
$$

and

$$
\begin{aligned}
\|z\|^2 &= \beta^2 + \sum_{i=0}^{n} \left(\gamma^2 x_i^2 + \delta^2 y_i^2 \right) \\
&\le \beta^2 \left(1 + (n+1) 2^{4w-2l} 2^{2l-4w} + (n+1) 2^{-2w} 2^{2w} \right) \\
&= \beta^2 (2n+3).
\end{aligned}
$$

Hence, for our lattice based approach to have a chance of succeeding, we must have

$$\sqrt{2n+3} \le 2^{(nw+w-l)/(2n+3)}.$$

In practice l is 160 and if d is much larger than 300, the computation of LLL reduced bases takes a prohibitively long time. If we assume reduction of 300 dimension lattices is both feasible and results in vectors close to the minimum (which is a very optimistic assumption), we are assuming that $n \approx 100$. We will recover the full secret if

$$3.83 \approx \log_2 \left(\sqrt{2n+3} \right) \le (101w - 160)/203.$$

i.e.

$$w \ge (3.83 \cdot 203 + 160)/101 = 9.28$$

Thus we expect 10 equal bits in consecutive positions to be sufficient in our problem.

5   Experimental Results

In order to get an idea of how successful this sort of attack might be, we ran a large number of experiments. Our initial goal was to sweep a reasonable area of the parameter space and determine a rough success rates for different combinations of window size and number of messages. However, as the number of messages grows the lattice dimensions and hence the time take to perform the attack also grows. This effect means that a great deal of processing time is required to perform attacks with a large number of messages. To enable completion of our experiments within a reasonable time frame, we distributed the workload across a network of around fifty Linux workstations each incorporating 2 GHz Intel Pentium 4 processors and around 512 Mb of memory. Using these machines we conducted one hundred runs of each combination of parameters and quote the success rate of these attacks in Table 1.

Table 1. A table showing the success rate of attacking a 160 bit exponent with variable window size and different numbers of messages. Note that window sizes below 9 and number of messages below 20 yielded no successful attacks. Also note that the number of messages is the dominant factor in how long each attack takes and that we measure the average time taken in minutes.

	Messages					
Window	10	20	30	40	50	60
5	0%	0%	0%	0%	0%	0%
6	0%	0%	0%	0%	0%	0%
7	0%	0%	0%	0%	0%	0%
8	0%	0%	0%	0%	0%	0%
9	0%	0%	0%	12%	26%	30%
10	0%	0%	41%	96%	99%	98%
11	0%	0%	100%	100%	100%	100%
12	0%	31%	100%	100%	100%	100%
13	0%	99%	100%	100%	100%	100%
14	0%	100%	100%	100%	100%	100%
Time	0.38	4.72	21.70	106.28	317.21	570.89

Each attack involved two successive LLL reductions. The first LLL application used a floating point implementation of the Schnorr–Euchner algorithm [15] using deep insertions. Due to floating point errors this only provided an approximation to an LLL reduced basis. To obtain a fully reduced basis the version of De Weger [19] was then applied to the output basis from the Schnorr–Euchner algorithm.

There are several interesting features in these results. Firstly, it is clear that window sizes below 9 and number of messages less than 20 yielded no successful attacks. In terms of window size this is unfortunate since we would expect real attack scenarios to utilise small windows, for example window widths of size 4 or

5, that correspond to table indices or addresses for example. Secondly, there is a fairly polar behaviour in terms of success in that an attack seems to either work either nearly all of the time or nearly none of the time. Again, this is unfortunate from a practical stand point since as an attacker we can tolerate probabilistic success if the parameters allow more realistic choices.

The polar behaviour is a common feature of LLL experiments. For each lattice Λ, we can consider the value

$$D(\Lambda, a) = |\{v \in \Lambda : 0 < \|v\| < a\}|$$

We shall call function D the *norm distribution* of Λ. In out attack, we looked at lattices of a particular form

$$L(n, \beta, \gamma, \delta, \boldsymbol{a}, \boldsymbol{b}, c, \boldsymbol{d})$$

in which we know the size of one of the non-zero lattice points is small; our target vector $\boldsymbol{z}$ is less than some number Z. For fixed w and n, our norm distribution $D(L, \cdot)$ changes very little from experiment to experiment. When $D(L, Z+\epsilon) = 1$, where ϵ is a small number that accounts for the LLL error as an SVP oracle, we expect the attack to succeed. Moreover we expect it to succeed for all the other experiments of the same w and n values. Similarly when $D(L, Z + \epsilon)$ is large, we expect failure every time. Probabilistic success occurs when $D(L, Z + \epsilon)$ is small but larger than 1. Compared to the huge number of lattice points we are dealing with dwarfs the number of experiments we were able to do, we see probabilistic success on only a few of the parameter choices.

Our results only seem to succeed for $n \leq 9$. We believe this to be the limit of attacks using this style of lattice. A different lattice style could have quite a different norm distribution and could respond better to LLL, reducing our ϵ error term. This could yield much more favourable results than those presented here and remains an open problem. Indeed in the DSA attacks with several known bits, the success rate has been raised by simply inputting the information in a different way, see [12] and [13].

To get a better idea of how the attack behaves when using parameters that are ideal from an attackers point of view, we started a second set of experiments that focus on a window size of four but with much larger number of messages. We expected this to be more suitable in practice since, as discussed in Section 2, four bit indices are often used in table driven exponentiation. If capturing relations between these indices is possible, we would therefore be interested in knowing their potential for use in an attack. Unfortunately, the results of these experiments were inconclusive due to the length of time and amount of memory required to complete each one. The bottleneck proved to be the efficiency of our LLL implementation which, with a large number of messages, required so much memory to store the lattice that the virtual memory system was unable to maintain an acceptable performance level. Although negative, this second result does provide us some information in the context of our investigation. That is, forcing an attacker to collect many signatures is clearly a good way to foil attack in a practical situation since performing the lattice reduction is too computationally hard.

6   Conclusions

We have presented an interesting extension of prior work on lattice reduction used in the context of side-channel attacks. We weaken the assumptions of previous work so that it is more probable that the profiling phase of an attack will recover useful information, even when defence measures are deployed against other techniques. By extending prior work that assumes an attack can obtain the value of secret information by allowing them simply to uncover relationships between different parts of said information. This is especially dangerous in the context of signature schemes such as DSA/EC-DSA where such leakage can totally reveal the underlying secret.

However, the results from our experimentation are not as positive as the initial attack scenario. We found that the attacker would need to collect relationships about a large number of bits in contrast with knowing the value of a small number of bits in previous work. Such large relationships would be difficult to collect with existing side-channel analytic techniques and, in this respect, further work is needed to extend the attack. We expect that continued research into physically obtaining bit relationships from a target device and more efficient implementations of the lattice reduction stage might make our attacker more feasible in the future.

References

1. M. Bellare and S. Goldwasser and D. Micciancio. "Pseudo-Random" Number Generation Within Cryptographic Algorithms: The DSS Case. In *Advances in Cryptology – EUROCRYPT '97*, Springer-Verlag LKNCS 1233, 277–291, 1997.
2. D. Bleichenbacher. On the generation of DSS one-time keys. Preprint, 2001.
3. D. Boneh and D. Brumley. Remote Timing Attacks Are Practical. To appear in *12th USENIX Security Symposium*, USENIX Press, 2003.
4. N. Howgrave-Graham and N.P. Smart. Lattice attacks on digital signature schemes. *Designs, Codes and Cryptography*, **23**, 283–290, 2001.
5. K. Itoh, T. Izu and M. Takenaka. Address-Bit Differential Power Analysis of Cryptographic Schemes OK-ECDH and OK-ECDSA. In *Workshop on Cryptographic Hardware and Embedded Systems (CHES)*, Springer-Verlag LNCS 2523, 129–143, 2002.
6. K. Itoh, T. Izu and M. Takenaka. A Practical Countermeasure Against Address-Bit Differential Power Analysis. In *Workshop on Cryptographic Hardware and Embedded Systems (CHES)*, Springer-Verlag LNCS 2779, 382–396, 2003.
7. P.C. Kocher. Timing Attacks on Implementations of Diffie-Hellman, RSA, DSS, and Other Systems. In *Advances in Cryptology – CRYPTO '96*, Springer-Verlag LNCS 1109, 104–113, 1996.
8. P.C. Kocher, J. Jaffe and B. Jun. Differential Power Analysis. In *Advances in Cryptology – CRYPTO '99*, Springer-Verlag LNCS 2139, 388–397, 1999.
9. A.K. Lenstra, H.W. Lenstra and L. Lovász. Factoring polynomials with rational coefficients. *Math. Ann.*, **261**, 515–534, 1982.
10. T.S. Messerges. Using Second-Order Power Analysis to Attack DPA Resistant Software. In *Workshop on Cryptographic Hardware and Embedded Systems (CHES)*, Springer-Verlag LNCS 1965, 238–251, 2000.

11. B. Möller. Parallelizable Elliptic Curve Point Multiplication Method with Resistance against Side-Channel Attacks. In *Information Security (ISC)*, Springer-Verlag LNCS 2433, 402–413, 2002.
12. P.Q. Nguyen and I.E. Shparlinski. The insecurity of the Digital Signature Algorithm with partially known nonces. *J. Cryptology*, **15**, 151–176, 2002.
13. P.Q. Nguyen and I.E. Shparlinski. On the insecurity of the elliptic curve digital signature algorithm with partially known nonces. *Designs, Codes and Cryptography*, To appear.
14. W. Schindler. A Combined Timing and Power Attack. In *5th Workshop on Practice and Theory in Public Key Cryptosystems (PKC)*, Springer-Verlag LNCS 2274, 263–279, 2002.
15. C.P. Schnorr and M. Euchner. Lattice basis reduction: improved practical algorithms and solving subset sum problems. In *Proc. FCT 1991*, Springer-Verlag LNCS 529, 68–85, 1991.
16. Y. Tsunoo, E. Tsujihara, K. Minematsu and H. Miyauchi. Cryptanalysis of Block Ciphers Implemented on Computers with Cache. In *International Symposium on Information Theory and Its Applications (ISITA)*, 2002.
17. Y. Tsunoo, T. Saito, T. Suzaki, M. Shigeri and H. Miyauchi. Cryptanalysis of DES Implemented on Computers with Cache. In *Workshop on Cryptographic Hardware and Embedded Systems (CHES)*, Springer-Verlag LNCS 2779, 62–76, 2003.
18. C.D. Walter and S. Thompson. Distinguishing Exponent Digits by Observing Modular Subtractions. In *Topics in Cryptology (CT-RSA)*, Springer-Verlag LNCS 2020, 192–207, 2001.
19. B.M.M. de Weger. Solving exponential diophantine equations using lattice basis reduction. *J. Number Theory*, **26**, 325–367, 1987.

How to Disembed a Program?
(Extended Abstract*)

Benoît Chevallier-Mames[1], David Naccache[1], Pascal Paillier[1], and
David Pointcheval[2]

[1] Gemplus/Applied Research and Security Center
{benoit.chevallier-mames,david.naccache,pascal.paillier}@gemplus.com
[2] Ecole Normale Supérieure/CNRS
david.pointcheval@ens.fr

Abstract. This paper presents the theoretical blueprint of a new secure
token called the *Externalized Microprocessor* (XμP). Unlike a smart-
card, the XμP contains no ROM at all.

While exporting all the device's executable code to potentially untrust-
worthy terminals poses formidable security problems, the advantages of
ROM-less secure tokens are numerous: chip masking time disappears,
bug patching becomes a mere *terminal update* and hence does not imply
any roll-out of cards in the field. Most importantly, code size ceases to be
a limiting factor. This is particularly significant given the steady increase
in on-board software complexity.

After describing the machine's instruction-set we introduce a public-key
oriented architecture design which relies on a new RSA screening scheme
and features a relatively low communication overhead. We propose two
protocols that execute and dynamically authenticate arbitrary programs,
provide a strong security model for these protocols and prove their security under appropriate complexity assumptions.

Keywords: Embedded cryptography, RSA screening schemes, ROM-
less smart cards, program authentication, compilation theory, provable
security, mobile code.

1 Introduction

The idea of inserting a chip into a plastic card is as old as public-key cryptography. The first patents are now 25 years old but mass applications emerged
only a decade ago because of limitations in the storage and processing capacities
of circuit technology. More recently new silicon geometries and cryptographic
processing refinements led the industry to new generations of cards and more
complex applications such as multi-applicative cards [7].

Over the last decade, there has been an increasing demand for more and
more complex smart-cards from national administrations, telephone operators

---

* The full version of this work can be found at [6].

M. Joye and J.-J. Quisquater (Eds.): CHES 2004, LNCS 3156, pp. 441–454, 2004.

and banks. Complexity grew to the point where current cards are nothing but miniature computers embarking a linker, a loader, a Java virtual machine, remote method invocation modules, a bytecode verifier, an applet firewall, a garbage collector, cryptographic libraries, a complex protocol stack plus numerous other clumsy OS components.

This paper ambitions to propose a disruptive secure-token model that tames this complexity explosion in a flexible and secure manner. From a theoretical standpoint, we look back to von Neumann's computing model wherein a processing unit operates on volatile and nonvolatile memories, generates random numbers, exchanges data via a communication tape and receives instructions from a program memory. We revisit this model by alleviating the integrity assumption on the executed program, explicitly allowing malevolent and arbitrary modifications of its contents. Assuming a cryptographic key is stored in nonvolatile memory, the property we achieve is that no *chosen-program* attack can actually infer information on this key or modify its value: only authentic programs, the ones written by the genuine issuer of the architecture, may do so.

Quite customizable and generic in several ways, our execution protocols are directly applicable to the context of a ROM-less smart card (called the Externalized Microprocessor or $X\mu P$) interacting with a powerful terminal (Externalized Terminal or XT). The $X\mu P$ executes and dynamically authenticates external programs of *arbitrary size* without intricate code-caching mechanisms. This approach not only simplifies current smart-card-based applications but also presents immense advantages over state-of-the-art technologies on the security marketplace. Notable features of the $X\mu P$ are further discussed in Section 7 and in the full version of this work [6]. We start by introducing the architecture and programming language of the $X\mu P$ in the next section. After describing our execution protocols in Sections 4 and 5, Section 6 establishes a well-defined adversarial model and assesses their security under the RSA assumption and the collision-intractability of a hash function.

2   The $X\mu P$'s Architecture and Instruction Set

XJVML. An executable program is modeled as a sequence of instructions $P = (INS_1, \ldots, INS_\ell)$ where INS_i is located at address i for $i \in 1, \cdots, \ell$ off-board. These instructions are in essence similar to instruction codes executed by any traditional microprocessor. Although the $X\mu P$'s instruction set could be similar to that of a 68HC05, MIPS32 or a MIX processor [10], we choose to model it as a JVML0-like machine [13], extending this language into XJVML as follows. XJVML is a basic virtual processor operating on a volatile memory RAM, a non-volatile memory NVM, classical I/O ports denoted IO (for data) and XIO (for instructions), an internal random number generator denoted RNG and an operand stack ST, in which we distinguish

- **transfer instructions: load** x pushes the current value of RAM$[x]$ (*i.e.* the memory cell at immediate address x in RAM) onto the operand stack. **store**

x pops the top value off the operand stack and stores it at address x in RAM. Similarly, load IO captures the value presented at the I/O port and pushes it onto the operand stack whereas store IO pops the top value off the operand stack and sends it to the external world. load RNG generates a random number and pushes it onto the operand stack (the instruction store RNG does not exist). getstatic pushes NVM$[x]$ onto the operand stack and putstatic x pops the top value off the operand stack and stores it into the nonvolatile memory at address x;

- **arithmetic and logical operations:** inc increments the value on the top of the operand stack. pop pops the top of the operand stack. push0 pushes the integer zero onto the operand stack. xor pops the two topmost values of the operand stack, exclusive-ors them and pushes the result onto the operand stack. dec's effect on the topmost stack element is the exact opposite of inc. mul pops the two topmost values off the operand stack, multiplies them and pushes the result (two values representing the result's MSB and LSB parts) onto the operand stack;

- **control flow instructions:** letting $1 \leq L \leq \ell$ be an instruction's index, goto L is a simple jump to program address L. Instruction if L pops the top value off the operand stack and either falls through when that value is the integer zero or jumps to L otherwise. The halt instruction halts execution.

Note that no program memory appears in our architecture: instructions are simply sent to the microprocessor which executes them in real time. To this end, a program counter i is maintained by the XμP: i is set to 1 upon reset and is updated by instructions themselves. Most of them simply increment $i \leftarrow i + 1$ but control flow instructions may set i to arbitrary values in the range $[1, \ell]$. To request instruction INS$_i$, the XμP simply sends i to the XT and receives INS$_i$ via the specifically dedicated communication port XIO.

SECURITY-CRITICAL INSTRUCTIONS. While executing instructions, the device may be fed with misbehaving code crafted so as to read-out secrets from the NVM or even update the NVM at wish (for instance, illegally credit the balance of an e-Purse). It follows that the execution of instructions that have an irreversible effect on the device's NVM or on the external world must be authenticated in some way so as to validate their genuineness. For this reason we single-out the very few machine instructions that send signals out of the XμP[1] and those instructions that modify the state of the XμP's non-volatile memory[2]. These instructions will be called *security-critical* in the following sections and are defined as follows.

Definition 1. *A microprocessor instruction is security-critical if it might trigger the emission of an electrical signal to the external world or if it causes a*

---

[1] Typically the instruction allowing a data I/O port to toggle.
[2] Typically the latching of the control bit that triggers EEPROM/Flash update or erasure.

modification of the microprocessor's internal nonvolatile memory. We denote by S *the set of security-critical instructions.*

As we now see, posing $S = \{\texttt{putstatic }\ x,\ \texttt{store IO}\}$ is not enough. Indeed, there exist subtle attacks that exploit i as a side channel. Consider the example below where k denotes the NVM address of a secret key byte $u = \text{NVM}[k]$:

$$P = (\texttt{getstatic }\ k,\ \texttt{if } 1000,\ \texttt{dec},\ \texttt{if } 1001,\ \texttt{dec},\ \texttt{if } 1002,\ \dots)\ .$$

The XμP will require from the XT a continuous sequence of instructions

$$\text{INS}_1, \text{INS}_2, \dots, \text{INS}_{u-1}, \text{INS}_u$$

followed by a sudden request of INS_{1000+u} and the value of $u = \text{NVM}[k]$ has hence leaked-out.

Let us precisely formalize the problem: a microprocessor instruction is called *leaky* if it might cause a physically observable variable (*e.g.* the program counter) to take one of several possible values, depending on the data (RAM, NVM or ST element) handled by the instruction. The opposite notion is the one of *data indistinguishability* that characterizes those instructions for which the processed data have no influence whatsoever on environmental variables. Executing a $\texttt{xor}$, typically, does not reveal information (about the two topmost stack elements) which could be monitored from the outside of the XμP. As the execution of leaky instructions may reveal information about internal program variables, they fall under the definition of security-criticality and we therefore include them in S. Following our instruction set, we have $S = \{\texttt{putstatic }\ x,\ \texttt{store IO},\ \texttt{if } L\}$.

3   Ensuring Program Authenticity

VERIFICATION PER INSTRUCTION. To ascertain that the instructions executed by the device are indeed those crafted by the code's author, a naive approach consists in associating a signature to each instruction *e.g.* with RSA[3]. The program's author generates a public and private RSA signature key-pair (N, e, d) and embeds (N, e) into the XμP. The code is enhanced with signatures $P = ((\text{INS}_1, \sigma_1), \dots, (\text{INS}_\ell, \sigma_\ell))$ where $\sigma_i = \mu(\text{ID}, i, \text{INS}_i)^d \bmod N$, μ denotes a deterministic RSA padding function[4] and ID is a unique program identifier.

Note that the instruction address i appears in the padding function to avoid interchanging instructions in a program. The role of ID is to guard against code mixture attacks in which the i-th instructions of *two* programs are interchanged. The XμP keeps the ID of all authorized programs in nonvolatile memory. We consider the straightforward protocol shown on Figure 1.

---

[3] Any other signature scheme featuring high-speed verification could be used here.

[4] Note that if a message-recovery enabling padding is used, the storage of P can be reduced.

0.	The XμP receives and checks ID and initializes $i \leftarrow 1$
1.	The XμP queries from the XT instruction number i
2.	The XT sends $(\mathsf{INS}_i, \sigma_i)$ to the XμP
3.	The XμP
(a)	ascertains that $\sigma_i^e = \mu(\mathsf{ID}, i, \mathsf{INS}_i) \bmod N$
(b)	executes INS_i
4.	Goto step 1.

Fig. 1. The Authenticated XμP(inefficient)

This protocol is quite inefficient because, although verifying RSA signatures can be relatively easy with the help of a cryptocoprocessor, verifying one RSA signature per instruction remains resource-consuming.

RSA-BASED SCREENING SCHEMES. We resort to the *screening* technique devised by Bellare, Garay and Rabin in [4]. Unlike verification, screening ascertains that a batch of messages has been signed instead of checking that each and every signature in the batch is individually correct. More technically, the RSA-screening algorithm proposed in [4] works as follows. Given a list of message-signature pairs $\{m_i, \sigma_i = h(m_i)^d \bmod N\}$, one screens this list by simply checking that

$$\left(\prod_{i=1}^{t} \sigma_i\right)^e = \prod_{i=1}^{t} h(m_i) \bmod N \quad \text{and} \quad i \neq j \Leftrightarrow m_i \neq m_j \ .$$

At a first glance, this primitive seems to perfectly suit our code externalization problem where one does not necessarily need to ascertain that all the signatures are individually correct, but rather control that all the code $(\{\mathsf{INS}_i, \sigma_i\})$ seen by the XμP has indeed been signed by the program's author at some point in time.

Unfortunately the restriction $i \neq j \Leftrightarrow m_i \neq m_j$ has a very important drawback as loops are extremely frequent in executable code (in other words, the XμP may repeatedly require the same $\{\mathsf{INS}_i, \sigma_i\}$ while executing a given program)[5]. To overcome this limitation, we introduce a new screening variant where, instead of checking that each message appears only once in the list, the screener controls that the number of elements in the list is strictly smaller than e (we assume throughout the paper that e is a prime number) *i.e.* :

$$\left(\prod_{i=1}^{t} \sigma_i\right)^e = \prod_{i=1}^{t} \mu(m_i) \bmod N \quad \text{and} \quad t < e \ .$$

This screening scheme is referred to as μ-RSA. The security of μ-RSA for $\mu = h$ where h is a full domain hash function, is guaranteed in the random oracle model [5] by the following theorem.

---

[5] Historically, [4] proposed only the criterion $(\prod \sigma_i)^e = \prod \mu(m_i) \bmod N$. This version was broken by Coron and Naccache in [9]. Bellare *et al.* subsequently repaired the scheme but the fix introduced the restriction that any message can appear at most once in the list.

Theorem 1. *Let (N, e) be an RSA public key where e is a prime number. If a forger $\mathcal{F}$ can produce a list of $t < e$ messages $(m_1, \ldots, m_t)$ and $0 \leq \sigma < N$ such that $\sigma^e = \prod_{i=1}^{t} h(m_i) \bmod N$ while the signature of at least one of $m_1, \ldots, m_t$ is not given to $\mathcal{F}$, then $\mathcal{F}$ can be used to efficiently extract e-th roots modulo N.*

The theorem applies in both passive and active settings: in the former case, $\mathcal{F}$ is given the list $\{m_1, \ldots, m_t\}$ as well as the signature of some of them. In the latter, $\mathcal{F}$ is allowed to query a signing oracle and may choose the value of the m_is. We refer the reader to [6, Appendix A.1] for a proof of Theorem 1 and detailed security reductions.

OPAQUE SCREENING. Signature screening is now used to verify instructions collectively as depicted on Figure 2. At any point in time, ν is an accumulated product of $t < e$ padded instructions $\nu = \prod_i \mu(\mathsf{ID}, i, \mathsf{INS}_i)$. Loosely speaking, both parties $\mathsf{X}\mu\mathsf{P}$ and XT update their own security buffers ν and σ which compatibility (in the sense of $\sigma^e = \nu \bmod N$) is checked before executing any security-critical instruction. Note that a verification is also triggered when exactly $e - 1$ instructions are aggregated in ν.

0.	The $\mathsf{X}\mu\mathsf{P}$ receives and checks ID and initializes $i \leftarrow 1$
1.	The $\mathsf{X}\mu\mathsf{P}$
(a)	sets $t \leftarrow 1$
(b)	sets $\nu \leftarrow 1$
2.	The XT sets $\sigma \leftarrow 1$
3.	The $\mathsf{X}\mu\mathsf{P}$ queries from the XT instruction number i
4.	The XT
(a)	updates $\sigma \leftarrow \sigma \times \sigma_i \bmod N$
(b)	sends INS_i to the $\mathsf{X}\mu\mathsf{P}$
5.	The $\mathsf{X}\mu\mathsf{P}$ updates $\nu \leftarrow \nu \times \mu(\mathsf{ID}, i, \mathsf{INS}_i) \bmod N$
6.	If $t = e$ or $\mathsf{INS}_i \in \mathcal{S}$ the $\mathsf{X}\mu\mathsf{P}$
(a)	queries from the XT the current value of σ
(b)	halts execution if $\sigma^e \neq \nu \bmod N$ (cheating XT)
(c)	executes INS_i
(d)	goto step 1
7.	The $\mathsf{X}\mu\mathsf{P}$
(a)	executes INS_i
(b)	increments $t \leftarrow t + 1$
(c)	goto step 3.

Fig. 2. The Opaque $\mathsf{X}\mu\mathsf{P}$ (secure but suboptimal)

As one can easily imagine, this protocol becomes rapidly inefficient when instructions of $\mathcal{S}$ are frequently used. For instance, `if`s constitute the basic ingredient of `while` and `for` assertions which are extremely common in executable code. Moreover, in many cases, `while`s and `for`s are even nested or interwoven. It follows that the Opaque XμP would incessantly trigger the relatively expensive[6] verification stage of steps 6a and 6b (we denote by CheckOut this verification stage throughout the rest of the paper). This is clearly an overkill: in many cases ifs can be safely performed on non secret data dependent[7] variables (for instance the variable that counts 16 rounds during a DES computation). We show in the next section how to optimize the number of CheckOuts while keeping the protocol secure.

4   Internal Security Policies

We now associate a *privacy bit* to each memory and stack cells, denoting by $\varphi(\text{RAM}[j])$, $\varphi(\text{NVM}[j])$ and $\varphi(\text{ST}[j])$ the privacy bit associated to RAM$[j]$, NVM$[j]$ and ST$[j]$. NVM privacy bits are nonvolatile. Informally speaking, the idea behind privacy bit is to prevent the external world from probing secret data handled by the XμP. RAM privacy bits are initialized to zero upon reset, NVM privacy bits are set to zero or one by the XμP's issuer at the production or personalization stage, $\varphi(\text{IO})$ and $\varphi(\text{RNG})$ are always stuck to zero[8] and one by definition and privacy bits of released stack elements are automatically reset to zero.

We also introduce simple rules by which the privacy bits of new variables evolve as a function of prior φ values. Transfer instructions simply transfer the privacy bit of their variable (*e.g.* getstatic 3 simultaneously sets ST$[s] \leftarrow$ NVM[3] and $\varphi(\text{ST}[s]) \leftarrow \varphi(\text{NVM}[3])$ where s denotes the stack pointer and ST$[s]$ the topmost stack element). The rule we apply to arithmetical and logical instructions is *privacy-conservative* namely, the output privacy bits are all set to zero if and only if all input privacy bits were zero (otherwise they are all set to one). In other words, as soon as private data enter a computation all output data are tagged as private. This rule is easily hardwired as a simple boolean OR for non-unary operators.

This mechanism allows to process security-critical instructions in different ways depending on whether they run over private or non-private data. Typically, executing an if L does not provide critical information if the topmost stack element is non-private. A CheckOut may not be mandatorily invoked in this case. Accordingly, outputting a non-private value via a store IO instruction does not provide any sensitive information, and a CheckOut can be spared in this case as well. In fact, one can easily specify a *security policy* that contextually defines the conditions (over privacy bits) under which a security-critical instruction may or may not trigger a collective verification. To abstract away the security policy chosen by the issuer, we introduce the boolean predicate

$$\text{Alert}: \mathcal{S} \times \Phi \mapsto \{\text{True}, \text{False}\}$$

---

[6] While the execution of a regular instruction demands only one modular multiplication, the execution of an INS$_i \in \mathcal{S}$ requires the transmission of an RSA signature (*e.g.* 1024 bits) and an exponentiation (*e.g.* to the power $e = 2^{16} + 1$) in the XμP.

[7] Read: non-((secret-data)-dependent).

[8] *i.e.* any external data fed into the XμP is considered as publicly observable by opponents and hence non-private.

where Φ denotes the set of all privacy bits $\Phi = \varphi(\text{RAM}) \cup \varphi(\text{NVM}) \cup \varphi(\text{ST})$. Alert($\text{INS}, \Phi$) evaluates as True when a CheckOut is to be invoked. We hence twitch our protocol as now shown on Figure 3.

0.	The XμP receives and checks ID and initializes $i \leftarrow 1$	
1.	The XμP	
	(a)	sets $t \leftarrow 1$
	(b)	sets $\nu \leftarrow 1$
2.	The XT sets $\sigma \leftarrow 1$	
3.	The XμP queries from the XT instruction number i	
4.	The XT	
	(a)	updates $\sigma \leftarrow \sigma \times \sigma_i \bmod N$
	(b)	sends INS_i to the XμP
5.	The XμP updates $\nu \leftarrow \nu \times \mu(\text{ID}, i, \text{INS}_i) \bmod N$	
6.	If $t = e$ or ($\text{INS}_i \in \mathcal{S}$ and Alert(INS_i, Φ)) the XμP	
	(a)	CheckOut
	(b)	executes INS_i
	(c)	goto step 1
7.	The XμP	
	(a)	executes INS_i
	(b)	increments $t \leftarrow t + 1$
	(c)	goto step 3.

Fig. 3. Enforcing a Security Policy: Protocol 1

5   Authenticating Code Sections Instead of Instructions

Following the classical definition of [1,11], we call a *basic block* a straight-line sequence of instructions that can be entered only at its beginning and exited only at its end. The set of basic blocks of a program P is usually given under the form of a graph $\text{CFG}(P)$ and computed by the means of control flow analysis [12, 11]. In such a graph, vertices are basic blocks and edges symbolize control flow dependencies: $\text{B}_0 \rightarrow \text{B}_1$ means that the last instruction of B_0 may handover control to the first instruction of B_1. In our instruction set, basic blocks admit at most two sons with respect to control flow dependance; a block has two sons if and only if its last instruction is an `if`. When $\text{B}_0 \rightarrow \text{B}_1$, $\text{B}_0 \Rightarrow \text{B}_1$ means that B_0 has no son but B_1 (but B_1 may have other fathers than B_0). In this section we define a slightly different notion that we call *code sections*.

Informally, a code section is a maximal collection of basic blocks $\text{B}_1 \Rightarrow \text{B}_2 \cdots \Rightarrow \text{B}_\ell$ such that no instruction of $\mathcal{S} \cup \{\texttt{halt}\}$ appears in the blocks except, possibly, as the last instruction of B_ℓ. The section is then denoted by $\text{S} = \langle \text{B}_1, \dots, \text{B}_\ell \rangle$. In a code section, the control flow is deterministic *i.e.* independent from program variables; thus a section may contain several cascading `goto` instructions. Code sections, unlike basic blocks, may share instructions; yet they have a natural graph structure induced by $\text{CFG}(P)$ which we do not use in the sequel. It is known that computing a program's basic blocks can be done in almost-linear time [12] and it is easily seen that the same holds for code sections. We refer to the full version of this work for an algorithm computing the set Sec(P) of code sections of a program P.

Given that instructions in a code section are executed sequentially, and that sections can be computed at compile time, signatures can certify sections rather than individual instructions. In other words, a single signature per code section suffices. The signature of a code section S starting at address i is:

$$\sigma_i = \mu(\text{ID}, i, h)^d \mod N \ ,$$

with $h = H(\text{INS}_1, \ldots, \text{INS}_k)$ where $\text{INS}_1, \ldots, \text{INS}_k$ are the successive instructions in S. Here, H is an iterative hash function recursively defined by $H(x_1, \ldots, x_j) = F(x_j, H(x_1, \ldots, x_{j-1}))$ and $H(x_1) = F(x_1, IV)$ where $F(x, y)$ is H's compression function and IV an initialization constant. We summarize the new protocol on Figure 4.

0.	The XμP receives and checks ID and initializes $i \leftarrow 1$	
1.	The XμP	
	(a)	sets $t \leftarrow 1$ (t now counts code sections)
	(b)	sets $\nu \leftarrow 1$
2.	The XT sets $\sigma \leftarrow 1$	
3.	The XμP	
	(a)	sets $h \leftarrow IV$
	(b)	queries the code section starting at address i
4.	The XT	
	(a)	updates $\sigma \leftarrow \sigma \times \sigma_i \bmod N$
	(b)	sets $j = 1$
5.	The XT	
	(a)	sends INS_j^i to the XμP
	(b)	increments $j \leftarrow j + 1$
6.	The XμP	
	(a)	receives INS_j^i,
	(b)	updates $h \leftarrow F(\text{INS}_j^i, h)$
7.	If $\text{INS}_j^i \in \mathcal{S}$ and (Alert($\text{INS}_j^i, \varPhi$) or $t = e$) the XμP	
	(a)	sets $\nu = \nu \times \mu(\text{ID}, i, h) \bmod N$
	(b)	CheckOut
	(c)	executes INS_j^i
	(d)	goto step 1
8.	Else if $\text{INS}_j^i \in \mathcal{S}$ then the XμP	
	(a)	sets $\nu = \nu \times \mu(\text{ID}, i, h) \bmod N$
	(b)	increments $t \leftarrow t + 1$
	(c)	executes INS_j^i
	(d)	goto step 3
9.	Else the XμP	
	(a)	executes INS_j^i
	(b)	increments $j \leftarrow j + 1$
	(c)	goto step 5.

Fig. 4. Authentication of Code Sections: Protocol 2

This protocol presents the advantage of being far less time consuming, because the number of CheckOuts (and updates of ν) is considerably reduced. The formats under which the code can be stored in the XT are diverse. The simplest of these consists in representing P as the list of all its signed code sections $P = (\mathsf{ID}, (1, \sigma_1, \mathsf{S}_1), \ldots, (k, \sigma_k, \mathsf{S}_k))$. Whatever the file format used in conjunction with our protocol is, the term *authenticated program* designates a program augmented with its signature material $\Sigma(P) = \{\sigma_i\}_i$. Thus, our protocols actually execute authenticated programs. A program is converted into an authenticated executable file via a specific compilation phase involving both code processing and signature generations.

6   Security Analysis

What we provide in this section is a formal proof that the protocols described above are secure. The security proof shall have two ingredients: a well-defined security model describing an adversary's goal and resources, and a reduction from some complexity-theoretic hard problem. Rather than rigorously introducing the numerous notions our security model is based upon (which the reader may find in [6], as well as the fully detailed reductions), we give here a high-level description of our security analysis.

THE SECURITY MODEL. We assume the existence of three parties in the game:

- a code issuer $\mathcal{CI}$ that compiles XJVML programs into authenticated executable files with the help of the signing key (N, d),
- an XμP that follows the communication protocol given in Section 4 and contains the verification key (N, e) matching (N, d). The XμP also possesses some cryptographic private key material k stored in its NVM,
- an attacker $\mathcal{A}$ willing to access k using means that are discussed below.

ADVERSARIAL GOALS. Depending on the role played by the XμP's cryptographic key k, the adversary's goals might be of different nature. Of course, inferring information about k (worse, recovering k completely) comes immediately to one's mind, but there could also be weaker (somewhat easier) ways of having access to k. For instance if k is a symmetric encryption key, $\mathcal{A}$ might try to decrypt ciphertexts encrypted under k. Similarly, if it is a public-key signature key, $\mathcal{A}$ could attempt to rely on the protocol engaged with the XμP to help forging signatures in a way or an other. More exotically, the adversary could try to *hijack* the key k e.g. to use it (or a part of it thereof) as an AES key whereas k was intended to be employed some other way. $\mathcal{A}$'s goal in this case is a bit more intricate to capture, but we see no reason why we should prohibit that kind of scenario in our security model. Third, the adversary may attempt to modify k, thereby opening the door to fault attacks [2,3].

THE ATTACK SCENARIO. Parties behave as follows. The $\mathcal{CI}$ crafts polynomially many authenticated programs of polynomially bounded size and publishes them.

We assume no interaction between the CI and $\mathcal{A}$. Then $\mathcal{A}$ and the $X\mu P$ engage in the protocol and $\mathcal{A}$ attempts to make the $X\mu P$ execute a sequence of instructions ξ that was not originally issued by the CI. The attack succeeds when ξ contains a security-critical instruction that handles some part of k which the $X\mu P$ nevertheless executes.

We say that $\mathcal{A}$ is an $(\ell, n, \tau, \varepsilon)$-attacker if after seeing at most ℓ authenticated programs $P_1, \ldots, P_\ell$ totalling at most $n \geq \ell$ instructions and processing at most τ steps, $\Pr[\mathcal{A}$ succeeds$] \geq \varepsilon$. In this definition, we include in τ the execution time $\mathsf{Time}(\xi)$ of ξ, stipulating by convention that executing each instruction takes one step and that all transmissions (instruction addresses, instructions, signatures and IO data) are instantaneous.

SECURITY PROOF FOR PROTOCOL 1. We state:

Theorem 2. *If the screening scheme μ-RSA is (q_k, τ, ε)-secure against existential forgery under a known message attack, then Protocol 1 is $(\ell, n, \tau, \varepsilon)$-secure for $n \leq q_k$.*

Moreover, when $\mu = \mathsf{FDH}$, outputting a valid forgery is equivalent to extracting e-th roots modulo N as shown in [6, Appendix A.1]. The following corollary is proved by invoking Theorem 1.

Corollary 1. *If μ is a full domain hash function, then Protocol 1 is secure under the RSA assumption in the random oracle model.*

SECURITY PROOF FOR PROTOCOL 2. We now move on to the (more efficient) Protocol 2 defined in Section 5. (μ, H)-RSA is defined as being the RSA screening scheme with padding function $(x, y, z) \mapsto \mu(x, y, H(z))$. We slightly redefine $(\ell, n, \tau, \varepsilon)$-security as the resistance against adversaries that have access to at most ℓ authenticated programs totalling at most n code sections. We state:

Theorem 3. *If the screening scheme (μ, H)-RSA is (q_k, τ, ε)-secure against existential forgery under a known message attack, then Protocol 2 is $(\ell, n, \tau, \varepsilon)$-secure for $n \leq q_k$.*

When $\mu(a, b, c) = h(a\|b\|H(c))$ and h is seen as a random oracle, a security result similar to Corollary 1 can be obtained for Protocol 2. However, a bad choice for H could allow the adversary $\mathcal{A}$ to easily find collisions over μ via collisions over H. Nevertheless, unforgeability can be formally proved under the assumption that H is collision-intractable. We refer the reader to the corresponding theorem given in [6, Appendix B]. Associating this result with Theorem 3, we conclude:

Corollary 2. *Assume $\mu(a, b, c) = h(a\|b\|H(c))$ where h is a full-domain hash function seen as a random oracle. Then Protocol 2 is secure under the RSA assumption and the collision-intractability of H.*

WHAT ABOUT ACTIVE ATTACKS? Although RSA-based screening schemes may feature strong unforgeability under chosen-message attacks (see [6, Appendix A.2] for such a proof for FDH-RSA), it is easy to see that our protocols cannot resist chosen-message attackers whatever the security level of the underlying screening scheme happens to be. Indeed, assuming that the adversary is allowed to query the code issuer $\mathcal{CI}$ with messages of her choosing, a trivial attack consists in obtaining the signature

$$\sigma = \mu(\mathsf{ID}, 1, H(\mathsf{INS}_1, \mathsf{INS}_2, \mathsf{INS}_3))^d \mod N$$

of a program P where ID is known to be accepted by the $\mathsf{X}\mu\mathsf{P}$ and the single-section program P is

$$P = (\texttt{getstatic 17, store I0, halt})$$

wherein $\mathrm{NVM}[17]$ is known to contain a fraction of the cryptographic key k, the value 17 being purely illustrative here[9]. Similarly, the attacker may query the signature of some trivial key-modifying code sequence. Obviously, nothing can be done to resist chosen-message attacks.

7   Deployment Considerations and Engineering Options

From a practical engineering perspective, our new architecture is likely to deeply impact the smart card industry. We briefly discuss some advantages of our technology.

CODE PATCHING. A bug in a program does not imply the roll-out of devices in the field but a simple terminal update. Patching a future smart card can hence become as easy as patching a PC. A possible bug patching mechanism consists in encoding in ID a backward compatibility policy signed by the $\mathcal{CI}$ that either instructs the $\mathsf{X}\mu\mathsf{P}$ to replace its old ID by a new one and stop accepting older version programs or allow the execution of new or old code (each at a time, *i.e.* no blending possible). The description of this mechanism is straightforward and omitted here.

CODE SECRECY. Given that the XT contains the application's code, our architecture assumes that the algorithm's specifications are public. It is possible to reach *some* level of secrecy by encrypting the XT's program under a key (common to all $\mathsf{X}\mu\mathsf{P}$s). Obviously, morphologic information about the algorithm will leak out to some extent (loop structure *etc.*) but important elements such as S-box contents or the actual type of boolean operators used by the code could remain confidential if programmed appropriately.

SIMPLIFIED PRODUCT MANAGEMENT. Given that a GSM $\mathsf{X}\mu\mathsf{P}$ and an electronic-purse $\mathsf{X}\mu\mathsf{P}$ differ only by a few NVM bytes (essentially ID), by opposition to smart-cards, $\mathsf{X}\mu\mathsf{P}$s are real commodity products (such as capacitors,

---

[9] The `halt` instruction is even superfluous as the attacker can power off the device right after the second instruction is executed.

resistors or Pentium processors) which stock management is greatly simplified and straightforward. Given the very small NVM room needed to store an ID and a public-key, a single XµP can very easily support several applications provided that the sum of the NVM spaces used by these applications does not exceed the XµP's total NVM capacity and that these NVM spaces are properly firewalled. From the user's perspective the XµP is tantamount to a key ring carrying all the secrets (credentials) used by the applications that the user interacts with but *not* these applications themselves.

A wide range of trade-offs and variants is possible when implementing the architecture described in this paper. Referring to the extended version of this work [6] for more, a few engineering options are considered here.

SPEEDING UP MODULAR OPERATIONS. While the multiplication of two κ-bit integers theoretically requires κ^2 operations, multiplying a random ν by $\mu(x)$ may require only $\kappa^2/4$ operations when μ is adequately chosen. Independently, an adequate usage of RAM counters allows to decrease the value of e without sensibly increasing the expected number of CheckOut on the average.

REPLACING RSA. Clearly, any signature scheme that admits a screening variant (*i.e.* a homomorphic property) can be used in our protocols. RSA features a low (and customizable) verification time, but replacing it by EC-based schemes for instance, could present some advantages.

CODE SIZE VERSUS EXECUTION SPEED. The access to a virtually unlimited ROM renders vacuous the classical dilemma between optimizing code size or speed. Here, for instance, one can cheaply unwind (inline) loops or implement algorithms using pre-computed space-consuming look-up tables instead of performing on-line calculations *etc.*

SMART USAGE OF SECURITY HARDWARE FEATURES. Using the Alert predicate, the XµP could selectively activate hardware-level protections against physical attacks whenever a private variable is handled or forecasted to be used a few cycles later.

HIGH SPEED XIO. A high-speed communication interface is paramount for servicing the extensive information exchange between the XµP and the XT. Evaluating transmission performances for a popular standard, the Universal Serial Bus (USB)[10], we found that transfers of 32 bits can be done at 25 Mb/s in USB High Speed mode which corresponds to 780K 32-bit words per second. When servicing Protocol 1, this corresponds approximately to a 32-bit XµP working at 390 KHz; when parallel execution and look-ahead transmission take place, one gets a 32-bit machine running at 780 KHz. An 8-bit USB interface leads to 830 KHz. There is no doubt that these figures can be greatly improved.

---

[10] Note that USB is unadapted to our application as this standard was designed for good bandwidth rather than for good latency.

8 Further Work

The authors believe that the concept introduced in this paper raises a number of practical and theoretical questions. Amongst these is the safe externalization of Java's *entire* bytecode set, the safe co-operative development of code by competing parties (*i.e.* mechanisms for the secure handover of execution from program ID_1 to program ID_2), or the devising of faster execution protocols.

Interestingly, the paradigm of signature screening on which Protocols 1 and 2 are based also exists in the symmetric setting, where RSA signatures are replaced by MACs and a few hash functions. Security can also be assessed formally in this case under adequate assumptions. We refer the reader to [6] for details.

This paper showed how to provably securely externalize programs from the processor that runs them. Apart from answering a theoretical question, we believe that our technique provides the framework of novel practical solutions for real-life applications in the world of mobile code and cryptography-enabled embedded software.

References

1. A. Aho, R. Sethi, J. Ullman, *Compilers: Principles, Techniques, and Tools*, Addison-Wesley, 1986.
2. E. Biham and A. Shamir, *Differential Fault Analysis of Secret Key Cryptosystems*, In Advances in Cryptography, Crypto'97, LNCS 1294, pages 513–525, 1997.
3. I. Biehl, B. Meyer and V. Müller, *Differential Fault Attacks on Elliptic Curve Cryptosystems*, In M. Bellare (Ed.), Proceedings of Advances in Cryptology, Crypto 2000, LNCS 1880, pages 131–146, Springer Verlag, 2000.
4. M. Bellare, J. Garay and T. Rabin, *Fast Batch Verification for Modular Exponentiation and Digital Signatures*, Eurocrypt'98, LNCS 1403, pages 236–250. Springer-Verlag, Berlin, 1998.
5. M. Bellare and P. Rogaway, *Random Oracles Are Practical: a Paradigm for Designing Efficient Protocols*, Proceedings of the first CCS, pages 62–73. ACM Press, New York, 1993.
6. B. Chevallier-Mames, D. Naccache, P. Paillier and D. Pointcheval, *How to Disembed a Program?*, IACR ePrint Archive, `http://eprint.iacr.org`, 2004.
7. Z. Chen, *Java Card Technology for Smart Cards: Architecture and Programmer's Guide*, The Java Series, Addison-Wesley, 2000.
8. J.-S. Coron, *On the Exact Security of Full-Domain-Hash*, Crypto'2000, LNCS 1880, Springer-Verlag, Berlin, 2000.
9. J.-S. Coron and D. Naccache, *On the Security of RSA Screening*, Proceedings of the Fifth CCS, pages 197–203, ACM Press, New York, 1998.
10. D.E. Knuth, *The Art of Computer Programming, vol. 1, Seminumerical Algorithms*, Addison-Wesley, Third edition, pages 124–185, 1997.
11. S. Muchnick, *Advanced Compiler Design and Implementation*, Morgan Kaufmann, 1997.
12. G. Ramalingam, *Identifying Loops in Almost Linear Time*, ACM Transactions on Programming Languages and Systems, 21(2):175-188, March 1999.
13. R. Stata and M. Abadi, *A Type System for Java Bytecode Subroutines*, SRC Research Report 158, June 11, 1998, `http://www.research.digital.com/SRC/`.

Author Index

Lecture Notes in Computer Science

For information about Vols. 1–3044

please contact your bookseller or Springer-Verlag